INSIDERS' GUIDE® TO

CAPE COD
& THE ISLANDS

EIGHTH EDITION

PATRICK CASSIDY

INSIDERS' GUIDE

GUILFORD, CONNECTICUT
AN IMPRINT OF GLOBE PEQUOT PRESS

All the information in this guidebook is subject to change. We recommend that you call ahead to obtain current information before traveling.

INSIDERS' GUIDE®

Copyright © 2004, 2007, 2010 Morris Book Publishing, LLC

Previous editions of this book were published by Falcon Publishing, Inc. in 1999 and 2000.

Project Editor: Ellen Urban
Layout Artist: Kevin Mak
Text design by Sheryl Kober
Maps by XNR Productions, Inc. © Morris Book Publishing, LLC

ISSN 1532-6462
ISBN 978-0-7627-5311-6

Printed in the United States of America
10 9 8 7 6 5 4 3 2 1

CONTENTS

CONTENTS

Directory of Maps

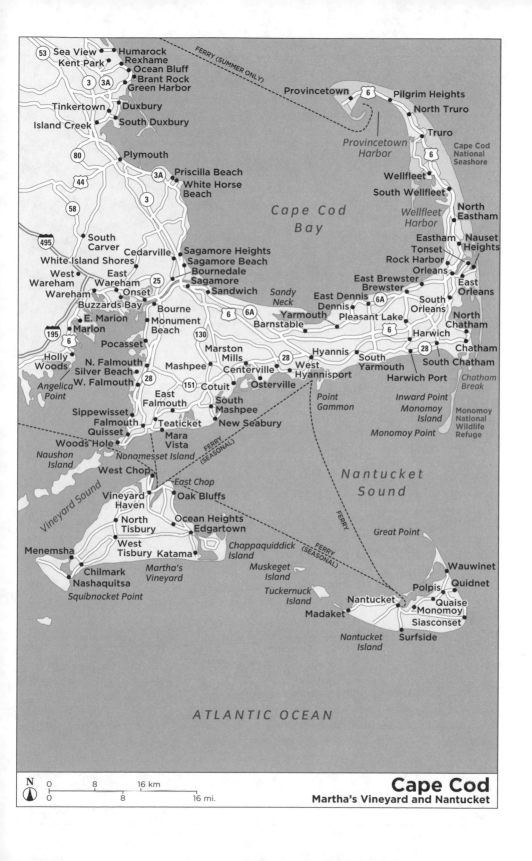

Cape Cod
Martha's Vineyard and Nantucket

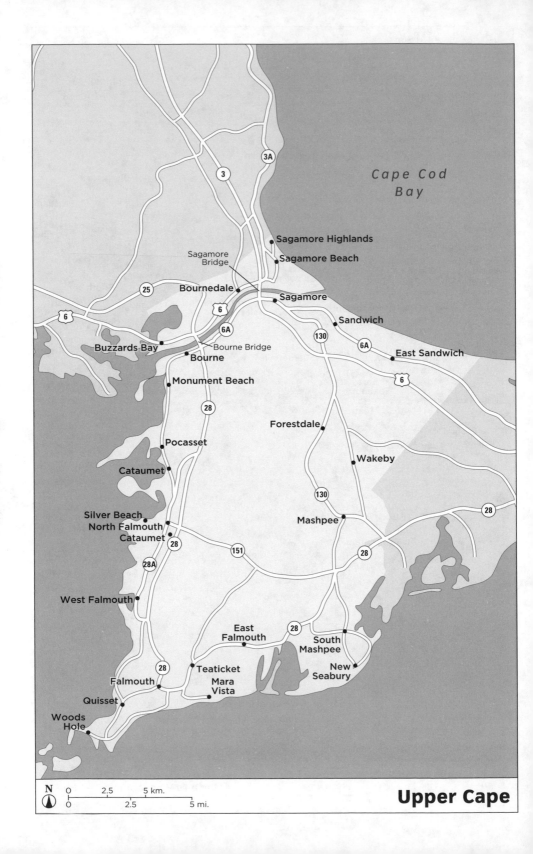

Cape Cod Bay

Sagamore Highlands
Sagamore Beach
Sagamore Bridge
Bournedale
Sagamore
Sandwich
Buzzards Bay
Bourne Bridge
Bourne
East Sandwich
Monument Beach
Forestdale
Pocasset
Wakeby
Cataumet
Silver Beach
North Falmouth
Cataumet
Mashpee
West Falmouth
East Falmouth
South Mashpee
New Seabury
Falmouth
Teaticket
Mara Vista
Quisset
Woods Hole

N

0   2.5   5 km.
0   2.5   5 mi.

Upper Cape

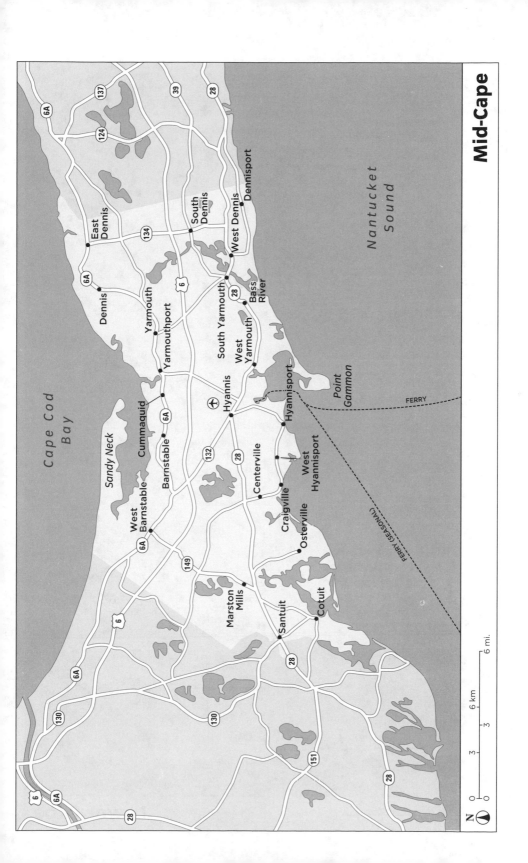

Mid-Cape

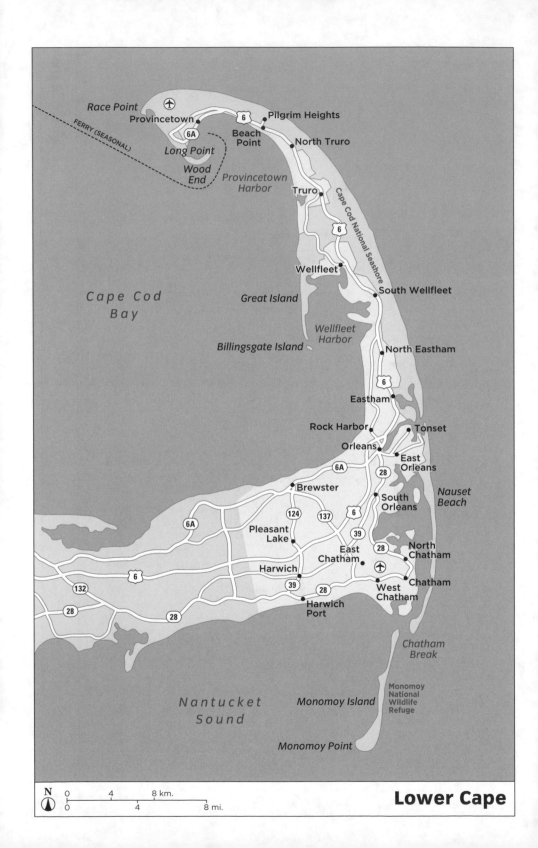

Lower Cape

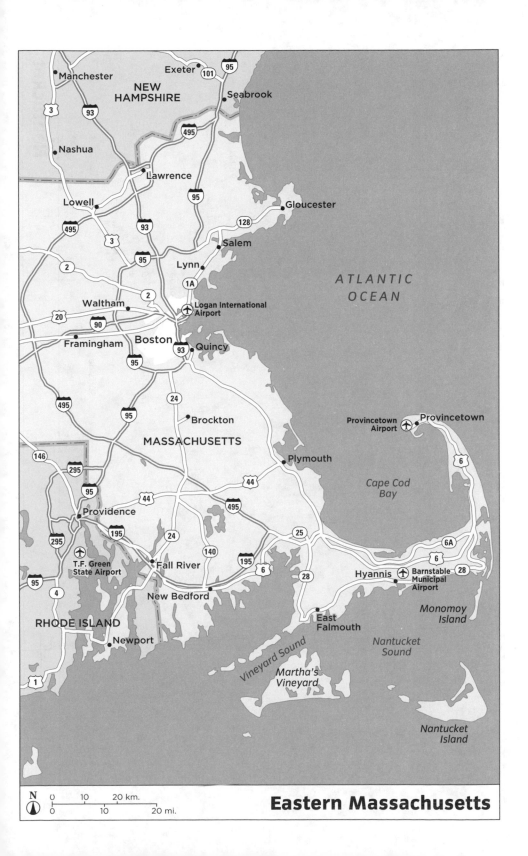

Eastern Massachusetts

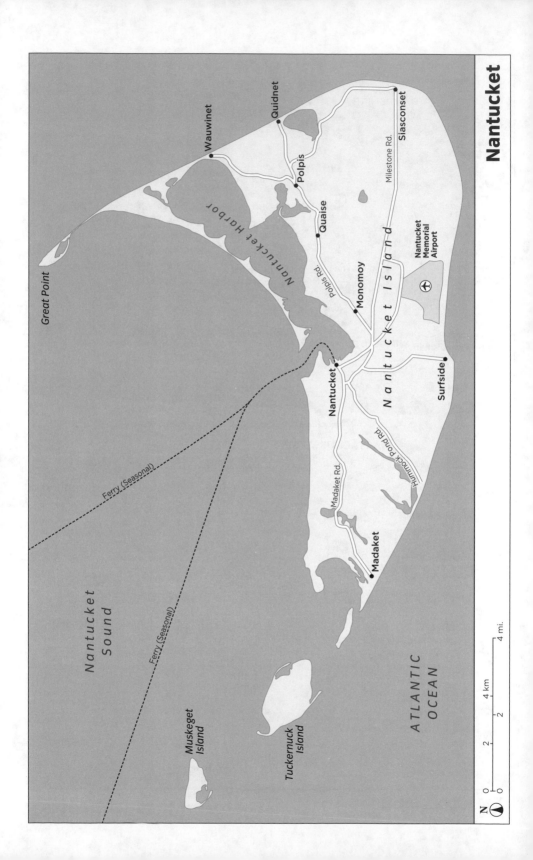

Nantucket

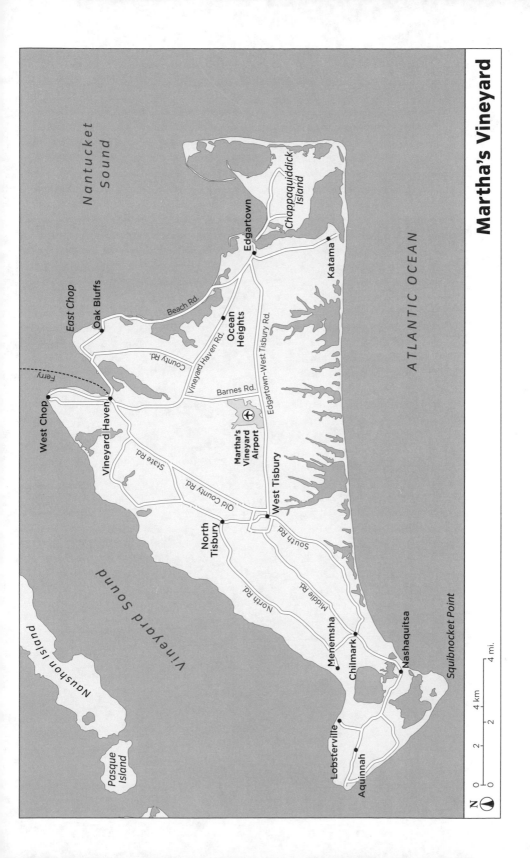

Martha's Vineyard

PREFACE

If there is a constant on Cape Cod and the islands of Martha's Vineyard and Nantucket, it is change.

Barrier beaches roll under themselves to reveal historic shipwrecks that disappear again beneath the sand with the unrelenting pressure of time. Nor'easters cross the surrounding waters to crash in an ever-changing mosaic like the waves of bay and ocean on the shores of this 70-mile sandy spit and its neighboring outcrops. Seasons pass one on the other with comforting regularity but also with an indifference that can be, at times, disconcerting.

Quaint cottages, sand dunes, and clam shacks still exist in abundance, but even Patti Page's "Old Cape Cod" has faded a bit, like a postcard from the mid-20th century tucked and forgotten behind a long-unmoved bookshelf. In place of the once seemingly immutable Cape Cod there is now an amalgamation of the old and new.

Trophy homes known as "McMansions" have replaced some of the cottages. The clam shacks are there but so too are chain restaurants and fine dining. Sweeping sand dunes and other picturesque scenes now compete with shopping malls and the march of development.

There are also places on the Cape and islands where even more unpleasant reminders of the modern world intrude. There is poverty and crime of every sort, although isolated and in limited amounts. The Cape and islands remain safe compared to cities and other, more urban areas of Massachusetts and the country. However, like everywhere else there are deadly accidents and occasional acts of violence, especially during the region's two extreme states of being: high summer when the population can triple with visitors and the deep winter when, despite typically mild temperatures, life on the peninsula can be chilled and lonely.

A visitor to the region is more likely to discover the area rich with natural beauty and pervaded with peacefulness. Salt marshes shelter quiet creeks and large harbors envelop and define quintessentially Cape Cod commercial areas and towns.

Each region of the Cape and islands has its own unique personality and split personalities. Provincetown can be rambunctious and reclusive. Yarmouth is divided between historic Route 6A—the "Old Kings Highway"—and the commercial tapestry of Route 28, an economic engine that sputters at times but always turns on for the summer hordes. Sandwich and Bourne are destinations unto themselves and simultaneously home for those who commute to work in Boston and beyond.

Traditionally divided into three main areas—the Lower, Mid, and Upper Cape—Cape Cod can just as easily be taken in chunks that have little to do with the borders of its 15 towns. The side of the peninsula closest to Cape Cod Bay tends to be quieter with smaller beaches and calmer waters. On the shores that border the Atlantic Ocean, the beaches tend to be larger and wilder, the waves and water temperatures of the Atlantic less forgiving. Sheltered from the open ocean by the islands and other land masses, the shores and waters of Nantucket Sound and Buzzards Bay fall somewhere in between these two extremes.

The Upper Cape is the westernmost portion of Cape Cod and includes Bourne, Sandwich, Falmouth, and Mashpee. Mid-Cape—located, as you've probably already guessed, in just about the middle of Cape Cod—consists of the towns of Barnstable, Yarmouth, and Dennis. The remaining towns of Brewster, Harwich, Chatham, Orleans, Eastham, Wellfleet, Truro, and Provincetown make up the Lower Cape. Another designation—the Outer Cape—includes the Lower Cape towns along the Atlantic, or back side, of the Cape: Eastham, Wellfleet, Truro, and Provincetown.

Nantucket is both a town and county unto itself. Martha's Vineyard is six towns: Tisbury, Oak Bluffs, Edgartown, West Tisbury, Chilmark, and Aquinnah, which together make up Dukes County.

Within the pages of this, the eighth edition of the *Insiders' Guide to Cape Cod and the Islands,* readers will find all they need to start to explore this inspiring region. While one book can never summarize all that is available here, it is the goal of this guide to point readers in the right direction and give them the basic information they need to find the rest out for themselves. We have attempted to remove overly effusive praise for one choice or the other and, instead, recommend you use this book as a beginner's manual and go with your gut.

Wherever visitors or new residents of Cape Cod and the islands find themselves, the sea is never far. The connection to the ocean, while tenuous at times in a world of cell phones and video games, is the heart of the region and connected to nearly every activity and endeavor that has ever taken place here.

Choose a harbor as the sun drops in the evening sky during the summer or fall and watch the fishing boats—commercial, charter, and recreational—return after a day on the water. As first mates fillet the day's catch and tourists gather to see the action, the night begins. The smell of the ocean wafts over the parking lot, soon to be replaced by the smell of its bounty cooking over a beachside bonfire. As much as things change, that which remains is worth the trip. This is Cape Cod.

HOW TO USE THIS BOOK

No doubt you have already flipped back and forth through the book, thumbing your way from Lodging to Restaurants to Vacation Rentals, maybe settling briefly on chapters such as Shopping or The Arts or some other chapter whose subject captured your interest. Or perhaps you're thinking of planning that perfect Cape Cod vacation and are in need of a more disciplined approach to your reading.

This guide is arranged to give you easy access to valuable information pertinent to Cape Cod and the islands of Martha's Vineyard and Nantucket. It's not necessary to read the chapters in order, as each chapter stands on its own. Depending on what you're looking for, other chapters such as Historic Cape Cod, Worship, or Retirement might be considered necessary reading as you make your plans.

If you plan to visit Martha's Vineyard or Nantucket, for a day or an extended period, read the introduction to those chapters to get the "lay of the land." An island day trip can be highly successful with just a little planning.

With a book this size and an area as diverse as Cape Cod and the islands, you'll find the Contents and the maps at the front of the book to be of great help. If you plan to do a lot of traveling around the Cape, consider picking up a more detailed map. The individual chapters themselves divide the Cape into the three principal regions outlined in the preface: Upper Cape, Mid-Cape, and Lower Cape, with the attractions for each being alphabetized.

All information concerning the islands (history, accommodations, restaurants, annual events, etc.) is in the island chapters toward the end of the book. All establishments on Martha's Vineyard are listed within the chapter in the following geographic order by town: Vineyard Haven (Tisbury) first, then Oak Bluffs, Edgartown, West Tisbury, Chilmark, and Aquinnah (formerly called Gay Head).

Each entry in the chapters includes the establishment's address, phone number, and Web site, if available. It is important to note that because each town has a number of villages, there exist many cases in which towns contain more than one Main Street or other streets with the same name. Dennis, for example, has a Main Street in both South Dennis and Dennisport. Barnstable has Main Streets in eight villages. Yarmouth contains four Pine Streets. In some towns, Route 6A along the north side is also known as Main Street, as is Route 28 running along the south side of other towns. In Yarmouth both Route 6A and Route 28 are known as Main Street. We have used route numbers wherever applicable to avoid confusion. Some roads change names. Willow Street in Yarmouth, for instance, becomes Yarmouth Road once it enters Barnstable. Even within a town, streets have been known to change names—Union Street in Yarmouthport, for example, becomes Station Avenue in South Yarmouth. Other streets are spelled slightly different from town to town, such as Setucket Road of Dennis, which is Satucket Road in Brewster.

We have endeavored to be as accurate as possible. Unfortunately businesses, organizations, and municipalities sometimes make decisions to change rates, hours, or policies in the spring, right before the busy season, after our press time. We have used the most up-to-date information available to us.

We have two final points to make. If, say, an inn in the Lodging chapter has a restaurant on-site that is written up in the Restaurants chapter, we'll reference it so you can flip to it for further information (and vice versa). Other types of entries that appear elsewhere in the book will be referenced in a similar fashion. Finally, there is an index at the back of the book to make looking up a particular entry very easy.

AREA OVERVIEW

Cape Cod is a spit of land thrust into the Atlantic Ocean like a sandy arm, with Provincetown at the "fist," Chatham at the "elbow," and Sandwich at the "shoulder." The Cape lies just south of Boston on the East Coast of the United States and is the premier vacation resort in New England.

For many longtime visitors the mere act of crossing either of the two bridges that connect the Cape to the mainland is enough to put them on "vacation time." For those who live here the transition can be even more dramatic, and the Cape Cod Canal can serve as a natural barrier between the outside world, its pressures, and hang-ups. Although the clear line between here and there has blurred in recent years, the Cape and islands remain a welcome respite from the world at large.

A LAND SURROUNDED BY SEA

The sea has shaped the land. Year by year, tide by tide, storm by storm, unseen currents, waves, and fierce winds driven by the sea have carved channels through barrier beaches and resulted in an ever-changing Cape Cod.

The sea has also shaped the way of life of the people who live here. It was an important economic resource for earlier inhabitants, helping to put food on the table and providing a living for fishermen, boat builders and chandlering. Many a headstone in our local cemeteries bears the simple words "lost at sea," which attest to a darker bond between the Cape's people and the ocean. Today, Cape Cod's population of approximately 220,000 year-round residents swells in the summer as visitors are drawn to the area's natural beauty, which in great measure comes from its proximity to the sea. So, in a sense, the sea is still the Cape's greatest economic resource. Tourism is the area's main industry now, with restaurants and lodgings the major employers of both year-round residents and a seasonal workforce.

HOW THE CAPE WAS FORMED

Cape Cod has been shaped by ice age glaciers and modern-day coastal erosion. About 22,000 years ago, mile-high glaciers made their farthest southerly advance into the lower New England area. As the front sections, or lobes, encountered warm temperatures, they began to melt. Over the next 4,000 years, the glaciers would recede, stop, advance, and then recede again with changing temperatures. Each time a glacier stopped, it deposited rocky debris gathered in its journey from the north. The hills along the northern coast of the Cape are made up of this debris. The coastline was gradually smoothed out by pebbles, stones, and rocks, and sand bars were formed around the Cape by drifting sand. The glaciers also left behind hundreds of ponds and lakes, called "kettle ponds," formed where huge chunks of glacial ice left depressions in the earth. There are about 360 of these kettle ponds on Cape Cod.

> **i** The Atlantic Ocean's coastal currents are constantly moving sand from the beaches along the Lower Cape and redepositing sand at the tip of the Cape at Provincetown and to the south at Monomoy Island. A fishing village existed on South Monomoy Island until the shifting sands filled the harbor and blocked off access to the sea, virtually eliminating the village.

A BRIEF HISTORY

Physical evidence suggests that the Cape's earliest inhabitants arrived 10,000 years ago. During the warmer months, they lived along the Cape's major waterways and estuaries and moved inland during the winter. In 1524, explorer Giovanni di Verrazzano spent several weeks exploring the area around Buzzards Bay and described an Algonquin-speaking people as being handsome, well dressed, and friendly.

In 1620, the Pilgrims arrived from England, making landfall at Provincetown, where they remained for about five weeks, exploring the area, before finally sailing on to Plymouth. While on the Cape they encountered native people who hunted, fished, and farmed, raising crops of corn, squash, beans, and tobacco. Within decades after the Pilgrims' arrival, a handful of Cape towns were settled: Sandwich in 1637, Yarmouth in 1639, and Barnstable in 1640. By the end of the 18th century, all of the Cape towns with the exception of Brewster, Mashpee, and Bourne, were incorporated. These three towns would all see incorporation during the 19th century.

Approximately two-thirds of the Cape's towns are named for English seaports, and all but two have English names (Orleans is named after a French city, and Mashpee is Wampanoag Indian). The Cape itself was named by English explorer Bartholomew Gosnold, who in 1602 arrived in the vicinity of the Elizabeth Islands off Woods Hole in Falmouth. He was impressed with the great number of codfish he saw in Cape waters. See our Historic Cape Cod chapter for more on the history of the Cape, as well as histories of the individual towns, which we describe here.

THE CAPE TOWNS

Upper Cape

Bourne, the town closest to the mainland, straddles the Cape Cod Canal. Bourne consists of nine villages, as well as the Massachusetts Military Reservation, totaling an area of 40 square miles and containing a population of about 19,500. The

village of Gray Gables in Bourne has the distinction of being home to the first summer White House of President Grover Cleveland in the 1890s. Monument Beach, Cataumet, and Pocasset are residential seaside villages off the beaten path; Bournedale, nestled between the two bridges on the mainland, has a country store and one of the Cape's herring ponds; Buzzards Bay is a commercial center, home to the Massachusetts Maritime Academy and views of Buttermilk Bay.

Lying just east of Bourne is historic Sandwich, which has a population of about 21,000 and is the oldest town on the Cape. Famous for the glass industry that thrived there in the 1800s, Sandwich is still home to a few glassmaking studios and the Sandwich Glass Museum. The village of Sandwich, its shady lanes dotted with antiques shops, historic inns, and a working Grist Mill, is the ideal place for a casual stroll.

Falmouth, situated south of Bourne and Sandwich, is the second-largest town on the Cape and has more shore and coastline than any other, with 14 harbors and numerous saltwater inlets reaching up like fingers from Vineyard Sound. With a year-round population of about 34,000, Falmouth is made up of eight villages. Falmouth Village, the center of the town, has a wonderful village green, a fascinating array of specialty shops, and includes Falmouth Heights, popular among summer visitors. East Falmouth, Hatchville, Teaticket, and Waquoit are residential areas. North and West Falmouth are known as the keepers of old Cape Cod. Their village centers were placed on the National Register of Historic Places because so many of their 18th- and 19th-century buildings remain.

The village of Woods Hole is home to three important scientific institutions: Woods Hole Oceanographic Institute (WHOI, or "hooey" to locals), the Marine Biological Laboratory, and the National Maritime Fisheries Service. This seaside village is also a starting point for ferries bound for Martha's Vineyard.

East of Falmouth is Mashpee, the town with the strongest ties to the Cape's Native American heritage. It's seen tremendous growth in the last decade; in fact it's become one of the fastest-growing areas of the state. It now has a year-round population of about 10,000.

Mid-Cape

Moving east to the Mid-Cape, Barnstable is the Cape's largest and most populated town with an estimated 49,000 residents in 60 square miles. It serves as the county seat, with a complex containing District and Superior Courthouses and the old county jail. In 2004 a new jail was opened in Bourne. Surrounding quiet, historic Route 6A, Barnstable Village is known for its lovely old houses and its harbor. Also on Route 6A is West Barnstable, which enjoys beautiful views of the salt marshes and barrier beach on Sandy Neck Conservation Area. Barnstable also contains Hyannis, which is the closest thing to a city on Cape Cod. Many residents of other Cape towns travel to Hyannis for shopping, medical services, or employment. Hyannis Harbor has two docks from which ferries depart for Nantucket and Martha's Vineyard. Hyannisport is famous for the Kennedy Compound, where President John F. Kennedy came to sail and enjoy the relaxed atmosphere of Cape Cod with his family in the "Camelot" days. Cotuit, Osterville, Centerville, and Marstons Mills make up the rest of Barnstable.

Stretching between Nantucket Sound and Cape Cod Bay is Yarmouth. On the north side of the Cape is historic, tranquil Yarmouthport along scenic Route 6A, and on the south side is Bass River and the bustling Route 28. If you're looking for a game of minigolf, a quick lunch, or a little nightlife, head for Route 28. If you're into antiquing and visiting historic sites, meander along Route 6A. Yarmouth's year-round population of about 25,000 grows to more than 50,000 in the summer months.

Dennis enjoys a great location and also stretches from the sound to Cape Cod Bay. Historic Route 6A wends through the quiet north side, and, to the south, Dennisport is very much a family-oriented summer resort with a breezy shoreline dotted with cottages and motels. Dennis spans 20 square miles and has a year-round population of about 16,000.

Lower Cape

Just east of Dennis is Brewster, often called the sea captains' town, because it was once home to many wealthy sea captains. Today many of its stately sea captains' homes have been converted into bed-and-breakfast inns. With a year-round population of about 10,000, Brewster is a family town, as evidenced by the high number of young children that required the town to build a second elementary school. Another sign of the town's growth—and its priorities—is the impressive remodeling of the Brewster Ladies' Library. Once the north parish of Harwich, Brewster has eight beautiful beaches and numerous freshwater ponds. It is also home to the Cape Cod Museum of Natural History, with its magnificent nature trails, and Nickerson State Park.

South of Brewster is Harwich, which boasts 16 saltwater beaches on Nantucket Sound, along with a number of freshwater ponds. Home to about 13,000 year-round residents, Harwich has seven villages, including bustling Harwich Port, quiet Pleasant Lake, historic North Harwich, and charming Harwich Center. Wychmere Harbor in Harwich Port is one of the most picturesque harbors on the Cape.

Tucked away on the "elbow" of Cape Cod is Chatham, almost a world unto itself. One thing that sets it apart is its geography; it's not on the way to any other town. With a picturesque Main Street of upscale shops along brick-lined sidewalks, Chatham exudes gentility and sophistication. It is also home to an active fishing fleet, which balances its affluent side. Chatham has just 7,000 residents, a high percentage of senior citizens and consistently votes Republican in presidential elections.

One of the most scenic drives on the Cape is Route 28 between Chatham and Orleans, a winding stretch of road filled with views of Pleasant Bay, inlets, and cranberry bogs. If you enter Orleans this way, you'll get a glimpse of woodsy, residential South Orleans and will pass the South Orleans General Store, which uniquely provides most of the necessary conveniences of a pleasant day trip. When you reach Orleans, which has a year-round population of nearly 7,000, you won't at first understand why this is called the hub of the Lower Cape—it's just a nice little downtown, you think, but most of what anyone would need is there. The town has many attractions, including the famed Nauset Beach on the ocean side and quaint Rock Harbor on Cape Cod Bay, home to a fleet of charter fishing boats.

The gateway to the Cape Cod National Seashore, Eastham is a town with a rural nature and both bay and ocean beaches. With about 5,500 residents, Eastham is predominantly a family town and has numerous summer cottages for rent clustered along the bay side. Roughly one-third of its 14 square miles are taken up by the Cape Cod National Seashore, established in 1961, and comprising Eastham's entire ocean coastline (see our Cape Cod National Seashore chapter).

Wellfleet is an art-lover's haven and a fishing community, a free-spirited individualistic community of about 2,700 year-round residents. The Cape Cod National Seashore extends the entire length of Wellfleet's ocean coastline, as well as its width as far as Great Island, a narrow strip of land that juts 8 miles into Cape Cod Bay and shelters Wellfleet Harbor. The harbor is home to an active fishing fleet and the famed Wellfleet oyster, which thrives in the murky but well-flushed water.

Laid-back and woodsy, with dramatic 80-foot beach cliffs overlooking the Atlantic Ocean and Cape Cod Bay, Truro is a haven for those who crave privacy but want proximity to someplace lively—and neighboring Provincetown fills that requirement perfectly. The least populated of all the towns with just 2,000 residents, Truro's downtown is hard to miss, with the post office, a seafood shop, and a seasonal convenience store the primary attractions.

Provincetown explodes on the senses with its fun-loving, artsy, carnival-like flavor that is counterbalanced by a fishing community of Portuguese heritage and incredible natural beauty. Well-known for its gay community, Provincetown is both colorful and sophisticated with lots of great restaurants, shops, and fine art galleries. Many of the town's summer residents are from Manhattan—which perhaps explains the undeni-able Greenwich Village flair. Some 3,500 people live here year-round, though the population swells to more than 30,000 in the summer. The Cape Cod National Seashore extends to the tip of Cape Cod at Long Point in Provincetown and encompasses the historic Province Lands, reserved as fishing grounds by the Pilgrim Fathers. The Province Lands are laced with thrilling bicycle trails and the Beach Forest walking trail. There's a visitor center set on a hill with magnificent views of the Atlantic Ocean and across the bay to Plymouth. Once a major whaling port, Provincetown is now home to the largest whale-watching fleet on the East Coast.

THE CAPE'S COMFORTABLE CLIMATE

One of the most interesting things about the Cape is its weather. On Cape Cod, you never know what you're going to get. You could be standing on Commercial Street in Provincetown, checking out the shops under sunny skies, while a little more than a half hour away in Chatham the clouds have rolled in, and people are packing up their beach gear to head to happy hour at the local watering hole.

It's not uncommon to see a 10-degree or more temperature difference between the north side of a town and the south side. It may be a downright sultry summer's day in Marstons Mills while lifeguards at Craigville beach are donning windbreakers against cool ocean breezes.

During winter, the atmospheric differences are even more pronounced. One winter's day may see the Lower Cape receiving 6 inches of snow, whereas the Mid- and Upper Cape receive only a dusting. Come the next storm, the tables could be turned.

Isolation from the land mass of New England and enclosure by ocean waters influences the weather on Cape Cod. The peninsula benefits from the warming effects of the ocean in winter and its cooling influences in summer. On the whole, the temperature on the Cape is moderate in all seasons. Consider the average monthly temperature range during summer months—

Town Halls

Barnstable
367 Main St., Hyannis
(508) 862-4000
www.town.barnstable.ma.us

Bourne
24 Perry Ave., Bourne
(508) 759-0600, (508) 759-0613
www.townofbourne.com

Brewster
2198 Rte. 6A, Brewster
(508) 896-3701
www.town.brewster.ma.us

Chatham
549 Main St., Chatham
(508) 945-5100
www.town.barnstable.ma.us

Dennis
485 Main St., South Dennis
(508) 394-8300
www.town.dennis.ma.us

Eastham
2500 U.S. Rte. 6, Eastham
(508) 240-5900
www.eastham-ma.gov

Falmouth
59 Town Hall Sq., Falmouth
(508) 548-7611
www.town.falmouth.ma.us

Harwich
732 Main St. (Route 39), Harwich
(508) 430-7514
http://harwichma.virtualtownhall.net

Mashpee
16 Great Neck Rd. North, Mashpee
(508) 539-1400
www.ci.mashpee.ma.us

Orleans
19 School Rd., Orleans
(508) 240-3700
www.town.orleans.ma.us

Provincetown
260 Commercial St., Provincetown
(508) 487-7000
www.provincetown-ma.gov

Sandwich
130 Main St., Sandwich
(508) 888-5144
www.sandwichmass.org

Truro
24 Town Hall Rd., Truro
(508) 349-7004
www.truro-ma.gov

Wellfleet
300 Main St., Wellfleet
(508) 349-0300
www.wellfleetma.org

Yarmouth
1146 Main St. (Route 28), South Yarmouth
(508) 398-2231
www.yarmouth.ma.us

June: high 71, low 56; July: 78 and 63; August: 76 and 61. In winter the temperature range is fairly constant: January has an average high of 40 and low of 25; for February, the averages are 41 and 26; March's highs and lows are 42 and 28. The temperatures during the shoulder seasons of spring and fall are comfortable—April: high 53, low 40; May: high 62, low 48; September: high 70, low 56; October: high 59, low 47. The average annual rainfall is about 44 inches, with roughly 3 inches per month falling during the summer and about 4 inches of precipitation per month in the winter.

The bracing waters of the Atlantic Ocean beaches are colder than the water along the south shore and in Cape Cod Bay—the perfect remedy for a hot summer's day!

GOVERNMENT BY THE PEOPLE

Most towns are run with the town-meeting style of government, with the exception of Barn-

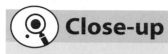

Close-up

Autumn on the Cape

Wish you could enjoy the Cape without the crowds? Consider scheduling your visit during September or October. As autumn falls over New England, you'll find that the summer crowds have left, traffic is flowing more smoothly, and year-rounders are breathing more easily. It's a great time of year for bargains: Prices for rooms and a round of golf have dropped, and stores are having end-of-season sales. Most seasonal attractions stay open until Columbus Day weekend, and the water is still relatively warm. You may even find that—wonder of wonders—you have the beach all to yourself. Whales continue to call the Cape's waters home until late October, and whale-watch trips are definitely less crowded (see our Whale Watching chapter for more information).

An autumn visit also means you get to enjoy a whole new set of seasonal pleasures on the Cape and islands. New England's famed autumn color reaches the Cape in mid-October. Call the Massachusetts Foliage Hotline at (800) 227-6277 for more information on how the color is progressing. For a closer view of the changing colors, consider hitting one of the many trails that crisscross the natural beauty of the Cape. Cape Cod's Walking Weekend, held in mid-October, is a great time to start. Guided walks and hikes are scheduled from Falmouth to Truro. Options may range from a beach walk in Eastham with a Cape Cod National Seashore ranger to a sunset stroll in Brewster with a Cape Cod Natural History Museum naturalist. Call for a schedule at (508) 362-3828.

Besides the leaves and sea grass changing hues, the Cape also offers the spectacle of acres and acres of cranberry bogs ripening from a deep green to a bright red. Cranberries are harvested from mid-September through mid-October using the wet method: Bogs are flooded so that the ripe berries float to the surface. Part of life on the Cape since the early 1800s, they are still celebrated as part of the region's heritage every year.

stable, which switched to a town council–based government in 1989. The other towns are run by boards of selectmen and town managers or town administrators. Each spring town meetings are convened to decide budgets, capital expenditures, zoning changes, and other matters. Most towns have fall meetings as well, along with special meetings to decide pressing issues. Often called the purest form of democracy, town meetings guarantee that all voting residents have a say in town affairs. There is a high level of citizen involvement in the towns, with reliance on volunteers who serve on town boards, such as finance committees and conservation commissions.

THE CAPE'S ECONOMY

Tourism is undeniably the number-one force in the area's economy. Many Cape Codders work in

the area's health care system or as professionals in the fields of law and education. Agriculture and commercial fishing, which used to play a major role in the economic base, have declined in prominence but farming, including aquaculture, has made a comeback in recent years. Technology is up and coming on Cape Cod, with many people working remotely from the area.

PROTECTING AND PRESERVING THE CAPE

The Cape Cod Commission, Barnstable County's land-use regulatory and planning agency, was created in 1990 to control growth on Cape Cod. The commission has one representative from each of the Cape's 15 towns and, under the Cape Cod Commission Act, has the power to regulate developments of regional impact. It also provides planning assistance to the towns, designates areas of critical concern, and maintains a database of demographic information.

The commission sprang from a general concern among residents that unrestrained growth could negatively affect the peninsula's sensitive environment. Land conservation is an important issue on the Cape, and conservation trusts have flourished in every town. With large tracts of shoreline, ponds, and wetlands on Cape Cod, conservation commissions in every town have authority under state and local laws to oversee development near the shoreline and wetlands.

There has been intermittent push back against the powers of the Cape Cod Commission. In 2006 a task force was formed to look at

Chambers of Commerce

Brewster Chamber of Commerce
P.O. Box 1241, 2198 Main St.,
Brewster 02631
(508) 896-3500
www.brewstercapecod.org

Cape Cod Canal Region Chamber of Commerce (covering Bourne and Sandwich)
70 Main St., Buzzards Bay 02532
(508) 759-6000
www.capecodcanalchamber.org

Cape Cod Chamber of Commerce
Routes 6 and 132, Hyannis 02601
(508) 362-3225, (888) 332-2732
www.capecodchamber.org

Chatham Chamber of Commerce
P.O. Box 793, 2377 Main St., Chatham 02633
(508) 945-5199, (800) 715-5567
www.chathaminfo.com

Dennis Chamber of Commerce
P.O. Box 1001, 242 Swan River Rd., South Dennis 02670
(508) 398-3568
www.dennischamber.com

Eastham Chamber of Commerce
P.O. Box 1329, Eastham 02642
(508) 240-7211
www.easthamchamber.com

Falmouth Chamber of Commerce
20 Academy Lane, Falmouth 02540
(508) 548-8500, (800) 526-8532
www.falmouthchamber.com

Harwich Chamber of Commerce
One Schoolhouse Rd., Harwich Port 02646
(508) 430–1165, (800) 442-7942
www.harwichcc.com

Hyannis Chamber of Commerce
P.O. Box 1321, 1481 Rte. 132, Hyannis 02601
(508) 775-2201, (877) 492-6647
www.hyannischamber.org

Mashpee Chamber of Commerce
P.O. Box 1245, 520 Main St., Route 130 Mashpee 02649
(508) 477-0792
www.mashpeechamber.com

Orleans Chamber of Commerce
P.O. Box 153, 44 Main St., Orleans 02653
(508) 255-1386, (800) 865-1386
www.capecod-orleans.com

Providence Chamber of Commerce
P.O. Box 1017, 307 Commercial St., Provincetown 02657
(508) 487-3424
www.ptownchamber.com

Truro Chamber of Commerce
P.O. Box 26, 2 Head of the Meadow Rd., North Truro 02652
(508) 487-1288
www.trurochamberofcommerce.com

Wellfleet Chamber of Commerce
P.O. Box 571, Wellfleet 02667
(508) 349-2510
www.wellfleetchamber.com

Yarmouth Area Chamber of Commerce
424 Rte. 28, West Yarmouth 02673
(508) 778-1008, (800) 732-1008
www.yarmouthcapecod.com

the agency's activities and provide recommendations for how it could function better without inhibiting necessary economic development. The commission was reorganized to focus more on planning, but some towns, especially Yarmouth, have continued to push for more reform.

In 1998, voters approved the creation of a land bank to fund town purchases of open space. Although the funding mechanism was hotly debated (the approved version uses a 3 percent increase in property taxes, after an earlier version that would have added to the tax on property transfers was defeated), just about everyone agreed on the need for a land bank.

One of the strongest proponents of the land-bank bill, and for years a champion of the Cape's environment, is the Association for the Preservation of Cape Cod, which is involved in a variety of environmental and preservation issues. With a membership of approximately 5,700, the APCC marked its 40th anniversary in 2008.

The land bank has now given way, for the most part, to the Community Preservation Act, which funds projects that include not only open

Vital Statistics

Governor: Deval Patrick

Congressional delegation: Senator John Kerry and Congressman William Delahunt

Capital: Boston

State motto: *Ense petit placidam sub libertate quietem* (By the sword we seek peace, but peace only under liberty)

Nickname: The Bay State

Major cities (in eastern Massachusetts): Boston, Worcester, New Bedford

Counties of the Cape and islands: Barnstable, Nantucket, and Dukes (Martha's Vineyard)

Permanent population: According to the 2000 U.S. Census, roughly 247,000 people: 222,230 in Barnstable County, 14,987 in Dukes County, and 9,520 in Nantucket County

Area: 396 square miles (Barnstable County), 104 square miles (Dukes County), and 48 square miles (Nantucket County)

Average Cape temperatures: July (high/low): 78/63; January (high/low): 40/25

Colleges: Massachusetts Maritime Academy, Cape Cod Community College

Major employment sectors: Retail, services, and local government

Major airports: Logan International Airport (Boston), Barnstable Municipal, Airport (Hyannis), Nantucket Memorial Airport (Nantucket), Martha's Vineyard Airport (Vineyard Haven)

Military bases: Massachusetts Military Reservation

Daily newspaper: *Cape Cod Times*

State sales tax: 6.25 percent

State rooms tax: 5.7 percent

Municipal hotel/motel surtax: 4 percent

State meals tax: 5 percent

space protection but also the development of affordable housing and historic preservation through a similar funding mechanism.

Historic preservation is nowhere more of an issue than on quiet Route 6A, which has maintained its historic charm largely thanks to the jurisdiction of the Old Kings Highway Historic District, which stretches from Sandwich to Orleans. Although some residents may grumble that they can't even paint their house without approval from the Historic District Committee, it's hard to argue with the apparent results: Route 6A is a lovely stretch of road and tasteful to a fault.

Another hot-button environmental issue on the Cape that has received international attention over the past eight years is an effort by a company called Cape Wind Associates, LLC, to build a 130-turbine wind farm in Nantucket Sound. The project has moved forward in fits and starts, garnering passionate opposition and support on and off Cape Cod. In 2009 the project had received many of the necessary permits required to begin construction but was still tied up in a myriad of lawsuits, with still more expected if the federal government approved a lease for the wind farm.

RESOURCES FOR MORE INFORMATION ON THE CAPE

Planning a visit to the Cape? Write or call chambers of commerce and other organizations for free brochures, travel packs, maps, and money-saving coupons. Once you're here, stop by chamber-sponsored information booths set up in many towns and villages for last-minute updates and ideas for things to do and see.

See also the listing of the addresses and telephone numbers of the Cape's town halls earlier in this chapter. Beach parking stickers are issued by the town hall in each town (see our Beaches chapter for details). The offices can also provide information about the laws and regulations that are in effect in the town, such as fishing regulations, zoning laws, etc.

FOR MORE INFORMATION ON VACATIONING ON THE CAPE

MASSACHUSETTS OFFICE OF TRAVEL AND TOURISM
10 Park Plaza, Suite 4510, Boston 02116
(617) 973-8500, (800) 227–6277
www.mass-vacation.com

GETTING HERE, GETTING AROUND

People flock to the Cape not only because of its beauty, but also because it's easy to get to from many places. New York, New Jersey, Pennsylvania, Washington, D.C., even Ohio and Canada are all within a day's drive. From New York City, it's about a five-hour drive, from Boston it takes one hour to reach the canal, and from there it's a further one hour and 20 minutes to reach Provincetown at the tip of the Cape.

By land, whether you arrive from the north or from the west, you will cross the Cape Cod Canal at either Bourne or Sagamore over one of two bridges, allowing for views of the canal below and Buzzards Bay or Cape Cod Bay.

Arriving by air in either Hyannis or Provincetown, a traveler by day will see the entire outline of the Cape and islands surrounded by blue sea and fringed with sand dunes; at night, the Cape sparkles with thousands of lights and the beams of the many lighthouses that mark the harbor entrances and the treacherous coastline. The short flight from Boston—about 20 minutes—is truly spectacular.

By sea, whether arriving at Martha's Vineyard or Nantucket, or Provincetown via Boston, the Cape emerges from a lush green horizon into a coastline of harbors and gray-shingled buildings, accented by the widow's walks of sea captains' homes and the soaring spires of old churches. These spires provided mariners of centuries past with visible landmarks as they made their way along the coast. Today that role is filled by water and communication towers.

Below we've listed your various transportation options.

BY CAR

From Boston and points north: Take I-93 to Route 3 South. Where the Sagamore rotary existed until 2006, motorists now drive straight over the $59 million flyover before crossing the Sagamore Bridge and US 6 (also called the Mid-Cape Highway), which extends the entire length of the Cape to Provincetown. Follow US 6 until you see the name of the town you wish to visit. Exits are well marked. If you wish to visit Falmouth or Woods Hole, you do not have to go over the Sagamore Bridge, but instead exit before the bridge and take the Scenic Highway just a few miles to the Bourne Bridge. Cross over the Bourne Bridge, and continue south on Route 28.

From Springfield, Massachusetts, and points west: Take the Mass Pike, I-90 East and follow it to exit 11A; take I-495 South. I-495 merges into Route 25. Follow this road over the Bourne Bridge. If you are going to Falmouth or Woods Hole, go halfway around the rotary where Route 28 leads you on your way. If you are heading to any other town, go three-quarters around the Bourne rotary, where you will see a sign for US 6 East. Follow Sandwich Road (Route 6A) alongside the canal to the first set of traffic lights, just before the Sagamore Bridge. Take a right at the lights to US 6 (Mid-Cape Highway), and follow this road until you reach your exit.

From New York, Connecticut, Rhode Island, and points south: Take I-95 to Providence, Rhode Island. Take exit 20 to I-195 East. Follow this to Route 25 South, which leads to the Bourne Bridge.

Most people do, in fact, come to the Cape by automobile—more than 95,000 vehicles arrive per day during the popular summer months. Major routes can be busy. The Friday evening and Saturday morning approach to the Cape toward both Sagamore and Bourne Bridges is usually quite busy, and often traffic will be brought to a crawl for several miles before the bridge. This is because vacation rentals turn over on Saturday mornings, occasionally resulting in a Saturday afternoon backup going off-Cape, but most folks find a way to stay on the Cape one more day, meaning that the Sunday afternoon traffic usually backs up 2 or 3 miles going off-Cape.

Most of the radio stations have "travel reports" airing frequently Friday through Sunday in the summer for your convenience (try WQRC, 99.9 FM). Another great way to avoid traffic before you leave the house or motel is to call SmarTraveler at 511 or (617) 374-1234 (7* gets Cape Cod traffic or go to www.smartraveler.com) for up-to-the-minute information on traffic. This service employs cameras and airplanes to determine current traffic problems.

US 6:
The Mid-Cape Highway

The Mid-Cape Highway, technically US 6, is the main traffic artery, running down the middle of the Cape as far as Orleans. It then continues as US 6 to Provincetown. From the canal to Dennis, the Mid-Cape Highway is a four-lane freeway; the speed limit is 55 mph. After Dennis (exit 9A/B Cloverleaf) the road becomes, for a 13-mile stretch to Orleans, a two-lane freeway (one lane going west, one going east), dubbed Suicide Alley by locals. As the highway narrows into this stretch, there's bound to be a bit of congestion, especially in the summer on a busy Saturday morning, so watch out for this area if you're traveling at that time. Posted signs suggest that you use your headlights as you travel this 50-mph stretch, even during the daylight hours, to increase visibility. At the Orleans rotary, the freeway ends and US 6 widens to a four-lane surface street through Eastham and North Truro. Through Wellfleet and South Truro, it is a two-lane road with shoulders, and from Provincetown to its terminus at Route 6A (the Cape Cod National Seashore) it resumes its status as a surface expressway. Because US 6 is the only major thoroughfare on Cape Cod, state

police patrol these routes routinely. Also, US 6 from Wellfleet to Provincetown is narrow and prone to accidents, so be careful, especially when making left-hand turns. If you choose to speed between the Orleans rotary and Provincetown, you can expect the attention of local law enforcement, especially in Eastham, which is well-known for its heavy police presence on US 6.

Cape Routes

Many side roads intercept US 6 and Routes 6A and 28; consult a good map to find shortcuts. Locals use several principal north-south state highways (below designated per local usage as routes) to travel between east-west routes. Here are a few:

Route 151 runs from Route 28 in Mashpee (at the Mashpee rotary) to Route 28 in North Falmouth

Route 130 from Route 6A in Sandwich to Route 28 in Mashpee (Route 130 connects with US 6 at exit 2)

Route 149 from Route 6A in West Barnstable to Route 28 in Cotuit (Route 149 connects with US 6 at exit 5)

Route 132 from Route 6A in Barnstable to Route 28 in Hyannis (Route 132 connects with US 6 at exit 6)

Route 134 from Route 6A in Dennis to Route 28 in West Dennis (Route 134 connects with US 6 at exit 9)

Route 124 from Route 6A in Brewster to Route 39 in Harwich and Route 28 in Harwich Port (Route 124 connects with US 6 at exit 10)

Route 137 from Route 6A in Brewster to Route 39 in East Harwich and continuing to Route 28 in North Chatham (Route 137 connects with US 6 at exit 11)

Route 39 from Route 28 in Harwich Port to Route 28 in Orleans

Route 28 handles traffic south of US 6 and Route 6A handles it to the north. Both these routes are more scenic and slower than US 6. Route 28 connects most of the Cape business districts along the south coast. Route 6A is more of a country road, leading to many of the Cape's cozy inns and antiques shops along the north shore. It has been rated one of the top scenic drives in the country (see our Tours and Excursions chapter). These three roads—US 6, Route 28, and Route 6A—originate at the canal bridges, spread out over the Upper and Mid-Cape, and then converge at the Orleans-Eastham rotary on the Lower Cape, with US 6 alone carrying you northward from Eastham to Provincetown.

In many towns Route 6A is also known as Main Street, as is Route 28 in some towns. But some towns have other Main Streets. To avoid confusion, we have decided to use route numbers throughout this book wherever possible.

Rotaries

The Cape has some notable traffic circles called rotaries—approximately 19 of them. For those not familiar with rotaries, also called roundabouts, here's an explanation: Their purpose is to provide you with an opportunity to continue on your way without having to stop at major intersections. The traffic in a rotary travels counterclockwise. In other words, you can only turn right into or off a rotary. The law dictates that you yield to a car already in the rotary, rather like merging onto the highway—wait for a gap in traffic, and then ease into that spot. Be patient when entering and driving around a rotary. Usually the signs are pretty good, and you can read each one quickly as you enter the rotary so you'll know which road you need to take. If you do get confused and miss your turnoff, don't panic! Instead of slamming on

i Don't be confused when you drive along scenic Route 28 between Chatham and Orleans. This route is marked "south" when you will actually be traveling north to Orleans and visa versa. The confusion: Route 28 South takes a turn at Chatham and heads north to Orleans Center.

your brakes (the last thing you want to do in a rotary!), simply drive around again in a circle.

BY PLANE

Perhaps the best way to get a real feel for the Cape is to approach it by air. On a clear day you can see it all. You'll notice the relationships between the Cape peninsula and the two islands to the south, Martha's Vineyard and Nantucket, and you may even be able to see Monomoy Island off Chatham and the Elizabeth Islands off Falmouth. Even Cape residents are surprised by just how narrow this land looks from the sky.

Barnstable Municipal Airport in Hyannis is the Cape's main airport. It should also be noted that this airport has no fancy boutiques and no food courts—just friendly local people willing and able to assist you with your travel questions. The Cape also has a few other smaller airports, sometimes just a runway or two, which, with the exception of the Provincetown Airport, only serve private planes. Once you arrive at Barnstable, there are plenty of car-rental options right at the airport.

Always call two hours ahead of your flight departure time to guarantee that your flight is taking off. Even with the most sophisticated flight equipment, the fog can sock you in for a couple hours.

Fly to Barnstable Municipal Airport in Hyannis on Cape Air from Boston and Providence, or on US Airways Express from Boston and New York.

Fly to Nantucket on Cape Air from Boston, New Bedford, Providence, Hyannis, Provincetown, and Martha's Vineyard; or on US Airways Express from New York, Boston, Hyannis, and Martha's Vineyard. To fly to Nantucket from Hyannis, you can take Nantucket Airlines and Island Airlines.

Fly to Martha's Vineyard on Cape Air from Boston, New Bedford, Providence, Hyannis, and Nantucket.

Fly to Provincetown on Cape Air from Boston. Most of the 18-minute flight is over Cape Cod Bay, and the views of the dune-studded Cape as the plane sweeps over its tip are great. While flying over the bay, be sure to keep your eyes peeled for whales, which come into the area to feed.

BARNSTABLE MUNICIPAL AIRPORT

Boardman-Polando Field, 480 Barnstable Rd., Hyannis
(508) 775-2020
www.town.barnstable.ma.us/Departments/
Airport/05/index.htm

Barnstable Municipal Airport, the Cape's major airport, is right in the middle of the peninsula in Hyannis (town of Barnstable). With two 1-mile runways, it is certainly not the largest airport you'll ever land at, but it is far from the smallest. President Kennedy's plane would land here when he was arriving for a Hyannisport vacation. For celebrity watchers, when the rich and famous fly to the Cape, more often than not, they'll come through Barnstable.

Four airlines service the airport, three on a full-time basis and one seasonally. Also, two local airlines, Island Airlines and Nantucket Airlines, provide service from Hyannis to Nantucket (see our Nantucket chapter for more details).

Cape Air (866-227-3247, www.flycapeair .com), offers the most daily flights into Hyannis from Boston and to the Cape and islands in the summer. On average, there are about seven flights a day year-round between Boston's Logan International Airport and Barnstable Municipal Airport. These flights take about 20 minutes; it seems once the plane reaches its cruising height, it's time to prepare for landing. The airline has many flights each day to Nantucket and Martha's Vineyard. Call ahead for your reservations. Cape Air and Nantucket Airlines also offer off-season specials in addition to discounted commuter tickets.

Island Airlines flies only between Barnstable Municipal Airport and Nantucket about 20 times a day, with fewer flights on the weekends. For more information on Island Airlines schedules and reservations, go to www.islandair.net or call (508) 228-7575 or (800) 248-7779.

Outside the main terminal there are normally a number of taxis waiting. If you plan on leaving your car at the airport overnight, there is a daily parking fee.

If you need to rent a car, you're in luck; there are four car rental companies located in the main terminal: Avis, (800) 331-1212; Budget, (800) 527-7000; Hertz, (800) 654-3131; and Enterprise, (800) 736-8222.

CHATHAM MUNICIPAL AIRPORT

240 George Ryder Rd., Chatham
(508) 945-9000
www.chathamairport.com

Chatham Municipal Airport has a 3,000-foot-long, 100-foot-wide paved runway with a grass strip running alongside. The airport is open to the public and offers sightseeing and biplane rides. There's a restaurant on-site as well as a full maintenance facility.

FALMOUTH AIRPARK

67 Airpark Dr., Waquoit
(508) 548–9617
www.falmouthairpark.net

This one-runway airport is the centerpiece of "Cape Cod's only fly-in community," a residential zone where many homes have hangars for their planes the way other people have garages for cars. The 2,400-foot paved airstrip is open to the public and charters. There is a wash-down station available.

OCEAN WINGS AIR CHARTER

14 Airport Rd., Memorial Airport, Nantucket
(800) 253-5039
www.flyoceanwings.com

Ocean Wings Air Charter offers 24-hour year-round charter service to and from airports throughout the Northeast. If it is necessary to travel quickly and on the spur of the moment in and out of Nantucket, Martha's Vineyard, or Cape Cod, Ocean Wings may fit in with your personal demands. This company has a private hangar and offers flight instruction.

PROVINCETOWN AIRPORT

Race Point Road, Provincetown
(508) 487-0241

Located at the Province Lands, Provincetown Airport has one 3,500-foot paved runway just down the road from Race Point Beach, a short taxi ride from the town center. Cape Air flies into

Provincetown from Boston on a daily basis. During the summer there are sightseeing flights. You can rent a car at Provincetown Airport through Enterprise, (508) 487-0009.

Other airports on Cape Cod are open to private planes:

BY BUS

There are buses running nearly every hour to Cape Cod and around the peninsula. Buses are a convenient way to take a day trip to Boston from Cape Cod if going in that direction interests you.

Plymouth & Brockton Street Railway Company (www.p-b.com) —P&B for short—provides hourly (sometimes half-hourly during certain times on weekdays), scheduled motorcoach service from Logan International Airport and downtown Boston to stops in Sagamore, Barnstable, and Hyannis. Plymouth and Rockland are also on this line.

To get to Barnstable or Hyannis from Boston, take the Plymouth & Brockton bus from Logan International Airport or downtown Boston (South Station Bus Terminal, 700 Atlantic Ave.).

Another option is Bonanza, now owned by Peter Pan, which operates a line that leaves Boston (both Logan and South Station) for stations in Barnstable, Bourne, Falmouth, and Woods Hole.

Bonanza/Peter Pan also addresses the needs of Cape-bound customers in New York City (Port Authority), Providence, Rhode Island (Kennedy Plaza and the Peter Pan Bonanza Terminal), Fall River (Nationwide Travel), and New Bedford (SRTA Terminal). These buses deposit passengers at stops in Barnstable, Bourne, Falmouth, Hyannis, and Woods Hole.

The Hyannis Transportation Center (www .capecodtransit.org), located at the intersection of Main Street and Center Street in downtown Hyannis, had its first full season of operation in 2003. It is the main hub for the Breeze buses and shuttles of the Cape Cod Regional Transportation Authority (see descriptions below), the Plymouth & Brockton buses, and Peter Pan/Bonanza buses. You can also book bicycles and taxis, or catch a shuttle to Provincetown. The center also has a

park-and-ride lot if you need to ditch your automobile for a while.

Cape transportation officials are trying to improve the practicality of public transportation, which already offers relatively low fares and decent service. Various beach shuttles are especially useful for tourists. Routes are described in more detail below, or you may consult www .smartguide.org, a Web site that provides information about car-free travel on the Cape.

B-BUS

**Hyannis Transportation Center,
215 Iyannough Rd., Hyannis
(508) 385-1430, (800) 352-7155**

Unique to the Cape is the B-Bus, a fleet of 33 minivans that will transport you door to door between any towns on the Cape Mon through Fri (and on weekends in some towns). Call in advance, between 11 a.m. and 5 p.m., to schedule a ride. Fees will be discussed when you schedule, but they are generally quite low.

PETER PAN BUS LINES, BONANZA DIVISION

**1 Bonanza Way, Providence, RI
(888) 331-7500 or (800) 343-9999
www.peterpanbus.com**

Peter Pan's Bonanza Division offers many daily trips from Boston to Barnstable, Bourne, Falmouth, and Woods Hole (you can hop a ferry from here to the islands). Connecting service to other points on the Cape is provided via the Plymouth & Brockton line, known locally as the P&B (see below). Peter Pan/Bonanza runs seven days a week, 365 days a year, with some seven trips a day from Boston's Logan International Airport and up to fourteen a day from South Station (downtown Boston). Tickets from Logan International Airport to Bourne run about $24 one-way and $42 round-trip. Peter Pan/Bonanza has local terminals at the following locations: Tedeschi Food Shop, 105 Trowbridge Rd., Bourne; Mobil Mart Store, 2155 Iyannough Rd., Barnstable; Steamship Authority Pier, Woods Hole Wharf, Woods Hole; Peter Pan Terminal, Bonanza Division, 59 Depot Ave., Falmouth; and the Hyannis Transportation Center, 215 Iyannough Rd., Hyannis.

PLYMOUTH & BROCKTON STREET RAILWAY CO.

8 Industrial Park Rd., Plymouth
(508) 746-0378
www.p-b.com

Plymouth & Brockton probably handles the most Cape travelers and commuters, as they service the entire US 6 stretch from Provincetown into Boston's South Station and on to Logan International Airport. From Logan International Airport to Hyannis, a one-way ticket runs $25 and round-trip fare is $45; from South Station the prices are $19 and $34, respectively. Traveling all the way to Provincetown from Logan International Airport costs $35; a round-trip ticket is $63. At Logan International Airport, your tickets may be purchased from the driver when boarding the bus. Reservations are not necessary. Ask about discounts for seniors and children. P&B also offers 10-ride commuter books at reduced rates. There are 12 bus stops on Cape Cod: Sagamore, Barnstable, Hyannis, Harwich, Orleans, Eastham, North Eastham, South Wellfleet, Wellfleet, Truro, North Truro, and Provincetown.

i Don't be fooled when you see a bumper sticker that reads CAPE COD CANAL TUNNEL PERMIT. There is no such tunnel. It's a local joke first developed in 1994 to cash in on naive tourists. Today there are three tunnel permit stickers in circulation that are almost identical and seen on vehicles throughout the Cape.

BY SHUTTLE

In the summertime, when the roads are busiest, several Cape towns offer shuttle rides to certain attractions, town centers, shopping centers, and area beaches. Passengers use them for plain old transportation and for sightseeing. You can flag one down at any point during a route, and you don't have to worry about getting tickets ahead of time because you can pay when you get on. All the shuttles we list below are run by the Cape Cod Regional Transit Authority, where you can also pick up a bus schedule. These are available at

local chambers of commerce too. See our Tours and Excursions chapter for more details.

BARNSTABLE VILLAGER BREEZE (YELLOW LINE)

Starting at the Hyannis Transportation Center, this year-round shuttle travels to the Barnstable County Complex, making stops at the Cape Cod Mall (see our Shopping chapter) and other shopping areas on Route 132 in downtown Hyannis. It also goes to the Barnstable Municipal Airport on request, and in summer months offers service to Barnstable Harbor, where passengers can catch a whale-watching boat (see our Whale Watching chapter).

CAPE COD REGIONAL TRANSIT AUTHORITY

Hyannis Transportation Center
215 Iyannough Rd., Hyannis
(800) 352-7155
www.capecodtransit.org

The CCRTA operates a number of shuttles in various towns, including Falmouth, Hyannis, Yarmouth, and Provincetown. Fares for fixed routes are $2 for adults and $1 for senior citizens and the disabled. Most of the shuttles are seasonal, but four color-coded routes are year-round: the Green Line (Hyannis to Orleans Breeze), the Yellow Line (Barnstable Villager Breeze), the Red Line (Hyannis Villager Breeze), and the Blue Line (the SeaLine Breeze). Below we describe the shuttles run by the CCRTA.

FALMOUTH'S WOODS HOLE WHOOSH TROLLEY

This ride takes in Main Street from the Falmouth Mall on Route 28 and goes right into Woods Hole, including the Woods Hole Steamship Authority, the aquarium, and the Shining Sea Bike Path. The service runs from the last weekend in May through the second weekend in October, with trolleys running daily from the last weekend in June through Labor Day. The fare is $2, or $1 for senior citizens and people with disabilities. Children five and younger, when accompanied by adults, ride for free. One-day $6 shuttle passes are available.

FLEX BUS

Anyone who's ever unsuccessfully run for a bus will appreciate the philosophy of Flex, a year-round mode of public transportation that answers to the needs of off-route passengers. Flex services main stops in seven Lower/Outer Cape towns (Harwich, Brewster, Orleans, Eastham, Wellfleet, Truro, and Provincetown), making occasional detours to in-between stops within ¾ of a mile of its usual route. Just call in advance for an off-route pickup or drop-off, or catch Flex at one of its regular stops and find out what all the buzz is about.

HYANNIS TO ORLEANS (H2O) BREEZE (GREEN LINE)

Between Hyannis and Orleans, there's "H2O," the Hyannis to Orleans Breeze that swings through West and South Yarmouth, West and South Dennis, Dennisport, Harwich Port, South Chatham, South Orleans, and Orleans. You can get on at regular stops or just flag the driver down. The entire round trip takes about an hour one-way.

HYANNIS VILLAGER BREEZE (RED LINE) AND HYANNIS BEACHES BREEZE

The Hyannis Villager Breeze traverses downtown en route to the Barnstable Senior Center, pausing for stops at Cape Cod Hospital, West End Rotary, and Star Market. In summer, this service is supplemented by the Hyannis Beaches Breeze, a seasonal shuttle with stops at Veterans Memorial Beach, Kalmus Beach, and the Hy-Line Cruises Ferry Dock.

ONSET WAREHAM LINK (OWL)

Greater Attleboro Taunton Regional Transit Authority (GATRA)
10 Oak St., Second Floor, Taunton
(508) 222-6106
www.gatra.org
In parts of Bourne and Buzzards Bay, bus service is provided by OWL, the Onset Wareham Link operated by the Greater Attleboro Taunton Regional Transit Authority (GATRA). Contrary to its name, OWL is no friend to the nocturnal, stopping at

6:30 p.m. on weekdays and 5:30 p.m. on Saturdays (no service on Sundays).

PROVINCETOWN/NORTH TRURO SHUTTLE

This is the most popular shuttle service on the Cape. It runs from the campgrounds in North Truro to Provincetown and Herring Cove Beach.

SEALINE BREEZE

A year-round bus service, the SeaLine runs between Hyannis and Falmouth, connecting with the Whoosh Trolley in summer and taking over the Woods Hole route when the Whoosh is not running. It makes stops in Centerville, Osterville, Marstons Mills, Mashpee Commons, South Cape Village, East Falmouth, Falmouth, and Woods Hole.

YARMOUTH TROLLEYBREEZE

This shuttle leaves the Hyannis Transportation Center and travels along Route 28, South Dennis, passing through Yarmouth to Seagull and Smugglers Beach.

BY BICYCLE

Cycling is a popular way to get around Cape Cod, especially in summer. One advantage is that the terrain is relatively flat. You can pedal through villages and towns or get away from vehicular traffic by taking one of the Cape's pretty bike trails (see our Biking section in the Hiking and Biking Trails chapter). The 28-mile Cape Cod Rail Trail, which follows the old rail beds, runs from South Dennis to Wellfleet and goes through Nickerson State Park. The Cape has dozens of bicycle rental businesses that can put you on two wheels; you can get mountain bikes, kid trailers, even bicycles built for two. Most bike rental places also sell bicycles, accessories, and parts, in addition to renting equipment such as helmets and child passenger seats.

Bicycling is a must on the islands during the summer, as well as in some towns on the Cape. The roads can get clogged, often bringing traffic to a standstill, especially on weekends and during special events. Falmouth, Chatham, and especially Provincetown are ideal for biking around, saving you the headache of finding a parking space.

BY RAIL

Years ago rail was the most common way to get to the Cape and to your town of choice. Today rail service is all but gone after Amtrak eliminated its Cape Codder line. Recent efforts at the local, state and federal level have inspired train buffs and transportation experts to imagine a day when regular passenger train service could return to the Cape. A remnant of the old Cape Codder line that runs from Hyannis to Sandwich hosts the Cape Cod Railroad for sightseeing trips with a dining car (see our Tours and Excursions chapter); it is a lovely ride that winds through cranberry bogs and woodlands through the untouched center of the Cape. The rail line is now maintained and operated by Massachusetts Coastal Railroad, whose president, John F. Kennedy—no direct relation to the president aside from having grown up in the same Hyannisport neighborhood—is a strong advocate for bringing more passenger service to the Cape. MassCoastal also operates the well-known "trash train" (Kennedy has chosen to rename it the "energy train"), which hauls most of the Cape's garbage to a waste to energy facility in Rochester.

BY BOAT

We've saved the best until last. Traveling to the Cape by water may be the most relaxing way to get here. Several ferry companies offer fast, reliable transportation between various ports to the Cape and islands. It is important to make a reservation, especially if you plan on crossing with your car, because ferries get booked in advance during peak season months. Summer reservations, for example, are often booked by early winter of the preceding year. There are last-minute cancellations, but be prepared to wait for hours. (Don't forget to book your return reservation as well.) All island-bound ferries offer sufficient pay-per-day parking.

BAY STATE CRUISE COMPANY
1200 Seaport Blvd., Boston
(877) 783-3779, (617) 748-1428
www.baystatecruises.com
Bay State Cruises offers two flavors of ferry service from Boston to Provincetown: fast and fun, or leisurely and fun. Choose the fast-ferry service aboard the *Provincetown III* if you are headed to P'town for, say, the weekend, and would rather unwind from the week on a smooth-sailing catamaran than the interstate. The *Provincetown III* offers three daily departures. Stake out a spot on the enclosed lower deck, with comfortable, climate-controlled seating, or choose the open upper deck (with windscreen) for a taste of sea breeze. Sailing time is 90 minutes to Provincetown. Those who think that getting there is half the fun might opt for the *Provincetown II*. It's Boston's largest passenger cruise ship and aims to evoke the grandeur of days of yore. Relax on the sundeck for the three-hour cruise while you plan the rest of your day in Provincetown. You'll have three hours to explore Provincetown if you just want a day trip, or you can buy one-way passage. Round-trip fares aboard the *Provincetown III* are $86 for adults, $82 for seniors, $58 for children, and $12 for bicycles. Aboard the *Provincetown II*, round-trip fares are $44 for adults, free for children, and $12 for bicycles.

CAPTAIN JOHN BOAT LINES
State Pier, off Water Street, Plymouth
(800) 225-4000(508) 747-2400
www.provincetownferry.com
If you can only spare time for a day trip, but you don't want to spend half your time in the car, this seasonal day-trip service from Plymouth to Provincetown may be perfect for you. Leave the State Pier in Plymouth and enjoy a narrated tour of the Plymouth Harbor, breakfast or drinks, and a one-and-a-half-hour sail across the bay. Once there, you are set free for five hours to explore Provincetown. You can't bring your car on the boat, but you can bring your bicycle along for $5. They offer one trip daily from mid-June through early Sept. It leaves Plymouth at 10 a.m. and returns at 6 p.m. Round-trip fare for adults is $40, seniors are $35, and children under 12 are $30.

FALMOUTH-EDGARTOWN FERRY
278 Scranton Ave., Falmouth
(508) 548-9400
www.falmouthferry.com
As the name implies, this ferry will take you directly to Edgartown (most ferry services take you to Oak Bluffs or Vineyard Haven). Sailing time aboard the *Pied Piper* is roughly one hour. They offer four round-trips daily in summer, with five on Friday. Mon through Thurs round-trip fares are $40 for adults, $25 for children 6 to 12, free for kids 5 and under, and $10 for bicycles. Fri through Sun round-trip fares for adults are $50, $30 for children 6 to 12, and free for children 5 and under. There is an $25-per-day parking charge. Reservations are recommended.

FREEDOM CRUISE LINE
702 Main St., Harwich Port
(508) 432-8999
www.nantucketislandferry.com
Sailing from Saquatucket Harbor in Harwich Port, Freedom Cruise Line offers daily passenger service to Nantucket, and you can bring along your bicycle and pet too. The trip takes about an hour and twenty minutes. A round-trip fare is $68 for adults and $51 for children; one-way fare is $39 for adults and $29 for children, children under 2 pay only $6 round-trip ($3 one-way), and bicycles are $12 round-trip. *Freedom* is an 80-passenger ferry, so reservations are recommended for day trips. There are also restrictions on how many "overnighters" the line can leave on the island, so reservations are necessary. There is free parking for day-trippers.

i Even if you're taking a ferry ride on an overcast day, be sure to wear layers and sunscreen. Even if you can't see the sun, you could be burned by the glare off the water—and the wind is certain to be chillier than it is on shore.

HY-LINE CRUISES
22 Channel Point Rd., Hyannis
(508) 778-2600, (800) 492-8082
www.hy-linecruises.com
Hy-Line offers a year-round high-speed ferry between Hyannis and Martha's Vineyard. The trip takes about an hour, with scheduled departures throughout the day, seven days a week. In season (late May to late Oct), a round-trip fare for Hyannis to Martha's Vineyard costs $69 for adults and $48 for children ages 5 to 12 (free for children four and under with boarding passes). The company also services the Hyannis to Nantucket route and offers interisland service between Nantucket and Martha's Vineyard. It takes less than two hours to journey by ferry from Hyannis to Nantucket. Round-trip fare is $43 for adults and $22 for children. Hy-Line's High Speed Ferry, the *Grey Lady*, makes the crossing from Hyannis to Nantucket in about an hour, and a round-trip ticket costs $75 for passengers 12 and older and $51 for children ages 5 to 12. It's a good idea to call ahead for reservations, especially if you plan to travel during a holiday weekend or during July and Aug. Ferries leave from Dock One, Ocean Street, Hyannis.

ISLAND QUEEN
75 Falmouth Heights Rd., Falmouth
(508) 548-4800
www.islandqueen.com
For $18 round-trip ($9 for children), you can take the 600-passenger *Island Queen* from Falmouth Harbor to Martha's Vineyard from Memorial Day weekend to Columbus Day. The trip is a leisurely 35 minutes each way, and food service is available on board, along with a full bar. The passenger-only vessel makes seven trips each day in summer, and reservations are not needed. The *Island Queen* is also available for charters. This ferry service does not take credit cards.

THE STEAMSHIP AUTHORITY
Woods Hole Wharf, Woods Hole
(508) 477-8600
(508) 693-9130 for vehicle reservations
(508) 495-3278 for high-speed ferry passenger reservations
www.steamshipauthority.com
The Steamship Authority is the only company offering year-round ferry service from Woods Hole to points on Martha's Vineyard, and from

Hyannis to Nantucket. It's also the only ferry that transports cars. Keep in mind that taking your car to the islands can be very expensive, and it's usually not necessary because you can rent one upon your arrival. Better yet rent a bicycle or moped (see our Martha's Vineyard and Nantucket chapters). We advise you to check the schedule for boat departures as they change seasonally. The one-way fare from Woods Hole to Martha's Vineyard is $7.50 for adults, $4.00 for children ages 5 to 12, and free for children younger than 5. Ferry service from Hyannis to Nantucket costs $14.00 one-way for adults, $7.25 for kids (5 to 12), and is free for those under 5. The Steamship Authority also offers a Fast Ferry to Nantucket from Hyannis and the cost is $65 round trip for adults, $49 for kids (5 to 12), and is free for those under 5.

VINEYARD FAST FERRY
Roger Williams Way, Quonset Point, North Kingstown, RI
(401) 295-4040
www.vineyardfastferry.com
If you're headed directly to Martha's Vineyard and want to avoid traffic congestion on the Cape, look into this seasonal fast-ferry service. It's ideal for vacationers coming from southern New England who would rather spend ninety minutes making the trip by water than waiting for hours in traffic. The dock at Quonset Point is roughly 15 miles from T. F. Green International Airport in Providence, Rhode Island, 15 miles from the Amtrak terminal in Kingston, Rhode Island, and about eight minutes from I-95. You'll ride aboard *The Millennium*, a 110-foot, high-speed, three-deck catamaran with sundeck seating, a climate-controlled interior, and a full-service bar. In season, two daily round-trips are scheduled for Mon through Thurs, four on Fri, and three on Sat and Sun. Schedules change according to seasons and holidays, to be sure to check their Web site before making a reservation. Round-trip fares are $69 for adults, $46 for children (4 to 12), $12 for infants (3 and under), $69 for seniors (60 and over), and $12 for bikes and surfboards for the 90-minute trip from Quonset to Oak Bluffs. There is a $10 charge to park your car. Reservations are strongly recommended.

HISTORIC CAPE COD

Open the pages of any American history book, and you will read the Cape's story, from the Viking explorations on these shores nearly one thousand years ago to the landing of the Pilgrims in Provincetown in 1620. Here was the first Thanksgiving, when a peace treaty was signed between the Wampanoag tribe and Plymouth governor John Carver, and the Pilgrims gave thanks for their first year in the New World. Here, on this curved sandbar, the seeds of democracy were sown when the Pilgrims, anchored in Provincetown Harbor, signed the Mayflower Compact, a precursor to the Constitution.

The Cape's harbors resonate with salty tales of sea captains and whaling merchants, pirates and moon-cussers. Writers such as Henry David Thoreau, John Hay, and Henry Beston have described the wonder and mystery of the Cape's natural beauty and its changing seasons. And the glamour and controversy of the Kennedy era, of Hyannisport and Chappaquiddick, have added to its allure.

The old times may have gone, but the legacy of Cape Cod remains visible everywhere. At any town meeting you will see that the Cape's history is of paramount importance to the Cape Codders who continue to fight for their identity, their independence, and the preservation of the Cape's natural environment and recognition of its unique heritage.

PEOPLE OF THE FIRST LIGHT

The history of the Wampanoag Indians—the word Wampanoag means "People of the dawn or first light"—far predates exploration of these sandy shores by Europeans. Some theories suggest that their ancestors traveled from Asia to North America via the Bering Strait at the end of the ice age. Others, because there is no linguistic link, dispel that idea. The best guess is that Native American Indians arrived upon this newly formed land about 10,000 years ago. We do know that somewhere between 7,000 and 9,000 years ago, a small band of Native Americans came to the eastern shore of the Upper Mill Pond in Brewster. In 1987, archaeologist Fred Dunford from the Cape Cod Museum of Natural History uncovered artifacts at this prehistoric archaeological site that have placed the native inhabitants in the Stony Brook Valley firmly within the Middle Archaic Period.

Ancestors of the present-day Mashpee Wampanoag were Algonquin-speaking people who shared cultural traditions with a number of groups in southern New England under the name of Massachusetts-Narragansett. As members of the Algonquin Indian Nation, the Wampanoag Indians of the Cape were broken down into five major tribes: Nausets of the Lower Cape; South Sea in the Barnstable and Mashpee areas; Suconessets of Falmouth; Shaumes of Sandwich; and the Manamets in the Bourne and Sagamore areas. These tribes were further broken down into subtribes, such as the Nobscusset Indians of Dennis, who were members of the Nauset tribe.

THE VIKINGS

There are many tales of Norse explorers arriving in this area beginning more than a thousand years ago, but there has yet to be definitive proof of such exploration. One such legend tells that Norsemen visited the Cape and islands around

i The Pilgrims were actually headed for the northern Virginia territory, which at the time stretched up to near the Hudson River, before they were forced to steer northward by ocean storms.

A.D. 986, though they did not make landfall. Bjarni Herjulfsson was the little-known explorer who made the journey, and if the story is true, then he discovered America about 500 years before Columbus. Upon his return to his native Iceland, Herjulfsson told his story, and it became incorporated into Norse lore. One of those listening to the tales was Leif Ericson, son of Eric the Red. Around the year 1000, Leif borrowed his father's ship and sailed south, past Newfoundland and Nova Scotia, to arrive at what some historians believe was Cape Cod. The story goes that he sailed his vessel up a river that flowed in two directions, possibly Bass River, and made his camp at an inland lake where he could anchor his vessel, possibly Follins Pond at the head of Bass River in Yarmouth/Dennis. Despite these explorations, however, Native Americans were the sole inhabitants of the area until the 1600s.

The first recorded description of these people was provided by Giovanni di Verrazzano, who, in 1524, spent several weeks exploring the area between Block Island and Buzzards Bay. "These people are the most beautiful and have the most civil customs that we have found on this voyage," Verrazzano wrote. "They are very generous and give away all they have. We made great friends with them and they painted and decorated their faces with various colors, showing us that it was a sign of happiness."

OTHER EARLY EXPLORERS

In 1602 the English explorer Bartholomew Gosnold landed at a number of places along the Cape and islands and discovered the treacherous shoals that guarded the easternmost section of the Cape. Gosnold and his crew chose one of the Elizabeth Islands off Woods Hole to establish a settlement, but it failed shortly thereafter. He noted that game, fish, and berries were plentiful, and they traded with Native Americans for tobacco, deerskins, and fish.

By far the most complete description of Indian life on the Cape comes from the journal of Samuel de Champlain, who in 1606 paid an extended visit to the area. He sailed along the

coast approaching Cape Cod from the north and followed the shoreline, recording the depth of the bays and the features of the land, finally anchoring in Stage Harbor, Chatham. It seems that Champlain felt less admiration for the Native Americans, because his party had several conflicts with the natives, resulting in the death of at least one sailor.

THE PILGRIMS

It was not until November 1620 that European explorers would try again to settle this virgin outpost. This was the month that the *Mayflower* arrived in Provincetown Harbor. The ship had been headed for Virginia, but was blown off course and landed well north of its intended destination. We call the voyagers Pilgrims, but they called themselves Separatists. The religious movement that brought them to America began in 14th-century England and was based on the premise that no man needed a priest between himself and God, no person should be involved in ritualistic worship, and everyone was under the obligation to lead his life as simply as possible.

After the *Mayflower* anchored in Provincetown Harbor and before explorations were initiated, the Mayflower Compact, a charter for a democratic settlement, was signed on board on November 11, 1620. Led by Captain Myles Standish, a group explored the coast and voyaged southward, coming ashore across the bay on the sand flats of Eastham, where they first encountered Indians. Today the beach is still called First Encounter Beach, to signify the spot where shots were fired and arrows launched. The Pilgrims rejected Provincetown as a place

i Three *Mayflower* passengers lie in Eastham's Old Cove Cemetery, located about a mile north of the Orleans-Eastham rotary on US 6. The graveyard is on the right just after Shore Road. Here you can see legible gravestones dating from the 1700s. Gravestone rubbing is not permitted without permission of the Eastham Historical Society. Call (508) 240-1247.

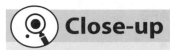 **Close-up**

The Cape Cod Canal

When William Bradford and Myles Standish were exploring the area around Plymouth in 1626, they discovered that two rivers, the Manomet on Buzzards Bay and the Scusset on Cape Cod Bay, were separated by only a short distance of land. The Pilgrims realized the advantage to trade and transportation of digging a canal that would connect the two bodies of water; however, the idea was not acted upon. In 1776, General George Washington, hoping to avoid a British blockade and to enhance security, sent an engineer to conduct the first feasible study of the area, but still no canal was constructed.

Well into the late 1800s, attempts to organize this mammoth construction project continued to be thwarted until 1904, when New York financier Augustus Belmont considered the project. He purchased the Boston, Cape Cod and New York Canal Company. By July 1907 his newly formed Cape Cod Construction Company moved its first shovelful of dirt, and digging was under way. Over the next seven years, the men and machinery removed earth. In 1912, two large dredges began digging toward each other from Bourne and Sandwich.

Workers completed the Buzzards Bay Railroad Bridge in September 1910 and finished the two vehicle bridges within the next two years. The finished canal became the world's widest sea-level canal at 480 feet across. It was 17.4 miles long and 34 feet deep. On July 29, 1914, exactly seven years to the day since work first began, the Cape Cod Canal officially opened, heralded by a parade of ships and boats, among them Augustus Belmont's private 80-foot yacht and the U.S. Navy destroyer *McDougall,* which carried Assistant Secretary of the Navy Franklin Delano Roosevelt. The Cape Cod Canal beat the opening of the Panama Canal by 17 days.

In 1915, canal traffic numbered more than 2,600 vessels, but it never achieved the volume of traffic that Belmont had hoped for. When a German submarine attacked and sank the *Perth Amboy* off Nauset Beach in Orleans, President Woodrow Wilson ordered a readily compliant Belmont to permit the government to operate the canal. Eventually, Belmont sold the canal to the American government for $11.5 million, and the Army Corps of Engineers took charge of its operation and maintenance. Although the canal was technically a success, it never brought the commercial prosperity to Upper Cape towns that its planners anticipated.

During the Great Depression the National Industrial Recovery Act of 1933 provided $4.6 million to build the present three bridges, employing some 700 workers for two years. These modern bridges were completed in 1935. The Bourne and Sagamore Bridges, with a span of 616 feet, became among the longest continuous truss bridges in North America. The railroad bridge, at 544 feet, remains the third-longest vertical-lift drawbridge on the continent. You can admire the workmanship of the bridges from the 7-mile paved service road that lines both sides of the canal.

If you are taking a boat ride through the Cape Cod Canal, you'll move along at a good clip in the direction of the tide but seem to be fighting an uphill battle when you go against it. One reason for this is that Cape Cod Bay waters are about 5 feet higher than Buzzards Bay waters, so a tremendous current is created as they merge and flow through the narrow passageway. Average high-tide waters move through the canal at 4 to 5 miles per hour. When high tides are accentuated by a full moon or other conditions, the water's speed can reach more than 7 miles per hour.

If you'd like to learn more about the canal, take a tour of the Corps of Engineers Field Office on Academy Drive in Buzzards Bay (508-759-4431), or stop by the visitor center at 60 Ed Moffitt Dr. in Sandwich. If you wish to read about the canal, we recommend *The Cape Cod Canal* by Robert Farson.

to settle because, despite the vast harbor, there was no readily available fresh water. They traveled across Cape Cod Bay as far as Plymouth, where they found a protected harbor with high ground overlooking it, suitable for a permanent settlement.

Most versions of American history start with the Pilgrims' arrival at Plymouth Rock on Christmas Day in 1620. But the hostile greeting they received from the Indians near Eastham suggests earlier activity in the area: It's thought that the Indians were retaliating, presumably for the Pilgrims' previous pilfering of corn reserves at a site in Truro now known as Corn Hill. One thing we do know: The Pilgrims would return to Cape Cod again and again. Many of these early settlers were instrumental in preparing the way for the settlement of the earliest towns in Sandwich and Eastham. Meanwhile, the Native American Indians were a race already in decline. Epidemics of smallpox, introduced by other groups of explorers just three or four years before the arrival of the Pilgrims, had reduced their ranks considerably. Natives unwittingly handed over large tracts of land for a pittance, not realizing their marks on the white man's strange parchment spelled out their demise.

Religion played a large role in the settlement of different towns. Though most of the earliest settlers were Congregationalists, there were also Quakers among them and, later, Methodists and Baptists. Though these settlers left other places to land here in search of religious freedom, many of them found themselves embroiled in the same old religious arguments. When the settlers were not arguing about religion, they were squabbling over land and debating where one person's property ended and another's began. With the building of a meetinghouse and the hiring of a minister to preach, a handful of families would form an application for incorporation. The church spurred incorporation, and incorporation spurred more settlers, and thus the towns were born and grew and prospered.

UPPER CAPE

Bourne

It was in Bourne that the Pilgrims established their first trading post in 1627. In a paradox of sorts, this township is both the oldest and the newest town on the Cape. Originally settled as part of Sandwich (established 1687), the present town of Bourne was incorporated in 1884, when it broke away from Sandwich after some two-and-a-half centuries of dissension. It is named for Jonathan Bourne, a prominent citizen who made his fortune and reputation in the whaling industry.

A largely agricultural and fishing community, Bourne's motions for separation from Sandwich never seemed to pass at town meetings, so aggrieved citizens in the outlying villages petitioned the state legislature. Because these areas attracted prominent summer visitors from New York, New Jersey, and Boston, there was no lack of advice and influence. When the towns separated, Sandwich lost its warm-water coast, harbors, shellfish beds on Buzzards Bay, and a number of industries, such as Keith & Ryder, which made stagecoaches and railroad cars.

One of the most important events of Bourne history was the building of the Cape Cod Canal and the Bourne Bridge, which spans this man-made waterway. The idea of building a canal was first raised by Governor William Bradford of Plymouth. He had noticed that the Manomet River from the south and Scusset Creek from the north nearly cut through the neck of the peninsula of Cape Cod. Indeed, local Indians took advantage of these waterways to traverse the Cape, carrying their canoes the short distance in between the two rivers. In 1627, the Plymouth settlers established Aptucxet Trading Post on the banks of the Manomet River for the purpose of trading with the Dutch from New Amsterdam (New York) to the south as well as with Indians in the area. The trading post was closed in the late 1650s (see our Attractions chapter for more information), but the idea of a canal resurfaced again and again. General Washington inquired about such a waterway during the American Revolution. The building of a canal would make the trip from New York to Boston by sea so much quicker and safer: A huge number of ships were shipwrecked around the treacherous shores of Cape Cod and the islands. Various plans were presented throughout the 19th century, but it was not until the early 20th century that shovel moved dirt and the canal was dug. (See the Close-up on the canal in this chapter.)

Like most Cape towns, Bourne consisted mostly of farmers and fishermen in the early years and, in the 19th century, industrial workers, who labored at grist and flour mills, a comb and button factory, and lumbering. Trade necessitated transportation, and the coming of the railroad to Buzzards Bay in the 19th century spawned a tourist industry that still thrives today, though passenger service from off-Cape is now defunct. The villages of Bourne were popular with wealthy people who summered there and built handsome estates along the beautiful shore. President Grover Cleveland purchased a summer house called Gray Gables, where he would come to relax and escape the pressures of Washington. Cleveland was an avid sportsman and loved hunting and fishing on the Cape with his good friend, renowned 19th-century actor Joseph Jefferson, who owned a summer home called the Crow's Nest on Buttermilk Bay.

Sandwich

The very first of Cape Cod's 15 towns to be incorporated was Sandwich, settled in 1637, when permission was granted to Edmund Freeman of Saugus to establish a settlement comprising 60 families. In that year, Freeman and nine other men from Saugus, north of Boston, arrived to tame this area known as Manomet, which was close to the Aptucxet Trading Post in what is now Bourne. These 10 men became known as the "10 men of Saugus" and were joined by some 30 other families from Plymouth, Lynn, and Duxbury.

Pilgrims Myles Standish and John Alden journeyed down from Plymouth in 1639 to establish the bounds of this growing settlement. The town became incorporated with the name of Sandwich because a number of its residents had originally come from Sandwich, England. At the time, the new township of Sandwich also included all the land that would later become Bourne.

The first settlers were largely Congregationalists, but Quakers came to town shortly afterward, seeking converts. Some settlers did convert, but the Quakers were persecuted in town, and many left for other parts. Pockets of Quakers remained in Sandwich, however, to take their place in the town's history, and are still there.

The earliest settlers were chiefly farmers who raised cattle and sheep. Because Sandwich lacked an adequate harbor, the maritime history of the town was limited to local fishing and reaping the harvest of the occasional beached whale. Local sailors and ship captains typically sailed from ports of other towns, such as neighboring Barnstable and Falmouth, each of which had good harbors. Sandwich did contribute with its share of saltworks, but the town remained mainly a farming community, earning its living from the soil rather than the sea.

The 19th century brought change and unthinkable prosperity to Sandwich. In 1825, Deming Jarves established the Boston and Sandwich Glass Works, which he figured would utilize two of Sandwich's more abundant natural resources: sand and trees. Unfortunately, the sand was found to be the wrong type for producing the glass Jarves had in mind. Sand had to be imported to Sandwich! By 1850, the plant employed 500 workers and was producing a half-ton of glassware each week. Besides standard glassware, the company also created artistic pieces. Jarves enticed some of the world's greatest glassmakers to relocate from Europe to Sandwich to fashion these intricate, decorative works of art.

The same year glassmaking came to Sandwich, Keith & Ryder opened for business to produce wagons, stagecoaches, and, later, railroad freight trains. This highly successful company remained in business for 102 years, employing many Sandwich residents, and produced the vehicles that helped America expand westward.

The 1880s saw Sandwich's future grow dim. In 1884, Bourne and her six villages separated from Sandwich, taking away residential tax dollars as well as the Keith & Ryder company. Four years later, in 1888, the major blow came when the glass company closed its doors because of competition. People were out of work, and Sandwich's economy crumbled. The ripple effect closed local businesses, which in turn put more people out of work, closing more businesses. A number of people moved away to start over elsewhere.

Fortunately, Sandwich has survived intact and remains a charming village that attracts many visitors with its numerous historical buildings. Visitors also come to see the Sandwich Glass Museum (see our Attractions chapter), which traces the history of the town's glassworks and displays one of the largest collections of blown, pressed, cut, and engraved Sandwich glass in the United States.

Falmouth

Falmouth was officially settled in 1660 by a dozen families led by Isaac Robinson and John Hatch, both Barnstable Congregationalists fed up with the religious persecutions of the day, particularly of Quakers. The original name for this area was the Indian term Suckanesset, or Succonessitt, which translated as "black clam" or "the place of the black shells." In 1690, the town was renamed Falmouth after an English seaport.

Falmouth was the site of a handful of small battles with the British during both the American Revolutionary War and the War of 1812, and in each case the Falmouth men prevailed. During the American Revolution, Falmouth was one of the few Cape towns fired on by the British. In 1779, the British attempted to loot the town of its supplies and weaponry, but their advances were repelled. Frustrated, the British decided to teach the Falmouth patriots a lesson by burning their town. The marauders were met by 200 members of the Cape militia, who prevented an attack. One year earlier, the waters off Falmouth saw perhaps the first naval victory in American

history. The British had been offshore capturing Falmouth ships, ransacking them, and confiscating their supplies. Colonel Joseph Dimmick, who had been training the Falmouth militia on the village green, took three whaleboats out against the British navy and won back a schooner that the British had hijacked.

During another war, in 1814, the British ship *Nimrod* sailed into waters off Falmouth. Its captain demanded the town's cannons, which were positioned in the village square. Captain Weston Jenkins of the Falmouth militia flatly refused to comply, and the pages of history state that his reply to the British was, "Come and get 'em!" This, of course, prompted heavy fire, and a number of buildings in town were hit, including the Elm Arch Inn and the Nimrod Inn. Both establishments proudly wear their battle scars today—a cannonball-size hole still exists in a wall at the Nimrod Inn.

The town was ideally suited to fishing and farming and a whaling fleet was based in Woods Hole, where there remains a stone building on Water Street that once made candles from spermaceti whale oil. Shipbuilding was an important maritime trade, and at one point Falmouth's 300 households included 148 headed by sea captains.

Agriculture thrived here, and cranberries and strawberries were leading crops. In fact, around the turn of the 20th century, Falmouth was the leading producer of strawberries east of the Mississippi. (Many Cape Verdeans who had come from the Portuguese islands off the coast of Africa to work in the fishing and whaling industry sought agricultural work here and eventually settled in the area.) Salt harvested from seawater was also an important "crop."

Falmouth set aside its village green in 1749 as common land for the town's 600 residents. Once used for grazing livestock and military training, the expanse now adds charm as well as its proud history to the town.

Across the street from the village green is the First Congregational Church, built in 1708. Its 807-pound bell was made by Paul Revere and cost the town of Falmouth $338.94. Falmouth is also home to Nobska Light, built in 1828; Marine Biological Laboratory, established in 1888; and Woods Hole Oceanographic Institution, established in the late 1930s.

Mashpee

The history of Mashpee reflects the white man's attempt to allow the native Indians of the area to "own" their own village and manage their own affairs. Though these intentions were probably good ones, in truth it is a tale of one race trying to decide what another race wants. The results, though not completely disastrous, were at best off the mark.

Centuries before the Pilgrims landed in Provincetown, the Wampanoag Federation was well established in southeastern Massachusetts. The federation consisted of approximately 30 tribes of peaceful people who had a complex social structure. These native Indians grew crops, hunted, fished, traded amongst themselves. Among these people, the Massipees of the South Sea tribe lived in the vicinity of the present town of Mashpee.

The town's history is complex and very different from the other 15 Cape towns', because it is the only one in which native people acquired legal title to their lands. As white settlers began to hoodwink the Indians out of their native lands, three missionary ministers stepped forward to level the playing field. Those men were Samuel Treat in Eastham, Thomas Tupper in Bourne, and Richard Bourne in Mashpee. Though not an ordained minister, Bourne arrived in Mashpee in 1660 in an attempt to convert the natives to Christianity and establish a native Indian church. Bourne had the background, contacts, and desire to help native people establish the "Kingdome of Marshpee." He concluded early on that the only way to gain rights for the Indians was to persuade them to adopt some of the white man's ways, primarily the church and an understanding of their law.

The year 1684 saw the building of the present Indian Meeting House (see the Attractions chapter), now standing as the Cape's oldest church. In 1685, the year of Bourne's death, the General Court voted that no property within the plantation could be sold without the consent of the native residents. Despite this, the Native Americans were not prepared for self-government within an essentially foreign society, and the overseer system imposed by Plymouth virtually made the natives slaves on their own lands. In the 1700s, the tribe numbers dropped critically. In 1767, the area had 21 shingled homes, 52 wigwams, and 291 people; 100 years later, the population stood at 331 people. During the American Revolution 70 Mashpee Indians were killed fighting against the British.

Throughout the remainder of the 18th and 19th centuries, the town of Mashpee sought its freedom from the oversight of Plymouth. Assisting in that cause were Indian pastors Blind Joe Amos and William Apes. In 1834, the district of Mashpee was established, but the overseer system remained in effect. Immigration in the form of blacks, natives of the Cape Verde Islands off the coast of Africa, and even captured Hessian soldiers who had fought with the British in the American Revolution added to the bloodlines and began to reduce the numbers of pure-bred Indians. Finally, in 1870, Mashpee was incorporated as the Cape's 14th town.

Freedom was still something to be achieved, despite the incorporation. Advisory boards, convinced that the natives could not manage their affairs, continued to meddle. The last of these advisory councils finally released its grip in 1970, the year of the town's centennial celebration. After years of effort the tribe finally received federal recognition in 2007. Since that time attempts by the tribe to open a gambling casino on land purchased in Middleboro, Massachusetts, have moved forward in fits and starts. In the past several years the tribe has also been racked by scandal. In May 2009 the former tribal chairman Glenn Marshall was sentenced to 41 months in federal prison for embezzlement and fraud.

Indian heritage is still a central part of Mashpee, and those who want to learn about it can visit the Indian Museum and Tribal Council on Route 130 (currently under renovation), the Indian church and cemetery on Route 28, and the town archives on Great Neck Road. Or you can attend the Pow Wow in July (see our Annual Events chapter). Plimouth Plantation in Plymouth is also a good source of information on the culture of the Wampanoag people.

i The town of Mashpee was originally set aside by the Plymouth Colony as an Indian village and designated as a plantation for the Wampanoag Indians displaced by the settlers building towns on their ancestral lands. Today you can visit the Archives Building, home of the Mashpee Historical Commission. For more information, contact the Mashpee Chamber of Commerce at (508) 477-0792.

MID-CAPE

Barnstable

Barnstable was one of the first three town settled on the Cape, incorporated in 1639 along with Sandwich and Yarmouth. Named for Barnstaple, England (the colonists were not known for their spelling), the town's many place names actually reflect the early presence of Native Americans of various tribes. The villages of Cotuit, Cummaquid, and Hyannis can trace their names to Indian roots. Hyannis, for example, is named for Iyanough (also spelled Iyannough, or Iyanno, or a number of other ways), the Cummaquid sachem who extended kind hospitality to early settlers. His grave, off Route 6A in Cummaquid along the north shore of Barnstable, is marked (look for the sign), and a bronze statue of him stands at the village green on Main Street in Hyannis.

Another statue in town is of statesman and patriot James Otis Jr. It stands in front of the Barnstable County Courthouse on Route 6A in Barnstable Village, in sharp contrast to the statue of Iyannough in the southern village. Though each man came from the same land, they lived in two entirely different worlds. The relationship between these two cultures was summarized well by local historian Donald Trayser, who observed, "Fear of the Indians was natural, but on the Cape unjustified." Even during the King Philip War of 1676–77, which saw Massachusetts and Rhode Island Indians fighting against white settlers, relations between white settlers and the Cape Indians remained friendly.

Though the first white man to settle in the area was a parson, John Hull of Weymouth, Massachusetts, the founding of Barnstable in 1639 is credited to the Reverend John Lothrop, a Congregational minister who had been persecuted and imprisoned in England before emigrating to America with 25 followers. The group originally settled in Scituate, and within five years moved to Barnstable, then known as Mattakeese, where the vast salt marshes at Great Marsh offered unlimited food and bedding for livestock. The settlement originally stretched as far west as to include Falmouth. The southern part of the town was settled in 1660, in the area of the village of Hyannis. In 1685, the county of Barnstable was established, with the town of Barnstable serving as the county seat. At the point of the town's bicentennial celebration in 1839, there were 4,000 residents. Imagine, a bicentennial in 1839, when 24 states had yet to be admitted to the Union!

Along Route 6A in Barnstable Village you can view a historic marker at Sacrament Rock, the site of the first communion served by Rev. Lothrop to his congregation. Unfortunately, the historic rock was dynamited to make way for Route 6A, but it has been cemented back together complete with historical plaque and relocated on the side of the road in Barnstable Village. Not far away is Lothrop Cemetery, where the good reverend's remains became one with the earth many years ago.

Another marker on Route 6A identifies the home of Thomas Hinckley, an original settler of Barnstable who was a colonial governor in 1681. Barnstable is distinguished by a number of individuals and families who influenced the region and, in some cases, the nation. A marker in West Barnstable shows the home of James Otis, a chief justice of the State Court during the Revolutionary War. His son, James Otis Jr., was credited with delivering a speech that set the stage for the great rebellion. He participated in many significant events in colonial history, such as protests against the Stamp Act and the Townshend Acts, and was a good friend of John Adams.

At the intersection of Routes 149 and 6A in West Barnstable is a cemetery containing the grave of Captain "Mad Jack" Percival, one of Barnstable's most famous citizens. Percival was captain of the warship *Constitution* ("Old Ironsides") from 1844 to 1847. The famous vessel is now on permanent display in Boston Harbor.

Like the other Mid-Cape towns, Barnstable was settled by farmers. In addition to livestock, early farmers raised corn, rye, onions, and flax. By the 19th century fishing, shipping, and coastal trading were the foundation of its economy. The town boasted some 800 shipmasters, 104 in the village of Centerville alone. Osterville's Crosby Boatyard is famous for the Cape Cod catboat designed there. The West Barnstable Brick Company was active from 1860 to 1927, producing 100,000 bricks a day.

Cobb's Hill West Cemetery in Barnstable is the burial site of many of the early families in the area, and the West Parish church built in 1717 along Route 149 in West Barnstable stands as a proud monument to the world of 18th-century Cape Codders.

Yarmouth

Next time you're feeling sorry for yourself, think about one of Yarmouth's founding fathers, Anthony Thatcher. Here was a man who lost everything, only to rebuild his life over again and again, and in the process help to build a town. Before leaving England he lost his first wife and five of his nine children. Remarried, he and his wife and his four remaining children set sail for the New World in 1635. Though they arrived without mishap, a subsequent boat ride from Ipswich to Marblehead ended in the loss of his four children. Of all those on board, only he and his wife survived. With everything lost, the Thatchers arrived at Yarmouth in 1639 to found that town along with Thomas Howes and John Crow. John Thatcher, Anthony Thatcher's son, born in 1638 at Ipswich, would father 21 children to help populate the new township. His house is

directly across the street from the Yarmouthport Post Office on Route 6A.

The lands of Yarmouth had long been settled by Indian of the Mattakeese and Nobscusset tribes before Pilgrim Stephen Hopkins came south from Plymouth to build a house here in 1638. The new town, which was most likely named for Great Yarmouth in England, was originally a huge area encompassing the present town of Yarmouth and Dennis. With its salt marshes, thick woodlands, and rich soil, the north side was settled first. Lands were quickly acquired from the Indians, and a sturdy community began to grow. The Indians found themselves being boxed in, and areas were set aside for them at Long Pond, Scargo Lake, and along Bass River and Parker River. Burial grounds at Long Pond and Scargo Lake are marked with plaques; the one at Long Pond reads: ON THIS SLOPE LIE BURIED THE LAST NATIVE INDIANS OF YARMOUTH.

Yarmouth was a farming community in the 18th century and was renowned later for its maritime activity until the locomotives came to Cape Cod and the age of steam eclipsed the age of sail. Many ships from Yarmouth were engaged in the Indo-China trade. Secum and Taylor shipbuilders built the legendary *Red Jacket,* which made a record transatlantic crossing in 13 days.

Saltworks and cordage works sprung up on the Bass River. Settled by a Quaker named David Kelly, South Yarmouth became known as Quaker Village or Friends Village, and the townsfolk erected a meetinghouse there around 1809. Though other towns were less tolerant of Quakers, Yarmouth eventually accepted the "heretics," and their settlement played a large part in the development of the town. As early as 1721, and east parish of the Yarmouth Congregational Church was established in the area now known as Dennis. In 1793, this east parish, all of Yarmouth east of the Bass River, separated from the town to become the town of Dennis.

With many of the 650 buildings in the town's two historic districts on the National Register of Historic Places, Yarmouth is an architectural historian's dream. The age of the area and the sophistication of its residents are reflected in its varied architectural styles: Federal, Gothic, Greek Revival, and Victorian. Of course, the traditional Cape house—full Cape, half-Cape, and three-quarters Cape—is well represented along the historic routes.

A final note on Yarmouth: It seems it also has a chapter in the Norse sagas. As the tale goes, Leif Ericson's brother Thorvald visited these shores at the beginning of the 11th century and met up with Indians at Bass Hole in the northern part of Yarmouth. In a battle with the Indians, Thorvald was killed and buried at the beach. Thorvald's grave has never been found.

Dennis

To understand the early history of the town of Dennis, you must first study the history of Yarmouth, for Dennis was settled as part of Yarmouth in 1639. Of Old Yarmouth's three earliest settlers, Anthony Thatcher, Thomas Howes, and John Crow, two of the three—Howes and Crow—settled in what would later become Dennis. In 1721, the east parish of Yarmouth was established in the area now known as Dennis Village, and four years later a minister came to this east precinct of Yarmouth to become the church's preacher. That young minister was Rev. Josiah Dennis, a Harvard graduate who was born in Northern Ireland and arrived in Massachusetts around the year 1700 at the age of seven. Josiah Dennis would preach at the east church until his death in 1763. His successor, Nathan Stone, was the minister at the time of the separation from Yarmouth and the town's incorporation in 1793. It was suggested that the new township be named Dennis in honor of its first minister, rather than Nobscusset for the Indians of the area. Coincidentally, the last Nobscusset Indian died in 1793, the year of incorporation.

Many of the early residents had been farmers in England and were attracted to the area by the abundance of salt-marsh hay for their cattle. Early settlers practiced shore whaling and utilized "drift whales" that floated ashore. As whale oil became more valuable, whales were methodically pursued. Watch houses were built at Sesuit

and Nobscusset harbors to provide an alert when the great creatures were in the bay. Long boats were sent out, and the whales were herded into shallow water, where they became stranded. As whaling grew into an industry, harpooning, a skill developed in Scandinavia, was employed from boats offshore.

Around the time of the American Revolution, large-scale farming dropped off for lack of land, and many people moved to western Massachusetts. As the deepwater harbors of Nantucket and New Bedford began to dominate the whaling industry, Dennis turned to fishing, coastal trading, and shipbuilding. Fishing wharves lined the southern coastline, and Dennisport basked in the sweet aroma of fish drying. Some 400 shipmasters hailed from the town. Shiverick Shipyards in East Dennis produced eight magnificent clipper ships, all of which were recognized in the Golden Age of Sail. Mastered and crewed largely by Dennis men, these vessels helped to open up routes to the Orient and brought much fame and fortune to the town and its residents. Important as a fast means of transportation, particularly around Cape Horn during the California Gold Rush, these hardworking vessels were often in service for 25 to 30 years. A marker on Sesuit Road denotes the site of the shipyard.

Two major Cape industries, cranberry cultivation and saltworks, were both pioneered in Dennis. During the time the British were blockading American ports, the Continental Congress offered a reward to anyone who could invent an efficient means of producing salt. Capt. John Sears of East Dennis stepped forward in the later quarter of the 18th century to invent and eventually patent a solar evaporation vat that actually distilled salt from seawater. Though the brunt of many a joke, his "odd" experiments worked, and a profitable industry grew from his backyard hobby. Very soon saltworks were everywhere, lining every available beachfront area around the Cape. Meanwhile, in 1816, Henry Hall of North Dennis observed that wild cranberries flourished in areas where sand blew over them. He replicated the conditions and is considered to be the first person to cultivate cranberries.

LOWER CAPE

Brewster

Much of the history of Brewster was made beyond the boundaries of the town on the oceans of the world. Brewster raised more deepwater ship captains per capita than all other 19th-century American towns. Many of these ship captains operated slightly outside the laws of the day. For instance, during the War of 1812, Brewster's seafaring men defied President Thomas Jefferson's embargo against Britain. There were fortunes to be made crossing the Atlantic, and these men of Brewster were not about to let a presidential decree stand in the way.

Brewster was originally settled as part of Harwich in 1656 by John Wing, formerly of Sandwich. Early settlement was in West Brewster, around Route 124, in the area of the present Brewster Stone. A church founded here in 1700 has pews still marked with the names of original members. By the mid-1700s, bad feelings existed between the north and south precincts of Harwich, as each end of town was so different in its makeup. The ship captains and the fortunes they made were on the north side, whereas the working class, including fishermen and farmers, dwelt on the south side. By 1803, each town went in its own direction, the southern part keeping the name Harwich, the northern part opting for the name Brewster to honor *Mayflower* Pilgrim William Brewster.

In the center of Brewster, an old cemetery behind the Unitarian Church is the final resting place of many notable historic figures, including Captain David Nickerson, who was in Paris during the French Revolution. According to local legend, he was handed a baby—supposedly the Lost Dauphin of France, the son of Marie Antoinette and Louis XVI. He was begged to bring the child to America and asked to name the child Rene Rousseau, which he did. The child grew up to be a sea captain and, at the age of 25, was lost at sea. It is Cape custom for a young man lost at sea to have his name inscribed on his father's headstone, so upon Capt. Nickerson's stone (he

was lost at sea a few years later) is also the name Rene Rousseau.

Brewster has more than one connection with France. During the French Revolution, 1794 to be exact, Captain Elijah Cobb's ship was seized. Cobb obtained an audience with Robespierre to plead his case for the release of his ship. Robespierre saw Cobb's side of the argument and released the ship just days before he himself was executed. Cobb would later become a prisoner of war during the War of 1812 and be released in a prisoner exchange.

In 1815, Brewster Captain Jeremiah May orchestrated plans to take Napoleon to America, but the plans fell apart when the former emperor was captured.

Although Brewster has a strong maritime history, the Cape Cod Museum of Natural History permits an unusual glimpse of prehistoric life in this town. The first people who lived in this area would have seen a vast plain covered with pine forests, grasslands, and rivers, with bogs where Cape Cod Bay is now, for the shoreline was miles away from its present location, nearly out to Georges Bank. As glaciers melted, the sea level rose and covered the land area, which is now the continental shelf. Prehistoric people settled around river mouths such as Stony Brook in Brewster. Stone tools, spears, knives, and hide scrapers have been found at the town's Upper Mill Pond. In 1619, a plague killed as many as 90 percent of the native people. Written history kept by the Pilgrims and early colonists in Plymouth and on Cape Cod reflects a decimated and vulnerable native culture; European settlers, on the other hand, were strong in numbers but considerably divided by economic and religious differences.

Brewster was in 1870 the birthplace of prolific Cape writer Joe Lincoln. Through his novels, many people were first introduced to Cape Cod and its history.

Harwich

Like all of Cape Cod, Harwich was home to local Indians, in this case the Nauset Indians, consisting of the Sauquatuckett tribe to the north and the Monomoyick tribe to the south. These Indians lived in unspoiled beauty, undisturbed for many centuries and even for the couple of decades after the settlement of Yarmouth to the west and Eastham to the east. This land was the Cape's last wilderness until white settlers began to arrive toward the end of the 1650s.

In 1656, John Wing became the first settler to tame these wilds. He was a converted Quaker from Sandwich who apparently tired of the persecutions in that town and left to build a life elsewhere. He settled in part of the old Harwich that would eventually become Brewster. Wing was followed by John Dillingham and, later, Gersham Hall, who in the 1660s became the first to settle in the southern area of old Harwich (the section that would remain the Harwich of today). More families followed and by 1690 there were enough living in the area to establish a church. In 1694, this area became incorporated as Harwich and contained the present towns of Harwich and Brewster as well as parts of Eastham and Orleans.

Harwich in the 18th century was a town in separation. Residents in the southern part of town grew weary of traveling to the church parish in the north, so in 1744 they appealed for the building of a church in the south. Two years later, permission was granted, and a church was built. This southern parish later saw itself being split into some 15 splinter churches as a religious revolution of sorts took place in town. These religious groups included Congregationalists, Baptists, New Lighters, Come Outers (those who "came out" against slavery), and Standpatters (those who were not abolitionists).

In the 18th century, the town itself began to come apart. The areas known as Portonumecot and Namecoyick became parts of Eastham in 1772, later becoming South Orleans. About a quarter of a century later, the remaining part of Harwich split in two, the northern part becoming Brewster in 1803.

The earliest settlers were farmers who occasionally shored a whale. Harwich would later become one of the Cape's major fishing ports, reaping huge harvests of cod and mackerel.

Other industries included fishing for alewives, or young herring, from a number of streams, as well as harvesting cranberries from the many bogs. This latter industry was developed in town by Alvin Cahoon, who was instrumental in making cranberries a harvestable crop. Meanwhile, Harwich's Major Nathaniel Freeman gave the saltworks industry on the Cape a big boost by utilizing windmills to pump seawater into the salt vats. So profound were Harwich's contributions to the industry that it became home to the Massachusetts Salt Works Company, established in 1797. The industry peaked during the 1830s, only to see its decline a decade later, when salt mining in the Midwest provided a more cost-effective alternative.

Two structures in Harwich of historical interest are the South Harwich Methodist Church on Chatham Road and the Captain James Berry House on Main Street, both on the National Register of Historic places. You can see other historic sites at the Herring River in West Harwich and Muddy Creek between Harwich and Chatham.

Chatham

If the 13th-century Flateyjarbok (Flat Land Book) does in fact provide an accurate account of Norse expeditions around A.D. 1000, then the first visitors to Chatham were most likely Vikings from Iceland. If these Norse sagas are true, then Bjarni Herjulfsson sailed right past these shores more than a thousand years ago. The earliest accepted historic record, though, indicates that Samuel de Champlain anchored in Stage Harbor in 1606 to repair a broken rudder. Though Champlain and his crew were only able to navigate the treacherous shoals with the aid of Monomoyick Indians of the area, fear between the two groups once Champlain's men had set up camp on shore resulted in bloodshed. With a fixed rudder, the French left the harbor to explore Canada. Champlain named the locale Port Fortune, after the misfortune he had encountered there.

Fourteen years later, Chatham provided the pilgrims with their first glimpse of land since leaving England. Shoals off Monomoy Island drove the ship to the north, diverting them from their intended route to Virginia. Chatham remained unsettled until 1664, when William Nickerson of Yarmouth arrived in the area to stay. Since 1656, Nickerson had been acquiring land from the Monomoyicks, though it wasn't until 1672 that he actually received a deed of any kind. By 1682, he possessed about 4,000 acres of land, which was nearly all of Chatham.

In Nickerson's time, the area was known as Monomoit, and he had a difficult time attracting settlers to this remote area of the Cape. Besides the Indians, there was also the threat of attack by pirates. The Monomoyicks turned out to be friendly neighbors to the settlers who determined to "brave the wilds." At one time it was considered under Yarmouth's jurisdiction and, later, under that of Eastham. Though not a town, this area of Monomoit was allowed to separate from Eastham in 1679 to become what was termed a "constabelwich," meaning Monomoit could collect its own taxes but had no representation in the Colony Court. Monomoit's only chance at incorporation was in establishing a church, and then attracting a minister to this wilderness outpost. After a number of preachers came and went (no less than eight, including one who drowned), Rev. Hugh Adams arrived in 1711, and, in June 1712, the town was incorporated. The stipulation was that the town had to be incorporated with an English name, so Chatham was chosen.

Chatham was the site of one of the worst smallpox epidemics on the Cape. During the winter of 1765–66 some 60 people, 10 percent of the population, contracted the disease. Thirty-seven people died, including the town doctor.

Chatham has one of the most dangerous coastlines in the Northeast. As Champlain learned in 1606, Chatham is guarded by treacherous shoals that have caused many a shipwreck over the centuries. In 1808, two wooden lighthouses were constructed at the mouth of the harbor to warn approaching ships. They crumbled over the eroded cliff and were replaced in 1841 and again in 1879 and 1881. Today one of the towers, Chatham Light, still serves as a navigational aid.

The other tower was moved north to Eastham to become Nauset Light. The terrible shipwreck called the Monomoy Disaster of 1902 took place just south of Chatham Light off the Monomoy Islands. Twelve men lost their lives on Shovelful Shoals in a fierce winter storm that March morning. Sole survivors Captain Elmer Mayo and Captain Seth Ellis became heroes, each man putting his own life in harm's way with the slightest hope of saving the life of another. Their tale of heroism is told on a monument standing in front of Chatham Light.

Orleans

The history of Orleans is sprinkled with French seasoning. Though it's not known for sure, the origin of the town's name seems to point to Louis Philippe de Bourbon, the Duke of Orleans in France. The Duke was in exile during the French Revolution and had visited America one month before the Cape town was incorporated. Thirty-three years later, he would become the king of France.

Originally settled as the south precinct of Eastham in 1710, the area was known as Pochet. The first meetinghouse was built in 1718 to become the South Parish of Eastham. Graves in the nearby cemetery date back to 1719. Orleans broke away from Eastham and was incorporated in 1797 to become one of only two towns on Cape Cod to not bear an English name (the other town is Mashpee). Before the white settlers, this land belonged to the Nauset Indians, more specifically the subtribes known as the Monomoyick and the Potonamiquoit (there are numerous spelling for this second tribe). Leif Ericson of the Norse sagas may have visited Nauset Beach along Orleans's Atlantic coast around the year 1000, Bartholomew Gosnold stopped here in 1602, and the French explorer Samuel de Champlain visited these outer shores in 1606.

The first recorded European shipwreck on the East Coast occurred off Nauset Beach in December, 1626, when the ketch *Sparrowhawk* wrecked in a storm. During the 19th century, the remains of the historic vessel emerged from the dunes and are now housed in a museum in Plymouth.

One of the smallest towns on the Cape, Orleans borders Cape Cod Bay to the northwest, the Atlantic Ocean to the east, and the waters of Pleasant Bay to the south. The land itself is marked by many bays, ponds, and creeks. The town is also the site of the Cape's first canal, Jeremiah's Gutter, a hand-dug trench that connected Boatmeadow River and Town Cove. Extremely high tides would flood the low-lying lands between the two bodies of water—in fact, Gosnold mistakenly concluded that the Cape north of this spot was actually an island cut off from the rest of the peninsula by this gulf of water. Dug in 1804, Jeremiah's Gutter (named for resident Jeremiah Smith, who owned the land through which it traveled) was useful during the War of 1812 when British ships were blockading Cape ports. After the war, its use diminished, and the canal was left to fill in with silt.

The French returned to Orleans in 1898 in the form of the French Cable Company. The company managed an undersea cable that con-nected the Cape town with Brest, France. A second cable then ran from Orleans to New York. Many important news items were received at Orleans first before being referred on to New York and the rest of the country, such as the loss of the steamer Portland in 1898, Lindbergh's flight across the Atlantic in 1927, and Germany's invasion of France in 1940. Along with the cable came workers from France to man the company's building. Many of these French remained in Orleans and raised families there.

Orleans has an extraordinary distinction—it has been attacked by both the British and the Germans. During the War of 1812, the HMS Newcastle anchored off Rock Harbor, and its captain demanded payment of $1,000 to spare the town's saltworks. The offer was refused, and so commenced the Battle of Rock Harbor. Brit-ish sailors attempted a landing but were driven away by the town's militia. The ransom was never paid.

On July 22, 1918, during World War I, a Ger-man U-boat surfaced off Nauset Beach to fire on

and sink three barges and a tugboat, the Perth Amboy. An estimated 146 rounds were fired in the one-sided exchange. At least one of the submarine's shells landed on the beach, the only assault on American soil during the war. When word of the attack was received at the Chatham Air Station, three planes were sent up to launch a counterattack. Without weaponry, the best the Yanks could do was to toss a monkey wrench at the fleeing sub.

In 1984, the 470-foot Maltese freighter Eldia grounded on Nauset Beach. It had unloaded its cargo of sugar in New Brunswick and was riding light off Cape Cod when high winds and heavy seas blew it onto shore. Although the 28-member crew was evacuated with no loss of life, few will forget the bizarre sight of a giant ship on Nauset Beach, a sight that hearkened back to the old days when this coastline snatched many a passing ship to wreck upon her shoals.

Eastham

The decade of the 1640s saw the Pilgrims in Plymouth considering their future and whether they wanted to stay in Plymouth. Some thought of relocating their settlement to the outer lands of Cape Cod, and in 1643 a committee was formed to investigate that very possibility. Among those in the party who journeyed to the outer Cape was Thomas Prence, who came across to the New World on board the vessel Fortune in 1621. Upon their return to Plymouth, the committee decided to pack up their belongings and take their chances in the land known as Nauset, now known as Eastham.

Settlement commenced in 1644. The bound-aries were vague at best, at first consisting of everything east of Old Yarmouth and includ-ing the towns of Brewster, Harwich, Chatham, Orleans, Wellfleet, Truro, and, of course, Eastham. The township was known as Nauset until 1651, when it was renamed Eastham. This land was reserved for the Old Comers, those Pilgrims who voyaged across the Atlantic on the first three ships to carry settler—the Mayflower, Fortune, and Anne. Joining Prence were John Doane, Nicolas

Snow, and Josias Cook, as well as Richard Higgins, John Smalley, and Edward Bangs. Eastham is the only Cape Cod town founded entirely by people from Plymouth Colony. It's interesting that Pilgrims should return to Eastham, as it was the site of their first contact with Native Indians at First Encounter Beach in December, 1620, just before they sailed the *Mayflower* across the Bay to settle at Plymouth. Founding father Thomas Prence would later become governor of Plymouth Colony from 1655 until his death in 1673.

The first meetinghouse was erected in 1646 on the north side of Town Cove. The much-loved Rev. Samuel Treat came to Eastham in 1693, and his ministry would span the next 45 years. Besides preaching to the white settlers, Treat also ministered to more than 500 Native Americans, or "Praying Indians," and wrote services in their language. He enlisted Native preachers and lived up to his name by treating the Indians with the respect they were owed.

Harwich, which at the time included Brewster, separated from Eastham very early on with its settlement in 1656. Chatham departed next, when that area became a constablewich in control of its own destiny in 1679. Truro broke away from Eastham in 1709. Around 1720, a north parish was established in the area of Wellfleet and a south parish at what was later to become Orleans. The divisions were made official in 1763, when Wellfleet became its own town and in 1797, when Orleans followed suit. Eastham, once the most populated town on the Cape, became the least populated. Over the century since its settlement, so many trees had been cut that the once-rich Eastham topsoil was stripped away by the savage ocean winds. Scrub pine took hold where vast forests of oak once stood. Farmers turned from their barren soils to the seas and became fishermen. Those who did remain behind on shore became dairy farmers.

Old Cove Cemetery is Eastham's oldest cemetery. Three Pilgrims are buried here. In the mid-1800s, a small plot was added nearby for the graves of many children who died when a terrible epidemic of smallpox struck the town. The small cemetery was so deeply associated with grief and

tragedy that people shunned it, and it became overgrown with weeds and briars and was long forgotten. Only recently have the 22 headstones dating from 1836 to 1892 been rediscovered.

Henry Beston's famous book, *The Outermost House,* published in 1928, relates the year he spent in his beach cottage on the Great Dune of Eastham. Although the cottage was destroyed by the blizzard of 1978, its place in literary history is commemorated by a placard at Coast Guard Beach.

Wellfleet

When the settlers arrived at Nauset in 1644 to purchase lands from the Indians of the area, they asked them who owned the northern lands from Wellfleet toward Provincetown. The Indians, perhaps not understanding the question and possibly not identifying with the European notion of ownership, answered "nobody." So the settlers announced, "Then we own it!" And so began the settlement of Wellfleet, known then as Billingsgate, at that time merely the north precinct of the town of Eastham.

The lay of the land at Wellfleet was much different than it is today. Land masses that are now attached to the mainland were actually islands back then. Other 17th- and 18th-century islands that once supported homes and communities are now gone, swept away by the tides. Such is the case with the island of Billingsgate, which over the years was devoured by the waves. Strangely, much of the settlement of the area occurred on the islands rather than on the mainland. A north parish meetinghouse was erected in the area in 1723. As early as 1734, the residents here applied for town status, but it would be another three

i From 1872 to 1914, 13 Lifesaving Stations were built approximately every 8 miles along Cape Cod's eastern shore. They provided rescue and shelter for shipwreck victims. Today you can visit the Beachcomber Restaurant in Cahoon's Hollow, Wellfleet, a converted lifesaving station on the bluffs overlooking the Atlantic Ocean.

decades before their application was approved. In 1763, the town was incorporated, briefly, as the town of Poole, later changed to Wellfleet. Some say that the name "Wellfleet" may have come from "Wallfleet," after the Wallfleet oyster bed located in Blackwater Bay in England. Samuel de Champlain, who visited these Wellfleet shores back in the early 17th century, named the harbor *Port aux Huitres* (no need to look to your French dictionary, *huitres* does in fact translate as oysters). Of course, "Wallfleet" (or Wellfleet) sounds a lot like "whale fleet" too—another possible source for the town's name.

It is only a mile between Wellfleet's shores on the outer beach of the Atlantic Ocean and Cape Cod Bay. Wellfleet Harbor was once known as Grampus Bay for the blackfish, or pilot whales, that stranded themselves there. When the oyster beds died off in 1770 because of an epidemic of some sort, Wellfleet men became commercial fishermen, lobstermen, and whalers. Seed oysters were imported after the Revolutionary War, and the beds thrived again, making Wellfleet the largest producer of oysters in the state. During the early 19th century, salt vats were big business, and the town had some 40 saltworks during the 1830s, producing roughly 18,000 bushels of salt on an annual basis. The Wellfleet wharf business grew during the mid-1800s, catering to the fishing industry.

In 1717 off the shores of Wellfleet, the pirate known as Black Sam Bellamy was returning to the Cape on board his vessel *Whydah* when the ship was caught in a storm and sank. The location of the wreck baffled salvagers and historians until, in 1982, a treasure salvager located the wreck of the infamous ship. The bronze ship's bell with THE WHYDAH GALLEY 1716 inscribed on it was brought to the surface, along with hundreds of pieces of gold and other treasures. Artifacts from the Whydah can be seen at a museum on Provincetown's MacMillan Pier.

Wellfleet is the site from which one of the first transatlantic wireless telegraph messages was sent in 1903. The year before, a huge station was built on the cliff overlooking the ocean. This miracle of science, which allowed messages to travel across the invisible airwaves, was the invention of Italian physicist Guglielmo Marconi, who began experimenting with sending wireless messages in his teenage years. Besides that first telegraph message of 1903 (from President Theodore Roosevelt to King Edward VII of England), the Wellfleet wireless station also received a distress message from the sinking *Titanic* in April, 1912.

The following are some of Wellfleet's other claims to fame: The steeple of Wellfleet's First Congregational Church is the only town clock in the world that keeps ship's time (see our Attractions chapter). In the 1870s, Captain Lorenzo Dow Baker of Wellfleet introduced bananas to the United States and established the L. D. Baker Company in 1881, which later became the United Fruit Company. Wellfleet resident Luther Crowell invented the square-bottom paper bag.

Truro

The history of Truro can be traced to three hills: Corn Hill, the Hill of Storms, and the Hill of Churches. In November, 1620, the *Mayflower*, with its passengers and crew, found its way to Provincetown Harbor. An expedition that included Captain Myles Standish and William Bradford explored the lands of this lonely outpost in search of food and water and possibly a good place to settle. In the area of Truro, upon a hill now known as Corn Hill, the Pilgrims stumbled across what appeared to be an abandoned Indian encampment. Here they found Indian gravesites and unearthed baskets filled with ears of corn. This corn became the seeds of the Pilgrims' first planting. Also in Truro, the Pilgrim expedition located their first fresh water supply since leaving England, at Pilgrim Spring, which can still be seen on a Cape Cod National Seashore walking trail.

Truro was originally settled as part of the Nauset tract in the mid-17th century, later incorporated as Eastham. A group known as the Pamet Proprietors bought the land from the natives in 1689, and by 1697 farms were established in this remote area of the Cape, first called Pamet after the Native American tribe there. Pamet was

i **The thin pieces of wood used in over-lapping rows that form the sides and roofs of Cape Cod houses are white cedar shingles. White cedar is preferred over red cedar by most Cape Codders because it takes on a handsome, silvery sheen, whereas red cedar eventually turns brown. White cedar is also lighter, softer, and easier to split and shave.**

granted municipal privileges in 1705 and called Dangerfield because of the treacherous coastline. When Dangerfield officially separated from Eastham in 1709, the township was renamed Truro for the English town in Cornwall, which, with its rolling hills and lonely moors, resembled this area. The first meetinghouse was built in 1710 on the Hill of Storms. This meetinghouse was dismantled in 1840. The hill is also the site of North Cemetery, where the town's oldest stones can be found.

Truro was primarily a fishing and whaling town. At first whaling was done from shore and later from boats. In the 18th century, Truro was a leader in this industry, with vessels visiting the African coast and the whaling grounds of the Pacific. One particular Truro whaler, *Ichabod Paddock,* was even recruited to teach Nantucketers his techniques. Truro's history has always reflected a relationship with the sea. It had two good harbors, Pamet River Harbor and East Harbor (which is now the freshwater Pilgrim Lake, where the Pilgrims were thought to have anchored when they first arrived). Pamet River Harbor was the site of a thriving wharf business that grew from Union Wharf, built in 1829. The town had a sail loft and a shipbuilding yard built in 1830 on the Pamet River, where brigs and many Grand Banks schooners were built. The successful Union Company Store, which specialized in ship chandlering and general merchandise, epitomized the flavor of this fishing haven, and many townsfolk owned shares in the store and thereby shared in the town's victories.

But a series of events would send the town into a downward spiral. First was the terrible gale of October 2, 1841, which would see the loss

of 57 Truro men (10 percent of the town's able seamen) and seven of the town's eight fishing vessels. Then, in the 1850s, erosion began to claim the harbor. Citizens saw that erosion could eventually allow the Atlantic Ocean to cut right through Truro, creating an island of North Truro and Provincetown (the North Truro we know today is well south of Pilgrim Lake, up on the hill; this area is now called Beach Point). To avoid this, the entrance of East Harbor was blocked to become a lake. Then came the big blow when the Union Store went out of business in 1860. A growing 1840 population of about 2,000 had been cut in half by 1880. Migration cut that number in half again to about 500 people by 1930 as residents moved away to earn a living elsewhere.

The Hill of Churches is the spot where the Methodists of Truro built their meetinghouse in 1826. Methodists had first arrived here in the 1790s. The Congregationalists then decided to build their new church on the very same hill in 1827. It was built on this high ground to serve as both a worship center and as a beacon for ships. Its bell was cast by Paul Revere's son and cost $320, and the windows were made of Sandwich glass. In 1830, the Town Hall, or Union Hall, was constructed on the same hill, and its architecture resembles that of a church. The spires of these buildings can still be seen among the trees as you drive through Truro on US 6.

Highland Light in North Truro, also known as Cape Cod Light, is Cape Cod's oldest lighthouse. The 80-foot tower, which sits atop a 120-foot cliff, was built in 1797 and rebuilt in 1857. Cliff erosion threatened the structure's future, so in 1996 the historic lighthouse was moved to its present location. In November, 1778, during the days of the American Revolution, the British man-of-war *Somerset* wrecked along the Truro coast at Dead Man's Hollow in a gale. Some 480 British sailors were saved as the vessel cleared the outer bars and wrecked along the beach. The people of Truro and Provincetown divided up the spoils of the wreck, stripping the vessel of all its cargo and equipment. The British were eventually marched to Boston to confront the revolutionary forces,

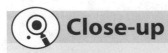 **Close-up**

Dune Shacks

One of the more evocative vistas on the Cape are the outer dunes that run between Truro and Provincetown. Over the years, these lovely, wild dunes have attracted all manner of artists, adventurers, and eccentrics. In the 1930s and '40s, squatters cobbled together numerous shacks out of driftwood and scraps in these dunes. Eighteen of these haphazard shacks have persisted to this day, largely because of the fascination many people have with their present and former inhabitants, and the fierce devotion to this singular way of life of those who still live among the dunes. Located along a 2-mile ridge of dunes, a few miles from bustling Provincetown, these austere lean-tos still have no power or water. Their extraordinary location and solitude have attracted an impressive roster of artists and writers over the years, from Eugene O'Neill and Tennessee Williams to Jackson Pollock, e.e. cummings, Norman Mailer, and Annie Dillard.

Seventeen of the shacks were added to the National Register of Historic Places in 1989 and now fall under the auspices of the Cape Cod National Seashore (CCNS). The CCNS and the Peaked Hill Trust, a nonprofit community organization, are responsible for maintaining nearly all of the shacks. When the National Park Service took over the shacks back in the early 1960s, they signed long-term leases with the current inhabitants. In 2006 the CCNS turned down an application to declare that the shacks have "traditional cultural significance."

If you're an artist or writer, you can apply for a brief, inspiring stay in one of the shacks. The Provincetown Community Compact manages one of them, called the C-Scape Dune Shack. You may contact them about applying at (508) 487-3684, or by writing P.O. Box 819, Provincetown, MA 02657. The Peaked Hill Trust runs another artist-in-residence program, which awards two-week stays to eligible artists in several other shacks. You may contact them at (508) 487-3635, or write them at P.O. Box 1705, Provincetown, MA 02657.

If a glimpse of the unparalleled light and views in the outer dunes is all you're after, you can access the area from Race Point Road or Snail Road. Off Snail Road follow a trail up to the top of the dunes, and you can see a few shacks in the distance. You can also view them if you hike east from Race Point Beach. An easier way to catch a glimpse is to visit the Cape Cod National Seashore's Province Lands Visitor Center (508-487-1256). It has a wraparound observation deck offering a 360-degree view, including several dune shacks. It's located on Race Point Road, off US 6 in Provincetown, and is open from May through Thanksgiving. An even easier option: Art's Dune Tours. Most vehicles aren't allowed on the dunes, but you can enjoy the views from the air-conditioned comfort of one of Art's Suburbans. They take groups on narrated, two-hour tours among the dunes, which include plenty of colorful history lessons about the shacks. Call (508) 487-1950, or visit www.artsdunetours.com. Tickets should be purchased in advance, and tours leave from the corner of Standish and Commercial Streets in Provincetown. Do remember, however, that these are either private residences or are being inhabited by artists in search of solitude.

and the Somerset's doctor is said to have stayed on in Truro and married a local woman.

Provincetown

At the very end of the Cape, at Provincetown, is where the history of Massachusetts began. Though English explorer John Smith sailed past this spot in 1614 without a thought of making landfall, Provincetown has the historic distinction of being the landing place of the *Mayflower*'s Pilgrims on November 21, 1620. The Pilgrims then went on to Plymouth, where they established a successful settlement. Perhaps even more historically significant is the fact that, while the vessel was moored in the harbor, the Pilgrims drafted and signed the Mayflower Compact, a document that became the foundation of democratic government in America. It spelled out the Pilgrims' plans for self-government. The Pilgrims spent five weeks in the Provincetown, Truro, Wellfleet, and Eastham area before they realized that the Cape's tip did not offer all they needed for settlement— namely fresh water and a protected harbor. Though some members wished to remain in this area, eventually all the Pilgrims got back on board the *Mayflower*, raised anchor, and continued along the coast to eventually land in Plymouth. Incidentally, several Pilgrims who had died on the crossing were buried in Provincetown.

Long before the Pilgrims came, however, the tip of the Cape had attracted native tribes and foreign explorers. Norse legends claim Vikings were the first discoverers of the New World, and Leif Ericson's brother, Thorvald, may have landed here during the first years of the 11th century to repair a damaged keel, naming the place Keelness.

Because of its remoteness, the tip of the Cape was one of the last parts to be settled. The area earned a somewhat unsavory reputation because of the smugglers, looters, and gamblers who came here before its actual settlement. No civil order was in place, and anyone who docked here to participate in whatever illegalities took place in the few coastal shacks did so in a land where laws simply did not exist. When nearby Truro was incorporated in 1709, this land to the north named "Cape Cod" was thrown into the package in an attempt to impose order. Eventually a permanent, though undisciplined, settlement did take hold. Law and order took hold as well, and this port town would quickly get down to business.

The township of Provincetown was incorporated in 1727, and the people immediately turned their attention to the sea and became expert fishermen and whalers. By 1760, a dozen whaling ships called Provincetown Harbor their home port. These whaling boats, always in search of good crews, found them in the Azores, Canary Islands, and Cape Verde islands. By the middle part of the century, Provincetown had a tremendous fishing and whaling fleet and was considered one of the most prosperous ports in

the country. Seventy-five wharves sprouted up along Commercial Street in this Cape Cod seaport, which was third behind only New Bedford and Nantucket in terms of whaling. The famous whaler *Charles W. Morgan,* now on prominent display at Mystic Seaport, Connecticut, was a Provincetown whaler that worked up until 1921, well after the quest for the leviathan had ended in most other ports. Experienced Portuguese fishermen joined the whalers who had made Provincetown their home, and by the turn of the 20th century, the port town had evolved into a flourishing fishing village with a Portuguese flavor. Today the annual Portuguese Festival, held the last weekend in June, celebrates the town's proud fishing tradition.

Provincetown also has the distinction of being the longest continuously running art colony in the country. In 1899, it became the site of an important art colony when Charles Hawthorne opened the Cape Cod School of Art. Art schools and galleries sprung up in this salty yet beautiful fishing village. That art legacy lives on in the many art schools and galleries in Provincetown today. This harbor community also attracted writers such as Eugene O'Neill, Sinclair Lewis, and John Dos Passos. In 1915, O'Neill, who in his early years worked on fishing boats, joined the Provincetown Players, a group who presented plays in an old fish house on Lewis Wharf in the East End of town. O'Neill went on to earn three Pulitzer Prizes and a Nobel Prize in 1936.

There are several historic monuments in Provincetown, the most impressive being the Cape Cod Pilgrim Memorial monument, constructed by the U.S. Army Corps of Engineers and funded by descendents of the Pilgrims. President Theodore Roosevelt laid its cornerstone in 1907, and President William Howard Taft attended its dedication ceremony in 1910. At 252 feet high, it is the tallest all-granite structure in the United States. A bronze plaque at the western end of Commercial Street commemorates the landing site of the *Mayflower's* Pilgrims in 1620, and the Pilgrim bas relief on Bradford Street behind Town Hall depicts the signing of the Mayflower Compact in Provincetown Harbor.

Today Provincetown's fishing industry is a shadow of its heyday in the 1850s, and the main source of income is tourism. Commercial Street attracts thousands of visitors each year to its many shops, fine restaurants, and exciting night-life. Provincetown is a colorful place, a vibrant mix of artists, fishermen, craftspeople, professionals, and retirees. An integral part of this mix is Provincetown's gay and lesbian population, who call this town home because of its accepting attitude, easy-going lifestyle, and respect for the individual.

Provincetown continues to be a fishing community boasting a proud Portuguese heritage. The Portuguese have played a large part in the town's history, as have the Norsemen who explored these shores nearly 1,000 years ago; the Pilgrims who landed in 1620; the smugglers and gamblers of the 17th century; the playwrights, artists, and bohemians of the last century; and the gay and lesbian population and the many washashores who have more recently made Provincetown their home—all have contributed to making Provincetown the fascinating place it is today. A trip to Cape Cod is not complete without a visit to the town at the tip.

LODGING

Cape Cod is a peninsula of great diversity, and that distinction holds true when it comes to the accommodations it offers its visitors. From elegant waterfront resorts to no-frills economy motels to quaint inns and cottages, there is a place for every budget and lifestyle.

Cape Cod has several large, contemporary, four-star resorts where you'll be awash in amenities, as well as hotels and motels that are moderately priced and offer fewer amenities but are perfectly acceptable. Many of the Cape's resorts, hotels, and motels offer suites in addition to rooms with the standard two double beds or one king-size bed.

For the most part, you will get what you pay for on the Cape. Private beaches, spacious rooms, and water views do come with a price. Still, bargains exist, especially in the off-season. Years ago, the Cape would shut down after Labor Day, but more and more people are discovering the Cape in the late fall, winter, and early spring, so many hotels, motels, and resorts are stretching out their seasons, with many staying open year-round.

Most facilities offer in-room televisions, telephones, and air-conditioning, but most accommodations do not allow pets. We do, however, make references to the ones that do welcome pets.

Autumn has become a popular season on the Cape. Visitors can enjoy the Cape's beauty at substantially lower prices, and there are plenty of packages available to make a stay even more attractive. Rates in the off-season can be as much as 50 percent less than summer rates.

In the first part of this chapter we present hotels, motels, resorts, and hostels for your consideration. In the second half of the chapter we provide information on other kinds of accommodations, including Bed-and-Breakfasts, Inns, and Cottages. See chapters on Vacation Rentals and Campgrounds and State Parks for still more options; we also provide a short section on kennels, should you need a place for your pet to stay. We've narrowed your search a bit, because there are thousands of rooms to choose from. Your best bet is to begin by deciding how you plan to spend your time while you're here; then pick the area that offers the activities you want.

If you plan on bringing bicycles, there are a number of accommodations on or near bike trails, such as the Cape Cod Rail Trail, which stretches from the Mid- to Lower Cape, or the Shining Sea Bike Path on the Upper Cape (see our Hiking and Biking Trails chapter). If you plan

on bringing a sailboard, there are hotels on the waterfront near Kalmus Beach in Hyannis, home to world-respected windsurfing and championship events weekly. If golf is your bag, many resorts and hotels offer golf packages. Of course cost is a consideration as well, so we've rated each entry for price (see the code at the beginning of this chapter for hotels and motels—inns and bed-and-breakfasts are priced slightly differently as is explained midway through the chapter).

It's best to make reservations before arriving on Cape Cod, as the area's accommodations fill up quickly, not only during the summer season, but also during weekends in spring and fall. This is especially true if you are planning to visit during special events, such as the Falmouth Road Race or our local sailors' favorite, Figawi Weekend. That's not to say you can't arrive without reservations and find a great room—it just might take a few stops.

One hundred and fifty years ago, travelers to various destinations on Cape Cod sought out lodging at day's end, seeking a hearty meal and a good night's rest. Today, travelers still look forward to the comfort of an inn at day's end, and many consider those inns to be destinations in themselves. Bed-and-breakfasts are usually private residences where the owners rent bedrooms (and sometimes suites) and offer a continental or full breakfast; inns are generally larger and often serve three-course gourmet meals for breakfast that could nourish you for the whole day. Because our bed-and-breakfasts and inns are often housed in older buildings, you get a firsthand taste of Cape history. It can be like stepping back in time but without giving up any modern comforts. In some cases, amenities and recent remodels include Jacuzzis, gas fireplaces, and wireless Internet access.

Another option on the Cape is to stay in a cottage. Cottage colonies are clusters of small, individual cottages or cabins that may share a common kitchen and gathering space or may be self-contained with private bathrooms and small kitchens. Families with young children may find that cottage colonies are a good choice because they aren't adorned with antique furnishings, as the inns often are, and there's plenty of space to run around in. Most are housekeeping cottages, meaning you clean up after yourself, and many require that you bring your own linens; be sure to ask exactly what the cottage supplies when you make your reservations.

Whatever type of accommodations you choose, you're likely to encounter a little history along with the hospitality. With the Atlantic Ocean to our east, Nantucket Sound to the south, and Cape Cod Bay to the north and west, it's no wonder that many of our historic homes were built by sea captains. In the 1700s and 1800s, young men often went to sea, and many traveled to the far corners of the world, returning with their wealth to build homes (estates in their day). Brewster, for instance, is referred to as the "Sea Captains' Town," where, it is said, 99 sea captains lived at one time. Towns like these also were dotted with large, rambling homesteads.

Today, many such homes are bed-and-breakfasts. Private bathrooms have been enlarged to include showers and tubs, and, in keeping with modern desires, Jacuzzis have been added to many homes. Furnishings range from antiques to period reproductions inside common rooms, and in the guest rooms, canopied and four-poster beds offer a romantic atmosphere. Wide-planked floors, narrow hallways, steep ship's staircases, and fireplaces add to the charm of each accommodation.

Historic houses with antique furnishings and civilized amenities such as crystal wine glasses and hand-stitched quilts don't mix well with boisterous children, so some bed-and-breakfasts don't allow children; others have age restrictions. We indicate those inns that welcome children and let you know which ones have age restrictions for their younger guests.

A few more Insiders' insights: Most inns and bed-and-breakfasts have cancellation penalties and restrictions. Calling to cancel less than two weeks before your arrival (especially in season) will almost guarantee that you won't get your deposit back (or that it will be applied to a future stay). Some establishments will give refunds in the event of cancellations only if they are able to re-rent your room. Most inns and B&Bs require a two-night minimum stay during the peak season, three nights on holiday weekends. Some, however, have minimum stays as long as five nights in July and August. Cottages are generally rented by the week in season. Innkeepers are much more flexible in the off-season—before June and after September, or anytime besides July and August, depending on the establishment—and off-season rates are usually drastically reduced.

The Cape offers a variety of accommodations beyond the conventional. Rates also vary; the ones we give here include either a full or continental breakfast. Some establishments offer what they call "hearty" or "extended" continental breakfasts, which usually means fresh squeezed juice, homemade muffins and breads, granola, and a fruit course. Some innkeepers are accomplished gourmet cooks who offer luscious breakfasts. The more ambitious ones offer multicourse gourmet treats that change each day of your stay and may include a main plate of elegant crepes, quiche, French toast, or whatever the innkeeper has chosen for the day.

Most bed-and-breakfasts and inns offer private bathrooms; the days of the shared bathroom seem to be in the past. Innkeepers are highly concerned about the privacy of their guests, and for that reason, some have in-room phones and televisions, whereas others pride themselves on being places where guests can escape ringing phones and the otherwise ubiquitous tube. Often, inns and bed-and-breakfasts compromise by offering TV and phones only in common areas. Most establishments do not allow pets, but we'll let you know if they do. Most innkeepers can make arrangements at a local kennel if you do need to bring your pet.

Remember that each establishment is as personal and unique as its innkeepers, most of whom are willing to share their expertise and knowledge with you. So ask them for recommendations about things to do in the area, places to visit, and the best restaurants. One good tactic: Ask your innkeepers where they go when they want to eat out and where they take friends who are visiting them from off-Cape. And don't be surprised if you find yourself developing a friendship with your hosts; Many such relationships have lasted from year to year.

If you'd like help booking accommodations, check out the reservation services listed at the end of this chapter. Many of them specialize in inns and bed-and-breakfasts.

The Cape's summer season is not only its busiest season but also its costliest. Many of the Cape's hotels and motels are only open during a handful of months (typically Memorial Day to Columbus Day) and have to reap a year's worth of income in less than a half-year's time. The July Fourth and Labor Day weekends are the bookends of what is usually a pretty steady tourist season. Still, June can be a very busy month, too.

You can nearly always expect to pay your bill with a major credit card; we let you know if an accommodation does not accept credit cards.

The trend has been toward entirely non-smoking facilities, but smokers can usually find someplace to light up. We mention in the listings below those hotels and motels that prohibit smoking on their grounds. However, if nothing is mentioned, assume smoking is permitted in certain areas. A number of places also have wheelchair-accessible facilities, and we indicate these in the entries below. Many old inns find it difficult to comply with wheelchair-accessibility codes because of the historic nature of their buildings, but if an inn has wheelchair-accessible features, we'll mention that.

HOTELS, MOTELS, AND RESORTS

Price Code

To help you select a hotel, motel, or resort in your price range, we have established the following key based on the average cost of a night's stay in a double-occupancy room during the season, minus tax and special charges. Massachusetts charges a state tax, as do the individual Cape towns, which equates to about 9.7 percent added to your bill.

$.................	**Less than $75**
$$	**$75 to $110**
$$$	**$111 to $175**
$$$$	**$176 or more**

Upper Cape

THE ADMIRALTY INN AND SUITES $$–$$$$
51 Teaticket Hwy., East Falmouth
(508) 548-4240, (800) 341-5700
www.theadmiraltyinn.com
The Admiralty Inn has wireless Internet access, satellite TV (free HBO, anyone?), and rooms that have been remodeled in recent years. The facility still has outdoor and indoor (heated) pools and a whirlpool. The Inn's central location makes it convenient to the beaches of Falmouth and the various island ferries that leave from Falmouth Harbor and Woods Hole. Open year-round, the Admiralty has 98 air-conditioned rooms, includ-

ing 28 townhouse suites. Eight of the rooms are wheelchair accessible. Rooms and suites feature private baths and include a wet bar, refrigerator, iron and ironing board, hair dryer, and coffeemaker. In addition to these basics, king Jacuzzi rooms and two-story townhouse suites offer Jacuzzis, microwaves, and VCRs.

BAY MOTOR INN $–$$$
223 Main St., Buzzards Bay (Bourne)
(508) 759-3989
www.capecodtravel.com/baymotorinn
Nestled in three acres of beautifully landscaped grounds, this family-owned and -operated motor inn has been providing vacationers with affordable accommodations since 1965. Bring your bike, fishing rod, and walking shoes, because just across the street is the famous Cape Cod Canal, with miles of paved trails alongside it. Popular with families, retirees, and especially fishermen, the Bay Motor Inn offers 17 clean units, among them poolside, efficiency, and cottage units. According to Fred, most guests favor the Cape "Coddages," freestanding cottage units complete with cable TV, air-conditioning, phones, and tiled bathrooms. You'll be close to a wide assortment of attractions and restaurants, or you can simply spend the day lounging by the wheelchair-accessible pool, playing tennis at the nearby courts, or just watching the boat traffic on the canal. Pets are allowed, but Fred and Irene ask that guests do not leave dogs unattended during the day (just down the road is a veterinary service that will watch your pet for a small fee). The Bay Motor Inn is open from Apr 1 to Nov 1.

BRIDGE-BOURNE HOTEL $$–$$$
100 Trowbridge Rd., Bourne
(508) 759-0800, (800) 675-0008
www.bridgebournehotel.com
Buses to and from Logan International Airport in Boston and the Woods Hole ferries to Martha's Vineyard depart practically from the front door of the hotel.

This 43-room hotel with modern rooms sits high above the Cape Cod Canal and features an indoor heated pool, hot tub, wireless Internet, complimentary continental breakfast, and eight deluxe suites with Jacuzzis and kitchenettes. Function rooms are available for weddings and other events, and the on-site dining is available at the Trowbridge Tavern & Ale House. Children 17 and younger stay free in their parents' room. It is open year-round.

THE COONAMESSETT INN $$$–$$$$
311 Gifford St., Falmouth
(508) 548-2300
www.capecodrestaurants.org
The tradition and charm of a New England inn is yours at the Coonamessett. Long adored by the locals for its beauty and grace overlooking Jones Pond, the 200-year-old inn is a Falmouth favorite for weddings, special occasions, and dining out. Known more for its fine restaurant (see our Restaurants chapter), the Coonamessett also offers spacious suites. Splendid views of gardens and the grounds meet you each morning. The inn is located near all the beauty and adventure the Cape has to offer. The inn is open year-round.

THE DAN'L WEBSTER INN $$$$
149 Main St., Sandwich
(508) 888-3622, (800) 444-3566
www.danlwebsterinn.com
One of the Upper Cape's most distinguished facilities, the Dan'l Webster Inn offers four dining rooms—the Music Room, the Heritage Room, the Conservatory and the tavern at the inn (see our Restaurants chapter)—an English-style tavern, and an outdoor swimming pool, all set in the midst of the historic Sandwich Village. This 48-room colonial inn is a reproduction of the original tavern, built in 1692, that served as a parsonage and Patriot headquarters during the Revolutionary War. It is named after statesman Daniel Webster who patronized the inn during the mid-19th century.

Guests have their choice of guest rooms and suites at the inn or in the Fessenden House on the property. Furnishings throughout are antiques or period reproductions. Dan'l Webster Inn offers many types of accommodations, ranging in style from the formally elegant Daniel Webster Suite with an outdoor balcony to two-bed "superior" rooms in the outdoor Fessendon Wing. All guest rooms are individually decorated and feature private baths; some have Jacuzzis. Pampering includes chocolates, turn-down service, free wireless Internet, and cable television. The Dan'l Webster is a nonsmoking inn, and it is open year-round.

THE EARL OF SANDWICH $$-$$$
378 Rte. 6A, East Sandwich
(508) 888-1415, (800) 442-3275
www.earlofsandwich.com
Built around a duck pond in a rural setting, the Earl of Sandwich has landscaped grounds, a pool, and rooms in the Old English Manor style. Many rooms have exposed beams and canopied beds, and all have air-conditioning, refrigerators, private baths, color cable TV, telephones and wireless Internet access. A complimentary continental breakfast is included with your stay. The Earl of Sandwich is located within a short drive from area beaches, shopping, and the many historical sites in nearby Sandwich. Be sure to call ahead if you plan on bringing the family pet. Pets are welcome but with some restrictions.

FALMOUTH INN $$-$$$
824 Rte. 28, Falmouth
(508) 540-2500, (800) 255-4157
www.falmouthinn.com
One of Falmouth's larger hotels, the Falmouth Inn is a single-floor facility catering to those who seek value and convenience. Located in the center of Falmouth on Main Street, the inn offers 123 spacious rooms that include color TV with free HBO, telephones, temperature control, a game room, and an outdoor courtyard. The retractable roof of the heated indoor-outdoor pool is unique for Cape Cod. On-site is the Captain's Dining Room restaurant and a cozy bar called the Shipwreck Lounge. Falmouth Inn is near Main Street shops, restaurants, beaches, Falmouth Harbor, and the *Island Queen* ferry. Inquire about getting a preferred tee time at the Falmouth Country Club's 18-hole championship golf course. The Inn is

open year-round and welcomes pets. There is no charge for children younger than 18.

GREEN HARBOR WATERFRONT LODGING $$$-$$$$
134 Acapesket Rd., East Falmouth
(508) 548-4747, (800) 548-5556
www.gogreenharbor.com
This East Falmouth beachfront fixture rests on the Green Pond inlet, which eventually empties into Vineyard Sound and is perfect for kayaking or canoeing. Green Harbor has 40 units. Each waterfront guest room offers one queen and one double bed, a private full bath, cable TV, telephone, microwave, refrigerator, and individually controlled heat and air-conditioning. Some are equipped with full kitchens as are certain beachside studios. There is also a three-bedroom cottage, which features three full baths, three televisions, a fireplace, and a fully equipped eat-in kitchen. The family-run facility has a heated outdoor pool as well as a 1-foot-deep kiddie pool. There are docking facilities available for your use if you plan to arrive on your own boat. Other on-site amenities include free wireless Internet access, charcoal grills, and a boating beach. Rowboats and paddleboats are also available for guest use. The lodge is open from mid-Apr to early Nov. Green Harbor allows pets as long as they are not left unattended in the room.

INN ON THE SQUARE $$$-$$$$
40 Rte. 28, Falmouth
(508) 457-0606, (888) 744-5394
www.innonthesquare.com
Boasting that it is "Falmouth's Premiere Hotel," this luxury inn has all the bells and whistles to merit the title—among them a heated indoor pool and private courtyard. The 72 guest rooms were updated in 2005. They include amenities such as spacious baths with granite vanities, cable TV, oversize towels, and gourmet coffee and tea stations. Situated within steps of the Shining Sea bike path and Falmouth's inviting gift shops, art galleries, eateries, and historic homes, the Inn on the Square is open all year and is wheelchair accessible with ADA-compliant rooms.

NAUTILUS MOTOR INN $$$–$$$$
539 Woods Hole Rd., Woods Hole
(508) 548-1525, (800) 654-2333
www.nautilusinn.com

This motor inn rests atop a hill overlooking Woods Hole Harbor, where ferries and oceanographic research vessels are ubiquitous. The views are spectacular (yes, that's Martha's Vineyard you see across the water). Situated close to Falmouth and the village of Woods Hole, which has great restaurants and marine-science attractions, this 54-room facility has a spacious sundeck, and tennis courts. All rooms have balconies or patios, some with lovely views of Vineyard Sound. Your morning coffee at the Nautilus is complimentary. The inn is open from early Apr through Oct.

SANDWICH LODGE & RESORT $$–$$$
54 Rte. 6A, Sandwich
(508) 888-2275, (800) 282-5353
www.sandwichlodge.com

Located in the oldest town on Cape Cod, the Sandwich Lodge & Resort is comfortable for the whole family and close to nearly all of Cape Cod's wonders. This affordable full-service hotel along beautiful Route 6A has 75 rooms, including pet-friendly standard rooms, one-room "suites," two-room "deluxe suites," and honeymoon-worthy "Jacuzzi suites." Set on six acres, the Sandwich Lodge & Resort offers both indoor and outdoor pools, outdoor barbecue facilities, complimentary wireless Internet access, a game room for the kids, a whirlpool, and meeting rooms for those mixing business with pleasure. Table tennis, billiards, badminton, volleyball, horseshoes, and shuffleboard fill the void between dips in the pools. In the morning, a complimentary deluxe continental breakfast awaits you in a meeting room adjacent to the indoor pool. On the grounds of the Sandwich Lodge & Resort is the British Beer Company, an Anglophilic pub that serves lunch and dinner. Sandwich Lodge & Resort is open year-round. Pets are allowed in standard rooms for an additional charge of $10 a night.

SEA CREST OCEANFRONT RESORT & CONFERENCE CENTER $$$–$$$$
350 Quaker Rd., North Falmouth
(508) 540-9400, (800) 225-3110
www.seacrest-resort.com

The Sea Crest has 700 feet of white-sand waterfront on Buzzards Bay. The facility offers you the opportunity to indulge in everything from tennis to swimming, dancing to dining. In season, kayaks, sailboards, and sailboats are available to let you explore the inlets of the bay. Windsurfing instruction is offered during the summer months.

Enjoy water-view dining in the Sea Crest's oceanfront dining room, or grab a bite at Oscars. If you'd rather soak up some rays, try the cabana bar, on a deck adjoining the outdoor pool. In addition you can enjoy the resort's indoor pool, exercise room, game room, whirlpool, sauna, and its two all-weather tennis courts. If you're bringing the kids, you'll be happy to know that during July and August, the day camp staff holds activities for children.

Many of the rooms have water views and balconies; all rooms come with double or king-size beds, irons and ironing boards, refrigerators, cable TV, telephones with data ports, wireless Internet access and hair dryers. Available space is sometimes limited by conferences. The resort has numerous conference rooms for those who have to work for a living. For those who can tear themselves away from the meetings and the beach, Falmouth's downtown and harbor are about a 10- to 15-minute drive away. Sea Crest is typically a year-round facility but will be closed for about five months at the end of the 2009 season for renovations.

SHADY NOOK INN & MOTEL $$–$$$
14 Rte. 6A, Sandwich
(508) 888-0409, (800) 338-5208
www.shadynookinn.com

One of the closest motels to the Shawme Forest and minutes away from Heritage Plantation, the Shady Nook Inn offers colorful flower beds, well-manicured lawns, and a lovely pool area. The 30 rooms, including seven efficiencies, include king- and queen-size beds and doubles, cable TV, data ports, and full baths. All rooms are spacious and have refrigerators. Convenient to historic Sandwich Village and nearby beaches, the Shady Nook Inn is open year-round.

SHORE WAY ACRES RESORT INN $$$–$$$$
59 Shore St., Falmouth
(508) 540-3000, (800) 352-7100
www.shorewayacresinn.com

In a classic New England setting on Shore Street, with its colonial homes and centuries-old elm trees, rests Shore Way Acres Inn. At one end of the street and only a few minutes walk away is the picture-perfect Surf Drive town beach, where you can look out across Vineyard Sound to Martha's Vineyard. The street's other end empties onto Main Street, where you will find, well, everything. Shore Way Acres offers several options for accommodations; among them four fully restored 18th-century sea captain's homes outfitted with antique furnishings and nautical accents. A less atmospheric but equally comfortable experience is available in the inn's two contemporary buildings, where simple guest rooms serve your needs with private baths, telephones with voice mail, cable TVs, refrigerators, coffeemakers, individual temperature controls, and other basic necessities. Many rooms offer special features such as full kitchens, decorative fireplaces, sitting areas, balconies, and private terraces. Besides men's and women's saunas and outdoor and indoor pools, there are also badminton, croquet, and volleyball courts; lawn swings; Victorian gazebos; umbrella tables; and barbecue grills on-site. If you need exercise, go outside or you can partake of membership privileges at a nearby fitness center. A nonsmoking facility, Shore Way Acres is open all year round and available for weddings, reunions, meetings, and other group activities. Breakfast is complimentary for all guests, and those with a yen for shellfish can place special reservations for a "Cook Your Own Cape Cod Lobster Clamboil."

SPRING GARDEN INN $$–$$$
578 Rte. 6A, East Sandwich
(508) 888-0710, (866) 345-5641
www.springgarden.com

The Spring Garden Inn is located along a quiet section of the Old Kings Highway at the east end of Sandwich. On a hillside overlooking a 2,500-acre conservation area, the inn offers views of marsh stretching out toward the Scorton River. Pine-paneled rooms with beam ceilings include private baths, coffeemakers, refrigerators, cable TVs, private phones, air-conditioning and wireless Internet access. The motel also features a two-room suite in the original living quarters of the inn, built in the 1940s, and two garden efficiency apartments. The efficiency studio features a queen bed, pull-out sofa, and a full-size, fully equipped kitchen. The one-bedroom efficiency apartment has a kitchenette and dining table, and leads to a garden patio area. Families will enjoy the swimming pool and a spacious backyard for the children. Scorton Creek is a great spot for canoeing and fishing. Complimentary continental breakfast is served each morning. The inn is open year-round.

SPRING HILL MOTOR LODGE $$$–$$$$
351 Rte. 6A, East Sandwich
(508) 888-1456, (800) 647-2514
www.springhillmotorlodge.com

The Cape Cod–style Spring Hill Motor Lodge has exceptionally well-maintained grounds spotted with colorful junipers. Its 22 rooms are equipped with color cable TVs, direct-dial telephones, coffeemakers, refrigerators, and individually controlled heat and air-conditioning. The lodge also features a heated pool and surrounded by a large sundeck, a lighted "tournament quality" tennis court, a basketball hoop, and a picnic area with tables. Bright one- and two-bedroom contemporary cottages feature custom kitchens, cathedral ceilings, French doors, and bay windows overlooking the manicured grounds. Spring Hill Motor Lodge is open all year.

Mid-Cape

THE ANCHOR-IN $$–$$$$
1 South St., Hyannis
(508) 775-0357
www.anchorin.com

You can't get much closer to Hyannis Harbor than the Anchor-In. The inn offers a great location with outstanding views, super rooms, immaculate grounds, and a delightful staff. Just 60 feet from the water's edge in downtown Hyannis, the Anchor-In is within walking distance of restaurants, island ferries, excursion boats, and shopping. Hyannis Marina, many boats, and a public boat launch are within sight. Most of the 42 rooms, whether standard, deluxe, or executive, have private decks and harbor views and sleep four comfortably. The inn used to have an extra room but that has been converted into a new common area—the Lewis Bay Library. Seven executive guest rooms bear the names of Barnstable's seven villages, and two of these qualify as "specialty suites." Typical of these lodgings are oversize 40-foot decks (the better to appreciate uniformly dazzling views of the harbor) and either Jacuzzis or marble tubs. All rooms are clean, comfortable, and attractively furnished; two rooms are fully wheelchair accessible. A large heated pool and lawn, complete with a huge grounded anchor to support the inn's name, overlook the harbor.

Open year-round, the Anchor-In completes its "Cape Cod hospitality" with a complimentary "deluxe" continental breakfast, served either in the sunroom, by the pool, or even on the deck in your own room.

BAYSIDE RESORT $$$–$$$$
225 Rte. 28, West Yarmouth
(508) 775-5669, (800) 243-1114
www.baysideresort.com

Refrigerators, cable TV with free in-room movies, and movies on demand make you feel at home. Many of the rooms have a sundeck and overlook Lewis Bay. They also offer Jacuzzi suites for two. There is a whirlpool and male and female saunas in the indoor pool area, which includes a fitness center. The Moby Dick Pub evokes the ambience of an old-school fisherman's bar. Outside, the picturesque pool area has a great view of Lewis Bay, and the large deck area is filled with plenty of lounge chairs for your relaxation. Among the other incentives to stay close are an outdoor beach, and a volleyball court. Complimentary continental breakfast is included as well as $6 dinner coupons. Bayside Resort is open year-round.

BLUE ROCK GOLF RESORT $$–$$$
39 Todd Rd., South Yarmouth
(800) 227-3263 (CAPE COD)
www.redjacketresorts.com

The Blue Rock Golf Course has 18 holes, a pro shop, golf school, driving range, and putting green (see our Golf chapter for more information). The Blue Rock is a 45-room motel with either double or deluxe king accommodations. Rooms have individual temperature control and panoramic views of the golf course. After you've hit the course you can hit the solar-heated outdoor pool, Grille Room restaurant, or on-site lounge. While you're waiting for your tee time, enjoy some tennis or a good book on your private patio or deck. Off site you have access to a nearby private beach (either at Blue Rock or one of three sister properties located on Nantucket Sound) and biking paths. This Red Jacket inn is open from Apr to the end of Oct. There are golf packages (and other packages) available.

BLUE WATER RESORT $$$–$$$$
P.O. Box 276, South Shore Dr.,
South Yarmouth
(800) 227-3263 (CAPE COD)
www.redjacketresorts.com

At this oceanfront hotel you can choose between two swimming pools, banana boat rides, a water trampoline, a putting green, and, of course, the waters of Nantucket Sound. This Red Jacket facility has a dining room lounge that serves breakfast and lunch. Rugosa roses and sand dunes enhance the attractive, well-kept grounds. In addition to 90 immaculate guest rooms, there are 24 cottages and family suites—among them the Sandpiper Townhouse, which can accommodate a party of eight. Some units are wheelchair accessible, others allow pets, and all accommodations are nonsmoking. During the summer, Blue Water offers supervised children's activities. Ask about the Blue Water's terrific package deals throughout the year. Children younger than 12 stay for free.

CAPE POINT HOTEL $-$$$$
476 Rte. 28, West Yarmouth
(508) 778-1500, (800) 323-9505
www.capepointhotel.com

Centrally located along West Yarmouth's popular Route 28, the Cape Point is an attractive accommodation with reasonably priced rooms for families and budget-conscious travelers. A waterfall in the lobby greets guests upon arrival. The facility includes a lovely outdoor pool, a regal indoor pool with a balcony overhead, a children's pool, Jacuzzi, exercise room, and game room to keep the kids entertained. Standard rooms have two queen-size beds, cable TV, refrigerator, and telephone. Deluxe rooms offer the same amenities but are approximately one-third larger and have a love seat–sofa that pulls out to a single bed. Two-bedroom family suites offer an extra special touch without taking an executive-size bite out of the family budget. Wheelchair-accessible accommodations are available. Open year-round, the hotel also has a breakfast cafe, a seasonal Cabana Bar and Grille, and a lounge, the Sports Loft, on-site.

CENTERVILLE CORNERS INN $$$-$$$$
1338 Craigville Beach Rd., Centerville
(508) 775-7223, (800) 242-1137
www.centervillecorners.com

A short walk from popular Craigville Beach on Nantucket Sound, Centerville Corners Inn is ideally located in the lovely whaling captain's village of Centerville. From here you are within minutes of the Kennedy Compound in Hyannisport, the ferryboats to the islands, elegant restaurants, and the Main Street historic district of Hyannis. Kayakers will delight in paddling the nearby Centerville River. Bring your bikes; from the motel you can pedal into Osterville or Hyannis with relative ease.

This smoke-free lodging blends colonial charm with modern amenities. Each spacious room is equipped with refrigerator, color cable TV, direct-dial telephone, ceramic-tiled bath, and individually controlled air-conditioning. Thanks to a recent update, all 17 efficiencies now feature kitchenettes, and every room has wireless Internet access. Each day, in season, a continental spread is served in the motel's breakfast room. The indoor heated pool and saunas overlook the large, private grounds, which you are free to use for picnics, barbecues, croquet, badminton, or just relaxing with your favorite book.

Additionally, Centerville Corners Inn is right across the street from the legendary Four Seas ice-cream parlor and just a short stroll to the 1856 Penny Candy Store and the Centerville Historical Society Museum. Dogs are permitted with prior approval and a $15-per-day charge. Golfers should ask about the motel's package deals.

COLONY BEACH MOTEL $$-$$$$
413 Old Wharf Rd., Dennisport
(508) 398-2217
www.colonybeachmotel.com

Choose from 44 rooms in this sound-side motel, including oceanfront and ocean-view efficiency units with fully equipped kitchen and dining areas, motel units, or nonefficiency suites with living rooms. There is a private beach, a game room, and a heated outdoor swimming pool. Children aged 2 to 12 may stay for an additional $5 plus tax per night. The Colony Beach Motel is open mid-May to mid-Oct.

THE CORSAIR AND CROSS RIP
OCEANFRONT RESORT $$$-$$$$
41 Chase Ave., Dennisport
(508) 398–6600, (800) 345-5140
www.corsaircrossrip.com

This three-acre family-owned and -operated Dennisport resort rests on Nantucket Sound. The resort includes two outdoor pools, two outdoor Jacuzzis, and two large sundecks overlooking the ocean. Recreation buildings across the street feature an indoor pool, a game room, a toddler area with plenty of toys, a barbecue area, and an outdoor play area for the kids. A recent update incorporated Wi-Fi access and an in-season coffee bar (in the lobby), offering caffeine to go with the resort's complimentary baked goods.

There are many types of rooms from which to choose. All rooms at the Cross Rip have kitchenettes. There are a variety of suites with more space—among them the two-floor Townhouse suite, which features ocean views, a galley kitchenette, and a semiprivate loft bedroom accessed by a spiral staircase. Open from mid-Apr to late Oct, the complex also rents out three fully furnished homes with access to the amenities.

DAYS INN HYANNIS $$-$$$$
867 Rte. 132, Hyannis
(508) 771-6100, (800) 329-7466
www.hyannisdaysinn.com

Open year-round, this 99-room Days Inn offers a central location convenient to shopping, restaurants, and the airport. Just down the road in one direction is the Hyannis Golf Course; in the other direction is downtown Hyannis with its Kennedy Museum and Memorial. On-site are two pools (indoor and outdoor), a whirlpool, and a fully equipped fitness room. All rooms bear the marks of a recent renovation, offering full baths, 25-inch color TVs with HBO, wireless Internet access, and balconies (on the upper level) or patios (on the lower level). Wheelchair-accessible rooms are available on request. A complimentary continental breakfast is also served. The inn is adjacent to the Cape Cod Mall and is popular with families and business travelers.

THE DUNES MOTOR INN $-$$$$
170 Seaview Ave., South Yarmouth
(508) 398-3062, (800) 237-5070
www.thedunescapecod.com

The Dunes has standard rooms and efficiencies; all decorated in Cape Cod scenes, as well as two-bedroom apartments for families. The rooms have two double beds (king- and queen-size beds are available at extra cost), private baths, air-conditioning, cable television, microwaves, and refrigerators. Efficiency units have two double beds along with a full kitchen set-up. A continental breakfast is available from 8 a.m. to 10 a.m. There's a heated outdoor pool, and the refreshing waters of Nantucket Sound are just a short walk away. It is open from May to Columbus Day.

GREEN HARBOR RESORT $$-$$$$
182 Baxter Ave., West Yarmouth
(800) 227-3263 (CAPE COD)
www.redjacketresorts.com

Because it is surrounded by salt water on three sides, there's really no sense in mentioning the wonderful water views. Almost as beautiful as the views are the lovely 7½-acre grounds of grass, sand, and gardens bursting with flowers. As for the accommodations, the 53 units here range widely in style from suites to cottages to villa town houses. Some units are in separate cottages; others are in the main motel building. Some rooms have decks and patios, and villas have decks overlooking the ocean. An oversize outdoor pool and deck offer a change of scenery for those who have been spending time down on the private beach. An on-site minigolf course keeps the kids in the swing of things, and bikes, canoes, and rowboats are all available. Of added interest to parents is the children's recreation program, which is complimentary in season. The angler in you will enjoy the jetties off the beaches. Or just pull up a chair and relax watching the tide rise and fall. Golfers take note: Green Harbor is a Red Jacket Resort. As their guest, you can take advantage of other Red Jacket Resort amenities . . . like the Blue Rock Golf Course (see our Golf chapter). Green Harbor is open mid-May to early Oct.

GULL WING SUITES $$
822 Route 28, South Yarmouth
(508) 394-9300
www.gullwingsuitescapecod.com

If you are looking for more room and want to stay in a suite, Gull Wing Suites has 136 newly renovated contemporary mini-suites, each with a sitting area, two color TVs, refrigerator, wet bar, microwave, mini-fridge, and individual temperature control. It is perfect for budget-conscious families who want extra room and deluxe treatment. Open year-round (on weekends only from Nov to Apr), the Gull Wing is a family resort with clean, comfortable rooms and a heated indoor pool, outdoor pool, whirlpool, sauna, Jacuzzi, arcade, playground, and brand-new fitness center. It also offers you a great location from which to visit area attractions, historical sites, and beautiful beaches. The Gull Wing welcomes children 18 and younger free when accompanied by adults.

HAMPTON INN SUITES ON CAPE COD
99 Main St., Route 28, West Yarmouth
(508) 862-9010, (888) 892-3844
www.capecodsuites.hamptoninn.com
This brand new Hampton Inn Suites opened for business in the spring of 2009 as part of an ongoing effort to revitalize Yarmouth's Route 28. The facility represents a new era for Yarmouth's hotels, which had fallen in stature after a building boom in the mid-1980s left the town awash in rooms for rent. The hotel has space for functions and was designed with a Cape Cod theme in mind, including black-and-white photographs of the Cape throughout. There are twelve types of rooms available, including those with two queen-size beds and studio suites for families with king-size beds, microwaves, a refrigerator and a queen-size pull-out couch. The hotel's construction incorporates the latest in energy efficiency, the newest rage in any new building on the Cape. There are also pools inside and outside and a whirlpool. Both wired and wireless Internet access is available in the hotel.

HARBOR HOUSE INN $$-$$$$
119 Ocean St., Hyannis
(508) 771-1880, (800) 211-5551
www.harborhouseinn.net
The Harbor House Inn is directly across the street from Hyannis Harbor, one of Cape Cod's busiest waterfront area. Consisting of 18 mini-suites and a honeymoon unit (the Harbor Suite), the inn boasts large tiled baths, fully equipped kitchens, and access to either a second-floor balcony or a

first-floor patio. Each unit contains a TV with DVD player (guests get their pick of free movies), and individualized temperature controls. The inn also offers free wireless Internet access. Each suite has windows with screens and a screen door should you wish to enjoy the salt breeze off the harbor. The inn is a nonsmoking accommodation. A continental breakfast is offered each morning. It is a very short walk to the ferries to the islands and there is a free on-demand shuttle to Kalmus Beach. The inn is open mid-Apr through late Oct.

HOLIDAY INN $$$-$$$$
1127 Rte. 132, Hyannis
(508) 775-1153
www.holidayinn.com/hyannisma
This 196-room Holiday Inn has a glass-walled pool area, , and right off the pool is an inviting lawn with lounge chairs and an attractive dining room that serves breakfast, lunch, and dinner. Its central location makes it convenient for shopping and fine dining. For those looking further afield the hotel's convenient location close to US 6 opens up the rest of the Cape for visitors to explore.

The hotel offers 20 post-and-beam design loft suites. There's a Jacuzzi, fitness room, and business center, and across the hall is a lounge with free wireless Internet. Home to the Madhatter restaurant for dinner and the Green House Grill for breakfast and dinner, the hotel is open year-round. Children under 12 get free breakfast and dinner.

HYANNIS HARBOR HOTEL $$-$$$$
213 Ocean St., Hyannis
(508) 775-4420, (800) 655-2047
www.hyannisharborhotel.com
Breathe in the salt air, bathe in the sun, and watch the boats sail in and out of Hyannis Harbor while you relax on the sundeck by the beautifully landscaped outdoor pool and Jacuzzi. If it's raining, how about a dip in the heated indoor pool and whirlpool, or a leisurely meal at the in-house Thirsty Tuna Restaurant and Bar? At the Hyannis Harbor Hotel, you're directly across Ocean Street

from picturesque Hyannis Harbor, just steps from the island ferries to Nantucket and Martha's Vineyard, as well as fishing charters and sightseeing excursions. You are also only a short walk to Veterans Beach, the John F. Kennedy Memorial, John F. Kennedy Museum, downtown shopping, and many harborside restaurants.

Recently renovated, many of the hotel's 136 rooms include award-winning decor, cable TV, and DVD players and offer balconies overlooking the scenic harbor and inviting outdoor pool area. Open from Apr to Oct.

HYANNIS INN MOTEL $$-$$$
473 Main St., Hyannis
(508) 775-0255, (800) 922-8993
www.hyannisinn.com

A good choice for visitors who appreciate the convenience of downtown Hyannis and an inexpensive Cape Cod vacation. Shops, attractions, island ferries, excursion tours, and whale watching are all within walking distance. The 77 rooms feature both standard rooms (cable TV and direct-dial phones with wireless Internet access) and rooms with outdoor decks. They have larger rooms with sofas and refrigerators, as well as a limited number of whirlpool rooms. Swim a few laps in the heated indoor pool, enjoy the sauna, or relax on the sundeck. You can start your day at Bluebird's Restaurant, which serves breakfast, and unwind later in the day at the Elbow Room Cocktail Lounge. They do have a wheelchair-accessible room. Children younger than 12 stay free. The motel is open from Mar to Nov.

HYANNIS TRAVEL INN
$$-$$$
18 North St., Hyannis
(508) 775-8200, (800) 352-7190
www.hyannistravelinn.com

With 83 rooms, indoor and outdoor pools, including an oversize whirlpool, this facility is a good value for couples and families who want to be close to the many Hyannis attractions. Minigolf, the Cape Cod Central Railroad, shops, restaurants, beaches, and the John F. Kennedy Museum

are all within a five-minute walk. Slightly longer walks will get you to the island ferries, the Hyannis waterfront district, and the Cape Cod Melody Tent (see our Arts chapter). Amenities include a continental breakfast with coffee, muffins, bagels, and juice. The motel is open from mid-Feb through Nov.

INTERNATIONAL INN $$-$$$$
662 Main St., Hyannis
(508) 775-5600, (877) SCUDDLE
www.cuddles.com

The International Inn is as centrally located as it is romantic: Just a short stroll from the Cape Cod Melody Tent (see the Arts chapter) on the west end of Main Street it is close to all the shops and sites along the popular main drag of Hyannis. A favorite spot for couples celebrating wedding anniversaries, the Inn's Plaza Suite is a sought-after getaway around Valentine's Day. This three-room suite includes a king-size canopied bed, a wet bar, and a 5-by-7 foot sunken Jacuzzi. Besides bubble-laden Jacuzzis, the International Inn boasts high-speed wireless Internet, the Gazebo Garden Room Restaurant, indoor and outdoor swimming pools, and saunas for men and women.

MARINER MOTOR LODGE $-$$$
573 Rte. 28, West Yarmouth
(508) 771-7887, (800) 445-4050
www.mariner-capecod.com

This L-shaped lodging has two pools (a heated 50-footer indoors and a heated 55-footer outdoors) in addition to a whirlpool, male and female saunas, a game room, and a picnic area. It has 100 air-conditioned rooms with in-room refrigerators and safes for valuables. Yarmouth's Sea Gull Beach is only a five-minute drive away, and Hyannis (and the island ferries) is no more than 10 minutes down Route 28. There are numerous dining opportunities within a couple of miles. The Mariner is open from Apr through Nov, and children under 18 stay for free. Wheelchair access is available for both standard and king rooms.

OCEAN MIST RESORT $-$$$$
97 South Shore Dr., South Yarmouth
(508) 398-2633, (800) 248-6478
www.capecodoceanresorts.com

Ocean Mist's 63 rooms are deluxe rooms with wet bars or efficiencies with full kitchens. All have individual temperature controls and remote-control cable television. Their loft suites feature cathedral ceilings and wet bars. Most have skylights and two private balconies with ocean views. Ocean Mist has a heated indoor pool, a hot tub, a private beach, and a cozy breakfast cafe.

RED JACKET BEACH RESORT $$$$
1 South Shore Dr., South Yarmouth
(800) 227-3263 (CAPE COD)
www.redjacketinns.com

The Red Jacket has everything, including a 1,000-foot sandy waterfront beach as well as frontage on Parker's River salt marsh.

If it's land sports that you prefer, the resort includes tennis, basketball, volleyball, and shuffleboard courts. The resort offers a supervised children's program of sports and activities. Kayaks and Jet Skis are available for rent, while thrill-seekers can opt for parasailing. If the water off the resort's private beach is too cold, both the outdoor and indoor pools are heated.

Among the resort's other amenities are a whirlpool spa, a sauna, on-site dining (now with all-new patio seating) and a zero-entry pool. Accommodations range from guest rooms to townhouses, many offering spectacular views of the ocean, Great Marsh, Nantucket Sound, or Parker's River. And, for partisans of pampering, there's the Spa at Red Jacket Beach, offering services such as massages, facials, and manicures.

i Check around for golf packages when looking for a place to stay on Cape Cod. Many hotels, motels, and resorts offer golf packages that include accommodations for two nights, two rounds of golf, and dinner discount certificates.

RESORT AND CONFERENCE CENTER AT HYANNIS $$$-$$$$
35 Scudder Ave., Hyannis
(508) 775-7775, (866) 828–8259
www.capecodresortandconference.com

Across the street from the Cape Cod Melody Tent, this resort features an 18-hole par 54 golf course—a spectacular 2,600-yard stretch of green called Twin Brooks. The full-service hotel/conference center pampers guests with private balconies (or patios) and four options for dining: Mulligan's, which serves breakfast and expertly prepared seafood; Coffee Cafe; Cabana Bar and Grill, a seasonal poolside cabana bar; and the Bogeys Sports Pub for those who need to watch the big game. Heated indoor and outdoor pools, a whirlpool, a spa, and a playground are among the extras you can expect from this year-round 224-room complex.

SURFCOMBER ON THE BEACH $$$$
107 South Shore Dr., South Yarmouth
(508) 398-9228
www.surfcombermotel.com

The Surfcomber provides peace and quiet right by the water's edge. Sunbathing and swimming at the private beach could be your occupation for the week, but if you tire of the salt water, there is a heated outdoor swimming pool within ear-shot of the ocean waves. Some rooms overlook Nantucket Sound, while others feature private balconies above the landscaped grounds and pool. Families or larger parties may opt for one of the motel's spacious efficiencies, which offer the convenience of kitchens with full-size ranges, refrigerators, coffeemakers, cookware, and utensils. Surfcomber is open from mid-May to Columbus Day.

TIDEWATER INN $-$$$
135 Rte. 28, West Yarmouth
(508) 775-6322, (800) 338-6322
www.tidewatercapecod.com

The 100-room Tidewater is on four acres bordering a conservation area overlooking Mill Creek Bay and Mill Pond. One mile east of downtown Hyannis, it provides a location central to the many attractions of Yarmouth, island ferries, and the airport. The lodge has a large indoor pool as well as an outdoor pool, hot Vita spa, hot tub, and a game room featuring table tennis, darts, and board games. Beaches are a short drive away, as is just about everything else, from movies, minigolf, and restaurants to outlets and shops. A large outdoor grassy area has picnic tables, a recreation area with volleyball net, sandbox, swings, and play equipment for the kids. The rooms feature remote-control cable TV, telephone, and individually controlled heat and air-conditioning. Enjoy one of their deluxe Jacuzzi rooms as your day comes to an end. The rooms are nicely furnished and have refrigerators. The property is entirely nonsmoking. Wheelchair-accessible rooms as well as bed-and-breakfast packages are available. There is no charge for children younger than 17 staying with an adult.

Lower Cape

BLUE SEA MOTOR INN $$$–$$$$
696 Shore Rd., Route 6A, North Truro
508-487-1041
www.blueseamotorinn.com
The owners of the Viking Shores Motor Lodge in Eastham also own the Blue Sea. The motor inn has 60 rooms and several efficiency kitchen units on the beach. The rooms have cable TV, heat and air-conditioning and refrigerators. The facility also has a private beach and an indoor swimming pool and hot tub.

CAPTAIN'S QUARTERS MOTEL AND CONFERENCE CENTER $$–$$$
5000 State Hwy., North Eastham
(508) 255-5686, (800) 327-7769
www.captains-quarters.com
With standard and deluxe rooms, an outdoor heated pool, courts for tennis (two) and beach volleyball, and complimentary use of bikes for the adjacent rail trail, this family-run facility has a lot to offer. Rooms all have refrigerators, phones, color cable TVs, and individual temperature control. Enjoy a complimentary continental breakfast in the lounge area, which features a delight-

ful hand-painted mural of nearby Nauset Light Beach. You can also help yourself to fresh popcorn later in the day. Families find this a good place to make their home base as they explore the Outer Cape. For business people, the Captain's Quarters offers conference facilities. It's open from late May to mid-Oct.

CHATEAU PROVINCETOWN $$–$$$
105 Bradford St. Ext., Provincetown
(508) 487-1286
www.chateauptown.com
High atop a hill at the west end of town, this 54-room facility enjoys sweeping views. The rooms are all done in classic Cape decor, and each has a large TV, data ports, and individual temperature control. All rooms are equipped with wireless Internet access and refrigerators, and most have private safes. There's a large heated pool, gardens, and a number of decks overlooking the water. Kids under 18 stay free and guests get complimentary morning coffee and muffins. It's open from early May to mid-Oct.

CHATHAM BARS INN $$$$
297 Shore Rd., Chatham
(508) 945-0096, (800) 527-4884
www.chathambarsinn.com
Built in 1913 as a hunting lodge by a wealthy Boston family, this resort still maintains its elegance and grandeur. The inn's impressive main house, which looks out over the water, has 40 rooms, complemented by an array of cottage rooms, cottage suites, and lavish master suites complete with wet bars and fireplaces. All the rooms are inviting and purposely understated—decorated with lots of wicker and floral prints and fabrics—and many feature balconies with breathtaking views of the Atlantic Ocean and Pleasant Bay. The 25 acres of grounds boast courts for every conceivable sport, from tennis to shuffleboard, along with a private beach and a heated outdoor pool. Wireless Internet access is available throughout the property, and a full fitness center is flanked by a private spa offering massage therapy, skin care treatments, and body treatments.

One finds an atmosphere for every mood at in-house restaurants, including the main dining room, the Chef's Table, the Tavern, and the Beach House Grill, and anglophiles can even partake of traditional afternoon tea in the inn's South Lounge.

CHATHAM SEAFARER $$$–$$$$
2079 Main St., Chatham
(508) 432-1739, (800) 786-2772
www.chathamseafarer.com
The Seafarer is family owned and managed. Rooms are hand-stenciled and furnished with one queen or two double beds. The property has a secluded garden and a large pool for guests who choose not to walk or bike the short distance to a nearby beach on Nantucket Sound. All the rooms are nonsmoking and guests are asked to limit smoking to the sitting area outside of their rooms.

The Seafarer is open Apr through Nov.

THE COVE ON THE WATERFRONT $$–$$$$
13 Rte. 28, Orleans
(508) 255-1203, (800) 343-2233
www.thecoveorleans.com
The sparkling waters of Town Cove lap at the shore of this attractive year-round complex, which features beautifully landscaped gardens and patios, a heated outdoor pool, and, of course, terrific water views. Many of the rooms have views of Town Cove, and many have private decks. All are equipped with king or queen beds, comfortable sitting areas, coffee stations, refrigerators, cable TVs (complimentary HBO and ESPN) and DVD players. The entire facility is non-smoking. Book a waterfront room or, for an extra special stay, a room at the Inn at the Cove. It has 10 rooms and suites (some with fireplaces, some with full kitchens), all warm and cozy with Shaker-style furnishings. Visit the waterfront gazebo, where you can commune with the terns and gulls, and watch sailboats tack by.

EAGLE WING GUEST HOTEL $–$$$
960 U.S. Rte. 6, Eastham
(508) 240-5656, (800) 278-5656
www.eaglewingmotel.com
All 19 rooms in this little gem, located near the Cape Cod National Seashore, have private baths, air-conditioning and heat, refrigerators, cable TV, and phones. Most have king-size beds. A back deck stretches the length of the building so guests can enjoy the quiet backyard, which borders a wetland sweet with birdsong in spring and summer. There's a large outdoor pool, and morning coffee is available, along with freshly baked muffins, tea, and orange juice. Ideal for couples and adults looking for quiet, clean, and comfortable surroundings, the Eagle Wing provides all the amenities of a large facility while maintaining the feel of a guesthouse or inn. The motel, which is completely nonsmoking, is open May through mid-Oct.

THE EVEN'TIDE RESORT MOTEL AND COTTAGES $–$$$$
650 U.S. Rte. 6, South Wellfleet
(508) 349-3410, (800) 368-0007 (Massachusetts only)
www.eventidemotel.com
This friendly, family-owned motel is set so far back among the woods that you may feel like you're vacationing in the middle of a forest—if forests came complete with a 30-by-60-foot indoor pool. All the rooms at this facility come with refrigerators, cable TVs, clock radios, coffeemakers, individual temperature control, and private, ceramic-tiled baths with tubs and showers. The most popular units are the queen-size rooms with their pretty custom-made oak furnishings. Eight cottages, five of them A-frames with wood-stoves, are also available, all with decks. An off-site property is also offered by the EvenTide—a surf-side cottage at South Wellfleet's LeCount Hollow Beach. Biking enthusiasts take note: The Cape Cod Rail Trail runs right through the backyard. In addition to an outdoor play area, complete with basketball court and horseshoe pit, guests can entertain themselves at the newly added minigolf course, shuffleboard court, or fitness facility. The EvenTide is open from May 1 through Nov 1.

FOUR POINTS HOTEL BY SHERATON
EASTHAM CAPE COD $$$$
3800 U.S. Rte. 6, Eastham
(508) 255-5000, (800) 325-3535
www.starwoodhotels.com/bestweb

The Four Points Hotel, part of the Sheraton chain, has 107 recently renovated guest rooms, including suites, all beautifully appointed. The indoor atrium and pool are a refreshing oasis at the end of a long day (there are also men's and women's saunas and an outdoor pool). The fitness room is stocked with up-to-date equipment. The on-site restaurant, Bellamy's Grille and Bar, serves breakfast and dinner, and room service allows you to dine on your private balcony or on Sheraton's trademark comfort bed. Four Points is open year-round and is great for families or business travelers.

HORIZONS BEACH RESORT $$$-$$$$
190 Rte. 6A, North Truro
(508) 487-0042, (800) 782-0742
(outside Massachusetts)
www.horizonsbeach.com

In a quiet, rural setting just a short drive away from Provincetown and only a mile from Cape Cod National Seashore, Horizons Beach Resort offers efficiency units, some right on the beach and the rest a short stroll away. All have cable TV, kitchens, and individual temperature control. Beachfront units have private decks with views of Cape Cod Bay. Relax on the 500-foot private beach on Cape Cod Bay, or take a dip in the beachside pool. Horizons also offers two-room condominium units with fireplaces and is open from early Apr to late Oct.

MAINSTAY MOTOR INN $$-$$$
2068 U.S. Rte. 6, South Wellfleet
(508) 349-2350, (800) 346-2350
www.mainstaymotorinn.com

The Mainstay is convenient to everything. Tennis courts are within walking distance, the Cape Cod National Seashore is a scallop shell's throw away, Wellfleet Harbor's marina is practically in the front yard, and whale-watching boats in Provincetown are a few miles away. When you're tired of sight-seeing, relax by the Mainstay's indoor pool, or soak in the Jacuzzi. Each of the 30 rooms here has a king- or queen-size bed or two double beds with a full bath, refrigerator, and outdoor deck. Some rooms are efficiencies with refrigerators and microwave ovens as well, and there is also a three-room cottage available for rent by the week in season. A complimentary continental breakfast is served daily in the coffee room, which also houses the Mainstay's free lending library. It's open from Apr through Nov.

MIDWAY MOTEL & COTTAGES $-$$$
5460 U.S. Rte. 6, North Eastham
(508) 255-3117, (800) 755-3117
www.midwaymotel.com

Right on the scenic Cape Cod Rail Trail bike path, in the heart of the Cape Cod National Seashore and close to the Wellfleet Bay Wildlife Sanctuary, this complex is made up of four separate buildings, nicely spaced and set back from the road. There are a total of nine motel units, an efficiency, a three-bedroom cottage that can sleep six, and a one-bedroom cottage that can accommodate two to four people. All rooms have full baths, cable TVs, air-conditioning, ceiling fans, coffeemakers, refrigerators, and microwave ovens. The three-acre property has a play yard with swings and a climbing tower for children, and, for all ages, volleyball, horseshoes, badminton, and shuffleboard. Complimentary coffee is served with newspapers each morning in the common room. The Midway is open Feb through Oct.

NAUSET KNOLL MOTOR LODGE $$$
237 Beach Rd., East Orleans
(508) 255-2364
www.capecodtravel.com/nausetknoll

Situated on a knoll overlooking Nauset Beach and the Atlantic, this accommodation's every room commands a view of the ocean. Four acres of manicured grounds ensure privacy. The Nauset Knoll consists of 12 spacious ground-level rooms with 8-foot picture windows facing the ocean. The simply decorated rooms offer ceramic-tiled bathrooms (tub and shower combination), color cable TV, and baseboard hot-water heat. Operated under the supervision of the National Park Service, the Nauset Knoll is the only motel on the Atlantic Ocean within the Cape Cod National Seashore. It is just a short drive to fine dining and the attractions of the lower Cape. We'll give you a tip about this place: Especially appealing to birders is autumn at the lodge when the best birding of the year can be enjoyed on the dune uplands. You'll have the beach to yourself, along with the warm waters that have heated all summer. Children are welcome at Nauset Knoll, which is open from mid-Apr to late Oct.

OCEAN EDGE RESORT AND CLUB $$$$
2660 Rte. 6A, Brewster
(508) 896-9000, (800) 343-6074
www.oceanedge.com
Ocean Edge is distinguished by its impressive Gothic and Renaissance Revival stucco mansion and stone carriage house on 400 acres of land. Once part of the vast Roland Nickerson estate, the main 400-foot-long mansion is as grand inside as out, with carved wood-paneled walls, a two-tiered Italian oak staircase, and Edwardian fireplaces crafted of marble and wood. The resort straddles Route 6A, evoking the ambience of old New England summer colonies. Attached to the mansion by enclosed walkways is a two-wing 90-room hotel. In addition to deluxe and superior guest rooms, visitors can choose from lavish corner suites; Bayside Villas; and Resort Side Villas.

People flock here for the world-class golf (see our Golf chapter), tennis schools and clinics, and for the abundance of other recreational activities. The resort has eight pools (four outdoor, two indoor, and two for toddlers) and a 700-foot private beach. Recently bought by ClubCorp, the Ocean Edge was updated in 2005 and now features state-of-the-art fitness facilities, a spa treatment room, and a USPTA-certified tennis complex. The 18-hole, par 72, USGA championship golf course reopened in May 2008 after an $8.5 million renovation and redesign. You could conceivably spend a week at Ocean View without dining at the same place, thanks to the availability of eateries including the Ocean Grille, Bayzo's Pub, the family-style Reef Café, and poolside cabanas catering to the Arbor, Fletcher, and Bay Pines complexes. The resort also offers children's activities in summer and year-round concierge service to enhance your trips off campus.

ORLEANS HOLIDAY MOTEL $$–$$$$
48 Rte. 6A, Orleans
(508) 255-1514
www.rodewayinnorleans.com
Open year-round in Orleans, the Orleans Holiday Motel has 43 contemporary, clean rooms in a great location just outside of town. The motel offers accommodations with two double beds, one queen-size bed, or two queen-size beds. Rollaway beds and cribs are also available. Each room is fully carpeted and includes air conditioning, heat, bath with tub and shower, direct-dial phones, color cable TV with HBO, and a refrigerator. Rooms also have ironing boards and wireless Internet access.

During the summer months, this is a great place to stay. The pool has an extra-large shallow section for children. The nicely landscaped backyard area is ideal for barbecues and picnics. It's close to family dining—next door to a local favorite, the Lobster Claw Restaurant. A complimentary continental breakfast is served in the motel lobby every morning from 7 until 10 a.m. All rooms are nonsmoking, and two "pets permitted" accommodations are available.

PLEASANT BAY VILLAGE RESORT $$$–$$$$
1191 Orleans Rd., Chatham
(508) 945-1133, (800) 547-1011
www.pleasantbayvillage.com
Painstakingly renovated by innkeeper Howard Gamsey, this 58-room facility is set on six acres of beautiful grounds, with oriental gardens, waterfalls cascading into a rock-lined koi pond, and inviting private woodland. Pleasant Bay Village's efficiencies and suites are furnished in contemporary style. Original art from some of Cape Cod's well-known artists adorns the walls, and every accommodation, from rooms to two-bedroom suites, is comfortable, private, and quiet. One room is wheelchair accessible. Wake up to complimentary morning coffee and newspapers. Full breakfasts are available, as is lunch beside the

outdoor heated pool (in season). Children are welcome for an additional nightly fee, and the facility, open from late May through Oct, is non-smoking.

SEASHORE PARK INN $$–$$$
24 Canal Rd., Orleans
(508) 255-2500, (800) 772-6453
www.seashoreparkinn.com

Centrally located, this 62-room, family-oriented resort features a large indoor pool in a huge glass-walled room that you may have a hard time tearing the kids away from. That is, until they realize how close this property is to area attractions. The Seashore Park Inn is near restaurants, shops, the Cape Cod National Seashore, and other beaches, as well as the Cape Cod Rail Bicycle Trail. A continental breakfast is served every morning in the sunny cafe overlooking the outdoor pool. Many of the rooms are efficiency units, with refrigerators, stoves, and a second sitting area with a sleep sofa. All the rooms are non-smoking and have telephones, cable TVs, private baths, and individual temperature control. Most rooms offer balconies or patios. Open from Apr through late Oct, the Inn offers off-season rates as well as money-saving weekly rates any time of year. Children younger than 17 stay free.

TOP MAST RESORT $$–$$$$
217 Shore Rd., North Truro
(508) 487-1189, (800) 917-0024
www. topmastresort.com

This resort is located directly on Cape Cod Bay and surrounded by conservation land and scenic views. Choose from 72 units: Beachfront motel rooms have a queen bed and couch, small fridge and microwave; beachfront one- and two-room efficiencies and cottages have double and/or queen beds, cooktops, sinks, refrigerators, microwave ovens, and more. All beachfront rooms have private balconies overlooking the groomed beach and are perfect for watching sunsets over the Provincetown skyline. The outdoor pool is surrounded by chaise lounges and picnic tables, and new to the property is a large indoor pool complex complete with a heated pool, hot tub,

kiddy pool, sauna, steam room, weight room, large outdoor deck area with a fire pit, frozen drinks, beverages, and snacks. Breakfast is served daily at the on-site Top Mast Cafe. Family owned and operated by the Silva family for over 35 years, the Top Mast is open from early May to late Oct.

VIKING SHORES MOTOR LODGE $$$
5200 U.S. Rte. 6, Eastham
(508) 255-3200, (800) 242-2131
www.vikingshores.com

Centrally located in the Cape Cod National Seashore, Viking Shores not only offers a relaxing atmosphere in a wooded natural setting, but also direct access to the Cape Cod Rail Trail bike path. Each of the modern rooms features cable TV, private baths, refrigerators, telephones, wireless Internet access, and individual temperature control. Outside, barbecue grills and picnic tables accommodate al fresco diners. Nauset Beach and Coast Guard Beach on the Atlantic Ocean are just minutes away. If you enjoy tennis, don't forget your racquet to play on their courts. And the heated pool offers you the opportunity to just sit back and relax. If that's not enough, your hosts, Deb and Scott Sverid, will make sure you enjoy yourselves. They are happy to suggest a nature trail, guided walk, or a local seafood restaurant. The Audubon Sanctuary at Wellfleet Bay is less than a mile from the Viking Shores, and Ben & Jerry's is just down the street—always a plus when on vacation. A complimentary continental breakfast is served each morning during the season. The Viking Shores Motor Lodge is open mid-May through early Oct.

WELLFLEET MOTEL & LODGE $$$–$$$$
170 U.S. Rte. 6, Wellfleet
(508) 349-3535
www.wellfleetmotel.com

With a total of 65 rooms, the Wellfleet Motel & Lodge is right on the Cape Cod Rail Trail bike path and just across the street from Audubon's Wellfleet Bay Wildlife Sanctuary (see our Hiking and Biking Trails chapter). All the rooms—40 in the lodge and 25 motel units—are equipped with refrigerators, coffeemakers, color cable TVs, and wireless Internet access. There's both an indoor and an outdoor pool, with a barbecue and picnic area beside the latter. The lodge has an eatery (Harrigan's Café) with a full breakfast menu, and the facility is open year-round.

WEQUASSETT INN $$$–$$$$
Route 28 at Pleasant Bay Rd., Harwich
(508) 432-5400, (800) 225-7125
www.wequassett.com
This resort is almost a village unto itself. The 23-acre estate, which takes its name from a Native American word that means "crescent on the water," comprises a slew of buildings, including one built in 1740. Each of the rooms and suites has views of Pleasant Bay, Round Cove, or the woods and is furnished in Early American or country pine. So exquisite is the decor that many rooms have won national design awards.

Tennis buffs can stay in one of the garden view villas, just steps away from four Har-Tru clay tennis courts. The inn also has its own dock and offers a sailing program for novices to salty-dog sailors. (The inn even has a rental fleet of Hobie Cats, Sunfish, and kayaks.) If you're not in the mood for salt water, take a dip in the awesome heated pool, recently renovated to include a dramatic entry, a new Jacuzzi, and a boardwalk of Brazilian wood.

Golfers will be happy to learn the Wequassett is affiliated with the exclusive nearby Cape Cod National Golf Club, allowing guests to arrange for tee times at the private course. Among the inn's other amenities are dining options from gourmet (Twenty-eight Atlantic) to everyday (Thoreau's and the seasonal Outer Bar and Grille and LiBAYtion, a second outdoor bar.) Parents will appreciate the children's fun club, which offers camp-style activities for kids from 4 to 12 (in July and August only).

The staff here is attentive but far from stuffy, and a concierge is available to help you with everything from dinner reservations to fishing excursions. The Wequassett is open from Apr through Nov.

BED-AND-BREAKFASTS, INNS, AND COTTAGES

Price Code

The following key to room rates should help you get a quick fix on the range of prices available. The key is based on the average cost of a night's stay in a double-occupancy room during the peak summer season, minus tax and special charges, if any. State and local room tax combined is generally 9.7 percent.

$	Less than $100
$$	$100 to $150
$$$	$151 to $200
$$$$	$201 or more

BED-AND-BREAKFASTS/INNS

Upper Cape

BAY BEACH   **$$$$**
3 Bay Beach Lane, Sandwich
(508) 888-8813
www.baybeach.com

Overlooking captivating Cape Cod Bay, Bay Beach is your private window onto a world of luxury and exceptional beauty. Recognized by the American Bed and Breakfast Association as one of the top inns in North America, Bay Beach is truly an exceptional accommodation. One of the keys to its success is the professionalism, hospitality, and superb taste of the innkeepers. Each of the three spacious rooms is exquisitely decorated for elegant comfort in wicker, rattan, and rich color. Each room has a private bath with Jacuzzi, air-conditioning, color TV, a stereo with CD player, a refrigerator; and a private deck. Two suites have fireplaces, and all have access to a private beach and daily indulgences like fresh flowers; refrigerators stocked with wine, cheese, and

fresh fruit; and morning papers delivered to the door. The views from this modern, oceanfront bed-and-breakfast are incredible—on a clear day you can see the Pilgrim Monument across the bay at Provincetown. This secluded, beachfront compound is just minutes from a wide variety of activities, including fishing, swimming, golf, biking, and walking trails. One room is wheelchair accessible. An extensive continental breakfast is served, featuring homemade breads and fresh fruits. Children 16 years of age and older are welcome at the Bay Beach, which is open from May to the end of Oct.

THE BELFRY INNE AND BISTRO   **$$$$**
8 Jarves St., Sandwich
(508) 888-8550, (800) 844-4542
www.belfryinn.com

The Belfry Inne (ca. 1860) exemplifies an era renowned for gentility and grace. From beneath a timeworn façade, innkeeper Chris Wilson has uncovered original cornerboards, fishscale scalloped shingles, and other artistry from the Victorian age. This stately structure, once a rectory, is captivating. Splendid period detail, such as the original Eastlake newel post, Sandwich-glass double door, and other architectural features, have been faithfully restored.

The Inne, which encourages respite and relaxation, comprises three restored period buildings—the Painted Lady, an 1882 Victorian manor house; the Abbey, a former church built in 1900; and the Village Inn, an 1830 Federal-style structure with a covered porch, perfect for rocking. The Painted Lady features nine bedrooms, working fireplaces, balconies, skylights, and private baths, some with whirlpools. The Abbey has been transformed into six bedroom suites named

Monday through Saturday. They feature gas fireplaces, ultra-massage whirlpools for two, king/queen beds, and balconies. Extra touches such as vaulted ceilings, skylights, vintage bathtubs, hand-selected antiques, and down-filled duvets increase the feel of elegance. From a queen-size iron bedstead to a mahogany shell–painted headboard, each furnishing in each room has been restored to its late 19th-century charm. All rooms at the Belfry have TV, and air-conditioning. The inn features a full restaurant, the Belfry Bistro, where diners can savor delicious international cuisine and enjoy piano music nightly. For contemporary comfort food, there's the Painted Lady Café, serving lunch and dinner in the Drew House from Apr through Dec. A full guest breakfast is served buffet style daily; specialties include house-made granola and Inne-baked pastries and breads. Added pampering is available thanks to the availability of in-room spa services from facials to 60-minute couples massages. A picture-postcard property in the heart of Sandwich center, the Belfry is close to all that historic Sandwich offers. Shops, museums, and the nature center are all within a short walk. The Belfry is open year-round. Children are welcome. Pets are allowed with advance notice.

CHAPOQUOIT INN $$$$
495 Rte. 28A, West Falmouth
(508) 540-7232, (800) 842-8994
www.chapoquoit.com
The entranceway to this inn surrounded by flowery gardens is a typical Greek Revival affair, with pilasters, entablature, and half-length sidelights. Windows are simply framed and contain the old six-over-six sash, and a wonderful old arched window is located in the gable. A sunlit breakfast room opens to a deck overlooking a gazebo and the gardens. Choose one of the spacious guest rooms, lovingly decorated for your comfort with linens, colorful quilts, and an abundance of pillows. Each room has a character all its own and is furnished with various antiques, family mementos, and beautiful prints of Falmouth by local artist Karen Rinaldo. The master bedroom has a canopied king-size bed. There are seven

rooms in total, and all have private full baths. Wake up to the aroma of freshly brewed coffee and a breakfast of fresh fruit, muffins, breads, and a hot specialty each day served cafe style. Spend your days at Chapoquoit Beach, within walking distance; Old Silver Beach; or one of the 10 other beaches in the area. The sunsets are glorious on the tidal creek across the street. The inn is close to Falmouth Center and the island ferries. Chapoquoit Inn is open year-round and is nonsmoking. Children 12 and older are welcome.

INN ON THE SOUND $$–$$$$
313 Grand Ave., Falmouth Heights
(508) 457-9666, (800) 564-9668
www.innonthesound.com
If you can imagine yourself awakening to a million-dollar view of Vineyard Sound with the island of Martha's Vineyard in the near distance, then the Inn on the Sound is for you. Eight of its 10 guest rooms have water views, and every room has its own individual character. The decor is casual contemporary, with natural oak features, ceiling fans, and the homey touch. All of the rooms have private baths; five have private decks. It's the perfect oasis for those phobic of the frills that beset most New England B&Bs, eschewing musty Victoriana in favor of sleek, stylish decor. Thoughtful touches include plentiful pillows, plush robes, and a basket of beach towels in case you forgot your own. A full breakfast is served in the dining room, though guests are welcome to take it "to go." The Inn on the Sound is located almost on the finish line of the Falmouth Road Race, up the hill from the beaches at Falmouth Heights, and close to fine dining.

ISAIAH JONES HOMESTEAD BED AND BREAKFAST $$–$$$$
165 Main St., Sandwich
(508) 888-9115, (800) 526-1625
www.isaiahjones.com
This 1849 Victorian in Sandwich Village is furnished almost entirely with antiques. Built at the height of Sandwich's 19th-century prosperity, the rooms here are named for important Sandwich citizens, such as Thomas Dexter, who

built the gristmill, and Deming Jarves, founder of the Sandwich Glass Factory. All seven rooms are elaborately appointed, some with canopied and four-poster beds, four with a whirlpool, and five with fireplaces. Each has a private bath. The Homestead serves a candlelit three-course gourmet breakfast that may include fresh scones, hot breads, fresh fruit, and juices. After breakfast retire to a chair on the front porch overlooking Main Street to make plans for the day, which may include many activities within walking distance. Children 12 and older are welcome at this year-round inn.

PALMER HOUSE INN $$$-$$$$
81 Palmer Ave., Falmouth
(508) 548-1230, (800) 472-2632
www.palmerhouseinn.com

This is a Victorian charmer on one of Falmouth's more secluded tree-lined streets. Lace curtains at the stained-glass windows, rich woodwork, polished hardwood floors, and antique furnishings create an overall sense of warmth. This large and immaculate facility has delightful touches pointing to a time of class and elegance (you'll love the scented fine linens and the plump pillows), but the inn also provides such modern-day amenities as bubbling whirlpool tubs and Posturepedic mattresses. The inn has 16 guest rooms: 12 in the Queen Anne–style main house and 4 (including one ADA-compliant room) in the neighboring guesthouse. The innkeepers also operate a two-bedroom cottage with a whirlpool tub, two televisions and a VCR, a mini-fridge, and a private deck and garden. All rooms are named after notable New England authors, with the Edith Wharton room evoking the Age of Innocence and the Henry David Thoreau cottage emphasizing seclusion and serenity. Guests can expect a few extras in addition to the usual amenities—among them whirlpool baths, four-poster beds, and triple sheeting with a 600 thread count. Breakfast is served in a sunny dining room, where fresh flowers and fine china set the scene for gourmet foods listed as recipes of the month on the Palmer House Web site. The inn is open year-round and welcomes children age 10 and older.

1750 INN AT SANDWICH CENTER $$$
118 Tupper Rd., Sandwich
(508) 888-6958, (800) 249-6949
www.innatsandwich.com

This vintage Federal-style house was built in 1750 and has, over the years, been beautifully restored and expanded. The airy, immaculate B&B is furnished with wonderful period pieces, including a beautiful oak hutch handcrafted locally by West Barnstable Tables. As the name implies, the Inn at Sandwich Center is conveniently located in town, just steps from the Sandwich Glass Museum, the Thornton Burgess Society Museum, Shawme Pond, and Heritage Plantation. The inn is listed in the National Register of Historic Places.

There are five guest rooms, all tastefully appointed, most with fireplaces, some with four-poster beds; all have private baths. Amenities include luxurious bed and bath linens; nightly turndown service; complimentary Wi-Fi access; access to cold drinks, bottled water, coffee, and tea throughout the day; a gazebo-enclosed hot tub; on-site spa services; and a nightly cocktail hour with port, sherry, and chocolates. There is a small library to browse through and, in the parlor, comfy chairs are available so that you may enjoy a good book. A full gourmet breakfast is served each morning.

The Inn at Sandwich Center is open seasonally and is nonsmoking. Children older than 12 are welcome.

WILDFLOWER INN CATERING AND ACCOMMODATIONS $$$-$$$$
167 Palmer Ave., Falmouth
(508) 548-9524
www.wildflower-inn.com

Four of the five rooms at this Victorian-style inn are named after flowers (Jasmine, Moonflower, Geranium, Beachrose, and Loft Cottage). Each room is different—a white wrought-iron bed in one room, a four-poster canopied bed in another. Some have antiques; all are filled with flowers. Each room has a private bath, and two rooms have whirlpools. The Loft Cottage is fashioned from the old stables, with a full kitchen, living room, and loft bedroom.

In keeping with its name, the Wildflower Inn specializes in "edible flower cuisine," harvesting blooms from its own gardens for its award-winning dishes. Guests can sample this floral fare in a homey gathering room warmed by a fireplace, sampling breakfast specialties that have earned mention on the PBS series Country Inn Cooking. Children over 12 are welcome, and those interested in staying a while should inquire about the availability of long-term rentals.

WOOD DUCK INN $$
1050 County Rd., Cataumet (Bourne)
(508) 564-6404
www.woodduckinnbb.com
If you are a nature lover, especially a birder, looking for a serenely private getaway, this is the place for you. The Wood Duck Inn Bed and Breakfast is located in Cataumet, a seaside hamlet and one of the "villages" of Bourne. It offers a country setting on a peaceful rural road that meanders past fields and cranberry bogs. From the spacious, well-manicured lawn, you'll have a bird's-eye view of a 17-acre working cranberry bog that connects with miles of wooded conservation land; if you walk farther out, you'll come to Red Brook Pond; beyond that you'll find Red Brook Harbor on Buzzards Bay. If you do walk through the grounds, or farther, you'll find the birding is great. But you don't necessarily have to go on a hike to spot wildlife. You might see foxes, coyotes, ospreys, or blue herons right from your guest-room window. The inn, built in 1848 by a sea captain's son, offers two suites and one comfy guest room, each with a private outside entrance—and easy access for the less mobile. The interior decor is tasteful and consists of charming country antiques, hand-made quilts, and stenciling. All rooms contain standard amenities including televisions, phones, and refrigerators, while the appropriately named Treetops Suite is more like a condo-efficiency, complete with a sitting room, balcony, kitchenette, microwave, games, and CDs to play on the stereo. The Garden Suite is ideal for romantic couples with its king-size antique featherbed and sweeping views of the bog and the inn's spectacular gardens.

Though the Wood Duck Inn is out in the country, it is just 10 minutes from Falmouth center and the island ferries, 90 minutes to Boston, and 90 minutes to Provincetown at the tip of the Cape. The suites are private and spacious enough to welcome "peaceful" children. It is also a fine location for a country-style Cape Cod wedding. The inn is open year-round. No credit cards.

WOODS HOLE PASSAGE
BED & BREAKFAST INN $$–$$$
186 Woods Hole Rd., Woods Hole
(508) 548-9575, (800) 790-8976
www.woodsholepassage.com
The Woods Hole Passage is a quiet retreat located along the road that connects Falmouth with Woods Hole. It's an ideal location if you are looking for an active, outdoor-filled visit. Woods Hole is just minutes away and offers fine waterfront dining, and Falmouth, with its great variety of fashionable stores and beaches, is a short distance away in the other direction. But if you're looking to get outside, take an easy stroll to Quisset Harbor and the elevated rock outcrop affectionately known as the Knob (see our Hiking and Biking Trails chapter). If you are looking to bike, the inn is down the road from the famous Shining Sea Bike Path. Your host, Deb Pruitt, has assembled a handy map that highlights the varied walking and bike paths nearby and the roads that lead to the local beaches. There are also complimentary bikes for guests to use.

Woods Hole Passage itself was originally part of the adjoining larger estate. It is a rustic, century-old carriage house with a newly renovated barn on spacious grounds surrounded by old shade trees, and it has a garden with a fishpond. The five guest rooms might be described as "country modern." All have small sitting areas, private baths, air conditioners, and queen-size beds.

Deb prepares a hearty homemade breakfast that might include home-baked breads, scones, fresh fruit, crème brûlée, French toast or strawberry shortcake, all served on small private tables in the guest room overlooking the expansive lawn (or on the patio in the summer). If you opt to venture to the islands for the day, a "breakfast-to-go" can be arranged. Woods Hole Passage is open year-round and it is a nonsmoking inn that welcomes children by prior arrangement.

The Inn is a quiet treat for visitors looking for a restful, peaceful, and soothing stay. Children 12 and older are welcome. The inn is open year-round.

Mid-Cape

ACWORTH INN $$–$$$$
4352 Rte. 6A, Cummaquid (Barnstable)
(508) 362-3330, (800) 362-6363
www.acworthinn.com

The Acworth, originally built in the 1860s, blends 19th-century traditional architecture with French country–style comfort. The five guest rooms are bright and airy, each with a private bath. Each room has its own special charm. Air-conditioning is available, and two of the rooms have working fireplaces. Three of the five rooms have TVs and four have refrigerators. All rooms have CD players and wireless Internet access. There is a large outdoor deck where breakfast is served.

The Acworth Inn is centrally located to fine dining, shopping, and outdoor activities. It is open year-round and is nonsmoking.

ASHLEY MANOR $$$–$$$$
3660 Rte. 6A, Barnstable
(508) 362-8044, (888) 535-2246
www.ashleymanor.net

A sweeping driveway invites guests to the lovely two-acre estate. The oldest part of the Manor is said to date from 1699, and, despite the many additions since, it still retains its link to its colonial past with wide-board floors, hand-glazed wainscoting on the walls, wide hearth fireplaces, a beehive oven, and even a secret passageway thought to have hidden Tories during the Revolutionary War. Spacious guest accommodations and six guest rooms, including two double-bed rooms and four suites, are carefully designed to conform to the age and history of the manor house. All have air-conditioning and private baths and feature striking period decor; all but one have a working fireplace; some of the rooms

have four-poster or canopy-draped beds, and all the suites feature whirlpool tubs. Rooms also have flat-screen TVs, DVD players, and wireless Internet access.

The Manor is furnished with handsome antiques, Oriental rugs, and graceful country furniture. A backyard gazebo and fountain garden highlight the parklike private grounds and a recently redone tennis court. Depending on the season, you may enjoy your complimentary breakfast before the dining room's crackling fireplace or on the breezy outdoor terrace. Within walking distance of Barnstable Village center and the harbor, the Ashley Manor is a gem of an inn and is open year-round. Children 14 years of age and older are welcome.

BEECHWOOD $$$–$$$$
2839 Rte. 6A, Barnstable Village
(508) 362-6618, (800) 609-6618
www.beechwoodinn.com

This Queen Anne–style home has been fully and authentically restored, hearkening back to an era of grace and elegance. Guests from around the world delight in the sprawling lawn, the 10-foot privet hedge, and century-old beech trees that lent the inn its name. The inn also features a wraparound veranda with comfortable rockers, and extravagant antiques in the six inviting guest rooms, three of which have working fireplaces. The rich tones of natural wood throughout the inn are set off beautifully by Oriental rugs, armoires, and antique furnishings. Built in 1853, this Victorian home has fireplaces in the dining room and in the parlor, where afternoon tea, coffee, and sweets are served in cooler months. All rooms have wireless Internet access, refrigerators, air-conditioning, and private baths. Innkeepers Ken and Debra Traugot serve a candlelit, three-course gourmet breakfast that draws rave reviews for dishes like raspberry bread, baked pears, and apple harvest pancakes. The Beechwood, which is just down the road from Barnstable Village, its harbor, and area beaches, is open year-round. The inn welcomes children age 12 and older.

'BY THE SEA' GUESTS
BED & BREAKFAST $$-$$$$
57 Chase Ave. (also Inman Rd. Ext.),
Dennisport
(508) 398-8685, (800) 447-9202
www.bytheseaguests.com

'By the Sea' Guests is one of the few Cape Cod bed-and-breakfasts with its own private beach. Family operated, this lovely 12-room, five-suite inn offers a quiet and comfortable beachfront lodging experience.

Helen and Dino Kossifos continue the tradition of family hospitality and friendly service that began in 1964. You can still awaken to a hearty continental breakfast served on the wraparound veranda overlooking Nantucket Sound. In addition to morning fare from pastries to apple crepes, homemade carrot cake, cookies, fresh fruits, and other snacks are available to guests throughout the day and evening.

Of the 12 rooms, four are oceanfront and four have ocean views. Three units are wheelchair accessible, and one is ADA compliant. All rooms are equipped with wireless Internet access and contain private ceramic-tiled baths, cable television with DVD/CD players, refrigerators, ceiling fans, and individual temperature control. Deluxe suites are housed in a separate building and feature fully equipped kitchens, living rooms with gas fireplaces, and private balconies. 'By the Sea' Guests is open from late Apr to Oct for the guest rooms, and the suites are available through Dec. They welcome well-behaved children and allow outside smoking only.

CAPTAIN FARRIS HOUSE $$$-$$$$
308 Old Main St., Bass River Village (South Yarmouth)
(508) 760-2818, (800) 350-9477
www.captainfarriscapecod.com

This house was built in 1845 in a historic section of South Yarmouth known as Bass River and is in the National Register of Historic Places. A perfect blend of antique and contemporary, the inn has 10 rooms, each one lovingly detailed with modern amenities; private baths, some with Jacuzzis; antique king- or queen-size beds; wireless Internet access and a loaner laptop; cable TVs with VCR and in-house videos; bathrobes; and air-conditioning. Three-course breakfasts are served either in the dining room or outside in the greenhouse garden courtyard. The inn is open year-round.

i Planning to bring your windsurfer? Consider any one of the fine accommodations along South Shore Drive in South Yarmouth. Here the warm waters of Nantucket Sound lap at the shore outside your door and the prevailing winds of summer offer world-class windsurfing right from the beaches in front of the Red Jacket Beach Resort, (508) 398-6941.

CROOK JAW INN $$-$$$
186 Rte. 6A, Yarmouthport
(508) 362-6111
www.crookjawinn.com

From the moment you step inside, there is a distinctive feeling to this ca. 1798 Cape Cod sea captain's house. It boasts a wealth of "early settler" details, seven fireplaces, pegged hardwood wide-planked floors, a ship's captain's staircase, and narrow hallways. The common room with fireplace and the dining room beckon you to relish the days when travelers gathered around to exchange tales. You will find modern conveniences here, including private baths, a whirlpool in the downstairs guest room, and air-conditioning. Each morning guests can linger over a breakfast of Crook Jaw Inn blend coffee, freshly baked muffins and scones, and other gourmet fare. Within walking distance are some great dining spots, including the oldest inn on Cape Cod, the Olde Yarmouth Inn (see our Restaurants chapter.)

The Crook Jaw, which is listed in the National Register of Historic Places, features featherbeds and Egyptian cotton linens, and the five guest rooms offer furnishings that span continents and centuries. The inn is open year-round.

HONEYSUCKLE HILL $$$-$$$$
591 Rte. 6A, West Barnstable
(508) 362-8418, (866) 444-5522
www.honeysucklehill.com

Built in 1810 in the Queen Anne style by the Fish and Goodspeed families, this inn, which is listed in the National Register of Historic Places, is surrounded by verdant lawns and English gardens. The guest rooms are laden with antiques, white wicker, featherbeds, and Battenburg lace. Each room is air-conditioned, equipped with wireless Internet access, a flat-screen TV and a DVD player, and has an oversize marble shower, complemented by English toiletries and fluffy terry robes. This comfortably renovated house has all the grace of its heritage: wide-planked floors, ship's captain's staircase, wonderful ceiling angles, and narrow halls. At Honeysuckle Hill you'll enjoy your morning coffee, complimentary newspaper, and a full breakfast in the dining room. The menu changes daily and offers such gourmet specialties as eggs Benedict or Grand Marnier French toast, accompanied by fruit and freshly baked muffins. Then you can retire to the front porch to plan your day or just sit and soak in an outdoor hot tub surrounded by flowers.

Your hosts, Freddy and Ruth Riley, are very gracious and take pride in offering excellent accommodations. The inn is open year-round and welcomes children age 12 and older.

THE JOSIAH SAMPSON HOUSE $$$
40 Old Kings Rd., Cotuit
(508) 428-8383, (877) 574-6873
www.josiahsampson.com
Built in 1793 in the Federal style of the times, the Josiah Sampson House offers six guest rooms, each with a private modern bath and most with fireplaces. Antiques and period reproductions evoke the era when English businessman Josiah Sampson was in residence at "Sampson's Folly," a nickname townsfolk bestowed on his home for its ostentatious elegance. Innkeepers Richard Thomas and Joe Gergyes have maintained the traditional names for the different rooms. The Library Room, which now has a queen-size bed, was in fact Josiah Sampson's library and still boasts a collection of books. The Queen's Room has two twin canopied beds and offers excellent views of the yard complete with romantic gazebo. The Rose Room, so called for its floral

decorating scheme, has a beautiful queen-size canopied bed. While there are no TVs in the individual rooms, there is a TV with satellite and a player piano in the common area. There is also wireless Internet access and a computer for guest use. A gourmet breakfast is served each morning in the dining room or on the garden-view porch. Guests can also relax in the hot tub. The Josiah Sampson House is open year-round.

THE LAMB AND LION INN $$$–$$$$
2504 Rte. 6A, Barnstable
(508) 362-6823, (800) 909-6923
www.lambandlion.com
Set back off historic Route 6A, this expanded 1740 home surrounds a central courtyard featuring a lovely outdoor pool with an all-season hot tub. It's a fun, airy inn with a Caribbean feel, until you enter the colonial-era common room of the main house and stand on the wide-board floors in front of one of the many fireplaces.

The Lamb and Lion Inn offers a variety of rooms, most opening onto the courtyard. Some have private entrances; others have private decks for afternoon lounging. They even offer a family-style suite, the "Barn-stable," in a converted barn with three loft sleeping areas, living room, kitchen, and barbecue deck. All the rooms are spacious, clean, and have private baths, cable TV, telephones with data ports, and wireless Internet access.

The Innkeeper's Pride, elegant accommodations set apart from the other guest rooms, offers a fireplace, sunken tub, kitchen, and a private deck. A "deluxe" continental breakfast is served on the sunporch. Children 10 years and older are welcome and the inn is pet friendly. The Lamb and Lion is open year-round. The inn also hosts family celebrations, catered luncheons, small wedding parties, and small group meetings.

LIBERTY HILL INN $$$–$$$$
77 Rte. 6A, Yarmouthport
(508) 362-3976, (800) 821-3977
www.libertyhillinn.com
Located in the heart of Yarmouthport, this inn is just a short, leisurely stroll away from picturesque

country lanes, outstanding restaurants, interesting antiques and gift shops, and a number of historical attractions. Built by a shipbuilder in 1825, the handsome Greek Revival building with nine guest rooms evokes the elegance of past centuries with its wide floorboards, chandeliers, and antiques. Some rooms have four-poster beds, some have lovely lace canopied queen-size beds, and all have private bathrooms and air-conditioning. Three rooms with whirlpools are available, and all four rooms in the carriage house feature working fireplaces. The inn was recently updated with a large new kitchen, additional gas fireplaces, new air-conditioning in the rooms, and central air in the main house. Also new are global positioning devices for guests to use, a cappuccino and espresso machine, and a wine fridge for guests. Your hosts serve a sumptuous breakfast under a crystal chandelier. The inn is open year-round, and children are welcome. One room is wheelchair accessible.

THE LIGHTHOUSE INN $$$$
1 Lighthouse Inn Rd., West Dennis
(508) 398-2244
www.lighthouseinn.com

The Lighthouse Inn began life in May 1855 as the Bass River Light, the Cape's 15th lighthouse. At that time it consisted only of the center section of the inn today. Though it closed briefly from 1880 to 1881, it remained an important south-side lighthouse until 1914, when the opening of the Cape Cod Canal made it obsolete. In 1989 it was recommissioned and is today a working lighthouse from May to Oct each year. The on-site dining room (the Lighthouse Inn—see our Restaurants chapter) seats 200.

The inn is situated all by itself down at West Dennis Beach. Accommodations run the gamut from basic rooms and suites in the main house to oceanfront cottages with decks, fireplaces, and comfortable furnishings that sleep as many as six people. Each room and cottage has a TV, telephone, refrigerator, in-room safe, hair dryer, and private bath.

On-site there is a tennis court, an outdoor heated swimming pool, a nightclub (the Sand

Bar, which is described in our Nightlife chapter), shuffleboard, volleyball, and miniature golf, and a private beach with a network of jetties for bluefish fishing. There are arts and crafts classes, sandcastle-building contests, and other daily, supervised activities for children ages three and older. The Stone family operates the inn from mid-May to early Oct.

SEA BEACH INN $–$$$
388 Sea St., Hyannis
(508) 775-4612
www.capecodtravel.com/seabeach

This inn was once a sea captain's home. Located within sight and sound Nantucket Sound on Sea Street Beach, the inn has five guest rooms in the main house and another four in the carriage barn. Three of the five rooms in the main house have private baths, and the rooms in the carriage barn area perfect for families. Wireless Internet access is available at no extra charge. The inn is an easy walk to some of Hyannis's best dining, as well as the Melody Tent for first-rate nightly entertainment. An efficiency unit is available, and a one-bedroom apartment can be rented on a weekly basis. Continental breakfast is offered between 7:30 and 9:00 a.m. The Inn is open from May through mid-Oct, and children are welcome.

SEA BREEZE INN $$–$$$$
270 Ocean Ave., Hyannis
(508) 771-7213
www.seabreezeinn.com

The Sea Breeze Inn is so close to the beach, you'll feel actual sea breezes firsthand. Besides the proximity to the beach, the inn is also near most Hyannis activities, including the Cape Cod Melody Tent, restaurants, golf, and island ferries. The 14 rooms in the main building feature shabby-chic antiques, televisions, wireless Internet access, private baths, and air-conditioning. The inn features a rooftop widow's walk with tables, chairs, and a beautiful view of Nantucket Sound. Larger parties may opt for the efficiency cottage, which has a queen-size bed and sleeper couch along with a refrigerator, stove, and microwave. A generous continental breakfast is served in the main house. The inn is open year-round, and children are welcome.

SIMMONS HOMESTEAD INN $$$$
288 Scudder Ave., Hyannisport
(508) 778-4999, (800) 637-1649
www.simmonshomesteadinn.com

The Simmons Homestead Inn is a historic sea captain's home built in 1820 by Lemuel Simmons. It was a private estate until 1987, when it was restored and converted into a country inn. The property is attractive, with a rolling backyard and a sitting porch. The interior decor is eclectic, reflecting the personality of its innkeeper, Bill Putnam. The inn has 14 rooms, some furnished with canopied four-poster beds, brass beds, or white whicker. Each room has a private bath, two have private decks, and two have working fireplaces. And if you like plants and animals of the brass and ceramic variety, you will be right at home. All the rooms have their own animal theme (as in giraffe, elephant, cat, etc.). There's even a hot tub and a spacious billiards room. There is a fleet of mountain bikes for guests to use. In the morning, guests will find a full country breakfast in the dining room (the late Dinah Shore once cooked breakfast here for the guests). A social hour with wine takes place every evening, and a single-malt "tasting hour" is staged on weeknights during the cooler months. Putnam is an avid collector and has perhaps the largest collection of single-malt scotch—542 brands at last count—in the country. He also has 55 classic red sports cars he keeps out back in "Toad Hall," along with 30 cats, although they are not allowed in the main house to avoid problems for those with allergies. The Simmons Homestead is the perfect setting for a Hyannis-based stay that will include shopping, dining, entertainment, beaches, and boat excursions, all within a short drive. Open year-round, the inn welcomes children and dogs.

ISAIAH HALL BED AND BREAKFAST INN $$-$$$
152 Whig St., Dennis
(508) 385-9928, (800) 736-0160
www.isaiahhallinn.com

The Isaiah Hall Bed and Breakfast is named for a 19th-century cooper, whose grandfather Henry is credited with developing cranberry cultivation on Cape Cod back in 1814. Isaiah Hall, realizing how successful cultivated cranberries would become, began producing barrels in large volume. Hall's barrel size is still the accepted unit of measure for cranberries that are bought and sold today on the open market.

This 1857 Greek Revival farmhouse has 10 rooms and the new Isaiah Hall Suite, a 775–square-foot room with a fireplace, a queen pillow-top bed, a 52-inch TV, and a Bose 1-2-3 sound system. All rooms have private baths, eight have queen-size beds that are canopied or boast bedsteads of white iron or brass, four have balconies, and two have fireplaces. Rooms are distributed throughout the main and carriage houses, the latter featuring stenciled walls, white wicker, and knotty-pine walls. All the rooms have air-conditioning, TVs, and VCRs. Wireless Internet access is available for free in most guest rooms and in the common Great Room.

An extended continental breakfast is served each morning at the dining room's gorgeous 12-foot cherry table. After breakfast, take a stroll through the wonderful gardens or perhaps down to Corporation Beach for a day of sun, sand, and surf. Later you can walk to America's oldest summer theater, the Cape Playhouse, or over to Dennis Village. The inn is open year-round and children are welcome.

Lower Cape

ALYCE'S DUNSCROFT BY-THE-SEA $$$-$$$$
24 Pilgrim Rd., Harwich Port
(508) 432-0810, (800) 432-4345
www.dunscroftbythesea.com

The Dunscroft, built as a private estate in 1925, exudes casual elegance. The bright rooms and cottage suite are furnished with fine linens, beautiful beds—canopied, four-poster, and sleigh beds—plump pillows, and lace curtains. All are air-conditioned and have private baths, some with Jacuzzis..

During her 22 years as owner and resident innkeeper, Alyce Mundy has named rooms for her mother and nieces, including Clara's Cottage, Penelope and Leona. Three units have fireplaces, two have patios, and three are accessed by private entrances. Guests enjoy a full breakfast in the dining room, and they can relax in a firelit gathering room. Select a book from the library and grab a seat by the baby grand piano, where spontaneous sing-alongs have been known to break out on summer evenings. The inn, which is near Main Street shops, is open year-round.

BRASS KEY GUESTHOUSE $$$–$$$$
67 Bradford St., Provincetown
(508) 487-9005, (800) 842-9858
www.brasskey.com
Expanded and renovated in 1997, the inn has a total of 43 rooms, all with Sealy pillow-top mattress sets and "pillow menus" (French goose or Swedish foam, anyone?), luxurious linens and duvet covers, plush robes, flat-screen cable TVs with DVD players, Bose clock radios, minifridges, electronic mini-safes, cordless phones, and DSL connections. Some rooms have private Jacuzzis, others have private decks or wrought iron mini-balconies, and a number of rooms have fireplaces. An elaborate continental breakfast is served each morning. The Brass Key has a heated infinity pool as well as a large, in-ground hot tub set in a gorgeous brick-lined courtyard; you can ask for one of the rooms that opens onto the hot tub or the pool. Although the complex, with six outbuildings and a gatehouse, has frontage on three streets, it still maintains its original intimacy. The Brass Key's new owner, Thomas Walter, has renovated parts of the Guesthouse since taking over. There is now a lounge, penthouse and cabana suites, remodeled bathrooms, and a large wooden pergola for weddings and other events.

Minimum-stay requirements are in effect during the busy season. There is one wheelchair-accessible room. The inn is open year-round and accepts no children younger than 16.

BREWSTER BY THE SEA
EUROPEAN INN & SPA $$$–$$$$
716 Rte. 6A, Brewster
(508) 896-3910, (800) 892-3910
www.brewsterbythesea.com
Brewster by the Sea offers the charm of an 1846 Federal-style farmhouse with modern amenities. Each of the eight guest rooms (two of them suites) has its own special charm. The distinctively decorated rooms have fine linens, down comforters, TV with HBO, temperature control, wireless Internet access, and private bathrooms with hair dryers, toiletries, and thick terry-cloth robes. Outside, beyond the spacious rear deck surrounded by hedges, hydrangeas, and gardens, there's a heated pool and a hot tub that can be used year-round. The two-acre property has an apple orchard and is right across the road from the historic windmill on the grounds of Drummer Boy Park, where Sunday evening band concerts are held in the summer. It is also just a short stroll to the nature trails at the Cape Cod Museum of Natural History.

Breakfast is a leisurely affair, served in the olde farmhouse or available "to go" on the poolside veranda. A full slate of spa services is also available in the inn, with everything from foot reflexology to hot lava stone treatments available on-site. Children older than 16 are welcome.

THE CANDLEBERRY INN $$$
1882 Rte. 6A, Brewster
(508) 896–3300, (800) 573-4769
www.candleberryinn.com
This restored 250-year-old house has a rich history, as evidenced by accents like the original wide floorboards, wainscoting, a fan window over the front entrance, and window glass with "bubbles and waves." Nineteeth-century author Horatio Alger was among the statesmen, seafarers, and heroines to call this house home. The eight guest rooms all have private baths; six, including one suite, are in the main house, and another two are located in the newer carriage house. The main house's atmospheric common areas are adorned with Oriental rugs and family heirlooms. Carriage house guests have access to

a shared deck overlooking the gardens. Beach chairs and towels are available for borrowing, and a guest refrigerator accommodates beverages beyond those provided by the innkeepers (coffee and tea in the morning, wine or mulled cider after dark). Guests are treated to a full breakfast in the 18th-century dining room or outside on the garden patio, which has a view of lush gardens. The inn is open year-round and children seven and older are welcome.

THE CAPTAIN'S HOUSE INN $$$$
369-377 Old Harbor Rd., Chatham
(508) 945-0127, (800) 315-0728
www.captainshouseinn.com

The stately white 1839 Greek Revival–style mansion, the attached carriage house, "Stables," and the 200-year-old bow roof cape, called the "Captain's Cottage," provide 16 luxuriously appointed guest quarters. Each has its own unique atmosphere; most have queen- or king-size canopied four-poster beds, sitting areas, and fireplaces; some have whirlpool tubs and TVs with VCRs and CD players; and all have private baths, air-conditioning, and telephones with voicemail and data ports. The inn also has wireless Internet access.

Enjoy a gourmet country breakfast and English afternoon tea served in the dining room, which overlooks the gardens. Tea is also available in the privacy of your room upon request. The in-house chef also pampers guests with poolside lunches and serves an evening snack in the kitchen. The whole complex is beautifully appointed with antiques and period wallpaper and furnishings. The Captain's House Inn is open year-round.

CARRIAGE HOUSE INN $$$$
407 Old Harbor Rd., Chatham
(508) 945-4688, (800) 355-8868
www.thecarriagehouseinn.com

Located a quarter mile from Pleasant Bay and the ocean in this picturesque seaside village, the inn is a traditional Cape home, furnished with antiques and period accents. There are six rooms and a guest suite scattered through the main house and adjacent carriage house, all of them deco-rated with the kind of thoughtful touches you'd expect to find in the home of an exceptionally tasteful friend. The main house rooms offer standard amenities like individual temperature control, cable TVs with DVD players, morning paper delivery, and luxurious towels, while the carriage house kicks it up a notch with fireplaces, private entrances, canopied and four-poster beds, and private outdoor sitting areas. Those that spring for the suite will enjoy indulgences like a walk-in closet, a roomy bathroom with two separate vanity sinks, beamed ceilings, a fireplace, and a private deck. Wireless Internet access is available only in the main house. Breakfast is served under the crystal chandelier in the formal dining room or at individual tables in the adjacent sunroom. The Carriage House Inn is open year-round and welcomes children age 10 and older. No pets are allowed, but seeing-eye dogs are welcome.

CHILLINGSWORTH $$
2449 Rte. 6A, Brewster
(508) 896-3640
www.chillingsworth.com

A well-kept secret on the Lower Cape is that the renowned restaurant Chillingsworth (see our Restaurants chapter) also has three elegant rooms furnished with antiques for rent. Two are large, with sitting areas, and all three have private baths, air-conditioning, wireless Internet access, and cable TV. Guests are treated to a full breakfast each morning and wine and cheese at the afternoon check-in. They're also within walking distance of a private beach—and, of course, steps away from elegant French cuisine served at Chillingsworth Restaurant. Guests get priority for lunch and dinner reservations, along with attentive service and luxuries like down puffs, fresh flowers, and extravagant furnishings. Chillingsworth is open from mid-May through Nov.

THE CRANBERRY INN $$$$
359 Main St., Chatham
(508) 945-9232, (800) 332-4667
www.cranberryinn.com

This is Chatham's oldest lodging, a grand 1830s Greek Revival building updated with modern comforts such as private baths, air-conditioning, cable television, and wireless Internet access. The decor evokes a Yankee farmhouse with its quilt-covered four-posters and period antiques. Fireplaces, wet bars, and private decks are among the extras available in certain rooms; others feature atmospheric accents like exposed beams and vaulted ceilings. The common rooms include a reception room with baby grand piano, fireplace, and fresh long-stemmed flower arrangements. The Tavern, with a wood-burning fireplace, is a cozy spot for evening cocktails. A full country breakfast is served in the cheerful dining room.

Directly behind the inn is a lovely, natural cranberry bog and nature trail leading to Old Mill Pond. Guests are welcome to walk with care and, in the winter season, may enjoy seeing the abundance of wildlife that migrates through this part of Cape Cod. The Cranberry Inn is open year-round and welcomes children age 12 and older.

CROWNE POINTE HISTORIC INN AND SPA $$$$
82 Bradford St., Provincetown
(508) 487-6767, (877) 276-9631
www.crownepointe.com

With the same owners as the Brass Key, the Crowne Pointe was originally built in the 19th century as a sea captain's home. The property has undergone extensive renovations in the past decade, although it has not been enough to rid the place of ghost stories, including one of a man who has been spotted on surveillance cameras moving through the lobby late at night, according to the innkeepers. Ghosts aside, the inn's many room types can accommodate a range of high-end tastes, including those looking to stay in the two-story Penthouse, complete with full kitchen, multiple flat-screen TVs, and a woodstove.

THE INN AT COOK STREET $$$$
7 Cook St., Provincetown
(508) 487-3894, (888) 266-5655
www.innatcookst.com

This cozy little inn, opened in 1996, offers four rooms, one suite, and two adjacent cottages, all with private baths and nice touches such as flowers, 800-thread-count Egyptian cotton sheets, and framed photographs taken by one of the innkeepers. All have TVs with DVD players and refrigerators, and some have decks, either private or shared; the cottages are equipped with gas fireplaces. Our favorite is the wisteria-draped Koi Cottage, where a vaulted ceiling shelters a cozy loft with a futon and skylights. Sit for a while and watch the goldfish in the small koi pond. Innkeepers Lisa Feistel and Doreen Birdsell serve up a hearty continental breakfast and genuine hospitality. The inn is open year-round and does not accept children.

INN AT THE OAKS $$$
3085 U.S. Rte. 6, Eastham
(508) 255-1886, (877) 255-1886
www.overlookinn.com

Nestled in the woods across from the Cape Cod National Seashore, this 1869 inn is beautifully decorated with imaginative colors blending nicely with antique furnishings. The inn has 10 rooms and suites, each with a private bath, individual temperature control, cable TV, DVD player, ceiling fan, telephone, and wireless Internet access. A renovated carriage house offers two "First Mates Suites" suitable for families of four or more; both accept pets for an additional fee of $30 per stay. With its wraparound porch, playground, hot tub, and toy-filled playroom, the Inn at the Oaks is that elusive Cape Cod commodity: a B&B that not only allows children, but caters to them.

Innkeepers Pam and Don Anderson stayed here on their honeymoon, arranged to buy the inn, and molded it to fit their growing family. Don's Danish heritage shines through in the country breakfast, which features a signature dish of Abelskivers (Danish pancakes) along with continental specialties like pancakes, parmesan baked eggs, and banana walnut French toast. The inn is next to the Cape Cod Rail Trail bike trail (see our Hiking and Biking Trails chapter) and a short pedal away from beaches and area attractions such as the Eastham Windmill. Check out the inn's "Family Fun Blog" online for up-to-date events and information, one of the better Web sites as of 2009. The inn is open year-round.

KALMAR VILLAGE $$–$$$$
674 Shore Rd., North Truro
(508) 487-0585, (617) 277-0091 (off-season)
www.kalmarvillage.com

In the same family since the 1960s, the "village" features a 400-foot private beach, a large freshwater pool, barbecue facilities, and well-maintained grounds awash in fragrant lilac and rosa rugosa. Kalmar is just steps away from the Provincetown border and close to the National Seashore. Rates include linens, towels, blankets, maid service, and cable TV, and there's even a laundry on the premises. Kalmar Village also has wireless Internet access.

LAND'S END INN $$$$
22 Commercial St., Provincetown
(508) 487-0706, (800) 276-7088
www.landsendinn.com

Land's End is a celebration of art and architecture. With sweeping water views as a backdrop, the interior is filled with an incredible collection of vases, woodcarvings, and Tiffany lamps. Oriental rugs and unusual antique furniture abound, and each of the 16 guest rooms—all with private baths—is unique. Perched on top of Gull Hill at the far end of Commercial Street and reached by climbing an enchanting brick path that twists and turns, the inn is a remarkable piece of architecture—sort of Victorian contemporary. The main building dates back to 1904, and a more recent wraparound porch and rear addition keep with the turn-of-the-20th-century feel of the place, as do the terraced gardens on the two-acre grounds. The inn is open year-round and allows pets in the French Country apartment, Wisteria Room, and the Gull Hill.

Kalmar has a total of 56 units but is extremely popular and usually gets booked at least a year in advance. If you can't finagle one of the cottages—the epitome of Cape Cod charm—consider one of the efficiency units. Kalmar Village is open May through Oct.

THE MOORLANDS $$–$$$
11 Hughes Rd., North Truro
(508) 487-0663
www.themoorlands.com

Built by Captain Atkin Hughes at the turn of the 20th century, The Moorlands has been restored to Victorian splendor and updated to include such modern amenities as in-room phones, ceiling fans, TVs, and refrigerators. A continental breakfast is served daily in the dining room. The Moorlands has a music room with a variety of instruments for guests to play, including a piano, organ, guitars, and bass. Accommodations at this year-round inn vary: Choose from several guest rooms (all with private baths), a two-room suite, a three-room apartment, two 1950s-style cottages, a penthouse apartment with a private deck and entrance, or an 18th-century restored carriage house, which has a full kitchen, TV and VCR, private bath, courtyard garden, and a five-person hot tub. Pets are welcome in the cottages.

THE NAUSET HOUSE INN $–$$$
143 Beach Rd., East Orleans
(508) 255-2195, (800) 771-5508
www.nausethouseinn.com

The Nauset House has 14 guest rooms, imaginatively yet simply done, and furnished with antique and hand-painted furniture. Besides the great decor the inn also has some of the best pricing that we've found, with rooms as low as $89 for couples. The large common room in this 1810 house is set up with several intimate sitting areas for sociable conversation or solitary reading by the fireplace. Past the brick-floored breakfast room is an enchanting greenhouse conservatory where ivy climbs the glass walls, fragrant camellias grow near wicker chairs, and grapes ripen on the arbor above the entrance.

Innkeepers John and Cindy Vessella and Diane Johnson serve a complimentary full breakfast, featuring fresh omelets and homemade granola. The inn is open mid-Apr through Oct and welcomes children 12 and older.

THE OLD HARBOR INN $$$$
22 Old Harbor Rd., Chatham
(508) 945-4434, (800) 942-4434
www.chathamoldharborinn.com

An easy stroll from Chatham attractions like the lighthouse, seasonal band concerts, and Cape

Cod League baseball games, this appealing B&B offers eight designer-furnished rooms named for local towns, harbors, inlets, and beaches. A recently added fitness room will help you work off the Inn's gourmet buffet breakfast.

All rooms offer comforts such as private, full baths; televisions with VCRs; CD alarm clocks; air conditioning; and fluffy bathrobes. For added luxury, you can opt for a luxury suite like the Stage Harbor, with its two Jacuzzis and king-size four-poster, or a deluxe room like the North Beach, featuring a cathedral ceiling, a king-size mahogany sleigh bed, and an in-room fireplace. Five rooms are equipped with refrigerators full of complimentary bottled water and soft drinks, refreshments that are available—along with snacks, popcorn, and your pick of the in-house video collection—to any guest for the asking. Open all year, the Inn welcomes children 12 and over.

OLD SEA PINES INN $–$$$
2553 Rte. 6A, Brewster
(508) 896-6114
www.oldseapinesinn.com

The Old Sea Pines Inn in Brewster was once the center of a 300-acre estate known as the Sea Pines School of Charm and Personality. It continued as a school until the 1970s, when innkeepers and owners Stephen and Michele Rowan envisioned this lovely mansion as a bed-and-breakfast inn. From the outset, they have carefully maintained its original turn-of-the-20th-century style and integrity. Besides the structure itself, the charming decor adds to the inn's appeal. Some of the inn's 22 rooms, especially the 5 with shared baths, are small, but they are a great bargain and still include the inn's full breakfasts. Some of the units have fireplaces, and a free night is offered to honeymooners booking a stay of four or more nights. Next to the spacious living room is the large, formal dining room, which opens onto a leafy outdoor dining deck overlooking the lawns and gardens.

Many couples choose to marry at the Old Sea Pines Inn or to hold their receptions here. The private setting of the Wedding Garden is perfect for ceremonies. The inn, open year-round, also does rehearsal dinners. Children over eight are welcome throughout the inn, while younger fry are accommodated in the inn's two family suites, which can sleep up to four guests comfortably.

OYSTER COVE BED & BREAKFAST $$$$
20 Partridge Way, Wellfleet
(508) 349-2994
www.oystercove.com

Dick and Sandy Nichols, built this large three-level deck home on waterfront property owned by their family since the 1930s. It offers you views of Indian Neck, Great Island, Chipman Cove, and of course Wellfleet Harbor, home of the world-famous Wellfleet oyster. Bring your kayak and explore to your heart's content. Or walk the shoreline of Ducke Creeke. Nature is at your doorstep. And when you're hungry for civilization again, you can head to the many art galleries in Wellfleet.

This spacious architect-designed home features French doors, open ceilings with exposed beams, and polished concrete floors. Each living area opens onto a large outside deck and includes cable TV with DVD and a CD/radio system. The three-room lower level Beach Suite features a large bathroom with two sinks and tub with shower, and a living/dining area with wet bar and kitchenette, making it ideal for couples, families, or groups of up to six people. All beds are queen size. The home is equipped with wireless Internet access and air-conditioning throughout.

A gourmet continental breakfast of muffins and scones, fresh fruit, and Green Mountain organic coffee is served daily, and wireless Internet access is available throughout the house. Oyster Cove is open year-round and welcomes children of all ages.

THE PARSONAGE INN $$–$$$
202 Main St., East Orleans
(508) 255-8217, (888) 422-8217
www.parsonageinn.com

Built around 1770, this house still has its original wide floorboards and the tranquil feel of the vicarage it became in the 1800s. The eight guest rooms, each with a private bath, are furnished with country antiques and decorated simply with hand-stenciling, quilts, and fresh flowers. Wireless and dial-up Internet access is available in all rooms, as is individual temperature control.

Innkeepers Ian and Elizabeth Browne serve a hearty morning meal in the charming little breakfast room or outside on the brick patio. You can also opt to take breakfast in your room. The offerings range from fruit salad with yogurt and granola to orange zest French toast with warm maple syrup. Later in the day, enjoy refreshments in the parlor, play the piano, or relax in front of the fire. Just a mile and a half from Nauset Beach, the Parsonage is also close to shops, restaurants, and galleries and is open year-round. Children older than six are welcome.

THE PENNY HOUSE INN & SPA $$$–$$$$
4885 U.S. Rte. 6, North Eastham
(508) 255-6632, (800) 554-1751
www.pennyhouseinn.com

This restored sea captain's house, set on two acres, includes a heated outdoor pool and in-house day spa. Combining the personalized service of a B&B with the upscale amenities of a boutique hotel, the Penny House pampers guests with extras like Matelasse covers, oversize bath towels, luxury linens, and toiletries from Baudelaire and Gilchrist and Soames. There is a full breakfast in the dining room, which features the home's original 1690 wide wood floorboards. The house has two sections—the old 1690 portion and the "new" section, which dates from 1750.

The rooms are of varying sizes and rates. All rooms have air-conditioning, cable TV and VCRs, private bathrooms, and free wireless Internet access. The Penny Serenade room has a private entrance and a private deck overlooking the terrace—a perfect honeymoon suite! If you want a fireplace, ask for suites that also include two-person whirlpool tubs. All guests enjoy access to the day spa and neighboring Willy's Gym, a deluxe wellness center equipped with an indoor saltwater pool, Pilates and yoga classes, racquetball courts, a rock-climbing wall, and other

enticements. After a shower try some afternoon tea accompanied by treats like brownies, homemade cookies, blueberry tarts, and sour cream coffeecake. The Penny House is closed over Christmas and New Year's. The inn is nonsmoking, and children older than eight are welcome.

THE QUEEN ANNE INN $$$$
70 Queen Anne Rd., Chatham
(508) 945-0394, (800) 545-4667
www.queenanneinn.com

Built in the 1840s by a sea captain for his daughter, the Queen Anne Inn has been an inn since 1874. Inspired by the "elegant simplicity" of early New Englanders, the innkeepers have kept many of the building's original furnishings and infused the guest rooms with an atmosphere that merges classic lines with contemporary design. In addition to a private bath, telephone, and cable television in each room, guests can opt for features including working fireplaces, private balconies with hot tubs, and canopied beds from the era when clipper ship captain Norman Howes' daughter was in residence.

In addition to its outdoor pool and indoor Jacuzzi, the Queen Anne has an exercise and massage room. The in-house restaurant, the Eldredge Room, emphasizes regional ingredients in its eclectic American cuisine. The inn closes from Jan through Mar. Children are welcome but smoking is not.

SHIP'S KNEES INN $$–$$$$
186 Beach Rd., East Orleans
(508) 255-1312, (888) 744-7756
www.shipskneesinn.com

This restored 1820 sea captain's home is just a short walk from Nauset Beach. The rooms are cozy and comfortable, with classic New England accents like braided rugs, hand-painted murals, four-poster beds, and vintage clipper ship models. But don't be misled by old-school touches like painted beams and ornamental wreaths—the rooms may look retro, but all are equipped with wireless Internet access, individual temperature control, refrigerators, and cable TV. Atmosphere to spare is available in the Master Suite, where a working fireplace anchors a courtyard-facing space outfitted with a queen bed and twin pull-out sofa bed.

A continental breakfast is served on the patio, which gets a lovely sea breeze, or indoors in the breakfast room or parlor. The inn has an outdoor pool, is open year-round, and welcomes children 12 and older.

SHIREMAX INN $-$$

5 Tremont St., Provincetown
(508) 487-1233, (888) 744-7312

Innkeeper Jack Barnett named his inn after his two Samoyed huskies, Shire and Max. Jack is a dog lover, and his inn in the quiet west end of town is one of only a handful of places that welcomes pets. (The inn charges an additional $5 per night per room for pets, and you must get approval in advance to bring your well-behaved pet.)

The seven units are large and homey and are stocked with everything from color TVs to beach chairs and towels. Four have private baths; three share. The room in the far back of the main house offers a private bath, private entrance, and sundeck. Two separate apartments are also available; each has a VCR and TV, telephone, full kitchen, and private sundeck. Guests are served an expanded continental breakfast on the deck, which is a great place to sunbathe in the afternoon. A minimum stay of five nights is required in July and Aug; the apartments are rented by the week. The ShireMax is closed from Nov through Apr.

THREE PEAKS INN $$

210 Bradford St., Provincetown
(508) 487-1717
www.threepeaksptown.com

Built in the early 1870s and renovated to conform to the original integrity of the period, Three Peaks is one of the most outstanding examples of Victorian architecture in Provincetown. The inn's entrance features gardens along a flower-lined walkway and a front porch with upholstered wicker rockers. Original wide double doors open on a foyer with high ceilings and an open staircase to the second floor. The three guest rooms have private balconies, color cable TV, minifridges, and either ceiling fans or in-season air-conditioning. A continental breakfast is served each morning. Three Peaks is open year-round and is a nonsmoking house, but the spacious porches accommodate smokers. Children are welcome, but no pets.

WHALEWALK INN $$$$

220 Bridge Rd., Eastham
(508) 255-0617, (800) 440-1281
www.whalewalkinn.com

Elegant and accommodating, the Whalewalk Inn offers 16 guest rooms and suites in six buildings, all beautifully decorated and furnished with antiques and reproductions, original art, baskets, throw pillows, and fresh flowers. Innkeepers Elaine and Kevin Conlin and their staff go out of their way to please you. Browse through the inn's library of books, menus from area restaurants, and other resources. In the morning, help yourself to coffee, then sit down to a full breakfast in the dining room. Some rooms have sitting rooms and private entrances, some have fireplaces, wet bars, kitchenettes, or whirlpools; all have air-conditioning and private baths.

Sharing the acreage of the main 1830s inn are a variety of other buildings ranging from suites for families to a converted barn and a spa penthouse. The three-and-a-half-acre grounds feature impeccable lawns with comfortable Adirondack chairs. Less sedentary guests can visit the spa and wellness center, where a heated indoor resistance pool, sauna, and hot tub accompany an impressive array of cardiovascular and weight-training equipment, including a 32 inch TV with the Wii video game system. Services from spa facials to Reiki massage are available by appointment.

The Whalewalk is open from Apr through early Dec (and select winter weekends) and welcomes children 12 and older. The Whalewalk's blog is another good Web site, focusing on specials and local events.

COTTAGES

You may want to consider staying in a cottage: usually a freestanding, small house that sits in a colony of look-alike units. Cottages provide a more rustic environment. Some provide a communal outdoor pool with recreation and barbecue area. Usually they come with a kitchenette, microwave, television, and a small yard area, and some may be on or near the water.

Upper Cape

PINE GROVE COTTAGES $-$$
358 Rte. 6A, East Sandwich
(508) 888-8179
www.pinegrovecottages.com

These 10 charming heated cottages sit side by side off Route 6A, with ample space between them to ensure privacy. In fact, you can have your own private Cape Cod one-room cottage, perfect for two people, for half the cost of an average motel room. Some deluxe cottages have two bedrooms, a living room with sleep sofa, TV, and a fully equipped kitchen. Pine Grove specializes in hosting families and accommodating reunions or other large gatherings.

The cottages rent by the night or the week. For less than $70 a night you can rent a rustic cottage with color TV and efficiency area. The complex has a swimming pool and a play area for young children, and they provide cribs, baby baths, barbecue grills, linens, and towels. Pine Grove Cottages are available from May through Nov.

Lower Cape

THE COLONY OF WELLFLEET $$$-$$$$
Chequessett Neck Road, Wellfleet
(508) 349-3761
www.thecolonyofwellfleet.com

Built as a private club in 1948 by one of the founders of Boston's Institute for Contemporary Arts, this collection of masonry and wood-frame duplexes, scattered along a wooded hillside overlooking the water, has been run as a cottage colony since 1963. With bedrooms that double as sitting rooms during the day, the cottages have fireplaces, galley kitchens, glass- and screen-enclosed dining porches, and patios or decks. One-bedroom cottages rent for $1,295 for a week or $195 per day with a three-day minimum stay. Two-bedroom cottages are about $500 to $1,000 more per week.

DAYS' COTTAGES $$$
271 Shore Rd., North Truro
(508) 487-1062
www.dayscottages.com

If these pretty-as-a-picture waterfront cottages look familiar, it's because they have been immortalized through the years by dozens of artists in countless paintings and postcards.

What began as nine cottages in 1931 has grown to 23—all exactly alike. These cottages are so popular with returning guests that it's nearly impossible to book one for less than a week during the season. The on-site market stocks everything you'll need, from postcards to pomegranates. The cottages are open May through the weekend after Columbus Day. No credit cards.

LINGER LONGER BY THE SEA $$-$$$
261 Linnell Landing Rd., Brewster
(508) 896-7714
www.lingerlongerbythesea.com

At the edge of Cape Cod Bay, the 1907 main building with its lawn ringed by a moss-covered stone wall conjures up visions of turn-of-the-20th-century seaside grandeur. It houses six apartments and is flanked by 10 cottages.

All units have fully equipped kitchens, color TVs, wireless Internet access, living rooms, bedrooms, and bathrooms with tubs and showers. Cribs and high chairs are provided on request. You'll have the benefit of a private beach, and the cottages have picnic tables and charcoal grills. Linger Longer is open from mid-Apr through Nov. Most of the units are winterized, so you'll be cozy and warm during off-season visits. Two cottages have fireplaces.

SURF SIDE COTTAGES $$$
Ocean View Drive, South Wellfleet
(508) 349-3959
www.surfsidecottages.com

For Surf Side's repeat customers, this oasis amid Wellfleet's sand dunes and pine trees is a perfect spot for families in search of the kind of summer community that does not exist in many other places. With two dozen cottages, including some that are a barefoot stroll from the Cape Cod National Seashore, this accommodating complex features knotty-pine interiors, outdoor showers, screened porches, fireplaces, kitchens, bathrooms, and barbecues. There are laundry facilities on the premises, and pets are allowed with advance notice (and an additional charge) before Memorial Day and after Labor Day. Surf Side is open from early Apr through Oct and requires one-week-minimum stays between Memorial Day and mid-Oct.

i Want to spend a night in a lighthouse? Race Point Lighthouse, located at the Cape's tip in Provincetown, has several bedrooms in the keeper's house that you can reserve for a night, a weekend, or longer. You'll need to bring your own bed linens, towels, food, and drinking water. Room rates are between $155 and $185 a night. Call (508) 487-9930 or visit www .racepointlighthouse.net.

RESERVATION SERVICES

Reservation services can make planning your vacation much easier. Instead of calling around to see which establishments have openings—especially if you haven't started planning way in advance—enlist the help of one of the Cape's reservation services. Most deal with hotels, inns, and bed-and-breakfasts, though some specialize in the latter. The following reservation services are among the best around. Most do not charge; others charge a modest fee. We indicate any fees in the individual write-ups.

BED AND BREAKFAST CAPE COD
16 Arey's Lane, P.O. Box 1312
Orleans, MA 02653
(508) 255-3824, (800) 541-6226
www.bedandbreakfastcapecod.com

In early 1998, Orleans Bed & Breakfast Associates merged with Bed and Breakfast Cape Cod to create a reservation service that represents inns and bed-and-breakfasts throughout Cape Cod, Martha's Vineyard, the South Shore, and Nantucket. Properties, which are all inspected and approved annually, range from modest to luxurious. There is a one-time $10 handling fee for the services here even if a customer does not use the service again for years.

HOSTELS

If you're a back-to-basics type of person who would rather spend money on, say, a nice dinner or some pricey souvenirs than empty your wallet on a fancy hotel, a hostel may be for you.

Beds are simple and often in dorm-like settings, and lock-outs (those times when you must vacate your room) and curfews are strictly enforced. Some American Youth Hostels (AYHs) have lock-outs timed between 10 a.m. and 5 p.m.; some have curfews of 11 p.m. Reservations are necessary. Check-in is between 3 and 10 p.m. All AYHs offer free on-site parking and bike storage.

The area has four AYHs—in Eastham, North Truro, Martha's Vineyard, and Nantucket—and non-AYH members can stay at them by simply paying the modest additional fee for an introductory membership (also see our Nantucket and Martha's Vineyard chapters). AYH accepts Visa and MasterCard and offers discounts to area attractions. There's also a privately owned hostel in Provincetown. Below we give descriptions of the Cape hostels.

HOSTELLING INTERNATIONAL $
75 Goody Hallet Dr., Eastham
(508) 255-2785, (888) 901-2085
www.capecodhostels.org
This hostel offers 46 beds in seven cabins ($32 Sun through Thurs and $35 Fri and Sat, plus $3 for nonmembers). Two family cabins, which offer two double beds and two bunk beds and sleep six, are also available.

Guests can use the screened-in porch common room, picnic tables, grills, communal kitchen and volleyball. The hostel is normally open late Memorial Day through the second week in Sept.

HOSTELLING INTERNATIONAL $
111 North Pamet Rd., North Truro
(508) 349-3889
www.capecodhostels.org
There's a reason this hostel is perched high atop the sand dunes: It was once a Coast Guard Station known as Little America. Now this hostel's known by that name too. Its location within the Cape Cod National Seashore will give you unbeatable views of the coastline, cranberry bogs, beaches, and beautiful Cape Cod sunrises. The 42 beds are set up in a multilevel house. Rates are $32 to $35. It's open from late June through early Sept.

OUTERMOST HOSTEL $
28 Winslow St., Provincetown
(508) 487-4378
www.outermosthostel.com
This privately owned hostel has 40 beds in five whitewashed cabins—nothing to write home about, but a steal at $25 per night. The hostel has a common living room and kitchen in one cabin. The expansive yard offers grills and picnic tables. The Outermost has no lockouts and no curfew. It's open mid-May through Oct.

KENNELS

If you need a place for your dog or cat to stay—perhaps you got your signals crossed on whether your chosen accommodation allows pets, or maybe you'd like to take a couple of days and visit the islands, sans pooch—the Cape has a number of kennels. Here are a few of the best.

THE ANIMAL INN
Route 130, Forestdale
(508) 477-0990
www.animalinncapecod.com
This veterinarian-owned facility has heated individual kennels, sheltered outdoor runs, and a separate kitty quarters. It offers grooming, obedience training, an on-premise vet clinic, and even a soothing sound system. The manager lives on

the property, so your pets are always watched over.

DERBYFIELD COUNTRY KENNEL
556 Depot St., North Harwich
(508) 432-2510
www.derbyfieldkennel.com
The owners reside at this kennel, which offers separate heated accommodations for dogs and cats and indoor/outdoor runs. Cats get extra-large, shelved "condos" so they can jump from level to level, and all pets get a treat at the nightly bed-check time. Grooming and training are also available, as are premium pet supplies; special diets can be accommodated.

NAUSET KENNELS
2685 Nauset Rd., North Eastham
(508) 255-0081
www.nausetkennels.com
In business since 1972, this reputable facility offers indoor and outdoor runs, three outdoor play yards, and separate quarters for dogs and cats, with insulated floors and even air-conditioning. Nauset Kennels also does grooming and offers day care for dogs. Staff members live on the premises.

PLEASANT BAY ANIMAL HOSPITAL
Route 137 and Queen Ann Road,
East Harwich
(508) 432-5500
www.pbah.com
This facility offers boarding and grooming as well as medical services. It has separate, air-conditioned accommodations for dogs and cats. Dogs get individual attention and are walked three times a day (or more if an owner chooses) on four and a half acres of property.

VACATION RENTALS

U ntil the downturn of 2008 and 2009, the Cape could best be described as an owner's market. Rentals were snatched up quickly, often before the season started in June. Although
scanning the newspapers can yield some good rental leads, your best bet is to contact local real
estate agents. Even if you're planning an off-season rental, prepare early. Many owners close
their property around Columbus Day. Sometimes renters can negotiate a better deal by agree-
ing to rent for the month or the season because it's much easier for the owners. One possibility
is to join together with some friends and agree to an extended rental. Each group can then take
a week or two weeks over the month or season.

The warm summer months provide a variety of rental properties, from cottages to houses
to condominium units. A rental cottage is usually a three-season small house. Many cottage
rentals, even long-term ones, do not supply linens (such as sheets or towels), paper goods, or
toiletries. Some offer housekeeping and laundry services for an extra fee. Almost all weekly
rental units of any kind rent from Saturday to Saturday.

When you think of condominiums and time-shares, think upscale apartments, almost
always fully furnished, and often part of a waterfront or water-view complex. Time-share units
are owned by a person or company who then rents out the unit for various periods of time.
Time-shares should only concern you if you plan on buying into one. If you do, make sure you
know what you are getting into as there have been issues with time-share owners feeling they
were ripped off.

If you do want to rent a cottage for a week, especially during July, plan on calling well in
advance. Many rental offices are busy in January and February booking rentals for the coming
summer season. In-season rates are the priciest; those in shoulder seasons (right before or
immediately following the busy summer season) can drop as much as 30 percent; off-season
rates (if the accommodations are available) can be as much as 50 percent off seasonal prices.

It would be impossible to mention all the resorts and rental agencies on the Cape, but we've
put together a list of those that offer the finest in vacation rentals. Keep in mind that many of
these agencies are also full-service real estate companies (see our Relocation chapter) and will
be more than happy to answer any questions—and perhaps sell you a property once you've
acquired a taste for Cape Cod.

Usually rental properties contain a fully equipped kitchen, but it is important to remember
that the Cape includes such a range of properties that "fully equipped" can mean different
things depending on the situation. For instance where a dishwasher may be considered standard issue for a year-round house, it is not always available in a small cottage that may have
been built 50 years ago, before dishwashers were an option. If a microwave oven, blenders,
electric can openers, and the like are considered a must, ask in advance.

Televisions, VCRs or DVDs, telephones, whether the cottage has a tub or just a shower
(families with small children who are used to taking baths will want to know) are all items to
be questioned before you send in your deposit. By the way, the typical deposit on a vacation
rental is 50 percent due upon making reservations, with the balance due before your arrival.
Before you book, always ask about cancellation policies and whether pets, visiting guests, and/
or smoking are allowed.

Finally, if you cannot find what you're looking for in this chapter, call the chamber of commerce in the town in which you're interested (chamber of commerce phone numbers are listed in the Area Overview chapter). The local chambers are more than happy to offer you more information.

UPPER CAPE

BEACH REALTY
133 North Shore Blvd., East Sandwich
(800) 886-4998
www.beachrealtycapecod.com
This office carries approximately 200 property listings in seven beach areas from Sagamore to Town Neck. Properties differ in size, and most of them rent by the week, though vacation rentals are available. Homes rent for $550 to $3,900.

i When contacting agents about vacation rentals, ask if they list any "quirky" ones. Sometimes you can find older cottages or homes with quaint or out-of-the-ordinary accommodations at bargain prices.

CAPE COAST REALTY
4 Barlows Landing Rd., Suite 1, Bourne
(508) 563-3332
www.capecoastrealty.com
You can choose from approximately 70 waterfront and water-view homes for rent in Bourne, Sandwich, and Falmouth. The rate for a small cottage is about $900 per week; a private luxury home rents for anywhere from $2,000 to $4,000 per week.

DONAHUE REAL ESTATE
850 Main St., Falmouth
(508) 548-5412
www.falmouthhomes.com
This active rental office lists approximately 250 rental properties from $700 to $8,400, including houses, condominiums, duplexes, and apartments, many with three, four, or even six bedrooms. Most of these properties are in Falmouth, and they are available for one week to a full season.

ERMINE LOVELL REAL ESTATE INCORPORATED
881 Palmer Ave., Falmouth
(508) 548-0703
www.francescaparkinson.com
With many inland and waterfront properties, including 8- or 11-bedroom houses, this more-than-70-year-old real estate office offers vacation rentals exclusively in the Falmouth and Woods Hole areas.

JOHN BARRETT REAL ESTATE
178 Rte. 28, East Falmouth
(508) 548-2000, (800) 339-6712
www.johnbarrettrealestate.com
With an inventory of 500 vacation rentals from cottages to waterfront homes, this office has listings in Falmouth, East Falmouth, and Mashpee, including Popponesset. Homes and condos are rented by the week or full season.

KINLIN GROVER GMAC REAL ESTATE
P.O. Box 2000, Brewster
www.vacationcapecod.com
(508) 896-7004, (800) 338-1851
Kinlin Grover GMAC is the leader in Cape Cod vacation rentals. Through their offices located across the Cape and various Web sites (also try www.kinlingrover.com), they service more visitors than any other rental company on the Cape.

i Sunday traffic going off the Cape is the worst. Most regulars say you have to be off the Cape before 10 a.m. to beat the backup at the bridges. We recommend extending your visit to Cape Cod and leaving after 6 p.m. when traffic is not so bad. It really depends on whether you want to get home tired or have some time to decompress before heading back to the daily grind.

NEW SEABURY RENTALS
12 Mallway St., New Seabury
(508) 477-8300, (800) 388-7686
www.newseaburyre.com/rentals.html

Nearly all the roughly 200 rental properties lie within the 2,000-acre New Seabury Resort, though separate services are available for Poponesset Beach (508-477-1143). Some are waterfront and range from two- to four-bedroom units. Country club, golf, tennis, and beach memberships are available. Membership includes pool and health club privileges.

REAL ESTATE ASSOCIATES
563 Rte. 28A (at Route 151),
North Falmouth
(508) 540-5545
www.uppercaperentals.com

Real Estate Associates has nearly 300 houses, condominiums, and cottages in waterfront, waterview, and beach locations. Within Falmouth, Bourne, Mashpee, Barnstable, and Sandwich, properties range from simple Cape Cod cottages to lavish luxury homes, with a price range of $800 to $6,000 per week.

MID-CAPE

CRAIGVILLE REALTY
648 Craigville Beach Rd., Craigville
(508) 775-3174
www.craigvillebeach.com

Craigville Realty has more than 200 rental properties, mostly homes and cottages in Centerville, Hyannis, West Hyannisport, and Craigville Beach. The offerings range from modest to exclusive, from $875 to $9,000 per week, including some waterfront.

ERA MARTIN SURETTE REALTY
563 Rte. 28, Harwichport
(508) 432-5499
http://capecodera.com

ERA Martin Surette Realty's Mid-Cape Rentals services Dennis, Harwich, Hyannis, Orleans, Sandwich, Yarmouth, Barnstable, and all related satellite towns (Dennisport, Yarmouthport, etc.). From cozy cottages to sprawling waterfront estates, every expectation is addressed in their extensive roster of properties. The agency also offers referrals for services including babysitters, housekeepers, transportation, caterers, and office facilities, easing the anxieties of clients with a variety of vacation needs.

PETER MCDOWELL ASSOCIATES
585 Rte. 6A, Dennis
(508) 385-9114, (888) 385-9114
www.rentcapecodproperties.com

This full-service real estate company offers about 200 summer rentals in the Mid-Cape, Harwich, and Brewster. Rental properties are available for a week, two weeks, a month, or for the whole summer season.

STEELE ASSOCIATES
1372 Rte. 134, East Dennis
(508) 385-7311
www.steelerealty.com

This family-owned company offers rental homes, cottages, duplexes, and condos in beach areas from Barnstable to Orleans. Rentals are weekly, monthly, or seasonal. Besides a busy summer rental season, Steele Associates also offers rentals during the off-season months of Sept and Oct. Summer weekly rentals range from $800 to $5,500 (for waterfront), and houses generally range from two to four bedrooms.

WATERFRONT RENTALS
20 Pilgrim Rd., West Yarmouth
(508) 778-1818
www.waterfrontrentalsinc.com

You can rent estates, homes, and condos from Falmouth to Truro through this established agency, which offers a wide selection of mid- and lower Cape properties. Over 160 properties are available for weekly, seasonal, or year-round rental and range from one- to nine- bedroom facilities. These rental properties range from $750 to $14,000 per week. Videos of properties can be viewed at the office.

LOWER CAPE

AMERICAN HERITAGE REALTY

414 Rte. 28, South Orleans
(508) 255-2069 (888) 296-4313
www.capecodforrent.com

American Heritage is one of the lower Cape's leading real estate and vacation rental firms. It serves Orleans, Harwich, Brewster, Chatham, Eastham, and Wellfleet.

BEACHFRONT REALTY

139 Commercial St., Provincetown
(508) 487-1397
www.beachfront-realty.com

Beachfront represents more than 50 accommodations for weekly rental and approximately 30 for seasonal rental in Provincetown. Weekly rates are from $900 to $4,000.

GREAT LOCATIONS REAL ESTATE

2660 Rte. 6A, Brewster
(508) 896-2090, (800) 626-9984
www.greatlocationsre.com

Great Locations offers exceptional vacation rentals, including a large selection of condominium rentals at Ocean Edge Resort in Brewster. Prices range from $900 to $3,900 per week in season, the latter being the price of a three-bedroom house on the water. Monthly and seasonal rentals are also available through this high-quality vacation rental outfit.

HARBORSIDE REALTY

154 Commercial St., Provincetown
(508) 487-4005, (800) 838-4005
www.harborside-realty.com

Harborside Realty handles 200 Provincetown properties, from basic quaint cottages at $800 a week to the most trendy four-bedroom private homes at about $4,000 a week. Properties are available by the week, month, and for the summer season.

KINLIN GROVER GMAC REAL ESTATE

P.O. Box 2000, Brewster
www.vacationcapecod.com
(508) 896-7004, (800) 338-1851

Kinlin Grover GMAC is the leader in Cape Cod vacation rentals. Through their offices located across the Cape and various Web sites (also try www.kinlingrover.com), they service more visitors than any other rental company on the Cape.

PAT SHULTZ AND ASSOCIATES

406 Commercial St., Provincetown
(508) 487-9550
www.patshultz.com

Pat Shultz and Associates promise to find the perfect rental for your needs—weekly, monthly, seasonally, or annually. Properties range from $600 studios and $900 one-bedroom apartments to $3,200 two-bedroom units and $6,000 waterfront houses.

PINE ACRES REALTY

20 Heritage Lane, Chatham
(508) 945-7443
www.pineacresrealty.com

Choose from nearly 220 Chatham properties rented by the week, season, or year. Rentals run from $800 to $5,000 for a waterfront estate.

THE RENTAL COMPANY AT WILLIAM RAVEIS

213 Main St., East Orleans
(508) 240-2222
www.capecodvacation.com

The Rental Company manages more than 450 vacation rentals in the Lower Cape towns, including Harwich, Brewster, Chatham, Orleans, Eastham, Wellfleet, and Truro. Their inventory of vacation homes, cottages, and condos rent from between $500 and $13,000 per week.

SYLVAN REALTY

1715 Rte. 28, Unit B, West Chatham
(508) 945-7222
www.sylvanrentals.com

This agency specializes in rentals of some 200 individually owned cottages and homes in the Chatham and Harwich areas. From fully furnished beach cottages to luxury homes, these properties are available on a weekly, monthly, and seasonal basis for $500 to $5,000 per week.

CAMPGROUNDS AND STATE PARKS

Cape Cod is a paradise for those who enjoy water sports, fishing, hiking, biking, and any of the other outdoor activities for which it is so well known. The Cape has a number of campgrounds and state parks that allow visitors to enjoy an outdoor experience in near unspoiled surroundings. Whether it's in a tent or an RV, camping Cape Cod style takes you out of the rhythm of everyday life—at least for a while. You'll go home refreshed—and you'll save scads of money because camping is the best deal going on the Cape. For less than $30 a night you can pitch a tent in a quiet, rustic environment on the edge of the dunes or deep in woodland.

In this chapter we've included information on both public and private campgrounds. Cape Cod has more than 4,500 campsites in 20 campgrounds and three state parks with over 800 campsites. As there is a diverse range of campgrounds, visitors will be sure to find accommodations to suit their style of camping. Reservations at most campgrounds are essential for camping during the Cape's peak season from mid-June through Labor Day.

TIPS TO GET YOU STARTED

Whether you are an experienced camper or a first-timer, decide on what kind of camping experience you want: back to nature, family oriented, in the woods, or close to town. Note that there is no wilderness camping on Cape Cod.

Second, consider your choices. Some people prefer to camp at smaller, more remote campgrounds and like to "rough it." In this case, consider the quiet solitude of the campgrounds near the National Seashore and surrounding areas in the Lower Cape. To others, camping is merely an affordable way to spend time on the Cape, and you may want to be near more lively areas, in which case the privately owned campgrounds in the Upper and Mid-Cape areas will probably suit your needs.

You'll always be close to water, so that shouldn't be a consideration, but there is a difference between the campgrounds on the Upper Cape and those located on the Lower Cape. Many campgrounds located in the Upper Cape have swimming pools, game rooms, and organized activities and tend to be more self-contained, while the smaller campgrounds on the Lower Cape may not have these amenities

but are closer to bike paths, hiking trails, and other areas of natural beauty. All campgrounds listed offer suitable tent sites and/or RV camping and provide flush toilets, and most offer electrical and water hookups. Although the listings below are as up-to-date as we can make them, you may want to use the phone numbers given to verify current fees and services.

CAMPGROUNDS

Upper Cape

BAY VIEW CAMPGROUND
260 Rte. 28 (MacArthur Boulevard), Bourne
(508) 759-7610
www.bayviewcampground.com
Perched on one of the highest points of land on Cape Cod, this 425-site campground is a good spot to enjoy sunsets and take advantage of the recreational opportunities in the area. Bay View is 20 minutes by car from both Falmouth and Sandwich. Walkers, runners, and in-line skaters will enjoy the nearby canal bike path, while bargain hunters will appreciate the proximity to factory outlet stores. Bay View is popular with families. The campground has a range of facilities

for every taste from shuffleboard to swimming pools. There is also a full-time recreation director who organizes daily activities, including teen dances and Wiffle Ball.

Each site has a picnic table, fireplace, and water hookups, electricity (full hookup sites have 30 amps), sewer, and cable TV. Facilities include showers and toilets, ice, gas, and wood. You can buy RV supplies such as hoses and awnings at the office. The Top Dog eatery serves concession-style foods in season and on weekends, and wireless Internet access is available at the campground's recreation building.

The campground is open from May to mid-Oct. Reservations are accepted in early Feb for the upcoming season. The in-season rate for two people is $55 plus $5 for children younger than 18 and $10 for those 18 and older. The off-season rate—for May and June and Labor Day to Oct—is $43.

i During peak weeks in the summer, most campgrounds require a reservation. Many also require a minimum length of stay during weekends in July and August. For instance, a minimum stay of two nights may be required over weekends, and a three-night stay might be required on holiday weekends. In July and August seven-night stays are required at some area campgrounds.

BOURNE SCENIC PARK
370 Bourne Scenic Hwy. (U.S. Route 6 and Route 28), Bourne
(508) 759-7873
www.bournescenicpark.com
Situated on the banks of the world's widest sea-level canal, this 450-site facility offers shady woods and proximity to shops and grocery stores. And the scenery is extraordinary: gigantic white cruise ships and tankers glide past your campsite along the canal and occasionally give a massive blast on their horns.

From the park, bikers and strollers have several access points to the popular canal bike path, where people push baby strollers, walk dogs,

bike, and in-line skate all day long. In the summer, the park offers a waterslide, pig roast, and live entertainment, including bands and DJs.

Operated by the Bourne Recreation Authority, the Scenic Park has electric and water hookups, a dump station, playgrounds, a recreation hall, a canalside picnic area, a basketball court, and activities for children throughout the summer. The country store sells basic supplies, including ice and wood.

In season the rates are $39 per day with electricity hookup and $32 without, or $234/$192 for a week. In the off-season, a week stay costs $170 with electricity.

DUNROAMIN' COTTAGES AND TRAILER PARK
5 John Ewer Rd., Sandwich
(508) 477-0859, (508) 477-0541
www.dunroamincottages.com or www .dunroamintrailerpark.com
A family-run business since 1952, Dunroamin' offers 66 trailer sites for self-contained vehicles, plus four cottages, on 30 acres next to Peter's Pond. The cottages, which book early, are right on the pond, which offers great freshwater fishing. Each cottage comes equipped with its own rowboat, oars, and life vests. There's a play area and a private sandy beach. Pets are allowed in the trailer park provided they're vaccinated, restrained, and kept off the beach. Trailer sites include hookups for water, electricity, and sewerage. Rates, based on a party of four, are $35 daily, $240 weekly, and $900 monthly. Cottages, which can accommodate five to six people, have weekly rental costs of about $895 to $935 in season, and between $695 and $740 in the off-season. The park is open mid-Apr to mid-Oct for trailers and mid-June to early Sept for cottage rentals.

PETER'S POND RV RESORT
185 Cotuit Rd., Sandwich
(508) 477-1775
www.peterspond.com
A 100-acre campground situated on a lovely freshwater lake, Peter's Pond Park offers swimming, fishing, and boating. It abuts a large conservation area

with walking trails and has playgrounds; playing fields for softball and volleyball; horseshoes; courts for bocce, shuffleboard, and badminton; a convenience store; and adult and teen recreation halls. The campground, which has been in the DeGraw family for more than 70 years, offers 411 large sites, accommodating both tents and RVs. There are also five cottages on-site. Wheelchair-accessible facilities are available. You can cook on individual charcoal and gas stoves. Pets are allowed if you abide by the park rules and have a valid rabies certificate for your animal.

The campground is open from mid-Apr until early Oct, and is $35 to $75, depending on location and hookups to electric and water.

SIPPEWISSETT CAMPGROUND & CABINS
836 Palmer Ave., Falmouth
(508) 548-2542
www.sippewissett.com
This campground has an activity center, a playground, and a volleyball area. Most of the 100 sites (accommodating both tents and RVs) are wooded, and all have picnic tables and fire pits. The shady campground offers 24-hour security, emergency assistance, and a coin-operated laundry. Dogs are not permitted here from late-May to Labor Day.

The nightly charge for families is $45 in season. Electric and water hookups are $5 extra per day. Tipis cost $63 per night. The off-season rate is $35 and $38 with water and electricity. Off-season rates apply at the beginning and end of the season, which runs from mid-May to mid-Sept.

WAQUOIT BAY NATIONAL ESTUARINE RESEARCH RESERVE
149 Waquoit Hwy., Waquoit
(508) 457-0495
www.waquoitbayreserve.org
Camping on the 300-acre Washburn Island in Waquoit Bay should be considered a privilege as well as a luxury. This beautiful island is now managed by the state, and campers must have permits (see information below). Eleven sites are available, nine for families and two for groups of no more than 25. The reserve offers a group rate of $25. Facilities consist of composting toilets and outhouses; the island has no electricity or fresh water. Only hibachis and Coleman-type stoves can be used for cooking. Access to the island across a narrow tidal channel is possible only by private boat—your own. Camping ends in mid-Oct.

Permits cost $8 per night for Massachusetts residents, $10 for out-of-staters.

i Most of the campgrounds that are in areas that allow campfires have wood available. For a few dollars you can get a good-size bundle that should last you a few nights.

Mid-Cape
CAMPERS HAVEN LTD. RV RESORT
184 Old Wharf Rd., Dennisport
(508) 398-2811
www.carefreervresorts.com
This place emphasizes family fun, including ice-cream socials, sing-alongs, story hours, candy bingo, beach barbecues, minigolf, bocce, shuffleboard, volleyball, basketball, horseshoes, potluck suppers, and two playgrounds, one for little tykes and another for older children. Some of the warmest waters on the Cape are just seconds away at their private beach on Nantucket Sound.

Choose from among 248 shaded sites. All include water, electricity, cable TV, and gray water disposal (many sites have full sewage disposal). Rates are $42 to $62 per day. The park is open from May 1 to Columbus Day and is limited to RVs and campers only. Dogs are not allowed between late June and Labor Day weekend.

Lower Cape
ADVENTURE BOUND CAMPING RESORT CAMP COD
48 Highland Rd., North Truro
(508) 487-1847, (877) 409-2267
www.abcapecod.com
This campground includes 330 tent, trailer, and RV sites surrounded by 22 acres of native pines and rambling hills, smack-dab in the middle of the Cape Cod National Seashore. Amenities include flush toilets, metered hot showers, a

Laundromat, private picnic tables, wireless Internet access, a fully stocked camp store, ceramic-tiled restrooms, and cable TV. Saunter over to the ocean or bay beach, both less than a mile away, or hike and bike the nearby trails.

The basic site fee is $36, plus $16 for complete hookup. Pets are allowed with certain restrictions. Open mid-Apr through Oct.

ATLANTIC OAKS
3700 U.S. Rte. 6, Eastham
(508) 255-1437
www.atlanticoaks.com
Just a half-mile from the Cape Cod National Seashore's visitor center, this modern campground meets the needs of RVers and tent campers alike (though the emphasis here is on the former). The 100 large wooded sites include drive-throughs with full electric and water hookups and cable TV. Other amenities include wireless Internet access, LP gas sales, free hot showers, laundry facilities, nightly movies during the summer, and, to keep the kids entertained, a playground. A 5,000-square-foot multipurpose building was added in 2006. Dogs are allowed for a nightly fee of $4 here, provided that they are taken with you when you're away from the camp. You might want to bring your bicycles, as Atlantic Oaks abuts the Cape Cod Rail Trail.

The grounds are protected (not that they need to be, in sleepy Eastham) by a 24-hour security gate. Rates are $38 to $63 per night at this campground, which is open May through Oct.

DUNES' EDGE CAMPGROUND
386 U.S. Rte. 6, Provincetown
(508) 487-9815
www.dunes-edge.com
Dunes' Edge, nestled beneath the shadow of Horses Head, one of the tallest hills in town, is well-suited for visitors who want to explore the Provincetown area and nearby beaches by bike or by foot.

Most of the 85 tent sites and 15 trailer spaces offer the utmost in privacy. The campground offers hot showers, a dumping station, laundry facilities, and a store, as well as close proximity to the Cape Cod National Seashore, which actually borders Dunes' Edge. The rates are $40 per day for one or two people in season and $30 in the off-season. The limit is six people per site. Your pet—one per site, welcome as long as it's leashed—stays free! Reservations are highly recommended. Open May through Sept.

MAURICE'S CAMPGROUND
80 U.S. Rte. 6, Wellfleet
(508) 349-2029
www.mauricescampground.com
The 240 tent, trailer, and RV sites, as well as several cottages and cabins, are set in the middle of a large pine grove, far from the hustle and bustle of US 6. Each site is spacious and has a picnic table. The general store offers pick-your-own lobster—perfect for a clambake! (Local ordinances forbid open fires in the area, but you can bring your own hibachi.)

The cottages, always in demand, can sleep two to four people and have insulated walls, fully equipped kitchens, air-conditioning, TV, and maple furnishings. The cabins, which can accommodate up to six people, are similar in construction to the cottages but do not accommodate cooking. Three utility buildings provide plenty of sanitary facilities, including modern restrooms and metered hot-water showers.

The site fee is $37 per day for two adults with no hookups. Electric, water, sewer, and cable hookups are an extra $5 to $8. Weekly rates for cottages start at $700; cabins rent for $95 nightly for two people. Reservations are strongly recommended for July and Aug. There is a no-pets policy. The campground is open late May to early Oct.

PAINE'S CAMPGROUND
180 Old County Rd., off U.S. Rte. 6, South Wellfleet
(508) 349-3007
www.campingcapecod.com
The emphasis here is on tent camping, and those who really want to get away from it all can choose a private "lug-in" tent site or opt for a reservation in the "quiet couples only" section. Both are secluded and no water or electricity is available.

Campers with children are placed in a family section. Many of these sites will accommodate multiple tents. Although Paine's preference is for tents, there are some hookup sites with water and 15-amp service; these are grouped together and suitable for tents, pop-ups, and pickup campers. Several sites have also been converted for RVs, with electric and water hookups, but there are no sewer hookups or dump stations. All hookup sites cost an extra $7 to $10 fee per day. Base rates are $40 per night for two people; add $15 per night for each extra adult and $5 per child. Larger group sites can accommodate family reunions and other small to large groups. No water or electric is available to the group sites. Reservations for any site are strongly recommended, and there is a no-pets policy. Paine's Campground is open from mid-May though mid-Oct.

SHADY KNOLL CAMPGROUND
1709 Rte. 6A, Brewster
(508) 896-3002
www.shadyknoll.com
With 100 wooded sites for tents and RVs, Shady Knoll offers free private hot showers, full hookups with wireless Internet access, fireplaces, laundry facilities, a playground, game room, lounge, and campground store. Campfires are allowed, and movies are shown nightly during the summer. Reservations are requested. Weekends in July and Aug require a three-night minimum stay. Shady Knoll is open May 15 through Columbus Day weekend. Rates are $38 to $54 a night, depending on whether you need electric, water, cable, or sewer hookup. Pets are allowed for an extra $4 a night, provided you take them with you when you leave your site.

SWEETWATER FOREST
Off Route 124, Brewster
(508) 896-3773
www.sweetwaterforest.com
One of the largest and oldest campgrounds on Cape Cod, Sweetwater is a sprawling spread of 250 sites on 75 acres of woodland bordering Snow's Pond. You can rent a canoe and cruise around the lake, fish off the dock, or play horse-

shoes on the beach—you can even arrange for a tractor-pulled hayride. There are five different playgrounds, as well as an 18-hole minigolf course. Free wireless Internet access is available. There is also a Memory Garden and play center.

Sites are available with partial or full hookups, and there's a separate area just for tents. Each site has its own picnic table and fireplace. Four modern comfort stations with free hot showers ensure that you won't have far to go when you have to go. Rates start at $32 per day for a family of four with no hookup, $46 for full hookup, which includes cable TV with the electric hookup. Reservations are recommended during the summer and on holiday weekends, and pets are allowed. Though the grounds officially close from Nov through Apr, self-contained camping is allowed during these months.

STATE PARKS

Within Massachusetts' state-owned campgrounds you'll discover some of America's best camping experiences. There are 28 exceptional state forests and park campgrounds in Massachusetts, and three of them are on Cape Cod—Scusset Beach State Reservation, Shawme-Crowell State Forest, and Nickerson State Park.

NICKERSON STATE PARK
3488 Rte. 6A, East Brewster
(508) 896-3491, (877) 422-6762 (ICAMPMA) (reservations)
www.reserveamerica.com
The 1,900-plus wooded acres that make up the bulk of the park once belonged to Roland Nickerson, a multimillionaire who founded the First National Bank of Chicago. The Nickersons, who lived farther west on Route 6A in an opulent estate now known as Ocean Edge Resort (see our Hotels, Motels, and Resorts chapter), had a hunting lodge on the acreage that now makes up the state park. The Nickersons hosted private hunts at their "Bungalow Estates," as they referred to their rustic playground. Nickerson's wife, Addie, donated the land to the state in 1934 in honor of their son, a victim of the 1918 influenza epidemic, and in honor of her husband.

The park features eight kettle ponds formed by ice-age glaciers. You can spot many rare species of plants and wildflowers growing around the edges of kettle ponds, but remember it's against the law to trample or pick them.

You could spend a month here and still find new things to do. Boat or swim in Cliff Pond, the largest in the park, or try your luck fishing at one of the four trout-stocked ponds. (Note there are no lifeguards.) Bird-watchers will be pleased to know Nickerson is a regular stop on the migration route of such feathered friends as larks, woodpeckers, wrens, warblers, and thrushes. It's also a watering hole for cormorants, Canada geese, great blue herons, ducks—even the occasional common loon. You may also spot owls, osprey, hawks, eagles, and such woodland animals as red foxes, skunks, chipmunks, white-tailed deer, and nonpoisonous snakes. The Cape Cod Rail Trail, which is great for bicycling, passes right through the park, with a few loops branching off through different areas of the park. Nickerson is also a winter wonderland, allowing visitors to ice-fish, ice-skate, and when there is snow, cross-country ski on marked trails. The park is an easy walk or drive from bay beaches, and beach walks are among the many interpretive activities led by park naturalists in season.

Nickerson State Park offers 420 camping sites at $17 per night for out-of-staters, but does not offer electric or RV hookups. The sites are large enough to handle two tents and two cars. The rate is for four adults per site. Reservations are required, and there is a $9.50 processing fee. Open late May through late Oct.

SCUSSET BEACH STATE RESERVATION
140 Scusset Beach Rd., Sagamore Beach
(508) 888-0859, (877) 422-6762
www.reserveamerica.com
A few hundred yards from a sandy Cape Cod Bay beach, Scusset Beach State Reservation offers walking trails and immediate access to the Cape Cod Canal bike path. Deer, foxes, upland game birds, and rabbits make their homes in the 330-acre preserve.

Fishing enthusiasts can cast their lines from a stone jetty at the end of the canal or from the banks of the canal, and there's also a wheelchair-accessible fishing pier. Scusset has 98 campsites, most in the open, including several wheelchair-accessible sites. Freshwater and dumping stations are nearby.

The campground is open year-round; however, after Columbus Day the water is turned off in the public facilities, and only self-contained vehicles are permitted until mid-Apr. The seasonal nightly rate is $15 for Massachusetts residents, $17 for out-of-staters. Large groups or clubs with self-contained RVs might be interested in reserving the spacious open field with grills and tables.

Stays are limited to no more than two weeks between Memorial Day and Labor Day, and reservations are required.

SHAWME-CROWELL STATE FOREST
Route 130, Sandwich
(508) 888-0351, (877) 422-6762 (reservations)
www.reserveamerica.com
The cool, wooded setting for Shawme-Crowell State Forest offers a summer haven for tent campers and RV owners. Just a half-mile away from scenic Route 6A, it's close to the canal bike path and Sandwich's marina, museums, and restaurants. Campers here have beach privileges at Scusset Beach on the opposite side of the canal.

Encompassing 742 acres, Shawme-Crowell is the fourth-largest park in Massachusetts. It has more than 285 sites, all with their own picnic tables and fireplaces. Scattered throughout are clean restrooms, hot showers, and sewage-disposal sites. The park has no on-site hookups for water or electricity. A convenience store carries firewood, ice, and other camping goods.

Overseen by friendly park rangers, this quiet, uncongested campground is open year-round for both tents and RVs—the first state park to adopt this year-round policy (previously, the park allowed only self-contained vehicles in winter). The nightly fee is $12 for in-state residents and $14 for out-of-state adults (children are free). Two vehicles are allowed per site. Pets are not allowed when camping in a yurt.

RESTAURANTS

There's a restaurant on Cape Cod to suit every mood, taste, whim, and budget. To help you choose the restaurant that suits your palate and your pocket, we've prepared descriptions of our favorite restaurants on Cape Cod. We'll tell you about places that offer such regional favorites as cod, Monomoy mussels, Wellfleet oysters, New England clam chowder—and of course, lobster. Although not all of the Cape's restaurants specialize in seafood, most serve lobster, and we highly recommend it, whether boiled, baked, broiled, stuffed, stewed, sautéed, served in salads, fried in cakes, or simmered the way we like it—with basil, wine, and tomatoes and served with clams, scallops, shrimp, and mussels.

If you're not in the mood for these regional dishes, there are many other choices. What's remarkable about the Cape is the incredible variety of eating establishments on this relatively small spit of land.

Most of the restaurants listed here accept major credit cards (we note the ones that don't), and, unless otherwise stated, all are wheelchair accessible. Many offer early-bird dinner specials, usually to those seated by 5:30 p.m., with discounts ranging anywhere from 10 to 30 percent off the regular price.

One of the nice things about eating out on the Cape is that most restaurants maintain a casual and comfortable "come-as-you-are" dress code, so to enjoy the relaxed atmosphere of these restaurants, you need dress no more formally than "Cape Cod casual," typically an ensemble of shirt, shorts, and sandals. Some restaurants, such as the Paddock in Hyannis or Chillingsworth in Brewster, afford you the opportunity to dress up more formally.

Many restaurants are packed during the height of the tourist season and on weekends and holidays. In summer, reservations are a must at fine restaurants, and a wait is common at those that maintain a first-come, first-served policy. You may even have to wait a bit when you've made reservations, because even the most efficient restaurant can get backed up with lingering diners.

Many restaurants now have Web sites with their menus for potential diners to peruse. Some Web sites even have video that shows chefs preparing the meals they serve.

Thanks to state legislation barring smoking in restaurants and bars, all of these restaurants are smoke-free.

We have followed our usual geographical order in presenting the restaurants in this chapter. Note that some entries are described as seasonal and are closed for the winter months, usually from late fall through April or May.

Price Code

The following price code is meant strictly as a guideline. The code is based on the average price of dinner for two, excluding appetizers, alcoholic beverages, dessert, tax, and tip. (Tipping is customarily 15 to 20 percent.)

$	Less than $20
$$	$20 to $35
$$$	$36 to $50
$$$$	$51 and more

UPPER CAPE

AQUA GRILLE $$
14 Gallo Rd., Sandwich
(508) 888-8889
www.aquagrille.com

Veteran Cape Cod restaurateurs the Zartarian family (the Paddock Restaurant in Hyannis) and German chef Gert Rausch have joined to create a quality dining experience with a global flair at moderate prices in a casual waterfront atmosphere. Aqua Grille is located at Sandwich Marina and Cape Cod Canal, and if you are in the mood for enjoying Cape Cod favorites such as native fish and lobster in a waterfront setting, this is your place. Appetizers are delicious and unusual (like the smoked chicken quesadillas, stuffed with cilantro and Vermont goat cheese, served with pico de gallo and ancho chile crème fraiche). Gert's special grilled-fish entrees are enhanced by chipotle aioli, sauce béarnaise, tomato and basil stew, dill mayonnaise, remoulade, and roasted red bell pepper sauce. Complementing the menu is an extensive wine and drink list. The Aqua Grille can also accommodate special functions such as rehearsal dinners and weddings. It's open daily for lunch and dinner. The restaurant is open only on weekends from Oct through the beginning of May.

THE BEE-HIVE TAVERN $$
406 Rte. 6A, East Sandwich
(508) 833-1184
www.thebeehivetavern.com

The day the Bee-Hive opened in 1992, it was so mobbed it ran out of food and had to close two hours early! Now under new ownership, the tavern has maintained the standards on which such success was built, offering cozy seating, reliably good food, and a personable staff. The menu offers a mix of specials, traditional entrees, and fresh seafood. Rolls and desserts are baked on-site, and the homemade Bee Sting ice cream makes a memorable dessert. The Bee-Hive is open daily year-round for lunch and dinner and serves breakfast on Sunday only.

BLEU $$$
10 Market St., Mashpee Commons, Mashpee
(508) 539-7907
www.bleurestaurant.com

The Loire Valley comes to Mashpee Commons courtesy of Frederic Feufeu, the French-born executive chef and owner of Bleu. The cool color scheme reflects the eatery's name, while the menu ranges from low-key brasserie classics (Black Forest ham and Gruyère buckwheat crepe) to boundary-pushing fusion (seared sea scallops with maple-grapefruit glaze, French beans tossed in walnut oil, with jasmine rice and crispy shrimp wraps).

BOBBY BYRNE'S PUB $$
Route 6A and Tupper Road, Sandwich
(508) 888-6088
Mashpee Commons, Mashpee
(508) 477-0600
www.bobbybyrnes.com

When locals are in a mood to relax, Bobby Byrne's is the place they head to, as this friendly pub lives up to its billing as "an eating, drinking, and talking establishment." Savory sandwiches, hamburgers, and nightly specials will certainly hit the spot, and their freshly made soups and lighter fare are always popular. Its casual atmosphere and reasonable prices, along with large bar and widescreen TV, draw fans of the Patriots, Red Sox, Celtics, and Bruins and friends who just want to get together to catch up on the latest. Bobby Byrne's serves lunch and dinner daily year-round. There's another Bobby Byrne's in Hyannis. (See the listing below in our Mid-Cape section.)

CAPTAIN KIDD BAR AND
WATERFRONT DINING ROOM $$$
77 Water St., Woods Hole
(508) 548-8563
www.thecaptainkidd.com

There's the Woods Hole Oceanographic Institute, then there's the other Woods Hole institution, the Captain Kidd, which opened shortly after Prohibition ended. You can settle down at the bar, in a lounge complete with a fireplace, in the waterfront dining room, or outside on the patio or dock overlooking Eel Pond. The menu features fresh seafood, including scrod, tuna, and lobster brought in by local fishermen. The Kidd serves lunch and dinner daily year-round.

CAPTAIN SCOTT'S $$
71 Tupper Rd., Sandwich
(508) 888-1675
www.captainscotts.com
If you are looking for casual dining, then try Captain Scott's, a small eatery with great food and prices easy on the wallet. You can stretch your dollar here with the daily specials, which usually run from about $6 to $15 per entree. You have your choice of indoor or outdoor seating, or you can order takeout. Captain Scott's, near the town marina, features early-bird specials and a daily special. In addition to the fish and chips and broiled scrod, the chicken and Italian entrees are very popular. Captain Scott's is open daily year-round for lunch and dinner.

CHAPOQUOIT GRILL $$
410 West Falmouth Hwy., Route 28A,
Falmouth
(508) 540-7794
This is a real locals' favorite, so you may have to wait to be seated, even on a weeknight. Our advice is to head for the bar, which is a delightful place, and start the evening off with a beverage. The food here is excellent, and the menu puts a spin on the concept of eclectic.

THE CHART ROOM $$
One Shipyard Lane, Cataumet (Bourne)
(508) 563-5350
This forty-year-old casual-style restaurant at Kingman Marina has an excellent reputation for consistency and good seafood—baked stuffed lobster, lobster salad, scrod, sole, bluefish, striped bass, halibut—in addition to steaks and chops. The freshly made quahog chowder is a good place to start—not too thick, not too watery, full of flavor. Desserts, such as apple pie and ice-cream puffs, are made locally. The Chart Room opens in mid-May for weekends only until mid-

June, then it's open daily through the summer; after Labor Day and up to mid-Oct it's open only on weekends. The Chart Room serves lunch and dinner and there's an afternoon bar menu as well. Call and ask for directions—this one's a little hard to find, but worth the trouble.

COOKE'S SEAFOOD $-$$
7 Ryan's Way, Mashpee
(508) 477-9595
www.cookesseafood.com
Cooke's has been serving award-winning broiled and fried seafood since 1977. Known for their excellent seafood platters, their fried clams consistently rank with the best on Cape Cod. There is another location in Hyannis and both are open daily from Mar through Nov for lunch and dinner.

THE COONAMESSETT INN $$$$
311 Gifford St., Falmouth
(508) 548-2300
www.capecodrestaurants.org/coonamessett
The Coonamessett has been a Falmouth favorite for decades. The restaurant has four attractive dining rooms, one with a fireplace, and two with lovely views of Jones Pond behind the inn. Popular menu items include traditional regional favorites, such as pan-seared Chatham cod, and freshly made soups, such as lobster bisque and roasted eggplant soup. There is also a choice of vegetarian entrees, and all desserts are freshly made. The Coonamessett Inn is open daily year-round serving lunch, dinner, and Sunday brunch.

THE DAN'L WEBSTER INN $$$
149 Main St., Sandwich
(508) 888-3622
www.danlwebsterinn.com
The award-winning Dan'l Webster (see our Hotels, Motels, and Resorts and Nightlife chapters) offers American cuisine, fine service, an exemplary wine list, and elegant ambience. We recommend dining in the Conservatory, a glass-walled area that offers views of the inn's linden tree and gardens. Seafood entrees are always delicious here, and carnivores consistently rave about the quality of the prime

rib. This year-round restaurant, open daily, serves breakfast, lunch, dinner, and Sunday brunch.

FIREFLY WOODFIRE GRILL AND BAR $$–$$$
271 Main St., Falmouth
(508) 548-7953
www.fireflywoodfiregrill.com

A wood-stone oven or wood-fire grill is account-able for most of the preparations at this aptly named eatery, where an open kitchen allows diners to see their cedar-planked salmon steaks and white pizettas hit the flames. Live entertain-ment, outdoor seating, and an extensive menu of domestic and international wines, beers, and microbrews are among the other draws at Firefly, which changes its menu and decor seasonally.

FISHMONGER'S CAFE $$
56 Water St., Woods Hole
(508) 540-5376
www.fishmongercafewoodshole.com

Where else besides Woods Hole could you enjoy a good ol' bowl of clam chowder beside a work-ing drawbridge? Watching the little bridge being raised and lowered for boat traffic passing into Eel Pond within a few feet of the restaurant is a fascinating pastime at Fishmonger's. In fact, all of Woods Hole's remarkable sights, marine and oth-erwise, are part of the view from this restaurant's windows. The casual gourmet menu focuses on natural foods, grains, fresh fish, and homemade soups, plus a number of vegetarian entrees—all excellent—as well as daily specials. The Fishmon-ger serves lunch and dinner daily and breakfast on the weekends during the season. Off-season breakfast is served daily.

FLYING BRIDGE RESTAURANT $$$$
220 Scranton Ave., Falmouth
(508) 548-2700
www.capecodrestaurants.org/flyingbridge

If you're looking for good food, outdoor seating, and views of Falmouth's busy inner harbor, you'll find it here. The menu offers a nice mix of native seafood, Italian dishes, steaks, burgers, sand-wiches, and chef's specialties. Lobster, swordfish, and fresh-caught tuna are always popular. This large restaurant, which is heavily booked for wed-dings and special functions, offers seating on two levels, and about half of its seating is outdoors. You can dine here daily in season for lunch and dinner, with late-night hours on weekends.

GOLDEN SWAN $$$
323 Main St., Falmouth
(508) 540-6580
www.goldenswanfineindiancuisine.com

For a quiet, moderately priced restaurant with authentic Indian food,, stop in at the Golden Swan. The restaurant offers a full bar and an ample wine and beer list. Golden Swan is open for dinner daily year-round.

HEMISPHERE $$$
98 Town Neck Rd., Sandwich
(508) 888-6166
www.hemispherecapecod.com

The former Horizons on Cape Cod Bay is now Hemisphere. Sit indoors or out on a deck, and order from a menu that's as casual as the atmo-sphere. You'll find the traditional seafood fare you'd expect from a place this close to the water. Hemisphere has a good selection of bar food and a children's menu, and most items are available on a take-out basis. It serves lunch and dinner daily from Apr to early Nov. The downstairs banquet room is open for special functions, but book it early.

LA CUCINA SUL MARE $$$
237 Rte. 28, Falmouth
(508) 548-560
www.lacucinasulmare.com

La Cucina Sul Mare serves generous portions of affordable northern Italian and Mediterranean specialties like zuppa de pesce, osso buco, and lobster fra diavolo. So join the line and wait for your turn under the tin ceiling: The food and service will make you glad you did.

THE LANDFALL $$–$$$
2 Luscombe Ave., Woods Hole
(508) 548-1758
www.woodshole.com/landfall

At the Landfall you can enjoy fresh seafood while you watch the sailboats and fishing vessels come and go in the harbor and the ferries pulling into their Woods Hole berth only a few hundred feet away. The restaurant's nautical decor complements its surroundings, and it makes sense to order fresh seafood here, especially the clam chowder, scallops, lobster, or seafood platter. The homemade apple crisp is a great way to round off your meal. It is open for lunch and dinner daily from Apr through Oct.

LOBSTER TRAP RESTAURANT $
290 Shore Rd., Bourne
(508) 759-3992
www.lobsters-online.com/lobstertrap/
Restaurant.asp
Open from May through Columbus Day, the Lobster Trap is a busy lunch spot and is packed at dinnertime. On the menu are popular dishes such as fish and chips, broiled haddock, chowders, steamers, and, of course, lobster, as well as many other kinds of broiled, boiled, and fried seafood. Special treats may include such tasty dishes as broiled swordfish tips. Burgers and chicken dishes are also served. The restaurant has a casual atmosphere—diners eat on paper plates with plastic forks on a large deck overlooking scenic Buzzards Bay. This seasonal restaurant is open for lunch and dinner seven days a week.

MARSHLAND RESTAURANTS $
109 Rte. 6A, Sandwich
(508) 888-9824
315 Cotuit Rd., Sandwich
(508) 888-9747
These local favorites might look inconspicuous, but their popularity is evident in the lines of regulars waiting to get inside. Daily specials, quick service, and booth seating make Marshland and Marshland Too popular places to meet friends, so expect a friendly hubbub in the restaurants. Everything on the menu is homemade, and the baked stuffed shells, lasagna, meat loaf, and broiled scrod with crab sauce are particularly good. If you're in a rush, you can grab some coffee and a fresh muffin or a cinnamon roll in the coffee

shop. They are open daily year-round. Breakfast, lunch, and dinner are served Tues through Sun, with breakfast and lunch only on Mon.

OYSTERS TOO $$–$$$$
876 Rte. 28, East Falmouth
(508) 548-9191
www.oysterstoo.com
This is another favorite restaurant among Falmouth locals. The atmosphere is relaxed, and the fireplace offers just the right ambience. There's live piano music on Fri and Sat evenings. The restaurant is open year-round, but closed on Mon and Tues during the winter.

PEKING PALACE $$
452 Main St., Falmouth
(508) 540-8204
www.pekingpalacefalmouth.com
This restaurant's pan-Asian cuisine is excellent, creatively prepared, and served in generous portions, even the takeout. The lunch and dinner menus focus on Mandarin, Szechuan, and Cantonese, with an assortment of chicken and beef dishes, plus a new sushi bar. Thai and Polynesian dishes are also available. Peking Palace is open daily year-round until 11 p.m., Fri and Sat until midnight.

PERSY'S PLACE $–$$
52 Falmouth Rd., Mashpee
(508) 477-6633
www.persysplace.com
If you or your companions are picky about breakfast or lunch, Persy's Place will be a treat for you. The menu features many made-from-scratch and hard-to-find specialties, such as Persy's own corn-beef hash and pan-fried codfish cakes. Most breakfasts come with a slab of their famous homemade cornbread and Boston baked beans. And don't forget their lunch menu, featuring homemade chowders, four quiches, and Dagwood-style deli sandwiches. Besides several off-Cape locations (a good stop on the way to or from the Cape perhaps), there is another Persy's in Hyannis. Both Cape locations are open year-round for breakfast and lunch.

i You may be surprised to learn that Cape Cod is host to a number of tea rooms. The Tea Shoppe in Mashpee Commons (508-477-7261), offers more than 40 choices of teas. At the Dunbar Tea Shop, located at 1 Water St. in Sandwich (508-833-2485), you can savor your tea while delighting in a cucumber and cream cheese sandwich.

THE QUARTERDECK $$-$$$
164 Main St., Falmouth
(508) 548-9900

The conch fritters, seafood, pasta, and vegetarian entrees are great. The Quarterdeck has a nautical decor, friendly staff, and a large choice of beers with a decent wine list, which includes Portuguese selections. It is open seven days a week for lunch and dinner year-round.

SEAFOOD SAM'S $-$$
6 Coast Guard Rd. on the Cape Cod Canal, Sandwich
(508) 888-4629
356 Palmer Ave., Falmouth
(508) 540-7877
www.seafoodsams.com

It was the summer of 1974 when "Sam's Seafood" first opened the doors to a restaurant so small there was no seating, only takeout. With a burgeoning chain of eateries on Cape Cod, the four Seafood Sam's can now seat between 50 and 350 people depending on which location you visit. The largest of the four is located on the Cape Cod Canal in Sandwich, the smallest in Harwich Port on Route 28. No matter which restaurant you visit, you will receive fast service, reasonable prices, and an offering of the best seafood, fresh daily, made to order. Specials are offered weekly, and all meals are served with your choice of rice pilaf or french fries and their own creamy coleslaw. The menu has been expanded over the years to include chicken, hot dogs, pasta, and veggies, to name a few items. The Seafood Sam's in Sandwich has a full liquor license and a large dining room in casual surroundings, perfect

for families. In Falmouth Seafood Sam's serves beer and wine. For more information on their other locations, please check the Mid-Cape and Lower Cape listings in the restaurant sections. All Seafood Sam's restaurants are open from Mar through Nov for lunch and dinner.

6A CAFE $
415 Rte. 6A, East Sandwich
(508) 888-5220

This cozy, personable diner-style cafe offers excellent food at unbelievably low prices. Adding to the fun atmosphere, an electric train circles the dining room overhead, not unlike the train that travels along the tracks crossing Route 6A not far from the cafe. You can order anything from pizza to burgers. 6A Cafe offers specials on weekdays. This comfortable, spotless cafe serves breakfast and lunch daily from 6 a.m. to 2:30 p.m.

SHUCKERS WORLD FAMOUS RAW BAR $$
91-A Water St., Woods Hole
(508) 540-3850
www.woodshole.com/shuckers

This is a super-casual place to meet, eat, and order a Nobska Light beer. Shuckers is a lively place, and everything is prepared on the premises. The bartenders are fun, and the seafood is exceptional—look for the twin lobster special and the mussel stew. Shuckers has a raw bar and outdoor seating overlooking Eel Pond and is open for lunch and dinner daily from May through Oct.

SIENA $$$
Mashpee Commons, Routes 28 and 151, Mashpee
(508) 477-5929, (877) 477-5929
www.siena.us

The contemporary, warmly tinted interior of this inviting restaurant is a great setting for enjoying its sophisticated Italian cuisine. The open kitchen, complete with charcoal grill, keeps the place lively. Garlicky mussels sounds like a good place to start, and the entrees range from Sangiovese wine-braised wild boar to "contemporary pastas" that include chicken, hot pepperoncini, and mild mascarpone. Open daily for lunch, dinner, or a late-night meal.

STIR-CRAZY $
570 MacArthur Blvd., Pocasset (Bourne)
(508) 564-6464
www.stircrazyrestaurant.com
If you enjoy Asian food, stop off for dinner or takeout at this small restaurant on MacArthur Boulevard (Route 28) for some Cambodian cooking. The food is filled with exotic flavors and spices and features healthy ingredients such as fresh vegetables, rice, and homemade noodles. Although the food can be spicy, it is not too hot unless you request it that way. It is open for dinner from Tues to Sun and serves lunch only on Fri. Stir-Crazy closes during the months of Jan and Feb.

i Nearly 16,000 people are employed by restaurants on the Cape during the high summer season. That's nearly 16 percent of the Cape's total workforce.

SWEET TOMATOES $
148 Rte. 6A, Sandwich
(508) 888-5979
www.sweettomatoesinc.com
From the crust to the creative toppings, these Neapolitan pizzas are full of flavor and healthy ingredients, and you can watch them being assembled. How about a white Greek pizza with feta cheese, spinach, and garlic, or maybe a white pizza with shrimp, garlic, onion, and capers? Whatever you decide, don't wait until you're hungry to call in an order because they often need half an hour to an hour to fill orders. Sweet Tomatoes is open Tues through Sun.

MID-CAPE

ACAPULCOS MEXICAN RESTAURANT $$
416 Rte. 28, West Yarmouth
(508) 771-6531
www.acapulcos.net

Acapulcos is simply good Mexican food for Cape Cod; nothing too fancy but consistently good burritos, chimichangas and fajitas. It's also a good place to meet over a Margarita. Acapulcos is open year-round for lunch and dinner.

ALBERTO'S RISTORANTE $$$–$$$$
360 Main St., Hyannis
(508) 778-1770
www.albertos.net
Serving fine Northern Italian cuisine featuring freshly made pasta, this restaurant has definitely made its mark on Main Street in Hyannis. The elegantly decorated restaurant is bright, comfortable, consistent, and well managed. Alberto's Italian hospitality will have you coming back again and again, whether for stuffed pasta, seafood dishes, or sirloin. Or perhaps you'd like to try the Seafood Alberto for Two, an oceanic feast filled with clams, calamari, muscles, shrimp, scallops, and a 1½-pound lobster. Daily and early-bird specials are offered. Alberto's is open daily for dinner year-round. Reservations are suggested.

ARDEO $$
Union Station Plaza, 23 Whites Path,
South Yarmouth
(508) 760-1500

81 Kings Circuit, Yarmouthport
(508) 362-7730

644 Main St., Hyannis
(508) 790-1115
www.ardeocapecod.com
The original Ardeo has spawned three other locations in Yarmouthport, Hyannis, and Brewster (see the Lower-Cape section), each focused on eclectic Mediterranean cuisine from kebabs and stuffed grape leaves to wood stone pizza and salmon Provençal. The family-owned eatery gets high marks from vegetarians and families in search of casual cuisine that goes beyond burgers and chicken fingers.

i Four Seas Ice Cream on South Main Street in Centerville is a Cape Cod institution, serving up award-winning ice cream for more than 70 years. Ice cream is made on the premises daily, using fresh ingredients.

BARNSTABLE RESTAURANT AND TAVERN $$–$$$$

3176 Rte. 6A, Barnstable
(508) 362-2355
www.barnstablerestaurant.com

Both a casual tavern and an upscale eatery can be found in this stately structure in Barnstable Village Center. Come on a Friday for live music in the patio, and ask for the Tavern Keeper's Special (a fresh-caught mélange of local seafood, served casserole-style).

BAXTER'S BOATHOUSE AND BOATHOUSE CLUB $$–$$$

177 Pleasant St., Hyannis
(508) 775-4490
www.baxterscapecod.com

When tourists ask the locals where to find a waterfront restaurant in Hyannis, the answer is often "Go to Baxter's." It's a perfect choice for a casual meal or cocktails in a waterfront setting. If you are arriving by boat, you can tie up at the small dock, or you can stay on your boat and be waited on. Fried clams are the most popular menu item, and, in addition to seafood, Baxter's also serves steaks, sandwiches, and burgers. Baxter's serves lunch and dinner daily from Apr through Columbus Day.

THE BLACK CAT $$–$$$

165 Ocean St., Hyannis
(508) 778-1233
www.blackcattavern.com

Many places advertise that they buy their fish fresh each day, but the Black Cat maintains that they buy their fish twice a day. Open year-round, seven days a week, the Black Cat features upscale, American-style food. Its large and varied menu covers seafood, pasta, and beef, and features several fried dishes. In the spring and fall, the Black Cat accepts reservations, but in the busy summer season, you may experience a slight wait for a table, as this restaurant is popular with both locals and tourists. It has an outdoor patio seating overlooking Hyannis Harbor and features live entertainment Thurs through Sun during the off-season and seven days a week during the summer.

BLUE MOON BISTRO $$$–$$$$

605 Rte. 6A, Dennis
508-385-7100
www.bluemoonbistro.net

Relatively new on the scene but already proven, Blue Moon Bistro's menu is a pleasure to choose from. Everything on it seems to live up to expectations as does the atmosphere inside the outwardly inconspicuous restaurant. Start with the herb-grilled shrimp and move on from there. Even when it doesn't seem like it can get better, it does. Blue Moon is open year-round.

BOBBY BYRNE'S PUB $

345 Rte. 28 and Bearses Way, Hyannis
(508) 775-1425
www.bobbybyrnes.com

This favorite Mid-Cape restaurant is open year-round, serving lunch and dinner daily, as well as brunch on Sunday. Specials are offered throughout the week. Bobby Byrne's has two other Cape locations, on Tupper Road in Sandwich and at Mashpee Commons in Mashpee. (See the write-up in the Upper Cape section of this chapter.)

BRAZILIAN GRILL $$–$$$

680 Main St., West End, Hyannis
(508) 771-0109
www.braziliangrill-capecod.com

Avid carnivores set their compass for this bustling churrascaria (Brazilian barbecue), which caters to the Cape's homesick Brazilian population with all-you-can-eat offerings of grilled chicken, sausage, beef, pork, and more. A comprehensive buffet of side dishes includes plantains, rice and beans, and authentic dishes like feijoada (black bean stew). Those who know tout the Grill's home-made flan as the best this side of Sao Paulo.

CAPTAIN PARKER'S PUB $$

668 Rte. 28, West Yarmouth
(508) 771-4266
www.captainparkers.com

Locals and visitors alike flock to Captain Parker's. Enormous portions, great-tasting food, and a huge list of specials are a few reasons this place is often crowded. Entrees include baked stuffed sole served with Newburg sauce and London broil, and don't leave without trying their award-winning chowder. Captain Parker's chowder won first place in so many chowder festivals that it basically stopped competing. Owner Gerry Manning makes customers feel at home when they walk through the doors while keeping the food coming out hot and good. Captain Parker's Pub is open daily year-round for lunch and dinner, and the prices are always reasonable.

CLANCY'S $$

8 Upper County Rd., Dennisport
(508) 394-6661
www.clancysrestaurant.com

Clancy's sits on the banks of Swan River, and the views are almost as good as the food. (The view of the water is spectacular off the sundeck—no extra charge!) Here you'll be able to get your fill without breaking the bank, even if you order the popular Steak Lucifer, a meld of sirloin, lobster, and asparagus topped with béarnaise sauce. Lunch and dinner are served daily, and there is a Sunday brunch as well as a children's menu.

COLOMBO'S CAFÉ

544 Main St., Hyannis
(508) 790-5700
www.colomboscafe.com

New on the scene with a good location on Hyannis's Main Street, this offering from David Colombo, owner of the popular Roadhouse Cafe, has attracted a crowd since it opened in 2008. The space does its job in bringing the feel of an Italian cafe to the Cape, including the luminescent glow from glass displays of treats for both the eyes and the mouth. The atmosphere alone is worth a visit.

COOKE'S SEAFOOD $-$$

1120 Rte. 132, Hyannis
(508) 775-0450
www.cookesseafood.com

Cooke's is one of those casual establishments that help define the Cape season—when Cooke's opens its doors in mid-March, you know the summer crowds aren't too far away. Cooke's has a reputation for serving great seafood, especially fried clams; also try the fish and chips and fresh scallops. Don't fret if you aren't a fish aficionado—Cooke's also has non-fish favorites such as burgers. They're open daily for lunch and dinner from Mar to the end of Nov. There's another Cooke's in Mashpee.

DIPARMA ITALIAN TABLE $$

175 Main St., West Yarmouth
(508) 771-7776
www.diparmarestaurant.com

A good place for families looking for a taste of Tuscany, DiParma was opened in 2008 and has been packed ever since. The atmosphere is casual but not too casual and the food is solid if not outstanding, with large portions that stick to the ribs. Whatever the draw, DiParma seems to fit the bill for plenty of discerning diners so far. DiParma is open for lunch and dinner year-round and serves pizza and a late-night menu from 10 p.m. to midnight.

THE DOLPHIN RESTAURANT $$

3250 Rte. 6A, Barnstable
(508) 362-6610

With low ceilings and a cozy fireplace, this third-generation family restaurant has changed little over the decades. The menu includes seafood, steaks, some veal and duck, sandwiches, burgers, and good daily specials. The calamari is also good, and so is the lively conversation at the bar, which can include informal legal debates spawned across the street in the Barnstable County court complex. The Dolphin is open daily for dinner and every day except Sun for lunch. Reservations are recommended.

ℹ️ You may notice that your waiter or waitress has an accent that is anything but local. Students come from around the world—many from Eastern Europe—for a "J-1 summer" on the Cape. J-1 is the name of the student visas they have in order to work in the United States.

EBB TIDE RESTAURANT $$$
94 Chase Ave., Dennisport
(508) 398-8733
www.ebbtiderestaurant.com
Within walking distance to the hotels and motels that line beach-fronted Chase Avenue, the Ebb Tide is a great place to enjoy traditional New England cuisine in a lovely setting. All-white linen with rich, royal blue accents, the restaurant's interior is elegant without being stuffy, and it's family friendly. The menu features lots of fresh seafood and steak. It's open for dinner May through Columbus Day.

FIVE BAYS BISTRO $$$$
825 Main St., Osterville
(508) 420-5559
www.fivebaysbistro.com
Cobalt blue glassware adorns the tables and vivid artwork lines the walls at this Osterville favorite, which evokes a Soho vibe with its sophisticated decor and intriguing cuisine. The antithesis of the usual Cape Cod seafood shanty, Five Bays accommodates style-starved city folk with a mix of timeless classics (pan-roasted Atlantic halibut) and out-of-the-box experiments (yellow fin tuna martinis). The sleek, pendant-lit bar serves specialty cocktails and stays open until midnight.

GINA'S BY THE SEA $$$
134 Taunton Ave., Dennis
(508) 385-3213
www.ginasbythesea.com
The minute you walk in the door of Gina's, you'll be greeted by the tantalizing aroma of garlic and marinara sauce. The menu features classic northern Italian dishes and comforting desserts. Chances are you'll have a bit of a wait, so relax at the laid-back bar or take a stroll on the beach, just steps away, until your table's ready. Open daily for dinner from Thurs through Sun, Gina's does not take reservations.

THE GOURMET BRUNCH $
517 Main St., Hyannis
(508) 771-2558
www.theoriginalgourmetbrunch.com
Not for the indecisive, this menu has over 100 omelets from which to choose. Or order waffles or a specialty item such as Brunch Supreme, which is made with puff pastry, ham, artichoke hearts, poached egg, cheese sauce, and crabmeat. Belgian waffles and quiches round out the breakfast selections, and a glass of champagne with strawberries makes for a festive brunch indeed. You can order breakfast at any time, but don't overlook the lunch menu. Soups, clam chowder, hot and cold sandwiches, and salads are standouts. The offerings continue beyond the menu with daily blackboard specials. The restaurant is open for breakfast and lunch daily year-round.

GRUMPY'S $$
1408 Rte. 6A, South Dennis
(508) 385-2911
www.grumpyscapecod.com
Expanded in 2004 to accommodate its growing cult, Grumpy's now serves home-cooked diner grub year-round. The South Dennis standby is open for breakfast and lunch. Ask for a seat overlooking the salt marsh and watch the locals come and go. No credit cards.

HEARTH 'N KETTLE $
Route 132 and Bearses Way, Hyannis
(508) 771-3000
1196 Rte. 28, South Yarmouth
(508) 394-2252
www.hearthnkettle.com
Locals and visitors to the Mid-Cape area can enjoy breakfast, lunch, and dinner at Hearth 'N Kettles in Hyannis and South Yarmouth. The restaurant closes only on Christmas Day and offers a menu steeped in traditional New England dishes with some surprises.

Both the Hyannis location and the South Yarmouth Hearth 'N Kettle are open year-round for breakfast, lunch, and dinner. Kids will enjoy watching ducks in the pond behind the South Yarmouth restaurant. You can find other Hearth 'N Kettle locations in Orleans as well as off-Cape in Plymouth, Weymouth, and Attleboro. (See our write-up in the Lower Cape section.)

INAHO $$-$$$
157 Rte. 6A, Yarmouthport
(508) 362-5522
www.inahocapecod.com
If you like great sushi, hot sake, and a good atmosphere to suck down both, this is the place to go. Inaho has been drawing rave reviews from locals and visitors alike for its beautifully prepared food, especially fish. The restaurant has a full sushi bar and is open for dinner year-round. It is closed on Sun. Reservations are recommended.

THE LIGHTHOUSE INN RESTAURANT $$$
1 Lighthouse Inn Rd., West Dennis
(508) 398-2244
www.lighthouseinn.com
Located within the Lighthouse Inn (see our Bed-and-Breakfasts, Inns, and Cottages chapter), this spacious restaurant is reminiscent of the classic Cape Cod restaurants of bygone years. Resting right on the water, the windows along the south-facing wall are many and offer breathtaking views of Nantucket Sound. The food here runs from the traditional (steamed lobster, filet of Chatham scrod) to such innovative and enticing delectables as cashew-encrusted halibut and grilled duck with red currant sauce. Situated on the site of the current West Dennis Lighthouse (formerly the Old Bass River Light; see our Attractions chapter), the Lighthouse Inn serves breakfast and dinner daily. Lunch is served during the high season. Reservations are suggested.

THE MARSHSIDE $$
28 Bridge St., East Dennis
(508) 385-4010
www.themarshside.com

We know of some people from just south of Boston who will make a day trip to Dennis just to have lunch at the Marshside. A stone's throw north of the intersection of Routes 6A and 134, this is a restaurant that attracts tourists as well as locals and maintains a passionate following. The restaurant was recently completely redone, as was the nearby culvert under Bridge Street. The former makes for a more elegant dining experience and the later for an improved marsh system.

For added atmosphere, ask for a table with a view of the marsh full of wildlife and Sesuit Harbor beyond. The Marshside serves lunch and dinner daily and is open year-round, so you can see the marsh during all four seasons.

THE NAKED OYSTER BISTRO & RAW BAR $$$
20 Independence Dr., Hyannis
(508) 778-6500
www.nakedoyster.com
This sleek eatery, secreted behind a bland exterior in a strip of office buildings, forsakes the nautical theme favored by legions of other Cape restaurants; all the better to focus squarely on fresh, excellent seafood. With its long mahogany bar, it feels like New York City and is perfect for a cocktail and oysters Rockefeller (oysters with Great Hill bleu cheese, caramelized barbecue sauce, and bacon).

The regular menu includes appetizers such as tuna sashimi and calamari marinara, and entrees like Baked Georges Bank Haddock, caught by a local fishing boat named *Tenacious* and served simply with lemon, roasted Yukon potatoes, and haricot verts. There are also several steak entrees and a few offerings for vegetarians. But people really come here for the raw bar: the "naked" dishes are considered the best offerings here, but the "dressed" options are also well done. Everything is complemented by an extensive list of wines by the glass. Open year-round for lunch Mon through Fri and dinner Mon through Sat.

OCEAN HOUSE $$$$
421 Old Wharf Rd. (end of Depot St.),
Dennisport
(508) 394-0700
www.oceanhouserestaurant.com
The Ocean House lives up to its name with windows flanking the shore of Nantucket Sound. Highlights of a meal here might include cornmeal-crisped local oysters, warm goat cheese and roasted beet salad, cedar plank–roasted teriyaki salmon, and warm Valrhona chocolate lava cake (with Chai ice cream and huckleberry plum sauce). Open every evening but Mon in season, the Ocean House closes for Jan and Feb.

THE PADDOCK $$–$$$
20 Scudder Ave., Hyannis
(508) 775-7677
www.paddockcapecod.com
The Paddock Restaurant has been serving elegant cuisine in a casual, friendly setting for more than 30 years. The Paddock offers a delicious menu and an extensive wine list. Owners John and Maxine Zartarian operate the restaurant (they met as college students working at the Flying Bridge in Falmouth), and their two sons are also involved in the family business. The menu offers a wide selection of seafood, poultry, steaks, and the house specialty—the two-pound baked stuffed lobster. The Paddock Restaurant can comfortably accommodate up to 150 people for cocktail parties or up to 125 people for dining. It is open from Apr through mid-Nov for lunch and dinner.

RED COTTAGE $
36 Old Bass River Rd., South Dennis
(508) 394-2923
Open all year for breakfast and lunch, the Red Cottage is famous for its home fries. No simple sliced-and-fried taters here. Instead the potatoes are tossed with ham, mushrooms, tomatoes, green peppers, and onion, then smothered with hollandaise sauce. Equally delicious are the crepes and Belgian waffles. The Red Cottage also features an extensive "lite side" menu, complete with a listing of fat grams per serving. Open daily except for Christmas, Thanksgiving, and Easter,

it's a busy place on weekend mornings but well worth the wait.

THE RED PHEASANT $$$–$$$$
905 Rte. 6A, Dennis Village
(508) 385-2133, (800) 480-2133
www.redpheasantinn.com
The Red Pheasant's menu is a delectable blend of game, lamb, beef, and seafood. Tables at the Red Pheasant, which is housed in a 200-year-old barn with wide pine floors and two fireplaces, are adorned with locally crafted pottery, glassware, and fresh flowers. The award-winning wine list (it has received the Award of Excellence since 1987 by *Wine Spectator*) is prodigious, and a new martini and wine bar features a signature drink called The Phez (pineapple-infused Ketel One vodka with splashes of chambord and champagne).

The Red Pheasant has great ambience any time of year, but the Garden Room is especially nice in summer, and in winter a table near the fireplace is cozy. The Red Pheasant serves dinner only, and reservations are strongly suggested.

THE REGATTA OF COTUIT $$$$
463 Rte. 28, Cotuit
(508) 428-5715
www.regattarestaurant.com
This sophisticated year-round dining establishment will delight you in the presentation, taste of your meal, and the impeccable service. The distinguished wine list is everything you would expect from a world-class restaurant. Chef and owner Weldon Fizell has created an attractive menu that includes caramelized jumbo sea scallops and seared filet of North Dakota buffalo tenderloin.

A full bar is offered in the small turn-of-the-20th-century piano bar. Reservations are encouraged. The Regatta is open year-round for dinner.

THE ROADHOUSE CAFE $$–$$$
488 South St., Hyannis
(508) 775-2386
www.Rd.housecafe.com
The Roadhouse is a favorite in downtown Hyannis. The lobster bisque has huge chunks of lob-

ster; the chicken homard, rolled with lobster and Swiss cheese, is manna from heaven; and some patrons say the cafe has better Italian cuisine than most Italian restaurants. The bistro tavern area looks a bit like backwoods Maine with its fireplace and beamed ceiling; you can sit at bar stools or booths, enjoy fabulous piano music, and order from either the bistro or the Roadhouse's menu. The Back Door Bistro presents the finest musicians on the East Coast as part of its Monday Night Jazz. The live entertainment adds a perfect touch to this fun restaurant (see our Nightlife chapter). The Roadhouse is open for dinner daily year-round; reservations are recommended.

SAM DIEGO'S $$
950 Rte. 132, Hyannis
(508) 771-8816
www.samdiegos.com
Sam Diego's has a fiesta atmosphere and a location convenient to the mall and other shopping. Free chips and salsa arrive shortly after you sit down, giving you something to munch on as you peruse the extensive menu and wait for a golden margarita. Sam Diego's offers an enjoyable and comfortable dining experience, reasonable prices, and plenty of parking. Sam Diego's is open for lunch and dinner daily year-round.

SCARGO CAFE $$
799 Rte. 6A, Dennis
(508) 385-8200
www.scargocafe.com
What was once a sea captain's house is now home to one of the Mid-Cape's finer casual restaurants. The cafe has two cozy dining rooms and a glassed-in atrium and greenhouse. The menu offers eclectic fare from tenderloin a la chèvre (with goat cheese and grilled portobello mushrooms) to shrimp and scallops Frangelico (in a buttery hazelnut sauce with tomatoes, scallions, and pistachio nuts). Scargo has great appetizers, such as tuna martini and stuffed artichokes. Children's and early-bird menus are also available. A limited number of reservations are accepted nightly. Scargo serves lunch and dinner daily year-round.

SEAFOOD SAM'S $-$$
1006 Rte. 28, South Yarmouth
(508) 394-3504
www.seafoodsams.com
A restaurant with delicious seafood, fast service, and reasonable prices, Seafood Sam's has been a favorite local eatery since 1974. With four restaurants conveniently located in the Upper, Mid-, and Lower Cape, each restaurant offers daily specials of the traditional fried summer seafood and burger variety. Eat in or call for takeout; Seafood Sam's is open daily for lunch and dinner from Mar through Oct.

SKIPPY'S PIER I $$
17 Neptune Lane, South Yarmouth
(508) 398-9556
Skippy's has a great view of Parkers River. It has seating for 250 people, including deck seating for 120. All the seats have water views, and the sunsets are gorgeous. Skippy's serves lobster ravioli, seafood from the raw bar, clams, scallops, steak, and pasta dishes. Open for lunch and dinner daily. The restaurant is closed from Nov through Feb.

LOWER CAPE

ABBA RESTAURANT $$$-$$$$
Old Colony Way and West Rd.,
Orleans
(508) 255-8144
www.abbarestaurant.com
Abba's pan-Mediterranean cuisine features flavorful dishes like pan-seared scallops in sage garlic sauce and grilled filet mignon in a morel mushroom sauce (with Jerusalem artichokes, asparagus, and pearl onions). Abba serves dinner only and is closed on Mon, but its adjacent cafe (Abba to Go) accommodates those in need of fulfilling gourmet food (including specialty pizzas, tabbouleh, and baked goods) on the fly.

ACADEMY OCEAN GRILL $$$-$$$$
2 Academy Place, Orleans
(508) 240-1585
www.academyoceangrille.com

This Orleans charmer holds the distinction of being the only Cape restaurant to showcase line-caught fish. In keeping with this specialty, the seafood here is exceptionally fresh and masterfully prepared, including standouts such as codfish Florentine (coated in spinach, Parmesan, and eggs) and wood fire-grilled swordfish with basil-Parmesan glaze. Ensconced in a property filled with flower gardens, the dining room is ringed with windows and decorated with tasteful maritime accents. Open six days a week in season, Wed through Sun in the off-season, and through the holidays. The Grill is closed from mid-Jan through Mar.

ADRIAN'S RESTAURANT $$
535 U.S. Rte. 6, Truro
(508) 487-4360
www.adriansrestaurant.com
Owners Adrian and Annette Cyr regularly travel to Italy, where they gather and fine-tune recipes for their loyal following. (The wood-fired brick pizza oven, in fact, was brought from Italy—brick by brick!) The homemade pastas are available in appetizer and entree sizes or try the Gorgonzola cappelletti, with a sage, butter, and Parmesan sauce. For dessert there is tiramisu or blueberry peach cobbler. During the season, Adrian's serves wonderful breakfasts, including huevos rancheros and cranberry pancakes with orange butter. You can have breakfast and dinner at Adrian's daily in summer. The restaurant is open from mid-May through mid-Oct, and in the spring and fall serves breakfast Sat and Sun, dinner Thurs through Sun.

ARDEO $$
280 Underpass Rd., Brewster
(508) 896-4200
www.ardeocapecod.com
The newest Brewster location for this local chain restaurant continues the tradition of Mediterranean cuisine, from kebabs and stuffed grape leaves to wood stone pizza and salmon Provençal. The family-owned eatery gets high marks from vegetarians and families in search of casual cuisine that goes beyond burgers and chicken fingers.

BAYSIDE BETSY'S $$–$$$$
177 Commercial St., Provincetown
(508) 487-6566
www.baysidebetsys.com
Great views are the draw at this window-lined restaurant on Provincetown Harbor, where classic comfort food is infused with French and Italian accents. Take a booth in the white plank-paneled dining room and order from the satisfying breakfast (lobster Benedict, homemade potato pancakes), lunch (fresh native scallop rolls, triple-decker club sandwiches), and dinner (sesame-crusted Ahi tuna, natured Long Island duckling with orange Triple-Sec demi-glace) menus. Bayside Betsy's is open daily in season and serves breakfast on the weekends from 9 a.m. to 4 p.m. Lunch is served every day from 11 a.m. to 4 p.m., and dinner is served from 5 p.m. to 11 p.m. on weekends and until 9 p.m. during the week. Betsy's is closed Tues and Wed from Feb through Apr.

THE BEACON ROOM $$$–$$$$
23 West Rd., Orleans
(508) 255-2211
www.beaconroom.com
Inviting in any season, this wood-beamed cottage offers adventurous cuisine in a homespun setting. Simple wood chairs and floral linens evoke the atmosphere of grandmother's house, but specials that change every night, such as the roasted half duck with the sauce of the day, are anything but old school.

BOOKSTORE AND RESTAURANT $$
50 Kendrick Ave., Wellfleet
(508) 349-3154
www.bookstorerestaurant.com
This comfortable eatery, which enjoys views of Wellfleet Harbor, is so popular we can almost guarantee that you'll have to wait for a table in summer and sometimes in the fall as well. Bring your appetite for baked stuffed lobster, Portuguese seafood stew, or fried Wellfleet oysters. There's a raw bar, and for landlubbers there are pastas, soups, sandwiches, and salads. In fine weather, try for a table on the deck, and enjoy

the gentle breeze off the harbor. It's open daily for breakfast, lunch, and dinner all year.

THE BRAMBLE INN $$$$
2019 Rte. 6A, Brewster
(508) 896-7644
www.brambleinn.com

This well-regarded restaurant offers fine dining in an intimate setting. Chef/owner Ruth Manchester's menu includes rack of lamb, filet of salmon Key West, and parchment-roasted boneless chicken breast served with a whole lobster and champagne sauce. Although there is no dress code, many patrons do show up in their best clothes, so you might feel more comfortable trading your jeans for something a bit dressier. Reservations are required. The restaurant is closed Mon and Tues. The twelve-seat Bayside Bar was recently added along with a bar menu.

BREWSTER FISH HOUSE $$$
2208 Rte. 6A, Brewster
(508) 896-7867
www.brewsterfish.com

This small, well-established restaurant serves some of the best seafood on the Cape, reasonably priced and delightfully innovative. Famous for its fresh fish specialties, the restaurant also features several nonseafood specials every night. The decor is simple but comfortable. Be forewarned: There is often a wait to get in because the restaurant has limited seating and does not take reservations. The Fish House serves lunch and dinner daily in season and is closed for about six weeks between Feb and Mar.

BREWSTER INN AND CHOWDER HOUSE $$
1993 Rte. 6A, Brewster
(508) 896-7771

As the name suggests, this restaurant serves some of the best chowder you'll ever taste. Winter specials include lean, juicy Yankee pot roast and flaky broiled Chatham scrod, and the burgers can't be beat. The dining room is small and homey, and the service friendly. During the summer there is music seven nights a week. The

Brewster Inn and Chowder House serves lunch and dinner daily year-round.

BUBALA'S BY THE BAY $$
183-185 Commercial St., Provincetown
(508) 487-0773
www.bubalas.com

This funky restaurant, open for brunch, lunch, and dinner, features an eclectic menu that ranges from burgers and quesadillas to seafood dishes like grilled tuna wasabi and West Indian roasted lobster. There are also vegetarian entrees, a children's menu, and a late-night menu. It has a heated patio on the water and a selection of signature drinks. Bubala's is open Apr through Oct.

CAPE SEA GRILLE $$$$
31 Sea St., Harwich Port
(508) 432-4745
www.capeseagrille.com

The Sea Grille's menu focuses on fresh seafood, seasonal produce, and sophisticated—not fried!—preparation. The beautifully restored sea captain's estate exudes casual elegance with its hardwood floors and an open, airy interior. From mid-May through Oct, dinner is served seven nights a week, while from Apr to mid-May the restaurant suspends service on Tues and Wed. The schedule changes again from mid-Oct through mid-Dec, when dinner is served Thurs through Sun.

CAPTAIN LINNELL HOUSE $$$$
137 Skaket Beach Rd., Orleans
(508) 255-3400
www.linnell.com

This classic 1840 mansion, on the road toward Skaket Beach, is well worth finding. Since 1988, owner/chef Bill Conway has been creating award-winning cuisine such as sautéed Wellfleet oysters in a champagne-ginger sauce, and shrimp and scallops sautéed in tarragon lobster butter. Open year-round, the restaurant serves dinner seven days a week in season, with a reduced schedule in winter; call for hours then. Reservations are required.

CHATHAM BARS INN $$$–$$$$
297 Shore Rd., Chatham
(508) 945-0096, (800) 527-4884
www.chathambarsinn.com

You can choose among three restaurants as well as other less formal seating areas. The seaside Beach House Grill is an ideal choice for an alfresco lunch of lobster rolls and chardonnay. Lunch features the typical Cape Cod staples: burgers, salads, and fried clams. You can dine here for breakfast and lunch daily during the season. The restaurant is open daily June through Sept, depending on the weather.

The Main Dining Room of the Chatham Bars Inn, plush and pricey, is your second choice for lunch and dinner. The restaurant offers a la carte classic New England cuisine that draws heavily on the bounty of coastal waters, which are right outside the dining room windows. Men are requested to wear jackets and ties. Dinner is served July through Oct. Check ahead because the Main Dining Room is also popular for weddings and other functions.

Less formal than the Chatham Bars Inn's main dining room is the chandelier-lit Tavern, where the food is as good as what's dished out in its pricier sister eatery. Relax over a casual lunch or dinner inside near the fireplace. Many people come here simply for coffee and dessert. The tavern is open daily year-round.

CHATHAM COOKWARE CAFE $
524 Main St., Chatham
(508) 945-1250

The perfect place to stop for a snack, or more, while shopping your way down Main Street. Filling breakfast sandwiches are served on Portuguese muffins, along with bagels, yogurt, and Danish. If there are any left when you stop by, opt for the vanilla nutmeg muffin dipped in butter. They also serve a range of thick sandwiches. Enjoy your purchases at a few air-conditioned tables inside, or carry it with you. They also have a freezer section of prepared foods that might come in handy if you need to throw a dinner together on short notice: salmon puffs, lobster strudel, spanakopita, and more. Duck in for breakfast or lunch daily.

CHATHAM SQUIRE $$
487 Main St., Chatham
(508) 945-0945
www.thesquire.com

Home to Chatham's oldest raw bar, the Squire offers an eclectic menu focused on fresh fish and shellfish. In addition to the dining room, the Squire has a large pub where you can get munchies. Locals have been eating here since 1968, and the waitstaff knows just about everyone by first name. It's open year-round for lunch and dinner.

CHILLINGSWORTH $$$$
2449 Rte. 6A, Brewster
(508) 896-3640
www.chillingsworth.com

Long considered the Cape's finest (and most formal) restaurant, Chillingsworth is the pinnacle of innovative French cuisine. Feast on at least a dozen variations of appetizers and entrees, including black and white truffle mac and cheese, and seared tuna tournedos with foie gras and morel sauce.

Jackets are preferred for men in the main dining room, and women will want to dress to the nines. Chillingsworth is open from mid-May through Nov. It serves dinner nightly in season and weekends only in spring and fall. In addition to fine dining in the elegant main restaurant, the Chillingsworth Bistro offers casual, a la carte bistro dining in the Greenhouse for lunch and dinner as well as Sunday brunch. Reservations are preferred.

For those who want to stay close to fine cuisine, Chillingsworth also offers elegant accommodations in three antique-appointed rooms (see our Bed-and-Breakfasts, Inns, and Cottages chapter).

CIRO & SAL'S $$$
4 Kiley Court, Provincetown
(508) 487-6444
www.ciroandsals.com

Ciro & Sal's is considered one of the better Italian restaurants on the Lower Cape, especially when it comes to such northern Italian delicacies as

Abruzzese (scallops, clams, shrimp, fish, mussels, and squid sautéed with plum tomatoes, fresh garlic, and herbs over pasta) and Vitello Scaloppine Al Marsala. For desserts nothing beats the tiramisu. And it would be hard to beat the atmosphere: Nestled in a low-ceilinged plaster- and brick-walled cellar off Commercial Street, Ciro & Sal's is filled with raffia-wrapped Chianti bottles hanging from the rafters and the sound of arias in the air. It's open for dinner every day during the busy season and weekends only from Oct through May, starting at 5:30 p.m.

COBIE'S CLAM SHACK $
3260 Rte. 6A, Brewster
(508) 896-7021
www.cobies.com
Launched in 1948, Cobie's is a veritable institution around here, and faithful patrons come back year after year for some of the best fried seafood anywhere. With white-clapboard, clam-shack ambience, this is one of the most comfortable outdoor eateries you'll find. Right off the Cape Cod Rail Trail near Nickerson State Park, Cobie's is a popular stop for seafood-craving cyclists and campers. Cobie's is open daily for lunch and dinner from late May through Sept.

COTTAGE STREET BAKERY $
2 Cottage St., Orleans
(508) 255-2821
www.cottageSt.bakery.com
Tucked away on a little street off Route 28, opposite the Christmas Tree Shop, this charming little bakery turns out scrumptious muffins, cookies, coffeecakes, and scones, among other specialties. Come here for the perfect birthday cake or just the perfect muffin. Try the Dirtbombs, generous sugar-smothered pastries. Sit down at a table or buy something to take home. The bakery is open daily year-round and does catering, wedding cakes, and mail order.

THE DUCK CREEKE TAVERN ROOM $$$
70 Main St., Wellfleet
(508) 349-7369
www.innatduckcreeke.com

The Duck Creeke Tavern Room offers an eclectic menu and entertainment, featuring piano, blues, and jazz ensembles. The Chart Bar, overlooking the pond at the rear of the building, has its walls decorated with local marine charts and is a favorite gathering place in the evening for regulars and newcomers alike (see our Nightlife chapter). You need not be staying at the Inn at Duck Creeke to eat in one of its two restaurants, the other being Sweet Seasons. We prefer this one for its simplicity in both food (seafood, steaks, chowders, and pasta) and decor. The tavern offers a children's menu and serves dinner Tue through Sun during the season; it's closed from mid-Oct through late May.

FINELY J.P.'S $$
554 Rte. 6, Wellfleet
(508) 349-7500
Since it opened in 1991, Finely J.P.'s has received rave reviews for dishes such as oven-poached salmon with ginger and soy sauce, Wellfleet paella, roast duckling with cranberry-orange sauce, and their famous Caesar salad. Vegetarians can try the farfalle with cannellini beans, escarole, and plum tomatoes.

Recently rebuilt from the ground up, the formerly boxy eatery now features an airy layout with a cedar-walled lounge and two split-level dining rooms. Al fresco diners are led over a bridge to a roof deck, where a new raw bar brims with Wellfleet oysters and other fresh-from-the-sea temptations. Despite this dramatic change in decor, the eatery's emphasis remains the same: It's all about fresh local ingredients, inventively prepared. Open seven days a week for dinner, Finely J.P.'s does not accept reservations.

400 EAST $$
1421 Orleans Rd., East Harwich
(508) 432-1800
www.the400.com
Ask anyone where to find the best burger in town, and you'll be pointed to 400 East in East Harwich. The scallop rolls and scrod picante are also quite good, but nobody makes a bigger, juicier, or tastier burger. The menu bulges with

dozens of other choices too. The restaurant is pub-like, with dark woods, captain's chairs, comfy booths, and friendly waitstaff. 400 East serves lunch and dinner daily year-round.

FRONT STREET $$$$
230 Commercial St., Provincetown
(508) 487-9715
www.frontSt.restaurant.com
One of the town's most popular and romantic restaurants—bistro may be a better word—Front Street is hidden in the brick-lined cellar of a Victorian house. Chef Donna Aliperti changes the menu weekly, showing off her culinary craft with such dishes as butternut ravioli, veal and shrimp piccata, and Tuscan calamari. The wine list is extensive, and the waitstaff knows just how to serve (they are there, but they never hover). Front Street serves dinner every day but Tues during the season.

HEARTH 'N KETTLE $
Route 6A and West Road
(at Skaket Corners), Orleans
(508) 240-0111
www.hearthnkettle.com
One of three Hearth 'N Kettle restaurants on the Cape, this Orleans location serves breakfast, lunch, and dinner year-round. The Orleans Hearth 'N Kettle is a favorite among locals. It's also child-friendly: Kids not only have their own menu, but get coloring books, crayons, and special cups as well! Other H&Ks are in Hyannis and South Yarmouth (see the listings in the Upper Cape and Mid-Cape sections). The restaurant has a full bar and is nonsmoking.

THE HOT CHOCOLATE SPARROW $
5 Old Colony Way, Orleans
(508) 240-2230
www.hotchocolatesparrow.com
The Sparrow is the hot spot in town for espresso, cappuccino, or just plain coffee. Even that is anything but plain—every day there are a half-dozen flavors from which to choose. In warm weather try one of their frozen coffee-chocolate drinks. There's an array of munchies to go with your coffee, including muffins, cookies, and coffeecake.

And then there's the chocolate. Homemade at the Sparrow's mother store in North Eastham are incredible truffles, fudge, caramels, toffee, and chocolates. All candy is sold by the pound or piece, and gift tins and packages are available as well. And, yes, they do mail orders. Open daily year-round, the Sparrow also serves ice cream, bagels, and panini sandwiches.

HUNAN GOURMET III $$
Bayberry Plaza, 225 Rte. 6A, Orleans
(508) 240-0888
Hunan Gourmet III is perhaps best-known for its all-you-can-eat buffet, a seemingly endless feast including sesame chicken, garlic noodles, vegetable lo mein, chicken with black bean sauce, shrimp and scallop medley, you-shell shrimp, dumplings, chicken teriyaki, pork fried rice, egg rolls, boneless ribs, fruit salad, almond cookies, and the ubiquitous Jell-O. You can order from the menu anytime from lunch to closing (later hours on Fri and Sat). Luncheon specials are also available daily, and the restaurant is open year-round.

IMPUDENT OYSTER $$$
15 Chatham Bars Ave., Chatham
(508) 945-3545
With a lively, friendly atmosphere, this restaurant is a favorite among locals. The oysters Rockefeller are a favorite as are the mussels in white wine sauce, the scallop roll, and the devils on horseback, bacon-wrapped scallops over toast points in a puddle of hollandaise sauce. The Impudent Oyster serves lunch and dinner daily year-round except for Thanksgiving and Christmas.

JAKE ROONEY'S $$
119 Brooks Rd., Harwich Port
(508) 430-1100
www.jakerooneys.com
Talk about an extensive menu—the one here is longer than some novels and caters to tastes both traditional and trendy. Along with fresh seafood, chicken, burgers, steaks, and pasta, the restaurant serves pizza, fajitas, and other international dishes. House specialties include aged Black Angus steak and sautéed clams Portuguese,

simmered with linguica, peppers, and onions in a hearty white wine broth. The restaurant has a casual publike atmosphere, with an old-school brass bar and an array of vintage paintings on the walls providing a nice touch. Jake Rooney's is open daily for lunch and dinner plus brunch on Sun year-round.

JAMS GOURMET GROCERY $
14 Truro Center Rd., Truro
(508) 349-1616

For many people Memorial Day marks the official start of the season on the Cape. It also marks the day Jams opens its door after months of hibernation. The sandwiches, named after Cape Cod sites and sights, are a bit pricey but mouth-watering and very filling. The Long Nook, for example, features tarragon chicken salad with lettuce and tomato; the Bikini has provolone, lettuce, tomato, onions, sprouts, and creamy Italian dressing. The newly renovated store also carries wine, coffee, newspapers, and toiletries. Jams offers breakfast, lunch, and takeout. It is open from 6:30 a.m. to 6 p.m. daily during the season and closes its doors in early Sept.

JOE'S BEACH ROAD BAR & GRILLE
AT THE BARLEY NECK INN $$$, $$(JOE'S)
5 Beach Rd., East Orleans
(508) 255-0212
www.barleyneck.com

This grand old 1857 sea captain's mansion was lovingly restored by Joe and Kathi Lewis, who stage weddings and other events in the Barley Neck's four intimate dining rooms and offer casual fare in Joe's Beach Road Bar and Grille, located in the attached barn.

The menu at either Joe's or the Barley Neck includes gourmet pizzas, pastas, an array of appetizers, and lots of native seafood. A huge fieldstone fireplace serves as the centerpiece of Joe's decor, which eschews nautical motifs in favor of denim tablecloths and World War II posters.

Joe's is open for dinner daily year-round. Dining room hours vary in the off-season, so call ahead. Reservations, in any case, are a good idea.

L'ALOUETTE $$$-$$$$
787 Rte. 28, Harwich Port
(508) 430-0405
www.lalouettebistro.com

Known for its sophisticated French food, L'Alouette also boasts a cozy, candlelit atmosphere and cordial, attentive staff. The pistachio-crusted roast rack of lamb with goat cheese soufflé is a particular favorite. For dessert try the crème brûlée, for which the restaurant is known, or the chocolate truffle cake with raspberry sauce. Open year-round, the restaurant has a celebrated wine list featuring small, handcrafted, estate-grown wines. Dinner is served Tues through Sun in season and Wed through Sun in winter. Reservations are requested.

LAND HO! $$
38 Main St., Orleans
(508) 255-5165
www.land-ho.com

This is a favorite haunt of locals, just as it's been since owner John Murphy took it over in 1969. This wood-paneled pub is a comfortable place to sit and chat over a meal and is brightened by red-and-white checked tablecloths and hundreds of original, wood-carved signs hanging from the ceiling. The blackboard specials are always good, as are the chowder, kale soup, and burgers. The Ho! is open for lunch and dinner daily all year. It's also a cool nightspot (see our Nightlife chapter), and serves a limited food menu until midnight.

LARRY'S P.X. $
1591 Main St., West Chatham
(508) 945-3964

Larry's P.X. opens at 6 a.m. for local fishermen and other early risers angling for a cup of joe or a hearty breakfast. You can also get lunch, with burgers, soup, and sandwiches. It's not fancy by any stretch, but it's comfortable, clean, and friendly. And if you want to know what's going on around town, this is a good place to come. You can order food until 2 p.m. Larry's P.X. is open daily year-round except Thanksgiving and Christmas.

LAURINO'S $$
3668 Rte. 6A, Brewster
(508) 896-6135

Here's a great place to bring the family. It offers huge portions of such Italian dishes as chicken Lauro (boneless chicken breast with scallops, sun-dried tomatoes, mushrooms, and tarragon cream) and linguine with mussels, served by super-friendly servers at penny-pinching prices. Laurino's also has a nice selection of pizzas and Italian grinders, and a children's menu. If that's not enough to keep the little ones entertained, Laurino's also has a playground equipped with a sandbox, swings, a slide, and a fort. Laurino's serves lunch and dinner daily year-round.

THE LIGHTHOUSE $$
317 Main St., Wellfleet
(508) 349-3681
www.mainst.lighthouse.com

This casual restaurant is one of those old stand-bys regulars return to again and again. The food is not fancy but good and reasonably priced, and the atmosphere is friendly. It's a great place to take kids. The young ones can get hot dogs and you can eat oyster rolls, cioppino, pesto pasta with shrimp, or one of the blackboard specials. The Lighthouse is open year-round for breakfast, lunch, and dinner.

THE LOBSTER CLAW $$
Route 6A, Orleans
(508) 255-1800, (800) 320-1802
www.lobsterclaw.com

This is seafood the way it should be served, from their chowder to the steamed clams, to the four varieties of lobster dinners (boiled, Lobster New-burg, deep-fried lobster meat, and baked stuffed lobster), all served with french fries and coleslaw. Other meals of chicken and steak are certainly available. The lunch menu includes American classics—hamburger, turkey breast sandwich, and hot dogs. The early-bird dinner special is served from 4 to 5:30 p.m., and you get a free chowder, beverage, and choice of ice cream or pudding with any regularly priced dinner. The Lobster Claw is open Apr through Oct, seven days a week, serving lunch and dinner from 11:30 a.m.

THE LOBSTER POT RESTAURANT $$$
321 Commercial St., Provincetown
(508) 487-0842
www.ptownlobsterpot.com

Ask anyone in town where to go for the best seafood, and everyone will tell you the Lobster Pot. The wait can be long in the summer because the Pot, as everyone calls it, doesn't accept res-ervations. The seafood is the freshest available, and Tim McNulty's clam chowder (now avail-able frozen for takeout) has won more "best of" awards than anyone can remember. The menu is extensive, but almost everyone orders lobster. The Lobster Pot is open daily for lunch and dinner Apr through Dec.

i **If you find yourself looking for a place to eat after 9 p.m. on the Cape—and you're not in Hyannis or Provincetown—your choices are limited. Most restaurants stop serving food at 9 p.m. The Land Ho!, right on Route 6A in Orleans, is a beacon at that point. It serves a full menu until 10 p.m. and serves appetizers, burgers, and soups until midnight. Call (508) 255-5165 for more information.**

LORRAINE'S $$$–$$$$
133 Commercial St., Provincetown
(508) 487-6074

If your taste runs toward Taco Bell, you may not appreciate the Latin cuisine at Lorraine's, where the enchiladas come with garlic shrimp and the tacos brim with blackened yellowfin tuna. Housed in an inviting cottage in Provincetown's West End, this local favorite also attracts discern-ing drinkers to its in-house bar, which boasts an encyclopedic list of premium tequilas. Open daily from June through Sept; call for off-season hours.

ℹ️ Summertime dining on Cape Cod is never complete without a visit to a local clam shack for heaping plates of fried clams, which are usually served whole, with their bellies—a pleasant surprise if you're used to clam strips. Arnolds on Route 6 in Eastham is a popular spot to get great fried clams. Call (508) 255-2575, or visit www .arnoldsrestaurant.com.

MAC'S SHACK $$–$$$
91 Commercial St.,
Wellfleet
(508) 349-6333
www.macsseafood.com

Brothers Mac and Alex Hay have solidified their reputation in the heart of Wellfleet with the success of Mac's Shack. Oceanic cravings are addressed by dishes like steamers, mussels, grilled fish, and fried clams, while carnivores can opt for a steak or burger. The sushi is a big draw, and the raw bar outside is usually crowded. The restaurant also has its liquor license so the days of BYOB are a thing of the past. Open for lunch and dinner from mid-June to mid-Oct, Mac's Shack sits on a small inlet just down the street from the more casual but equally fun Mac's Seafood on the harbor.

MOBY DICK'S RESTAURANT $$–$$$
U.S. Rte. 6, Wellfleet
(508) 349-9795
www.mobydicksrestaurant.com

You can't miss this eatery along Route 6. As the name might suggest, there is plenty of seafood to choose from, but there's also the requisite amount of burgers, chicken sandwiches, BLTs, and more. Open early May through Columbus Day and serving lunch and dinner from 11:30 a.m. to 10 p.m. in season (and until 9 p.m. in the spring and fall).

MONTANO'S $$
481 U.S. Rte. 6, Truro
(508) 487-2026
www.montanos.com

This great family-oriented restaurant serves creative Italian specialties, fresh seafood, and great steaks. Hearty appetites will be satisfied here, as entrees come with unlimited garden salad, potato or pasta, and homemade bread. Chef/owner Bob Montano includes some innovative chicken and veal dishes among the many menu offerings. Montano's is open daily year-round for dinner.

NAPI'S $$
7 Freeman St., Provincetown
(508) 487-1145, (800) 571-6274
www.napis-restaurant.com

Napi's is a work of art, with walls built from pieces of discarded Boston factories and decorated with salvaged stained-glass carousel horses, artwork, and antiques. The menu is nearly novella length, offering international dishes such as Brazilian shrimp, scallops Provençal, Russian oysters, and Thai chicken and shrimp.

Napi's serves dinner nightly from 5 p.m. Oct through Apr, Napi's also serves lunch starting at 11:30 a.m. An early-bird menu is available from 5 to 6 p.m. daily. You'll find free, limited parking adjacent to the restaurant on the corner of Bradford Street.

NAUSET BEACH CLUB $$$–$$$$
222 Main St., East Orleans
(508) 255-8547
www.nausetbeachclub.com

The Nauset Beach Club specializes in northern Italian fare and locally caught seafood. The restaurant, housed in a former duck-hunting cottage on the way to Nauset Beach, has a warm atmosphere, with terra-cotta walls, an upstairs fireplace and downstairs wood-burning oven, and low lights. Dinner is served every evening year-round.

OLD JAILHOUSE TAVERN $$
28 West Rd., Orleans
(508) 255-5245
www.jailhousetavern.com

Occupying the former home of Orleans constable Henry Perry (the stone room was actually used as a jail), the Jailhouse is popular with the locals. You'll find all the basics here: seafood salads and lobster rolls, burgers and Reubens, veal medallions and prime rib. Then there's the menu's most unusual dish: toast Nelson, which is French bread smothered with bacon, onion, shrimp, scallops, crabmeat, and hollandaise sauce. The Jailhouse is open year-round for lunch and dinner.

THE ORLEANS WATERFRONT INN $$$
3 Old Country Rd., Orleans
(508) 255-2222, (800) 863-3039
www.orleansinn.com

Right on Town Cove, the Orleans Inn enjoys water views from its lovely dining room and handsome bar area. The 1875 building, once home to the Snow family, has been restored to its former grandeur by the Maas family and is truly a pleasure to visit. The view from the dining room is breathtaking in any season, and the decor is elegant yet understated. The menu features well-prepared classics like pepper-crusted duck breast, steamed lobster, fried clams, and the inn's signature dish, sole stuffed with seafood and served with a lobster cream sauce.

During summer, the inn offers outdoor dining overlooking Town Cove with a view of Nauset Marsh in the distance.

The lunch menu stars tempting sandwiches, wraps, and seafood rolls. You can order lunch until 4 p.m.

Spend some time downstairs in O'Hagan's Irish Pub, where the martinis are famous and the ambience friendly (see our Nightlife chapter for details). Orleans Inn is open daily year-round for lunch and dinner.

PATE'S RESTAURANT $$
1260 Main St., Chatham
(508) 945-9777
www.patesrestaurant.com

In business since 1957, this restaurant still cooks its food in an open hearth, exactly as it's been doing since it opened. Most locals will tell you to order the native swordfish or prime rib. Legend has it that this was summer-resident Tip O'Neill's favorite restaurant. From the cars parked outside each summer, you can tell it's a favorite of a lot of people. Pate's serves dinner and is open nightly from April to Jan.

PEARL $$$
250 Commercial St., Wellfleet
(508) 349-2999
www.wellfleetpearl.com

From the creator of Roobar, the Pearl takes the place of the former Captain Higgins Restaurant on Wellfleet Harbor and is probably best known so far for its eco-friendly approach in its construction and operation. The menu includes the obvious—seafood—as well as steaks, sandwiches, and burgers. Pearl is open daily at 11 a.m. for lunch and dinner.

P.J.'S FAMILY RESTAURANT $$
2616 U.S. Rte. 6, Wellfleet
(508) 349-2126

A local institution since 1971, P.J.'s serves great chowder, homemade kale soup, and onion rings, along with broiled scallops, fish and chips, hot dogs, and lobster. Try one of their huge fish sandwiches followed by some soft-serve ice cream. The take-out window at P.J.'s is always bustling; place your order, and sit outside at a picnic table. Or you can sit inside in the comfortable dining room. During the high season the restaurant serves lunch and dinner from 11 a.m. to 9 p.m. on weekends and until 3 p.m. during the week. It is open from mid-Apr through mid-Oct.

THE PORT $$$–$$$$
541 Rte. 28, Harwich Port
(508) 430-5410
www.theportrestaurant.com

The horseshoe-shaped bar is always hopping at this cozy storefront cafe, which aims to import urban flair to downtown Harwich Port. But don't be misled by the orange walls, black banquettes, and hand-blown light fixtures: the decor may evoke the city, but the menu is straight from the shores and fields of New England. The recipient of several culinary awards since its inception in 2004, The Port puts a contemporary twist on regional seafood, serving specialties like pistachio-encrusted halibut and Thai salmon (with cucumber-cilantro yogurt sauce). Serving dinner only, from May through Nov.

RASPBERRIES $

30 Earle Rd., Harwich
(508) 432-1180, (800) 368-1180
www.commodoreinn.com

This is an ideal place to go for breakfast, especially for hearty appetites. The breakfast buffet here is bountiful and affordable. Indulge in pancakes, scrambled eggs, French toast, home fries, eggs Benedict, ham, quiche, pastries, muffins, fresh fruit . . . the list goes on and on. Raspberries is open for breakfast from mid-June through mid-Sept.

RUSS AND MARIE'S MARCONI BEACH
RESTAURANT IT-IL-DO BBQ $$-$$$

545 Rte. 6, South Wellfleet
(508) 349-6025
www.marconibeachrestaurant.net

Russ and Marie's specializes in southern-style wood-smoked barbecue. The wood-beamed, red-walled interior sets a warm stage for Russ's "famous" grilled specialties, among them ribs, chicken, pulled pork, chicken, and a full complement of fresh-caught seafood. Or try the raw bar, or one of the hearty home-style pastas (Wellfleet seafood fra diavolo is a special favorite). They serve lunch and dinner from Apr through mid-Nov.

SALTWATER GRILLE $$$

20 South Rte. 28, Orleans
(508) 255–5149
www.capecodswg.com

Formerly the Arbor Restaurant and Binnacle Tavern, the Saltwater maintains many of the Binnacle Tavern favorites, including pizzas, salads, and pastas. The layout is comfortable and friendly, with a horseshoe bar at the center of the action and tables and other rooms radiating outward. The atmosphere isn't quite the same as the eclectic feel the Binnacle was famous for, but it's not a bad place to hang out and have a drink or a bite to eat. The Saltwater is open for dinner year-round.

SEAFOOD SAM'S $-$$

Route 28, Harwich
(508) 432-1422
www.seafoodsams.com

Seafood lovers will want to visit this small roadside clam shack. Since 1974, Seafood Sam's has been serving Cape Codders and visitors the tastiest and healthiest seafood dinners, either broiled or fried (in low-fat oil). Seafood Sam's has three other locations in the Upper Cape and Mid-Cape; please check listings in those sections. They are open daily for lunch and dinner.

TERRA LUNA $$$$

104 Shore Rd., Truro
(508) 487-1019
www.theterraluna.com

With its cathedral ceiling, barn-board walls, exposed beams, tin-and-wood roof, and whimsical pieces of art, this eatery knows the importance of being different. And it shows on the menu and blackboard specials, which feature New American and Mediterranean cuisine. Terra Luna serves dinner daily from late May through mid-Oct.

TWENTY-EIGHT ATLANTIC AT THE
WEQUASSETT INN $$$-$$$$

2173 Rte 28, Harwich
(508) 430-3000
www.wequassett.com

This place is posh and serves sophisticated New England cuisine with international touches and views of Pleasant Bay. Try appetizers like the Chatham "day boat" scallops or entrees such as the caramelized black cod with candied fennel-onion fricassee and lobster fumet. They also have some of the more inventive vegetarian options around. Reservations are accepted, and dress is "smart casual." Twenty-Eight Atlantic is open year-round for lunch and dinner.

VAN RENSSELAER'S RESTAURANT &
RAW BAR $$

1019 U.S. Rte. 6, South Wellfleet
(508) 349-2127
www.vanrensselaers.com

VR's, as most locals call it, serves wholesome food in a casual setting at reasonable prices. Popular breakfast items include the Homegrown—scrambled eggs with fresh basil and tomato, served with fresh fruit. The dinner menu, enhanced by a terrific salad bar, lists specialties such as mixed seafood grill, seafood linguine, and steak tenderloin au poivre. The menu also includes a number of vegetarian dishes, and there's a children's menu too. Van Rensselaer's is open May 15 through the end of Oct for breakfast and dinner, daily in season, and on weekends in the fall. All items are available for takeout. Early-bird specials are from 4:30 to 5:30 p.m., and a new raw bar happy hour runs from 4 to 6 p.m.

VINING'S BISTRO $$$
595 Main St., Chatham
(508) 945-5033
www.viningsbistro.net

The Bistro features an unusual, ever-changing menu with an emphasis on local ingredients. No dish is ordinary here, where the innovative cuisine supplements native dishes with international entrees like Bangkok clay pot (a flavorful cauldron of shrimp, mussels, scallops, fish, and Asian vegetables, steeped in Thai green curry coconut sauce and served with jasmine rice and fresh pineapple). Of course there are seafood dishes like skillet-roasted, Portuguese-style Chatham scrod and pan-roasted Cape sea scallops with applewood-smoked bacon, mixed mushrooms, and caramelized red onion confit. The Bistro is open daily for dinner during the summer.

THE WELLFLEET BEACHCOMBER $-$$
1120 Cahoon Hollow Rd., Wellfleet
(508) 349-6055
www.thebeachcomber.com

When you mention the word Comber on Cape Cod, everyone knows you are talking about the Beachcomber in Wellfleet. This Cape Cod institution serves up great beach food and live music (see our Nightlife chapter) in the unique setting of Cahoon Hollow overlooking the Atlantic Ocean. Featuring Wellfleet oysters and steamers at the raw bar on the patio and a complete menu

with daily specials, plus a kids' menu and arcade, the Beachcomber is the place to be. A take-out window allows you to climb the dune path from the beach, order your lunch, and return to Cahoon Hollow Beach, in the Cape Cod National Seashore. The Beachcomber is open from Memorial Day weekend to Labor Day from 11:30 a.m. to 1 a.m.

WELLFLEET DAIRY BAR & GRILL $
U.S. Rte. 6, Eastham-Wellfleet line
(508) 349-7176
www.wellfleetcinemas.com

Be sure to ask about their dinner and movie special. It couldn't be any easier here, as the Wellfleet Dairy Bar & Grill is located at the Wellfleet Cinemas and Wellfleet Drive-In Theater. A casual family dining spot, it's a great place to meet friends before or after the movies or any other time. There's always something for the kids on their kiddy menu, like hamburgers, chowdah, or fish and chips. The parents can sip a beer, while the kids kick back with root beer floats. Order your dinner to go, and eat it under the stars at the Drive-In Theater (see the Arts chapter). The Grill is open every day in the summer from 11:30 a.m. Call for take-out orders and off-season hours.

THE WHITMAN HOUSE $$
Corner of Route 6 and Great Hollow Road, Truro
(508) 487-1740
www.whitmanhouse.com

For starters cheese and crackers, along with homemade bread, are brought to the table before you order at the Whitman. The menu has something for everyone including prime rib au jus, char-grilled swordfish, and broiled salmon with a New York sirloin. The 175-seat Whitman House Restaurant serves dinner daily beginning at 5 p.m.; lunch is served in the casual Bass Tavern and offers an early-dinner menu and a pleasing slate of children's selections.

THE WICKED OYSTER $$$
50 Main St., Wellfleet
(508) 349-3455

Bivalves are only part of the charm at this increasingly popular restaurant, which eschews clam shack kitsch in favor of understated style and original art. Housed in a gray clapboard building big enough to hold the crowds it attracts in season, the Wicked Oyster offers breakfast, lunch, and dinner and cedes its walls to revolving exhibits. Whether you drop by in the morning for smoked salmon Benedict or come at night for pan-fried sole with lemon caper butter, you'll appreciate the addition of this year-round eatery to the Lower Cape dining scene. The Wicked Oyster is closed on Wed.

WILD GOOSE TAVERN $$$
512 Main St., Chatham
(508) 945-5550, (800) 242-8426
www.wildgoosetavern.com

The Wild Goose Tavern at the Chatham Wayside Inn serves lunch and dinner; it also serves breakfast for guests of the inn. Lunch might be crab cakes or chicken francaise, but if you're in the mood for simpler fare, order a scallop roll, sandwich, or fish and chips. Dinner could be rack of lamb, lobster-scallop ravioli, or grilled swordfish. The restaurant is closed on Mon and Tues in the off-season.

WINSLOW'S TAVERN $$$
316 Main St., Wellfleet
(508) 349-6450
www.winslowstavern.com

This Federal-style captain's house was built in 1805 and now features five atmospheric dining rooms, where you can dine on simply prepared seafood (oven-roasted Chatham cod with tomato-garlic confit, scallop and shrimp skewers with basil-crushed peas and mixed mesculin greens) and homemade pasta (fettucine tossed with lightly creamed roast mixed cherry tomatoes and whole basil, three-cheese mac and cheese). Serving lunch from noon to 3 p.m. and dinner from 5:30 to 10 p.m. from mid-May through mid-Oct.

THE YARDARM $-$$
Route 28, Orleans
(508) 255-4840
www.yardarmrestaurant.com

The Yardarm is an eating and drinking pub. A favorite with locals and visitors, the Yardarm is famous for its seafood chowder, fish and chips, and signature fisherman's special, codfish cheeks. It's open year-round, serving lunch beginning at 11:30 a.m. and dinner at 5:30 p.m., featuring creative "whiteboard" specials and a kids' menu.

NIGHTLIFE

In the night, the Cape shows many faces: the magic of Lower Cape lighthouses piercing the fog to reveal treacherous shoals; convivial banter and quiet music in a fishing village tavern; the elegance of fine dining and dancing at a stylish resort; the intimacy of a quiet stroll along the beaches under the expanse of the Milky Way; and, of course, the energy of live bands and frenzied dancing at the nightclubs that dot Route 28.

As wonderful as it sounds, a Cape Cod evening is good for more than just strolling down to the local ice-cream shop. After the little ones are tucked into bed and darkness settles across the beaches and lakes and ponds, Cape Cod's wilder side comes out to play. As day becomes night, and dinner crowds become evening crowds, nightclubs and restaurants open their doors to locals and visitors. The Cape has some nightclubs and taverns that are only open for three months of the year, but in that time they pack enough excitement, not to mention paying customers, to last the year. Balancing these hot spots are the more reserved, but equally casual, environs for those looking only to unwind.

From relaxing piano bars to hopping clubs playing the latest pop music to casual bars with a couple of acoustic guitars in the background, there is a lot to cover in such a short time. Some towns are less nocturnally active, satisfied in offering just a few after-dark spots to keep things interesting.

Throughout Massachusetts, bars are required by law to close at 1 a.m., and some close earlier, especially on weekdays or during the off-season. Last call varies anywhere from 15 minutes to a half-hour before closing. Wine and beer are sold only in package stores (the Cape term for liquor stores) and at some convenience stores. Throughout most of Massachusetts, including the Cape, package stores must close by 11 p.m. Many Cape liquor stores close by 10 p.m.

Bring your ID because you will be carded if you look anywhere near 21. The legal blood-alcohol limit in Massachusetts is .08 percent. That's understood to be about the equivalent of one beer an hour for the average person. If you refuse a breath test for your blood alcohol, your license can be revoked for up to 180 days.

One thing the Cape doesn't have is an abundance of public transportation. Unlike nightlife in a more urban atmosphere, you won't find a line of cabs or a subway stop in front of the local clubs at closing time. If you want to try cabbing it, be sure to call ahead and set up a pickup time. However, a designated driver often is the best option for getting to and from your destination.

The cozy, back-roads charm of the Cape requires full attention for drivers, especially as there are few streetlights. With many people riding bikes or walking, even late into the evening, the Cape is no place to drink and drive. In recent years, Massachusetts has stepped up efforts to curb drinking and driving. During summer months, Cape police add dozens of officers to their departments, in part to increase traffic enforcement during the peak season.

For those interested in exploring Cape nightlife, we present here some of the bright spots you'll find from Bourne to P-town. Listings in this chapter predominantly cover bars, clubs, and restaurants that offer live entertainment. See our Arts chapter for theater, concerts, and other evening activities, and check local newspapers for special events such as dances and dinners sponsored by local churches and fraternal organizations. Because many of the nightspots we mention are also great dining establishments, look for more details on their cuisine in our Restaurants chapter.

UPPER CAPE

THE COURTYARD RESTAURANT AND PUB
1337 County Rd., Cataumet (Bourne)
(508) 563-1818
www.courtyardrestaurantandpub.com
Open year-round, the Courtyard Restaurant pushes back the dinner tables at 9:30 p.m. from Wed to Sun to make way for dancing and live entertainment that runs the gamut from contemporary jazz and blues to light rock and Top 40. The crowd, which ranges in age from late 20s to early 50s, takes in the music of local groups.

LIAM MAGUIRE'S IRISH PUB AND RESTAURANT
273 Main St., Falmouth
(508) 548-0285
www.liammaguire.com
At this Irish pub and restaurant, you'll get lively entertainment nightly in season when owner Liam Maguire takes the stage with his guitar to perform traditional and contemporary Irish folk music and requests such as "Danny Boy," "Green Fields," and "My Wild Irish Rose." International Irish music greats Tommy Makem and Paddy Reilly usually appear once a year to the delight of those of us who wear their green and orange with pride. The restaurant is open year-round and serves food until 10 p.m.

THE NIMROD
100 Dillingham Rd., Falmouth
(508) 540-4132
www.thenimrod.com
This colonial tavern still bears scars from British cannon fire (it's in what is now the men's room, if you're interested). Such reverence to history hasn't kept the Nimrod from staying with the times, however. It offers live music, mainly jazz, nightly. It also serves solid lunches, dinners, and a $12.95 brunch that includes a Bloody Mary or mimosa. As for the name? We're told the Nimrod was a fearless warrior of the biblical era. To this day the name is awarded to the British Navy's most powerful weapon. Open for dinner daily. Lunch is served Wed through Fri.

SANDWICH TAVERNA
290 Rte. 130, Sandwich
(508) 888-2200
www.sandwichtaverna.com
Restaurant by day and evening, the Sandwich Taverna morphs into a music club at night, featuring DJs, line dancing, karaoke on weeknights, and live acts on the weekends. Beef connoisseurs will admire the assortment of carnivorous entrees on the menu, which also offers kid-friendly plates from chicken fingers to macaroni and cheese. Open year-round, the restaurant serves lunch and dinner daily.

SILVER LOUNGE
412 Rte. 28A, North Falmouth
(508) 563-2410
The Silver Lounge in North Falmouth has been a favorite hangout for years and is one of the few that serves a full menu until 11:45 p.m. Eat in the railroad caboose, then join the crowd at the piano bar in the lounge, always a focal point for local gatherings. The pianist plays Thurs through Sat, and the Silver Lounge is open all year-round.

SURF LOUNGE AT THE SEA CREST RESORT
350 Quaker Rd., North Falmouth
(508) 540-9400
This oceanfront resort is a great place for an evening out if you want a romantic dinner overlooking Buzzards Bay, followed by some music and maybe a little cheek-to-cheek dancing. Most nights during the high season, there is live music that includes everything from a disc jockey to bands performing blues, show tunes, or Top 40.

WOODS HOLE COMMUNITY HALL
Water Street, Woods Hole
no phone
www.woodsholecommunityassociation.org
The Woods Hole Community Hall is a nice place to spend an evening of contra dancing, watching theater (see our Arts chapter), or listening to great folk music. The intimacy of the Community Hall permits you to sit within feet of performers. There's no central phone number to call for information, so you'll have to check their Web site or watch local papers for upcoming events.

MID-CAPE

HARRY'S BLUES BAR
700 Main St., West End, Hyannis
(508) 778-4188
www.harrysbluesbar.com
If you like your nights red hot and blue, pull up a stool at Harry's Blues Bar, where live blues, folk, and zydeco provide a soundtrack for satisfying Cajun and Creole cuisine. In business for more than 20 years, Harry's recently moved to a larger space just steps up the street. It still has all the same assets regulars have come to love—among them jumbo shrimp jambalaya, chicken and sausage gumbo, and a slate of great local and national entertainers.

IMPROPER BOSTONIAN
Route 28, Dennisport
(508) 394-7416
www.myspace.com/impboston
This summertime-only venue is open Thur through Sun from Memorial Day to Labor Day weekend and offers live bands at least two nights a week, usually Fri and Sat, and a DJ the rest of the time. The music is a meld of jazz, rock, pop, and blues. The Saturday afternoon happy hours are very popular. The Improper Bostonian attracts a young—early 20s to late 30s—crowd. It recently opened a downstairs area: the Proper Bostonian.

THE 19TH HOLE
11 Barnstable Rd., Hyannis
(508) 771-1032

The 40-and-younger crowd flocks to the 19th Hole, a happening sports bar with darts, pool, and a jukebox.

OLIVER'S AND PLANCK'S TAVERN
Route 6A, Yarmouthport
(508) 362-6062
www.oliverscapecod.biz
Oliver's in Yarmouthport (see our Restaurants chapter), near the town line with Dennis, hosts live entertainment and karaoke in its lounge Fri through Sun throughout the summer and Fri and Sat during the off-season. The late-30s to 50s crowd comes to dance to music from the 1970s and '80s.

O'SHEA'S OLDE INNE
348 Main St., West Dennis
508-398-8887
www.osheasoldeinne.com
This classic Irish pub features live music every night and a traditional Irish session every Sunday. The updated music calendar online gives a good feel for this Mid-Cape favorite. The menu is standard Irish pub fare, including Irish stew and a baked stuffed haddock.

THE PADDOCK
20 Scudder Ave., Hyannis
(508) 775-7677
www.paddockcapecod.com
The lounge at the Paddock (see our Restaurants chapter) hosts entertainment—including popular local jazz singers and pianists—on the weekend during the summer. The restaurant can hold up to 150 people and serves lunch and dinner daily.

PUFFERBELLIES ENTERTAINMENT COMPLEX
183 Iyanough Rd., Hyannis
(774) 259-1083
www.pufferbellies.net
From teen nights to DJs to bikini clad mud wrestlers, Pufferbellies has a popular mix of entertainment for the younger crowd and is also a favorite with the Cape's large Brazilian community and visitors or workers from European countries. The

crowd may be a little rough and ready, but if that's what you're looking for, there are only a few places to find anything similar on the peninsula. Pufferbellies is open year-round.

THE ROADHOUSE CAFE
488 South St., Hyannis
(508) 775-2386
www.Rd.housecafe.com
For another guaranteed good time, try the Roadhouse Cafe. Owner Dave Columbo's dad, Lou, is a highly regarded jazz musician, so it's no surprise that the Lou Columbo & Dick Johnson Jazz Ensemble takes the floor here on a regular basis. Top area pianists are featured on weekend evenings.

RUM RUNNER'S BAR AND GRILL
243 Lower County Rd., Dennisport
(508) 398-5673
www.rumrunnersbarandgrill.com
If you're looking for a hot nightspot with a young and sometimes wild crowd, Rum Runner's—formerly the Captain's Club—offers Boston-based and local blues and classic rock bands year-round. It's open nightly from Memorial Day to Labor Day and Fri and Sat off-season.

SUNDANCER'S
116 Rte. 28, West Dennis
(508) 394-1600
www.sundancerscapecod.com
This casual venue attracts a youngish crowd and features local rock bands most nights in season. On summer Sundays (and Tues during the high season) the focus is live reggae music. In the off-season, the entertainment is usually limited to weekends, and Sundancer's suspends service from Dec to Feb.

TOMMY DOYLES
334 Main St., Hyannis
508-862-9430
www.tommydoyles.com
When Tommy Doyles took over the former Hooters on Main Street in Hyannis, it filled a hole in the hub's night life. Although there is plenty of Irish next door at the 19th Hole and clubbing available elsewhere, the combination of an Irish pub and late-night entertainment appears to be a success so far. The restaurant can appear empty at times but that's partially because it is so big. The food is standard pub fare with Irish themes throughout the menu. Open seven days for lunch and dinner. At night live entertainment in the back room draws big crowds after 10 p.m.

LOWER CAPE

THE BEACHCOMBER OF WELLFLEET
1120 Cahoon Hollow Rd., Wellfleet
(508) 349-6055
www.thebeachcomber.com
Ask any local where to find the best music on the Lower Cape, and you will be pointed to the Beachcomber. The former 1897 lifesaving station sits almost at water's edge and attracts a collegiate crowd, especially after a day on the beach. The music here ranges from loud to louder, with popular acts including local favorites the Incredible Casuals, and surf legend Dick Dale. It's open from mid-May to early Sept, with acts almost nightly in July and Aug and less frequently (mostly on weekends) in the off-season. There is a cover charge for most live acts, though admission is free with a season pass.

THE BOATSLIP RESORT
161 Commercial St., Provincetown
(508) 487-1669
www.boatslipresort.com
This all-inclusive resort is the home of a popular P-town tradition: the Tea Dance, touted as "an afternoon of hot bodies, good friends, and great dance music" on a sprawling deck overlooking the ocean. Staged daily in season (from 4 to 7 p.m.), this al fresco disco is a magnet for local and visiting singles—both gay and straight. Open Apr through Oct, the Boatslip tapers its entertainment schedule in the off-season, holding tea dances on weekends and the occasional holiday (Women's Week, Halloween).

ℹ️ Hungry after a night of clubbing? With its Emack & Bolio's ice cream, specialty coffees, and backyard garden, Spiritus Pizza attracts a convivial crowd between last call and 2 a.m. It's in the center of P-town at 190 Commercial St. (508-487-2808 or www.spirituspizza.com). Open daily Apr through Oct from 11:30 a.m. to 2 a.m.

BOOKSTORE AND RESTAURANT
50 Kendrick Ave., Wellfleet
(508) 349-3154
www.bookstorerestaurant.com
This popular restaurant (see our Restaurants chapter) across from Mayo Beach features occasional live music. Downstairs is the Bomb Shelter Pub, which has a jukebox, darts, pool tables, large-screen TV, and a local, sports-loving crowd. It's open year-round.

BUBALA'S BY THE BAY
185 Commercial St., Provincetown
(508) 487-0773
www.bubalas.com
Open mid-April through Oct, this funky restaurant has live entertainment nightly in July and Aug, usually jazz, but sometimes folk rock.

CAMPARI'S BISTRO BAR & GRILL
323 Rte. 28, North Chatham
(508) 945-9123
www.camparis.com
Campari's is one of the few dining establishments on the Lower Cape that features contemporary and classic jazz on most evenings year-round. The restaurant is divided into two sections, the elegant bistro and bar to one side and a more casual, family-friendly grill to the other. Campari's is open Tues through Sun starting at 5 p.m.

CAPE COD'S IRISH PUB
126 Rte. 28, West Harwich
(508) 432-8808
www.capecodsirishpub.com
Irish superstars such as Tommy Makem and the Clancy Brothers have been known to stop in at the Irish Pub, located right next to the Herring River Bridge. The pub, which sponsors an Irish Pub Road Race in August, is open from May to Sept and features nightly entertainment in season. From Irish-American ensembles to karaoke nights, it's a musical melting pot on stage, the beat generally goes on between 9:30 p.m. to 1 a.m.

CHATHAM BARS INN
Shore Rd., Chatham
(508) 945-0096, (800) 527-4884
www.chathambarsinn.com
All summer, the Chatham Bars Inn holds a dinner dance on Sat nights. Jackets are required, and the ability to waltz, fox trot, and cha-cha-cha doesn't hurt. Slightly more casual, family-oriented events are held in the Beach House Grill in summer.

THE CHATHAM SQUIRE
487 Main St., Chatham
(508) 945-0945
www.thesquire.com
Half tavern and half nice restaurant, the Squire has several bars, with the tavern side being the liveliest. Although the Squire has live bands only occasionally, it has a jukebox and pool tables. This year-round establishment has a congenial atmosphere that lures the locals in the off-season.

FIRST ENCOUNTER COFFEEHOUSE
220 Samoset Rd., Eastham
(508) 255-5438
www.firstencounter.org
Many big names, including Wellfleet's own Patty Larkin and Livingston Taylor (James' brother), got their start and still perform at this well-known coffeehouse located in a church. The building itself is an 1899 yellow clapboard and stained glass church. Concerts are twice each month during the off-season. The coffeehouse is closed during Dec and May. During the summer concerts are once a month. If you're late, you won't stand a chance of getting in—the seating is limited to 100 people.

GOVERNOR BRADFORD
312 Commercial St., Provincetown
(508) 487-2781
Right in the center of town, this local hangout has chess and backgammon sets, pool tables, and pinball machines along with live entertainment just about every night in season. Open year-round, the Governor Bradford has a schedule saturated with drag karaoke, DJ nights, and live music acts.

JAKE ROONEY'S
119 Brooks Rd., Harwich Port
(508) 430-1100
www.jakerooneys.com
This year-round restaurant (see our Restaurants chapter) has live entertainment six or seven nights a week in summer and on weekends in the off-season. The mix includes karaoke, sing-alongs, and oldies bands.

> **i** Between 1945 and 1957, five drive-in theaters opened on Cape Cod. Today the large outdoor screen at the Wellfleet Drive-In is the only one remaining. It opened in 1957 with a screening of *Desk Set* starring Spencer Tracy and Katharine Hepburn.

JOE'S BEACH ROAD BAR & GRILLE AT THE BARLEY NECK INN
5 Beach Rd., East Orleans
(508) 255-0212
www.barleyneck.com
This high-ceilinged, barn-like lounge at the Barley Neck has a beautifully redone mahogany bar and a great old stone fireplace. Local musicians are featured Fri through Sun in season. You can also get great munchies here—see our Restaurants chapter.

LAND HO!
Route 6A and Cove Road, Orleans
(508) 255-5165
www.land-ho.com
This popular pub, hung with hundreds of original signs, has live bands two or three nights a week—

the nights vary. When there's no live music, the well-stocked jukebox is always playing.

THE MEWS RESTAURANT AND CAFE
429 Commercial St., Provincetown
(508) 487-1500
www.mews.com
In summer this year-round waterfront restaurant offers live entertainment, usually a cabaret act, on Fri, Sat, and Sun. Oct through May, the Mews hosts an open-mike coffeehouse. Make sure to try some of their international vodkas, reportedly the largest selection in New England.

PIED BAR
193A Commercial St., Provincetown
(508) 487-1527
www.piedbar.com
Many people consider this the quintessential lesbian dance club; *Time* named it one of the best women's bars in the country. The recently revamped bar is all about the dance floor: new sound, new lights—quite a scene. Open Memorial Day to mid-Oct, the Pied Bar features an after-tea dance every evening at 6:30 p.m. in season, and theme nights like "Bust Lust" and "Scanty Panties" into the fall.

THE WOODSHED
1989 Rte. 6A, Brewster
(508) 896-7771
Open from late May to mid-Oct, the Woodshed is a great place to unwind and take in some local color, along with great acoustic rock. As its name implies, this is a rustic venue and definitely casual. The Woodshed is open nightly during the summer; weekends in the off-season. Among the bar's other assets is its adjacent restaurant, the Brewster Inn and Chowder House, where you can find affordable comfort food and martinis worthy of 007.

SHOPPING

Although there are some large chain stores, the majority of retail shopping on Cape Cod is done in scores of smaller, independent shops that populate the peninsula.

The latest fashions are available, but Cape clothing stores are especially strong in classic designs and offbeat clothes just right for artistic types. We've got gourmet shops, jewelers, outdoor shops, shoe stores, bookshops, and gift shops. Many gift shops double as galleries, making it easy to find that one-of-a-kind wall hanging, basket, vase, or planter. (If you're in the market for art, be sure to check our Arts chapter for galleries.)

There are a few sizable retail centers besides Cape Cod Mall, which completed a massive renovation in 2000. Busy Route 132 in Hyannis is home to three other shopping plazas right nearby. On the Upper Cape the open-air Mashpee Commons has more than 90 shops plus several banks and eateries. There's also the Falmouth Mall with 20 stores. These large centers certainly come in handy, but shopping local is just as easy to do on the Cape. Although towns on the Outer Cape such as Truro, Wellfleet and Eastham do not have large downtowns, most other areas of the Cape have something to offer in the way of small walkable shopping areas. Even on the outer Cape there is Provincetown, with one of the most unique downtown experiences anywhere and small shops spread throughout the other three towns.

Provincetown's Commercial Street is as funky and colorful as Greenwich Village—only with a small-town, seaside flavor. This is the place to go for the offbeat and the outrageous, along with the artistic and spiritual. Wellfleet has a nice downtown, with an emphasis on galleries mixed with a few choice shops. Eastham's shopping scene is a bit scattered geographically, so you do need a car.

Orleans is the real retail hub of the Lower Cape. Many residents of surrounding towns come here regularly to do their grocery shopping, pick up dry cleaning, buy flowers, and just shop. It's the kind of town where you're bound to run into someone you know. It has a nice downtown area where you can park your car and stroll down the brick-paved sidewalks in some areas.

Chatham is also a good walking town, though there are shops beyond the downtown area you may want to drive to. Main Street Chatham has a genteel, relaxed feel—no hustle-bustle here. Harwich is sprawling, with shops all along Route 28 and in other areas of town. Harwich Port is a good place to start, because much of it is walkable. Brewster, likewise, has a couple of little centers, with a cluster of shops near the Brewster General Store, another cluster a mile or so east (including Brewster Book Store), and the Lemon Tree complex of shops to the west.

Shopkeepers accept many forms of payment—cash, personal checks (with proper ID), travelers' checks, and credit cards. Not all shops take all credit cards, but most accept at least one or two.

Although most stores are open seven days a week during the season (Memorial Day to Labor Day), many shops—especially those on the Lower Cape—have sporadic off-season hours or are open only on weekends in winter. We'll let you know if that is the case and, of course, we'll tell you when a shop is closed in the off-season. Otherwise, you can assume the store is open all year. It's always a good idea to call first during January, February, and March; even shops that are open all year sometimes close for a week or two in the dead of winter for cleaning, painting, or redecorating so they'll be ready for another busy summer.

GENERAL SHOPPING

Upper Cape

BEAN & COD
140 Main St., Falmouth
(508) 548-8840

This is a combination gourmet deli and gift store. Attractive and appetizing gifts are everywhere: Houseware items, such as glasses, trays, place mats, and lamps, adorn the walls and displays; intriguing gourmet food baskets, custom-filled with cheese, crackers, teas, coffees, and regional products adorn the sandwich deli counter, where you can choose from a menu of salads, sandwiches, and baked goods.

The Bean & Cod will ship wherever you want. It's open daily all year. The store also carries cookbooks, food mills, and other cooking equipment.

THE BLACK DOG GENERAL STORE
214 Main St., Falmouth
(508) 495-6000, (800) 626-1991
www.theblackdog.com

In 2003 this Martha's Vineyard cottage industry (see our Martha's Vineyard chapter) established a presence on the mainland (here in Falmouth, out in Provincetown, and, most recently, in Chatham). This store, modeled after the Vineyard Haven mother-ship emporium, features all the Black Dog apparel and accessories you —and your dog—will ever need.

CAPE COD FACTORY OUTLET MALL
1 Factory Outlet Rd., Sagamore
(508) 888-8417
www.capecodfactoryoutlet.com

This is a nice collection of well-known manufacturers, including Bass, Oshkosh B'Gosh, Samsonite, and Reebok. The mall also has a food court and is open daily year-round. It is just off exit 1 on US 6 westbound.

CHRISTMAS TREE SHOPS
Route 6A, Sagamore
(508) 888-7010
www.christmastreeshops.com

This growing chain was started by a Cape family in Yarmouthport, and it's been a draw for locals and tourists alike ever since. The Christmas Tree Shops carry a huge, ever-changing inventory of gifts and housewares, including lamps, lawn furniture, greeting cards, food and gourmet items, paper goods, linens, and, of course, Christmas items, all at near-wholesale prices. The Sagamore shop, with its unusual thatched roof and attached windmill, is a regional attraction; other Christmas Tree Shops are located in Falmouth, Hyannis, West Dennis, West Yarmouth, and Orleans. The shops are open daily.

HOWLINGBIRD STUDIO
91 Palmer Ave., Falmouth
(508) 540-3787
www.howlingbird.com

This silk-screening studio, which hand prints on canvas bags, long- and short-sleeve T-shirts, sweatshirts, and hats, is popular with Woods Hole Oceanographic Institute scientists and tourists alike. The animal and organism-themed prints tend toward the scientific rather than cutesy—a nice change of pace. Howlingbird is open daily year-round, with shorter hours in winter. Its retail shop on Water Street in Woods Hole is open May through Christmas.

MASHPEE COMMONS
At the Mashpee Rotary between Routes 28 and 151, Mashpee
(508) 477-5400
www.mashpeecommons.com

With more than 90 businesses, including banks, realtors, eateries, and several nationally known chains, Mashpee Commons has been praised in national design magazines for its attractive, functional, and unique retail shopping area. Some of its best-known businesses include Gap, Williams-Sonoma, Puritan of Cape Cod, Pottery Barn, Regal Cinemas, Talbot's, Banana Republic, and Ann Taylor, along with a cigar shop and the 360 Surf Cycle Store. Between shop-hopping, recharge at Starbuck's coffee house. Dining options range from down-home (the Uncommon Cafe) to upscale (Bleu, a classic French bistro). Mashpee Commons sponsors an annual array of outdoor concerts and activities throughout the year, including hayrides, Christmas caroling, and pops symphony performances. Mashpee Commons is open daily all year, with longer evening hours in summer. Check the Web site for a list of other stores at Mashpee Commons.

PAIRPOINT GLASSWORKS
851 Rte. 6A, Sagamore
(800) 899-0953
www.pairpoint.com

Established in the 1800s by Boston & Sandwich Glass Co., Pairpoint produces and sells beautifully fashioned handblown and pressed glass. Pairpoint makes vases, candlesticks, sun catchers, cup plates, and stemware, along with authentic reproductions of early American glass originals found in museums. You can watch glassblowers at work Mon through Fri; the shop is open daily.

SANDWICH LANTERN WORKS
157 Main St., Sandwich
Industrial Park
(888) 741-0714
www.sandwichlantern.com

Handmade on the premises, the handsome brass and copper onion lights sold here are replicas of those once carried on whaling vessels. Pre-1800s lanterns, wall sconces, and chandeliers to hang indoors or outdoors are also available. This shop is open Mon through Sat.

SOFT AS A GRAPE
251 Main St., Falmouth
(508) 457-7480
www.softasagrape.com

This well-established business carries T-shirts, shorts, and other casual apparel, including floral limited-edition designs in dresses, hats, tees, and sweaters. The store, which also carries accessories, is open daily year-round. You'll find other Soft as a Grape shops in Mashpee, Hyannis, Chatham, and Edgartown.

TITCOMB'S BOOKSHOP
432 Rte. 6A, East Sandwich
(508) 888-2331
www.titcombsbookshop.com

This four-decade-old bookstore's three floors have all manner of cozy places to sit and peruse the large selection of new, used, and historical books. Titcomb's specializes in rare books, local authors, and regional history, and their wide range of children's selections includes the popular American Girl series. It's open daily.

UNCLE BILL'S COUNTRY STORE
412 Rte. 28A, North Falmouth
(508) 564-4355

This store carries a little bit of everything—greeting cards, collectibles, homemade jams, penny candy, and jewelry. Special collections include Byers Choice carolers,

Old World Christmas, and decorations for all holiday seasons, especially Christmas. The store has a huge variety of teddy bears and also stocks a large number of cranberry and cranberry-design products, among them linen, pottery, food, cookbooks, and children's toys. Open every day except Thanksgiving and Christmas.

UNDER THE SUN
22 Water St., Woods Hole
(508) 540-3603
www.underthesunwoodshole.com

Under the Sun has been in business in Woods Hole for more than 30 years and has always emphasized local artists and artisans who make jewelry, glassware, pottery, and other functional and aesthetic pieces. They also carry a selection of comfortable shoes: Birkenstocks, Tevas, Danskos, and others. The shop is open daily in season. Call for hours during the off-season.

Mid-Cape

ANDI CAROLE A CASA VEINTE
20 Sea St., Hyannis
(508) 771-7539

This classy boutique sells gorgeous designer clothing for women—clothes by small designer

 **Close-up**

Made on Cape Cod

If you want to take home a piece of Cape Cod, seek out products that are made here. Besides being a vacation destination, the Cape is home to many creative and enterprising people whose products have achieved success from local venues to the worldwide stage. Here is a sampling of some of our favorite Cape-made products:

Cape Cod Potato Chips: Made in Hyannis, these goodies are probably the best-known Cape product. Founded by the late Steve Bernard of Chatham in 1980, the company was later bought by Eagle Snacks, then a division of Anheuser-Busch. When that firm decided to downsize in 1996, Bernard bought his old company back and became a local hero, because his action saved the plant from closing. For a fun field trip, take the kids on a free tour of the Cape Cod Potato Chips factory on Breed's Hill Road between 9 a.m. and 5 p.m. Mon through Fri. You may also call them at (508) 775-3358 or look them up on the Web at www .capecodchips.com.

Barnstable Bat Company: These bats are used by the Cape Cod Baseball League as well as some big name major leaguers (among them Nomar Garciaparra, Jason Varitek, and Trot Nixon). They make great gifts for nonpros, too, especially because you can have them engraved. Made of maple, ash, and birch, the bats bear the Cape Cod logo and start at around $55 for an adult bat (engraving included) and $45 for a youth bat. The company, launched in 1992, is located at 40 Pleasant Pines Avenue in Centerville, where the showroom is open Mon through Fri and varied hours on Sat. Call them at (888) 549-8046 to check hours or request a brochure. They do a lot of mail-order business, and you can also order off their site at www.barnstablebat .com.

Cape Cod Beer: For those looking for the perfect adult beverage for a Cape Cod summer day, head over to the Cape Cod Beer and Cape Cod Homebrew Supply at 1336 Phinney's Lane in Hyannis. The beer—India Pale Ale, Red, Porter, and seasonal varieties—is brewed right on site in their newly renovated brewery. Nothing says Cape Cod like a growler ($10 plus $2 deposit for a 64-ounce bottle, $7 to $8 refill) of Cape Cod Beer. Open noon to 6 p.m. Mon through Fri, 11 a.m. to 2 p.m. Sat. Tours Tues at 11 a.m. and Sat at 1 p.m. Call (508) 790-4200 or go online at www.capecodbeer.com.

Cape Cod Lavender Farm: A little-known treasure on the Lower Cape is the Cape Cod Lavender Farm in Harwich. Tucked away down a bumpy dirt drive off a dead-end road off Route 124 (look for the lavender sign about a block north of Harwich Center and don't be confused by your GPS—the farm is located about a half mile off Weston Woods Road), this family-run business produces soaps, oils, lotions, and candles, all scented with lavender. Take home a lavender scented pillow, or choose a lavender sachet, or a bouquet of dried lavender. If you can't get there, call (508) 432-8397 for a brochure or order from their Web site at www .capecodlavenderfarm.com.

labels you won't find anywhere else. One of those designers is Andi Carole herself, a talented lady known locally for her crusade against litter and for her beautiful dresses with clean, flattering lines. She uses European fabrics with an emphasis on natural fibers, and the quality of the material shows in each piece. Andi Carole a Casa Veinte is open Mon through Sat.

THE BARN & CO.
574 Main St., Route 6A, Dennis
(508) 385-2100
www.barnandco.com
The Barn & Co. may have moved but it's basically the same as it was in its former Yarmouthport location. You'll find bamboo root ducks and slate welcome signs, Brewster native Mary Beth Baxter's primitive cards and prints, Marstons Mills' Dust of

the Earth pottery, dried floral arrangements, and a dazzling children's section stocked with books, plush toys, and decorative items. Local artisans produce handsome baskets in Shaker, traditional, and Nantucket lightship designs. The shop is open daily, year-round.

CAPE COD MALL
7691 Yannough Rd. (Route 132), Hyannis
(508) 771-0200
www.simon.com
The largest mall on the Cape, the Cape Cod Mall is anchored by Macy's and Sears, along with mini-anchor Best Buy and Marshalls. Major retailers at the mall include Bath & Body Works, J. Crew, Gap, Gap Kids, Eddie Bauer, Ann Taylor Loft, Abercrombie & Fitch, and Victoria's Secret. Their 400-seat international Food Court features D'Angelo, Manchu Wok, McDonald's, Sarku Japan, and Freshens Yogurt. There's also a Regal Cinemas 12 theater-megaplex.

Cape Cod Mall is a totally nonsmoking facility. The stores are open Mon through Sat 10 a.m. to 9 p.m., Sun 11 a.m. to 6 p.m.

CLAIRE MURRAY
770 Rte. 6A, West Barnstable
(508) 375-0331, (800) 252-4733
www.clairemurray.com

867 Main St., Osterville
(508) 420-3562, (800) 252-4733
www.clairemurray.com
Claire Murray offers beautiful, distinctive, handmade rugs; needlepoint; gift items; home accessories; and cotton throws in its shops both here and in Mashpee, Dennis, Chatham, Nantucket, and Martha's Vineyard. Also available are rug-hooking and cross-stitch kits, as well as lessons. Open daily.

COLUMBIA TRADING COMPANY
1 Barnstable Rd., Hyannis
(508) 778-2929
www.columbiatrading.com
If it has anything to do with boats, you'll find it here. This shop, right near the corner of Main Street, deals in out-of-print and rare nautical books,

marine antiques, ship models, and marine artifacts. They offer thousands of new, used, and rare books on whaling, shipwrecks, Coast Guard history, boat building, sailboat racing, and navigation. It also has marine art for sale. The shop is open Mon, Tues, Thurs through Sat, and occasional Sundays in season (and from Thanksgiving to New Year's), and only on Mon, Tues, Fri, and Sat in the off-season.

THE DEAD ZONE
845 Route 28 (Boch Village), South Yarmouth
(508) 760-5823
www.deadzoneonline.com
Since 1990, the Dead Zone has been paying homage to the legion of Deadheads—devout followers of the band the Grateful Dead. Inside you'll find reminders of the '60s and '70s: tie-dyed clothes in wild colors, irreverent bumper stickers, incense, and love beads. Jerry Garcia may be gone, but his spirit lives on—accompanied by the spirit of Bob Marley, as evidenced in the wide selection of reggae merchandise. The shop is open "almost every day" in and out of season.

1856 COUNTRY STORE
555 Main St., Centerville
(508) 775-1856, (888) 750-1856
www.1856countrystore.com
As the local children know, if you've only got a nickel in your pocket, you can still buy something sweet at this historic country store in the heart of Centerville. Whether you're after penny candy, a daily paper, or a souvenir, you'll find it here. The Country Store is open daily.

JOAN PETERS OF OSTERVILLE
885 Main St., Osterville
(508) 428-3418
www.joanpeters.com
Interior designer Joan Peters brings together the elements of her own original paintings, wall coverings, hand-painted furniture, sinks, and tiles to create a distinctive, coordinated look. Peters custom designs carpets, and her hand-painted sinks and tiles are not only designed and painted on-site but also fired in kilns at the studio. Open Mon through Sat.

LADY BUG KNITTING SHOP

612 Rte. 6A, Dennis
(508) 385-2662
www.ladybugknitting.com

In business since 1982, this shop concentrates on knitting only. In the Kings Grant complex, the shop carries lots of yarn, needles, supplies, shawl pins, and books on knitting. Owner Barbara Prue offers knitting classes for all levels. The shop is open year-round, daily in summer and Mon through Sat the rest of the year.

LINDA BURKE

633 Rte. 6A, Dennis
(508) 385-8102

Linda Burke specializes in clothing that is classic and comfortable. The store maintains a customer registry that makes wardrobe-building easier and gift-giving error proof. Owner Linda Burke does all the alterations herself—you won't find this kind of service in larger stores. The shop is open year-round.

THE MILL STORE

42 East Main St. (Route 28), West Yarmouth
(508) 775-3818
www.millstores.com

This store has a large selection of unfinished furniture and craft items and is simply a fun place to explore if you are feeling creative or thinking it's time to make some changes in your personal space. Prices are excellent, and the store is open daily. The Mill Store has other locations in Dennisport and West Harwich.

OAK & IVORY

1112 Main St., Osterville
(508) 428-9425
www.oakandivory.com

This shop is owned and operated by a sixth-generation Nantucketer who makes classic Nantucket baskets on the premises. It also carries antique reproductions of tables, chairs, hutches, chests, and side chairs. The shop is open daily in summer and in Dec and closed Sun the rest of the year.

PARNASSUS BOOK SERVICE

Route 6A, Yarmouthport
(508) 362-6420
www.parnassusbooks.com

Housed in an 1840s building, Parnassus is a book-lover's dream come true. There are books everywhere—filling the floor-to-ceiling shelves, stacked on the wooden floor, piled in boxes. The shop carries extensive collections in such subjects as maritime history, fine arts, antiques, and Cape Cod and colonial American history; it also carries many publications you won't find anywhere else, such as old town reports. It is open Mon through Sat year-round.

THE PICKET FENCE

4225 Route 6A, Cummaquid
(508) 362-4865

Behind a picket fence is the Picket Fence, a great old barn and 1880s carriage house filled with unique decorative items and collectibles. You'll find hand-painted furniture, pottery, antique dolls, and a terrific assortment of holiday decorations. In Nov, you will often find free hot cider and cookies greeting you.

The shop closes after Christmas and opens again in spring.

PONDSIDE GIFTS & BOUTIQUE

1198 Main St., Route 28, South Yarmouth
(508) 760-1190
www.pondsidegifts.com

This unique gift store and boutique is located in the Hearth 'N Kettle Plaza on Route 28 (see our Restaurants chapter) and offers a great selection of gifts and accessories. Their lovely pilgrim glass vases and lamps are made with gold and lead crystal and have a beautiful cranberry color. In the boutique they've got evening bags and attractive angora coats and cardigans. The store is open year-round Mon through Sat.

PURITAN CAPE COD

408 Main St., Hyannis
(508) 775-2400, (800) 924-0606
www.puritancapecod.com

This family-owned retail clothing store represents three generations of commitment to Cape Cod and has a very traditional feel. Puritan carries a complete line of men's and women's clothing, including sportswear and performance shoes. Puritan also rents and conditions skis.

The company introduced its own beautiful four-color Cape Cod tartan plaid several years ago and offers men's and women's clothing in this handsome material. Puritan has other locations in Chatham, Falmouth, and Mashpee Commons. The stores are open Mon through Sat (except for the store in Mashpee Commons, which is open on Sun).

ROSS COPPELMAN JEWELERS
1439 Rte. 6A, Dennis
(508) 385-7900
www.rosscoppelman.com
Ross Coppelman's unusual and classic gemstones are displayed in striking settings, many of them inspired by ancient Egyptian, Aztec, and Roman designs but with a contemporary flair. Just west of the Route 134 junction, the shop has two showrooms of gold and silver jewelry and a workshop where it is created. Coppelman, who opened his business in 1971, designs and produces custom jewelry, including wedding rings, and also resets stones. The shop is open year-round.

THE SHOE SALON
837 Main St., Osterville
(508) 428-2410
www.theshoesalon.com
You'll find shoes by Cole Haan, Kate Spade, and Stuart Weitzman, along with accessories such as jewelry, handbags, and even a few select sweaters. In addition to dressier shoes, the store carries men's and women's Mephisto walking shoes, which have been handmade in France for more than 30 years. The shop is open daily during the season but closed on Sun during the winter. A second Shoe Salon is located on Main Street in Chatham (508-945-0292).

THE SILVER UNICORN
941 Rte. 28, South Yarmouth
(508) 394-8401
www.silverunicorncapecod.com
The Silver Unicorn has an extensive line of nautical jewelry—bracelets, charms, rings, and earrings in gold and sterling silver—with a Cape Cod theme (maps, lobster traps, and whale tails). The shop also sells nautical glass sculpture, Spencer Collins lighthouse replicas, and other maritime mementos. It's open daily.

TOBEY FARM
352 Rte. 6A, Dennis
(508) 385-2930
Tucked inside this more-than-300-year-old working farm—one of the best stops on the Cape for fresh fruits and vegetables—is a small shopping area featuring exquisite, reasonably priced dried floral wreaths and centerpieces made from lavender, eucalyptus, rosebuds, and yarrow. Freshly baked pies and a variety of locally bottled jams and jellies are irresistible. It's open year-round. Don't miss their Halloween celebration, which includes hayrides for children.

WEST BARNSTABLE TABLES
2454 Rte. 149, West Barnstable
(508) 362-2676
www.westbarnstabletables.com
Stephen Whittlesey and Richard Kiusalas produce handmade custom furniture in a primitive style that retains and emphasizes the color and texture of the natural wood, much of which is about 100 years old, salvaged from New England houses, barns, and boats. The shop also converts antique windows into frames for mirrors. Trestle, Shaker, farm table, and pedestal legs accent the distinctive tables. They display unique folk art cupboards created from antique wood and found pieces such as ship portholes. The large, year-round showroom is open daily.

THE WHIPPLETREE
660 Rte. 6A, West Barnstable
(508) 362-3320

Housed in a beautiful, 18th-century barn, the Whippletree is filled with gifts and home accessories with a country flavor, including cotton coverlets, dried flowers and wreaths, greeting cards, candles, and hand-carved birds. Some popular collectible lines include Christopher Radko, Charming Tails, and the Boyds Collection. You can also select gifts for the holidays and items for children and babies. The Whippletree is open seven days a week from June to Dec and Thurs through Sun, with a gradual return to a seven-day schedule, in the spring. The Whippletree is closed in Jan, Feb, and Mar.

WILD BIRDS UNLIMITED
1198 Rte. 28, South Yarmouth
(508) 760-1996
www.wbu.com
Bird lovers flock here for bird feeders (priced from $3 to $300) and plenty of seed and suet. The bird-themed paraphernalia goes on and on: hand-carved birds, jewelry, music boxes, clothing, songbird tapes, videos, books, and all kinds of educational materials. Wild Birds Unlimited has standing and hanging baths in wood, iron, concrete, ceramic, and plastic that can be hung from trees, mounted on a deck, or placed in your gardens. The store is open seven days a week.

YANKEE ACCENT
23 Wianno Ave., Osterville
(508) 428-2332
www.yankeeaccent.com
A cross between a gift shop and a gallery, this more-than-30-year-old business with a nautical focus carries prints and originals by well-known local artists such as Kathy O'Neil and Nancy Braginton-Smith. It also carries gifts for the home and books by New England authors. The store is open Tues through Sat from May to Jan and on Sat only the rest of the year.

YANKEE CRAFTERS SCANDINAVIAN IMPORTS INC.
48 North Main St., South Yarmouth
(508) 394-0575
www.yankeecraftersinc.com

Going once . . .

A great way to pick up antiques, art, and collectibles is at auction. If you're unfamiliar with the auction scene, attend one or two as a spectator before going to bid. The Robert C. Eldred Company on Route 6A in Dennis is the oldest auction house on the Cape. The company holds at least 12 sales throughout the year; call (508) 385-3116, or visit www.eldreds.com for a free schedule. The Sandwich Auction House (508-888-1926, www.sandwichauction.com) holds auctions every Saturday, and almost every Wednesday in July and August.

Thousands of pieces of handcrafted wampum (cylindrical beads made from shells, once used by Native Americans as ornaments and currency) jewelry—rings, pins, earrings, and bolas—are offered at very reasonable prices. Also among the collections are Scandinavian jewelry, linens, calendars, crystal, and Norwegian trolls. The building is listed on the National Register of Historic Places. Yankee Crafters is open daily.

Lower Cape

ALLEN HARBOR NAUTICAL GIFTS
335 Lower County Rd., Harwich Port
(508) 432-0353, (800) 832-2467
www.capecodnauticalgifts.com
Even landlubbers will enjoy the incredible selection of items found here. There are jigsaw puzzles and calendars commemorating various Cape Cod landmarks, T-shirts, watches, books, jewelry, doormats, and decorative household treats. Allen Harbor also sells a great selection of tide clocks and wind and weather instruments. The shop, which also does mail order, is closed weekends during the off-season except at Christmastime.

ATLANTIC SPICE COMPANY
2 Shore Rd., North Truro
(800) 316-7965
www.atlanticspice.com
This warehouse sells row after row of spices and herbs, from allspice to vanilla beans and everything in between. You can buy in bulk (one- or five-pound packages) or, if you're unsure of the potency of a particular spice, you can buy a smaller sampler bag or ask for a taste. Atlantic also sells a wide range of teas (loose and in tea bags), shelled nuts, seeds, potpourri, and baking items. The shop is open daily year-round.

THE BASEBALL SHOP
26 Main St., Orleans
(508) 240-1063
www.baseballshoporleans.com
The store stocks more than 1,000 different baseball caps, as well as trading cards, bumper stickers, autographed material, and select clothing. It's open year-round, daily in season and closed Tues in winter.

BEN FRANKLIN
631 Main St., Chatham
(508) 945-0655
www.benfranklinchatham.com
This old-fashioned five-and-dime store carries a wide variety of merchandise, from art supplies and toys to greeting cards, mugs, and T-shirts. Kids gravitate to this shop because it sells baseball cards, model kits, and classics like Play-Doh and Silly Putty, and adults like it because it sells grown-up essentials such as desk blotters, calendars, and magazines. The shop is closed Sun in the off-season.

BETH BISHOP SHOP
45 South Orleans Rd., Orleans
(508) 255-0642, (800) 287-0642
www.capecod-orleans.com/bethbishop
Locals will tell you that Beth Bishop "is always in style." Known for its service and wide selection of fine-quality dresses, sportswear, beachwear, sleepwear, and outerwear, it's been a favorite Cape-wide clothing store since 1955. The shop is open year-round, seven days a week.

BIRD WATCHER'S GENERAL STORE
36 Rte. 6A, Orleans
(508) 255-6974, (800) 562-1512
www.birdwatchersgeneralstore.com
Since 1983 owner Mike O'Connor's entire focus is on the needs of both birds and bird-watchers. This is the place to buy a bird feeder—the store carries more than 100, not to mention tons of bird feed to fill them! You can't be a bird-watcher without binoculars, and Bird Watcher's carries some 40 types. It also stocks a comprehensive selection of bird books and T-shirts, socks, door knockers, welcome mats, sun catchers, magnets, gift wrap, and note cards. Tell the super-friendly staff a joke, and they'll give you a gift. The shop is closed Thanksgiving and Christmas, and the rest of the year you'll find the daily hours (often down to the second) posted on a board out front.

BOOKSMITH/MUSICSMITH
Skaket Corners
Route 6A and West Road, Orleans
(508) 255-4590
This is a great place to shop if you're into books and your other half is into music. You'll both be happy browsing here, as half the store is devoted to hardcover and softcover books, and the other half is compact discs and tapes. The store also sells calendars, magazines, and videos and has a great children's corner in back. It's open daily year-round.

BREWSTER BOOK STORE
2648 Rte. 6A, Brewster
(508) 896-6543
www.brewsterbookstore.com
This delightful little shop is filled to the brim with hardcover and paperback books, with a strong local-author and local-interest section and a terrific children's section. It also sells unusual cards and stationery. The shop holds regular book signings, especially with local authors, and offers weekly story times for little ones. It's open daily.

THE BREWSTER STORE
1935 Rte. 6A, Brewster
(508) 896-3744
www.brewsterstore.com

Erected as a Unitarian church in 1852, the Brewster Store is a landmark and a tradition. Revered by locals and visitors alike, it's a take-your-time kind of place where you grab a cup of coffee, a doughnut, and a newspaper and sit out on the porch and watch the world go by. You can buy linens, mugs, teapots, cookbooks, jams, and T-shirts, among other items. Children love coming in to pick out penny candy and put dimes in the turn-of-the-20th-century player piano, which gives the place a rollicking ragtime sound. The shop is open daily.

CABOT'S CANDY
276 Commercial St., Provincetown
(508) 487-3550
www.cabotscandy.com
The Cicero clan began making fudge and saltwater taffy on the premises in 1969. Stand inside or in front of the huge picture window and watch as a massive spool of taffy is tamed into individually wrapped bite-size pieces. (Ask for a free sample.) The flavors sometimes change, but you can be sure of finding cranberry, grape, chocolate, cherry, piña colada, licorice, orange-pineapple, and their signature flavor, molasses peanut butter. Cabot's also sells sugar-free taffy, but sweet tooths may prefer options including fudge (made in 16 flavors), peanut brittle, and caramel honey crunch popcorn. It's open only holidays and weekends in the off-season.

CHATHAM CANDY MANOR
484 Main St., Chatham
(508) 945-0825, (800) 221-6497
www.candymanor.com
People from all over the world have visited Chatham Candy Manor for the caloric concoctions that they make in small batches, then hand-dip every day in the same tradition started more than 50 years ago by the store's founder, Naomi Turner. The selection is endless: chocolate-dipped fruits (including apricots, pears, and pineapples in dark or milk chocolate), hazelnut puree and chocolate treats shaped like scallops, and cranberry cordials (fresh fruit melded with bonbon crème

and liqueur, then covered with pure chocolate). Even the barley lollipops are kettle cooked and poured by hand. Mail order is available; call for a brochure and price list. The shop is open daily.

CHATHAM GLASS COMPANY
758 Main St., Chatham
(508) 945-5547
www.chathamglass.com
Glassblower Jim Holmes is the force behind the vibrant contemporary glass pieces you'll find here. The bud vases evoke jeweled candied apples, and the kaleidoscopic bowls and sleek candlesticks would liven up any table. Holmes's work is carried by several fancy department stores and featured in the collections of museums like the Philadelphia Museum of Art and the Corning Glass Museum. If your taste is more traditional, this is also the place to order the small, colonial-style "bulls-eye" glass window panes that you may have been admiring in local historical homes. Look in on the working studio if you want to see how it's all done. Open Mon through Sat.

CHATHAM JAM AND JELLY SHOP
10 Vineyard Ave., West Chatham
(508) 945-3052
www.chathamjamandjellyshop.com
This shop, in a residential area just off Route 28, sells more than 75 varieties of homemade preserves, and several concoctions (wild beach plum, cranberry, and wild blackberry) are from fruit handpicked on Cape Cod. The shop offers taste sampling, so you can't go wrong. Gift sets and mail order are available. Open Mon through Sat in season, and Thurs through Sat in the off-season.

COLLECTOR'S WORLD
4100 U.S. Rte. 6, Eastham
(508) 255-3616
www.collectorsworldcapecod.com
This shop carries both antique and new collectibles, including dolls, Bosson wall heads, model cars, lighthouses, and cottage figurines. It also sells quality jewelry and unusual wooden toys for children. The shop is open Mon through Sat (and

"Sunday by chance") year-round, but during the winter it is best to call ahead.

CRAZY HORSE TACK AND GIFT SHOP
125 Rte. 6A, Orleans
(508) 240-2244, (800) 243-4003
www.equestrian-tack.com

This shop sells all sorts of equine products, from saddles and bridles to riding apparel, jewelry, and toys. There's a selection of gift items such as coffee mugs, key chains, and books, so if you've got a horse lover on your gift list, this is the place to go. The shop sells both English and western tack and apparel and also carries plenty of horse-care products. It's open year-round Mon through Sat.

THE ECLECTIC COMPANY
14 Commercial St., Wellfleet
(508) 349-1775
www.wellfleeteclectic.com

This aptly named shop offers a diverse assortment of unusual home accessories, clothing, and jewelry. You'll find hand-painted furniture, colorful ceramics, linens, and unique accents for your home, such as garden accessories. It's open daily in summer and on weekends in spring and fall; the shop closes after Columbus Day and reopens again in Apr.

EXUMA FINE JEWELRY
283 Commercial St., Provincetown
(508) 487-2746
www.exumajewelry.com

Exuma specializes in custom jewelry, creating classic and modern designs in 14- and 18-karat gold and platinum. Rings are big here—gorgeous settings of sapphires, rubies, emeralds, and diamonds glitter in the cases. Jeweler and craftsman Gunter Hanelt, originally from Germany, favors clean, uncomplicated designs that never go out of style. The showroom, located diagonally across from Town Hall, is open year-round, daily in summer, six days a week (closed Wed) through Christmas, and on weekends only from Jan through Mar.

i For an out-of-the-ordinary shopping treat, visit Marine Specialties at 235 Commercial St. in Provincetown. This small warehouse stocks a broad range of stuff, from army-navy surplus items, to camping and sailing supplies.

FOCALPOINT STUDIO
Post Office Square, Main Sreet, Orleans
(508) 255-6617, (800) 696-6617
www.focalpointstudio.com

Focalpoint specializes in family portraits, which are often done at the beach. Local photographer/owner Bob Tucker has created traditional portraits for hundreds upon hundreds of families and is also adept at restoring precious heirloom photographs. Focalpoint will also produce photo images on T-shirts, mouse pads, and other items. They offer framing services, color laser copies, and fax service. It's open year-round.

THE GLASS EYE
3 Main St., Unit A, Eastham
(508) 255-5044

All the stained-glasswork displayed in the gallery is by owner John Knight, but the shop also carries blown glass, handcrafted jewelry, and gift items from a variety of other artists, many of them local. In addition to glasswork, the gallery sells wonderful handmade paper creations by co-owner Donna Knight, who often offers papermaking demonstrations. Be sure to visit the working stained-glass studio downstairs. Scrap glass is free for the asking, and you can even take lessons in the off-season. The shop is open daily through Christmas and closed on Sun from Jan to spring.

GOOD SCENTS
351 Commercial St., Provincetown
(508) 487-3393
www.goodscentsptown.com

This small store is filled with all you need to pamper yourself (or someone else)—lovely scented soaps, shampoos, and lotions, along with bath brushes, luxurious robes, and massage oils. Choose from a variety of skin-care products, and lotions, shampoos, and bath gels custom-scented with essential or perfume oils. The shop happily makes up gift baskets and does mail order. It's open daily in season and weekends during the off-season.

THE GOOSE HUMMOCK SHOP
15 Rte. 6A, Orleans
(508) 255-0455, (508) 255-2620 (boat store)
www.goose.com
Outdoor enthusiasts find the Goose Hummock Shop ideal for one-stop shopping. From bait and fishing equipment to camping gear, firearms, clothing, canoes, kayaks, and bicycles, it's all sold and serviced by a knowledgeable staff either here or in the store right behind the main one. The shop is open daily.

GREAT CAPE HERBS
2628 Rte. 6A, Brewster
(508) 896-5900, (800) 427-7144
www.greatcape.com
This all-natural herbal apothecary has an encyclopedic assortment of Western and Chinese herbs stored in glass containers on rough-hewn shelves. You'll also find books on herbs and natural healing. Vegetarian alert: Peta's Place, an on-site cafe, serves up organic, vegetarian lunches, and for caffeine devotees, the Great Cape Espresso Cafe offers organic lattes and fresh pastries from Confectionately Yours. The shop is open daily.

HANDCRAFT HOUSE
3966 Rte. 6A, Brewster
(508) 240-1412
www.handcrafthousegallery.com
One of our favorites, Handcraft House serves as a showcase for owner Eileen Smith's beautiful watercolors, many of them Cape landscapes. It also carries a variety of fine, handcrafted items largely by New England craftspeople. You'll find colorful hand-woven scarves, iron-forged candlesticks, wood marquetry boxes, glass sun catchers, and jewelry, among many other items. The shop is open daily in season, on weekends in late fall, and is closed from Jan to mid-Apr.

HERRIDGE BOOKS
140 Main St., Wellfleet
(508) 349-1323
The books here are in such great shape that many customers cannot believe they are used. Don't miss the lower level, reached via a yellow stairway with an unusual handrail made from an oar; you'll find some wonderful old volumes there. Bird lovers will relish the limited-edition Audubon prints that are based on originals and sanctioned by the Audubon Society. Herridge Books is open daily during the summer and open sporadically throughout the off-season. Call for hours.

HOPKINS HOUSE
2727 Rte. 6A, Brewster
(508) 896-9337, (508) 896-3450 (bakery)
You may have a hard time distinguishing between the old and the new in this shop, located in a historic home and filled with a blend of antiques, reproductions, and folk art by owner Mary Beth Baxter, who has a knack for creating paintings that look as if they've been waiting a century for you to discover them. The attached bakery, run by Baxter's daughter, sells irresistible scones, muffins, sticky buns, and breads. The shop is open Tues through Sun through Christmas and closed Jan to mid-May.

JULES BESCH STATIONERS
15 Bank St., Wellfleet
(508) 349-1231
Proprietor Michael Tuck's store bears testimony to his belief that letter writing need not be a lost art. Glorious blank and versed cards for everyday and special occasions line the aisles of his store, along with beautifully colored blank stationery sold by the sheet. Wooden racks hold luxurious wrapping paper, also sold by the sheet. The shop also offers calligraphy services and carries an array of inkwells and ink and fountain and quill pens. It's closed Dec through Mar and open daily during the summer. Call for hours during the remainder of the year.

KEMP POTTERY
9 Rte. 6A, Orleans
(508) 255-5853
www.kemppottery.com
Here's your chance to see a potter at work, as this is not only Steve Kemp's store but also his studio and has been since 1978. His varied designs, often inspired by nature, include lamps, sinks, tiles, bird feeders, fountains, and sculpture, and many of them are made with Nauset Beach sand. Kemp also does unique bas relief signs, several of which can be seen at the Cape Cod Museum of Natural History in Brewster. His functional pieces, including dinnerware, are lead-free and safe for the oven, dishwasher, and microwave. Open daily in season, Mon to Sat off-season.

KID & KABOODLE
115 Rte. 6A, Orleans
(508) 240-0460
www.cribrentalscapecod.com
Whether you need a gift for a baby shower, play clothes for your toddler, or a christening gown for your grandchild, this is the place to come. If you're shopping with little ones, they can play with the toys in the back room while you browse. Kid & Kaboodle also carries maternity clothes and rents baby furniture. It's open daily.

ℹ️ Every Saturday from mid-May through mid-October, you can buy the freshest Cape Cod–grown fruits and vegetables, cultivated mushrooms, local honey, herbs, and flowers—even freshly caught fish—at the Orleans Farmers' Market, Old Colony Way, near the Dunkin' Donuts.

LEMON TREE VILLAGE SHOPS
Route 6A, Brewster
Located in west Brewster, this complex is one-stop shopping for everything from kids' toys to pastries to cookware. The 15 shops and two cafes include La Bodega (508 896-7340, www.capelabodega.com), for unusual women's clothing, jewelry, and gifts; Lemon Tree Pottery (508 896-3065, www.lemontreepottery.com) for pot-

tery, ceramics, jewelry, and lawn ornaments; The Village Toy Store (508 896-8185, www.thevillage toystorebrewster.com), with everything for kids of all ages; and The Cook Shop (508 896-7698, www.cookshopcapecod.com), with cookware, coffeemakers, waffle irons, and obscure kitchen utensils like truffle slicers and lemon zesters. Upstairs in the Cook Shop is the tabletop shop, with dinnerware, cutlery, containers, baskets, linens, and every other necessity for the nicely set table—even the tables and chairs themselves. Grab a cup of joe and a sweet for breakfast at Cafe Alfresco. Shops are open daily.

LINDA'S ORIGINALS
220 Rte. 6A, Brewster
(508) 385-2285, (800) 385-2284
See The Yankee Craftsman on page 135.

MAD AS A HATTER
360 Commercial St., Provincetown
(508) 487-4063
Though Mad Hatter sells jackets, shirts, and scarves, people head here for the crowning touch. Choose from zany headgear, such as a multicolored beanie with a propeller, or more traditional, classic designs. You can also get custom-made hats here. The shop is open year-round.

MONAHAN AND COMPANY
540 Rte. 28, Harwich Port
(508) 432-3302, (800) 237-4605
www.monahanjewelers.com
Monahan and Co. designs and manufactures hundreds of styles of nautical and seashore-related jewelry. They also custom-design nautical pieces in 14- and 18-karat gold and platinum. Other specialties include Claddagh rings, brass ball markers for stylish golfers, wind indicators, and the distinctive Cape Cod line of jewelry, silver and gold pieces accented with 14K balls. Monahan and Co. is open daily May through Oct and weekends in the off-season.

NORTHERN LIGHTS HAMMOCKS
361 Commercial St., Provincetown
(508) 487-2385
www.northernlightshammocks.com

The friendly staff at Northern Lights Hammocks will try to get you to sample the swinging, swaying merchandise, whether it is made of rope, cotton, hemp, silk, Textilene, or canvas. Some of the hammocks here are true works of art. One award-winning Danish model features a teak and stainless steel stand that could harmonize with the decor of even the chicest home. The shop is open daily in season and weekends only off-season.

NOW VOYAGER BOOKSTORE & GALLERY
357 Commercial St., Provincetown
(508) 487-0848
www.nowvoyagerbooks.com
Best known for its collection of gay and lesbian books, Now Voyager also has the latest in fiction and nonfiction and a large mystery section. It has a sampling of CDs, cassettes, and videos as well as used books and has expanded to include a gallery featuring works by international artists. The shop closes for the month of Jan.

OCEANA
1 Main St. Square, Orleans
(508) 240-1414
www.oceanacapecod.com
Oceana carries lovely jewelry, candlesticks, nature books, and original art, wall hangings, rugs, and hand-painted tables, along with many other items. Oceana Kids, located next door, is filled with nature-oriented toys, rubber stamps, and mariposa bunny utensils. Don't miss these shops; they are open daily.

ORLEANS WHOLE FOOD STORE
46 Main St., Orleans
(508) 255-6540
www.orleanswholefoodstore.com
This is a true health food store, where you can buy grains and cereals in bulk and purchase freshly ground peanut butter, vitamins, and a wide variety of organic products, including produce. It's also a great place to grab a quick lunch, as the store makes healthy sandwiches, soups, and sometimes pizza. This good-for-you shop carries a nice selection of books, with an emphasis

on spiritual topics, self-help themes, and cooking; lovely, unusual greeting cards; and Crabtree & Evelyn soaps and lotions—not to mention calendars and T-shirts. It's open daily with extended hours in the summer.

PENTIMENTO
584 Main St., Chatham
(508) 945-0178
This shop has wonderful ambience—maybe it's the fact that it sells indulgent items such as luxurious clothing from designers like Sigrid Olsen and Eileen Fisher, pretty blank journals, fine stationery, scarves, and jewelry. It also carries whimsical picture frames, bejeweled sandals, clever totes, and home accessories. Call for hours during the off-season.

PEWTER CRAFTER OF CAPE COD
791 Rte. 28, Harwich Port
(508) 432-5858
www.capecodpewter.com
Artist and craftsman Ron Kusins reveals the simple beauty of a metal that is often overlooked. The shop features unique decanters, candlesticks, vases, plates, cups, and other items done in traditional and contemporary styles that are both decorative and functional. It's open weekends; calls are welcome for appointments.

THE POTTED GERANIUM
188 Rte. 28, West Harwich
(508) 432-1114
www.pottedgeranium.com
Every room of this old Cape Cod house is filled with wonderful home accessories, folk art, crafts, and gifts. You'll find pewter bookmarks made in Chatham, locally produced weathervane Christmas ornaments, hand-painted mirrors, baskets, ceramics, linens, Vera Bradley bags, and even paper jewelry. If a new mom or baby is on your gift list, visit the baby room for blankets, layettes, clothes, and wooden toys. Or check the kitchen for flavored teas and coffees, kitchen utensils and linens, and a sampling of jellies and jams from the Chatham Jam and Jelly Shop. Open daily in season.

PROVINCETOWN BOOKSHOP
246 Commercial St., Provincetown
(508) 487-0964
Open since 1964, this year-round shop is filled floor-to-ceiling with hardcover and paperback books, everything from poetry and plays to best sellers, with a good selection of Cape Cod books. It's open daily.

SALTY DUCK POTTERY
115 Main St., Wellfleet
(508) 349-3342
Katherine Stillman's wheel-thrown pottery has a free and easy quality to it. Many of the plates and cups are designed with free-form pears and abstract designs. All her wares are lead-free and can go from oven to dishwasher. We also give Katherine credit for her open-door policy: If you want to buy something and she's not there, simply leave cash or fill out a charge slip. Her trust is as beautiful as her pottery.

THE SECRET GARDEN
321 Main St., Wellfleet
(508) 349-1444
This two-story garden is overrun with charming garden art, folk art, twig love seats, garden goodies, crushed-velvet hats, birdhouses, animal marionettes, and an eclectic selection of jewelry. Open Apr through Dec.

THE STRAWBERRY PATCH
2550 Rte. 6A, Brewster
(508) 896-5050
www.brewsterstore.com/strawberry_patch .php
This red-shuttered old horse barn is the exclusive home of Hand-tiques, the name owner Mary Anne Boyd coined for her unique array of gifts. Many of the goods are displayed in antique display cases: A cast-iron stove holds cookie cutters, and old post office boxes cradle candles.

The shop carries U.S.-made cotton throws, pillows, and tablecloths, along with kitchenware, dolls, gifts, candy, and Christmas decorations. The Strawberry Patch is open daily.

SUSAN BAKER MEMORIAL MUSEUM
46 Rte. 6A, North Truro
(508) 487-2557
www.susanbakerart.com
Everyone has a right to his or her own idiosyncrasies, and Susan Baker is no exception. Not wanting to wait until she dies to have her own memorial museum, she opened this pop palace in 1984. Once you spot Susan's work, you won't forget her startling and brightly colored pieces, which are sometimes three-dimensional, sometimes satirical, sometimes in the form of printed booklets. The shop is open daily in season and erratically off-season (ring the bell at the side door if you'd like to see the collection in the off-season).

SYDENSTRICKER GALLERIES
490 Rte. 6A, Brewster
(508) 385-3272
www.sydenstricker.com
The glass made here is so dazzling that several American embassies serve dessert to their guests on Sydenstricker plates, inspired by the art of ancient Egypt. Choose from dishes in various sizes (some with a signature rippled edge), complete place settings, rectangular serving plates, candy dishes, even ashtrays. Two showcases are filled with glass paperweights. You can watch the glass being made Tue through Sat from 10 a.m. to 2:30 p.m. The shop is open daily.

THE WHALE'S EYE
653 Route 28, Chatham
(508) 945-3084
Housed in an old barn, the Whale's Eye has an array of beautifully hand-painted furniture and mirrors. All the work is by Suzanne and John Rocanello, who opened the shop in the barn adjacent to their home in the late 1970s and soon after began marketing their creations at craft shows all over the Cape (see our Annual Events chapter). At the shop you'll see chests, boxes, tables, and mirrors, many painted with nautical scenes. The Rocanellos do a lot of custom work, and if you bring in a fabric swatch or wallpaper strip, they'll be happy to use colors that will work

with your decor. The shop is open daily in summer and a bit sporadically in spring and fall. It's open by appointment only in the winter.

WELLFLEET FLEA MARKET
**U.S. Route 6, within the Wellfleet
Drive-in, South Wellfleet
(508) 349-2520, (508) 349-0541
www.wellfleetfleamarket.com**

This outdoor extravaganza and Cape Cod institution since 1957 features more than 200 vendors selling everything from imported dresses, leather bags, and fleece vests to used books, antiques, and handmade furniture. It's open from 8 a.m. to 3 p.m. Sat and Sun mid-Apr through Oct. During July and Aug the Flea Market is open Sat, Sun, Wed, and Thurs. It's also open on holiday Mondays. Admission is $1 to $2 per carload, depending on the day. If you stay long enough to get hungry, you can grab a bite at the snack bar. There are restrooms for your convenience, too. Many of the vendors accept credit cards; many are also open to price haggling.

THE WHITMAN HOUSE QUILT SHOP
**U.S. Route 6 at Great Hollow Road, North
Truro
(508) 487-3204, (877) 487-3204
www.whitmanhousequilts.com**

This store is housed in a former schoolhouse that is the oldest structure in Truro. The specialty here is Amish quilts, new and old. The two floors also showcase modern-day cranberry glass, teddy bears, a profusion of potpourri, brass beds, and dolls. It's closed in the off-season.

THE YANKEE CRAFTSMEN
**220 Rte. 6A, Brewster
(508) 385-4758, (800) 385-4758**

Perched side by side on a hill, these two stores have been delighting collectors for a more than a decade. Linda's Originals carries a wide range of hand-painted clothing and handcrafted items and the largest selection of afghans on the Cape. The store is also home to the Cats Meow, a captivating collection of miniature handcrafted buildings.

The Yankee Craftsmen abounds with collectible items made by crafters, both local and worldwide. It has one of the largest collections of Byers Choice Carolers in the country, as well as Harbour Lights lighthouses. In the summer, be sure to visit the lavish, award-winning flower gardens. The shops are open daily.

YANKEE DOODLE SHOP
**181 Rte. 28, West Harwich
(508) 432-0579
www.yankeedoodleshop.com**

Room after room of finished and unfinished quality country furniture, all made right on the premises, are offered at prices so low you'll question the price tag. Yankee Doodle markets a wide selection of onion lamps and decorative storage boxes, hand-painted bureaus, and cast aluminum eagles—even authentic spinning wheels. In the off-season it's open Sat and Sun only. During the season they are generally open daily but call for hours.

YANKEE INGENUITY
**525 Main St., Chatham
(508) 945-1288, (888) 945-9123
www.yankee-ingenuity.com**

Half gallery, half gift shop, Yankee Ingenuity carries unusual items in a wide range of prices, making it an ideal place for gift-shopping. You'll find sports ball banks, cunning lighthouse ornaments, unusual mirrors, beautiful Cape Cod photography, clocks, desk accessories, oversize stuffed animals, even Tiffany-style lamps. The shop is filled with interesting and beautiful things, from Impressionist-print umbrellas to jewelry, letter openers, and desk sets fashioned from shells. It's open daily.

YELLOW UMBRELLA BOOKS
**501 Main St., Chatham
(508) 945-0144, (800) 471-0144
www.yellowumbrellabooks.com**

Yellow Umbrella has been offering locals and tourists the latest in fiction and nonfiction best sellers, used books, and works by local authors since 1979. The store also has an extensive section of books about Cape Cod. It carries rare and out-of-print books, used hardcover and paperback books, and they will do special orders. Be sure to visit the outdoor bargain racks—any book is a buck. It's open daily year-round.

ANTIQUES

There are those who come to the Cape not only for its lovely beaches, but also for its proliferation of great antiques shops. Every town has more than a few places to browse among old things, with some dealers specializing in certain items such as pattern glass, early American furniture, or old tools, and others carrying a smattering of diverse items. A number of antiques cooperatives and centers have sprung up on the Cape for those who like variety.

Listing every antiques shop could easily fill a whole book, so we've focused on a few favorites here. You're sure to find others as you travel the Cape, particularly on the north side, where historic Route 6A is an antiques-lover's paradise. Hours can vary, so to be safe call ahead.

Upper Cape

AURORA BOREALIS ANTIQUES
194 Lakeview Ave., Falmouth
(508) 548-8280

Here you'll find a quality line of Staffordshire, Orientalia, prints, furniture, nautical pieces, lamps, silver, and glass, along with ephemera and books. The shop is open by appointment and for antique shows.

HORSEFEATHERS ANTIQUES
454 Rte. 6A, East Sandwich
(508) 888-5298

Owner Jeanne Gresham has created a distinctly Victorian and feminine feeling in this lovely shop, which carries table and bed linens, antique lace and trim, and a mix of everyday and special items such as china teacups and paper valentines. Antique christening gowns and other children's clothing are usually available. Call ahead for an appointment.

i If you want to get the most out of your antiquing adventures, contact the Cape Cod Antiques Dealers Association for a listing of their members. Visit them online at www.ccada.com.

THE WEATHER STORE
146 Main St., Sandwich
(800) 646-1203
www.theweatherstore.com

This store is filled with antique weather instruments such as weather vanes, barometers, thermometers, books, and compasses, along with marine antiques such as spyglasses and 19th-century maps. The store is open Mon through Sat from Apr through Christmas and by appointment other times.

Mid-Cape

ANTIQUES CENTER OF CAPE COD
243 Rte. 6A, Dennis
(508) 385-6400
www.antiquecenterofcapecod.com

This huge center has more than 160 dealers selling everything from wooden iceboxes to old dolls. With four massive buildings situated on four acres of land, this is easily the largest antiques center on the Cape. It's open daily all year except Jan through Mar, when it's closed on Wed.

SOW'S EAR ANTIQUE COMPANY
4698 Rte. 28, Cotuit
(508) 428-4931
www.sowsearantiqueco.com

The Sow's Ear is in a 1729 house that is considered the oldest in Cotuit. This period home is filled with 18th- and 19th-century furnishings and accessories. Here you might find unusual furniture, rugs, baskets, dolls, decoys, vases, silver, folk art, or other treasures. Blended among the antiques are some new items, such as candles and light fixtures. The shop is open year-round, Tues through Sun, 10 a.m. to 5 p.m.

STANLEY WHEELOCK
870 Main St., Osterville
(508) 420-3170

This established Osterville business is known for its comprehensive line of American, English, and Continental furniture, decorative accessories, china, glass, and fine prints. It is open Mon through Sat from Apr through Dec and by chance or appointment from Jan through Mar.

Lower Cape

THE FARMHOUSE ANTIQUES ETC.
U.S. Route 6 and Village Lane, South Wellfleet
(508) 349-1708
www.farmhouseantiques.com
This old farmhouse is jammed with cast-iron cookware, vintage linen, decorative pieces, and more postcards, trading cards, advertising ads, and magazines than you'll know what to do with. You can also find restored antique lamps, lighting fixtures, and original pieces by local artist Diane Vetromile, who has been known to cover an entire table with buttons to fabulous effect. The shop is open daily in season, closed Tues during the winter.

HARWICH ANTIQUES CENTER
10 Rte. 28, West Harwich
(580) 432-4220
www.harwichantiquescenter.com
This two-building complex has more than 140 dealers displaying furniture, paintings, Lionel trains, model ships, art deco, Griswold, Orientals, primitives, vintage dolls, old radios, and other intriguing antiquities. There's a large assortment of majolica, along with porcelain, dinnerware, linen, and quilts. The center is open daily all year.

HOUSE ON THE HILL
17 Seaview St., Chatham
(508) 945-2290
You'll find a delightful collection of baseball cards and sports memorabilia, political pins, toys, old advertisements, postcards, and Cape Cod memorabilia here, along with glass, china, and small furniture. The shop keeps regular hours from Memorial Day to Labor Day, usually until dusk, and is open by chance or appointment the rest of the year.

MAPS OF ANTIQUITY
1409 Rte. 28, Chatham
(508) 945-1660
www.mapsofantiquity.com
Maps of Antiquity mostly offers 19th-century maps, but it also has some earlier ones, including those of Massachusetts townships and other New England states. European and world maps, railroad maps, coastal charts, and early U.S. maps are also part of the collection. If you can't find a specific map in their inventory, the store may be able to order it. The shop is open seven days a week year-round.

PLEASANT BAY ANTIQUES
540 Rte. 28, South Orleans
(508) 255-0930
www.pleasantbayantiques.com
This shop, housed in a Victorian farmhouse and attached 18th-century barn, is filled with early American furniture, including tables, highboys, tiger maple desks, and four-poster beds. You're likely to find grandfather clocks, elegant secretary desks, and dining tables. Don't miss the decoy room, and be sure to visit the woodshed, which showcases marine antiques. The shop is open year-round Mon through Sat.

THE SPYGLASS
2257 Rte. 6A, Brewster
(508) 896-4423
This fascinating shop specializes in 18th- and 19th-century marine antiques. You'll find barometers, globes, sextants, writing boxes, maps, and navigation charts, as well as early American furniture and folk art. Open daily. Call ahead during the winter months.

ATTRACTIONS

In this chapter, we cover those destinations that reveal the Cape's rich history, natural beauty, and unique charm. These are historic landmarks, museums, and attractions dedicated to promoting an awareness and enjoyment of Cape Cod.

From Aptucxet Trading Post along the Cape Cod Canal to Pilgrim Monument in the heart of Provincetown, interesting, fun, educational, and inspiring places beckon. There are hundreds of organizations across Cape Cod that offer the visitor a glimpse into the past or provide a better understanding of the Cape's heritage. Among them are historic homes, sea captain's mansions, and historical buildings, including windmills, churches, meetinghouses, and homesteads.

Following is a list of Cape Cod's many attractions, including a walk through the pages of the Cape's history as provided by the many museums and historic sites scattered about the old carriage routes of the Cape's 15 proud towns. But don't forget to turn to other chapters—Kidstuff, Sports and Recreation, Beaches, and Boating and Water Sports, to name a few—for other interesting stops along the way.

UPPER CAPE

APTUCXET TRADING POST
24 Aptucxet Rd., Bourne
(508) 759-8167
www.bournehistoricalsoc.org
Aptucxet (pronounced Ap-tuc-set) is the site of a Pilgrim trading post, the first of its kind in the New World. Situated on the banks of what is now the Cape Cod Canal, this replica trading post (built in 1930) has displays that include a collection of prehistoric tools from the Wampanoag tribe and a rune stone supposedly chiseled by Vikings. Also on the grounds is a Victorian railroad station built by the Old Colony Railroad in 1892 for President Grover Cleveland (President Cleveland had a summer place in Bourne) and a Dutch-style Jefferson windmill shipped here from the Netherlands and once owned by 19th-century actor and Bourne resident Joseph Jefferson. The trading post is open Tues through Sat 10 a.m. to 4 p.m. and Sun 2 to 5 p.m. from late May through Columbus Day, and by appointment in early May and late Oct. Groups of 10 or more can arrange special tours. Admission is $4.00 for adults, $3.50 for senior citizens, and $2.00 for children ages 6 to 18.

BENJAMIN NYE HOMESTEAD & MUSEUM
85 Old County Rd., East Sandwich
(508) 888-2368
www.nyefamily.org
The Benjamin Nye Homestead offers a peek into the lives of the Pilgrims and the many generations that settled on the Cape after them. The house dates back to at least 1685, but many believe the structure first went up in the 1670s. The original structure was expanded into a salt-box-style house and then enlarged into a colonial dwelling. It was a private residence until 1958 and has been operated as a museum since 1972. On occasion, the museum offers special demonstrations of hearthside cooking, spinning, and candle making. To this day, the Nye Family Association, which runs the museum, makes new discoveries in the house, uncovering old floors and locating other original items that have been tucked away over the centuries. The museum is open from mid-July through mid-Oct (Tues through Sat, except holidays, noon to 4:30 p.m.), and an admission fee of $3.50 is charged for adults and $1.00 for children.

BOURNE FARM
881 Palmer Ave., West Falmouth
(508) 548-8484
This 1775 farm is a former working farm that has been beautifully restored so that you can enjoy and learn about the early days of farming in Falmouth. Call to make an appointment for a tour. They offer seasonal guided walks, special nature programs, and an annual Pumpkin Day Festival the Saturday of Columbus Day weekend (see our Annual Events chapter).

BRIGGS-MCDERMOTT HOUSE AND BLACKSMITH SHOP
22 Sandwich Rd., Bourne
(508) 759-6120
www.bournehistoricalsoc.org
This Greek Revival–style house, furnished with 1830-1910 period furniture, is maintained by the Bourne Society for Historic Preservation. On the National Register of Historic Places, the house is located across from the Bourne Public Library and is significant because it features a dazzling Charles Raleigh–painted ceiling, as well as some of his paintings. An adjacent blacksmith shop—a restored shop with working forge, artifacts, tools, and wagons—is said to be where President Grover Cleveland had his horses shod. The house and working blacksmith shop are open for tours from late June through the end of Aug on Tues and Sat from 1 to 4 p.m.

DEXTER GRIST MILL
Town Hall Square, Town Hall, Sandwich
(508) 888-4910
A working 17th-century gristmill with primitive wooden gears, the Dexter Grist Mill features a 54-inch French Buhr millstone. For the first 15 years after the incorporation of Sandwich, the residents of this first Cape Cod town had to travel to Plymouth to have their corn ground. Thomas Dexter of Sandwich remedied that situation by building a mill on this site in 1654 to the delight of all residents. A stream running through the village was dammed to create a picturesque pond and herring run, which give migrating herring a pathway from Cape Cod Bay to Shawme Pond.

Dexter Mill offers a tour and sells fresh ground corn on the premises. It is open daily 10 a.m. to 4 p.m. in the summer, with limited hours in Sept and Oct. After Columbus Day, the mill closes until June 15. Admission is $1.50 for adults and 75 cents for children.

FALMOUTH HISTORICAL SOCIETY
55-65 Palmer Ave., Falmouth
(508) 548-4857
www.falmouthhistoricalsociety.org
The historical society maintains and operates the Julia Wood House and the Conant House & Garden at this site, the latter offering a display of memorabilia of Katharine Lee Bates, who penned the poem "America the Beautiful." You will also find antique glass, silver, china, Revolutionary War exhibits, and whaling memorabilia. The Julia Wood House is a Georgian-style building that is furnished as a house museum. The Conant House features displays on Falmouth's coastal trading and whaling eras, and the Hallett Barn houses other exhibits. Both houses are on the National Register of Historic Places and are open late June to early Sept, Tues through Fri from 10 a.m. to 4 p.m. and Sat from 10 a.m. to 1 p.m. The Historical Society also offers guided walking tours in the summer. Admission to the two museum houses is $5 for adults and free for children under 13.

HERITAGE MUSEUMS & GARDENS
67 Grove St., Sandwich
(508) 888-3300
www.heritagemuseumsandgardens.org
This immaculately maintained museum complex has 76 acres of grounds with outdoor gardens, paths, sprawling lawns, and the renowned Dexter collection of rhododendrons. The grounds also feature the Old East Windmill, which was built at Orleans in 1800 and moved to Heritage Plantation in 1968. The complex has a gift shop and cafe and hosts numerous special events and outdoor concerts. A shuttle bus with a wheelchair lift provides transportation around the grounds. The museum is open 10 a.m. to 5 p.m. daily, from Apr through Oct, and features an evening "spectacle of lights" during the holiday season (Thanksgiving to New

Year's). The admission fee is $12 for adults, $11 for senior citizens (65-plus), $6 for children ages 6 to 16, and free for children 5 and younger.

HOXIE HOUSE
Route 130, Sandwich
(508) 888-1173

The Hoxie House is Cape Cod's oldest saltbox-style house and is a classic historic home, built around 1675 for the Reverend John Smith, his wife Susanna, and their 13 children. It is named for Abraham Hoxie, a Sandwich whaling captain who bought it in the 1850s. Remarkably its occupants lived without electricity, plumbing, or central heat until the early 1950s. In the late 1950s, the town purchased the Hoxie House, restored it to its original condition, and added period furnishings. The museum is open 10 a.m. to 5 p.m. Mon through Sat and 1 to 5 p.m. Sun from June through mid-Oct. Admission is $3 for adults and $2 for children 5 to 15 years old. Children under 5 get in free. The Hoxie House has a combination ticket with the Grist Mill that is $5 for adults and $3 for children.

i Rhododendrons, known for their large flowers and splendid colors, are considered native to Cape Cod and bloom the last week in May and the first few weeks in June. They may be seen throughout the Cape, but especially at the Heritage Museums & Gardens in Sandwich, where Charles O. Dexter used between 5,000 and 10,000 seedlings to produce new varieties known as Dexter Rhododendrons.

JONATHAN BOURNE HISTORICAL CENTER/ BOURNE HISTORICAL SOCIETY
30 Keene St., Bourne
(508) 759-8167
www.bournehistoricalsoc.org

This is a late 19th-century colonial Revival building of architectural significance, designed as a library by noted architect Henry Vaughn (1845-1917). There is an exhibition gallery with changing exhibits relating to the history of Bourne, including paintings, photographs, furniture, and other artifacts. The building also houses the Bourne Archives, which makes Bourne one of the few towns on the Cape with its own archive building. The house is open Mon and Tues from 9 a.m. to 2:30 p.m. and on Wed from 6:30 to 8:30 p.m. There is no admission fee.

MARINE BIOLOGICAL LABORATORY
Water Street, Woods Hole
(508) 289–7623, (508) 548-3705
www.mbl.edu

A one-hour tour includes a video followed by a meet-and-greet with marine animals used in MBL research. You can also take a walking tour of the campus. Free tours are held Mon through Fri from late June through Aug. Children younger than 5 are not admitted in the Marine Resources Center, though they are welcome to view the video. Reservations are required one week in advance of your visit because tours are limited to 15 people. The tours are free and are scheduled for 1 and 2 p.m.

MASHPEE WAMPANOAG INDIAN MUSEUM
Route 130, Mashpee
(508) 477-0208

This building was erected by descendants of Richard Bourne, the 17th-century minister and missionary who undertook the cause of the Native Mashpee Indians. The recently renovated museum contains local artifacts and a diorama depicting Wampanoag home life. Guides are all Wampanoag Indians, and the tribe runs the museum. Next to it is a herring run that helps migratory saltwater herring make their way up the Mashpee River to Mashpee Lake. The museum is open year-round, Mon through Fri, 9 a.m. to 4 p.m., and Sat by appointment. Admission is free, although donations are accepted.

OLD INDIAN MEETINGHOUSE AND BURIAL GROUND
Route 28 and Meeting House Road, Mashpee
(508) 539-1438
www.mashpeewampanoagtribe.com

Dating back to 1684, this structure is the oldest church building on Cape Cod. It was built by a Native American congregation of "Praying Indians" in Santuit, and the wood for it was hauled by oxcart from Plymouth. It was moved to the present location in 1717 and the ancient cemetery surrounding it has a number of old headstones. The church is open in the summer for worship and memorial services. Otherwise it is open only by appointment. Call the Mashpee Wampanoag Tribal Council (508-477-0208) to make an appointment and to determine any fees.

SANDWICH FISH HATCHERY
164 Rte. 6A, Sandwich
(508) 888-0008
www.masswildlife.org
Half a million fish, primarily trout, are raised here to stock the state's various ponds. You can track the stages of fish development and even feed them. Admission is free. The hatchery is open year-round from 9 a.m. to 3 p.m. daily.

SANDWICH GLASS MUSEUM
129 Main St. at Tupper Rd., Sandwich
(508) 888-0251
www.sandwichglassmuseum.org
In 1825, Deming Jarves arrived in Sandwich to open the Boston and Sandwich Glass Company. Over the next 60 years, this company provided many Sandwich residents with jobs and brought much prosperity to the town. This museum contains one of the largest collections of blown, pressed, cut, and engraved Sandwich glass in the United States. It provides a wonderful picture of the glassmaking industry and the town during its heyday through artifacts, equipment, old photographs, and records. The museum has a museum shop featuring reproductions of items from the collection, many of them in glass from the in-house studio. Among the excellent exhibits and demonstrations offered throughout the year is a "hot glass show," showcasing the talents of professional glass blowers. It is open Apr through Dec from 9:30 a.m. to 5:00 p.m. daily; Feb through Mar it's open Wed through Sun 9:30 a.m. to 4:00 p.m. Adults enter for $5.00 and children 6 to 16

years of age for $1.25. It closes for the month of Jan. Groups of 10 or more are eligible for a group discount—call for details.

THORNTON BURGESS MUSEUM
4 Water St. (Route 130), Sandwich
(508) 888-6870
www.thorntonburgess.org
The Thornton W. Burgess Museum is located on beautiful Shawme Pond in the center of Cape Cod's oldest town. Thornton W. Burgess, born in Sandwich in 1874 and renowned author of some 170 books, penned the popular children's series *Old Mother West Wind*, as well as *The Adventures of Peter Cottontail*. Although it is geared toward children (see our Kidstuff chapter), the museum's collection of Burgess books, photographs, and memorabilia should also be fascinating to adults. The museum also offers an activities-packed summer program for kids. There is a gift shop stocked with educational toys and games, Green Briar Jam Kitchen products, storybooks, and other enticements. The museum is open daily from May through Oct (Mon through Sat 10 a.m. to 4 p.m. and Sun 1 to 4 p.m.). Both the museum and the Green Briar Nature Center & Jam Kitchen are run by the Thornton W. Burgess Society. The society requests a donation for admission to the museum.

i During his lifetime Paul Revere made only 37 church bells. The First Congregational Church on Main Street in Falmouth boasts one, cast in 1796, by the famous patriot.

WOODS HOLE HISTORICAL MUSEUM
573 Woods Hole Rd., Woods Hole
(508) 548-7270
www.woodsholemuseum.org
This museum is actually a complex of three buildings, the main one being the William Bradley House, the third-oldest house in the village of Woods Hole. It was owned by 19th-century ship captain William Bradley, who was lost at sea. The structure houses the Woods Hole Historical Collection of paintings, portraits, photographs, and

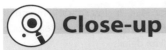 **Close-up**

Cape Cod Lighthouses

Extending more than 50 miles into the Atlantic Ocean, Cape Cod has always been difficult to navigate because of its rugged coastline, dangerous sand bars and rip tides, and few safe harbors to enter in a storm. Over the past 300 years, there have been more than 3,000 shipwrecks on the Cape, mainly along the treacherous outer shore between Provincetown and Chatham.

Cape Cod has had more than 20 lighthouses operating along its shores during the past 200 years. Before the days of the Cape Cod Canal, during the 19th-century heyday of busy shipping between Boston and New York, lighthouses were essential to protect ships from dangerous shoals. Lighthouse keepers were needed to tend the kerosene lamps, and the brave men of the U.S. Lifesaving Service manned lifeboats in an attempt to save lives when ships foundered in storms off the Cape Cod coast, often called the Graveyard of the Atlantic. Today, seven lighthouses still operate, and several decommissioned lights still stand along the coastline.

Chatham Light, Chatham

Today Chatham Light is also Chatham Coast Guard Station, a very important lifeboat station along this dangerous shore. There is ample parking at this site for a magnificent view of the Atlantic Ocean and the North Beach break, known as Chatham Spit. The beach is easily accessible by stairs leading down from the parking lot. The area is very dangerous for swimming, so take notice of any signs that forbid entering the water. To get to Chatham Light, drive east on Main Street, Chatham, to the junction with Shore Road. Turn right, and drive ½ mile.

Highland Light, Truro

Also known as Cape Cod Light, this is the Cape's first lighthouse, built in 1797 at the request of George Washington. The light was rebuilt in 1857, and this is the 66-foot tower that you see today. One of the most important lights on the East Coast for mariners, it too was moved away from eroding dune cliffs in 1996 and 1997 to save it from falling into the ocean. The current beacon, with more than 620,000 candlepower, is the most powerful light in New England and shines about 20 miles to sea. You can get to Cape Cod Light from US 6 in North Truro. Turn onto Highland Road, which is more than 3 miles north of Truro Center. At the end of Highland Road, turn right onto Lighthouse Road, and you'll see the parking lot.

Mayo Beach Lighthouse, Point Montara, California

That's right. There's a Cape Cod lighthouse in California. Thought to have been destroyed in 1939, a small lighthouse that once overlooked Wellfleet Harbor was discovered in 2008 at a hostel on a rocky shoreline south of San Francisco. The lighthouse had apparently been moved across the country instead of being razed, making it potentially the furthest any lighthouse has ever been moved by the U.S. Coast Guard and the only lighthouse known to have watched over both the Atlantic and the Pacific oceans.

Monomoy Point Light, Chatham

Monomoy Point Light is at the southern tip of Monomoy Island some 8 miles from the mainland. The Friends of Monomoy is the only organization that can give you permission to enter the lighthouse and enjoy the expansive view of the entire island from atop the lighthouse tower. The Island is accessible through the "Rip Ryder" ferry service (508-237-0420, www.monomoyislandferry.com). The light itself is at the south end of the 5-mile-long island.

Nauset Light, Eastham

Nauset Beach Light was, until recently, located atop a bluff overlooking the Atlantic Ocean. In 1996 it was moved just west of its former site on property of the Cape Cod National Seashore to protect it from encroaching beach erosion. This working lighthouse is visible 15½ miles out to sea. It's not tough at all to get to Nauset Light. Take US 6 through Eastham, and at the traffic lights at Cape Cod National Seashore Visitor Center, turn right onto Nauset Road. Follow Nauset Road, and it will merge with Doane Road; follow Doane to the intersection with Ocean View Drive. Bear left onto Ocean View Drive; 1 mile down the road is Nauset Light Beach parking lot.

Nobska Point Light, Woods Hole

Nobska Point Light Station towers over the waters of Vineyard Sound. It serves as a beacon for Woods Hole Harbor and as a guide for mariners traveling between Cape Cod and Martha's Vineyard. To get to Nobska Point Light from Falmouth, turn left at the intersection of Route 28 and Woods Hole Road, and follow Woods Hole Road about 3 miles to Church Street. Turn left, and Nobska Lighthouse will appear about 1½ miles on the left. Limited parking is available opposite the light.

Race Point Lighthouse, Provincetown

Built in 1876, this lighthouse was manned by a lightkeeper until 1972, when the light station was automated. After the light station was automated (it now runs on solar power), the lightkeeper's house fell into disrepair. In recent years the New England Lighthouse Foundation has completed a renovation of the house, which is now used as a retreat for scientists and artists. It is not easily accessible; you can only reach it by four-wheel-drive vehicle or on foot, if you want to enjoy a ramble along the outermost shoreline. It takes some extra effort to get to the Race Point Light. From US 6, turn right at the traffic lights onto Race Point Road, follow it to the end, and park in the parking lot at Race Point Coast Guard Station. Heading west, you must walk along the beach for about 2 miles.

Stage Harbor Light, Chatham

This light used to serve as a beacon for Chatham's "Old Harbor," or Stage Harbor. In 1933 the original tower was disconnected and sold to the government. It is private property today but is occasionally opened during specially scheduled events. Stage Harbor Light is inaccessible by road. Off Route 28 in Chatham, turn right at Barn Hill Road, and continue ½ mile to Harding Beach Road. Turn right, and continue to Harding Beach parking lot. You'll walk more than 1 mile along the beach to the light. Or you can view it from the end of Champlain Road in Chatham.

Three Sisters Lighthouses, Eastham

Nauset Beach Light Station was first established in 1839 with the construction of three small brick towers. Because of the three separate structures, the light station has always been known as the "Three Sisters of Nauset." The Three Sisters have been moved back about ¼ mile from the shore and are arranged in an attractive parklike setting, standing as a monument to all lighthouses still in existence. Directions: Same directions as to Nauset Light. Park in the beach parking lot and walk inland along a paved trail parallel to Cable Road. You'll find the Three Sisters at the end of the trail.

records. The two other buildings, moved to the grounds in 1996, are a boat barn (the Swift Barn, a small boat museum) and an 1890s workshop that at one time belonged to a doctor with various hobbies, including etching and fly-tying. Mid-June to mid-Oct the houses are open Tues through Sat from 10 a.m. to 4 p.m.; closed late Oct to mid-June. Admission is free, though donations are gratefully accepted.

WOODS HOLE OCEANOGRAPHIC INSTITUTE'S EXHIBIT CENTER
15 School St., Woods Hole
(508) 289-2663, (508) 289-2252
www.whoi.edu

See videos of deep submersible *Alvin,* explore interactive exhibits about whale and dolphin research, and watch colorful footage of the creatures that live along deep-sea hydrothermal vents. Then step into a full-size model of *Alvin's* inner sphere and imagine your own life aquatic on the ocean floor. The exhibit center is open Apr through Dec: by appointment only in Apr; Mon through Sat, 10 a.m. to 4:30 p.m., from May through Oct; and Tues through Fri, 10 a.m. to 4:30 p.m., Nov and Dec. Donations are requested. From late June to early Sept, you can also take a guided tour of the WHOI dock area and other research facilities. These tours leave from the WHOI Information Office at 93 Water Street Mon through Fri at 10:30 a.m. and 1:30 p.m., and last about 75 minutes. Call to reserve a spot because space is limited.

MID-CAPE

BARNSTABLE SUPERIOR COURTHOUSE
3195 Main St., Barnstable
(508) 362-2511
www.barnstablecounty.org

This granite building, constructed in 1832, has two cannons on the front lawn that were hauled to Barnstable by oxen to defend the town's saltworks during the War of 1812. Also on the front lawn is a life-size statue of James Otis Jr., who was known as "the Patriot" because of his speeches that rallied people to the Patriot cause before the American Revolution. Otis, who was a good friend of President John Adams, delivered a number of speeches in Boston and elsewhere that helped to move the colonies closer toward revolution. Otis is joined on the county courthouse's front lawn by his sister, Mercy Otis Warren, a writer who has been called the "First Lady of the American Revolution" because of her works that included a pamphlet calling for a bill of rights in the Constitution and a history of the American Revolution. Six buildings compose the governmental complex of Barnstable County (including the former county jail), which has been the seat of the county court since 1685.

CAHOON MUSEUM OF AMERICAN ART
4676 Rte. 28, Cotuit
(508) 428-7581
www.cahoonmuseum.org

Located in a 1775 Georgian colonial farmhouse, the Cahoon Museum is best known for its collection of fanciful primitive paintings by the late Ralph and Martha Cahoon. The building—worth a visit in itself with its wide-planked floors, narrow doorways, and ship's captain's staircase—was actually the Cahoons' home and studio for 37 years. In addition to the Cahoon paintings, the permanent collection features 19th- and early 20th-century American art by the likes of Ralph Blakelock, William Bradford, and William Matthew Pride. The museum also offers special exhibitions, gallery talks, classes, and a gift shop. It is open Tues through Sat, 10 a.m. to 4 p.m., and Sun, 1 to 4 p.m., year-round, except January, when it closes for a month. Admission is $5 for adults, $4 for seniors and students, and free for children under 12.

CAPTAIN BANGS HALLET HOUSE
11 Strawberry Lane (off Route 6A), Yarmouthport
(508) 362-3021
www.hsoy.org

Owned and operated by the Historic Society of Old Yarmouth, the oldest section of the Captain Bangs Hallet House was built in 1740. The main section was then added in 1840. The site is named for Capt. Bangs Hallet, who lived here after retiring from the China trade and acquiring the house from Captain Allen H. Knowles in 1863. Tours of the building take place Thurs through Sun at 1, 2, and 3 p.m. from June through mid-Oct. Call ahead to arrange group tours. Admission is $3.00 for adults and 50 cents for children.

CENTERVILLE HISTORICAL SOCIETY
513 Main St., Centerville
(508) 775-0331
www.centervillehistoricalmuseum.org
Founded in 1952 this society maintains the Mary Lincoln House with late Victorian displays, including a child's room, a doll and quilt room, and a colonial kitchen. Also on view are the personal collections of Charles Ayling, including Sandwich glass, military collections, Dodge MacKnight paintings, Elmer Crowell bird carvings, and furniture. Other displays include marine artifacts, including tools, excerpts from ships' logs, and the wheel from the steamer *Portland,* which was lost on Nov 27, 1898, in a gale subsequently called the Portland Gale after the steamer. The Centerville museum also hosts temporary exhibitions and is noted for its fine collection of period clothing, including shoes, jewelry, and accessories. The house is open from noon to 4 p.m., Tues through Sat, early May through Dec. Admission is $6 for adults, $5 for seniors and students, and free for children under 12.

CAPE MUSEUM OF FINE ARTS
Route 6A, Dennis
(508) 385-4477
www.cmfa.org
The Cape Cod Museum of Fine Arts is home to a growing public collection of paintings, sculpture, and works on paper by a wide variety of artists associated with Cape Cod. The collection features artwork by Hawthorne, Diehl, Gammell, Hofmann, Vickrey, Hunter, McCurl, and others. A gift shop is on the premises. The museum is open year-round. Adult admission is $8; people younger than 18 enter free. Admission by donation all day Thurs. (See the Arts chapter for more information on their gallery shows.)

CONGREGATIONAL CHURCH OF SOUTH DENNIS
218 Main St., South Dennis
(508) 394-5992
www.southdennischurch.org
Known as the Sea Captain's Church because so many of its members were shipmasters, this church was built in 1835. The south parish of the Dennis church was established here in 1794 and later broke away from the north in 1817. The current church replaced a small meetinghouse built in 1794. The church features the oldest operating pipe organ in the country and a chandelier of Sandwich glass that was once fueled with whale oil. The organ, built in 1765, was installed in the mid-19th century and attracts pipe organ enthusiasts from around the world. Behind the church is a cemetery with many stones bearing the names of ship captains as well as the words lost at sea.

CULTURAL CENTER OF CAPE COD
307 Old Main St., South Yarmouth
(508) 394-7100
www.cultural-center.org
The Cultural Center of Cape Cod opened its doors at the former headquarters of the Bass River Savings Bank in 2007. Since then the building has hosted artists, musicians, dancing, and any other form of creative outlet one could imagine. It is an elegant venue for everything from weddings to artist receptions to forums on important issues of the day such as homelessness. It is centrally located in South Yarmouth, where town officials have pushed for more of a village center feeling. Call or go online for a schedule.

THE EDWARD GOREY HOUSE
8 Strawberry Lane, off Route 6A, Yarmouthport
(508) 362-3909
www.edwardgoreyhouse.org
Edward Gorey, a prolific and distinctive artist, illustrator, and author, lived out the last years of his life here, in what he called the "Elephant House." It is now a small museum dedicated to preserving his work and introducing it to fresh

eyes. Best known for his animated opening credits to the PBS series *Mystery* and for dark curios like *The Gashlycrumb Tinies,* Gorey was an engaging talent. You'll see countless drawings, adolescent diaries—even his favorite yellow sweater. You'll also learn about his work in the Cape theater community and at least one room will be a hit with the little ones: Gorey was an ardent advocate of animal welfare, so one room is devoted to animals and suitable for kindergartners. Open Wed through Sun (hours vary in the off-season). Admission is $5 for adults, $3 for students and seniors, $2 for ages 6 to 12, under age 6 free.

IYANOUGH'S GRAVE
Off Route 6A, Cummaquid
Monuments to the American Indian Sachem Iyanough appear all around Barnstable. The village of Hyannis and the section of the village of Osterville known as Wianno are both derivations of his name. The village green in Hyannis features a statue of the chief. Another monument to Iyanough is his gravesite, just north of Route 6A in the village of Cummaquid. In 1621, when he was in his mid-20s, the chief died of exposure after being chased into a swamp by Pilgrim Myles Standish, who at the time believed Indians were endangering settlers. Iyanough, however, had displayed only good relations with the settlers. In the mid-19th century, a farmer plowing his field discovered Sachem's grave. A sign along Route 6A marks the spot.

JOHN F. KENNEDY HYANNIS MUSEUM
397 Main St., Hyannis
(580) 790-3077
www.jfkhyannismuseum.org
The John F. Kennedy Hyannis Museum is a multimedia exhibit designed to open a window on the days that JFK, a Hyannisport summer resident, spent on Cape Cod. Opened in 1992, the museum features an 80-photo collection, a video narrated by Walter Cronkite, and oral histories from friends of the 35th president. The museum is near the John F. Kennedy Memorial (see the listing below), the Kennedy Compound in Hyannisport, and St. Francis Xavier Church, where the Kennedy family has worshiped since the 1930s.

The museum is open daily during the summer, but hours vary at other times of the year so call ahead or go online for specifics. The museum is closed in Jan. Admission is $5.00 for adults and $2.50 for children ages 10 to 17; children younger than 10 are admitted free.

JOHN F. KENNEDY MEMORIAL
Ocean St., Hyannis
(508) 790-6320
This monument to our fallen president and fellow Cape resident was unveiled in 1966. Situated along a quiet section of Ocean Street in Hyannis, it looks out over Lewis Bay. The memorial is a stone monument adorned with Kennedy's image and a fountain where visitors can remember our 35th president.

JOSIAH DENNIS MANSE AND OLD WEST SCHOOLHOUSE
77 Nobuscusset Road at Whig Street, Dennis
(508) 385-2232, (508) 385-3528 (for tours)
This 1736 saltbox was the home of the town's founding father, Rev. Josiah Dennis, who lived here until his death in 1763. The manse is now a museum featuring artifacts of early Dennis life, with a children's room and spinning and weaving exhibit. A maritime room holds models, paintings, and equipment from the Shiverick Shipyards, which produced eight large clipper ships during the mid-19th century. On the grounds is a 1770 one-room schoolhouse. The museum, which is owned by the town, is closed from mid-Sept to late June but, in season, welcomes guests on Tues morning (10 a.m. to noon) and Thurs afternoon (2 to 4 p.m.). Admission is free, but donations are accepted.

JUDAH BAKER WINDMILL
River St., South Yarmouth
(508) 362-3021
www.hsoy.org
Resting along the banks of the Bass River at the end of Willow Street on River Street is the Judah Baker Windmill, built in 1791. It wasn't always located in South Yarmouth. It was once a Dennis windmill built near Grand Cove. After changing

hands a few times during the course of the 19th century, it eventually landed in the hands of Capt. Braddock Matthews, who moved the windmill to its current South Yarmouth location in 1863. It remained in operation until 1891.

NOBSCUSSET INDIAN BURIAL GROUND
Route 6A, East Dennis

Although this burial ground is rather difficult to locate, it's well worth the effort. Along the banks of Scargo Lake, known to the Native Americans as Nobscusset Pond, lies the Nobscusset Indian burial ground. There are no stones to see, only a plot of land encircled with a granite and iron fence, and a plaque that identifies the spot as the burial ground for the Nobscusset tribe of Indians. The tribe's 17th-century sachem, Mah-antampaine, is buried here. To find the burial ground, look for a clearing in the bushes a few hundred feet west of the Scargo Lake town landing on Route 6A.

THE OLDE COLONIAL COURTHOUSE
Rendezvous Lane at Route 6A, Barnstable
(508) 362-8927
www.talesofcapecod.org

Built in 1772, this courthouse is where the seeds of independence were planted. At this site on Sept 27, 1774, more than 1,500 people disrupted a court session to protest a British ruling determining how jurors were to be selected. The building also served as a Baptist church for more than a hundred years. Today the building is the home of Tales of Cape Cod, an organization dedicated to the preservation of local history. There are no set hours; in fact the building is only open for special events or by appointment by calling the number listed above. Admission is free.

OSTERVILLE HISTORICAL SOCIETY
Parker and West Bay Roads, Osterville
(508) 428-5861
www.ostervillemuseum.org

The Osterville Historical Society operates a colorful museum within the Jonathan Parker House, which was built as a half-house in 1824. The exceptional displays include a large painting of George Washington at Valley Forge by Jean Baptiste Adolphe Gilbert, a Victorian Room, and a children's room that contains dolls, toys, and two beautiful doll houses, one made in 1870. Behind the Jonathan Parker House rests a boathouse containing historic Crosby catboats and Wianno Seniors and Juniors—all these styles of boats were designed in Osterville. Also on the grounds is the mid-18th-century Cammett House, which is the second-oldest house in Osterville and provides a look at early architecture, including a root cellar and beehive oven. From mid-June to mid-Sept, the historical society museum is open Wed through Sat, but hours and activities vary so it is best to call ahead.

SCARGO TOWER
Off Scargo Hill Road, East Dennis

Scargo Tower is a 28-foot-high brick observatory sitting atop the 160-foot-high Scargo Hill, so you can imagine the view on a clear day. Provincetown Monument across Cape Cod Bay can be seen, as can the white cliffs of Plymouth. In perfect atmospheric conditions you can just make out a suggestion of Nantucket to the south. Built in 1902 and called Tobey Tower to honor early settler Thomas Tobey, it was given to the town of Dennis in 1929 and renamed Scargo Tower in favor of the Nobscusset Indian Princess of the same name. Below the tower and hill rests Scargo Lake, which during the summer hosts swimmers, sailboats, and canoes. Scargo Tower is open to the public and is a great place to stargaze.

STURGIS LIBRARY
3090 Rte. 6A, Barnstable
(508) 362-6636
www.sturgislibrary.org

Believed to be the oldest library building (ca. 1644) in the country, the Sturgis Library has a number of special collections documenting the rich history of Cape Cod and the islands, including the Henry Crocker Kittredge Maritime Collection, the Lothrop Genealogy and Local History Collection, the Cape Cod History Collection, and the Sturgis Library Archives. The library is open year-round; hours are Mon, Wed, Thurs, and Fri 10 a.m. to 5 p.m.; Tues 1 to 8 p.m.; and Sat 10 a.m. to 4 p.m. It is closed Sun and holidays.

WEST PARISH MEETINGHOUSE
2049 Meetinghouse Way (Route 149), West Barnstable
(508) 362-4445
www.westparish.org
When the first Congregationalists arrived to the settlement of Barnstable in 1646, they set to work on building a meetinghouse on Cobb Hill at Barnstable Village. Though this original building no longer exists, the West Parish Meetinghouse, built in 1717, attests to a flourishing congregation that divided itself into east and west parishes. Paul Revere cast the bell, and the 1723 gilded cock weather vane earned the church its nickname the "Rooster Church."

WINSLOW CROCKER HOUSE
240 Rte. 6A, Yarmouthport
(508) 375-9183
www.hsoy.org
A Georgian design, this 1780 house was built in West Barnstable and moved to Yarmouthport. It has elaborate paneling, a large central chimney, a bowed roof, and a fine collection of decorative arts from the 1600s to 1800s. Owned and operated by Historic New England, the newly restored Winslow Crocker House is open the first Sat of each month from June to Oct. Hourly tours begin at 11 a.m., with the last tour beginning at 4 p.m. Admission is $4.

LOWER CAPE

ATWOOD HOUSE AND MUSEUM
347 Stage Harbor Rd., Chatham
(508) 945-2493
www.chathamhistoricalsociety.org
Built in 1752, the Atwood House is one of the oldest houses in Chatham. Since 1926, the house has been the home of the Chatham Historical Society. The museum's eight rooms, containing many historic collections and furnishings, include the Joseph C. Lincoln Room, which is a repository of the prolific Cape author's books and memorabilia. The museum also holds murals by 20th-century artist Alice Stallknecht, an antique Fresnel lens from Chatham Light, antiques, Sandwich glass, and an international collection of seashells and artifacts. It is open from early June to the mid-Oct, Tues through Sat from 1 to 4 p.m. (except in July and Aug, when hours are extended to 10 a.m. to 4 p.m.).

BROOKS ACADEMY MUSEUM
80 Parallel St. (at Routes 124 and 39), Harwich
(508) 432-8089
www.harwichhistoricalsociety.org
The Harwich Historical Society operates this museum, which is named for its builder, Sidney Brooks. It offers a comprehensive exhibit on cranberry history and culture in addition to collections of Native American artifacts; Sandwich glass; early tools, implements, and toys; and historical documents, including genealogical information. Brooks Academy was known in the 1840s as the Pine Grove Seminary and was one of the first schools of navigation in the country. The building was sold to the town of Harwich in 1869 and used as a public school. The museum offers scheduled walking tours during the season and in the off-season by appointment. Admission is free, but donations are welcomed.

BREWSTER HISTORICAL SOCIETY MUSEUM
3171 Rte. 6A, East Brewster
(508) 896-9521
www.brewsterhistoricalsociety.org
The Brewster Historical Society's museum has exhibits honoring the maritime history of Brewster and features memorabilia relating to the town, including an early-20th-century barbershop, a ca. 1860 dollhouse, and much more. It's open mid-July to Sept, Thurs through Sat, 1 to 4 p.m., and admission is free.

The historical society also operates the Old Higgins Farm Windmill (see our listing below) and Harris-Black House, both at 785 Main St., Drummer Boy Park, Route 6A in West Brewster. Both are open during the same hours as the Brewster Historical Society Museum.

CAPE COD MUSEUM OF NATURAL HISTORY
869 Rte. 6A, Brewster
(508) 896-3867
www.ccmnh.org

With two floors of exhibits, this museum provides visitors with a good idea of the flora and fauna of Cape Cod. Here you can discover the nature of Cape Cod through interactive exhibits, live animals, fresh and saltwater aquaria, a tidal pool, and a new honey bee observation hive. Learn about coastal erosion, the archaeology of Cape Cod, and whales. Behind the museum is a vast salt marsh. The museum has walking trails, lectures, a library, a gift shop, an aquarium with more than 65 marine animals, and a wave tank. The museum is open daily in the summer (June through Sept) from 9:30 a.m. to 4 p.m. Call for off-season hours. Admission is $8.00 for those ages 13 and older, $7.00 for seniors, $3.50 for children 3 to 12, and free for youngsters age 2 and younger.

CAPE COD NATIONAL SEASHORE SALT POND VISITOR CENTER
U.S. Route 6, Eastham
(508) 255-3421
www.nps.gov/caco

The Salt Pond Visitor Center, part of the Cape Cod National Seashore, is generally open daily year-round from 9 a.m. to 4:30 p.m. It offers park-related films in a state-of-the-art theater equipped with a digital audio-visual system. An on-site store stocks maps, puzzles, games, books, and other local interest items, and the seasonal schedule includes highlights from hikes to campfire chats. For more information about the Visitor Center, see our chapter on the Cape Cod National Seashore.

i For a real treat take in a movie at the Cape Cinema at 35 Hope Lane (just off Route 6A) in Dennis. Get there early to admire the colorful interior ceiling designed by Rockwell Kent, then settle in for the screening, which is usually of the independent variety. This is where *The Wizard of Oz* premiered in 1940. For more information call (508) 385-5644, or visit www.capecinema.com.

CHATHAM FISH PIER
Aunt Lydia's Cove (off Shore Road), Chatham

Just down the road from the Chatham Light is the Chatham Fish Pier, where there's always a small crowd gathered on the visitor deck. Not only does the pier offer a great view of Chatham's harbor and outer beach with the Atlantic beyond but, when the fishing boats unload their catch, both children and adults get a fascinating glimpse of the Cape's best-known industry.

CHATHAM LIGHT
Shore Road, Chatham

In 1808, two wooden lighthouses were built on a cliff in Chatham east of the location of the current Chatham lighthouse—a cliff that no longer exists. These first two Chatham lights were range lights, meaning they were movable and could be aligned in such a way that mariners approaching Chatham by sea could find the channel to the harbor by lining up the two lights. By 1841, the cliff had eroded so much that both lighthouses tumbled to the beach below. Another pair of lighthouses—these made with brick and mortar—were constructed to replace the old ones, but the cliff continued to erode at a rate of 20 feet per year until these were also destroyed in 1879 and 1881. To replace this second set, two iron lighthouses were built. One is the current Chatham Light; the other was moved to Eastham in 1923 to become the current Nauset Light. Chatham Light overlooks the Chatham Break, a mile-wide hole in the barrier beach that stretches back to the mainland and Nauset Beach in Orleans. The break occurred in early 1987 during a fierce nor'easter.

CHATHAM RAILROAD MUSEUM
153 Depot Rd., Chatham

On the appropriately named Depot Street is Chatham's Railroad Museum. It was built in 1887 and operated as a train depot until 1937, servicing more than 20,000 passengers per year. It was donated to the town in the 1950s and is today a museum offering a wide variety of railroad-related items that are sure to delight railroad buffs. The building, listed in the National Register of Historic Places, offers displays of antique equipment and memorabilia as well as a caboose dating from 1910. It is open Tues through Sat, 10 a.m. to 4 p.m., mid-June through mid-Sept. There is no admission fee, though donations are accepted.

CROSBY MANSION
Crosby Lane (off Route 6A), across from Nickerson State Park, Brewster
(508) 896-1744, (508) 394-6113
Many consider the Crosby Mansion to be one of the Cape's hidden gems, wrapped in a love story more than a century old. This gracious home was built in 1888 by Albert Crosby for his wife, Matilda. Aside from being a residence, the building has been used as a music school, a summer camp, and for weddings. A continuous slide show, exhibits, and tour allow you to learn about the Crosby family and life in the 1890s. Local volunteers put countless hours into preservation of the building. The house is maintained by the Friends of Crosby Mansion, and there are no set hours, though it is generally open between April and November and there are open houses held on Sunday during the summer. The house is also opened for the Brewster in Bloom weekend, usually the last weekend in Apr or the first weekend in May (see our Annual Events chapter). You can call the number above to arrange a tour of the building; there is no fee to tour the house.

EASTHAM GRIST MILL
U.S. Route 6, Eastham
(508) 240-5900 (Town Hall)
On the town green in Eastham is the oldest and most widely known of all the Cape Cod windmills. The Eastham Grist Mill was built in Plymouth in the 1680s, which means that the corn it ground most likely found its way into the mouths of the sons and daughters of Pilgrims. It was later moved to Truro during the end of the 18th century by floating it across Cape Cod Bay. In 1793 it was moved to Eastham and landed on its present site in 1808. The mill remained in operation until the turn of the 20th century. It was first opened to the public in the 1930s, and was restored in

the 1960s. Nowadays it is open weekdays and Sat from 10 a.m. to 5 p.m. and Sun 1 to 5 p.m. during July and Aug when visitors can see its original wooden machinery, still operating today. Admission is free, but donations are accepted.

i Combine the magic of a Cape Cod vacation and the thrill of a train ride as the Cape Cod Central Railroad (508-771-3800 or www.capetrain.com) takes you on a ride from downtown Hyannis to the Cape Cod Canal. The train travels through beautiful bogs and past natural woodlands and lush marshes. The train offers great meals along with the vistas.

EASTHAM SCHOOLHOUSE MUSEUM
U.S. Route 6 at Nauset and Schoolhouse Roads, Eastham
(508) 255-0788
www.easthamhistorical.org
This one-room schoolhouse was built in 1869 as an elementary school. Around the turn of the 20th century, the town had three such one-room schoolhouses. These were later joined to form the Eastham Central School, which operated until 1936. After two of the original schoolhouses deteriorated in the mid-1900s, the old original schoolhouse was restored to its late-19th-century one-room status and serves as a museum of the Eastham Historical Society. It still has two doors marked as separate entrances for boys and girls. Exhibits include farming and household implements, Native American artifacts, and displays pertaining to area history. The museum is open July and Aug from 1:00 to 4:00 p.m. Tues and Wed and 10 a.m. to 4 p.m. Thurs and Fri. Admission is free, but donations are welcome.

EDWARD PENNIMAN HOUSE
Fort Hill Road, Eastham
(508) 255-3421 (Salt Pond Visitor Center)
Located within the boundaries of the Cape Cod National Seashore, the Penniman House in the Fort Hill area of Eastham showcases the fortunes made by the Cape's whaling captains. Retiring from the sea in 1876, Captain Edward Penniman

built this impressive Victorian mansion on a knoll with a cupola overlooking the Atlantic Ocean. In front of the house, a gateway made of two huge whale jawbones marks the entrance to the property. You can tour the house during the summer season. The Penniman House is open from May through Sept, Tues through Thurs from 1 to 4 p.m. Just call ahead to register if you plan on visiting. Guided tours are available twice weekly (Mon and Sat at 11 a.m.) by reservation only. Admission is free.

EXPEDITION *WHYDAH* MUSEUM
16 MacMillan Wharf, Provincetown
(508) 487-8899
www.whydah.com

The museum is devoted to the only pirate ship ever discovered and authenticated. The story of pirates unfolds as the museum tells the story of the wreck of the *Whydah,* its discovery by local diver Barry Clifford, and the priceless artifacts recovered from the wreck found off Wellfleet, Cape Cod. Call for hours as they change throughout the year. Adults are charged $10, children (6 to 12) and seniors cost $8, and children younger than 6 enter free.

FIRST CONGREGATIONAL CHURCH
200 Main St., Wellfleet
(508) 349-6877
www.uccwebsites.net/wellfleetfirstcongma
.html

This church holds the distinction of being the only church in the world known to keep ship's time, thus revealing Wellfleet's proud history as a seafaring town. For those not familiar with ship's time, the 24-hour day is divided up into six four-hour segments, representing a four-hour watch on board a ship. The first watch begins at 12 and concludes at 4, when the second watch begins. On each half hour during the watch, the bells chime: one bell at 12:30, two bells at 1, three bells at 1:30, and so on until eight bells are chimed and then the cycle begins again. Wellfleet's First Congregational Church was built in 1850 and contains an 1873 Hook and Hastings organ. Call to arrange a visit.

FIRST ENCOUNTER BEACH
Samoset Road, Eastham
(508) 255-0788
www.easthamhistorical.org

At First Encounter Beach along the Cape Cod Bay side of Eastham's shore is a granite boulder with a plaque marking this location as the site of the Pilgrims' first encounter with Native Americans. Unfortunately, this first encounter was not a friendly one. The Pilgrims, on their third day of exploring this new land, awoke to a volley of arrows that they answered with a volley of musket fire. Both parties departed, uninjured. Future relations between the two peoples would be much more cordial.

FRENCH TRANSATLANTIC CABLE STATION MUSEUM
Corner of Cove Road and Route 28, Orleans
(508) 240-1735
www.frenchcablestationmuseum.org

Built in 1890, this is the U.S. terminal for the first transatlantic cable laid between the United States and France via Newfoundland. The cable was 3,000 miles long and was used to transmit news of such important events as Lindbergh's transatlantic flight in 1927 and the invasion of France by the Germans in 1940. Many of the original French cable operators immigrated to this country and settled in the area. The cable station was guarded by Marines during World War II because it provided an important link with U.S. operations in Europe. The station was closed in 1959, but all the original cables, instruments, and other equipment are still in place. It is open during July and Aug, Mon through Sat from 1 to 4 p.m.; June and Sept, Fri through Sun 1 to 4 p.m.; and at other times by special request. No admission fee is charge, although donations are accepted.

HIGHLAND LIGHT (CAPE COD LIGHT))
27 Highland Rd., Truro
(508) 487-1121
www.trurohistorical.org

This is the nation's first lighthouse. The original Cape Cod Light first stood watch on these sandy cliffs in 1797 and was lit by whale-oil lamps.

By 1857, the tower was in danger of falling down, so the current Highland Lighthouse was constructed that year. Remarkably, the original whale-oil lamps were in use until the turn of the 20th century, when they were replaced by a modern lamp system. The light system was updated with electricity in 1932. Sitting atop the cliffs of Truro and with a range of some 20 to 30 miles, the light is the first seen by transatlantic mariners as they approach the northeast coast. The 80-foot tower was moved back from the cliff in 1996 and thus saved from erosion threatening to destroy it.

Highland Light is open mid-May through mid-Oct, 10 a.m. to 5:30 p.m. daily. Admission is $4 for the tower, and $6 for the tower and adjoining museum. Children must be 48 inches tall to tour the tower.

JENNY LIND TOWER
Off Lighthouse Road, North Truro
In the mid-1800s, Jenny Lind was a legendary opera singer dubbed the "Swedish Nightingale" because of her sweet soprano voice. Legend has it that a Lind concert in Boston was so oversold that crowds rioted, forcing Lind to sing (for free) high atop a 55-foot stone tower at the Fitchburg Railroad Depot. In 1927, when it was announced that the tower was going to be destroyed, a wealthy Boston attorney shipped it, piece by piece, to a parcel of land he owned in North Truro. Today the tower and the land are part of the Cape Cod National Seashore. Though the tower is not officially open to the public, you can see it from the parking lot of the Highland Light as well as from the Highland Golf Links.

i **The 10-team Cape Cod Baseball League is a popular draw on late summer afternoons throughout the Cape. The players hail from colleges and universities around the country, use only wooden bats, and take aim for the big leagues. Games are played from mid-June to mid-August and are free. For more information visit www.capecodbaseball.org.**

JONATHAN YOUNG WINDMILL
Route 6A, Orleans
(508) 240–1329
www.orleanshistoricalsociety.org
This windmill was built in 1720 in South Orleans and moved in the mid-1800s to Orleans Center. It was then bought by a private interest in 1897 and relocated again, this time to Hyannisport. In 1983, the windmill was donated to the Orleans Historical Society and moved back to Orleans and its current place at Town Cove Park, where it was restored. The windmill is open to the public daily from 11 a.m. to 4 p.m. from June to Sept. No admission fee is charged.

MARCONI STATION SITE
Marconi Site Road (off U.S. Route 6), Wellfleet
(508) 771-2144
Many believe this to be the site of the initial transatlantic wireless message; in fact, the first such message was sent from England to Greenland in 1901, more than a year before the South Wellfleet Wireless Transmitting Station sent its first message. Regardless, this site, now known locally as the Marconi Wireless Site or Marconi Station, does hold its place as the site of the first wireless message sent across the Atlantic from the United States. On Jan 19, 1903, the airwaves crackled atop this windswept Wellfleet cliff—helping to change long-distance communications forever. Developed by the Italian physicist Guglielmo Marconi, the first Wellfleet telegraph transmitted a message from President Theodore Roosevelt to King Edward VII of England. On the evening of Apr 14, 1912, the station received the distress call from the Titanic. The station at South Wellfleet would only be in service until 1917, as cliff erosion was already threatening. Although erosion has destroyed much of the site, a plaque commemorates its former use, and you can still view the footings of some of the towers (these towers stood more than 200 feet high) as well as a model of how the station looked in 1903.

NAUSET LIGHT
Beach Road, Eastham
(508) 240-2612
www.nausetlight.org

Highland Light to the north had one tower. Chatham Light to the south had two towers. So, to mark the cliffs of Eastham, Nauset was given three lights. The first three lighthouses built on the cliff here were small brick towers constructed in 1837. These three lighthouses surrendered to cliff erosion in 1892, and their remains can be seen along Nauset Beach from time to time. Three new towers, taller and made of wood, were constructed on the cliff to replace the original towers and were known as the Three Sisters. Two of these lighthouses were sold to private interests in 1918; otherwise they would have fallen over the rapidly eroding cliffs. The third light worked the cliff alone until 1923 when it, too, was sold. During that year, the site saw the installation of the current Nauset Light, formerly one of the Chatham Twins. In 1996, Nauset Light was moved back from the cliff, as it was about to suffer the fate of the original brick lighthouses. As for the Three Sisters, they have been reunited and are now on display along Cable Road, just up the street from Nauset Light. Nauset Light is open for Sunday tours from July through Oct, as well as select dates in May and June. In July and Aug, tours are also offered on Wed. Call for times.

OLD GODFREY WINDMILL
Near Chase Park, Chatham

This wind-powered grist mill was built along Stage Harbor Road in 1797 by Colonel Benjamin Godfrey. The mill ground corn until 1898. Over the course of the 20th century, it was twice damaged by storms and was closed until 1956, when it was given to the town. The mill was then moved to its current location at Chase Park. It is open every day except Tues throughout July and Aug. This is one of those look-see attractions with no admission fee charged.

OLD HARBOR LIFESAVING STATION
Race Point Road, Provincetown
(508) 771-2144

Race Point is now home to the Old Harbor Lifesaving Station that once protected the shores of Chatham. Built in 1897, it was one of 13 stations that lined the outer Cape beaches from Provincetown to Monomoy Point until the Lifesaving Service became part of the Coast Guard in 1914. The Old Harbor Station was decommissioned in 1944 and sold off to private interests. It was acquired by the National Park Service in 1973 and moved up the coast on a barge in the winter of 1978, just ahead of that year's devastating blizzard. Now it rests at Race Point overlooking the Atlantic. Its boat room contains a surf boat and various lifesaving apparatus. The station is open to visitors during July and Aug from 1:30 to 3:30 p.m. daily and 6 to 8 p.m. Thurs for its popular demonstration of a "breeches buoy" rescue (see our Cape Cod National Seashore chapter).

OLD HIGGINS FARM WINDMILL
785 Rte. 6A, Brewster
(508) 896-9521
www.brewsterhistoricalsociety.org

Built in 1795, this smock-type windmill was moved from Ellis Landing in Brewster to its current location at Drummer Boy Park in 1974. It is maintained by the Brewster Historical Society, which opens it to the public from mid-June to mid-Oct. The windmill is open Thurs through Sat, 1 to 4 p.m. The visit is free, but donations are welcome.

ORLEANS HISTORICAL SOCIETY MUSEUM AND MEETING HOUSE
3 River Rd., Orleans
(508) 240-1329
www.orleanshistoricalsociety.org

Opposite Orleans Town Hall, this Greek Revival–style meetinghouse is a former Universalist church built in 1834. Acquired by the Orleans Historical Society in 1971, it now houses collections of historic photographs, paintings, toys, costumes, china, and farm implements. It also has displays of Native American artifacts and Coast Guard lifesaving equipment, as well as items salvaged from one of the most infamous New England shipwrecks, the November 1898 wreck of the *Portland,* which resulted in the loss of all 176 people aboard. One of the many interesting items here is a letter from Capt. Richard Raggot of the British Navy dated September 30, 1814, containing the British demand for $1,000 to protect the town's saltworks from destruction (see our Historic Cape Cod chapter). The museum is open from mid-June through Sept, Thurs through Sat, from 10 a.m. to 1 p.m. or by appointment. Admission is free.

i Centuries ago, Route 6A was no more than a cart path for early settlers. As towns flourished and commerce grew, Route 6A became an extension of the Kings Highway and now is the major route for those traveling the north side of Cape Cod. Ranked among the country's top scenic byways, Route 6A extends 34 miles from Bourne to Orleans.

PILGRIM MONUMENT AND PROVINCETOWN MUSEUM
One High Pole Hill Road, Provincetown
(508) 487-1310
www.pilgrim-monument.org
The tallest granite structure in the United States, this 252-foot tower commemorates the Pilgrims' arrival in this town in 1620. It was completed in 1910 and features a granite block from every state in the union at the time. Theodore Roosevelt attended the laying of the cornerstone in 1907. This is a beacon for the area, visible from the Cape Cod Canal on a clear day. For a spectacular view of Cape Cod Bay and the area, you can climb the 116 steps and 60 ramps to the top. The museum has displays of Native American artifacts and antique china, pewter, and silver. Other items of particular interest pertain to expeditions by Antarctic explorer Admiral Donald MacMillan, a native son of Provincetown, and to the life of playwright Eugene O'Neill, whose plays were first performed in this town. The museum is open from mid-Apr through Oct at 9 a.m. each day. Last admission is at 4:15 p.m. in the off-season and 6:15 p.m. in July and Aug, and the doors close 45 minutes later. Parking is free; an admission fee

of $7.00 is charged adults; children's admission is $3.50 for those ages 4 to 14, and seniors and students (15 and older, with ID) pay $5.00.

PROVINCETOWN ART ASSOCIATION AND MUSEUM
460 Commercial St., Provincetown
(508) 487-1750
www.paam.org
The Provincetown Art Association and Museum was established in 1914 during the early years of Provincetown's art colony. Its galleries feature exhibits by established and emerging Outer Cape artists, as well as Art Association members. Also on display are works from the very impressive 2,000-piece permanent collection, including works by Hawthorne, Motherwell, Knaths, Hensche, Hofmann, Moffett, Bultman, and other painters associated with Provincetown. There is a museum store, library, artists' archives, and a museum school on the premises. It's open during the off-season Thurs through Sun from noon to 5 p.m. From Memorial Day through Sept, the hours are 11 a.m. to 8 p.m., Mon through Thurs, 11 a.m. to 10 p.m. Fri, and 11 a.m. to 5 p.m. Sat and Sun. An admission fee of $7 is charged for nonmembers.

RACE POINT LIGHTHOUSE, LONG POINT LIGHTHOUSE, WOOD END LIGHTHOUSE
Province Lands, Provincetown
(508) 487-9930
www.racepointlighthouse.net
Provincetown has three lighthouses guiding ships along its dangerous coastline toward the safety of Provincetown Harbor. All three are at the farthest reaches of Cape Cod, where roads give way to ever-shifting dunes of sand. Race Point Light was built in 1876, replacing the original lighthouse built here in 1816. The current Race Point Lighthouse is 41 feet tall. Long Point Light, at 36 feet, was originally installed along this lonely shore in 1827 and was replaced by the current Long Point Lighthouse in 1875. Today it is powered by solar energy. Between Race Point and Long Point rests the 45-foot-tall Wood End Light, which was built in 1873. Its light is also solar powered. All three

have foghorns, which make for an interesting sound in foggy weather. You can spend a night, weekend, or week at the keeper's house at Race Point Light, and the Whistle House is also open for stays of up to seven nights. Public tours are offered on designated Saturdays from May to Oct. Call for prices and availability.

STONY BROOK GRIST MILL & MUSEUM AT THE HERRING RUN
1002 Stony Brook Rd., Brewster
This area was home to many mills over the centuries, beginning with the very first gristmill built by Thomas Prence in 1663. Near Prence's gristmill, a fulling mill was also built in the 1600s. The fulling mill burned down in 1760, and the gristmill did the same in 1871. The country's first factory-produced woolen cloth was produced at a woolen mill built here in 1814. A new gristmill was constructed over the remains of the original in 1873, and it is this mill that today sits alongside Stony Brook. The museum is open to the public and the mill grinds corn June through Aug on Sat and Sun, 10 a.m. to 2 p.m. Adjacent to the mill is the Brewster herring run, where the annual migration of herring, also called alewives, occurs each spring (mid-Apr to early May).

SWIFT-DALEY HOUSE AND RANLETT TOOL MUSEUM
U.S. Route 6, Eastham
www.easthamhistorical.org
Built in 1741 by Joshua Knowles, this bow-roofed home has wide floorboards, a minister's cupboard, original wainscoting, and an 8-foot-wide fireplace. The house once belonged to Nathaniel Swift, one of the principals of the Swift Meat Packing Company. It is open weekdays from 10 a.m. to 1 p.m. in July and Aug, and on Sat from 10 a.m. to 1 p.m. in Sept. The Ranlett Tool Museum behind the Swift-Daley House has a display that includes numerous tools and implements collected in the area, including remnants of saltworks and cranberry-growing operations. The hours are the same as those for the Swift-Daley House. Admission to both is free.

TRURO HISTORICAL SOCIETY MUSEUM AT THE HIGHLAND HOUSE
Highland Light Road, North Truro
(508) 487-3397
www.trurohistorical.org
A turn-of-the-20th-century hotel (built in 1907) houses the Truro Historical Society's collections. These include Native American artifacts, items dating from the 17th century, lifesaving equipment, 17th-century weaponry, antique fishing and whaling equipment, household items, shipwreck items, Sandwich glass, historic photographs, and a pirate's chest! The museum is open June through September, 10 a.m. to 4:30 p.m. Mon through Sat and Sun from 1 to 4:30 p.m. Admission is $4; children younger than 12 are admitted free. The museum is just a stone's throw from the Highland Lighthouse and can be toured in tandem with it for an additional $2.

TRURO VINEYARDS OF CAPE COD
Route 6A, North Truro
(508) 487-6200
www.trurovineyardsofcapecod.com
Take a break from sightseeing and indulge in a few sips of local wine. Tour the vineyard, which thrives on the Cape's sandy soils and temperate breezes, and the winery. Tastings remain casual affairs, but they are now held under the vineyard's new "tasting pavillion" behind the lovely 1830s farmhouse, which houses the gift shop. It carries their wines, as well as cooking oils, marinades, jams, and all the wine accoutrements you could ever need. Open daily during the season, weekends in Apr and Dec. Call or go online for hours.

WELLFLEET HISTORICAL SOCIETY MUSEUM
266 Main St., Wellfleet
(508) 349-9157
www.wellfleethistoricalsociety.org
Wellfleet Historical Society Museum is located in a mid-19th-century general store. Its collection, focusing on the town's history, includes lifesaving equipment and medals, oystering displays, and information on early medicine. The exhibits highlight prominent Wellfleet residents, such as

Lorenzo Dow Baker, founder of the United Fruit Company empire, who was the first to import bananas into the United States in 1870; Luther Crowell, who invented a machine that made the square-bottomed paper bag; Sarah Atwood, one of the country's first female lighthouse keepers; and Clarence John Bell, a horse-and-buggy era doctor who delivered 2,500 babies in Wellfleet.

The museum is open from late June through early Sept (1 to 4 p.m. Wed, Thurs, and Sat, 10 a.m. to 4 p.m. Tuesday and Friday) and during the Oyster Festival in mid-October (10 a.m. to 5 p.m.). Walking tours are offered Tues and Fri at 10:15 a.m. Call for a schedule of walking tours. Admission is free, though a nominal fee of $1 is encouraged for those over 12.

KIDSTUFF

Cape Cod is a wonderful place to be a kid. We've met countless adults who say their idyllic childhood vacations here are part of why they return to the Cape—sometimes permanently.

Obviously there are the beaches. Everyone—not just children—loves running in the sand, splashing in the surf, building sandcastles, and hunting for seashells and beach rocks. Cape Cod kids have their own giant sandbox to play in year-round. But there's plenty to do on the Cape beyond beaches, from bumper cars and miniature golf to nature centers and museums.

There's so much for kids to do on the Cape that to detail everything would take a whole book. So we decided to simply offer a selection of what we consider to be the best and the brightest. We know you'll already be planning trips to museums (see our Attractions chapter), so we reserved this space for places especially geared toward children.

Check out the Hiking and Biking Trails chapter, our Beaches chapter, or our Arts chapter for still more ideas for what to do with children on the Cape.

Also included in this chapter are descriptions of summer camps, sports clinics, and creative centers that have become dependable outlets for youthful curiosity and energy.

If you and your other half must get away for some time alone, babysitting services are available (see our Education and Child Care chapter). Most hotels and accommodations keep a list of reliable sitters they've recommended in the past. The Children's Place (508-240-3310; www.capecodchildrensplace.com), a regional family resource center in Eastham (serving the Lower Cape towns from Brewster to Provincetown), keeps a list of recommended babysitters. And if you're staying on the Lower Cape (namely Provincetown), the Council on Aging (508-487-7080) also offers a babysitting service. Senior citizens will watch your kids (either in their homes or at your place) for a reasonable hourly rate, which depends on the number of children and the amount of notice given. It's not an all-day arrangement, but perfect for parents who want to get away for a few hours of sightseeing or dinner.

AQUARIUMS AND ANIMAL FARMS

Upper Cape

SANDWICH FISH HATCHERY
Route 6A, Sandwich
(508) 888-0008

Fishing around to do something really different? Adults and kids alike will enjoy the Sandwich Fish Hatchery, where more than half a million fish are raised to stock the state's various ponds. Kids will be able to track the stages of fish development and feed the critters (bring quarters!). Admission is free. It's open year-round, 9 a.m. to 3 p.m. daily.

WOODS HOLE SCIENCE AQUARIUM
166 Water St., Woods Hole
(508) 495-2001
http://aquarium.nefsc.noaa.gov

The public aquarium of the Northeast Fisheries Science Center encourages children to touch the specimens. They can feel around three touch-tanks and pick up such deep-sea wonders as sea cucumbers, lobsters, and starfish. They can also look at creatures close up under a magnifier and go eye-to-eye with marine life through the glass of 16 display tanks. They can see seals too: Feedings are held at 11 a.m. and 4 p.m. Student volunteers are on hand to answer kids' queries in summer.

The aquarium is open Mon through Fri 11 a.m. to 4 p.m. during the school year, and in summer Tues through Sat (11 a.m. to 4 p.m.). Admission is free, though donations are appreciated.

Mid-Cape

ZOOQUARIUM
674 Rte. 28, West Yarmouth
(508) 775-8883
www.zooquariumcapecod.net

Half zoo, half aquarium, the ZooQuarium has displays and exhibits of all things native to our area. But there's so much more. One large room houses tanks of local pond and sea-life exhibits. Outside there is a petting zoo with llamas and sheep. The ZooQuarium is open daily from mid-Apr through Sept. Call or go online for hours in the offseason. Admission is $10 for visitors ages 10 and older and $7 for children ages 2 to 9 (see our Kidstuff chapter for more information).

MUSEUMS AND NATURE CENTERS

Upper Cape

CAPE COD CHILDREN'S MUSEUM
577 Great Neck Rd. South, Mashpee
(508) 539-8788
www.capecodchildrensmuseum.org

Here families can have fun together while discovering new things about the world around us. The museum offers daily programs, a planetarium, a 30-foot pirate ship, a puppet theater, a toddler play area, and a museum store. It's the perfect rainy-day activity. Open year-round, the summer hours are 10 a.m. to 5 p.m. Mon through Sat, and noon to 5 p.m. on Sun. Admission is $6 for those ages 1 through 59 and $5 for seniors 60 years and older (see our Kidstuff chapter).

GREEN BRIAR NATURE CENTER AND JAM KITCHEN
6 Discovery Hill Rd., East Sandwich
(508) 888-6870
www.thorntonburgess.com

You're still in Thornton Burgess country here: The Old Briar Patch comes to life at this nature center, which abuts 57 acres of conservation land. Kids can visit frogs and turtles at the Smiling Pool and wander on the nature trails to look for signs of other critters. The Jam Center, established in 1903, is a kitchen nestled back in the woods where jams and jellies are still made the right way—by hand. Take a tour of the kitchen and see them being made, then buy some to take home. You can also take one of the center's regularly offered jam-making classes—available for both children and adults—and take home the fruits of your own labor. Green Briar is open daily Apr through Dec (10 a.m. to 4 p.m. Mon through Sat, 1 to 4 p.m. Sun), Tues through Sat (10 a.m. to 4 p.m.) Jan through Mar. Admission is by donation.

HERITAGE MUSEUMS & GARDENS
67 Grove St., Sandwich
(508) 888-3300
www.heritagemuseumsandgardens.org

This is a perfect outing for parents and the kids-in-the-stroller set. You'll get to see everything—lush gardens and some magnificent collections including 32 antique cars and folk art—while giving the little ones a good workout. The old-fashioned, hand-carved 1912 indoor carousel gives free rides with paid admission. Admission is $12 for adults ($11 for those older than 65), $6 for ages 6 through 16, and free for children 5 and younger. Admission is free for members of Heritage Plantation. It's open daily 10 a.m. to 5 p.m. from Apr through Oct.

THORNTON BURGESS MUSEUM
4 Water St., Sandwich
(508) 888-6870
www.thorntonburgess.org

The life and career of the Sandwich native and children's author who wrote thousands of stories and 170 books, including *The Adventures of Peter Cottontail* and the beloved *Old Mother West Wind* series, is chronicled here through memorabilia and exhibits. The cottage where the museum is housed was the home of Burgess's eccentric aunt, a teacher who talked with plants and wildlife. So it's only natural that this is a place where kids can also get close to plants—in the touch-and-smell herb garden. Story hours (Burgess's tales, of course) are given on the front lawn regularly throughout the summer. The museum is open daily May through Oct; hours are 10 a.m. to 4 p.m. Mon through Sat, and 1 to 4 p.m. on Sun. The museum requests a donation for admission.

i The National Marine Life Center cares for stranded marine animals. Its visitor center, with exhibits and activities about whales, dolphins, seals, and sea turtles, is worth the trip, and admission is free. Open to visitors daily from late May to Sept. Call (508) 743-9888, or visit wwwnmlc.org.

Lower Cape

CAPE COD MUSEUM OF NATURAL HISTORY
896 Rte. 6A, Brewster
(508) 896-3867
www.ccmnh.org

Although this wonderful facility is great for people of all ages, it is family-oriented and very child-friendly. Take the little ones downstairs to a room full of hands-on exhibits, fish tanks, and demonstrations that will entertain them for hours. They can observe the world of nature up close through whale displays, marine life exhibits, and window bird feeders. The museum offers walking trails and numerous classes, programs, and tours. The museum is open daily in the summer (June through Sept) from 9:30 a.m. to 4 p.m. Call for off-season hours. Admission is $8.00 for those ages 13 and older, $7.00 for seniors, $3.50 for children 3 to 12, and free for youngsters age 2 and younger.

i They're strange looking, they're harmless, and they're more closely related to spiders than to true crabs. Horseshoe crabs are recognized by their brown, rounded shell and spinelike tail or telson. The horseshoe crab has inhabited the earth for 200 to 350 million years and has remained essentially unchanged in form.

WELLFLEET BAY WILDLIFE SANCTUARY
291 U.S. Rte. 6, South Wellfleet
(508) 349-2615
www.wellfleetbay.org

This Outer Cape treasure offers many fascinating programs that let you sample the Cape's different habitats, from coastal heathlands to meadows, from fresh and saltwater inlets to barrier beaches. Both on-site programs at the sanctuary and off-site programs that include nearby Nauset Marsh and Monomoy Island are offered. Programs include interactive field trips, guided walks, cruises, and informative lectures by Audubon naturalists. You can sign up for an organized program or just come to walk the beautiful trails or the tidal flats at low tide. The sanctuary trails are open 365 days a year from 8 a.m. to dusk (8 p.m. in the summer). The nature center is open daily, 8:30 a.m. to 5 p.m. from Memorial Day through Columbus Day, and closed Mondays after Columbus Day. Admission is free for Massachusetts Audubon members. The fee for nonmembers is $5 for adults, $3 for kids 3 to 12 and younger and senior citizens, and free for those under 3.

MINIGOLF AND AMUSEMENTS

Mid-Cape

PIRATE ADVENTURES
Ocean Street Dock (Slip #4), Hyannis
(508) 394-9100
www.pirateadventures.com

Pirate Adventures is pure fantasy—it's an old-fashioned, swashbuckling adventure your children will remember for years to come. With costumed pirate actors, painted faces, and sailor sashes, the little mates aboard the pirate ship Sea Gypsy cast off on a pirate adventure. There's underwater treasure to find and a secret map that leads you there. But before the crew gets to pull up the booty, they may have to fire the water cannons in order to save the ship and capture the treasure. There is lots of fun to be had, as the crew sings sea chanteys, takes the time-honored oath of loyal sailors, and participates in storytelling and a gang effort to find the treasure. This

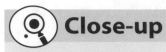 **Close-up**

Rainy Day Doings

The gardeners among us welcome rainy days, knowing that without enough moisture the Cape would be bereft of many of the plants and flowers that make it beautiful. For those on vacation, however, a rainy day can be challenging, especially if there are children involved. Here are a few of our favorite rainy-day activities; many of them are listed in this chapter.

Libraries: Every town has one, and on rainy days, the children's librarians expect crowds and often schedule extra activities accordingly. See the Yellow Pages in the phone book or call town hall (see our Area Overview chapter for contact information for each town) for the library nearest you.

Bookstores: We love to browse in bookstores on rainy days. Try Parnassus Books in Yarmouthport (great for old books) or the Armchair Bookstore in Dennis (which has an especially appealing children's section).

Cape Cod Museum of Natural History: This Brewster museum will keep children—and adults—amused for hours. It is busier than usual on rainy days, but the plus side is that you're sure to meet other families to chat with.

Cape Cod Mall: Expect crowds at this Hyannis mall on rainy days, but at least it's a diversion. There are plenty of shops, plus three anchor stores (see our Shopping chapter) and a lively food court.

Arcades: If you can stand the noise, bring your kids to Ryan Family Amusements, located in Cape Cod Mall; Main Street, Hyannis; South Yarmouth; and Buzzards Bay.

Beaches: As long as it's not stormy, there's nothing wrong with a walk at the beach in the rain. We especially like going to the beach when there's a light mist falling, and fog gives the shoreline a mystical, ethereal look. Best of all, there are no crowds.

popular adventure runs frequent trips from the Ocean Street Docks in Hyannis, beginning mid-June and running through Labor Day. There are eight excursions daily, running every hour and 15 minutes starting at 9 a.m.

Reservations are required. Admission is $20 per person.

i Strawberry season on the Cape usually begins around the second week of June, though it's very dependent on spring weather. Check with Andrews Farm (508-548-4717), 394 Old Meeting House Road, East Falmouth, or Coonamessett Farm (508-563-2560), 277 Hatchville Rd., East Falmouth, to see what's ripe for picking. Picking on the first day of the season will get you the largest, plumpest berries.

PIRATE'S COVE ADVENTURE GOLF
723 Main St., South Yarmouth
(508) 394-6200
www.piratescove.net

This two-course attraction even has a pirate ship in a fake pond, surrounded by waterfalls and cliffs. Kids can win fun prizes in keeping with the theme, such as pirate eye patches, tattoos, and flags. Pirate's Cove is open daily from mid-Apr through Oct. Admission is $7.95 per course ($6.95 for ages 12 and younger). In the summer, Pirate's Cove is open from 10 a.m. to 10 p.m.; in the fall and spring it's usually open 10 a.m. to 7 p.m.

RYAN FAMILY AMUSEMENTS
Cape Cod Mall, Route 132, Hyannis
(508) 771-1120
441 Main St., Hyannis
(508) 775-3411

1067 Route 28, South Yarmouth
(508) 394-5644
200 Main St., Buzzards Bay
(508) 759-9892
www.ryanfamily.com
Ryan Family Amusements offers all kinds of arcade games, pinball, Skee-Ball, and video games along with children's games such as ride-on horses, air hockey, and basketball.

Lower Cape

BUD'S GO-KARTS
364 Sisson Rd., Harwich
(508) 432-4964
Unique to the Lower Cape, this long-established go-kart center, easy to find on the corner of Route 28 and Sisson Road, rings all summer with the delighted shrieks and shouts of children going fast and loving it. You can get on the course for $6. In the summer it's open daily from 9 a.m. to 11 p.m..

CAPE ESCAPE ULTIMATE ADVENTURE GOLF
14 Canal Rd., Orleans
(508) 240-1791
www.capeescapeadventures.com
Right near the Orleans Rotary, this minigolf center features 18 holes set in nautical surroundings, complete with waterfalls, boats, a koi pond, and a water wheel. Cape Escape Mini-Golf is open daily from 9 a.m. to "late" in July and Aug and 10 a.m. to "late" from Apr through June. The cost is $8.50 for ages 13 and older and $8.00 for seniors and children 12 and under.

GRAND SLAM ENTERTAINMENT
322 Rte. 28, Harwich Port
(508) 430-1155
www.capecodbumperboats.com
Batting cages are ready and waiting for your little sluggers. There are also bumper boats and arcade games. Activities are priced by tokens— one token, for example, buys you 10 pitches in the batting cage. Tokens purchased singly cost $1.50, but in multiples they cost less: $1.25 when you buy five, $1.00 if you buy 10, and 90 cents if you purchase 22. Grand Slam is open 9 a.m. to 10 p.m. daily, mid-Apr through Sept.

i For a twist on the normal sightseeing tour, try Cape Cod Duckmobiles. They offer narrated tours of downtown Hyannis and Hyannis Harbor on restored U.S. military amphibious vehicles—taking you from land to sea and back to land. Tours leave from 437 Main St., Hyannis. Tickets are $17 for adults, $14 for seniors and students, and $5 for children younger than age five. Call (888) 225–3825, or visit www.duckmobile.com.

POITS LIGHTHOUSE MINI-GOLF
5270 Rte. 6, North Eastham
(508) 255-6321
www.poitslighthouseminigolf.com
This high seas–themed minigolf course is the newest addition to the Poit's entertainment complex. It encompasses 18 holes, a winding river, a fountain, a pond with geysers, three lighthouses, and the pièce de résistance: a wraparound waterfall that gushes from a height of 16 feet. Poit's also includes a snack bar, a video arcade, and an ice-cream concession serving treats from Garelick Farms. Open from mid-Apr through mid-Sept. Daily in-season hours are from 10 a.m. to 10 p.m. In the shoulder months, Poit's is open weekends only from 10 a.m. to 6 p.m.

TRAMPOLINE CENTER
296 Rte. 28, West Harwich
(508) 432-8717
Kids will have a great time jumping to their hearts' content. A dozen large trampolines in a fenced-in outdoor area are set at ground level, so even the smallest of small fry can fly high. Remember to follow the two rules: no shoes and no flips. The center is open 9 a.m. to 10 p.m. (or 11 p.m. if lots of people are bouncing) daily from mid-June through Labor Day. The cost is $5 for 10 minutes.

SUMMER CAMPS AND CREATIVE CENTERS

Many a Cape Cod resident has childhood recollections of learning to swim and sail at a Cape Cod summer camp. With its numerous beaches, ponds, and woods, this area is ideal for providing youngsters with outdoor education and recreation. The Cape also has outlets for youthful energies at its sports clinics and art-fostering creative centers. One affordable alternative to day camps are the recreation programs sponsored by each town. Offerings vary from town to town, but generally include arts and crafts, swimming, tennis, and other sports. Some even have golf and sailing. Each town varies in its policy for allowing participation by nonresidents, but most allow nonresidents to sign up, with lower fees for residents. Fees vary as well, but most other towns charge at least nominal fees. Contact your local town recreation department for specific information.

Upper Cape

CAMP BURGESS FOR BOYS–CAMP HAYWARD FOR GIRLS
75 Stowe Rd., South Sandwich
(508) 428-2571
www.ssymca.org

Set on over 300 acres of land in an area that encompasses three ponds, these two camps—Burgess for boys and Hayward for girls—are traditional overnight camps for children ages 7 to 15 run by the South Shore YMCA. The waterfront facility allows for sailing, windsurfing, waterskiing, basketball, volleyball, and tennis. The camps feature a 30-foot climbing tower and offer low- and high-ropes courses. Also offered are classes in arts and crafts, photography, mountain biking, and horseback riding. Sessions run from one to two weeks in June and Aug and cost $1,325 per camper for two weeks ($665 for one).

CAMP FARLEY 4-H OUTDOOR EDUCATION CENTER
615 Rte. 130, Mashpee
(508) 477-0181
www.campfarley.com

This 32-acre camp on beautiful freshwater Mashpee-Wakeby Pond has both day and overnight programs for children ages 4 to 15. Activities range from arts and crafts to boating, canoeing, and horseback riding. Environmental and nature programs are also included. Day camp is $275 per week for kids in grades 1 to 7, and the camp offers weeklong sessions for $425 to overnight campers in grades 3 to 10.

CAMP LYNDON CAPE COD YMCA
117 Stowe Rd., South Sandwich
(508) 428-9251
www.ymcacapecod.org/lyndon.htm

A day camp for boys and girls from ages 4 to 15, Lyndon offers archery, games, sports, sailing and boating, a ropes challenge course, arts and crafts, kickball, and soccer. Swimming (including instruction) and horseback riding (ages 6 to 15) are part of the program. Camp Lyndon and its sister camp, Camp 132 in West Barnstable, are very popular and fill quickly. We advise contacting Camp Lyndon in March if you'd like your child to participate in one of their two-week summer programs. Bus transportation is available.

Mid-Cape

CAMP WINGATE-KIRKLAND
79 White Rock Rd., Yarmouthport
(508) 362-3798, (888) 714-2267
www.campwk.com
Since the late 1950s, this coeducational overnight youth camp has offered sports, water activities, arts and crafts, camp craft, music, and drama. Children can choose from a seven-week session or one of the two three-and-a-half-week sessions, paying either $8,550 for the full season or $5,450 for a half session.

CAPE COD GYMNASTICS
334B Hokum Rd., Dennis
(508) 385-8216
www.capecodgymnastics.com
Open year-round with a variety of classes, Cape Cod Gymnastics offers five-week sessions and summer camps for cheerleading, skateboarding, and general gymnastics. Classes are available for children as young as preschool ages, including one (My Buddy) for preschoolers and parents to take together. Go online or call for various rates and schedules.

FAIR ACRES COUNTRY DAY SCHOOL
35 Fair Acres Dr., Marstons Mills
(508) 420-3288
With pretty Shubel Pond at its doorstep, this day camp for children ages four to nine offers certified Red Cross swimming instruction, arts and crafts, nature studies, sports, tennis, and drama. Call Mon through Fri for details.

YMCA CAMP 132
2245 Rte. 132, West Barnstable
(508) 362-6500
www.ymcacapecod.org
The Y offers a weeklong summer day program for children ages 5 to 10 at its well-equipped facility. Children participate in arts and crafts, archery, sports, swimming (including lessons), and Friday field trips (to the Boston Aquarium or to whale watch, for example). Tuition is $198 per week, and overnights are offered to 7-to-10-year-olds for an extra fee of $30 per night. YMCA membership is not required, but you save 5 percent by belonging to the association.

Lower Cape

ACADEMY OF PERFORMING ARTS
5 Giddiah Hill Rd., Orleans
(508) 255-5510
www.apacape.org
More than 35 instructors teach classes ranging from dance (ballet, jazz, world, modern, ballroom, and tap) to drama and music for children and adults. How about hip-hop classes? There's even a slate of "early childhood" offerings, among them primers on "creatures movement" and "story dance." Courses run two weeks in July and Aug with a graduation ceremony—a public performance to show off newfound talent.

BREWSTER DAY CAMP
3570 Rte. 6A, Brewster
(508) 896-6555
www.brewsterdaycamp.com
Set on a four-acre campus near Nickerson State Park, the Brewster Day Camp offers art, archery, boating, exploring, field sports, games, nature activities, Red Cross swimming lessons, and sailing. There are off-campus trips and children can opt for lessons in horseback riding, golf, and tennis. One to five-day programs are offered (with a few overnights) for children from kindergarten through eighth grade. Sign up by the week, with the full session running for eight weeks from late June through mid-Aug. The weekly rate is $490.

BREWSTER WHITECAPS BASEBALL CLINIC
Community Center Field, Brewster
(508) 896–3424
www.brewsterwhitecaps.com
From mid-June through July the Brewster Whitecaps team sponsors weeklong clinics. Kids learn everything from how to bunt to how to hit a home run. Open to children ages 6 to 13, the clinics meet at Cape Cod Regional Technical School field, the home field for the Brewster Whitecaps. Cost is $65 for the first week (subtract $5 per week thereafter).

CAPE COD MUSEUM OF NATURAL HISTORY
869 Rte. 6A, Brewster
(508) 896-3867
www.ccmnh.org
From late June to mid-Aug, the museum offers one- to nine-week nature day programs for children in grades 1 through 7, in which they learn about everything from birds to dinosaurs. They even get to set up their own freshwater and saltwater aquariums. CCMNH also offers age-appropriate, three- to five-day sessions for kids ages three and four and for those up to grade seven for a total of eight months in summer. Typical activities include catching insects, building bird feeders, making sun clocks, and learning about bird banding, coyote tracking, geology, and astronomy. Call for a schedule.

CAPE COD SEA CAMPS
3057 Main St., Brewster
(508) 896-3451
www.capecodseacamps.com
Established in 1922, Cape Cod Sea Camps is the oldest residential camp on the Cape. With beautiful grounds that stretch to Cape Cod Bay, it offers a three-and-a-half- or seven-week residential camp for ages 8 to 17 and a day camp for ages 4 to 17. Instruction covers all sorts of water sports, including sailing, swimming, windsurfing, waterskiing, and canoeing. They offer both day and overnight programs.

CREATIVE ARTS CENTER
154 Crowell Rd., Chatham
www.capecodcreativearts.org
Budding da Vincis and Cassatts will love the year-round classes in drawing, painting, pottery, photography, sculpture, and jewelry making. Classes are flexible and open to a wide range of ages and skill levels. Price varies per program.

ORLEANS FIREBIRDS BASEBALL CLINIC
P.O. Box 504, Orleans, MA 02653
(508) 255-0793
www.orleanscardinals.com
The weeklong morning clinics for boys and girls ages 6 through 13 begin in mid-June and continue through the first week of Aug. Cost is $70 for the first week and $65 for each additional week. This fee includes a Firebirds clinic T-shirt.

WELLFLEET BAY WILDLIFE SANCTUARY
291 U.S. Rte. 6, P.O. Box 236, South Wellfleet, MA 02663
(508) 349-2615
www.wellfleetbay.org
Kids who are avid about nature will appreciate the Natural History Day Camp Programs at this Massachusetts Audubon site. The activities are calibrated to different ages, but they all have an intense focus on animals and their habitats. Each week focuses on different marine or animal life, their habitats, and the children's exploring and observing skills. Younger kids learn about animal tracks, older kids go on canoe trips and snorkel in Cape Cod Bay. The camp runs from mid-June through Aug for children in preschool programs through grade eight.

WOODSONG FARM EQUESTRIAN CENTER
121 Lund Farm Way, Brewster
(508) 896–5800
www.woodsongcentral.com
If your child is crazy about horses, check out Woodsong Farm's summer programs. For beginners there's Pony Kids, offered two, three, or five days a week for ages 5 to 14. Experienced riders ages 9 to 18 can enroll in Horsemasters. Both programs cover all aspects of horsemanship. Lessons are available year-round at the center, which also boards horses and has its own tack shop. Check their Web site for current schedules and dates.

ANNUAL EVENTS

Before you decide when to visit Cape Cod, take a look at what's going on. Cape Cod is no longer just a summer playground. Now it's a year-round vacation resort with events planned for all twelve months.

Arrive in May and you'll find yourself at the largest sailboat regatta on the East Coast, the Figawi Race from Hyannis to Nantucket (be sure to make early reservations for their posh charity ball). In June, Cape Cod Heritage Week will lead you through the towns of the Cape, where you'll discover a treasure chest of cultural, historical, and environmental riches. Flip the calendar to December, and you'll find yourself strolling amid merry crowds through some of America's most charming colonial villages decked out in Christmas card perfection.

Perhaps no event on Cape Cod surpasses the joyousness of the Portuguese Festival held in Provincetown the last weekend in June. In July Independence Day fireworks, patriotic banners, and parades mark the official start of summer, when arts and crafts fairs abound and village greens around the Cape host evening concerts. The circus and fairs come to town, and the annual Wampanoag Pow Wow brings together Native American Indians from across the nation for three days of tribal dances and events. The second weekend in August transforms Falmouth into a race track for thousands of runners who compete in the famous Falmouth Road Race.

Autumn is a truly magical time here—more so if you're visiting Bourne for its Farm Pumpkin Day or Falmouth for Harvest Day. Museums and sanctuaries also offer an opportunity to explore the seasonal changes through programs and activities every day of the year.

Also occurring throughout the year, Cape Cod's many charity events help maintain institutions vital to the social fabric of the Cape and give you great opportunities to have fun. You can golf with stars on the greens of Willowbend Country Club or listen to the Boston Pops Esplanade Orchestra at the Village Green in Hyannis.

We suggest that you call the Cape Cod Chamber of Commerce, or the chamber of commerce in the town you will be visiting, for an up-to-date listing of weekly events. A competition fomented recently over who could provide the most information about what to do on Cape turned out to be a boon for tourists. Check out the results in the Cape's only year-round daily, the *Cape Cod Times,* and feel free to consider this a shameless plug for the author's day job.

The following listing of events is arranged chronologically by month and then roughly by geography, so Provincetown festivals, for example are listed toward the end of the month. The year begins, appropriately, with New Year's celebrations.

JANUARY

Upper Cape

CAPE AND ISLANDS ORCHID SOCIETY SHOW
Resort and Conference Center at Hyannis,
35 Scudder Ave.,
Hyannis
www.caios.org

This annual show is sponsored by the Cape and Islands Orchid Society the last weekend in Jan. It includes exquisite blooming orchid displays, informative demonstrations on growing orchids and building greenhouses, and, of course, orchids for sale. The aroma alone is worth the price of admission. It is usually held at the Sea Crest Resort and Conference Center in Falmouth, but due to renovations there it is scheduled for the Sea Crest's sister facility for at least 2010.

FEBRUARY

Mid-Cape

HYANNIS MARATHON, HALF MARATHON, 10K, RELAY
Hyannis
www.hyannismarathon.com
This event, usually held in late Feb, starts and finishes at the Resort and Conference Center at Hyannis. Some 300 marathoners, 1,500 half marathoners, 500 10Kers, and 50 relay teams wend their way along a scenic course that passes Craigville Beach, Hyannis Harbor, Lewis Bay, the John F. Kennedy Memorial, and the Kennedy Family Compound. The marathon is a Boston Marathon qualifying event.

PRESIDENTS' WEEKEND ANTIQUE SHOW AND SALE
Barnstable High School Field House
West Main Street, Hyannis
(508) 775-2280
www.hyannislibrary.org
Scheduled each year for the Sat and Sun of Presidents' Day weekend, this show features more than 50 regional dealers who offer an array of antique furniture, glass, silver, jewelry, postcards, paintings, rugs, maps and prints, and china. The doors open at 10 a.m. This is a major fund-raiser for the Hyannis Public Library. Admission is $6.

i If you are lucky, you can sometimes spot whales from land. April is one of the best times for seeing humpback and finback whales. Race Point or Hatches Harbor in Provincetown are good places to look. Whales can also be seen occasionally right inside Provincetown Harbor. For more information call the Provincetown Center for Coastal Studies, (508) 487-3622.

APRIL

Upper Cape

WOODS HOLE MODEL BOAT SHOW
Woods Hole Historical Museum, 579 Woods Hole Rd., Woods Hole
(508) 548-7270
www.woodsholemuseum.org
You don't have to be an enthusiast to enjoy yourself at this event, held in mid-Apr. Stroll through an indoor exhibit of large model boats, or join the enthusiasts down at Eel Pond for regattas featuring radio-controlled models of vintage yachts from the 1930s.

Mid-Cape

DAFF O'VILLE DAYS
Various sites in Osterville
(508) 428-6327
Sponsored by the Osterville Business and Professional Association, this village-wide celebration takes place during the last week in April. Events include an Arbor Day celebration, Mad Hatter Tea Party, bagpipe music, wine tastings, and a book sale. The fun continues with outdoor grills, a fashion show, and an antique car display.

Lower Cape

BREWSTER IN BLOOM
Various locations in Brewster
(508) 896-3500
www.brewsterinbloom.org
An annual and eagerly awaited spring event, Brewster in Bloom started as a small festival celebrating Brewster's beautiful daffodil display. The festival is now three days of fun and games, including such activities as a chowder contest, dance, flea market, golf tournament, road race, parade, band concert, arts and crafts fair, ice-cream social, inn tour, and children's activities. And all the while there are more than 100,000 blooming daffodils lining the streets. The event takes place the last weekend in Apr, sometimes falling into the first days of May. Tickets are required for certain events, like the golf tourney and the dance; otherwise, most of Brewster in Bloom activities are free.

MAY

Cape-wide

CAPE COD MARITIME DAYS

Various sites throughout the Cape
(508) 362-3828
www.ecapechamber.com/maritimedays

Maritime Week is a major Cape-wide event that highlights the landmarks and sites comprising Cape Cod's wealth of maritime history. This mid-May celebration is coordinated by the Cape Cod Commission, which arranges lighthouse tours, Coast Guard open houses, special cruises, walks, and lectures throughout the week. In Yarmouthport, a village that was once a major port, you can take self-guided walking tours of sea captains' homes and attend open houses at museums, getting from place to place via the free trolley service. All events are free.

Upper Cape

RHODODENDRON'S BLOOMING

Heritage Museums & Gardens, Grove and Pine Streets, Sandwich
(508) 888-3300
www.heritagemuseumsandgardens.org

One of the largest and best collections of rhododendrons is found in Sandwich, and many are in bloom the last week in May and during the first two weeks in June. You may participate in tours and lectures, shop for plants at the plant sale, and, of course, view the multitude of beautiful rhododendron colors. Admission to Heritage Museums & Gardens is $12, seniors $11, ages 6 to 16 $6, ages 5 and younger free.

GREEN BRIAR HERB FESTIVAL

Green Briar Nature Center, 6 Discovery Hill Rd., East Sandwich
(508) 888-6870
www.thorntonburgess.org

Benefiting the Thornton Burgess Society, this free event held over three days in mid-May offers lectures on herbs, special demonstrations, exhibits, and wildflower garden walks. You can get a taste of the herbs at a wonderful luncheon (reserva-tions are required) and buy plants just in time to start your own herb garden.

WOODS HOLE ILLUMINATION WEEKEND

Woods Hole
(508) 548-8500

This event, held over a weekend in late May, provides a great introduction to charming Woods Hole. Harbor tours, carriage rides, Coast Guard rescue enactments, and music under the stars will keep you occupied while you're waiting for the main attraction: nightly illuminations of boats and businesses throughout Woods Hole Village, Eel Pond, Great Harbor, and Little Harbor, all free.

Mid-Cape

FIGAWI SAILBOAT RACE & CHARITY BALL

Hyannis
(508) 221-6891
www.figawi.com

The Figawi regatta, which takes place over Memorial Day weekend, is a great Cape Cod celebration that kicks off the summer season in style. Generally considered the largest sailboat race on the East Coast, the Figawi usually draws more than 200 boats in a highly competitive race from Hyannis to Nantucket. A cocktail party greets contestants at Nantucket, and the following day is filled with an awards ceremony, an afternoon clambake, and evening Memorial Day party. The reverse Figawi from Nantucket to Hyannis is followed by another party and another awards presentation. And if you'll be here earlier, you can join the fun a whole week earlier at the black-tie Figawi Charity Ball, the kickoff event held the preceding weekend at the Resort and Conference Center at Hyannis. Proceeds aid local charities.

Lower Cape

SPRING FLING

Downtown Chatham
(508) 945-5199, (800) 715-5567
www.chathamcapecod.org

Chatham gets a little crazy with spring fever in May with its annual Spring Fling. There's a wild and crazy hat parade, clowns, jugglers, a pet show, and face painting. Sponsored by the Chatham Merchants Association, this family-oriented event is held on the Saturday of Mother's Day weekend.

ARTS AND CRAFTS SHOWS
Nauset Middle School, Route 28, Orleans
www.artisansguildcapecod.org
The Artisans' Guild of Cape Cod hosts six arts and crafts shows during the year; the first takes place on Memorial Day weekend (the others are held in early July, early and late Aug, early Oct, and late Nov). Some shows are held on the front lawn of Nauset Middle School, others in the school's gymnasium, and the late Aug show is at Cape Cod Academy. There is plenty of parking available at the schools and no admission fee.

JUNE

Upper Cape

STRAWBERRY FESTIVAL
St. Barnabas Church, Falmouth
(508) 548-8500
www.stbarnabasfalmouth.org
About a century ago, Falmouth was one of the largest producers of strawberries in the eastern United States. The tradition continues as seemingly everyone in town shows up on the Village Green across from the St. Barnabas Church to feast on fresh strawberries from Tony Andrews' Farm in East Falmouth. You can also buy crafts and baked goods throughout the day.

> **i** In the spring Pilgrim Heights in Truro is one of the best places on Cape Cod to see hawks. Look for broad-winged hawks, sharp-shinned hawks, American kestrels, and northern harriers. You might spot red-tailed hawks too, which are present year-round. Wellfleet Bay Audubon Sanctuary (508-349-2615) leads hawk walks through the spring months.

Mid-Cape

ANNUAL WCOD CHOWDER FESTIVAL
Cape Cod Melody Tent, West Main Sreet, Hyannis
(508) 775-5678
www.106wcod.com
Sample delicious chowders cooked up by some of Cape Cod's best restaurants at the Annual WCOD 106FM Chowder Festival, but be sure to get to the Melody Tent before the chowder buckets run dry. The event is usually held toward the end of June, but the exact date depends on the Melody Tent entertainment schedule. Call for a schedule and the price of admission.

Lower Cape

BREWSTER HISTORICAL SOCIETY ANTIQUES FAIR
Drummer Boy Field, Route 6A, Brewster
(508) 896-9521
www.brewsterhistoricalsociety.org
You're bound to find something special to purchase among the more than 70 dealers selling their wares at this very popular show and sale. It's held on the last Saturday of June on the Drummer Boy Park grounds and, as a special bonus, the on-site Old Higgins Farm windmill is open free to the public for the event. The fair runs from 9 a.m. to 4 p.m. and admission is $5; ages 12 and younger are free.

PORTUGUESE FESTIVAL
Provincetown
(508) 246-9080
www.provincetownportuguesefestival.com
Provincetown celebrates its Portuguese and fishing heritage with a festival the last weekend of June. There is music galore, a kids' fishing derby on Fri from 10 a.m. to noon, a parade at 3 p.m. on Sat, and live music and dance performances throughout the weekend. The blessing of the fleet occurs on Sun, and that event begins with a noon procession from St. Peter's Church to MacMillan Pier. Parking is limited in Provincetown, but you should be able to find a place in one of the town parking lots if you get there early. There is

no charge to attend the parade and the blessing of the fleet; however, donations are requested for some of the activities.

JULY

Cape-wide

INDEPENDENCE DAY FIREWORKS AND EVENTS
Various locations throughout the Cape
Many towns across the Cape offer spectacular fireworks displays to celebrate Independence Day. Plan to arrive by dusk at one of the following locations: Falmouth Heights, Hyannis Harbor, Orleans Rock Harbor, and Provincetown Harbor. Hyannis also hosts a July 4th boat parade in the harbor, Falmouth has a blessing of the fleet, and Harwich has a July 4th Family Fun Day with a craft fair and entertainment. Chatham, Orleans, Wellfleet, and Provincetown have parades.

Upper Cape

CONCERTS IN THE PARK
Buzzards Bay Park, Buzzards Bay
(508) 759-6000
www.capecodcanalchamber.org
The music ranges from country and western to jazz and from show tunes to rock 'n' roll at this music series held at Buzzards Bay Park gazebo. Bring a blanket or lawn chair and join the fun every Thurs night from 6:30 to 8:30 p.m. during July and Aug. Admission is free.

BARNSTABLE COUNTY FAIR
Route 151, East Falmouth
(508) 563-3200
www.barnstablecountyfair.org
A Cape Cod tradition for more than 160 years, the Barnstable County Fair regularly attracts more than 100,000 people for nine days packed with fun, food, and education. There are incredible exhibits, amazing entertainment, awesome animal shows, and food and craft events at which adults and children win prizes for baked goods, canned goods, homegrown fruits and vegetables, quilts, and other handiwork as well as for

the best sheep, pigs, cows, rabbits, poultry, and so on. Top-name entertainment fills the evenings. A petting zoo, carnival rides, and games make the Barnstable County Fair really exciting for kids. The fair is held the third week in July. Regular admission is $10 for those 13 and older; $8 for seniors and soldiers with valid military ID; and free for kids 12 and under admitted with a paid adult. Check out the three-day pass for $25. Rides cost extra.

ANNUAL ARTS & CRAFTS STREET FAIR
Main Street, Falmouth
(508) 548-5600
Hosted by the Falmouth Village Association, this event features more than 200 artisans and craftspeople displaying their wares. Booths line both sides of Main Street, and they close the street to vehicle traffic. You'll also find plenty of food and fun entertainment throughout the day. The Street Fair, held on a Wed during early July, starts at 10 a.m. and goes until 5 p.m.

MASHPEE WAMPANOAG POW WOW
Barnstable County Fair Grounds, Route 151, Mashpee
(508) 477-0208
www.mashpeewampanoagtribe.com
Open to the public, this event is sponsored by the Mashpee Wampanoag Tribal Council and features tribal dances and other activities, such as the native fireball game, princess contests, a road race, traditional clambake, and American-Indian crafts. This popular three-day event attracts American Indians from many other states and always takes place the first weekend in July. An admission fee of $8 is charged; $6 for children and seniors.

ANNUAL SANDCASTLE COMPETITION
South Cape Beach, Mashpee
(508) 477-0792, (508) 539-1400 ext. 519
www.mashpeeleisureservices.com
South Cape Beach is the site of this annual sandcastle competition sponsored by Leisure Services from 9 a.m. until noon the second Sat in July. There are five categories. Contestants are allowed three hours to produce their masterpieces; judg-

ing is at noon. The competition is free, though preregistration is requested.

MASHPEE NIGHT AT THE POPS
Mashpee Commons, Mashpee
(508) 539-2345
www.mashpeepops.com

The Cape Cod Symphony Orchestra, featuring conductor Royston Nash, and a fireworks display. Just bring your own chair. It's sponsored by the Mashpee Community Concert Committee. It's generally held at 7 p.m. on the last Sat in July. Admission is free.

Mid-Cape

ST. GEORGE'S GRECIAN FESTIVAL
St. George Greek Orthodox Church, Route 28, Centerville
(508) 775-3045
www.stgeorge-capecod.com

This three-day fair in mid-July features fantastic food like you've never tasted before. Besides the wonderful Greek food, there's a great crafts fair and bake sale as well as high-spirited dancing and a guided tour of the majestic domed Greek Orthodox Church. There are different booths and food tents. Free admission and parking.

Lower Cape

BAND TIME IN CHATHAM
Kate Gould Park, off Main Street, Chatham
(508) 945-5199
www.chathamcapecod.org

This is good old-fashioned Cape Cod family fun. On Fridays from July 4 through Labor Day, Kate Gould Park fills with thousands of people who happily listen to the Chatham Band play various traditional tunes, including such favorites as the "Bunny Hop" and the "Hokey Pokey" for the kids. Bring a blanket, lawn chairs, and maybe some bug spray. The music is free, but you may want to purchase balloons and refreshments. Concerts start at 8 p.m.

AUGUST

Upper Cape

PETER RABBIT'S ANIMAL DAY
Thornton Burgess Museum, Route 130, Sandwich
(508) 888-6870
www.thorntonburgess.org

The Thornton Burgess Society sponsors this fair geared to younger folk, who will love the live animal exhibits, pet rabbit show, music, story times, refreshments, and games. Burgess items are available for purchase. There is no admission fee to the fair, which takes place the second weekend in Aug.

FALMOUTH ROAD RACE
Falmouth
(508) 540-7000
www.falmouthroadrace.com

Three decades ago, a group of runners decided to run from Woods Hole to a bar in Falmouth Heights. Thus began what has become an international road race that is second only to the Boston Marathon in New England popularity. The Falmouth Road Race attracts thousands of onlookers and some 10,000 runners from across the country and around the world to sample its challenging 7.1-mile course the second weekend of Aug. The race starts at 10 a.m. (see our Sports and Recreation chapter for more information).

Mid-Cape

CENTERVILLE OLD HOME WEEK
Various sites in Centerville
(508) 790-6220
www.centervillelibrary.org

Among the special moments of the Centerville Old Home Week are a reunion dinner, an ice-cream social with legendary Four Seas ice cream, lectures, a road race, band concerts, and a bonfire at the beach. A good time is always had by all. Old Home Week takes place in mid-Aug, and proceeds benefit the Centerville Library.

WEST BARNSTABLE VILLAGE FESTIVAL
Various locations in West Barnstable
(508) 428-8754

Look for fun and community spirit with book sales, children's games and activities, raffles, mini-train rides, horse-drawn wagons, and plenty of food. This event is held the third Sat in Aug, and most activities are free.

POPS BY THE SEA
Hyannis Village Green, Hyannis
(508) 362-0066
www.artsfoundation.org/pops-by-the-sea

The Boston Pops Esplanade Orchestra comes to town with conductor Keith Lockhart to perform some wonderful late-afternoon music, both classical and popular tunes as well as patriotic marches and sing-alongs. Held at the Hyannis Village Green, the concert usually takes place on the first Sunday of the month and is sponsored by the Arts Foundation of Cape Cod. Lawn seats cost $15 ($20 the day of the concert, $5 for children 6 to 12), and premium seats cost $50.

Lower Cape
CRAFTSMEN FAIR
Drummer Boy Park, Route 6A, Brewster
(508) 385-2970

The Society of Cape Cod Craftsmen has been sponsoring this popular juried crafts showcase for half a century, making it the second-oldest crafts organization in New England. The three-day craft celebration features about 50 craftspeople. It is held the second Tues, Wed, and Thurs in Aug, from 10 a.m. to 5 p.m. the first two days and until 7 p.m. on Wed. Admission is free.

ANNUAL POPS IN THE PARK
Eldredge Park, Orleans
(508) 225-1386
www.popsinthepark.com

Grab your lawn chair or blanket, pack a picnic dinner, and enjoy the music. The Annual Pops in the Park, held at Eldredge Park in Orleans, is an outdoor concert by the Cape Cod Symphony Orchestra, conducted by the symphony's newest

maestro, Jung-Ho Pak. The concert is held the third or fourth Saturday of the month. Tickets cost $75 for table seats, $20 for field admission, and $10 for children ages 6 to 17 (all prices are increased the day of the event; check the Web site for details).

FINE ARTS WORK CENTER ANNUAL BENEFIT AUCTION
24 Pearl St., Provincetown
(508) 487-9960
www.fawc.org/auction/index.shtml

You'll find a little bit of everything here—from works of fine art to jewelry to furniture to clothing. Merchandise and services are donated to this live auction by area merchants and residents. The event is held in mid-Aug, and proceeds help support the Work Center's fellowship programs. Admission to the auction is free.

CARNIVAL WEEK
Various locations in Provincetown
(508) 487-2313, (800) 637-8696
www.ptown.org

Just when you thought you had seen it all in P-town, along comes Carnival Week. Sponsored by the Provincetown Business Guild, this week-long celebration, usually held the third week in Aug, features musical productions, guesthouse parties, balls, drag bingo, karaoke, tea dances, nightclub entertainment, and an outrageous parade complete with floats and entertainers. Be careful as the festivities have been known to get a little out of hand, but for some that's the draw.

SEPTEMBER

Upper Cape
BOURNE SCALLOP FEST
Buzzards Bay Park, Buzzards Bay
(508) 759-6000, ext. 10
www.bournescallopfest.com

For more than 30 years Bourne has hosted the largest scallop festival on the East Coast during the third weekend in Sept. Thousands converge on Buzzards Bay Park over three days to sample the seafood and attend the crafts fair. There are children's games, rides, plenty of live entertainment, and, of course, scallops. It's $5 to enter (free for kids under 12), and there are plenty of things to spend your money on, like great food and local handmade crafts.

CRANBERRY CLUSTER DOG SHOW
Barnstable Fair Grounds, Route 151,
East Falmouth
www.cranberrycluster.com
(508) 362-6506

This four-day event is held by both the Cape Cod Kennel Club (www.capecodkc.org) and the South Shore Kennel Club (www.southshorekennelclub. org). Any AKC-licensed dog that meets eligibility requirements is allowed to enter and applications must be submitted three weeks before the show. More than 1,000 dogs representing more than 125 breeds compete. Spectator tickets are $5 for adults and $2 for children ages 12 and younger.

Mid-Cape

CAPE COD GLASS SHOW
Corpus Christi Church, Sandwich
(508) 888-0251
www.sandwichglassmuseum.org

The Sandwich Glass Museum has sponsored this mid-Sept glass show for two decades. Nearly 50 glass dealers from throughout the United States display samples of antique and contemporary glass. Proceeds from this event benefit the Sandwich Glass Museum. Admission is $6.

Lower Cape

PROVINCETOWN AIDS SUPPORT GROUP ANNUAL LIVE AND SILENT AUCTION
Fishermen's Wharf, Provincetown
(508) 487-9445
www.asgcc.org

This Provincetown auction is held every Labor Day weekend and is attended by tourists, residents, and even some celebrities who bid on everything from works of art to furniture and jewelry. Proceed benefit the town's AIDS support programs. Nearly every Provincetown artist contributes artwork to this worthy cause.

HARWICH CRANBERRY FESTIVAL
Various locations in Harwich
(508) 430-2811
www.harwichcranberryfestival.org

Since it started as part of the National Bicentennial Celebration in 1976, the Harwich Cranberry Festival has grown into a town-wide extravaganza. In 2009 financial restraints led to the announcement that the festival would be canceled, but a smaller version was planned. Best to check with the festival committee and Web site to see if it is going to happen in the future.

A TASTE OF HARWICH
Cape Cod Regional Technical School
Route 124, Harwich
(508) 432-1600

Get a taste of Harwich, all under one roof. This evening event, sponsored by the Harwich Chamber of Commerce, allows you to sample fine cuisine from a number of Harwich restaurants. A Taste of Harwich takes place in early Sept.

EASTHAM WINDMILL WEEKEND
Various locations in Eastham
(508) 240-7211
www.easthamwindmillweekend.com

Windmill Weekend is a community celebration, featuring a parade, road race, games, sand art competition, entertainment, antique car show, kids' activities, a chowder contest, a pancake breakfast, square dancing, and an arts and crafts show. The whole event focuses on the Eastham gristmill, which was built in Plymouth way back in the 17th century. The celebration usually takes place the weekend after Labor Day. US 6 is closed for a few hours for the parade, so pay attention to the date if you are planning on passing through.

TRURO TREASURES WEEKEND
Truro
www.trurotreasures.org

This celebration of Truro has been going on since 1991 and seems to get bigger every year. It takes place during a long weekend in mid-Sept and features a historic home tour, a classic and antique car exhibit, an arts and crafts fair at the

Truro Central School, a flea market at Atlantic Spice, a pancake breakfast, a croquet tournament on the village green, grape stomping at the Truro Vineyards and Winery, a treasure hunt and face-painting for the children, and is topped off with a favorite local tradition: the "Dump Dance," complete with live music.

GREAT PROVINCETOWN SCHOONER REGATTA
Provincetown
(508) 487-3424
www.provincetownschoonerrace.com
Honoring the importance of 19th- and 20th-century schooners to the economy of Provincetown, this stunning regatta involves vessels up to 110 feet long. Held on a weekend in early Sept, it starts off with a Parade of Sail along the Provincetown waterfront, followed by the noon start of the regatta.

PROVINCETOWN ART ASSOCIATION ANNUAL CONSIGNMENT AUCTION
460 Commercial St., Provincetown
(508) 487-1750
www.paam.org
Every year since 1979, this auction has been an art-lover's dream come true. The items put on the block here are consigned by collectors, ensuring only first-rate works of art by area artists. Dealers and collectors from around the country attend. There is no charge to attend this mid-Sept auction. Proceeds help fund the Provincetown Art Association's programs and exhibitions.

OCTOBER

Upper Cape

ANNUAL HARVEST DAY CELEBRATION
Main Street, Falmouth
(508) 548-5600
www.falmouthchamber.com
The Cape Cod Farmers Market, face painting, pumpkin totem pole, pumpkin decorating, scarecrow making, balloon animals, free cider and donuts—they all add up to autumn fun. The Village Association sponsors the Annual Harvest Day Celebration the first Saturday of the month.

CAPE COD MARATHON
Falmouth
(508) 540-6959
www.capecodmarathon.com
This marathon, which begins and ends at Falmouth's Village Green, attracts between 600 and 2,000 participants. Sponsored by the Falmouth Track Club and run the last week in October, it's considered a Boston Marathon–qualifying event (see our Sports and Recreation chapter). The race starts at 8:30 a.m.

MASHPEE OKTOBERFEST
Mashpee Commons, Routes 151 and 28, Mashpee
(508) 539-1400, ext. 519
www.mashpeeleisureservices.com
Mashpee adds to the autumn fun with its very own Oktoberfest complete with an arts and crafts show and rides for the children. There are sidewalk sales, a parade, car show, authentic German food and music, and live entertainment. The festivities are presented by Mashpee Leisure Services, Mashpee Commons, and the Mashpee Chamber. This great family event is held early in Oct from 10 a.m. to 5 p.m. Admission is free.

Mid-Cape

YARMOUTH SEASIDE FESTIVAL
John Simpkins Elementary School
Route 28, South Yarmouth
(508) 778-1008, (800) 732-1008
www.yarmouthseasidefestival.com
Come enjoy a seaside parade, pumpkin decorating contest, arts and crafts, plenty of food, music, children's rides, demonstrations, races, competitions, and a fireworks display. The festival is held Columbus Day weekend.

Lower Cape

WELLFLEET OYSTER FESTIVAL
Wellfleet
www.wellfleetoysterfest.org

Main Street is closed to cars the weekend after Columbus Day to accommodate this two-day food and crafts fair. Shell fishermen and -women serving up their local specialties are the main attraction, but the arts and crafts fair, live music, 5K road race, kayak race, historic walking tours, museum talks, and a town-wide parade keep everyone busy. It culminates with the Sunday finals of a two-day "Shuck-Off" competition, in which shellfish harvesters show off their speed and skills.

WOMEN'S WEEK
Various sites in Provincetown
www.womeninnkeepers.com
Women's Week, usually held in early Oct near Columbus Day, is a weeklong festival of music, comedy shows, readings, fashion shows, auctions, and a Saturday night prom. Many art galleries also hold events and exhibitions honoring women. Women's Week is sponsored by the Women Innkeepers of Provincetown.

NOVEMBER

Upper Cape

HOLIDAYS-BY-THE-SEA WEEKEND
Various sites in Falmouth
(508) 548-8500
www.falmouthchamber.com
Falmouth's Holidays-by-the-Sea is a gala seasonal celebration that extends from mid-Nov through New Year's Day. It features Christmas caroling at Nobska Lighthouse, concerts and other performances, bazaars, and Santa's arrival by boat. The festivities include the annual Christmas Parade down Main Street to the Village Green on Sunday.

Lower Cape

HOLIDAY CRAFT FAIR
Cape Cod Regional Technical High School, Route 124, Harwich
(508) 432-4500, ext. 232
Held annually at the Cape Cod Tech, this craft fair features more than 125 artisans from up and down the East Coast. The fair, which features all handcrafted items, takes place over two days, and admission is free.

ANNUAL LIGHTING OF THE MONUMENT
1 High Pole Rd., Provincetown
(508) 487-1310
www.pilgrim-monument.org
Every winter, volunteers drape Provincetown's Pilgrim Monument with some 5,000 lights, turning the world's tallest granite structure into the world's tallest granite Christmas tree (more than 250 feet tall—see Attractions chapter). The monument is lit the day before Thanksgiving, and remains lit nightly through New Year's Day. Carols and refreshments at the town hall complete the scene.

DECEMBER

Cape-wide

CHRISTMAS STROLLS
There's perhaps no more wonderful way to catch the holiday spirit than a Christmastime stroll through one of the Cape's picturesque villages. The museums, historic homes, bed-and-breakfasts, and stores all open their doors to the public with good holiday cheer. Expect to see Santa commanding the attention of wide-eyed children and to hear carolers filling the air with traditional holiday song. Besides getting you in the spirit, the strolls are also a great way to get your holiday shopping done.

Many towns and villages have Christmas strolls; they are generally planned for early Dec. Here are some of them:

Sandwich Stroll (during Christmas in Sandwich)
Falmouth Christmas Stroll (during Christmas by the Sea)
Hyannis Christmas Stroll and Harbor Lighting
Barnstable Village Christmas Stroll
Dennis Christmas Stroll
Yarmouthport Christmas Stroll
Osterville Village Christmas Open House
Harwich Stroll (during Christmas Weekend in Harwich)
Chatham Christmas Stroll

NEW YEAR'S EVE CELEBRATIONS
Various sites throughout the Cape
(508) 362-0066

Almost every town on Cape Cod, including Falmouth, Mashpee, Hyannis, Orleans, and Provincetown, have fireworks displays, costume parades, and fun for the whole family. Chatham has one of the largest First Night events, appropriately named Chatham First Night, with a celebration of the arts from noon until the midnight fireworks go off. Cape-wide celebrations have been in high demand. You can purchase First Night buttons at the local chamber of commerce (listed in our Area Overview chapter), at participating community stores, or by calling the Arts Foundation at the number above. For more information on Christmas strolls and holiday activities in a particular town, check with the town's chamber of commerce or town hall.

THE ARTS

Cape Cod offers visitors and residents alike a varied and rich cultural experience with a cosmopolitan twist. Cape Cod is famed for its summer theater, whose illustrious history begins with the first performed play of Eugene O'Neill and continues with spectacular productions at places such as the marvelous Cape Playhouse in Dennis, which has attracted (and continues to attract) world-class talent like Helen Hayes, Julie Harris, and Tallulah Bankhead. If you're a music lover, you can enjoy hot sounds at the Beachcomber and Jazz by the Sea or soaring symphonies at various venues when the Cape Cod Symphony Orchestra performs.

You'll find that the Cape is rich in the visual arts too. The spectacular landscape, the laid-back lifestyle, and the unique light have been an irresistible draw for painters. Craftspeople and artisans have come too. Fine art galleries abound, such as Tree's Place in Orleans or the Blue Heron Gallery in Wellfleet.

Indeed the Cape is one of New England's largest centers of the arts. It has some 125 different arts organizations, according to the Arts Foundation of Cape Cod.

If you're an artist yourself, be sure to check out the opportunities for workshops and classes here on the Cape, which we offer in our Education and Child Care chapter. But first, for you and for everyone else who loves art, we offer a broad overview of the Cape's cultural offerings. We start by taking a look at the theater scene, then music, dance, art galleries and art museums, and movie theaters that show more than box-office hits. There's plenty here to lure you off the beach—take a break from the sun and bathe in creativity instead.

THEATER

Theater has played a starring role in the Cape's history since the summer of 1915, when a group of "wash-ashores," including writers John Reed and Susan Glaspell, gathered in Provincetown to write, produce, and stage plays. A year later an aspiring playwright named Eugene O'Neill arrived in town, determined to make his mark on theatrical history. On July 28, 1916, his first play, *Bound East for Cardiff*, was staged in a waterfront fish house to tremendous acclaim. Two years later the group named themselves the Provincetown Players and moved to New York City to continue their work, where the theater bearing their name still remains.

Provincetown continues its theatrical tradition with several theater groups, but the rest of the Cape has much to offer at other theatrical venues, and many of them perform year-round. In any given season you can see musicals, comedy, original works, and reworked classics, performed by the likes of the Harwich Junior Theater, the Monomoy Theatre in cooperation with the Ohio University players, and WHAT—Wellfleet Harbor Actors' Theater. Ticket prices are a fraction of what you might pay in Boston or New York to see a production of equal caliber.

Here, the curtain goes up on a town-by-town stage sampling.

Upper Cape

THE CAPE COD THEATRE PROJECT
Various venues
(508) 457-4242
www.capecodtheatreproject.org
Since the introduction of Jeff Daniels's play *The Vast Difference* in 1995, this professional group has staged readings of new plays in July only, usually at the Woods Hole Community Hall or Falmouth Academy. Some of the works originally read here have gone on to Broadway.

FALMOUTH THEATRE GUILD
Highfield Drive, Falmouth
(508) 548-0400
www.falmouththeatreguild.org

The Falmouth Theatre Guild puts on three or four shows a year at Highfield Theater. Favored as one of the best local theater companies, they eschew heavy dramas in favor of musicals, comedies, and other feel-good fare.

During the summer the College Light Opera Company (www.collegelightopera.com) moves in and stages nine musicals, each running a week. The shows begin the last week of June and run through the last week of Aug. Expect some Gilbert and Sullivan and plenty of Broadway classics.

WOODS HOLE THEATER COMPANY
68 Water St., Woods Hole (Falmouth)
(508) 540-6525
www.woodsholetheater.org

Established in 1974, this company presents three or four shows a year at the Woods Hole Community Hall and sponsors occasional productions by other theatrical troupes. The company aims to provide a wide variety of theater for the community. Included in each season are comedy, drama, and musicals.

Mid-Cape

BARNSTABLE COMEDY CLUB
3171 Rte. 6A, Barnstable
(508) 362-6333
http://home.comcast.net/~rkenneally/bcchome.html

The nation's third-oldest continuously operating theater, the Barnstable Comedy Club has been offering audiences the best in comedy, drama, and music since 1922. The group stages four major productions a year, with 10 performances of each show. Though the performers are all volunteers and nonprofessionals, remember their names: Past "nobodies" have included Geena Davis and Kurt Vonnegut.

CAPE PLAYHOUSE
820 Route 6A, Dennis
(508) 385-3911, (877) 385-3911
www.capeplayhouse.com

For more than 80 years, the legendary Cape Playhouse has been bringing Broadway actors to Cape Cod. The Cape Playhouse has attracted so many stars since it opened in 1927 that it is often referred to as the "Birthplace of the Stars." Young unknown Bette Davis first worked as an usher before returning the following summer to act. Humphrey Bogart, Shirley Booth, Robert Montgomery, and Gregory Peck made their early appearances at the Cape Playhouse before going on to win Academy Awards. As a student, young Jane Fonda even appeared one summer with her father, Henry.

America's oldest professional summer theater, the Cape Playhouse offers first-rate theater each summer. Evening performances are offered Mon through Sat, and matinees are on Wed and Thurs afternoons. On Thurs and Fri mornings, the Cape Playhouse Children's Theatre is a terrific way to introduce young people to the wonder and magic of live theater designed especially for them. Tickets are sold individually or by subscription. The season begins in June and runs to early Sept, with two-week runs of six plays, ranging from musicals and comedies to mysteries. In addition to the Cape Playhouse, the 26-acre complex is home to the Cape Cinema (see the Cinema section later in this chapter), the Cape Cod Museum of Art (see the Art Museums section later in this chapter), and the Center Stage Cafe.

COTUIT CENTER FOR THE ARTS
4404 Rte. 28, Cotuit
(508) 428-0669
www.cotuitcenterforthearts.org

This busy arts organization broke ground on a new performance center in June 2002, and the glossy new space stages three to four productions a year. The eclectic schedule ranges from Oscar Wilde to Edward Albee. In addition to performances, the Cotuit Center for the Arts offers drama and arts classes for children, teens, and adults (see our Education and Child Care chapter).

ℹ The Arts Foundation of Cape Cod publishes an annual calendar of special
events presented by the Cape's heritage,
cultural, visual, and performing arts organizations. To receive the guide, call (508)
362-0066.

Lower Cape
ACADEMY OF PERFORMING ARTS
120 Main St., Orleans
(508) 255-1963, (508) 255-3075
www.apacape.org
Founded in 1975, the academy stages an impressive schedule of productions throughout the
year—musicals, dramas, comedies, and everything in between—many of them works by
local and regional playwrights. The building itself
dates to 1873 and once served as the Orleans
Town Hall. General admission tickets for a main
performance are $20. A children's theater show
is presented Fri from July through Aug at 10 a.m.
General admission to the children's show is $10.
The academy also offers a plethora of courses in
dance, music, and acting at its teaching facility
on Giddah Hill Road (see our Education and Child
Care and Kidstuff chapters).

CAPE COD REPERTORY THEATER COMPANY
3379 Rte. 6A, Brewster
(508) 896-1888
www.caperep.org
Cape Rep operates the Cape's only outdoor theater, a beautiful venue among the pines across
from Nickerson State Park in East Brewster, just off
Route 6A. The group has an indoor theater at the
same site, and there's usually something going
on at both venues from late spring to early fall.
The group's offerings include musicals, original
plays, and, at the outdoor theater, family-oriented
productions. The company stages children's theater on Mon and Wed mornings from late June
through Aug; reservations are a must, as these
shows sell out fast. Tickets for the children's theater are $8 for both adults and children. The price
for indoor performances is $22 to $28.

CHATHAM DRAMA GUILD
134 Crowell Rd., Chatham
(508) 945-0510
www.chathamdramaguild.org
The guild does four major shows a year in fall,
winter, and spring. Productions range from musicals to comedy and mystery. *Chathamania*, a
brand-new old-fashioned variety show, as well
as more traditional productions such as Ibsen's *A
Doll's House*, were featured during past seasons.
Over the years the guild has staged productions
in conjunction with Chatham High School, making an educational experience for the students as
well as a grand experience for the general audience. Call for tickets and pricing.

HARWICH JUNIOR THEATRE
Corner of Division and Willow Streets,
West Harwich
(508) 432-2002, ext. 4
www.hjtcapecod.org
Founded in 1952, this year-round company
stages delightful family shows including dramas, musicals, comedies—even Shakespeare.
Although the plays staged here are always great
for children—*Man of La Mancha, HMS Pinafore,
A Christmas Story*—they can also be enjoyed by
people of all ages. Performances are held Fri and
Sat evening at 8 p.m. and on Sun at 2 p.m. (usually). Tickets are between $20 and $25 ($15 for
those under 21). The Harwich Junior Theatre also
offers a full curriculum of inspiring and fun classes
taught by theater professionals.

MONOMOY THEATRE
776 Main St., Chatham
(508) 945-1589
www.monomoytheatre.org
Monomoy Theatre's season kicks off in June with
a delightful mix of musicals, comedies, dramas,
thrillers, and an annual Shakespeare play. Since
1957 the theater, operated by the Ohio University
School of Theater Arts, has combined talented
students with visiting professors, faculty, and
professional guest artists. The season usually
begins with a two-week musical followed by
seven one-week plays. Season subscriptions are

available. Theater tickets range between $18 and $25, depending on the showing.

PROVINCETOWN REPERTORY THEATRE
238 Bradford St., Provincetown
(508) 487-7487, (800) 791-7487
www.ptowntheatrecompany.org
This group stages performances of American plays and music May through early Nov. In partnership with the Provincetown Theatre Company, the Provincetown Repertory Theatre recently completed construction of a new 180-seat building with state-of-the-art staging, audio and lighting systems. Here you will find fare ranging from Eugene O'Neill (*Long Day's Journey into Night*) to *Streakin' A Musical Flashback to the 1970s* (or *Revue* produced by the new Provincetown Players). They also host a Fall Playwright's Festival in mid-Sept and a Woman's Week New Play Festival in Oct.

WELLFLEET HARBOR ACTORS THEATER (WHAT)
1 Kendrick Ave., Wellfleet
2357 Rte. 6, Wellfleet
(508) 349-9428, (866) 282-9428
www.what.org
WHAT cofounder and artistic director Jeff Zinn brings something different to the theater experience on Cape Cod, providing an alternative to more traditional theaters. The original theater by the harbor only seats 90 people, but the Julie Andrews Stage that was dedicated in 2007 next to the Wellfleet Post Office has room for more than double that number. The group stages up to nine shows a year from May through early Nov. The box office is at the Julie Andrews Stage.

MUSIC

From Big Band to Broadway, blues to bebop, reggae to rockabilly, there is always some form of music on the Cape, especially during the summer when crowds gather in a celebratory atmosphere that just cries out for accompaniment. Many towns offer weekly free outdoor concerts during July and August that feature some of the best local musicians. Just bring your lawn chair and head toward the music. Some annual events are so popular that many visitors plan their vacations around them (such as Pops in the Park—see our Annual Events chapter—and Jazz by the Sea). The Cape Cod Melody Tent is the place to go for big-name entertainment in summer. It is a seasonal outdoor tent—a huge one with stadium seating—and it's a terrific place to see a concert. If you are looking for alternative music, you've come to the right place—because the Cape is within a few hours' driving time of Boston and Providence, Rhode Island, area nightclubs are able to draw some of the best national touring bands to their small venues. (Our Nightlife chapter will provide you with a sample of restaurants and bars that offer live entertainment.) Here's a listing of some of the best musical venues on the Cape. Check local newspapers for exact dates and concert schedules.

Upper Cape
COLLEGE LIGHT OPERA COMPANY
Highfield Theater, Highfield Drive, Falmouth
(508) 548-0668
www.collegelightopera.com
The College Light Opera Company stages nine musicals a summer, each running a week, from the last week of June through the last week of Aug. Shows include operettas by Gilbert and Sullivan and heaps of Broadway classics.

> **i** **Summer Concerts on the Green is a series of free concerts held Friday nights at Peg Noonan Park in Falmouth throughout the summer. These family-oriented concerts start at 6 p.m. and feature a variety of local professional musical talent from Irish folk music to swing. For more information contact the Arts Foundation of Cape Cod (508-362– 0066), or visit www.artsfoundation.org.**

WOODS HOLE FOLK MUSIC SOCIETY
Woods Hole Community Hall, Water Street, Woods Hole (Falmouth)
(508) 540-0320
www.arts-cape.com/whfolkmusic

From Oct through Apr, the Woods Hole Folk Music Society stages concerts on the first and third Sundays of the month. The programs often attract nationally known performers such as Bill Staines, Peggy Seeger, Roy Bookbinder, Oscar Brand, David Mallett, Aoife Clancy, and Kim and Reggie Harris. Admission is $15, with discounts for members, seniors, and children.

Mid-Cape

CAPE COD MELODY TENT
21 West Main St. and West End Rotary, Hyannis
(508) 775-5630
www.melodytent.com

The Cape's premier summer showcase, the Cape Cod Melody Tent is one of only 10 outdoor performance tents in the country. Many big names in show business have appeared here, including Willie Nelson, Aretha Franklin, and Tony Bennett, to name a few. The big tent is pitched in early June and is taken down in early Sept. Shows sell out fast; check the box office for last-minute seat cancellations. Ticket prices vary, so go online or call for specific shows.

The Melody Tent also features popular children's theater and musical productions every Wednesday morning during the season.

i Just about every town on the Cape offers free outdoor summer concerts. Check with the town's chamber of commerce or town hall (see the Area Overview chapter) for more information.

CAPE SYMPHONY ORCHESTRA
712A Main St., Yarmouthport
(508) 362-1111
www.capesymphony.org

The award-winning Cape Symphony Orchestra performs classical, pops, and educational concerts at the Barnstable High School Performing Arts Center in Hyannis from Sept through early May. Two hugely successful outdoor summer pops concerts are performed at the Mashpee Commons at the end of July and at Eldredge Park in Orleans in mid-Aug. Music Director Royston Nash stepped down in 2008 but still conducts from time to time. The new director and artistic director of the Cape's only symphonic orchestra, Jung-Ho Pak, also conducts the San Diego Chamber Orchestra, the World Symphony Orchestra, and the Summer Orchestras at the Interlochen Center for the Arts. Go online or call for ticket prices.

Lower Cape

CAPE COD CHAMBER MUSIC FESTIVAL
Various venues
(508) 945-8060
www.capecodchambermusic.org

Launched in 1980, the Cape Cod Chamber Music Festival hold concerts in various venues for three weeks in August, with special events other times. The roster includes chamber music concerts, programs for young people, evenings of jazz, and the annual screening of a music-themed film. Concert tickets average $28 to $40, depending on when you purchase and what you are going to hear ($15 for college students, free for those 18 and under).

GREAT MUSIC SERIES ON SUNDAYS AT 5
Unitarian Universalist Meeting House, 236 Commercial St., Provincetown
(508) 487-9344
www.ptownmusic.com

Nearly 10 years old, this series is organized by the Meeting House Instrument Trust, a group working toward restoring the historic Universalist Meeting House organ housed in this 1851 Greek Revival gem. Concerts are varied programs of classical music and Broadway show tunes, featuring virtuoso vocalists and talented local musicians. Concerts are held from late June through mid-Oct on Sun at 5 p.m. Tickets are $15 (free for kids 12 and under); the group also welcomes donations.

DANCE

Mid-Cape

CAPE DANCE THEATER OF CAPE COD
2240 Community College
Route 132, West Barnstable
(508) 375-4044

Made up of faculty, students, and area residents, this innovative dance troupe focuses mainly on modern dance, though it has broadened its scope in recent years to include such traditional fare as ballroom dancing. The troupe usually stages three annual shows at the college's Tilden Arts Center.

COASTAL DANCE COMPANY
49 John Maki Rd., West Barnstable
(508) 362-3111
www.capecodballetsociety.org
This company produces a Nutcracker gala each Dec; recently the production was a joint venture with the Cape Cod Symphony Orchestra at the new performing arts center at Barnstable High School in Hyannis. A second major performance of each year is staged in the spring. Ticket prices range from $15 to $25. A dance academy is also associated with the company and gives lessons to students of all ages.

Lower Cape
STUDIO 878
878 Main St., Chatham
(508) 945-8780
Studio 878 is a nonprofit educational organization that has become known for its unusual and exploratory performance collaborations. It offers professional training in dance from beginning through professional levels.

ART GALLERIES

The Cape is home to a diverse selection of world-class art galleries.

Museum-quality installations grace the walls of art galleries like Jan Collins Selman's Fine Art Gallery in Falmouth, Tree's Place in Orleans, and the Left Bank Gallery in Wellfleet. Much of the art is generated by local artists, but not always—many of these galleries represent nationally and internationally known artists, as well as New York artists who summer on the Cape. Cape Cod attracts talented artists whose work ranges from contemporary realism and impressionism to postmodernism. Much of the art is inspired by the stunning natural beauty of the Cape,

rendered in many different styles, from realistic to impressionistic and abstract. Because the Cape Cod lifestyle is largely unassuming, the art is too—in many cases, it is inspired by the solitude of the outer beaches, sunrise over a salt marsh, and, yes, fishing boats in quaint harbors.

Ask any artist why he or she prefers Cape Cod and almost each of them says the same thing: the light. The Cape's unique light and natural beauty was drawing artists here even before Charles Hawthorne founded the Cape Cod School of Art in Provincetown in 1899. And it continues to attract painters, sculptors, and other artists, including Edward Hopper, who summered in Truro from 1920 to 1967. The profusion of galleries here, particularly in the Lower Cape towns of Wellfleet and Provincetown, attests to our high population of visual artists. Many galleries are run by these artists, and you can often catch a glimpse of them at work while you're browsing in galleries with attached studios.

Here are some of our favorite galleries. Remember that hours vary greatly during the off-season, so it's best to call in advance.

Upper Cape
GALLERY 333
333 Old Main Rd., North Falmouth
(508) 564-4467, (617) 332-5459 (off-season)
www.gallery333.com
Housed in an 1800 home, this gallery has three rooms of paintings, drawings, limited edition prints, glass, sculpture, ceramics, and photography, representing a range of styles from representational to abstract. The gallery focuses on distinguished local and New England artists. Open Wed through Sun from mid-June to mid-Sept, and by appointment in the off-season (by calling the number above), Gallery 333 offers five or six shows each summer, with Sat evening receptions opening each show.

JAN COLLINS SELMAN FINE ART
317 Main St., Falmouth
(508) 457-5533
www.jancollinsselman.com

Jan Collins Selman is an award-winning artist best known for her pastels and oils of Cape Cod, Martha's Vineyard, and Nantucket. Here you can purchase her work in oil, pastel, monotype, woodcuts, etchings, and prints, as well as the work of many other award-winning artists. The gallery also displays lovely works in ceramics, sculpture, photography, etching, and printmaking. The gallery is open year-round.

WOODRUFF'S ART CENTER
1 North Market St., Mashpee Commons, Mashpee
(508) 477-5767
www.woodruffsartcenter.com
Here you'll find watercolors, acrylics, oils, and pastels by John Richardson Woodruff and his wife, Amy Rice Woodruff, along with reproductions of works by other artists. The Woodruffs also offer custom framing and a wide range of art supplies. The gallery is open daily year-round.

WOODS HOLE GALLERY
15 School St., Woods Hole (Falmouth)
www.arts-cape.com/whgallery
Since 1963, Edie Bruce, owner of the Woods Hole Gallery, has been cultivating the newest and freshest talent in the world of art. The collections here are superb, representing only New England artists in a range of media including pastels, watercolors, oils, and acrylics. Bruce, an artist herself, also restores paintings and teaches art. The gallery is open Thurs through Mon during July, Aug, and Sept; call for off-season hours.

Mid-Cape
BIRDSEY ON THE CAPE
12 Wianno Ave., Osterville
(508) 428-4969
This friendly gallery, housed in an old building with lots of character, represents more than 40 artists. You can pick up a framed print here for a mere $35, or you could spend as much as $3,500 for an original painting. Some of the popular artists whose work graces Birdsey's three rooms include Jane Shelly Pierce, Vern Broe, Susie

McLean, and Neil McAuliffe. The gallery is open seven days a week but closed Jan through Apr.

CAPE COD ART ASSOCIATION
3480 Route 6A, Barnstable
(508) 362-2909
www.capecodartassoc.org
The nonprofit Cape Cod Art Association was established in 1948, and offers year-round monthly art exhibitions, some for members only, and others open to area residents. Some shows are juried, and artists are always present at openings. The CCAA also hosts classes and workshops year-round.

COTUIT CENTER FOR THE ARTS
4404 Rte. 28, Cotuit
(508) 428-0669
www.cotuitcenterforthearts.org
In addition to staging performances and offering art and drama classes, the recently expanded Cotuit Center features frequent exhibits of artwork by students, teachers, and other established artists year-round.

GUYER BARN GALLERY AND ARTS CENTER
250 South St., Hyannis
(508) 790-6370
www.town.barnstable.ma.us/GuyerBarn
This restored 1865 barn, owned by the town of Barnstable and adjacent to the town hall complex and the library, shows the work of local artists, both recognized and new. The nonprofit gallery, sponsored by the Barnstable Cultural Council, is open Apr through Oct and hosts two special holiday craft show fairs in Nov and Dec.

HIGGINS ART GALLERY
Cape Cod Community College, 2240 Rte. 132, West Barnstable
(508) 362-2131, (508) 375-4044
www.capecod.mass.edu
Housed in the Tilden Arts Center of Cape Cod Community College, the Higgins Art Gallery features a variety of works. It is open to the public Mon through Fri, 10 a.m. to 5 p.m., with several special shows a year. Due to its school affiliation, the gallery closes from mid-Apr to Sept.

Lower Cape

ADDISON HOLMES GALLERY
43 Rte. 28, Orleans
(508) 255-6200, (877) 291-5400
www.addisonart.com
The Addison Holmes Gallery represents a number of acclaimed fine artists, including Laura Griffith, Ann Trainor Dominque, and Garry Gilmartin. The two-level gallery, in a former home on Town Cove, is bright and inviting. It's open year-round, with shorter hours in winter.

ART HOUSE GALLERY
38 Thad Ellis Rd., Brewster
(508) 896-5557
www.arthousecapecod.com
The couch at the Art House Gallery is comfy and offers a good view of featured works by more than 20 artists from the Cape and beyond, including some from Europe. Cape artists featured here include lithographer Richard Pargeter and pastel artist Joan Ledwith. The gallery is open weekends noon to 5 p.m.

BLUE HERON GALLERY
20 Bank St., Wellfleet
(508) 349-6724
www.blueheronfineart.com
The Blue Heron has one of the largest collections around, featuring representational contemporary art in a range of mediums, including oil, egg tempera, watercolor, pastel, acrylic, photography, etchings, sculpture, and limited-edition prints. The gallery's roster of artists from around the United States is impressive, and many have been displaying their work here for years. With rooms on two floors, this gallery has a light, clean look and a relaxed atmosphere that makes viewing art here a particular pleasure. Open daily Mother's Day through the middle of Oct, Blue Heron hosts artist receptions on most Sat evenings in July and Aug, offering new art and the opportunity to meet the artists.

COVE GALLERY
15 Commercial St., Wellfleet
(508) 349-2530
www.covegallery.com
Cove Gallery displays works by such internationally recognized artists as Leonard Baskin and children's book illustrator Tomie de Paolo. Also look for the bold, semi-representational paintings of John Grillo. The rooms are airy and uncluttered and include one room devoted to illustrated children's books, where you may also purchase children's illustrations, including works by Barry Moser. Out back is a peaceful garden overlooking Duck Creek. The Cove also does custom framing. It's open year-round, daily in summer with reduced hours in the off-season, so call ahead.

CREATIVE ARTS CENTER
154 Crowell Rd., Chatham
www.capecodcreativearts.org
The nonprofit Creative Arts Center has two galleries hosting several shows a year, alternating exhibitions of students, members and faculty with regional displays featuring other Cape Cod organizations. The center, open daily in summer (and on weekdays from Sept through May), also offers a wide range of classes.

DNA GALLERY
288 Bradford St., Provincetown
(508) 487-7700
www.dnagallery.com
Ever since the DNA (for Definitive New Art) opened in 1994, it has been a welcome artistic refuge for those seeking the leading-edge exhibitions in a wide range of media. DNA, which represents some 30 emerging and established artists, also morphs its openings into "happenings," merging them with dance pieces, theatrical readings, films, and musical events, usually held on weekends. It's open daily May through Oct.

JACOB FANNING GALLERY
25 Bank St., Wellfleet
www.jacobfanningcapecod.com
This bright gallery in an 1865 building displays the work of some 20 artists, including environ-

mental sculptor Stephen Thomas, who creates whimsical creatures such as cockroaches and crickets using recycled metal painted bright colors. He even makes potted flower arrangements using outdoor faucets and other materials to charming effect. The gallery is open daily May through Oct, then Sat only (and Thanksgiving weekend) in Nov.

KELY KNOWLES ROCK HARBOR ART GALLERY
104 Rock Harbor Rd., Orleans
www.capewatercolors.com

This beautiful barn, just a few doors down from Rock Harbor, houses the works of talented husband-and-wife artists Kely and David Knowles. Kely Knowles exhibits her luminous, shimmering watercolors along with pen-and-ink renderings and greeting cards. Her husband carves unique wood sculptures, including unusual fish wall hangings. The gallery is open most of the time in summer and often in spring and fall or by appointment any time of year.

KENDALL ART GALLERY AND WELLFLEET FRAME SHOP
40 Main St., Wellfleet
(508) 349-2482
www.kendallartgallery.com

This gallery represents more than 40 contemporary artists. Artist-in-residence Walter Dorrell creates his Wellfleet watercolors in his "floating" studio, a canoe he takes into the town's kettle ponds. The gallery is open May through Oct, daily in summer and Mon through Sat in spring and fall.

LEFT BANK GALLERY
25 Commercial St. and 3 West Main St., Wellfleet
(508) 349-9451 and (508) 349-7939
www.leftbankgallery.com

Left Bank represents more than 50 local and nationally known artists, such as Rosalie Nadeau, Jim Holland, and Gail Bessette. It also hosts changing exhibitions. Check out the Potter's Room, filled with American crafts, and the out-door sculpture garden. The gallery is open year-round, daily from Memorial Day to Columbus Day, Thurs through Sun during the winter. Also check out the gallery's second location, Left Bank Small Works and Jewelry (at 3 West Main Street), and its newest location in Orleans (see listing below).

LEFT BANK GALLERY
8 Cove Rd., Orleans
(508) 247-9172
www.leftbankgallery.com

For many years an institution in Wellfleet, the Left Bank's opening of an Orleans location was welcomed by local art lovers. In addition to paintings, sculpture, textiles, and ceramics by local, regional, and nationally known artists, you'll find gorgeous handcrafted jewelry. The gallery also has a third room, which is filled with the works of a new slate of artists. The gallery is open seven days a week year-round, with reduced hours in the off-season.

MADDOCKS GALLERY
1283 Rte. 6A, Brewster
(508) 896-6223
www.jamesmaddocksgallery.com

Working primarily in acrylics, Jim Maddocks creates Cape Cod scenes filled with flowers, sandy lanes, and views of the bay. His paintings have a dreamy quality that lulls and charms the viewer. A bonus: Very often you can catch the artist at work in his studio/gallery, located in a carriage house adjacent to his historic home. It's open most days in season; call for off-season hours.

RICE/POLAK GALLERY
430 Commercial St., Provincetown
(508) 487-1052
www.ricepolakgallery.com

Also in the East End is the Rice/Polak Gallery, where you'll find contemporary artworks in various media by local and other artists. It's open May through Dec, daily from May through Sept and weekends from Oct through Dec.

RUDDEFORTH GALLERY
3753 Rte. 6A, Brewster
(508) 255-1056
www.ruddeforthgallery.com
Debra Ruddeforth's oils and watercolors are soft, lush, and inviting; they include many Cape landscapes as well as florals and still lifes. A full selection of limited-edition reproductions is available as well. Open daily year-round 10 a.m. to 5 p.m., the gallery also displays the still-life and fine-arts landscape photography of Tom Ruddeforth.

STRUNA GALLERIES
3873 Rte. 6A, Brewster
(508) 255-6618
www.strunagalleries.com
Timothy Struna's pen-and-ink renderings feature Cape landscapes and old houses and perfectly capture the essence of the Cape. He also works in watercolors and acrylics, and we highly recommend a visit to his cozy gallery, near the Orleans line. It's open daily all year. There is another location of Struna Galleries on Main Street in Chatham.

TREE'S PLACE
Routes 6A and 28, Orleans
www.treesplace.com
The collection of paintings in the gallery space at Tree's Place couldn't have been better coordinated. Several rooms house pieces of art, many oversized, and all beautifully hung; the effect is a museum-like ambience. Featured artists include Sam Barber, Robert Vickrey, Robert Douglas Hunter, and Sam Vokey, among other artists. Tree's Place presents weekly exhibitions throughout July and Aug, including exhibitions during the first few weeks of Sept. There is often an exhibition the week after Thanksgiving, featuring in-house artists and selected guests. Opening nights are usually Sat evenings from 5 to 7 p.m. Tree's Place is open daily in summer, and suspends service on Sun in spring, fall, and winter.

UNDERGROUND GALLERY
673 Satucket Rd., Brewster
(508) 896-3757
www.karennorthwells.com

The Underground Gallery is an architectural wonder supported by tree trunks and nestled under 250 tons of earth. But the real attractions are the vivid, distinctive watercolors by Karen North Wells. The works of her husband, architect and artist Malcolm Wells (who designed the gallery), are also on display, as is a selection of books and a collection of greeting cards reproduced from Ms. Wells's paintings. It's open year-round, Wed through Sat from noon to 5 p.m., and Sun by appointment.

WINSTANLEY-ROARK FINE ARTS
744 Rte. 6A, Dennis
(508) 385-4713
www.masterfulart.com
This gallery features the luminous oils and pastels—portraits, landscapes, and still lifes—by Robert K. Roark and the fine art photography of Anita Winstanley-Roark. They also host the work of about 20 other artists. Open daily in summer, the gallery is open Tues through Sun in the spring and fall and by chance or appointment in the winter months.

WOHLFARTH GALLERIES
432 Commercial St., Provincetown
(508) 487-6569
www.wohlfarthgalleries.com
Wohlfarth Galleries features both photography and fine art, and represents past and present students of the Cape Cod School of Arts (see our Education and Child Care chapter) established by Charles Hawthorne. The gallery is open May through Dec.

ART MUSEUMS

The Cape's three art museums are treasures not only for their wonderful collections but also for their very existence, as they preserve much of what is important to Cape Codders. In addition to making art accessible to the public, these institutions hold keys to both the past and the future, showing the legacy left by early artists and encouraging a new generation.

Mid-Cape

CAHOON MUSEUM OF AMERICAN ART
4676 Rte. 28, Cotuit
(508) 428-7581
www.cahoonmuseum.org
Located in a 1775 Georgian colonial farmhouse, the Cahoon Museum is best known for its collection of fanciful primitive paintings by the late Ralph and Martha Cahoon. The building—worth a visit in itself with its wide-planked floors, narrow doorways, and ship's captain's staircase—was actually the Cahoons' home and studio for 37 years. In addition to the Cahoon paintings, the permanent collection features 19th- and early 20th-century American art by the likes of Ralph Blakelock, William Bradford, and William Matthew Pride. The museum also offers special exhibitions, gallery talks, classes, and a gift shop. It is open Tues through Sun (10 a.m. to 4 p.m., Tues through Sat, 1 to 4 p.m. on Sun) year-round, except Jan, when it closes for a month. Admission is $5 for adults, $4 for seniors and students, and free for children under 12.

CAPE MUSEUM OF FINE ARTS
Route 6A, Dennis
(508) 385-4477
www.cmfa.org
The Cape Museum of Fine Arts conveys the important role that Cape Cod and the islands have played in American art. Founded in 1981 by a group of artists, educators, and community activists, CMFA focuses on the works of artists who have been influenced by the Cape environment, its people, and the interactive exchange of artistic ideas. The museum houses a collection that ranges from the late 1800s to the modern era, with more than 800 works by such icons as Charles Hawthorne, Paul Resika, Martha Cahoon, and Chaim Gross.

The museum sponsors frequent classes, trips, a fine-arts auction, and a film series. The museum is open year-round. Adult admission is $8; people younger than 18 enter free. Admission is by donation all day Thurs.

Lower Cape

PROVINCETOWN ART ASSOCIATION AND MUSEUM
460 Commercial St., Provincetown
(508) 487-1750
www.paam.org
The Provincetown Art Association and Museum was established in 1914 during the early years of Provincetown's art colony. Its galleries feature exhibits by established and emerging Outer Cape artists, as well as Art Association members. Also on display are works from the very impressive 2,000-piece permanent collection, including works by Hawthorne, Motherwell, Knaths, Hensche, Hofmann, Moffett, Bultman, and other painters associated with Provincetown. There is a museum store, library, artists' archives, and a museum school on the premises. It's open during the off-season Thurs through Sun from noon to 5 p.m. From Memorial Day through Sept, the hours are 11 a.m. to 8 p.m. Mon through Thurs, 11 a.m. to 10 p.m. Fri, and 11 a.m. to 5 p.m. Sat and Sun. An admission fee of $7 is charged for nonmembers.

CINEMA

Moviegoers have some unique options on the Cape. Although multiplex movie theaters are sprinkled throughout the Cape (in Mashpee, Hyannis, Dennis, Falmouth, Wellfleet, and Harwich), there are a few theaters that offer alternatives to the current box-office hits. If you prefer art and foreign films to the latest thriller, or you like the idea of watching a movie in an unconventional setting, check out these unique venues. Also, join in the fun at the annual Provincetown International Film Festival, which takes place each June and brings stars to town.

Mid-Cape

CAPE CINEMA
Cape Playhouse grounds, Route 6A, Dennis
(508) 385-2503
www.capecinema.com

Insiders know that the Cape Cinema, built in 1930, is the place for serious movie watching. The theater shows the finest in foreign, independent, and art films from Apr through early Jan.

Getting there early will not only guarantee you a seat, but also give you time to bask in the building's beauty. The exterior was designed in the style of the Congregational Church in Centerville, and the interior ceiling is covered with a 6,400-square-foot mural of heavenly skies designed by Rockwell Kent and executed by Jo Mielziner. (Kent also designed the stage's golden sunburst curtain.)

i The Provincetown International Film Festival (www.ptownfilmfest.com) is a mid-June, five-day festival showing more than 70 movies that reflect the diversity and commitment to creativity for which Provincetown is known. A Filmmaker on the Edge award is also given to honor filmmakers who have consistently pushed the boundaries of filmmaking. Recent award-winners have been Todd Haynes (*Far From Heaven*) and Gregg Araki (*Mysterious Skin*).

Lower Cape

WELLFLEET CINEMAS
Route 6 at the Eastham-Wellfleet line
(508) 349-7176
www.wellfleetcinemas.com
Wellfleet Cinemas, built in 1986, is independently owned and operated. The cinemas have four screens equipped with Dolby Stereo and offer weekly first-run moves. The cinemas are open for matinees every day all summer long. The Wellfleet Cinemas is open 365 days a year. Next door to the indoor screens is the Wellfleet Drive-In, where the family can take in an old-school flick on the 100-foot-by-44-foot screen. Enjoy first-run double features almost every night.

HIKING AND BIKING TRAILS

Though most people tend to associate Cape Cod with its spectacular beaches, many visitors do not realize the Cape is also graced with inland beauty from Bourne to Provincetown.

There's a good reason why Cape Cod is paradise for people who love the outdoors, and that reason is the miles of maintained hiking and biking trails that meander throughout our meadows and uplands and through Cape Cod's many public areas.

One of the most impressive trails is the Cape Cod Rail Trail, 22 miles of paved surface running parallel to US 6 beginning just south of Patriot Square Mall in Dennis on Route 134, through Nickerson State Park, and ending in Wellfleet behind the South Wellfleet General Store. The former route of the Cape Cod railroad is a smooth and mostly flat surface providing bicyclists with a private universe where they can roll along merrily at whatever speed they choose. Additions are planned and other railroad routes on the Cape have been made into bike paths, including a newly paved 7-mile section of the Shining Sea bike path in Falmouth.

Hiking through Cape Cod's conservation and parklands is still the best way to see some of the Cape's most spectacular sights. The many walking trails of Cape Cod lead nature lovers and the casual stroller to every corner of the Cape, through woodlands, over cedar swamps, into open salt marsh, and onto open shorelines.

If you want to discover what it's like to walk the whole Cape from end to end, try Elliot Carr's *Walking Cape Cod;* it's a good source and a good read. The Cape Cod National Seashore also offers invaluable trail information. There you can find maps, updates on trail status and condition, and information about which of the trails in the National Seashore are best suited to your particular interests and experience.

On the trail you'll want extra water, a good pair of shoes, and most important, common sense. Tell someone where you are going and when you expect to be back. Now, grab your camera, and if you travel quietly enough, maybe you'll see an otter swimming in the salt marsh, seals basking on the seashore, or a deer feeding under a crabapple tree.

HIKING TRAILs

Upper Cape

There are a variety of stunning walking trails in the Upper Cape area, such as the trail along the Cape Cod Canal between Bourne and Sandwich. The 7-mile paved path runs along both sides of the canal and is relatively level. You'll see cormorants diving for fish while sailboats and tugs towing gigantic tankers pass by within a few hundred yards. Or for something completely different, journey into the woodlands of Beebe Woods in Falmouth in search of glacier boulders and kettle ponds that dot the grounds.

ASHUMET HOLLY WILDLIFE SANCTUARY
Ashumet Road, East Falmouth
(508) 362-1426
www.massaudubon.org
Owned by the Massachusetts Audubon Society, the Ashumet Holly Reservation and Wildlife Sanctuary, off Route 151 (signs are posted) on Currier Road and Ashumet Road, is a popular 45-acre preserve that is open from sunrise to sunset all year. The grounds include 65 varieties of holly trees, as well as Franklinia trees, which are actually a type of tea plant named in honor of Benjamin Franklin. The sanctuary offers workshops, bird walks, and field trips throughout the year. Admis-

sion to the Ashumet Holly Reserve is $3 for adults and $2 for seniors and kids 3 to 12. Maps are available at the visitor center at the sanctuary.

BEEBE WOODS
Off Depot Avenue, Falmouth
(508) 457-2536
Beebe Woods was a generous gift to the town of Falmouth from benefactor Josiah K. Lilly in 1966. Located at the end of Depot Avenue, the wooded grounds of the nearly 400-acre estate have extensive trails and are open to the public for walking, cross-country skiing, horseback riding, and bird-watching. Four large kettle ponds dot the woodlands, as do glacier boulders and wetlands. If you are looking for a serene outing, a 1.6-mile walk to Ice House Pond at the end of the trail is as peaceful as it gets on Cape Cod.

BOURNE FARM
881 Palmer Ave., West Falmouth
(508) 548-8484
www.saltpond.info
The 49-acre Bourne Farm is owned and operated by Salt Pond Area Bird Sanctuaries, Inc. In July and Aug you can take an afternoon tour (by appointment—call the number above) of the 1775 farmhouse and a barn with an old cattle tunnel. This former working farm has hiking paths and a parking area. A free nature program geared to children is given every Tues afternoon during July and Aug at 3 p.m. The trails are open year-round.

BOYDEN FARM CONSERVATION LANDS
Cotuit Road, Sandwich
(508) 833-8054
Boyden Farm is a 48-acre conservation area that fronts Peter's Pond and features walking trails and a wildlife management area. Bring your binoculars to the wildlife field, where you may spot deer, hawks, and wild turkeys, which have been successfully released through the management program of the Sandwich Conservation Commission. Parking is west of Cotuit Road and just south of Farmersville Road.

THE BRIAR PATCH
Route 6A, East Sandwich
(508) 888-6870
The Briar Patch is a 166-acre conservation area off Route 6A in East Sandwich. This pleasant area of white pine, black locust trees, and meandering trails was a source of inspiration to Thornton W. Burgess, who wrote *Old Mother West Wind* and many other popular children's books in the early 20th century. Two trails loop through the abandoned pastures and groves of black locust and white pine. Enter the trailheads on Discovery Hill Road off Route 6A behind the Green Briar Nature Center.

DENORMANDIE WOODS CONSERVATION AREA AND BROYER AND ROBINSON CONSERVATION AREA
Red Brook Road, Bourne
(508) 563-2884
The DeNormandie Woods Conservation Area comprises nine acres of wooded upland with a $2/3$-mile trail connecting the 30-acre Broyer and Robinson Conservation Area. Watch out for lady slipper orchids and rhododendrons, which bloom spectacularly in the late spring and early summer. Enter either by Shore Road between Red Brook Harbor Road and County Road or along Red Brook Road between Scraggy Neck Road and Parker's Boat Yard.

FOUR PONDS PARK AND TOWN FOREST
Barlows Landing Road, Bourne
(508) 759-0615, option 6
Trails around Freeman Pond, Upper Pond, the Basin, and Shop Pond, and then through the Town Forest, comprise this roughly 300-acre conservation area maintained by the Bourne Conservation Department. Laced with marked hiking trails, the area also has marked points for pickerel and trout fishing. Although no prominent structure remains, the area used to be part of the Pocasset Iron Works. You can park in the lot on the right of Barlows Landing Road about a mile from MacArthur Boulevard.

i The historic character of Olde Kings Highway, also known as Route 6A, makes it a unique experience for bicyclists and walkers. Once a Native American trail, the road between Plymouth and Province-town is America's largest designated historic district. Heavily traveled by cars, it is suited to experienced bicyclists. This route is brimming with art galleries, dining establishments, antiques and gift shops, and boutiques.

FRANCES A. CRANE WILDLIFE MANAGE-MENT AREA
Ashumet Road, Falmouth
(508) 759-3406
www.300committee.org/cranewildlife.htm
The Frances A. Crane Wildlife Management Area is a 1,700-acre reserve regulated by the Massachusetts Division of Fisheries and Wildlife. The land is an extensive sand plain with mostly pitch pine and little deciduous growth. It is stocked with game during the fall hunting season and should not be considered safe for recreational activities at that time. At other times of the year, it is a popular place for walking and horseback riding.

GOODWILL PARK
Palmer Avenue, Falmouth
(508) 457-2543
The 85-acre Goodwill Park is a spacious wooded area with a lovely pond. The park is open daily from 8 a.m. to 4 p.m. for hiking, swimming, Frisbee, and canoeing. With a lovely freshwater beach, restrooms, barbecue grills, and play equipment, this is a good place for families and picnickers. To bring a large group call the parks department at the above number to reserve the pavilion area.

JOHN'S POND PARK
Hooppole Road, Mashpee
(508) 539-1400
John's Pond Park is a 258-acre park with a trail system and a 1,200-foot sandy beach. Nature lovers can watch herring swim up the Quashnet River in the spring and fall and explore an extensive area of cranberry bogs. As you head toward North Falmouth, you'll find the park off Route 151 past the Barnstable County Fairgrounds; turn right onto Currier Road, then right on Hooppole Road and right again onto Back Road. John's Pond Park is just beyond the trailer park.

LOWELL HOLLY RESERVATION
South Sandwich Road, Mashpee
(508) 679-2115
www.thetrustees.org
At the Lowell Holly Reservation, marked by a small sign on Sandwich Road, you'll find a delightful ½-mile trail among American beech, huge holly, white pine trees, and rhododendron. Birders have spotted eagles, ospreys, and hawks here. Once owned by James Lowell, the former president of Harvard University, this 135-acre property is maintained by the Trustees of Reservations. The parking fee on summer weekends is $6.

MAPLE SWAMP CONSERVATION AREA
Service Road, Sandwich
(508) 833-8054
Maple Swamp Conservation Area is a network of dirt roads and paths spreading out over 500 acres along a service road parallel to US 6 between exits 3 and 4. It is closed to vehicles and has numerous trails and roads for walking (no biking). The kettle-hole ponds and irregular terrain are typical of the topography that glaciers created thousands of years ago. The elevation ranges from 40 feet above sea level to 250 feet at one of the highest points on the Cape.

MASHPEE RIVER RESERVATION
Quinaquisset Road, Mashpee
(508) 679-2115
www.thetrustees.org
The 400-acre Mashpee River Reservation has 2 miles of hiking trails along the Mashpee River, a protected waterway that is perfect for canoeing, bird-watching, and walking. Coming from the Mashpee Rotary, follow Route 28 toward Hyannis to the first right, Quinaquisset Road.

MURKWOOD CONSERVATION AREA
Route 6A, East Sandwich
(508) 833-8054

To explore the 79-acre Murkwood Conservation Area, park at the East Sandwich Fire Station on Route 6A and walk across the street. A peninsula, this former farmland abuts Scorton Creek, and you might be fortunate enough to see eagles, osprey, shorebirds, and white-tailed deer. The area's several miles of trails pass through swampy areas and pinewoods, and the view of Scorton Marsh, especially at sunset, is breathtaking.

NIVLING-ALEXANDER RESERVE
Shore and Thaxter Roads, Bourne
(508) 563-2884

Also known as the Red Brook Pond Conservation Area, the Nivling-Alexander trail is a half-mile circular wooded trail through pitch pine and hardwoods (vibrant in the fall), passing through 40 acres of land along Red Brook Pond and working cranberry bogs. The entrance is at Shore Road and Thaxter Road.

PINE BARRENS
Great Neck Road, South, Mashpee
(508) 539-1400

The Pine Barrens is a 300-acre reserve that has about 4 miles of marked walking trails and sandy roads. To get there, turn right off Great Neck Road onto the dirt road opposite Punkhorn Point Road.

RYDER CONSERVATION AREA
Cotuit and South Sandwich Roads, Sandwich
(508) 833-8054

The lovely 243–acre Ryder Conservation Area is accessible from Cotuit and South Sandwich Roads and offers about 5 miles of walking trails. Wakeby Pond has fishing areas and a boat ramp and is an excellent area for canoeing and swimming. Nature lovers will appreciate the large holly trees (some more than 100 years old), the beech/pine tree groves, and the old abandoned cranberry bogs. Lifeguards are on-site during the summer months (Ryder Conservation Area is open May to Oct). A local beach sticker is required

during the summer months between 9 a.m. and 4 p.m. A daily pass may be purchased for $10 at the Sandwich Town Hall ($60 for the season). There are several parking areas and entrances off the west side of Cotuit Road between Harlow Road and Boardly Road.

SCUSSET BEACH STATE RESERVATION
Scusset Beach Road, Sandwich
(508) 888-0859
www.mass.gov/dcr/parks/southeast/
scus.htm

Scusset Beach Reservation, on the north side of the canal (see our Campgrounds and State Parks chapter), is a large state-run park that is mostly used for camping, but hiking and fishing are permitted. A 1-mile trail through Scusset leads to Sagamore Hill, which offers a panoramic overlook of Cape Cod Bay. Take Meetinghouse Road east off the Sagamore Rotary to Scusset Beach Road to the trail entrance opposite the pier. A daily parking fee is charged.

SHAWME-CROWELL STATE FOREST
Route 130, Sandwich
(508) 888-0351
www.mass.gov/dcr/parks/southeast/
schr.htm

This large 742-acre state-run park is used mostly for camping and offers an abundance of wildlife, flora, and fauna. This quiet campground at the beginning of Cape Cod has 285 campsites, and toilets and hot water are available for a nightly fee (see our Campgrounds and State Parks chapter). The park also has 15 miles of roads and trails that provide excellent hiking and biking access to the pitch pine and scrub oak forests. You can view all of Cape Cod Bay from the summit of Mr. Perry inside the park. A camping permit allows campers to use Scusset Beach.

SOUTH CAPE BEACH STATE PARK
Great Neck Road, Mashpee
(508) 457-0495
www.mass.gov/dcr/parks/southeast/
socp.htm

At the end of Great Neck Road is South Cape Beach, where the state maintains a public beach, parking lot, and conservation land with 3 miles of sandy roadways suitable for hiking. Here you can explore both freshwater and saltwater wetlands. There is a $7 fee for parking. For more information about South Cape, contact the Waquoit Bay National Estuarine Research Reserve at the above number.

TALBOT'S POINT CONSERVATION LANDS
Old County Road, Sandwich
(508) 833-8054
Talbot's Point Conservation Lands on Old County Road has a relatively level trail system through a red pine forest planted for soil control by the Conservation Corps during the Great Depression. Its 112 acres abut a saltwater and freshwater marsh, and walkers may see shore and upland game birds as well as osprey. The area features a freshwater bubbling spring. Park on the wide sandy road north from Old County Road, about 1 mile east of Hoxie Pond.

WASHBURN ISLAND
Waquoit Bay, East Falmouth
(508) 457-0495
www.waquoitbayreserve.org
Washburn Island is a 334-acre wooded island in Waquoit Bay managed by the state Department of Conservation and Recreation. It is only accessible by boat and has no fresh water. If you wish to camp on the island, you must purchase a permit (see our Campgrounds and State Parks chapter). Call the Waquoit Bay National Estuarine Research Reserve at the number above for more information.

i You've come to the right place if you want to walk. Cape Cod Pathways is our ever-expanding network of trails that link open space with all 15 towns. Pick up a map of trails from the Cape Cod Chamber (508-362-3225), or most town chambers. You may also call Cape Cod Pathways at (508) 362-3828.

Mid-Cape

BASS HOLE (GRAY'S BEACH)
Center Sreet, Yarmouthport
(508) 398-2231, ext. 1283
Bass Hole, also called Gray's Beach, at the end of Center Street, is the place to stroll along the boardwalk, put your toes in the water, and enjoy the beach, playground, and barbecue facilities.

BRIDGE CREEK CONSERVATION AREA
Route 149, West Barnstable
(508) 862-4093
To reach Bridge Creek Conservation Area, you can park at either the fire station on Route 149 or at Church Street (which can be found off Route 6A). This large 246-acre conservation area has 2½ miles of well-cleared trails for you to explore. Maps are available at the trailhead.

BURGESS PARK
Route 149, Marstons Mills
(508) 790-6345
Burgess Park is a 17-acre park with an 18-"hole" Frisbee golf course, walking trails, a playground, volleyball court, croquet area, horseshoe pits, and barbecue grills. The park overlooks Hamblin Pond, and it's an easy walk to the pond's beach. Parking is $12 on weekdays, $15 on weekends and holidays.

CALLERY-DARLING CONSERVATION AREA
Center Sreet, Yarmouthport
(508) 398-2231, ext. 1283
The Callery-Darling Conservation Area is a great place to spot woodland and water birds, such as the great blue heron, the largest heron in North America, which fishes in both fresh and salt water. There is a trail system here comprising some 2.4 miles wandering through lands where foxes, rabbits, and deer make their home.

CONSERVATION AREA
New Boston Road, Dennis
(508) 760-6123
Simpkins Neck and the Romig-Jacquinet Conservation Area are two connected parcels of land

that are largely surrounded by marshlands. Once you find the entrance (off New Boston Road, two houses past Berrien Studios on your left), you can follow the trail to the edge of the marsh. It's 1.5 miles round-trip.

CRAB CREEK CONSERVATION AREA
North Dennis Road, Yarmouthport
(508) 398-2231, ext. 1283
Blue crabs (Callinectes sapidus) are abundant here, and their presence gave this conservation area its name. A 500-foot trail follows a creek that joins Follins Pond with Mill Pond; it is a prime fishing spot and features a dock just for that purpose.

CROCKER NECK CONSERVATION AREA
Santuit Road, Cotuit
(508) 862-4093
The 97-acre Crocker Neck Conservation Area in Cotuit is a peninsula created by Shoestring Bay, Popponesset Bay, and Pinquickset Cove. It is wooded and has an interpretive trail with permanent numbered markers and an observation deck overlooking tidal pools. The area also has saltwater marshes. You can park in a lot off Santuit Road.

CROWE'S PASTURE
South Street, East Dennis
(508) 760-6123
Nature lovers will relish Crowe's Pasture, a bayfront site of more than 50 acres off South Street at the end of Quivet Cemetery. Follow the dirt road (about 2½miles round-trip), and revel in an oasis barrier beach with marsh hawks and wild apple and cherry groves.

DENNIS POND CONSERVATION AREA
Willow Street, Yarmouthport
(508) 398-2231, ext. 1283
As its name suggests, this conservation area is adjacent to Dennis Pond and features a 1,325-foot trail that leads through woodlands of red maple,

white pine, and sweet pepperbush. There's a small parking area out on Willow Street where you begin your journey.

HATHAWAY'S POND RECREATION AREA
Old Phinney's Lane, Barnstable
(508) 862-4093
The Hathaway's Pond Recreation Area in Barnstable has oak and pine forests, two ponds, an interpretive trail, and a picnic area within its 94 acres. The entrance is on Phinney's Lane off Route 132.

HORSE POND CONSERVATION AREA
Higgins Crowell Road, West Yarmouth
(508) 398-2231, ext. 1283
Located near the Mattacheese School, this ¾-mile hilly trail is marked by pitch pines, white oaks, sassafras, and blueberry and huckleberry bushes. Though the trail is joined by side trails that lead off toward longer journeys, the main trail keeps Horse Pond within sight.

INDIAN LANDS CONSERVATION AREA
Main Street, South Dennis
(508) 760-6123
Some of the Cape's most awesome flora and fauna abound in Indian Lands Conservation Area, a 2-mile walk that hugs the banks of Bass River. Birders can easily spot kingfishers and blue herons in the winter. You know summer is around the corner when the lady's slipper orchids start sprouting in May.

LONG POND CONSERVATION AREA
Santuit-Newtown Road, Cotuit
(508) 862-4093
A community garden with two observation decks overlooking the 37-acre Long Pond are features of Long Pond Conservation Area. An interpretive network of trails totaling 2 miles passes through fields and woodlands. A parking entrance on Newtown Road is about 2½ miles from Route 28.

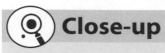 **Close-up**

Birding on Cape Cod

One of the best spots along the Northeastern seaboard to view birds is Cape Cod. During the migration seasons, more than 260 different species of birds may make a stop on Cape Cod to feed on marine worms, insects, crustaceans, and mollusks before continuing their long journey, which may have started in the Arctic Circle to end in South America, 12,000 miles away. Cape Cod lies about halfway along this busy flyway, and places like Monomoy Island and Nauset Marsh are regular stopovers for these birds, perfect areas to feed and rest before flying either north or south in the spring and fall.

Birds can, for the sake of simplicity, be divided into three main categories: backyard birds, shorebirds, and raptors. It's no surprise that shorebirds top the list of birds on Cape Cod. Among the many varieties of shorebirds found around these shores are dunlins, sanderlings, gulls, ducks, mergansers, sandpipers, and Canada geese.

Birding is terrific on Cape Cod no matter what the season, though spring is the best time to view migrating birds, and August is best for observing shorebirds. Many gulls and terns, having bred in June and fledged their young in July, become roving flocks in August. From mid-July to Labor Day, great concentrations of shorebirds can build up around feeding grounds. September is a good month for birding because of the possibility of a rare sighting. If a Nor'easter hits the Cape, sometimes migrating birds such as shearwaters, northern gannets, loons, and petrels become trapped near land and instinctively turn to the Cape. If you set up watch in the morning after a storm at a beach such as First Encounter Beach in Eastham, you'll have an excellent chance of observing some rare birds. September is also a wonderful month when many migrating birds linger on these shores, delaying their flights south for as long as possible. These birds tend to concentrate near their favorite food source before continuing on their journey.

Winter birds are plentiful, too. Herons, egrets, and sandpipers, all birds associated with wetland habitats, are abundant this time of year. A variety of waterfowl—including buffleheads, common eiders, canvasbacks, and goldeneyes—make the Cape their home during different months in the winter. A winter walk along a salt marsh, beach, or tidal flat will give good opportunities to observe these birds feeding and resting.

MEADOWBROOK ROAD CONSERVATION AREA
Meadowbrook Road, West Yarmouth
(508) 398-2231, ext. 1283
Meadowbrook Road Conservation Area is a pretty walking area with a short boardwalk over a freshwater marsh that leads to a scenic overlook of Swan Pond.

NATURE TRAILS
Route 6A, Yarmouthport
(508) 362-3021
www.hsoy.org
The Nature Trails behind the Yarmouthport Post Office on Route 6A are owned by the town and maintained by the Historical Society of Old Yarmouth. There is a gatehouse at the beginning of the trail where you can pick up a trail map and where a donation is requested. The main trail is approximately 1 mile long, and the pond trail around Millers Pond adds another half-mile to the trek.

RAYMOND J. SYRJALA CONSERVATION AREA
Winslow Gray Road, West Yarmouth
(508) 398-2231, ext. 1283
The Raymond J. Syrjala Conservation Area is about a half-mile from Route 28. The 3,540–foot trail encircles a kettle-hole pond that serves as a

great frog pond. The trail itself is spongy because it's made up of decaying leaves and pine needles. Many species of vegetation, such as red maple, pitch pine, and blueberries, are marked.

SANDY NECK RECREATION AREA
Off Route 6A, West Barnstable
(508) 862-4093
The Sandy Neck Recreation Area has about 5 miles of sandy trails bordered by wildflowers and cranberries. It's a nice place to canoe and fish. You can plan your hike from a trail map at the beach guard station. Parking is available, and a small fee is charged during the summer.

SIMPKINS NECK ROMIG-JACQUINET FRESH POND CONSERVATION AREA
Route 134, South Dennis
(508) 760-6123
Fresh Pond Conservation Area, right on Route 134, is 27 unspoiled acres of blueberries and wild cranberries. You can occasionally spot ducks and red-tailed hawks here while you walk one of four informal trails ranging from a 15-minute loop to a leisurely 45-minute walk.

WEST BARNSTABLE CONSERVATION AREA
Route 149, West Barnstable
(508) 862-4093
West Barnstable Conservation Area is an extensive 1,114-acre area with 15 miles of trails. A good number of the trails are geared toward mountain biking. You'll find limited parking at the intersection of Popple Bottom Road and Route 149 or off the service road.

Lower Cape
The Lower Cape is dominated by the expansive Cape Cod National Seashore, one of America's most beautiful recreational shorelines (see our Cape Cod National Seashore chapter). Adding to this bounty of natural areas are other excellent parks and wildlife refuges, including Nickerson State Park in Brewster, the Massachusetts Audubon Society's Wellfleet Bay Wildlife Sanctuary, and the magnificent Monomoy National Wildlife Refuge.

BELL'S NECK ROAD CONSERVATION AREA
Off Bell's Neck Road, Harwich
(508) 430-7538
One of the finest bird-watching sports on the Lower Cape, this is a magnificent 245-acre utopia of marshlands, herring runs, reservoirs, and tidal creeks.

THE CAPE COD NATIONAL SEASHORE
Salt Pond Visitor Center, U.S. Route 6, Eastham
(508) 255-3421

Province Lands Visitor Center, Race Point Road, Provincetown
(508) 487-1256

Park Headquarters, Marconi Station off U.S. Route 6, Wellfleet
(508) 771-2144
www.nps.gov/caco
With some 27,700 acres of federally protected undeveloped uplands, bogs, pitch pine forests, sand dunes, and ponds in six towns (Chatham, Orleans, Eastham, Wellfleet, Truro, and Provincetown), the National Seashore takes up almost half of the town of Wellfleet and about 70 percent of Truro. In addition to six ocean beaches, comprising nearly 40 miles of seashore on the Atlantic coast (see our Beaches chapter), the Cape Cod National Seashore boasts nine hiking trails that meander through varied terrain. You can get free maps at the Salt Pond Visitor Center in Eastham, which is open all year (daily except Jan and Feb, when it's open on weekends only) and shows free interpretive videos in addition to hosting a variety of interpretive programs.

Right behind the Salt Pond Visitor Center are several trails, including the quarter-mile Buttonbush Trail, which has a guide rope and Braille map interpretations along the way. It's a good trail not only for the sight impaired, but for people who want to experience what life is like without the sense that most of us take for granted. Close your eyes and try it. Another nearby trail takes a wooded route out to the 1.2-mile Salt Pond trail, which passes by the Salt Pond, along Nauset Marsh, and circles back to the visitor center; you can also walk or bike on the 2-mile bike trail that leads out to Coast Guard Beach, past Doane Rock—a good place to stop and picnic.

One of our favorite walking spots is the National Seashore's Fort Hill in Eastham, where 1½ miles of trails meander through fields with stunning water and marsh views, through woods and a cedar swamp. You're likely to spot rabbits, birds, and other wildlife, but watch out for poison ivy. We're also partial to the Seashore's longest and most difficult trail, Great Island in Wellfleet. Accessible by driving out past the harbor to the parking area, the trail is a hilly 8 miles (round-trip) through soft sand, pitch pines, and marshes that offer breathtaking views of Wellfleet Bay. Be sure to check the tides, because much of the trail is flooded at high tide. In Provincetown check out the 1-mile-long Beech Forest trail, where you'll circle a freshwater pond as you walk among American beech trees, sheep laurel, yellow and gray birch, and swamp azaleas. There's a lot more to the National Seashore, so check in with the Park Service at the Salt Pond Visitor Center for more information.

MONOMOY NATIONAL WILDLIFE REFUGE
Monomoy Island, Chatham
(508) 945-0594
www.fws.gov/northeast/monomoy
Accessible from Chatham only by boat in good weather conditions, Monomoy is a 7,600-acre, two-island wilderness area, one of only four remaining between Maine and New Jersey. Acquired by the federal government in 1944 and now under the administration of the U.S. Fish and Wildlife Service, Monomoy has no electricity, no human residents, no vehicles, no paved roads—and more than 285 species of birds inhabiting saltwater and tidal flats, bayberry and beach plum thickets, freshwater ponds, and a 9-mile-long barrier beach. There is also a nonworking lighthouse (built in 1823, restored in 1988). Beach areas are closed from Apr to mid-Aug so that the nesting areas of piping plovers and terns won't be disturbed.

Quiet is the best word to describe Monomoy. In the winter, thousands of seals take harbor here. Monomoy is an important stop along the North Atlantic flyway, and in May and late July migrating waterfowl and shorebirds stop here for a rest. Monomoy was once attached to the mainland; a 1958 storm severed the relationship. Twenty years later, another storm divided the island in two. The Cape Cod Museum of Natural History (508-896-3867), and Wellfleet Bay Wildlife Sanctuary (508-349-2615), offer regular guided tours; see our Tours and Excursions chapter. Morris Island, a 40-acre island accessible by car and foot, is home to migrating warblers, and tidal flats provide food for oyster-shucking birds.

NICKERSON STATE PARK
Route 6A, Brewster
(508) 896-3491
This 1,779-acre wonderland has 8 miles of bike trails that link with the Cape Cod Rail Trail as well as miles of hiking trails that meander through the woods. Some wind past the park's two main attractions, Flax Pond and Cliff Pond. The trails are also great for cross-country skiing in winter. Hike out to Higgins Pond, a major migration stop for endangered birds such as ospreys and peregrine falcons. You'll also see cormorants, wrens, hawks, owls, warblers, thrushes, great blue herons, Canada geese, and the common loon. Nickerson also has bayfront land on the north side of Route 6A (an easy walk from the park's entrance on the south side of the road) and offers ranger-guided interpretive programs and informative walks explaining plant and wildlife in a variety of habitats. Call for program schedules, or check the big board in the main parking lot.

PUNKHORN PARKLANDS
Run Hill Road, Brewster
(508) 896-3701
Here you'll find a maze of 45 scenic trails throughout more than 800 acres of rugged parkland made up of marshes and meadows, quarries and woodland, pine and oak—a tranquil paradise interrupted only by warbling birds, howling coy-

otes, and the occasional mountain bike. Along the paths you'll spot old pumps once used by cranberry growers to flood these former bogs.

SPRUCE HILL CONSERVATION AREA
3341 Route 6A, Brewster
(508) 896-3701
This 25-acre parcel, hidden behind the Brewster Historical Society Museum on the eastern end of town, features a ½-mile former carriage road leading to Cape Cod Bay and an expansive beach. Rumor has it that bootleggers used the trail during the time of Prohibition. Fragile plant life is abundant here, so please, as always, stay on the official path.

Steer Clear of Deer Ticks

Hiking and biking trails crisscross the most beautiful areas of the Cape and islands—which are also the habitat of the deer tick. These ticks are known to carry Lyme disease and should obviously be avoided. They are at their most plentiful May through July. Some helpful hints for a worry-free walk: Wear light-colored clothing (to spot ticks more easily), tuck your pant legs into your socks, and use insect repellant containing DEET (though not on infants). Inspect yourself, your children, and your pets after the walk just to be sure. If you find a tick, remove it within 24 hours. Use tweezers to dislodge the tick. Pull straight out with steady pressure, save the tick, and contact the Barnstable County Department of Health and the Environment at (508) 375-6617 so they can identify the tick for you and let you know if you should seek treatment.

WELLFLEET BAY WILDLIFE SANCTUARY
U.S. Route 6, Wellfleet
(508) 349-2615
www.wellfleetbay.org
The Massachusetts Audubon Society operates this 1,000-acre-plus tract of salt marsh, woodland, beach, tidal flats, and moorland. What was once a turnip and asparagus farm is now a haven of self-guided nature trails and superb bird-watching, along with a natural history day camp for children and weeklong field trips for older folk. Guided walks, canoe cruises through Nauset Marsh, Monomoy cruises, and seal- and whale-watching trips are regularly sponsored. The excursions are extremely popular and book fast. The 1½-mile Goose Pond Trail, part of the 5 miles of trails, offers a look at a diversity of habitats and leads to the shore. It's an excellent place for viewing shorebirds, hawks, and herons. In keeping with the theme of preservation, the visitor center uses passive solar heating and composting toilets. It's open year-round. A donation is requested: $5 from adults and $3 from seniors and children from 3 to 12 (those under 3 enter free). Of course if you are a member of the Massachusetts Audubon Society, the donation is waived.

i Coyote sightings on the Cape have been reported since the late 1970s, and coyotes have been spotted in each Cape town. There's little to fear from them: They are evasive creatures who are not interested in you (though they may cast an eye toward small pets). Absolutely do not try to feed them.

BIKING

Whatever your biking abilities, you can choose an abundance of trails throughout the Cape. In this section we highlight paved trails, though we mention some dirt trails, and also let you know about bike shops that provide maintenance and rentals.

Biking Trails
Upper Cape
CAPE COD CANAL AREA
Buzzards Bay to Cape Cod Bay
(508) 759-4431

Owned and operated by the U.S. Army Corps of Engineers, this 8-mile-long paved surface rolls gently along both sides of the Cape Cod Canal area in Bourne and Sandwich. The path is used every day in every season by bikers—from new-comers to experienced bicyclists—and by in-line skaters, walkers, and dog owners. As sunsets are usually spectacular along the Cape Cod Canal, you might want to plan your ride along the canal at sundown.

The path can be accessed at many points along its length. Those access points along the north side of the canal are northeast of Bourne Bridge, Herring Brook Fishway in Bournedale, Scusset State Park, and at the east side of Saga-more Bridge. South side accesses are along Pleas-ant Street in Sagamore, the southeast side of the Bourne Bridge, and the Boat Basin off Freezer Road in Sandwich. The access roads are marked, so you should be able to find your way.

SHINING SEA BIKE PATH
Woods Hole to Falmouth
(508) 548-7611

A favorite with bikers, walkers, and in-line skat-ers is the Shining Sea Bike Path, named in honor of Katherine Lee Bates, who wrote the lyrics of America the Beautiful and was born in Falmouth in 1859 in a house that still stands today at 16 Main Street. The bikeway is a level, 10.7-mile paved path and was built over the old Penn Cen-tral Railroad tracks. It overlooks Vineyard Sound as it passes alongside marshland and then gently winds by Nobska Point Lighthouse, on its way from North Falmouth to Woods Hole. The path was only 3 miles long until 2009 when more than 7 miles were tacked onto it. As the route follows the shore, it provides a great opportunity to take a swim, so bring your bathing suits.

As you pass Nobska Point, you can get a good view of the island of Martha's Vineyard, just 5 miles off the coast. Here you'll be about as close as you can get to the island without sailing toward it. Cross a few vintage wooden bridges, travel past the Coast Guard Station, and you're gliding into the quaint seaside town of Woods Hole. The trail also connects with paths that take you to other beautiful areas, such as Quisset Harbor.

Lower Cape
CAPE COD NATIONAL SEASHORE
U.S. Route 6, Eastham
(508) 771-2144, (508) 255-3421
www.nps.gov/caco

The Cape Cod National Seashore maintains three bicycle trails ranging from 1½ miles to just over 7 miles long. The trails are relatively flat with only a few hills in the dune areas where you might need to walk. Bike maps of the National Seashore are available at the visitor center in Eastham.

At the visitor center right near the Cape Cod Rail Trail (exit the trail at Locust Road, and cross US 6 at the traffic light, if you are on a bike) is the Nauset Trail, a lovely 2-mile trail that goes out to Coast Guard Beach on the Atlantic Ocean. The highlight of the ride comes when the trail opens to a wide vista of Nauset Marsh with the Atlantic Ocean in the distance. Although it's only a 15-minute ride to the beach from the visitor center, you parallel Nauset Marsh the entire way, through groves of cedar and locust trees.

The Head of the Meadow Trail is 2 miles long and wanders straight through the marshlands and dunes of the North Truro highlands. You can access the trail at High Head Road or at the Head of the Meadow Beach parking area. During July and Aug there is a nominal fee to park in the Head of the Meadow lot. We recommend you start at High Head Road and bike south toward Head of the Meadow. If you wish to venture further than just the 2-mile trail, it's easy. From Head of the Meadow head by bike to US 6, and head south a short distance to Highland Road and up the paved road through the dunes to a vista that takes in both the Atlantic Ocean and Cape Cod Bay.

In Provincetown, the Seashore has miles of trails. The Province Lands Trail, is a 7-mile loop that winds up and down dune hills, past lily ponds and bogs, through woods and sand dunes to the beaches at Race Point and Herring Cove. The trail starts at either Beech Forest at one end or Herring Cove at the other. Again there is a parking fee in season. The trail may also be picked up at the Province Lands Visitor Center, where there is no parking fee.

CAPE COD RAIL TRAIL
Dennis to Wellfleet
(508) 896-3491

Here is a great ride for bike enthusiasts who want to sample all the fun biking can offer. This 22-mile paved trail offers you a glimpse of the heartland of Cape Cod as it runs from Dennis to Wellfleet, following an old railroad bed. The trail is fairly straight and sweeps by sweet-smelling cedar and pine forests and includes long straight stretches between roadway intersections; they are all well marked with a post situated in the middle of the path separating bike and car traffic.

The trail enters Nickerson State Park in Brewster, where you will find just the right mix of pathway and off-road biking if you are looking for more of a challenge. There are not many restrooms along the route, but there are facilities at Nickerson State Park in Brewster and a composting toilet in Eastham.

Parking areas for trail access are in Dennis on Route 134; in Harwich on Headwaters Road near Route 124; in Brewster on Route 137 at Nickerson State Park off Route 6A; in Orleans Center; in Eastham at the Cape Cod National Seashore Visitor Center; and at the National Seashore trailhead on LeCount Hollow Road in South Wellfleet.

NICKERSON STATE PARK
Route 6A, Brewster
(508) 896-3491

If you are in search of new terrain for off-roading, you'll find that Nickerson State Park is practically the only place on the Lower Cape to ride a moun-

> **i** Rubel Bike Maps publish great detailed maps for trails on the Cape and islands. Check www.bikemaps.com.

tain bike. Service roads wind along the perimeter of the park, offering some fun dirt paths to play on; weave in and out of pine forests, and suddenly you've left the paved world behind. And, once you do that at Nickerson, the possibilities are endless.

The park has 8 miles of paved biking trails that connect to numerous freshwater ponds and picnic areas. If you want the park to yourself, come here in late fall, winter, or early summer before the campers arrive. A map is available at the entrance.

Bike Rentals

The Cape has plenty of shops that rent and sell bicycles and cycling equipment. Below, we list a few that are close to the major bike routes.

Upper Cape
HOLIDAY CYCLES
465 Grand Ave., Falmouth Heights
(508) 540-3549

If you're vacationing in Falmouth, you'll want to spend some time on the Shining Sea Bike Path. Stop by Holiday Cycles for bike rentals and any equipment you might need.

Mid-Cape
BARBARA'S BIKE AND BLADE, INC.
430 Rte. 134, South Dennis
(508) 760-4723

BARBARA'S BIKE SHOP #2
Route 6A, Brewster
(508) 896-7231
www.barbsbikeshop.com

Barbara's is right at the parking lot at the beginning of the Cape Cod Rail Trail. They rent bicycles by the hour, day, or week for all members of the family, from toddlers to teenagers to grandparents. They also rent in-line skates by the day for $15. When in Brewster, check out their second store on Route 6A.

ℹ️ Mountain bike enthusiasts may want to take on the "Trail of Tears" off Race Lane in Marstons Mills. It's an 18-mile loop, appropriate for those with experience. Pick up a map of the area at Barnstable Town Hall in Hyannis.

Lower Cape
ARNOLD'S WHERE YOU RENT BIKES
329 Commercial St., Provincetown
(508) 487-0844

Located in the center of Provincetown, Arnold's is known as the place "where you rent any kind of bike." From children's 20-inch coaster brake bikes to Fuji and Speed Royce bikes, you can rent by the hour, half-day, day, or week. They also specialize in bike repairs, tires, tubes, and accessories. Arnold's is open seasonally.

IDLE TIMES BIKE SHOP, INC.
4550 Rte. 6, Town Center Plaza, North Eastham
(508) 255-8281

188 Bracket Rd., North Eastham
(508) 255-5070

2616 Rte. 6, Wellfleet
(508) 349-9161

29 Main St., Orleans
(508) 240-1122
www.idletimesbikes.com

With two shops in Eastham, one in Wellfleet, and one in Orleans, Idle Times boasts the largest fleet of rental bikes on the Cape. They also sell bikes and accessories. The Town Center Plaza shop is open year-round.

LITTLE CAPISTRANO BIKE SHOP
341 Salt Pond Rd., Eastham
(508) 255-6515
www.capecodbike.com

This friendly shop is just across US 6 from the Cape Cod National Seashore Visitor Center, right near the Cape Cod Rail Trail and the Seashore bike trails. It offers rentals, sales, accessories, and repairs. It's open early Apr through Oct, and by appointment only from Halloween through Mar.

RAIL TRAIL BIKE & KAYAK
302 Underpass Rd., Brewster
(508) 896-8200
www.railtrailbikeshop.com

With direct access to the Rail Trail and only minutes from Nickerson State Park, Rail Trail Bike & Kayak may be one of the most convenient locations to enter the Rail Trail. There is plenty of all-day parking available at Bike & Kayak, so you can hop on one of their rental bikes and spend the whole day exploring Nickerson State Park and the Lower Cape.

TOURS AND EXCURSIONS

The Cape is beautiful from any perspective, whether it's riding in a car or walking on a beach. But to truly experience its many charms, try switching viewpoints. Get out on the water in a cruise ship or sailboat; take a train that chugs through country farms and hidden fields; or get a bird's-eye view from a plane or glider. Or combine exercise with education by taking a walking tour.

Here are some of our favorite tour and excursion companies, arranged by mode of transportation: boat, train, trolley, and plane. Keep in mind that most of these tours are only offered in season, and reservations may be required. We've given times wherever possible, but they are subject to change. It's best to call ahead to check. Check out our Getting Here, Getting Around chapter for more cruise ideas.

BOAT CRUISES

Upper Cape

CAPE COD CANAL CRUISES
Onset Pier, Onset
(508) 295-3883
www.hy-linecruises.com
This is a great way to explore Buzzards Bay and the Cape Cod Canal. As you travel the length of the 7-mile canal, you may pass tankers, sailing yachts, fishing boats, or plush cruise ships. A division of Hy-Line, Cape Cod Canal Cruises offers trips daily in summer, departing from Onset Pier in Onset. There are a variety of cruise options, including two- and three-hour cruises, a sunset cruise, a moonlight and music cruise, and a jazz cruise. Call or go online for more information.

OCEANQUEST HANDS-ON DISCOVERY CRUISES
100 Water St., Woods Hole
(508) 385-7656, (800) 376-2326
www.oceanquestonline.org
This information-packed cruise includes a hands-on science lesson for all ages. "It is geared to the general public—the nonscientist," says OceanQuest founder and director Kathy Mullin, a marine biologist who has worked on whale-watching boats for more than a decade. "We take a sample of the ocean, and with that we look at temperature, depth, salinity, density, the pH, and we talk about the greenhouse effect and global warming." Passengers also get a chance to practice with a plankton tow, a trawl, microscope, and lobster trap. Cruises are offered weekdays July through Aug. The cost is $22 per adult ($17 for kids 4 to 12, and $5 for those younger than 4; infants are free). Group rates are also available.

PATRIOT PARTY BOATS
227 Clinton Ave., Falmouth
(508) 548-2626, (800) 734-0088
www.patriotpartyboats.com
Patriot Party Boats is a family-owned and -operated business started nearly half a century ago. Docked at the entrance of scenic Falmouth Harbor, Patriot Boats operates fishing and charter boats, scenic sunset cruises, and operates the *Liberté*, a 74-foot schooner.

Liberté makes three cruises a day at 10:30 a.m., 2 p.m., and 6:30 p.m. The fare for an adult is $20 to $30 ($15 to $20 for children 12 and younger). This two-hour sail on the *Liberté* is only offered during July and Aug.

Equally appealing are the deep-sea fishing charters, which offer a great time and the possibility of catching sea bass, flounder, tautog, and scup. You can get detailed information about these in our Fishing chapter. Patriot Boats offers overnight, long-term parking at $15 a day for those utilizing their fast ferry to Martha's Vineyard. They also operate a 24-hour water taxi and offer private charter fishing excursions; call for more information.

Mid-Cape

CATBOAT RIDES
164 Ocean St. Dock, Hyannis
(508) 775-0222, (800) 308-1837
www.catboat.com

The classic catboat *Eventide* makes several trips daily out of Hyannis Harbor from early May through mid-Oct. Avid birders might opt for a nature cruise to the Pine Cove Wildlife Sanctuary in Lewis Bay. Other cruises include a Hyannisport cruise; a blue-water cruise; a sunset cocktail cruise, and a starlight cruise. The 34-foot *Eventide,* which has a 38-foot sloop-rigged mast, carries up to 22 people. It can sail in only 30 inches of water, allowing it to get very close to the shore and attractions such as the Kennedy Compound and local lighthouses. Cruise prices are $30 for adults, $25 for senior citizens, and $10 for children less than 90 pounds. Call ahead for reservations and schedules. The *Eventide* is available for private parties and corporate parties up to 20 people.

HYANNISPORT HARBOR CRUISES
Ocean Street Dock, Hyannis
(508) 778-2600, (800) 492-8082
www.hy-linecruises.com

Hy-Line offers cruises of Hyannisport Harbor on board the *Patience* or the *Prudence,* 1930s Maine coastal steamer replicas. You'll see the Kennedy Compound in Hyannisport as well as Squaw Island, Great Island, the Hyannis Yacht Club, and Point Gammon Lighthouse. Depending on the season, the schedule includes four to 17 trips a day between mid-Apr and late Oct. Call or go online for prices and schedules, including information on ferry service to and from Martha's Vineyard and Nantucket.

STARFISH BASS RIVER CRUISES
109 Rte. 28, West Dennis
(508) 362-5555
www.capecoDr.rcruise.com

The only river cruise on Cape Cod, Bass River Cruises takes you over the gentle waters of the Bass River, Grand Cove, and Weir Creek on the *Starfish,* a custom-built, flat-bottomed vessel. You'll see Cape wildlife such as egrets, herons, and terns, along with gorgeous riverfront estates, windmills, and a lighthouse. Cruises run from Memorial Day weekend through Columbus Day. Refreshments are available on board, including a full bar. The cost for a 90-minute cruise is $18 for adults and $7 for children. Group rates are available. Reservations are strongly recommended, and you should plan on arriving 20 minutes before the boat is scheduled to depart to claim your tickets.

Lower Cape

BAY LADY II
20 Berry Lane, MacMillan Wharf,
Provincetown
(508) 487-9308
www.sailcapecod.com

This 73-foot vessel, which boasts 2,230 square feet of sail, will take you on a two-hour jaunt across Provincetown Harbor and into Cape Cod Bay. Choose from morning, afternoon, and sunset sails, priced at $20 ($12 for children) in the daytime and $25 ($12 for children) at dusk. Sailing times are 10 a.m., 12:30 p.m., 3:30 p.m., and sunset. The schooner sails daily from mid-May to late Oct; reservations are recommended.

BEACHCOMBER BOAT TOURS
Stage Harbor or Ryder's Cove, Chatham
(508) 945-5265
www.sealwatch.com

Chatham's surrounding islands are home to numerous species of shorebirds, and Beachcomber's exciting 90-minute cruise is a perfect way to see them. An onboard naturalist will fill you in on these and other creatures living in or near the beautiful Stage Harbor and the Monomoy Island Wildlife Refuge. The list of creatures includes seals too. Tickets are $27 for adults and $23 for children 3 to 15 years old. Children younger than 3 ride for free, and seniors pay $25. Reservations are recommended. Parking is limited at Stage Harbor, so the Beachcomber offers a shuttle from Crowell Road, Chatham.

Beachcomber Boats also offers a boat-to-the-beach, a shuttle service between the town fish pier on Shore Drive and Chatham's outer beach on the Atlantic Ocean. Shuttles leave from the fish pier docks regularly every 15 minutes throughout the day in July and Aug. A round trip shuttle costs $15.

CAPE SAIL
Saquatucket Harbor Marina, Route 28, Harwich Port
(508) 896-2730
www.capesail.com
Captain Bob Rice offers three-hour, six-hour, and overnight charters aboard the 35-foot Southern Cross cutter *Sabbatical* along with lessons of six to nine hours (on either the *Sabbatical* or a 16-foot O'Day Day Sailer named *Renata*), from May to Oct. He also offers multiday trips to Nantucket, Martha's Vineyard, and other popular destinations.

i **Remember, all water cruises and tours are dependent on the weather. If in doubt, call ahead to make sure your trip hasn't been canceled.**

ERIN-H
Wellfleet Harbor Marina, Wellfleet
(508) 349-9663, (508) 237-1960
www.virtualcapecod.com/erinh
Captain Robert Hussey runs five- and eight-hour and all-day charters on his 36-foot *Erin-H* from mid-May through the end of Sept. Up to six passengers are taken at a time; call for rates.

FLYER'S BOAT RENTALS, INC.
131A Commercial St., Provincetown
(508) 487-0898
www.sailnortheast.com/flyers

In business more than half a century, this boatyard offers hourly shuttles between town and Long Point, the very tip of the Cape (see our Beaches chapter), on a 24-foot float boat. The cost is $15 round-trip or $10 one-way. Shuttles run daily in summer.

NAVIATOR
Town Marina, Wellfleet Harbor, Wellfleet
(508) 349-6003
www.naviator.com
In addition to fishing charters (see our Fishing chapter), Captain Rick Merrill offers seasonal evening harbor cruises, off-season seal and seabird cruises (weekends throughout the fall and spring), and a weekly marine-life cruise in conjunction with the Wellfleet Bay Wildlife Sanctuary (see below) on his 49-passenger vessel. Call for the schedule.

OUTERMOST HARBOR MARINE
83 Seagull Rd., Chatham
(508) 945-5858
www.outermostharbor.com
This is the place to go for seal cruises and shuttles to South Beach and Monomoy from late June through mid-Sept. The shuttle to South Beach, which runs on demand from 8 a.m. to 5 p.m. daily, costs $20 per adult and $10 per child (under 12) for a round trip. The shuttle to North Monomoy costs $20.

SCHOONER HINDU
MacMillan Wharf, Provincetown
(508) 487-7333, (888) 666–HINDU
www.theschoonerhindu.com
An 80-year-old replica of the seaworthy schooners that sailed out of Provincetown during the 19th and early 20th centuries, the *Hindu* offers four two-hour sails a day in summer on Cape Cod Bay, at 10 a.m., 1 p.m., 3:30 p.m., and sunset, plus romantic moonlight cruises during full-moon periods from June through Oct.

WELLFLEET BAY WILDLIFE SANCTUARY
291 U.S. Rte. 6, Wellfleet
(508) 349-2615
www.wellfleetbay.org

In the summer, the sanctuary offers naturalist-led marine-life cruises aboard the *Naviator*. Cruise from Wellfleet Harbor into Cape Cod Bay to look at some of the marine creatures that live in the sea.

Two-hour tours of Nauset Marsh are offered from May through Oct. For hands-on fun, take the kids on the family cruise around Nauset Marsh. This two-hour trip, offered several times a week, is done at low tide, so you can get out of the boat and explore tidal pools, dig for shellfish, and see other sea life.

Wellfleet Bay also offers tours of North Monomoy Island from May through Nov; travel time is 20 minutes round-trip, with two-and-a-half hours spent walking around the island. From Apr through Nov, the sanctuary offers frequent seal cruises off Chatham, during which you can explore the coasts of South Beach and the Monomoy Islands for harbor seals and gray seals (the latter are more common in summer). Seal cruises are also available all year long; call for details. Also call for prices and specific times for any of the above-mentioned cruises, as schedules vary according to the day of the week.

TRAIN TOURS

Mid-Cape

CAPE COD CENTRAL RAILROAD
Main Street, Hyannis
(508) 771-3800, (888) 797–7245
www.capetrain.com
Climb aboard the Cape Cod Central and feel the thrill as the whistle blows and you begin your fun-filled adventure from Hyannis to Sandwich and back. You'll pass cranberry bogs, natural woodlands, lush marshes, and more as you make your way to the Cape Cod Canal. The scenic trains operate daily in July and Aug, and less regularly in late May, June, Sept, and Oct. The ride takes about 50 minutes to get to the canal, with a 10-minute stopover to gather passengers, and another 50 minutes back to Hyannis. The train leaves one or two times a day from the Hyannis station at Main and Center Streets and can also be picked up in Sandwich at the Jarves Street station.

The railroad also operates the dinner train, a three-hour gourmet excursion. Imagine you're riding the Orient Express while you enjoy a five-course gourmet meal served on crisp white linen. The three-hour trip departs at 6:30 p.m. (6 p.m. from September through December) from the Hyannis Station. Proper dress and reservations are required.

Cape Cod Central also offers a fun and affordable dining experience for the whole family too. While the kids dine on "wacky mac & cheese" and chicken fingers, parents enjoy a more refined menu of their own. This two-hour dinner trip departs from the Hyannis Station at 6:30 p.m. and days vary month to month. Call or go online for rates.

SIGHTSEEING TROLLEY

Lower Cape

PROVINCETOWN TROLLEY
37 C. Court St., Provincetown
(508) 487-9483
www.provincetowntrolley.com
Take a ride on an old-fashioned open-air trolley for a 40-minute narrated tour through picturesque Provincetown. The trolley runs along Commercial Street's waterfront and out to the Province Lands Visitor Center and National Seashore. The fare is $9 for adults, $8 for senior citizens, and $5 for those ages 12 and younger. Trolleys depart daily from in front of the town hall every half-hour from 10 a.m. to 4 p.m. as well as hourly between 5 and 7 p.m. from mid-May through late Oct.

AIR TOURS

Mid-Cape

CAPE COD SOARING ADVENTURES
114 Lovells Lane, Martsons Mills Airport,
Race Lane and Route 149, Barnstable
(508) 420-4201
www.capecodsoaring.com
Fly with hawks and eagles during one of three different aerial tours of varying lengths up to 40

minutes. A 20-minute flight costs $105, a 25- to 35-minute flight is $140, and a 30- to 40-minute flight is $175. Tours are available year-round and can be tailored to your tastes. Instruction and rentals are also available.

Lower Cape

CAPE AERIAL TOURS

Chatham Municipal Airport, 240 George Ryder Rd., Chatham
(508) 945-2363

Cape Aerial Tours offers two tours, a 25-minute sightseeing flight for $125 for three people, and a 55-minute flight for $195 for three people. There's also a "Photo Specific Flight" with an onboard photographer. Trips take you over Chatham, the Monomoy Islands, and Pleasant Bay as you fly along the shores of Cape Cod. Cape Aerial Tours operates year-round except for Christmas.

RACE POINT AVIATION

Provincetown Airport, Race Point Road, Provincetown
(508) 873-2342
www.racepointaviation.com

Race Point Aviation offers sightseeing flights of 20, 35, and 65 minutes for individuals or groups of up to three people. Owner-aviators Russ Kimball and Roger Putnam also offer flight instruction and are available year-round. Be sure to call a couple days in advance to arrange a flight.

UNIQUE LAND TOURS

Lower Cape

ART'S DUNE TOURS

4 Standish St., Provincetown
(508) 487-1950, (800) 894-1951
www.artsdunetours.com

Since 1946, the Costa family (first Art, now Rob) has piled people of all ages into four-wheel-drive vehicles for an hour-long journey to the outer reaches of the Cape Cod National Seashore. You'll get to see the beach shacks of yesteryear, where many famous writers and artists lived, and have a chance to get out and stretch and snap some photos. The most popular tours are the sunset ones; reservations are a must for these. Ask about Art's New England clambake tours—you'll enjoy a delicious meal and a sunset. Dinner culinary options include barbecue and sushi. Tours are given from Apr through Oct and depart throughout the day. Tours start at $25 for adults and at $17 for children ages 6 to 11. Reservations are required for the two-hour special sunset tours. Children younger than six usually ride for free.

i In southeast Massachusetts, some 11,000 acres of cranberry bogs thrive in the area primarily because of the sandy, acidic soil and good supply of clean water. The bogs lie amidst extensive forestland. Besides being home to cranberries, these lands shelter wildlife. They also lie near reservoirs filled with many varieties of fish.

PILGRIM MONUMENT AND PROVINCETOWN MUSEUM

High Pole Road, Provincetown
(508) 487-1310
www.pilgrim-monument.org

In conjunction with the Cape Cod National Seashore, the museum offers weekly walking tours through Provincetown in summer. Led by a National Seashore ranger and a museum staffer—both of whom are very knowledgeable about the area and its history—the tours are very educational and really great fun. It's a good way to get your bearing geographially, and you'll pick up all sorts of interesting bits of history and trivia. Tours, which begin at the monument at 9 a.m. sharp on Tues mornings, last about two hours, usually a little longer.

BEACHES

Cape Cod has some of the most unspoiled beaches in the world, in part because of the fore-sight of President John F. Kennedy, who signed a bill on August 7, 1961, making the Cape Cod National Seashore a reality. Stretching the entire length of Cape Cod's Atlantic shoreline from Chatham to Provincetown, the National Seashore operates ocean beaches through six towns along this coast. Called the "outer beach" by locals, the surf-washed sands and ocean rollers are bordered by a continuous sweep of sandy cliffs and windswept dunes.

Of course the National Seashore isn't the only place to enjoy a beautiful beach. The Cape has more than 150 saltwater and freshwater beaches, offering something for everyone. Some Cape beaches have rough-and-tumble waves great for surfing, such as Coast Guard Beach in Eastham or LeCounts in Wellfleet; others are gentle and quiet, like Corporation Beach in Dennis or Old Silver Beach in North Falmouth. Some are broad, like Nauset Beach in Orleans; and others are narrow, such as Nobska in Falmouth. Some are rocky, like Town Beach in Sandwich; and some are all sand, like Craigville Beach.

The beaches of Cape Cod Bay, crooked in the inner curve of Cape Cod's bent arm from Dennisport to South Wellfleet, are fast tidal flats that can be up to a mile wide at low tide. A long walk on the flats out to the water's edge will afford you the opportunity to view many creatures of sea and shore life in the intertidal zone such as moon snails, hermit crabs, starfish, and horseshoe crabs. One of the best starting points for a walk along the flats is from Paine's Creek in Brewster, but be sure to check the tide charts before you leave, or you might get caught too far out on the flats when the tide starts coming in (we provide more information on tides under the section on Beach Safety, below).

Cape Cod's bay beaches are naturally calmer and safer for young children, and to the south of the Cape, the warm waters of Nantucket Sound play host to families with kids and the younger adults who gather at Craigville Beach in Centerville and along the Falmouth Heights Beach. The bays and sounds are relatively shallow bodies of water and warm up faster than the Atlantic Ocean. In the height of the summer, average temperatures in Cape Cod Bay on the north side are in the high 60s, whereas the beaches on the south side in Nantucket Sound reach the high 60s and mid-70s. Ocean temperatures on the east side linger in the high 50s, rarely getting higher than the low 60s.

There are also many freshwater lakes and ponds that have calm waters and small sandy beaches, many with picnic facilities.

BEACH SAFETY

As you venture into the water, here are some things you should know to make your days at the beach safe and serene. Lifeguards are posted at many beaches from mid-June through Labor Day to oversee hundreds of swimmers, but their watchfulness should not be a replacement for adult supervision of children. Be aware of the waves, the currents, the undertow, and the tide.

Waves

The ocean surf provides an experience completely different from the conditions found in Cape Cod Bay, Nantucket Sound, or any nearby pond or lake. At sea, powerful forces generated by water movements are continuously at work. Ocean waves crest and become more rounded as they move in from the open ocean and before they break on shore.

When a wave breaks in shallow water, a vigorous suction is caused both by the breaking wave and by the backwash of the previous wave. Those unfamiliar with this ocean action should know that a person can be swept off his or her feet and actually be pulled into the oncoming wave. If this should happen to you, don't panic. Push under the water and toward the oncoming wave, and curl your body to form a smaller mass; this will allow you to withstand the force of the wave. Once the wave has passed, you will pop up on the other side.

Currents

A lateral current, also known as a long-shore current, runs parallel to the beach and perpendicular to the direction at which waves approach the shore. This current is usually strong enough to move you sideways along the shoreline. Again, don't be alarmed if after an extended period of time swimming in the ocean you notice that you don't recognize any of the beach umbrellas or landscape on shore. You have probably moved with the current and are in a new position relative to shore. Those who pay no attention can be swept sideways into a rip current and beyond the breaking waves.

Rip currents occur when waves breaking over an offshore sandbar spill into a trough on the shoreward side of the sandbar, pile up, and then exit quickly through any break in the mound of the sandbar that had trapped the water. Water seeking a seaward outlet through the trough may move faster than a swimmer can swim, sweeping him or her out with it. Although rip currents can vary greatly in appearance, as a general rule they look especially rough or choppy, may have the dark color of deeper water, and may or may not have foam. Considering the seriousness of a rip current, it is clear that any swimmer caught in one should stop, look, and study a rip before making his or her next move. There is usually no

suction, so remain calm. If you feel you can swim across the current, parallel to the shore, you can work yourself back to the beach at an angle. A rip current can also be escaped when you relax and allow it to carry you to the outermost limit, which is usually not far beyond the breakers. After judging the width of the rip current, you can swim parallel to the beach in the relative calm water outside the breakers, reenter the surf at the end of a set, and then swim safely to shore and your beach blanket.

Undertow

At surf beaches, we were told, the greatest percentage of drownings result from persons exhausting themselves fighting currents and waves. By understanding how a wave works, you will understand how to react to certain circumstances when they occur. For instance, when a wave breaks on the beach and returns back to sea, it gains momentum and can knock individuals off their feet and sweep them swiftly into the surf. If you are carried out, don't resist. The undertow will subside once it hits the surf line. Swimmers get in trouble in the undertow when they panic. The ocean is a great place to be if you know what to look for and how to react if caught off guard.

Tides

The tides are an essential consideration when planning your day in or around the bay, sound, or ocean. Visiting a bayside beach during low tide when the flats extend out for more than a mile can be a dangerous situation as the tide can sometimes rush in over the flats quicker than you could walk back to the shoreline. Cape Cod, like most places on the coast, experiences semidiurnal tides, meaning that two high and two low tides occur daily. Each tide, controlled by lunar movements, takes place fifty minutes later than the previous day. The moon completes a full circle around the earth every 24 hours and 50 minutes, causing the variation of tidal timing from day to day. Translated, this means that if high tide is at 10 a.m. on Tuesday, it will be high at

10:50 a.m. on Wednesday. To make matters more confusing, because Cape Cod is surrounded by the Atlantic Ocean, the canal, the bay, and the sound, the tides vary in time difference by as much as two hours between the Upper and Lower Cape. Ask for a tide chart when you arrive for your visit.

Child Safety

Children should not take water toys such as boogie boards, flotation rings, or rafts into the ocean because they can quickly be carried out to a depth that's over their heads, or even be swept far away by offshore breezes. And, though many of us remember digging in the sand to "bury" each other as children, that activity can be dangerous as well, which is why notices at the Cape Cod National Seashore warn against it. The sand can easily collapse and trap a child. Each year we hear of a child being buried while digging in the sand and having to endure a life-threatening experience that could have easily been avoided. Also, don't forget sunscreen. And while you're protecting your child with it, don't forget yourself.

Wheelchair Accessibility

Most towns now have beaches that are wheelchair accessible; several have purchased special beach wheelchairs that are available for those who request their use, and many beaches are equipped with heavy rubber mat planks that make it easy to bring a wheelchair out onto a sandy expanse. The individual beach entries later in this chapter give phone numbers that you can call for more information.

PARKING

Parking is a big consideration when you're planning a day at the beach. Many beach lots fill quickly on nice summer days. Most beaches either charge admission or require a parking sticker, generally available at town halls or, in some cases, at the beaches themselves. Requirements differ from town to town and, within

towns, from beach to beach, with some beaches offering parking by sticker only and others staffed with attendants who sell daily passes. We've detailed the procedure in each town in this chapter's listings. A note of caution: If you park illegally, you will be ticketed and fined. Sometimes public transportation is an option. Or ride a bike—admission to most beaches is free for those who walk or bike in. Also keep in mind that the rates printed here are subject to change; when towns decide to raise their beach parking rates, they usually do so in the spring at annual town meetings.

Some towns have beaches that are designated for residents only. This means the beach is town-owned and supposed to be reserved for the use of resident taxpayers. In most cases, this designation is made because these beaches are small and have very limited parking. Generally "resident only" means you must have a resident/taxpayer sticker on your car to park in these areas, but there's nothing to stop you from walking or biking there. So we have included these beaches in the listings for each town with the caveat that they are intended for residents only. Please, don't try parking at such beaches without a resident sticker—you will be ticketed and in some cases towed. And respect the rules at all beaches.

PRIVATE BEACHES

Yes, there is such a thing, though this issue has been and will continue to be debated, particularly in reference to shell-fishing rights. Unlike most other states, in Massachusetts, waterfront property owners may own the beach in front of their home to mean low tide—an imaginary line between high tide and low tide. This line obviously varies with the moon, season, and atmospheric conditions. (See our section on tides in this chapter.) What it boils down to is an archaic law we have all learned to live within. It actually dates back to colonial times, when the king granted waterfront deeds that specified the owner had ownership of the beach to high tide rather than low tide. Someone then came up with the phrase "mean low tide," and it's impossible to generalize with any certainty how close you should hug the waterline when passing in front of private property. The law reads that access across beaches is allowed for "fishing, boating, and waterfowling," so you might want to carry a fishing pole just in case. What you need to know is that many of the public beaches are alongside private beaches and, as inviting as that nearly empty beach past the public beach may appear, you don't have the right to spread your blanket on it. These private beach areas are usually marked with small no trespassing or private property signs. Most waterfront property owners understand the lure of the open beach, and they certainly relish a beach walk. If you pass with respect, they won't get upset—some of our best walks are across miles of bay beach, both public and private.

PETS ON THE BEACH

Cape beaches operate a dog ban generally between mid-May and mid-September, though the length of the ban can vary by town. It doesn't matter if your dog is on a leash or under control of your command: Taking a dog on the beach during these months is punishable by a fine of up to $50. Some beaches like Nauset Beach in Orleans and Craigville in Centerville will not permit you entrance to the parking area if a dog is in your vehicle. At the smaller beaches, signs are posted at the entrance path to the beach area.

If you bring your dog during the off-season, when the crowds have gone and the rules are more relaxed, be sure your dog is under your control at all times. Remember, it's not just humans your pet can disturb—it's nesting birds or stranded seals. The Endangered Species Act provides penalties for taking, harassing, or harming the piping plover, for example. It's likely that if your dog disturbs a plover's nest or otherwise disturbs one of the protected species, someone will be waiting for you in the parking lot upon your return.

Also, please remove your dog's waste from the beach. It's a form of pollution that contaminates shellfish beds, as well as the wetlands. Most trails and beaches offer some sort of doggie

"dispoza-scoop." The Cape Cod Canal Bike Path offers a pooper-scooper bag at the end of the trailhead that is convenient to use. Other mittlike contraptions are available.

CAPE COD BEACHES

Below we introduce you to some of our most beautiful Cape Cod beaches. Those included have lifeguards during the summer unless otherwise noted. Many have restrooms and changing facilities, whereas some only have portable toilets; we've noted available facilities in each entry.

So pack up your picnic basket (though you'll want to leave glass containers at home—they're not allowed on National Seashore and many town beaches). If you chance to forget it, though, all is not lost. Some beaches have snack bars, and virtually all are included in routes of local ice-cream trucks, whose bells call children in from the water faster than you can say Creamsicle.

Upper Cape

The Upper Cape towns have coastlines along the waters of Cape Cod Bay, Buzzards Bay, Vineyard Sound, Nantucket Sound, and the Cape Cod Canal. The waters of the south side are generally calm and warm, with water temperatures in some spots reaching the 70s during the summer, whereas the bay beaches in Sandwich are influenced by a different tidal system and are colder. Another influence on Sandwich beaches is the Cape Cod Canal, a structure that, since it was dug, has interrupted the natural sweep of wind-carried sands along the curve of the shore. As a result, Sandwich beaches tend to be rockier than others, but they are distinctly charming.

Bourne

Bourne is home to a number of fine saltwater beaches stretching across its more than 50 miles of coastline along Buzzards Bay. The town also has about 2 miles of frontage on Cape Cod Bay to the north, as well as a couple ponds available for freshwater swimming. Like many Cape towns, Bourne holds a tight guard on parking at its beaches. The only beach with public parking is Monument Beach, near the southern mouth of the Cape Cod Canal. There is also the state-owned Scusset Beach, which straddles the Bourne-Sandwich line to the north. You can park here for $7 a day. To park at any other beach in Bourne you need a sticker, given only to residents or those who can prove they are staying in Bourne, such as those staying at a campground or renting property. Weekly beach parking stickers are required if you want to park at a town beach and can be picked up for $40 at the Natural Resources Office, Bourne Town Hall, 24 Perry Ave., Buzzards Bay, (508) 759–0621. Bourne does not have a daily parking fee.

Electric Avenue Beach on Buzzards Bay rests at the entrance to Buttermilk Bay near the Buzzards Bay rotary at the west end of the Cape Cod Canal. Lifeguards are on duty at this beach.

Monument Beach along Shore and Emmons Roads has public parking and looks out upon the Bourne entrance to the Cape Cod Canal and the Monument Beach Marina. Lifeguards are on duty.

To the southwest of the entrance to the Cape Cod Canal you will find **Gray Gables Beach** in the village of Gray Gables. Gray Gables has lifeguards, portable toilets, and concessions.

A popular north side option is **Scusset Beach** on Cape Cod Bay. This large, clean, state-run beach is predominantly in the town of Sandwich, yet you approach it by taking Meetinghouse Road off the Sagamore Rotary just before the Sagamore Bridge. From Meetinghouse take Scusset Beach Road into Sandwich to the beach parking area where you'll pay a $7 fee (or $35 for a Massachusetts resident season pass, $45 for a nonresident season pass). This beach has a snack bar and bathhouse available.

Sagamore Beach at the Sagamore Highlands is really three interconnected beaches on the mainland side of the Cape Cod Canal. These north-side beaches can be found off Samoset Road. Though there are no concession stands at these beaches, there are lifeguards on duty and portable toilets available.

Off Barlows Landing Road in Pocasset is the appropriately named **Barlows Landing Beach.**

Overlooking beautiful Pocasset Harbor, this beach has lifeguards and portable toilets, but no concession stands.

Hen Cove Beach, also known as Pocasset Town Beach, is on Hen Cove in Pocasset, which empties into Red Brook Harbor. The beach is well protected by both the cove and harbor, making it a nice place for the kids. There are lifeguards on duty and portable toilets but no concession stands.

Another well-protected beach is **Squeteague Beach** at Cataumet's Squeteague Harbor. There are no lifeguards or concessions at this beach, though there is one portable toilet.

Freshwater swimming can be found at **Queen Sewell Pond** in Buzzards Bay, just south of Little Buttermilk Bay. There are lifeguards and portable toilets at this beach, but you'll need a sticker to park.

Another freshwater pond open to swimmers is **Picture Lake,** located off Williams Avenue between County Road and Route 28 in Pocasset. This beach has lifeguards but no bathroom facilities. You'll need a sticker to park.

Sandwich

Sandwich has saltwater access along the north side of the town that borders Cape Cod Bay. A portion of this north shore lies on the other side of the Canal (the mainland side). Although deprived of the large harbors, coves, and bays present in many of the other Cape towns, Sandwich features a number of fine freshwater ponds in the southern portion of the town, including Peters Pond and Snake Pond. Sandwich also has frontage on a portion of Mashpee's Wakeby Pond, just enough to sneak in a beach.

You need a sticker to park at all beaches in Sandwich. The resident sticker costs $30. The nonresidents must pay $75, and the sticker will not get you to Sandy Neck, Peters Pond, and the resident-only Snake Pond area, but will get you everywhere else. All stickers are sold at the Sandwich Town Hall Annex (508-888-4910). One-day parking passes are also available at the beaches, with the aforementioned exceptions, for $10.

Town Neck Beach, at the end of Town Neck Road, offers a good spot to watch boat traffic pass on the Cape Cod Canal. Though there are no lifeguards on duty, there are restrooms and a concession stand.

Town Beach rests at the entrance to Sandwich Harbor. This Sandwich beach can be reached by taking Town Neck Road to Freeman Avenue. Nearby is the famous Sandwich boardwalk crossing Mill Creek, which winds through the picturesque marshes long the north side of Sandwich. Town Beach offers concession stands and restroom facilities but no lifeguards.

East Sandwich Beach, also known as Springhill Beach, is off Route 6A at the end of Ploughed Neck Road where it empties into North Shore Boulevard. Just to the east is Scorton Harbor and beautiful Scorton Creek. The parking area accepts permits only. The beach has no lifeguards, concession stands, or toilet facilities.

Sandy Neck Beach is a beautiful beach with high sand dunes that stretches for miles along Cape Cod Bay off Route 6A at the extreme eastern boundaries of the town. This beach lies within both Sandwich and Barnstable and offers lifeguards, concession stands, and bathroom facilities. Many people enjoy taking a four-wheel-drive vehicle onto Sandy Neck Beach for a day of fishing and swimming; this requires buying a permit through the Town of Barnstable. Your four-wheel-drive vehicle must undergo an inspection at the gatehouse for proper emergency equipment such as a tow rope, shovel, and spare tire. For weekly or monthly parking passes for the public beach, call the Recreation Department at (508) 790-6345. For four-wheel-drive permits, call the Sandy Neck Gatehouse (in season) at (508) 362-8300. The beach is open year-round and parking is $10.

Sandwich has a beach on the Wakeby portion of the beautiful Mashpee-Wakeby Pond. The beach, which can be found off Sandwich-Cotuit Road, has a large parking area, restrooms, and a big gazebo for grilling and picnics. Lifeguards are on duty.

Falmouth

Falmouth offers more miles of coastline than any other Cape town. The southern shoreline borders Vineyard Sound and the western side overlooks Buzzards Bay.

If you plan to park at any but three of these beaches, you need a sticker, given only to residents or guests who can show they are staying in Falmouth. Stickers are available at the Surf Drive bathhouse. Guest stickers cost $200 per year, $60 for one week, $70 for two weeks, $80 for three weeks, and $90 for four weeks. Three beaches—Surf Drive, Old Silver, and Menauhant—have daily passes available for anyone. For more information about Falmouth beaches, call the Falmouth Beach Committee at (508) 548-8623. Wheelchairs are available for all beaches.

Along Vineyard sound, **Surf Drive Beach** is the closest beach to Falmouth village center. This beach offers lifeguards, a bathhouse with showers, and a concession stand. The waters here are warm and calm with wonderful views of Martha's Vineyard across the sound and Nobska Light nearby. A small inlet to the north of the beach is popular with families who have little kids. Surf Drive is one of the three beaches in town where you can park without a sticker for $10 a day.

Old Silver Beach in North Falmouth is as popular as it is beautiful. The Buzzards Bay waters here are warm and ideal for youngsters. A creek splits the beach in two; one side is for residents and the other side is for visitors to the town. Lifeguards watch over the swimmers, and a concession stand keeps hunger at bay. Portable toilets and showers are available. You don't need a sticker to park here, but you do need to buy a $20 pass.

Another North Falmouth beach is **Megansett Beach** on Buzzards Bay. Like Old Silver Beach, the waters here are warm. The beach has lifeguards but no concession stands or bathhouses. Parking is by resident sticker only.

Chapoquoit Beach rests along Buzzards Bay just south of West Falmouth Harbor off Chapoquoit Road. This residents-only beach has lifeguards and toilet facilities.

> **i** If you can't get to the beach before 10:30 a.m., most likely you'll have to wait in line to get a parking space. If you go after 4 p.m., you won't have to pay.

Wood Neck Beach can be found at the mouth of the saltwater Little Sippewisset Lake in West Falmouth. Its waters are warmed by Buzzards Bay. Wood Neck has portable toilets on-site as well as lifeguards. Parking is by sticker only.

Falmouth Heights Beach overlooks Vineyard Sound and Martha's Vineyard, and the waters are warm and inviting. There are lifeguards on duty and portable toilets available, and though there are no concession stands, there are a number of places nearby to go get something to eat.

Two other wonderful Vineyard Sound beaches are **Menauhant** and **Bristol.** Both south-side beaches have lifeguards, concession stands, and portable toilets. Menauhant also has showers. Bristol Beach is accessible by sticker only. There is a $10-per-day parking fee at Menauhant for those without a sticker.

Grews Pond is a wonderful little freshwater pond in Goodwill Park off Gifford Street just north of Falmouth center. The pond has lifeguards on duty, and toilet facilities are available.

Mashpee

The southernmost portion of Mashpee touches Nantucket South, Waquoit Bay, and Popponesset Bay. Within the town are a number of large ponds: Ashumet and John's Ponds in the west, Santuit Pond in the east, and the connected Mashpee and Wakeby Ponds along the northern border with Sandwich. Parking at all but one beach requires a Mashpee resident sticker obtained at the town hall on Great Neck Road; call the Mashpee Town Hall at (508) 539–1400 for more information. If you're not a resident, or more appropriately, do not have a resident parking sticker, South Cape Beach at the southern tip of Mashpee is run by the state and allows anyone to park for a fee.

South Cape Beach on Nantucket Sound is a great, unspoiled place to enjoy sand, sea, and sun. About 3½ miles from the Mashpee Rotary at the end of Great Neck Road South, the beach is operated by both the town, which has a parking lot and requires a resident sticker, and by the state Department of Environmental Manage-

ment, which has a large parking lot and charges nonresidents of Mashpee $7 per day. Lifeguards are on duty, and toilet facilities are available.

For freshwater swimming go to **Attaquin Park** on the 729-acre Mashpee-Wakeby Pond. The park, off Route 130 at the southern end of the pond, has a swimming area, lifeguards, toilet facilities, and a state boat ramp with parking available.

Another popular freshwater spot is **John's Pond** at Hooppole Road off Route 151 and Currier Road. It has a public beach complete with lifeguards and toilet facilities.

Mid-Cape

The beaches of the Mid-Cape can be found on two separate bodies of salt water—Nantucket Sound to the south and Cape Cod Bay to the north. These have the Cape's warmest waters. Nantucket Sound is fed by warm southern waters, and its relatively shallow depth of about 40 feet—sandbars stretch as far as Nantucket—allows it to hold its warmth. On the bay side the tidal flats of the Mid-Cape heat up the north-side waters as they ebb and flow over the sand, which has been baking in the sun. The best time to swim in these waters is when high tide occurs late in the day and the sun has had all day to warm the sands. On the whole beaches in this long middle area of the peninsula are not as affected by currents and rips as the Lower Cape. There are also a number of beautiful lakes and ponds offering freshwater options.

Barnstable

Cotuit has three fine beaches, all requiring resident stickers to park. Beach stickers are available at the National Guard Armory at 225 South St. Resident stickers are $30 per season, nonresident stickers are $50 per week. **Oregon Beach** off Main Street has no lifeguards or restrooms, nor does **Ropes Beach,** located in the protected Cotuit Bay. Cotuit's **Loop Beach,** also off Main Street does have lifeguards and bathroom facilities. Neighboring Osterville has a saltwater residents-only beach on Vineyard Sound at the end of Wianno Avenue called **Dowses Beach.**

Lifeguards oversee Dowses Beach, and toilet facilities and concessions are available.

The often-crowded Craigville Beach off **Craigville Beach** Road in Centerville is a favorite with sunbathers and swimmers. On Nantucket Sound, this beach has a large parking lot and a bathhouse with outdoor showers. There are lifeguards on duty.

Two nearby residents-only parking beaches in Centerville are **Covells Beach** along Craigville Beach Road to the east of Craigville Beach and **Long Beach** on Long Beach Road to the west. Covells has lifeguards and restrooms; Long Beach has neither.

Hyannis has four beaches—East Beach, Kalmus Beach, Sea Street Beach, and Veterans Beach. **East Beach,** just west of Hyannis Harbor, has residents-only parking with no food or bathroom facilities and no lifeguards on duty.

As a windsurfing beach, **Kalmus Beach** at the end of Ocean Street in Hyannis is considered by some to be the best on the Cape. One of two beaches in Hyannis Harbor, Kalmus has a windsurfing area, snack bar, bathroom facilities, and a picnic area; and the beach is protected by lifeguards.

Sea Street Beach at the end of Sea Street is the second public beach in Hyannis Harbor and is within walking distance of many accommodations in Hyannis. This beach has a bathhouse, snack bar, and picnic area; lifeguards are on duty in season.

Veterans Beach on Ocean Street in Hyannis is a popular place where families enjoy picnics and cookouts shaded by a pine grove. The facilities include a bathhouse, snack bar, picnic area and playground, and lifeguards. The Kennedy Memorial (see our Attractions chapter) is adjacent to Veterans Beach.

Six-mile-long **Sandy Neck Beach,** north of Route 6A in West Barnstable, is the town's longest beach. The road that leads to the beach, Sandy Neck Road, actually connects with Route 6A just over the town line in East Sandwich. Sandy Neck Road then works its way north into West Barnstable before reaching the beach parking lot. This beach offers swimming, fishing, camping, and hiking. Facilities include indoor restrooms, showers, and a snack bar; lifeguards work this beach.

Next to picturesque Barnstable Harbor at the end of Millway along the north shore of town is Millway Beach. This beach offers a great view of the boat traffic entering and leaving the harbor, but parking is for residents only. **Millway Beach** has lifeguards and restrooms. Across the waters is Sandy Neck with its decommissioned lighthouse at the point.

For freshwater swimming, there is the residents-only **Hamblin Pond** off Route 149 in Marstons Mills with lifeguards, restrooms, and a picnic area. Another Marstons Mills pond is **Lovells Pond** off Newtown Road, with lifeguards and rest rooms. **Joshua's Pond** on Tower Hill Road in neighboring Osterville has bathroom facilities and a playground for the kids, as well as lifeguards.

Lake Wequaquet, also residents-only, on Shoot Flying Hill Road in Centerville, is a freshwater playground. The lake is almost 2 miles long and roughly a mile wide. Bathroom facilities are on-site, as are lifeguards.

Hathaway's Pond off Phinney's Lane in Barnstable has restrooms and a picnic and playground area. Lifeguards are on duty. Parking is $5 weekdays, $6 on weekends.

i "Shark sightings" are common during summers on the Cape. They are nearly always harmless sharks, of the brown, thresher, or basking varieties. If you're worried about encountering sharks, stay near shore, and swim with groups.

Yarmouth

Yarmouth has coastlines to the north on Cape Cod Bay and to the south on Nantucket Sound and Lewis Bay. The east side of the town borders Bass River to the south and Garden Creek to the north. The north side of the town on Cape Cod Bay is only about 1½ miles long and is largely marshland, save for a small beach at Bass Hole on the east end. The south side has beaches, and all but four require a parking sticker. Sea Gull, Sea View, Parker's River, and Bass River beaches all allow daily parking for a $15 fee if you do not have a sticker. Two beaches in Yarmouth—Dennis Pond and South Middle Beach—require a resident parking sticker. Nonresidents can obtain a sticker for $70 a week or $175 a season. Stickers are available at beach entrances. Call the town clerk's office (508-398-2231, ext. 1216) for more information.

Off Sea Gull Road, which is off South Sea Avenue in West Yarmouth, is where you'll find **Sea Gull Beach.** Offering plenty of parking spaces, this is Yarmouth's largest and most popular beach, especially with high school and college students. Sitting just west of Parker's River, it has lifeguards, toilet facilities, a few picnic tables, and concessions. There is a daily parking fee at Sea Gull Beach of $15.

From **Bay View Beach,** at the end of Bay View Street in West Yarmouth near the town line with Barnstable, you have a good view of Lewis Bay and the thousands of boats that enter Hyannis Inner Harbor every year. Bay View Beach has lifeguards on duty (on weekends only) and bathroom facilities. Parking is $15 daily.

Colonial Acres Beach at Lewis Bay is at the end of Standish Way in West Yarmouth. It has portable toilets and a bridge to the beach.

Englewood Beach, also in West Yarmouth on Lewis Bay, is at the end of Berry Avenue. Englewood has restrooms and lifeguards. The town's sailing program is based at Englewood Beach.

On the east side of the mouth of Parker's River is **Sea View Beach** off South Shore Road in South Yarmouth. This south-side beach is protected by lifeguards, it has a picnic area and portable toilets.

To the east of Sea View Beach, along the Cape's southern shore, is **Parker's River Beach,** which lies along the warm waters of Nantucket Sound. The beach has restrooms, a concession stand, outdoor showers, swings, good parking, and lifeguards. It costs $15 a day to park.

South Middle Beach on South Shore Drive in South Yarmouth is a residents-only beach offering a large parking lot and restrooms. Lifeguards keep an eye on the activities out on Nantucket Sound.

Smugglers Beach (also known as Bass River Beach) is a good family beach with a fishing pier,

a large parking area, and a snack bar. This beach, located at the mouth of the Bass River in South Yarmouth, also has lifeguards and bathroom facilities. A daily parking fee of $15 is required.

About a half-mile up Bass River is where you'll find **Windmill Beach** off River Street. It is a small beach with no lifeguards or toilet facilities, but the views of the river are spectacular. Nearby is the Judah Baker windmill, built in 1791.

Wilbur Park and its beach area are about 4 miles up Bass River, where Highbank Road Bridge connects South Yarmouth with the village of South Dennis. Though there are no lifeguards or bathroom facilities, Wilbur Park has a picnic area and a boat ramp.

The only beach on the north side is **Bass Hole,** also known as Gray's Beach. It is at the end of Center Street off Route 6A in Yarmouthport and is considered by many to be one of the great spots on the Cape to watch the sun going down. Bass Hole is at the mouth of Garden Creek and has a long boardwalk that extends over the salt marsh and offers an excellent view of coastal plant and marine life. Across the river is Dennis's Chapin Beach. Bass Hole Beach is rather small and, at low tide, has very little water, which makes it perfect for small children (just pay attention to the tidal current in the creek). Bass Hole Beach has a large picnic area complete with a pavilion and bathroom facilities. There are lifeguards on duty.

In addition to its wealth of saltwater beaches, Yarmouth also has four public beaches at freshwater ponds. Sandy Pond off Buck Island Road in West Yarmouth offers not only a beach for swimming but also playing fields for softball, basketball, and soccer; tennis courts; and a playground. The beach has lifeguards on duty and a comfort station.

Long Pond is off Indian Memorial Drive in South Yarmouth. Lifeguards are on duty on weekends, and portable toilets are available. The beach also has a playground on-site and free parking.

Also in South Yarmouth **Flax Pond Recreation Area** has picnic areas, tennis and volleyball courts, and softball fields. Toilet facilities are provided, and lifeguards are on duty on weekends.

i **Lose your wedding ring on the beach? Hoping to find buried treasure? Rent a metal detector from J & E Enterprises, located at Old Main Street and Forest Road in South Yarmouth. Call (508) 760-2100 for more information.**

Dennis Pond off Summer Street in Yarmouthport requires a town beach parking sticker. You'll find lifeguards and toilet facilities at this pretty pond, located just a stroll from Yarmouthport village.

Dennis

With great beaches on both the north and south sides of town, it's no wonder that so many tourists make Dennis their vacation destination. There are eight beaches on Cape Cod Bay and another eight on Nantucket Sound. If you prefer freshwater swimming, Scargo Lake offers two beaches. Residents pay $30 for a parking permit, whereas nonresidents pay $300 for the season. A seasonal pass can be acquired for $135 by those who can produce a rental lease for four or more weeks. Weekly stickers run $60, and daily parking fees are $15 during the week and $20 on the weekends. Stickers can be obtained at the Dennis Town offices on Main Street in South Dennis at (508) 760–6159.

Chapin Memorial Beach on Chapin Beach Road at the northwest corner of Dennis is a favorite among owners of four-wheel-drive vehicles. At low tide, those looking for shellfish will delight in being able to walk more than a mile out on the tidal flats of Cape Cod Bay. The beach has lifeguards and no restrooms, but portable toilets are available. Across the water are Yarmouth's Bass Hole and Gray's Beach.

Also on Cape Cod Bay is **Mayflower Beach** at the end of Beach Street. In addition to restrooms and concessions, this beach features a boardwalk that stretches from the large parking lot over the dunes to the beach below. Mayflower Beach is staffed with lifeguards.

Bayview Beach at the end of Bayview Road is a residents-only beach. Though there is a boardwalk leading to the beach, there are no restrooms or concession stands, but lifeguards are on duty.

Crescent-shaped **Corporation Beach,** off Corporation Road and hugging Cape Cod Bay, is a popular spot on hot summer days. The curve of the beach forms a tidal pool that's perfect for children. Corporation Beach has lifeguards, a concession stand, restrooms, and even a swing set for children set on a bluff overlooking the bay.

Howes Beach is a small public beach off Howes Street, just east of Corporation Beach. Howes has a boardwalk and lifeguards, but no restrooms.

Two East Dennis residents-only beaches are on each side of Sesuit Harbor. On the west side is **Harborview Beach,** which has no facilities, although a lifeguard is present. **Cold Storage Beach** on the east side of the harbor has restrooms and lifeguards.

The last public beach on the north side is **Sea Street Beach** at the end of Sea Street in Quivet (East Dennis). There is a boardwalk leading to the beach, as well as lifeguards and portable toilets.

There is perhaps no more popular Mid-Cape beach than **West Dennis Beach,** off Davis Beach Road in West Dennis. Situated on a narrow patch of sand on Nantucket Sound just east of the mouth of Bass River, the beach stretches for more than a mile. Beachgoers begin to arrive here by 10 a.m., but because the parking lot has room for more than 1,000 cars, you'll rarely have to worry about finding a space. The eastern end of the beach is reserved for Dennis residents; the western end, however, is less crowded and open to everyone. A well-equipped snack bar concession, restrooms, and showers provide all the comforts, and 10 lifeguard stations make this a safe, secure haven. At the beach is the Old Bass River lighthouse (see our Attractions chapter). Parking is $15 a day.

About three-quarters of a mile east of West Dennis Beach is **South Village Beach,** a residents-only beach, by the mouth of Swan River. Toilet facilities and lifeguards are on-site, but there are no concession stands.

A number of Dennisport beaches are available for the visitors who rent cottages in this south-side village. **Haigis Beach** lies where Ocean Drive meets Old Wharf Road. Lifeguards are on duty, toilet facilities are available, and there are concession stands.

Farther down Old Wharf Road is **Glendon Beach,** opposite Glendon Road. Like Haigis Glendon has lifeguards, toilet facilities, and a concession stand.

Sea Street Beach at the end of Sea Street in Dennisport is perhaps a half-mile east of Glendon Beach. Like Glendon and Haigis, the Nantucket Sound waters here are warm, and the beaches are marked with rock jetties. Sea Street Beach has restroom facilities, concessions, and lifeguards on duty.

The next two beaches do not have lifeguards, restrooms, or concessions. **Raycroft Beach** is at the end of the short Raycroft Parkway off Old Wharf Road. To the east about a couple hundred yards is **Depot Street Beach** at the end of (you guessed it) Depot Street.

At the end of Inman Street (off Chase Avenue) is the final saltwater beach in Dennisport. Flanked by motels with private beaches on either side up and down the popular Chase Avenue, **Inman** is a public beach that offers toilet facilities and concessions. Lifeguards keep tabs on what's going on out in the water.

Scargo Lake is a 50-plus-acre freshwater sandy-bottomed kettle hole—nearly 50 feet deep—nestled at the bottom of Scargo Hill. The lake is home to two popular beaches: Princess Beach, off Scargo Hill Road, and Scargo Beach, off Route 6A. **Princess Beach** has restrooms and a picnic area as well as lifeguards. **Scargo Beach,** narrow and tree lined, also has toilet facilities and a lifeguard.

Lower Cape

Beaches in this area are on Cape Cod Bay, Nantucket Sound, and the Atlantic, plus numerous freshwater ponds. The Cape Cod National Seashore (CCNS, 508-771-2144) has great beaches in Eastham, Wellfleet, Truro, and Provincetown. Admission to any CCNS beach from late June to Labor Day is $15 per car; admission is $3 for walkers or bikers. For $45 you can get a season pass good at all CCNS beaches—a wise invest-

ment if you'll be staying a while or visiting often over the course of the summer. Those older than age 62 can get a Golden Age Passport, good at all national parks. And anyone, regardless of age, can get a Golden Eagle pass for a fee, good at all national parks for one year. Lower Cape beaches, as a rule, are relatively undeveloped; most have no real restroom facilities but usually have portable toilets. National Seashore beaches, however, do have restrooms and shower facilities. Most Lower Cape beaches do not have concession stands; we've noted the exceptions.

i Join National Park Service rangers on a Cape Cod National Seashore interpretive program and learn more about the nature and history of Cape Cod. Ranger-led activities range from guided canoe trips to historic house tours and backcountry nature hikes. The hikes and house tours are free; there is a small fee for canoe and surf-casting lessons and trips. Call (508) 255-3421, or visit www.nps.gov/caco.

Brewster

Brewster has eight public beaches on Cape Cod Bay, plus a couple of beaches on freshwater ponds, the largest being Long Pond, which lies half in Brewster and half in Harwich. Parking permits for town beaches are available in the lower level of the Brewster town office Building/Visitor Information Center on Route 6A, at the rear entrance, (508) 896-4511, from 9 a.m. to 3 p.m. daily. The cost is $15 a season for residents, and for nonresidents its $15 a day, $50 a week, or $125 for the season—very reasonable rates. Facilities are limited at Brewster beaches. There are no snack bars, though the ice-cream truck cruises the beach parking lots on summer days. Portable toilets are the best you'll do for bathrooms. The only lifeguarded beach is at Long Pond, where the town holds its swimming instruction program.

Going from west to east, **Paine's Creek** is the first town beach on the bay. As its name implies, it is fed by a creek and is perfect for children. Parking is limited, though portable toilets are available. Off Lower Road, **Robbins Hill Beach** and **Saint's**

Landing Beach are both pretty and quiet and, like all Brewster beaches, are huge at low tide when the flats seem to go on forever. **Breakwater Beach** is a popular spot for families. At the end of charming Breakwater Road off Route 6A by the Unitarian Church, the beach is bordered by grassy dunes, and there is plenty of parking. **Point of Rocks Landing** is nice and quiet, but has virtually no parking. **Ellis Landing** and **Crosby Landing** are both great beaches; Crosby is larger and has more parking and is walkable from **Nickerson State Park** across Route 6A. Within Nickerson State Park you'll find **Flax Pond** and **Cliff Pond,** both great for swimming and picnicking.

Harwich

Harwich has many beautiful beaches on Nantucket Sound, plus four on freshwater ponds. Stickers are required for parking and are available at the Harwich Community Center, 100 Oak Street (508-430-7638), between 8:30 a.m. and 4 p.m., Mon through Thur (and 8:30 a.m. to noon on Fri). Residents get stickers for $20 a season. The cost for nonresidents, who must show proof of renting in Harwich, is $55 for a week and $125 for a season. The exception is Red River Beach, off Depot Road in South Harwich, where you can park daily for $10 on weekdays, $15 on weekends and holidays. The town's larger beaches—**Red River** and **Bank Street**—have lifeguards and restrooms; a few of the smaller ones like **Earle Road** are equipped with portable toilets. Other small beaches on Nantucket Sound in Harwich are **Jenkins Beach,** right next to Saquatucket Harbor, and **Merkel Beach,** tucked next to Wychmere Harbor.

Harwich also has five freshwater beaches: **Bucks Pond,** off Route 39; **Sand Pond,** off Great Western Road; **Hinckleys Pond** and **Seymour Pond,** both off Route 124; and **Long Pond,** off Long Pond Drive. Sand Pond, the site of the town's recreation program's swimming lessons, does have restrooms.

Chatham

Parking permits are required at most of Chatham's nine beaches; the exceptions are Jackknife Harbor and Oyster Pond beaches, which have limited but free parking. School House Pond accepts only resident beach stickers. Stickers good at the other beaches can be obtained at the Permits Department at 283 George Ryder Road. Daily parking is $15, a one-week sticker is $60, and a season sticker is $125. Residents and property owners can get season stickers for $25 at the Permits Department on George Ryder Road (508-945-5180). Only five beaches have lifeguards: **Hardings, Cockle Cove, Ridgevale, Oyster Pond,** and **Schoolhouse Pond.** Those beaches also have restrooms; other town beaches have portable toilets.

Jackknife Harbor Beach is located on Pleasant Bay, off Route 28 on the Harwich/Chatham line. It's a popular beach, but there are no restrooms.

Cockle Cove Beach, off Cockle Cove Road, is the best choice for families with little ones, because it has lifeguards. It also has restrooms, and parents will appreciate the calm waves and long stretches of soft sand. **Hardings Beach,** off Hardings Beach Road, has a concession stand for snacks, restrooms, and quietly pounding surf. **Ridgevale Beach,** between Hardings and Cockle Cove (at the end of Ridgevale Road), also has lifeguards, restrooms, and a concession stand in summer.

Also on Nantucket Sound are **Pleasant Street Beach** (where you don't need a sticker to park) and **Forest Beach Road Beach.** Those seeking solitude should head over to Atlantic Ocean–fronted North Beach. Located at the southern end of Orleans's Nauset Beach, it's accessible only by boat. Area water taxis will take you there (and bring you back) for a small round-trip fee per adult.

The remote **South Beach,** off Morris Island Road just beyond the Chatham Light, and also on the Atlantic, provides solitude without requiring a boat. It has no parking lot, so you'll have to walk or bike there. The most desolate stretches take quite a hike, but the quiet and grandeur cannot be beat.

Oyster Pond, an inland saltwater pond off Stage Harbor Road that's connected to Nan-

Sea Turtle Migration

Cape Cod Bay is considered the normal northern extent of the Kemp's Ridley turtle, the world's most endangered sea turtle. Following warm-water currents, the Ridley and other sea turtles move north from feeding grounds along the eastern seaboard to Cape Cod Bay, where they feed during the summer and early fall. Normally the cooling temperatures of fall signal the turtles to head south for the winter. Each fall, about a dozen Kemp's Ridley turtles are found stunned by cold water and air temperatures, having floated helplessly on the surface, carried ashore by the tides and winds. If you find a sea turtle on the Cape Cod Bay beaches in the fall, do not remove the turtle. Rather cover it with seaweed or some blankets, and call the town authorities.

tucket Sound via Stage Harbor and Oyster Creek, is calm and relatively warm and has a lifeguard in season; it also has restrooms. Schoolhouse Pond, situated on Schoolhouse Road in West Chatham, is also worth a visit for its tranquility, but note that parking is limited to Chatham residents.

Orleans

Orleans has only a few public beaches, but when one of them is beautiful Nauset Beach, famous for its wide expanse, big Atlantic Ocean surf, and lovely dunes, and the other is Skaket Beach on Cape Cod Bay, one of the best places to watch a sunset, who could ask for more? Residents get beach stickers for free; renters (who must show proof of renting in Orleans, such as a lease or rent receipt) can get stickers for $50 a week, or $110 for the season. People who are renting in nearby towns can get a season sticker for $150. Call (508) 240-3780 for beach sticker information. A $15 fee is charged for parking at Skaket and Nauset

beaches, paid at the tollbooth upon entering. The one-day permit entitles you to go to either beach—or both—during that day.

Nauset Beach, at the end of Beach Road in East Orleans (just follow Main Street east), has lifeguards, a snack bar, and restrooms. You can rent beach chairs and umbrellas, too. Four-wheel-drive vehicles are permitted on one section of the beach, except when plovers and other birds are nesting, but you must have a permit from the Orleans Parks and Beaches Department, 18 Bay Ridge Lane, (508) 240-3775.

Over on the bay side, **Skaket Beach,** off Skaket Beach Road, is just as popular as Nauset and also has restrooms. Parking is limited, and the lot fills up fast. At low tide, people flock here for the chance to walk a mile or so onto the flats. At high tide it's great for frolicking in the calm water.

If you don't want to swim but just want to get your feet wet, stop at the little beach at **Rock Harbor,** another great place for sunsets. One secret gem is the tiny beach that is reachable by walking down the trail at Paw Wah Point Conservation Area, off Namequoit Road. You'll even find a few picnic tables scattered here and there.

Orleans has a freshwater pond worth visiting: **Pilgrim Lake,** off Kescayogansett Road, features a lifeguard in season as well as changing rooms, picnic areas, a small beach, and even a dock should you decide to moor your boat while taking a dip.

ℹ **When people or animals trample beach grass, the dunes in turn begin to fall apart or erode. This is why it is important not to take shortcuts through the dunes to get to the beaches. Beach grass, which holds the sand on the dunes, can withstand the most powerful winds, but can die if stepped on more than once.**

Eastham

Parking at Eastham town beaches requires a sticker, available at the Natural Resources building on Old Orchard Road (508-240– 5976). Stickers are $20 for residents; for nonresident renters the cost is $55 for one week and $150 for the season. Visitors can park for $15 a day. But note that although Eastham resident stickers are good for both town and National Seashore beaches, visitor stickers purchased from the town are good only at town beaches and not Seashore beaches.

The National Seashore beaches have lifeguards in season, but Eastham town beaches do not, with the exception of **Great Pond Beach,** on Great Pond Road, and **Wiley Park,** on the other side of Great Pond off Herringbrook Road. Wiley Park also has a small playground and restrooms and is great for families. Eastham beaches have no concession stands, but the ice-cream truck visits each one periodically all day long. Town beaches that dot the bay side include **First Encounter,** which is beautiful but can get crowded. To get away from it all, drive beyond the main parking lot and find a spot down by the river, where the beach is lovely and the water is calm. First Encounter is one of the few beaches in Eastham with real restrooms, the other two being Wiley Park and Cook's Brook; the others have portable toilets.

Moving up the bay coast, you'll find **Thumpertown Beach,** which is nice but has limited parking and a stairway down to the beach. Just north of Thumpertown is **Campground Beach,** which has a larger parking lot and easier access to the beach but can get cramped at high tide. **Cook's Brook** is quiet and pretty, as is **Sunken Meadow;** both have limited parking and are frequented largely by the occupants of nearby cottages.

On the ocean side are two popular Cape Cod National Seashore beaches. They're easy to find—just turn east at the visitors center off Route 6, and keep driving. **Coast Guard Beach** has virtually no parking at the beach, but there is a large lot just a half-mile away that is serviced by a frequent shuttle bus. Or park at the Doane Rock picnic area, and hike through the woods and over the boardwalk—a pretty walk, but long if you're carrying much gear or have young children. Just to the north is **Nauset Light Beach,** whose namesake lighthouse was moved back from an eroding cliff in 1996. The lot here fills up fast. If you're really desperate, you can park at the high school on Cable Road, but it's a hearty walk

from there. You may want to note that Nauset Light Beach features a towering stairway that leads down to the beach, so if your party includes someone who has difficulty with stairs, choose Coast Guard Beach instead, as it has a gentle ramp leading down to the sands.

Wellfleet

Many of the beaches in Wellfleet require a town sticker; renters can buy one at the town pier for $35 for 3 days, $70 for a week, $120 for two weeks, and $225 for the season. These include the bayside **Duck Harbor,** at the very end of Chequessett Neck Road; **Indian Neck Beach,** off Pilgrim Spring Road; nearby **Burton Baker Beach; Powers Landing,** off Chequessett Neck Road; and, on the Atlantic side, **Newcomb Hollow Beach** and **LeCount's Hollow Beach** (also called Maguire Landing).

With the exception of Duck Harbor, all the bayside beaches are really on the harbor, with views of Great Island, which juts into the bay. Great Island is National Seashore territory and more for hiking than beaching (see our Hiking and Biking Trails chapter), but if you really want to get away from it all, put on your backpack and hiking shoes and trek out to Great Island's remote shores. Indian Neck Beach is perhaps the nicest of all, with its soft, sandy stretch looking out over the harbor and the bay beyond. Adjacent Burton Baker Beach is the only town beach that allows windsurfing, but only at certain times of the day. Sailboarders should pick up a copy of the regulations at the beach sticker booth at Wellfleet Harbor.

Beach stickers are also needed to park at Great Pond (off Cahoon Hollow Road), **Gull Pond** (off Gull Pond Road), and **Long Pond** (off Long Pond Road). Just past the harbor on Kendrick Avenue is **Mayo Beach,** perfect for families with children. Here you can see boats heading in and out of the harbor, and you can actually park for free here if you can get a space. Right across the street is a terrific playground, so even if the kids get restless and bored with the beach, you can take them over to Baker's Field for some swinging, climbing, and sliding. Parking is free, and you'll also find full restrooms there. Other town beaches have portable toilets.

On the Atlantic side **Cahoon Hollow Beach** attracts a big college crowd, who later in the day flock to the beach-side Beachcomber bar and restaurant (see our Nightlife chapter). The lot fills up quickly, and you can opt to use a beach sticker or pay a daily parking fee of $15. The same goes for White Crest Beach, just to the south. The waters at **White Crest Beach** (also called Four Mile Beach and Surfer's Beach) are rougher, making it ideal for the surfers who flock here. Please note that White Crest is not a place to bring young children, senior citizens, or people requiring wheelchairs, as a steep dune path with no staircase leads down to the beach.

The National Seashore's **Marconi Beach** will take your breath away. Parents will appreciate the easy access from the parking lot to the beach itself. In season facilities here include full restrooms and outdoor showers.

Truro

You'll need a sticker, available to renters in the Beach office in Truro Center, to gain access to just about all of the beaches in Truro. The cost is $10 a year for residents; for nonresidents it's $30 a week or $150 for the season. All the town beaches are equipped with portable toilets. If you want the real facilities, go to the National Seashore portion of **Head of the Meadow Beach** on the ocean side—Head of the Meadow Beach is owned half by the town and half by the Seashore. Both sides have lifeguards in season, so this is a good choice for families with children. Another plus is that the ice-cream truck cruises this lot. If you don't have a beach sticker, you can park at the town portion of Head of the Meadow for a $10 fee. The same goes for Corn Hill Beach on the bayside; all other Truro beaches require stickers to park.

Also on the ocean side, **Ballston Beach** and **Long Nook Beach** are very popular, so get there early to get a parking space. Long Nook is quiet and banked by dune cliffs; Ballston requires some walking to get out to the beach, so, if you have lots of gear, carrying it can be awkward. Another Truro beach on the ocean side is **Coast Guard Beach** (not to be confused with the National Seashore beach by the same name in Eastham). On the bay side Corn Hill (also on the ice-cream truck's route) has plenty of parking and is popular with families. This picturesque beach is right at the mouth of the Pamet River, and you'll see boats heading in and out of the harbor.

At the southern end of town, also on the bay side, is **Ryder Beach,** which has been something of a well-kept secret. It's a lovely beach but not heavily frequented, so it's a nice choice for those who want to get away from crowds. Just north of that is **Fisher Beach,** which is nice but has only a tiny parking lot. North of Corn Hill is **Great Hollow Beach,** which is lovely and quiet, and then **Cold Storage Beach,** also called Pond Village, which is very popular, so get there early in the day.

Provincetown

Provincetown is unique in that it has no real town beaches—and thus, there is no such thing as a Provincetown beach sticker. The two main beaches here are both part of the National Seashore: **Herring Cove** and **Race Point.** The waters are warmer and calmer at Herring Cove, but sun worshippers often prefer Race Point because it faces north and gets sun all day long. Still, everyone agrees that the sunsets at Herring Cove are unparalleled on the entire Cape, because the sun actually seems to set into the ocean, unusual for the East Coast. National Seashore beaches have lifeguards, full restrooms, and outdoor showers. It's $15 to park, $3 to walk or bike in. Season passes are available for $45.

The Harbor Beach, running parallel to Commercial Street alongside the bay, is ideal for those more interested in a walk at water's edge than a swim. There's no beach lot per se, but the closest parking is in the town lot at MacMillan Wharf, which has hourly rates. There are also various town landings along the entire length of Commercial Street that give beach access.

If you really want to get away from it all, head for the very tip of Cape Cod: **Long Point,** where Long Point Lighthouse signals the entrance to Provincetown's busy harbor. You can get there by two routes—one by land, the other by sea. Walk across the breakwater at the western end of Commercial Street adjacent to the Provincetown Inn. It's about two hours—but it seems like a longer walk back. Or hop aboard a water shuttle from Flyer's Boat Shop at 131A Commercial Street (508-487-0518). The shuttle leaves every hour or so, with the last return around 5 p.m., and costs $10 one-way, $15 round-trip.

ℹ️ Piping plovers and least terns are threatened species under Massachusettes state law. Pay special attention to signs posted around beaches and beach parking lots. Sometimes plovers decide to nest there, necessitating the closure of parts of beaches and parking lots. Rules about staying away from nesting areas are enforced.

Hatches Harbor, off Herring Cove, is a natural harbor reachable only two ways: either by a long walk along Herring Cove Beach or by a short drive with a four-wheel-drive vehicle over the sand. Its remoteness makes Hatches a perfect spot for those seeking solitude. On any given day there's usually just a handful of visitors, most of them townies picnicking or fishing from their four-wheel-drive vehicles. The area surrounding Hatches Harbor was once home to early fishing settlements. Race Point Lighthouse is nearby, adjacent to the newly renovated light-keeper's house, which you can rent for a weekend, a week, or more.

WHALE WATCHING

Cape Cod provides visitors with the opportunity to observe the largest creatures on earth in their natural habitat. Nothing is quite as thrilling as seeing these enormous mammals gliding smoothly through the water. Often you'll see whales in pairs or threesomes, either a mother and her calf or these two accompanied by another adult whale acting as guardian. The whales are visitors here too: they come to the area annually to feed on Stellwagen Bank, which lies roughly 6 miles northeast of Provincetown. Predictably, this city on the tip of the Cape offers some of the most appealing excursions, because trips from this location offer more time to look at whales and less time getting there and back.

"There" of course is Stellwagen Bank, an 842-square-mile section of the shallows in the open ocean lying in the Gulf of Maine just off the mouth of Cape Cod Bay. Long a prime fishing area, Stellwagen's unique conditions and topography enable it to support a tremendous diversity of marine life, from single-cell organisms to great whales. But it wasn't always that way. The shallow platform known as Stellwagen Bank was once dry land where mastodon and mammals roamed. It is believed that about 12,000 years ago, the bank stood well above sea level and may have been connected to Lower Cape Cod. Early humans arrived in New England about 11,000 years ago, and they may have witnessed the beginning of the final chapter in the history of Stellwagen Bank. By then, as waters from the melting glaciers continued to raise the level of the sea, Stellwagen Bank slipped beneath the waves. Today it is covered by at least 65 feet of water and attracts a wide variety of sea life, including huge quantities of plankton (tiny single-celled plants that float in the water) and many species of fish and marine mammals who feed on them.

A protected National Marine Sanctuary since 1992—the first area in the Northeast to receive that designation—Stellwagen Bank attracts the whales that migrate here because of its abundant food supplies. Many types of whales are found here, including finback (the largest), humpback (the most playful), right (the most endangered), sei, minke, killer (also known as Orca), and pilot whales (also known as black fish). Each species has its own distinct habits, but generally the whales begin arriving in this area in early spring and leave for warmer waters in early winter.

Although the whales may be busy feeding underwater at Stellwagen Bank, they'll take time out to flirt with the whale-watching boats and will often voluntarily approach the boats and swim alongside and underneath them for hours. Humpback whales are the most popular species to watch because they are inquisitive enough to come close to the boats and have an engaging tendency to perform. Humpbacks feed for about six or seven months in the waters of Stellwagen Bank, which is rich with plankton, squid, herring, sand lance, and other sea life, and then leave the area, fasting until they return the following year from their wintering ground in the West Indies, where they breed and give birth.

Different species of whales feed on different types of sea life. Right whales, for instance, feed mostly on plankton. Whales follow the food sources, and whale-watching boats follow the whales, so when you're out on one of these boats, you'll often find yourself zipping around a bit until the boat operators get a handle on exactly where the whales happen to be. If you leave from either Barnstable or Provincetown, you'll generally see whale-watch boats from Plymouth and Boston approaching from the other direction.

Despite the fact that whaling was, for centuries, an important New England industry (see our Historic Cape Cod chapter), it was the 20th century that brought some species close to extinction. Between 1910 and 1963 140,000 humpback whales were killed; today only a few thousand survive. The right whale, so named because it is relatively slow-moving and floats when killed—therefore the "right" whale to take—is practically extinct; researchers estimate there are now between 350 and 400 northern right whales left in the Atlantic Ocean, and those numbers are sometimes reason for dispute among those who calculate them.

In 1975, a group of schoolchildren took the first whale-watching tour on the East Coast, conducted by Captain Al Avellar of the Dolphin Fleet out of Provincetown. More than 25 years later, the concept of peacefully watching whales, rather than killing them, has caught on, and now tens of thousands of people leave every summer from Plymouth, Barnstable, and Provincetown to visit the summer homes of the whales. During whale-watching trips, staff members (often naturalists or marine biologists) provide commentary about the natural history of the area, especially the whales and their habitat. When the scientists spot whales, the excitement in their voices is genuine; for many it's like encountering old friends. Those who have worked around whales for a long time can identify individual whales by distinctive markings on the flukes of the whale's tail, underside, body, or head, and often know specific details of their lives, from their offspring to their travel patterns.

The most exciting moment during a whale watch comes—if you are lucky, that is—when one of the whales shoots straight up out of the water and splashes down again into the sea in a move known as "breaching." After that you'll be hooked, finding yourself telling your friends that they absolutely must experience a whale watch and offering to accompany them so you can experience it again.

The issues and restrictions that accompany whale-watching tours are far more complex than those for other types of tours. State and federal agencies have developed guidelines for the whale-watching industry that are based as much on safety for the marine mammals as for the humans. For example, boats are prohibited from coming within more than 300 yards of most whales and 500 yards of the endangered right whale.

Whale watching is now a $100 million industry in New England—an important part of the Cape's tourist economy, having extended off-season business in areas such as Provincetown. Because whale watching begins in April many seasonal shops, restaurants, and other businesses in Provincetown open then rather than waiting for Memorial Day.

In this chapter we acquaint you with several of the organizations that conduct whale-watching excursions. Always call ahead to make sure the trips haven't been canceled because of adverse weather or rough sea conditions. Reservations are a must in summer, and a good idea even in spring and fall—both great times to experience the Cape. Whale-watch tours run from mid-April through the end of October and usually last between three and four hours. Most companies offer three trips a day: The morning boat ride is ideal for families with small children, the afternoon trip is usually the most crowded, and the sunset trip is most romantic and beautiful, though it can be tough to see the whales at dusk.

All charters guarantee sightings; in the rare chance no whales are spotted, you'll be given a rain check to use at another time.

CHARTERS

Mid-Cape

HYANNIS WHALE WATCHER CRUISES
Barnstable Harbor
(508) 362-6088, (800) 287-0374
www.whales.net

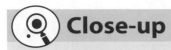

Close-up

Seal Sightings

Seals are carnivorous aquatic mammals with front and hind feet modified as flippers, or fin-feet. The name seal is applied broadly to any of the fin-footed mammals, or pinnipeds. The two species of seal predominantly found along the Cape and islands' shorelines are the harbor and gray seal. These are sometimes joined in these waters by other species of seals—harp, hooded, and, most rarely, ringed seals.

It is believed that seals evolved from animals that once lived exclusively on land. Some 30 million years ago, as the climate gradually changed and the water cooled, the ancestors of the animals that would become seals abandoned the land for the sea. Though their true ancestry ties them to bears, harbor seals are most commonly compared with dogs. Gray seals have also been compared with horses, because their head is horselike and massive compared with the head of the harbor seal. In fact, they're sometimes called horsehead seals. A male gray seal can reach 8 feet in length and weigh as much as 800 pounds; while the female is smaller, reaching only 7 feet in length and weighing 550 pounds.

Cape Cod is a great spot to see seals. It is estimated that as many as 3,000 to 5,000 seals inhabit the waters of Cape Cod year-round, and because these waters surround our peninsula, there are lots of places where you can see them without ever leaving land. The best time to spot them is November through April. Chatham is a popular viewing spot, because the majority of our seals spend time along South Monomoy Island and most recently have been moving to nearby North Beach, Tern Island, and Aunt Lydia's Cove, which is across from the Chatham Fish Pier. You can also see seals around Wellfleet, Provincetown, and Woods Hole. Nantucket Sound and Vineyard Sound have been seeing more seal activity too.

The best time to view seals is at low tide. When the tide goes out and the sandbars are left exposed, seals generally haul themselves out on land to rest, conserving energy and gaining body heat from the sun. Generally, between September and October the large population of gray seals begins to arrive in the waters of Cape Cod. The breeding season, especially for gray seals, runs from late September through early March. During this time the pups are born on the barrier beaches or the Monomoy Island shore.

Of course you can also see them in the water too. A seal cruise is a great way to view these elusive marine mammals. At first they will appear way off in the distance as black dots bobbing in the surf or like dark rocks protruding from the water. But as the boat draws closer, you'll see that these dark spots are seals, and that they are everywhere. There's nothing quite like hearing the bark and chatter of seals as they frolic in the water, and you'll certainly have a better appreciation for these sleek mammals after seeing their big brown eyes inquisitively looking your way.

If a seal cruise interests you, there are a number of tours that leave from Stage Harbor in Chatham during the summer months and out of Ryder's Cove in North Chatham from October through May. You can inquire at Beachcomber Boat Tours, (508) 945-5265, www.sealwatch .com, or the Monomoy Island Ferry, 508 237-0420, www.monomoyislandferry.com.

About 3 miles north of Hyannis in Barnstable Harbor, next door to Mattakeese Wharf Restaurant, the Hyannis Whale Watcher Cruises run excursions across Cape Cod Bay to the Stellwagen Bank area. The company's 120-foot jet-powered cruiser has open upper and lower deck viewing areas and two enclosed cabins. Travel time to reach the whales is often less than an hour, and trips last three to four hours. The boat has a full galley serving food and beverages.

The cost is $45 for adults, $40 for adults 62 and older, $26 for children ages 4 to 12, and free for children 3 and younger. Trips run May through Oct.

Group rates for 20 or more are available. The boats are wheelchair accessible. For educational groups, Hyannis Whale Watcher Cruises also offers a two-hour floating classroom trip for students that make nature trips into Cape Cod Bay.

i No matter how hot the weather, don't forget to bring a jacket on a whale watch. The temperatures at sea are always cooler.

Lower Cape

DOLPHIN FLEET
MacMillan Wharf, Provincetown
(508) 240-3636, (800) 826-9300
www.whalewatch.com, www.provincetown whalewatch.com
Originator of the whale-watching industry on the Eastern Seaboard, the Dolphin Fleet always has a naturalist on board to provide informative and entertaining commentary about the whales. We like the fact that whale watches on this line are small; although the boats can hold more, the number of passengers is limited to 145. It also helps that the vessels were designed with stability in mind. The central cabin is heated, and the galley serves breakfast, lunch items, and snacks. During peak season the Dolphin Fleet offers eight trips a day, and it offers trips from mid-Apr through Oct. The cost is $39 for adults and $31 for children ages 5 to 12. Children four and under ride free.

i Humpback whales measure from 40 to 60 feet in length and weigh as much as 40 tons. On your excursion you may see them breaching—that is, rising from the ocean's depths and leaping straight out of the water into the air. Scientists don't know what it means or why they do it.

BOATING AND WATER SPORTS

In this chapter we explore the different ways you can safely get out on the water for an enjoyable day of power boating, sailing, kayaking, surfing, Jet-Skiing, or diving.

Boating for pleasure is well suited for relaxing get-togethers, family celebrations, or a carefree day out on the water with a friend. With the advent of summer, present-day Cape Cod sailors in pleasure boats follow in the watery wake of their earlier ancestors who went to sea to earn a living.

Whether you're bringing your own boat, or plan on renting one here, you'll be happy to know that each Cape town has numerous boat ramps, marinas, and boatyards, as one would expect in a land surrounded by water. If you are renting a boat, be sure you are qualified to handle it. Boat rentals are dwindling, primarily because of increased insurance costs; that should serve as warning enough that handling a sail or powerboat is no simple matter. Not to worry though—the Cape still has plenty of rentals available and a number of instructors to help you find the boating experience that best suits you. Another delightful way to explore the Cape's many inlets and creeks is by kayak or canoe. Paddling is an increasingly popular sport on Cape Cod, and there are many guides and rental opportunities from which to choose—or bring your own kayak or canoe and launch it from one of the Cape's many boat ramps.

Water sports have become the rage for those who like to push the edge of the watery envelope. The Cape has some of the best windsurfing beaches on the East Coast, and the surfing is superb on the Outer Cape's ocean-side beaches. For an unusual water sport adventure, how about diving for shipwrecks in the untamed Atlantic?

Jet-Skiing is another popular sport—and also a red-hot topic here. Personal watercraft have been prohibited from certain areas to protect sensitive marine life and its habitats. If you plan to bring a Jet Ski or other personal watercraft on your vacation, remember that you are considered a boater and are required to follow boating regulations. We can't tell you here what you can and cannot do on a personal watercraft, so we recommend that you check with the local authorities before launching yours. You'll want to avoid areas that are habitats for shorebirds and marine mammals.

Also, whether you're in a small personal watercraft or large boat, remember to keep lifejackets and first-aid supplies on hand. Carry emergency supplies, and make sure they're in working order. If you're cruising the coast, carry an accurate navigation chart, because the Cape's sandy coastline can change with just one storm. Keep an eye on the weather, and don't take any chances if you see fog rolling in. The waters around the Cape, especially along the Outer Cape and the Buzzards Bay and canal areas, can be a little tricky.

BOATING

If your vision of a Cape Cod vacation includes a ride on a sailboat tacking across a gleaming bay, you'll be glad to know that sail cruises, boat rentals, and sailing lessons are readily available. If you are a seasoned boater or cruising the coastal waterways in your own boat, the following will help you find a marina for refueling, pumping out, or simply getting ice.

Sailing Instruction

There are more than 40 yacht clubs and sailing associations around the Cape and islands that offer sailing lessons to members and nonmembers. The instructors at many of these places are seasoned locals, many of them having learned to sail at the clubs where they now teach.

Because junior sailing programs are very popular here, early registration is recommended. After an initial instructional period and sailing with an instructor, you'll soon be sailing around in a dinghy. Instructors may then move you up to the bigger 16-foot day sailers, boats specifically designed for a day of sailing in local bays and coves. In no time you'll be a master of terminology and seamanship, helming and crewing, rigging and docking. In short, you'll have mastered the basic fundamentals of navigation and, even more importantly, you'll know about safety on the sea.

A number of towns offer instruction, including Barnstable (508-790-6345), Falmouth (508-457-2567), Harwich (to residents), (508-430-7553), Sandwich (508-888–4361), and Yarmouth (508-398-2231). Here are a few other possibilities to get you out on the water.

Upper Cape
THE BUZZARDS SAILING SCHOOL
99 South Rd. on Wings Neck, Pocasset
(508) 563-9757
www.buzzardssailing.org

The Buzzards Sailing School is a more than 40-year-old nonprofit instructional sailing program for people ages 8 to 18. All classes, which run from late June through mid-Aug, emphasize fun and enjoyment of the water as well as water safety and the learning of sailing skills. All groups are taught in Widgeons, 420s, and Optimist dinghies. Those who enroll for the four-week minimum or take the full eight-week program will benefit most. Four classes per week cost $140.

Mid-Cape
WIANNO YACHT CLUB
101 Bridge St., Osterville
(508) 428-2232
www.wiannoyc.com

The Wianno Yacht Club has a junior sailing program dedicated to teaching kids how to sail in a fun and encouraging environment. From the Seamen level (ages 7 to 9), to Mates (ages 8 to 10), Ensigns (ages 10 to 13), to Advanced Sailing for nonracers and the Racing Team, which practice skills in 420s, Wianno Yacht Club offers a program for everyone. The summer is divided into two four-week sessions, and you may register for one or both of them. The full eight-week program is $800 for members, $900 for nonmembers; each of the two four-week sessions costs $450 for members, $500 for nonmembers. For adults who want to join a sailing program, the Wianno Yacht Club offers lessons on Thurs evenings from early July to early Aug.

Lower Cape
AREY'S POND BOAT YARD SAILING SCHOOL
Arey's Lane, South Orleans
(508) 255-0994
www.by-the-sea.com/areyspondboatyard

APBY operates on Pleasant Bay all summer long. Under the guidance of experienced instructors, APBY Sailing School specializes in teaching folks of all ages, from those just starting out to those brushing up to those interested in learning racing techniques. If you're a beginner, you'll take the tiller and sail a boat during your first lesson. Private lessons start at $132 for two-hours, $12 for each additional person.

CAPE SAIL
Saquatucket Harbor, Route 28, Harwich
(508) 896-2730
www.capesail.com

Bob Rice shares his more than 20 years of sailing experience in an extensive, hands-on six- or nine-hour course. His "classrooms" are either a small boat (the 16-foot *Renata* at Brewster's Town Landing, Upper Mill Pond) or a large boat (the 35-foot *Sabbatical* in Saquatucket Harbor in Harwich Port). He promises to have the patience of a saint with novices; intermediate sailors may choose his overnight learning excursions on Nantucket Sound. Lessons are held from Memorial Day to early Oct. For more information on charters, see the entry in our Tours and Excursions chapter.

CHEQUESSETT YACHT & COUNTRY CLUB
680 Chequesset Neck Rd., Wellfleet
(508) 349-3704
www.cycc.net
In season from July through early Sept, Chequessett Yacht & Country Club offers eight weeks of junior sailing clinics at a cost of $160 for each two-day session, $275 for a four-day session. Private instruction for adults is also available.

Marinas and Boatyards
When it comes to boating, there isn't much that you can't get with one stop at a local marina or boatyard. You'll find necessities like fuel, launch services, repair workshops, and, in most cases, a retail store that carries marine essentials.

Cape Cod boasts more than 40 marinas, nestled in protected harbors and coves in some of the most picturesque parts of the peninsula. Most have repair service and an extensive array of full-service conveniences. You'll also find boatyards and boat builders not only right on the water but scattered about in industrial parks and along major roadways miles from the nearest waters. Take advantage of their knowledge. Marina personnel and boat builders understand the demands the sea makes on a boat. Many can incorporate the best designs and techniques into restorations, modifications, and repairs, whereas others offer new construction and sales of new boats, to which they often add their name. For instance, Nauset Marine, with a location in Orleans (508-255-0777, www.nausetmarine.com) is one of the largest Boston Whaler distributors in the country. Arey's Pond Boat Yard (see entry above and below), builder for the world-renowned APBY catboats, is a wooden boat center. Crosby Yacht Yard in Osterville (see entry below), in business since 1850, builds a classic gaff rigged sloop, the Wianno Senior. Function, quality, and durability—what else would you expect from Cape Codders?

Upper Cape
BOURNE MARINA
101 Academy Dr., Buzzards Bay
(508) 759-2512
In town within easy walking distance of shops, restaurants, and family recreational facilities, Bourne Marina has 144 slips and can accommodate 60-foot boats with a 6-foot draft. It has fuel, water, 30- and 50-amp electrical service, and pump-out facilities, as well as restrooms, showers, lockers, and a laundry area. You'll have use of a community lounge, a pressure washer, and pump-out, and a marine and grocery store. The marina is open from May through Oct.

BREWER FIDDLER'S COVE MARINA
42 Fiddler's Cove Rd., North Falmouth
(508) 564-6327
www.byy.com
Well located for access to the Cape Cod Canal, Fiddler's Cove is a marina and boatyard with complete marine service. The facility has no moorings, but it has 105 seasonal slips and offers power, fuel, water, and cable. It can accommodate boats up to 80 feet in length and up to a 7-foot draft. The marina has a 35-ton travel lift for launching or hauling. It also has a laundry, showers, clubhouse, and a picnic area with grill. The marina is open year-round.

EAST MARINE
89 Falmouth Heights Rd., Falmouth
(508) 540-3611
www.eastmarine.com
North Marine and East Marine offer gas and diesel fuel, repair service for inboard and outboard motors, and hauling services. East Marine is a Yanmar engine dealer, while North Marine deals in Yamaha and Mercruisers.

FALMOUTH MARINE
Falmouth Inner Harbor, 278 Scranton Ave., Falmouth
(508) 548-4600
www.falmouthmarine.com
Falmouth Marine has 30 slips and 16 moorings. It can accommodate boats up to 90 feet with

an 11-foot draft and haul boats weighing up to 70 tons. A full-service yacht yard with stock room, gas and diesel fuel, electrical hookups, and pump-out service, Falmouth Marine also offers passenger ferry service to Edgartown. The year-round facility is within walking distance of restaurants and shops. Note that the fuel dock closes for the winter.

i Keep our waters as clean as possible. If you come across the discharge of oil or oily waste, or notice a film or sheen upon the surface of the water, call the local harbormaster's office or the U.S. Coast Guard.

FALMOUTH TOWN MARINA
180 Scranton Ave., Falmouth
(508) 457-2550
www.town.falmouth.ma.us/depart
.php?depkey=harbor
This marina has seasonal and transient slips, but there is a waiting list for seasonal slots. The marina accepts boats up to 100 feet. It offers water, electricity, and shower facilities, and you can get fuel nearby. The marina is open from the beginning of Apr to the end of Oct.

KINGMAN YACHT CENTER
One Shipyard Lane, Cataumet (Bourne)
(508) 563-7136
www.kingmanmarine.com
The 235 dock slips here can accommodate vessels up to 120 feet long. The marina offers water, 110- and 220-volt outlets, and fuel. There are also restrooms, a laundry, shops, and a marina store. The marina is open year-round.

LITTLE RIVER BOAT YARD
Seconset Island, Mashpee
(508) 548-3511
Little River Boat Yard is a full-service marina that does repairs, sells gas and ice, and rents ice eaters (things that keep ice from forming around docks). It is open year-round.

MACDOUGALLS' CAPE COD MARINE SERVICE
145 Falmouth Heights Rd., Falmouth
(508) 548-3146
www.macdougalls.com
MacDougalls' is a full-service boatyard with a sail loft and an engine shop. It rents 100 deep-water docks and moorings, has electrical service, gas, ice, and a marine store, as well as a railway and a 50-ton travel lift. The facility is open year-round and offers storage, laundry, and showers.

NEW SEABURY MARINA
135 Daniels Island Rd., New Seabury (Mashpee)
(508) 477-9197
www.newseaburyrealestate.com
New Seabury has five transient slips and gas, water, and electrical service, as well as a marina store. It can accommodate boats up to 39 feet in length. The marina is close to tennis, golf, and restaurants. It is open from May to Oct.

NORTH MARINE
53 Falmouth Heights Rd., Falmouth
(508) 457-7000
See East Marine on page 228.

PARKER'S BOATYARD
Red Brook Harbor, 68 Red Brook Harbor Rd., Cataumet (Bourne)
(508) 563-9366
www.parkersboatyard.com
Located in picturesque Red Brook Harbor, Parker's Boatyard carries both gas and diesel fuel and has 130 seasonal and transient moorings and slips with launch service and limited overnight dock space. The facilities include bathrooms, showers, and a picnic area with grills. A complete boatyard that specializes in sailing yachts, Parker's does repairs, repowering, awl-grip work, rigging and spar work, hauling, launching, and winter storage. Though the boatyard is open year-round, the marina is closed for the winter months.

THE SANDWICH MARINA
25 Ed Moffitt Dr., Sandwich
(508) 833-0808 (harbormaster)
www.sandwichmarina.com
This marina on the Cape Cod Canal has more than 200 commercial and recreational slips and offers water, electricity, and diesel fuel as well as showers, parking, a playground area, a boat ramp, and winter storage. Stores are within walking distance. Open year-round, the marina can accommodate boats as long as 80 feet.

WOODS HOLE MARINE
91A Water St., Woods Hole
(508) 540-2402
www.woodsholemarine.com
Woods Hole Marine has a full-time mechanic available and can handle boats up to 65 feet long with about 40 moorings and 22 slips. Facilities include dinghy docks, showers, toilets, and a pump-out boat that services five harbors in the area. The facility has water and 30-amp electrical service and is within walking distance of a convenience store, shops, and restaurants. It's open from early spring to the end of Oct.

Mid-Cape
BARNSTABLE MARINE SERVICE
Barnstable Harbor, Off Mill Way,
Barnstable
(508) 362-3811
Barnstable Marine, on Cape Cod Bay, has 45 slips. It sells diesel fuel and gasoline, has showers and restrooms, bait and tackle, ice and snacks, haul-out facilities with a 20-ton travel lift, and full mechanical, carpentry, finishing, and repair services. It is open year-round and is a short walk from village shops and stores.

BASS RIVER MARINA
140 Main St., West Dennis
(508) 394-8341
www.bassrivermarina.com
Bass River Marina is open year-round and offers 160 slips. This Mid-Cape marina on the beautiful Bass River has gas and pump-out facilities, showers, a restaurant, and ice. It is open year-round.

CROSBY YACHT YARD INC.
72 Crosby Circle, Osterville
(508) 428-6900
www.crosbyyacht.com
A popular rendezvous place for yacht clubs and boating groups, Crosby Yacht Yard can accommodate power- and sailboats up to 120 feet. It has both slips and moorings, shower and laundry facilities, fuel, water, ice, electricity, and a marine store. Repair service is available seven days a week. The facility has travel lifts, marine railways, inside and outside storage, and launch service. The home of the Cape Cod catboat, Crosby's is also a boat builder and an authorized dealer for Scout, Sealine, and Uniesse Marine Boats, and offers full brokerage services. There is a restaurant on the premises. Crosby Yacht Yard is open year-round.

HYANNIS MARINA
1 Willow St., Hyannis
(508) 790-4000
www.hyannismarina.com
Offering a calm, sheltered refuge, Hyannis Marina has 180 slips, diesel fuel and gasoline, water and electrical hookups, and a complete parts and service department. The marina can accommodate everything from motor boats to mega-yachts up to 200 feet. It has a full restaurant and bar; swimming pool; cabana bar; courtesy and rental cars; showers; dockside telephone, Internet, and TV service; a coin-operated laundry; and game room. The facility also includes an electronics and canvas shop, valet rack service, a marine store, and emergency service. It is open year-round.

NAUTICUS MARINA
339 West Bay Rd., Osterville
(508) 428–4537
www.nauticusmarina.com
This marina is open from May to Nov and can accommodate boats up to 120 feet with a 6-foot draft. It has 1,000 feet of rental dock space, including 15 slips for seasonal use. Electrical, water, and cable service are available, but the marina has no gas, nor does it offer repair service. The marina is within walking distance of village shops and restaurants.

NORTHSIDE MARINA
Sesuit Harbor, 357 Sesuit Neck Road,
East Dennis
(508) 385-3936
www.northsidemarina.com
This northside marina on Sesuit Harbor offers 120 slips, storage, gas, diesel, pump-out facilities, showers, and a restaurant. The marina is open year-round.

OYSTER HARBORS MARINE
122 Bridge St., Osterville
(508) 428-2017
www.oysterharborsmarine.com
Oyster Harbors Marine has 110 slips and 30 moorings; it can accommodate boats from 8 to 100 feet long and has gas and diesel fuel, pump-out facilities, a 55-ton travel lift, and storage. This full-service boatyard offers a marine store, restrooms, showers, carpentry, and mechanical and electronic repairs, as well as sales for yachts and outboard motors. It is open year-round.

SHIP SHOPS BOATYARD
Pleasant St., South Yarmouth
(508) 398-2256
www.shipshops.com
Ship Shops is a full-service boatyard in South Yarmouth with a limited number of transient slips and moorings in Dennis and Yarmouth. It sells gas and diesel fuel and has a marine shop. Ship Shops is open year-round.

Lower Cape
ALLEN HARBOR MARINE SERVICE
335 Lower County Rd., Harwich Port
(508) 432-0353
www.allenharbor.com
This year-round facility on picturesque, protected Allen Harbor was founded in 1927 and is another full-service yard, offering slips and moorings, a gas dock, repairs, sales, and storage (they'll shrink-wrap your boat for the winter). Next to Allen Harbor Marine is a town-owned docking ramp.

AREY'S POND BOAT YARD
Arey's Lane, South Orleans
(508) 255-0994
www.by-the-sea.com/areyspondboatyard
This year-round boatyard has 60 protected moorings off Pleasant Bay that can accommodate boats up to 30 feet. It also offers custom wooden boat building and repairing, and sells new and used boats and skiffs.

CHATHAM YACHT BASIN
99 Squanto Dr., Chatham
(508) 945-0728
www.chathamyachtbasin.com
Open year-round, Chatham Yacht Basin has 30 moorings and 70 slips on pretty Oyster River. Chatham Yacht Basin is a full-service marina.

HARWICH PORT BOATYARD, ON WYCHMERE HARBOR
4 Harbor Rd., Harwich Port
(508) 432-1322
www.harwichportboatyard.com
A year-round facility, Harwich Port Boat Works offers a handful of guest mooring spots both here and in the inner harbor. This is a full-service marina, offering storage, gas and diesel fuel, boat and engine sales, and repairs. The yard is renowned for its restoration work; wood and glass are its specialties. Tie-ups are short-term only.

> **i** The hurricane season coincides with prime boating time. To prepare your boat for bad weather, seal hatches, portholes, windows, doors, and vents with duct tape. At a slip or tie-up, make the lines as long as possible, set extra anchors, and add extra fenders and chafe protection. Most importantly do not stay on board during a hurricane.

NAUSET MARINE
Off Barley Neck Road, Orleans
(508) 255-3045
www.nausetmarine.com
Open year-round, this marina has 55 slips, 45 moorings, and 40 dry-rack storage spaces. Gas and pump-out facilities are available.

OUTERMOST HARBOR MARINE
83 Seagull Rd., Chatham
(508) 945-2030
www.outermostharbor.com
Outermost Harbor Marine offers slips and moorings. It has a gas facility, hauling and launch service, storage facilities, and a marine hardware and supplies shop. It also specializes in fiberglass repairs. The facility is closed Jan and Feb.

OYSTER RIVER BOATYARD
Barn Hill Lane, Chatham
(508) 945-0736
www.oysterriverboatyard.com
Oyster River Boatyard accommodates boats up to 34 feet in its slips and moorings. Full mooring service (including setting, maintaining, and inspections) is available. The year-round boatyard also has a gas facility and repair service.

PROVINCETOWN MARINA
9 Ryder St. Extended, Fisherman's Wharf, Provincetown
(508) 487-0571
Smack in the middle of town, Provincetown Marina has more than 200 berths and 100 moorings, with launch service from 7 a.m. until midnight (later on weekends in season). Three launches operate from Memorial Day through Columbus Day weekend. The marina also has a pump-out station, trash Dumpster, and gas dock, as well as showers, telephones, soda machines, and a coin-operated laundry. Information is provided 24 hours a day on Channel 9. The marina is open from Memorial Day through Columbus Day weekend.

ROCK HARBOR
Rock Harbor Road, Eastham
(508) 240-5972
There are nearly 40 municipal town slips at Rock Harbor, but you can expect a wait—up to a decade—for a slip. There are a few transient slips available through the Eastham Natural Resources office on a reservation basis.

RYDER'S COVE BOATYARD
Town Landing, 46 Ryder's Cove Rd., North Chatham
(508) 945-1064
www.ryderscoveboatyard.com
Ryder's Cove, in Pleasant Bay, has 36 slips and 73 moorings. The marina offers gas and seasonal rack storage. Ryder's Cove is open throughout the year.

SAQUATUCKET HARBOR
Municipal Marina, 715 Main St. (Route 28), Harwich Port
(508) 430-7532
www.vsv.cape.com/~harharb/saq.html
The marina, a quarter-mile from the village, has 192 slips and a dozen visitor slips, making it the largest municipal marina on the Cape. Services and amenities include washers, dryers, restrooms, showers, pump-out service, and 20/30-amp/110-volt electrical service. The marina is open from early May to mid-Nov.

STAGE HARBOR MARINE
80 Bridge St., Chatham
(508) 945-1860
www.stageharbormarine.com
Stage Harbor Marine has 33 slips and 33 moorings, gas, hauling and storage facilities, and a first-rate repair shop. Stage Harbor is open year-round.

WELLFLEET MARINE
Town Pier, Wellfleet
(508) 349-2233
This year-round marina offers seasonal mooring by the night, week, and month on a first-come, first-served basis. It has a gas facility as well as diesel; pump-out is done via the harbormaster's boat. Several slips are available through the harbormaster.

Boat Rentals

If you're in the mood to do a little sailing or motoring upon the waves and you've got some prior experience, you may want to consider renting a boat. There are several rental outfits across the Cape to help you out, and some of them are listed below. Those people looking for charters and cruises, where you can sit back and enjoy the sights while someone else does the sailing, should refer to the Tours and Excursions chapter. Or, if you wish to mix in a little fishing, see the Fishing chapter.

Mid-Cape

CAPE COD WATERWAYS BOAT RENTALS
16 Rte. 28, Dennisport
(508) 398-0080
www.capecodwaterways.com
You can rent manually powered and electric paddleboats, canoes, and kayaks here and, because it is located right on Swan River, between Swan Pond and Nantucket Sound, renters can enjoy a variety of nearby Cape waters. The shop is open from May through Oct, and rentals are flexible in terms of hours, days, or weeks.

Lower Cape

FLYER'S BOAT YARD
131A Commercial St., Provincetown
(508) 487-0898, (508) 487-0518
www.flyersrentals.com
Since opening its doors in 1965, Flyer's has satisfied the needs of all kinds of boaters because it has one of the largest rental fleets on the Cape. Here they offer ocean kayaks, powerboats (ranging from 8- to 50-horsepower) and sailboats from a Sunfish to a 19-foot Rhodes. There is a two-hour minimum on rentals, with options for renting by the day or week.

JACK'S BOAT RENTAL
Nickerson State Park, Route 6A, Brewster
(508) 349-9808
www.jacksboatrental.com
Almost nothing beats sailing on Flax Pond on a warm summer day, and Jack's Boat Rental is the place for one-stop shopping. It's all here: Sunfish, sailboards, seacycles, pedal boats, canoes, and kayaks. Jack's also offers windsurfing and sailing lessons. Jack's has other locations at Gull Pond in Wellfleet and a retail shop on US 6 in Wellfleet. They are open late June through Labor Day.

WELLFLEET MARINE
Town Pier, Wellfleet
(508) 349-2233
From mid-June to mid-Oct, Wellfleet Marine rents (by the hour or day) Stur-Dee Cat 14-foot sailboats, 14-foot skiffs (with 6-horsepower motors), 19-foot Rhodes sloops, and 21-foot MacGregor sloops for use in Wellfleet Harbor.

Waterway Access

Cape Cod boat ramps come in a variety of forms: sand, gravel, and asphalt. Some town landings provide free use, whereas others require a sticker, so you'll want to inquire at the local town hall (phone numbers are listed in our Area Overview chapter). You'll find public boat ramps are very busy during the summer. Try to arrive before 10 a.m.; otherwise you may not find a place to park your vehicle and trailer.

KAYAKING AND CANOEING

As you glide through the water in a kayak or canoe, you'll find a peace and stillness most of us rarely experience. On Cape Cod you'll find beauty too, whether you're in a river inlet full of colorful sponges that reflect off the bottom or in the mooring fields of some boatyard. You'll be seeing Cape Cod's natural beauty from a different angle, too.

Getting Started

To kayak or canoe? That is the question. You may want to try both, preferably on the protected waters of a pond, lake, or bay. Here are a couple things to consider as you make your decision. In a kayak you sit closer to the water, where you're snug in the cockpit and not as easily disturbed by wind and rolling waves. In a canoe you sit higher up, on a bench, so this kind of craft can be less stable, especially in choppy waters. You propel a canoe by a single-ended paddle that you stroke first on one side of the craft and then the other. The high gunnels catch the wind, the upcurved bow pounds the surf, and all this translates into

Paddling in Red Brook Harbor

Red Brook Harbor in Buzzards Bay offers great variety to a paddler. Open, calm water, island vistas, and jagged shoreline highlight your trip. Start at the boat landing at Barlow's Landing off Red Brook Road in Cataumet. Gliding in and out of a mooring field, head north toward Bassett Island. You'll see a variety of nesting birds and might get a glimpse of a fox, a coyote, or an osprey. Shoreline rocks make the paddling more challenging. Turn around at the abandoned lighthouse and head back to Red Brook Harbor. The return distance is about 2 miles.

the sport, and whether you'll be going alone or with a friend.

If you're renting a kayak, look for a relatively flat bottom for stability. It should be shorter than 15 feet and be between 2 and 2½ feet wide. In this size kayak you can go just about anywhere on Cape Cod comfortably. In addition, you may want to consider getting a spray skirt, which covers the cockpit and prevents water from dripping off your paddle onto your clothing.

You'll also need a personal flotation device (PFD). A whistle is a good idea too; it might prove useful if you run into a creeping fog. Also consider purchasing a Loran map of the area you are paddling; these mark channels and depth of water.

Many people enjoy kayaking in the quiet waters of Waquoit Bay, where they can explore Washburn Island. Other good spots to start include Barnstable Harbor and Little Pleasant Bay in Orleans. Once in the water, cruise the shoreline and enjoy the sense of freedom you will experience in your kayak. Once you've gotten the hang of the sport, you may move up to a more seaworthy vessel that is usually 16 to 20 feet in length, but narrower, from 22 to 24 inches wide. These longer kayaks move through the choppy waters with more ease.

Before you begin any outings, be sure to check the tides and wind conditions, and take these into account when deciding how far you'll venture. Kayaks are capable of covering 1 to 2 miles in a couple of hours with a steady "touring" stroke. With the tide and wind at your back, you could increase that distance to 3 miles quite easily, but when you have to turn around and paddle against the tide and wind, you'll be going much slower and you'll be testing your stamina.

First-time canoeists will find excellent opportunities in the Cape's many marshes and tidal inlets. The Herring River in Harwich is a perfect place to start a canoe adventure. There is easy access to the river from the parking area on the east side of the Herring River Bridge on Route 28 in West Harwich. Once on the water, head upriver, where the water winds gently for miles past the salty scent of marsh peat. You may see

more work over less distance traveled. In a kayak, on the other hand, you use a two-ended kayak paddle, and you'll move through the water much more efficiently than in a canoe, so you can travel greater distances. Still, canoes provide advantages that kayaks don't, and one of them is space. This isn't so much a factor for those into solo canoeing, but it is an attraction for people who want to bring along fishing gear, a cooler, and definitely the dog. And although some people think of a kayak's easy maneuverability as an advantage over canoes, others are attracted to the challenge of successfully maneuvering a canoe. They say canoeing is more "interesting."

Whatever you decide, don't rent a fancy watercraft just because it looks cool. You may want to talk to enthusiasts of both sports, then try out crafts based on where and how you intend to pursue your sport of choice.

Canoes, like kayaks, come in solo and tandem versions and in various weights and sizes, so make your decision based on where you'd like to go, how seriously you intend to pursue egrets, great blue herons, and ospreys. To get the most out of your excursions, the best time to paddle the Herring River is at high tide. This will assure that you'll be able to see above the lush green marsh grasses that line the waterway.

Nickerson State Park's Cliff Pond also offers the first-time paddler a way to explore coves and hidden beaches in the shelter of lake surroundings. From Route 6A in Brewster, go through the park entrance, drive on the main road approximately 1.6 miles, and take a left onto the dirt road at the fisherman's landing sign. The sandy beach launching area makes getting in and out of your canoe in water easy.

Canoe and Kayak Tours and Rentals

Whether you choose a guide, interpretive paddling tour, or solo boat rental, the Cape has more than 60 paddling routes to explore. We recommend that you contact any one of the paddling tour companies listed below for professional instruction led by a trained guide. Tour guides offer a different tour every day through a different habitat. Be sure to call ahead for reservations, and ask specifically what you might see on the tour. In cases when a street address is not listed, assume the truck and boat trailer is the company's office during the summer months as they travel from location to location.

Upper Cape
CAPE COD KAYAK
Route 28A, Cataumet (Bourne)
(508) 540-9377
www.capecodkayak.com
Cape Cod Kayak provides a full range of activities for the kayak enthusiast out of various locations in the Upper Cape area. They offer tours that range from two to three hours. The cost is $35 to $75 for the kayak, paddle, spray skirt, PFD, and brief, basic instruction. Though they will deliver kayaks to most locations throughout the Cape, they primarily run kayak tours in the Upper Cape area, such as along the Mashpee River, in Wild Harbor and West Falmouth Harbor, and Scorton Creek in Sandwich, to name a few. Besides offering a different tour each day during the summer months,

Cape Cod Kayak also offers daily, weekend, and weekly rental options on kayaks, and they don't charge for delivery. Rental prices start at $35 for up to 24 hours for a solo kayak.

Mid-Cape
CAPE COD WATERWAYS BOAT RENTALS
16 Rte. 28, Dennisport
(508) 398–0080
www.capecodwaterways.com
This company rents canoes and kayaks for use on Swan River, Swan Pond, and Nantucket Sound. A solo kayak rents for $18 per 90 minutes; a tandem is $29. Canoes rent for $29 for 90 minutes. Daily rentals are $40 for a solo kayak and $50 for a tandem kayak or canoe. Safety equipment is included with the rental price. The shop is open from the beginning of May through Sept.

EASTERN MOUNTAIN SPORTS
1513 Rte. 132, Centerville (Hyannis)
(508) 362-8690
www.ems.com
Open year-round on Route 132, this store has access to sit-on-top kayaks, which have no cockpit and are often used by scuba divers. The store also carries flat-water kayaks, which are shorter, and sea kayaks, which range in length from 15 to 22 feet and are used for touring, because they have a lot of storage capacity. Eastern Mountain Sports also has a full range of paddles, flotation vests, safety equipment, maps and charts, camping and backpacking equipment, and clothing for sale in their retail store. EMS recently started to offer an occasional basic kayak tour for beginners to intermediates. Call for a schedule and rates.

Lower Cape
AUDUBON SOCIETY WELLFLEET BAY WILDLIFE SANCTUARY
291 U.S. Rte. 6, Wellfleet
(508) 349-2615
www.wellfleetbay.org
Audubon Society Wellfleet Bay Wildlife Sanctuary offers guided canoe and kayak trips with an environmental slant from the beginning of Apr through the end of Oct. Trips through marshes

and ponds, from Chatham to Provincetown, are the specialty here, and you won't find more knowledgeable guides anywhere else on the Cape. Learn about the natural history of this area, and practice your canoeing skills. The fee is $35 for nonmembers and $30 for members ($25 and $20 for canoes), and reservations are necessary.

CAPE COD MUSEUM OF NATURAL HISTORY
869 Rte. 6A, Brewster
(508) 896-3867
www.ccmnh.org

The Cape Cod Museum of Natural History offers guided natural history tours of Cape waterways. You can explore different locales all over Cape Cod—in ponds, rivers, and marshes—and learn the basics of paddling and water safety. Trips include rest stops and drinking water, and some include a short hike. Tours run daily from April through October, and reservations are necessary. Call the museum for times and details.

THE GOOSE HUMMOCK SHOP
Town Cove, 15 Rte. 6A, Orleans
(508) 255-2620
www.goose.com

The Goose Hummock Outdoor Center is a great place to start your Cape kayaking experience. Located on the sheltered waters of Town Cove in Orleans, just off the US 6 Rotary on the Orleans/Eastham town line, this outdoor center is the Lower Cape's number-one resource for paddling. The Goose offers the largest selection of kayaks and accessories for sale on Cape Cod. There's also a large selection of canoes and kayaks for rent, from $25 to $45 for three hours and $50 to $75 for full days up to $300 a week. The store is open year-round, but only offers rentals during the summer months.

The Goose Guides offer instruction and guided tours during the summer as well. Basic coastal kayaking instruction is $65 per person. Tours range from $45 to $80 depending on length of tour.

i Keeping beaches sanitary is hugely important on the Cape. The Barnstable County Department of Health and the Environment conducts weekly surveillance of the water quality at more than 250 beaches on Cape Cod during the summer. To check the status of your favorite bathing spot, access the town directory of public marine and freshwater beaches at www.barnstablecountyhealth.org.

JACK'S BOAT RENTAL
U.S. Route 6, Wellfleet
(508) 349-9808
www.jacksboatrental.com

You can explore the Outer Cape's hidden ponds, inlets, and marshes on guided kayak tours from this location. Tours are given from Memorial Day through Columbus Day weekend. Because no experience is needed, beginners and children are especially welcome. Note that times vary because of the fluctuating tides. Jack's, which also has locations at Nickerson State Park in Brewster (508-896-8556) and Gull Pond in Wellfleet (508-349-7553), also rents single and double kayaks and canoes for $50 to $60 per day.

WATER SPORTS

Surfing and Windsurfing

The ocean-side beaches of the Lower Cape cater to the surfing crowd, but, for the most part, the waters of Nantucket and Vineyard Sounds are too calm even for a boogie board. Primarily surfers tend to gather at Nauset Beach in Orleans and the Wellfleet beach triumvirate of LeCount Hollow, Cahoon Hollow, and Newcomb Hollow. The waves along this coast will never rival those of Hawaii and Southern California, but surfers travel from all over New England to surf the waves of a good nor'easter wave surge.

Don't be frightened if you are a beginner, for on most days the seas are relatively calm and ideal for getting caught up in the sport or for sampling the surfer lifestyle. There are a number of shops around the Cape that cater to the surfing crowd, and these can tell you where the surf is best and set you up with good equipment. Beware of a nasty undertow present at many of the outer beaches, and no matter the time of year, you'll want to pack a wet suit. The waters of the ocean side of the Lower Cape can be quite chilly, even in mid-August, especially if you are in the surf bobbing on your board for hours on end.

Windsurfing, sometimes called sailboarding, requires you to maneuver a sail that pivots 360 degrees on top of a rudderless board. The calm waters that make the southern waters off Cape Cod poor for surfing combine, however, with steady winds to make for great windsurfing. Still, the water can get choppy enough at times for experienced windsurfers to try some aerial maneuvers.

Considered to be one of the best places for sailboarding in the United States, and a past host of the national competitions, Kalmus Beach is well protected and has steady winds that usually blow 10 to 20 knots. Chapoquoit Beach on Buzzards Bay in Falmouth has also been the site of national competitions and is popular with advanced- intermediate to advanced windsurfers. Old Silver Beach on Buzzards Bay in North Falmouth and most of the Vineyard Sound shore are well suited to basic sailboarding skills. Other popular beaches where you can ply the waters include Chapin and Corporation Beaches in Dennis on Cape Cod Bay, and West Dennis Beach on Nantucket Sound. Pleasant Bay, with beach access in both Orleans and Chatham, provides a good mix of calm water and stiff breezes.

The following establishments sell and rent equipment or make repairs.

Upper Cape

CAPE COD WINDSURFING
350 Quaker Rd., North Falmouth
(508) 801-3329
www.capecodwindsurfing.com
On beautiful Vineyard Sound, this outfit rents watercraft such as kayaks, pedal boats, Sunfish, and sailboats. It also has windsurfing and sailboarding equipment and instruction available. The shop is located on Old Silver Beach at the Sea Crest Hotel.

Mid-Cape

BOARDING HOUSE SURF SHOP
302 Main St., Hyannis
(508) 778-4080
This year-round Hyannis shop sells everything to do with the three sports of surfing, skateboarding, and snowboarding. They offer all the clothing and accessories you'll need as well as videos to help you learn the techniques, and also a repair service.

Lower Cape

JASPER'S SURF SHOP INC.
U.S. Route 6, Eastham
(508) 255-2662
www.jasperssurfshop.com
Jasper's has a large selection of surfboards and equipment and sells some sailboards, swimsuits, wet suits, and lifeguard equipment. Repairs are done in the summer only. In the off-season, the shop takes mail orders via telephone.

MONOMOY SAIL AND CYCLE
275 Rte. 28, Chatham
(508) 945-0811
www.gis.net/~monomoy
Monomoy Sail and Cycle rents sailboards for use on Nantucket Sound and Pleasant Bay. Remember that, although Pleasant Bay offers calm, delightful waters, Southern Pleasant Bay, in Chatham, is much rougher—and potentially dangerous.

NAUSET SURF
Route 6A, Orleans
(508) 255-4742
www.nausetsurfshop.com
This year-round shop rents and sells the latest in wet suits, boards (sail, surf, skim, and body), and essential windsurfing and surfing equipment.

THE PUMP HOUSE SURF COMPANY
9 Cranberry Hwy. (Route 6A), Orleans
(508) 240-2226, (508)-240-2229 for surf report)
Offering a complete line of surfboards as well as clothing, swimwear, and eyewear, the Pump House is an ideally located Lower Cape surf shop

convenient to the Atlantic-side beaches. It provides a repair service, a surf report, and rentals, and also offers lessons. The Pump House is open weekends from early Apr to the end of May, stays open seven days a week from the end of May until Oct, and then reverts to weekend hours from Oct to Dec. It's closed Jan through March.

Diving

Beach diving is popular on the Cape, especially at Corporation Beach in Dennis and Sandwich's Town Beach, which is considered safe and easy for divers because the current is light and the rocky bottom is interesting. Divers see plenty of striped bass, bluefish, tautog, flounder, sea robins, sea urchins, and starfish.

Several books about underwater exploration in the area are available, including three by Donald L. Ferris and Bill Dubiel: *Beneath the Waters of Cape Cod, Beneath the Waters of Massachusetts Bay,* and *Exploring the Waters of Cape Cod: Shipwrecks and Dive Sites,* which has information on 94 dive sites, complete with maps, photos, and Loran numbers.

The ocean beaches of the Lower Cape have more currents and shoals than the bay. This is the untamed Atlantic, and you have to exercise caution, especially when near the shore. The waters of the bayside Cape are calmer and warmer, and the warmest waters tend to be those of Nantucket and Vineyard Sounds. The visibility also tends to be better in Cape Cod Bay and on the southern sounds than in Buzzards Bay. Just as winds alter the landscape, currents cause underwater changes, so you should consult the staff at local dive shops for suitable areas and current conditions for diving.

Check with one of the following dive shops for instruction, information, or gear before entering the water.

Upper Cape
AQUA CENTER
2 Freezer Rd., Sandwich
(508) 888-3444
www.aquacenter.com

Aqua Center is open year-round and has diving equipment, masks, snorkels, and fins. It also offers instruction and equipment rental.

> **i** There are around 365 freshwater ponds on Cape Cod. Most of them are kettle ponds. They were formed when ice blocks from glaciers created depressions in the land. These depressions were deep enough to reach the groundwater. Several fine kettle ponds are located within Cape Cod National Seashore.

Mid-Cape
CAPE COD BAY CHARTERS
Barnstable Harbor, Mill Way (off Route 6A), Barnstable
(508) 362-1249
www.ccbcharters.com

Charter the *Lucky Lady* for an ocean dive out of Barnstable Harbor, where you can choose wreck or reef dives. Scallop and lobster dives are also popular (you must have a Massachusetts lobster license in order to take a lobster). Six certified divers are needed for each charter. Call or go online for rates and more information.

THE DIVE LOCKER
237 Falmouth Rd., Hyannis
(508) 775-1185
www.capedivelocker.com

This store offers full scuba and snorkel gear rentals, swimming supplies, and scuba instruction classes and leads local dives and charters. Call ahead to reserve equipment or schedule a dive during the summer months. Open daily year-round.

SEA SPORTS
195 Ridgewood Ave., Hyannis
(508) 790-1217
www.capecodseasports.com

A full-service scuba-diving shop, Sea Sports caters to snorkeling. Sea Sports organizes an informal dive club and night dives, and also has a full-service surf shop. The shop is open year-round.

FISHING

Cape Cod is one of the best places to fish along the East Coast. And it's no secret why: It has more than 360 freshwater ponds and sports a coastline loaded with jetties, inlets, tidal rivers, and flats. It lies just west of the very fertile Stellwagen Bank and is along the migratory route for stripers and blues moving from southern waters to the Gulf of Maine.

Fishing has a rich history on the Cape, literally. The majority of the large homes and estates that line the main roads of the Cape almost certainly belonged at one time to fishing or whaling captains who prospered greatly from the sea. Of course it wasn't always an ocean of opportunity. Remember, the folks who arrived here in 1620 had crossed the ocean with the thought that they'd be farmers in what we now call Virginia. The crops yielded by the Cape's sandy soil were not as bountiful as these settlers had hoped, so they had to explore other ways to supplement their diet and provide a means of support. They soon realized that money could be made by venturing offshore to harvest fish from the sea.

Centuries later the Portuguese arrived here and added another layer to the Cape's fishing heritage. Provincetown, where many of the Portuguese settled, became a major fishing port during the 19th and early 20th centuries.

Though commercial fishing still exists, recreational fishing has grown to a point that it now rivals its commercial cousin, mainly because of the many restrictions placed on commercial fishing these days.

In this chapter, we give you an overview of the sport, along with places to go and people to see to help make your fishing experiences memorable. A word of advice: Familiarize yourself with the many local regulations. The Massachusetts Division of Marine Fisheries (617-626-1520, www.mass.gov/dfwele/dmf) can be reached Monday through Friday from 8:30 a.m. to 5 p.m. It can provide current information about species availability and regulatory restrictions, which often change.

Fly fishing is especially attractive here, because of the Cape's geography. Saltwater anglers go after striped bass, blues, bonito, false albacore, Spanish mackerel, cod, and fluke, whereas freshwater anglers find trout, small- and largemouth bass, and yellow perch.

Starting in 2010, to the consternation of fishermen who had enjoyed a free ride until then, saltwater fishing requires a saltwater fishing license. Freshwater licenses—the norm in Massachusetts—can be obtained from any town clerk and at many tackle shops around the Cape.

Shellfishing for mussels, clams, and quahogs is also quite popular around the Cape. Get a license and a clam rake or just a trowel and dig for your chowder. Types of shellfish available, regulations, and licensing fees vary from town to town. Contact the individual town for more information. Also, eels for family use or for bait, or seaworms for bait, are covered by local regulations, and permits are required.

To land the right fish, or any fish for that matter, you have to use the right bait. That's just one more reason to start your Cape fishing at a bait and tackle shop. You may also want to consider a local guide. The sandy shores of the Cape change constantly, especially after a rough winter or during the later summer hurricane season, and an experienced guide will get you into the right place. See our recommendations later in this chapter.

FRESHWATER FISHING

The most popular freshwater fish on the Cape are trout and small- and largemouth bass. More than 50 of our 360-plus ponds and lakes and a dozen streams give Cape Cod the reputation for top-notch freshwater angling. Bass, pickerel, white and yellow perch, brook, rainbow and brown trout, as well as other species, such as sunfish, catfish, and crappie, all grace our inland waters. Additionally, about four dozen streams and ponds are stocked with trout each year. Stocking usually takes place in March, though ice fishers have been known to land some large leftovers from the previous year.

As for fishing advice the best is to just get out there and try your luck. Any fisherman on any given day will probably have a different idea or bit of advice so talk to them all. Check at the local tackle shop near the pond you plan to fish for the best information.

Remember, a license is required to fish the Cape's freshwater ponds, lakes, streams, and rivers. State fishing licenses may be obtained at town halls or at certain bait and tackle shops. Typically licenses are not required for children younger than 15. If you are a Massachusetts resident, the annual fee for adults is $27.50. For ages 5 to 17 it costs $11.50. Nonresidents can buy a three-day license for $23.50.

Freshwater Fishing Spots

Upper Cape

Flax Pond in Bourne is a good place to catch both bass and pickerel. This shallow pond with a maximum depth of 6 feet can be accessed from the northwest off Old County Road.

Lawrence Pond is Sandwich's largest pond at nearly 140 acres. It has a maximum depth of 27 feet and a boat ramp at the southeastern corner off Great Hill Road. Here you can fish for white perch, pickerel, and bass.

Peters Pond, Sandwich's second-largest body of water, is stocked with trout, though pickerel and white perch can also be found here. A boat ramp is at the extreme eastern shore off John Ewer Road. The depths of this pond exceed 50 feet.

Safety in Waders

Local experts recommend that if you're fishing in waders, you should wear a personal flotation device (PFD) and tell someone where you're going and when you expect to be back. When in the water shuffle and slide your feet to move your body. But always keep both feet on the ground. If your waders fill with water and you're wearing a PFD, roll onto your back and paddle toward shore. Also carry a knife so that if you aren't wearing a PFD, you can cut off the waders.

Snake Pond in Sandwich is more than 30 feet deep. Bass and pickerel can be caught here. Access is from the south off Snake Pond Road.

Spectacle Pond in Sandwich is stocked with trout and is also home to numerous white perch, bass, and pickerel. Access can be made from the southwest shore off Pinkham Road. Two other Sandwich ponds stocked with trout are Pimlico Pond and Hoxie Pond. Scorton Creek is also stocked with trout, and you may also find some good-size bass in it as well.

Deep Pond in Falmouth is a bit misleading, as there are several deeper ponds in town. At a maximum depth of nearly 30 feet, the pond is stocked with trout. You can access the pond from the southwest off Sam Turner Road.

Grews Pond is another trout-stocked Falmouth pond. A boat ramp south of the pond provides access. Maximum depth is 35 feet. Childs River in Falmouth has been known to yield big trout.

Jenkins Pond, between Goodwill Park Road and Pumping Station Road in Falmouth, has a maximum depth of more than 50 feet and is home to bass, white perch, and pickerel. Much of this nearly 90-acre pond is more than 20 feet deep.

Ashumet Pond in Mashpee is stocked with trout and is also full of bass and pickerel. The pond has a maximum depth of 65 feet. Access can be found along the western shore off Currier Road in Falmouth.

Johns Pond in Mashpee achieves a maximum depth of 60 feet where stocked trout, pickerel, white perch, and bass swim. There is a boat ramp to the east off Hooppole Road providing access to this large body of water, more than 300 acres.

Mashpee Pond and Wakeby Pond in Mashpee are connected and, when combined, create a body of water of more than 700 acres. Mashpee Pond is the deeper of the two at nearly 90 feet. Both ponds are stocked with trout and also harbor bass, pickerel, and perch. Access Mashpee Pond at a boat ramp on its southern shoreline just north of Route 130.

Mid-Cape

Hamblin Pond in Marstons Mills is stocked with trout and also provides good bass and pickerel fishing. There is easy access from Route 149 by taking the road adjacent to the small cemetery.

Hathaway Pond in Barnstable is stocked with trout and has a maximum depth of nearly 60 feet. A boat ramp can be found on the southern shore off Phinney's Lane near the intersection of Route 132.

Lovells Pond in Marstons Mills is larger than 50 acres and is stocked with trout, as well as bass and pickerel. Access can be found along the southern shoreline off Newtown Road.

Shallow Pond in Barnstable lives up to its name—the maximum depth is less than 8 feet over its nearly 70 acres. This is mainly a pickerel pond. It sits between Route 132 and Huckins Neck Road.

i Barnstable's 3,400-acre **Great Marsh** is home to snowy egrets, mute swans, oystercatchers, hawks, eider ducks, and much more. It's an excellent place for exploring by kayak. The guides at Great Marsh Kayak Tours will take you on a tour. Stop for a picnic, stake out prime bird-watching areas, or learn to fly fish—by kayak. For more information call (508) 775-6447, or visit www.greatmarshkayaktours.com.

Wequaquet Lake, between Centerville and West Barnstable, is a huge lake by Cape Cod standards—650 acres—though its depth rarely exceeds 25 feet. This lake is stocked with northern pike and is also home to many bass, white perch, and plenty of pickerel. Access can be found along the northern shore off Shootflying Hill Road.

Dennis Pond in Yarmouthport is a great place to fish for pickerel and bass because it is a shallow pond that averages a depth of 10 feet. Access is along the east side off Summer Street.

Long Pond in South Yarmouth is stocked with trout. You can also catch bass, white perch and pickerel in this largely shallow pond with a maximum depth of 30 feet. There is a boat ramp on the south side of the pond north of the point where Route 28 and Wood Road intersect.

Fresh Pond in South Dennis is a shallow pond—about 5 feet deep—with access on its east side off Route 134. Pickerel can be caught here.

Scargo Lake in East Dennis achieves a maximum depth of about 50 feet over its 50-plus acres. The lake, which is stocked with trout, also has white perch and bass. Two access points can be found, one along the north side off Route 6A and another at the northeast corner off Scargo Hill Road.

Lower Cape

Cliff Pond in East Brewster is stocked with trout to swim in its nearly 200 acres. Access can be gained from the east off Nook Road and the west off Pond Road, both within Nickerson State Park. Nearby Little Cliff Pond is also trout stocked.

Flax Pond in East Brewster is trout stocked. It is more than 70 feet at its deepest point, and its waters are home to bass and pickerel. Access is from the northwest off Deer Park Road within Nickerson State Park.

Long Pond on the Brewster Harwich town line is very large, spanning nearly 750 acres. In some spots, the waters exceed 50 feet in depth, with just more than 60 feet being its greatest depth. Here you'll find plenty of bass fishing, along with white perch and pickerel. Access is from the east off Route 137 and south off Long Pond Drive as well as from the north off Crowells Bog Road (east of Route 124).

Sheep Pond is a 150-acre Brewster pond stocked with trout. Bass and pickerel also swim in its depths, which exceed 60 feet. Access is from the southwest off Route 124 (take Fisherman's Landing Road).

Seymour Pond on the Brewster/Harwich line has pickerel, bass, and white perch. It is about 180 acres in area and about 40 feet at its deepest point. It can be accessed from the east off Route 124.

Goose Pond in Chatham is trout stocked. Access to this 50-foot-plus pond is gained from the north off Old Queen Anne Road to Carriage Drive.

Schoolhouse Pond in Chatham is a small 20-acre pond stocked with trout. Maximum depth is about 50 feet. Access can be gained from the northwest off Old Queen Anne Road.

Bakers Pond in Orleans is trout stocked. A small pond at 28 acres, its maximum depth approaches 50 feet. Access is from the east off Bakers Pond Road.

Crystal Lake in Orleans has bass and pickerel along with stocked trout. Access points can be found along the northwest off Route 28 and southeast off Monument Road.

Great Pond is Eastham's largest pond at 110 acres. Bass and pickerel can be caught here. Access is off Great Pond Road.

Herring Pond of Eastham reaches a maximum depth of about 35 feet. Its 40-plus acres are trout stocked, and bass, white perch, and pickerel can also be found here. Access to the pond is from the southwest off Crosby Village Road.

Gull Pond in Wellfleet is stocked with trout, though you'll also catch bass, pickerel, and perch here. There is a boat ramp along the west side of the 100-plus-acre pond off Schoolhouse Hill Road. Maximum depth here exceeds 60 feet.

Long Pond in Wellfleet is like two ponds, the east side dropping to more than 30 feet and the west side going a bit deeper, more than 50 feet. Access to this bass and pickerel pond can be found along the northwest side off Long Pond Road.

Great Pond in Truro is a small trout-stocked pond that drops to greater than 35 feet in its center. There is access at the southwest tip just off US 6.

Gull Pond, just off Gull Pond Road in Truro, has been known to yield some good-size trout and bass. The Pamet River is also stocked with trout each year.

Pilgrim Lake in North Truro, on the right of US 6 just before entering Provincetown, is a bit deceiving for its size. Its total area is 350 acres, but its deepest waters are scarcely 6 or 7 feet. White perch and pickerel can be found here. Access is from the south off High Head Road.

SALTWATER FISHING

The entire Cape coastline is potential fishing ground. At any given hour on any given day during spring, summer, and fall, you are bound to find somebody casting from a jetty or dropping a line off a bridge. When the blues are running, the beaches are lined with surf casters hoping to snag a big one.

Today the most popular saltwater fish on the Cape is the striped bass, followed figuratively and literally by the bluefish. The bass usually first appear near Martha's Vineyard in mid-spring. A week or two later, they start showing up in the waters off the shores of the southern Upper Cape. The bluefish usually follow a week or two behind them. Stripers follow the Gulf Stream as it pushes its way north in the spring. (The Gulf Stream is one reason the water on the southern side of the Cape seems like bathwater in mid-August and the water on the east side feels like ice water.) The stripers, the blues, and others traveling north for the summer come by Martha's Vineyard first and then head along the southern shore of the Upper Cape.

Once the water temperature reaches into the 70s, around July, the stripers head for cooler water, right up the eastern forearm of Cape Cod. Monomoy Island off Chatham proves to be a nice block for the stripers and blues trying to navigate the Cape's elbow. But beware: Fish aren't the only ones caught by Monomoy. The shifting sands in the area and shallow flats have been known to strand a few boaters as well. Once past Monomoy, it's a clear run up the Cape to Provincetown and then onto the Gulf of Maine. During the late summer and early fall, Cape Cod's National Seashore becomes one of the best places anywhere for a surf caster to land a large striped bass as they return after a summer of good feeding in northern waters.

As previously mentioned, a license is required for saltwater fishing starting in 2010. In the first year it is expected to be merely a registration, with fees imposed in 2011. There are limitations and restrictions on certain saltwater fish: minimum size, number of fish you can take in a day, and, in some cases, what month of the year you can take them. There are also rules on how you can catch a particular species.

Regulations are known to change from year to year, so it's best to contact the Massachusetts Division of Marine Fisheries at (617) 626-1520 for the latest rules and regulations. Or visit a bait and tackle shop—they should be able to help out.

Below is a quick listing of some of the more popular coastal fishing locations from Bourne to Provincetown.

Saltwater Fishing Spots

Upper Cape

If you're in Bourne, try the pier at Shore Road in Pocasset or anywhere along the Cape Cod Canal.

In Sandwich, the jetty at the Sandwich basin is a good spot, or else the jetty or pier at Scusset Beach, the jetty at Sandwich Beach, or along Scorton Creek off Route 6A.

Falmouth, with its long coastline and many finger inlets, has a lot of great locations, including the bridge at Green Pond and the jetties at Falmouth Harbor, Woods Hole, and Great Pond.

Mashpee Neck Road and South Cape Beach in Mashpee are also great spots, as is the jetty at Dead Neck.

i **Except for bluefin tuna, which require going to sea, striped bass, bluefish, flounder, and mackerel are all available from shoreline locations just about everywhere on Cape Cod. If you are looking for surf-casting locations in the Falmouth area, try Chapoquoit Beach off Chapoquoit Road in West Falmouth, or Nobska Point off Church Street in Woods Hole.**

Mid-Cape

In Barnstable, give Barnstable Harbor, Craigville Beach, and Sandy Neck Beach a try.

Bass Hole (Gray's Beach) in Yarmouthport is a wonderful spot to kill a couple of hours (even if the fish aren't biting). Other spots in the town of Yarmouth are Sea Gull Beach, the jetty at Bass River Beach, and the Bass River Bridge linking Yarmouth with neighboring Dennis.

Dennis has a number of hot spots, including jetties at Corporation Beach, Davis Beach, Cold Storage Beach, and Sesuit Neck Beach. Chapin Memorial Beach is also a good spot.

Lower Cape

Cast your line at Paine Creek and Point of Rocks in Brewster, or at Bridge Street, Harding Beach, or Nauset Beach in Chatham. Monomoy Island off Chatham is great for boat fishing or even wading in the flats, and another good spot nearby is South Beach near the Chatham break—both these areas are right on the path of stripers and blues. The mouth of Pleasant Bay has been known to be a hot spot to catch a variety of saltwater species, including an occasional flounder.

Rock Harbor in Orleans is a nice spot, and so is Nauset Beach.

When in Eastham, take your rod over to Sunken Meadow Beach and First Encounter Beach on the bayside, and Coast Guard Beach and Nauset Light Beach on the ocean side.

Wellfleet's town pier is a popular fishing spot. Also in Wellfleet are Cahoon Hollow, Duck Harbor Road, and the jetty at Indian Neck.

Head of the Meadow Beach, Highland Light Beach, and the jetty at Corn Hill Beach in Truro are all spectacular spots.

In the fishing port of Provincetown, you can cast your line off historic MacMillan Wharf or at various spots along Provincetown's 3-mile-long harbor beach.

SHELLFISHING

There's perhaps nothing more relaxing than an early morning's jaunt to the local shellfish beds to dig for tasty critters hiding in the mudflats.

Regarding all shellfish: You need to consult the local town hall for restrictions and permits. Regulations and minimum-size requirements can be a little confusing at first. The minimum size of a good oyster is one with a certain shell diameter, whereas a minimum quahog size is measured in shell thickness. Conch is measured in shell width, and sea scallops must meet a certain shell height.

Each town has its own restrictions in terms of possession limits. You'll also want to find out which beds are open and which are closed and what types of shellfish are available for the taking. Contact the local town hall for local regulations and limits. (See the list of town halls in our Area Overview chapter.)

SPORTFISHING CHARTERS

While shore fishing is a big attraction on Cape Cod, to get a shot at some of the bigger fish, namely tuna, you need to head to sea. It also helps to heed the guidance of someone that knows the area and current regulations.

That's why a fishing charter is a great idea—whether you're looking for a family activity or an afternoon of competitive fishing among friends, you'll be able to find a boat and captain to accommodate you and your party.

Most charters include bait and equipment and provide some kind of instruction for beginners. Some will also rent you a rod and reel for a nominal fee. However, most are not staffed to provide supervision for children, so if you're coming as a family, you'll need to be the one to help your young anglers handle their rods and reels.

You will also find that boats vary greatly in size. Most small-group charters take a maximum of six guests, and in several cases the captain will charge you the full rate even if there are less than six in your party, or he will at least try to pair you with other folks so that he has a full boat. The larger-party boats vary greatly in the number of people they can take. Larger boats generally are less expensive per person, but you don't get the individual attention you receive on a small charter.

Most of the common game fish are found within an hour's ride from a Cape port. Many are found considerably closer, and, of these, some can be taken from skiff or shore. But whatever fish you wish to chase, there are experienced charter skippers who can guide you. Below is a list of recommendations.

Upper Cape

EASTWIND SPORTFISHING CHARTERS
Falmouth Town Marina, Falmouth Inner Harbor, Falmouth
(508) 420-3934
www.capecodstripers.com
Catching stripers is the *Eastwind*'s specialty. The *Eastwind* is a 35-foot Duffy sportfisherman and is fully equipped with Coast Guard–approved safety devices, state-of-the-art electronics, and top-of-the-line fishing tackle. Four-, six-, and eight-hour charters are available for up to six passengers starting around $125 per hour.

LEE MARIE SPORT FISHING
Falmouth Inner Harbor, Falmouth
(508) 548-9498
www.lee-marie.com
Do you enjoy sportfishing but not the cramped quarters on small boat charters? Try Lee Marie Sport Fishing. For more than 20 years, Don Oliver has been bringing fishing enthusiasts to the bass, blues, and bonito in the waters off the South Cape and islands. His 31-foot boat, complete with living quarters, won't leave you feeling confined. Don can take a maximum of six people on four-, six-, or eight-hour charters, depending on how much fishing you want to do. The boat operates out of Falmouth Inner Harbor from May to Nov.

PATRIOT BOATS
227 Clinton Ave., Falmouth Inner Harbor, Falmouth
(508) 548-2626, (800) 734-0088
www.patriotpartyboats.com
These family-owned and -operated boats depart from the entrance of Falmouth Harbor for full- or half-day deep-sea fishing trips with bait and tackle included. The fleet includes three party

boats, the *Minuteman,* the *T.G.,* and the *Patriot II.* These boats take anywhere from 36 to 49 passengers. There is plenty of room, outside seating, and a snack bar. You may want to book a Patriot Boats charter, which takes up to six people.

Mid-Cape

HY-LINE FISHING TRIPS
Ocean Street Docks, Hyannis
(508) 778-2600
www.hy-linecruises.com
Hy-Line offers a variety of fishing trips that leave throughout the day. Within a 45-minute cruise into Nantucket Sound, you will find yourself in one of the best areas on the East Coast for bottom fishing. This is your chance at the scup (porgy), fluke, and tautog found in these waters. Vessels are equipped with fish-finding electronics, and though they can't guarantee you a catch, we will assure you that it's fun for the whole family. Call for current prices. Rods can be rented.

Lower Cape

THE *BANSHEE* SPORTFISHING COMPANY
Stage Harbor Marina, Bridge Street, Chatham
(508) 945-0403
The *Banshee* is owned and operated by Captain Ron McVickar, who has more than 40 years of fishing experience, 30 of them doing charters. The 32-foot Banshee takes groups of six after striped bass, bluefish, and the occasional bonito. McVickar specializes in light tackle, with no line heavier than 30-pound test. The Banshee operates from May to early Nov.

THE *HEADHUNTER* FISHING CHARTER
Stage Harbor Marina, Chatham
(508) 430-2312
www.capecodfishingcharters.com
Captain Bob Miller has more than 20 years' experience fishing the waters around Chatham and Nantucket. He is patient with novice anglers and can challenge an expert. He fishes all year round, so he knows what is happening and where to go. His boat, *The Headhunter,* is fully equipped and accommodates a six-person charter easily.

THE *NAVIATOR*
Town Pier, Wellfleet
(508) 349-6003
www.naviator.com
Some say the star of the *Naviator* is its captain, Rick Merrill, a seasoned veteran of Cape Cod waters. Others say it's the 60-foot, 49-passenger boat herself. Four-hour fishing trips leave Wellfleet from late June through Labor Day twice a day at 8:30 a.m. and 1 p.m. The Naviator departs on weekends only in May and offers one trip daily during June and Sept.

ROCK HARBOR CHARTER SERVICE
Rock Harbor, Rock Harbor Road, Orleans
(508) 255-9757
www.rockharborcharters.com
With its 18 boats, Rock Harbor is home to one of the Cape's largest charter fleets. Ranging in size from 35 to 42 feet, each boat can take parties of six. They will also pair smaller groups into six to help spread the cost. From mid-May through mid-Oct, U.S. Coast Guard–licensed captains offer four- and eight-hour bluefish and striped bass fishing expeditions.

FISHING GUIDES

Inquire at local bait and tackle shops for the names and numbers of guides who know the waters well. Guides provide the expertise and the equipment needed for fly or spin fishing for striped bass and bluefish, as well as other species such as tautog, fluke, mackerel, scup, cod, shark, and tuna. Call ahead to schedule your outing. Prices depend on the length of the season. Most guides will take only one or two people, and often it is the same price regardless of whether you are alone or with a friend.

FISHING THE CAPE
Harwich Commons, 120 Rte. 137, East Harwich
(508) 432-1200
www.fishingthecape.com
Learn saltwater fly fishing from Orvis-trained guides. Two-day courses are offered May through

Aug for $470 per person (including lunch, bait, and the use of equipment). Lessons include distance casting, saltwater fly selection, big-game knots, leader rigging, fish feeding habits, "reading the surf," and safe wading practices. This outfit also employs 10 Orvis-endorsed fishing guides who lead flats-fishing, rip-fishing, and wading trips mostly in the Monomoy Flats area.

BAIT AND TACKLE SHOPS

If you're ready to go after the big ones, you'll want to first stop at one of the following bait and tackle shops to stock up on the tools of the trade. You'll want to get your hands on a current tide chart, and these are generally available free or for a nominal price at bait and tackle shops.

Upper Cape

EASTMAN'S SPORT & TACKLE
783 Main St., Falmouth
(508) 548-6900
www.eastmanstackle.com
Open year-round, this large Upper Cape shop carries all types of fresh- and saltwater fishing tackle, including extensive fly-fishing gear. At Eastman's you can obtain Massachusetts, New Hampshire, and Maine fishing licenses, as well as clamming equipment and tide charts.

RED TOP SPORTING GOODS
265 Main St., Buzzards Bay
(508) 759-3371
www.redtoptackle.com
With the Cape Cod Canal at its doorstep, this shop is just a few steps from one of the richest sources of saltwater fish—striped bass, bluefish, flounder, tautog, and mackerel—in the region. This year-round shop (hours are limited in winter) sells fishing tackle and other outdoor gear. It also handles fishing licenses and has tide charts.

SANDWICH SHIP SUPPLY
68 Tupper Rd., Sandwich
(508) 888-0200, (800) 555-8805
www.sandwichship.com

This shop carries an extensive line of equipment, bait and tackle, safety gear, flags, clothing, maps, anchors, chains, ropes, and other nautical necessities.

Mid-Cape

RIVERVIEW BAIT & TACKLE
1273 Rte. 28, South Yarmouth
(508) 394-1036
This store, just a half-mile west of Bass River, sells offshore tackle, bait, custom rods and reels, nautical charts, and fly-fishing supplies. It also rents equipment and offers rod and reel repair. It's open year-round.

SPORTS PORT
149 West Main St., Hyannis
(508) 775-3096
One of the Cape's oldest tackle shops still run by its original owners, Sports Port sells all salt- and freshwater tackle as well as shellfishing gear and fly-tying equipment. This shop is open year-round.

TRUMAN'S
608 Main St., West Yarmouth
(508) 771-3470
Open year-round, Truman's supplies fishing tackle, fly-fishing equipment, shell-fishing gear, and provides rod and reel repair. Also available are live bait, tide charts, and fishing licenses.

Lower Cape

THE GOOSE HUMMOCK SHOP
Route 6A, Orleans
(508) 255-0455
www.goose.com
For almost 60 years, Goose Hummock has been catering to the needs of Lower Cape anglers. This shop carries a full line of fishing equipment, including major brands of fly-fishing equipment, outdoor clothing, hunting and hiking gear, canoes, and kayaks. Goose Hummock is open year-round, offers fishing licenses, and has an extensive inventory in both sales and rentals. Goose Hummock fishing guides conduct trips of three hours and longer.

GOLF

Cape Cod's top-rated golf courses attract many visitors. The Cape today offers some of the most scenic and diverse layouts found anywhere in the United States. There are no less than 46 courses scattered around this scenic peninsula and its neighboring islands.

You'll encounter a full variety of conditions and hazards on the Cape. From the wide fairways of Falmouth Country Club to the tree-lined routing of Dennis Pines, and from the pot bunkers of Ocean Edge to the postage stamp greens of Bass River Golf Course, golf course architects seem to have thrown a bit of everything at the golfer. Water hazards may include Vineyard Sound, Bass River, or even the Atlantic Ocean. A hook may land you in a conservation area; a slice may send you into a pine forest. Of course the most prevalent hazard on the Cape is the wind. What might play as a seven-iron one day turns into a two-iron with a shift in the wind.

On paper, the back tees at Falmouth's Ballymeade Country Club appear to be the toughest public layout on the Cape, but most local players consider New Seabury's Ocean Course the Cape's best challenge, in part because of the ocean wind on its back nine. Other courses that will satisfy golf masochists include Bayberry Hills, Quashnet Valley Country Club, Cranberry Valley, Dennis Pines, Ocean Edges, and the Captains' Course. All these tracts have USGA slopes of about 130 from the back tees. (The slope system reflects a course's difficulty, measuring from 55 for the easiest to 155 for the hardest, with a course of average difficulty scoring 113.) Most beginners and casual players won't want to venture too far into the 120s. But that's the beauty of Cape courses—they all offer tees of varying lengths and slope ratings. In many cases there are more than 1,200 yards (not to mention several slope rating points) difference between the front and back tees at these top-ranked tracts. No matter what your ability might be, both you and your playing partners can enjoy the same course.

The best season for Cape golf is the fall, when the crowds have cleared, leaving open tee times and uncrowded courses. Many layouts drop their rates after the summer season, and the temperatures dip to a more comfortable 60- to 70-degree range after the heat of summer. New England golfers also recognize that fall is the prime time for course conditions, as the turf springs back from the summer traffic. And don't forget the foliage, too—inland courses, such as the Quashnet Valley Country Club, burst into color in mid- to late October.

Although the Cape might not enjoy the same reputation as the West Coast or the South, it nonetheless has made its mark on the golf world. Cape Codders Paul Harney, Carri Wood, Sally Quinlan, Jim Hallet, and John Curley have all played on the professional tours. The Cape is also home to some great local golf schools. The best time to take advantage of these packages is in the shoulder season, especially in the spring, when the courses and resorts are looking for business and you'll be looking to get your game in shape.

Driving ranges can be found at about half the Cape's courses and at dedicated facilities such as the Longest Drive in Dennis or T-Time in Eastham. Town-owned courses such as Cranberry Valley in Harwich and Bass River and Bayberry Hills in Yarmouth offer relatively inexpensive memberships to town residents, and many courses feature free or inexpensive golf clinics during the summer. Nearly all of the courses charge reduced greens fees if you sign up for a "twilight" tee time (after 2, 3, or 4 p.m., depending on the course).

And, if you yearn for a view of the first tee from your own backyard, the Cape is home to several golfing communities where luxury homes and condominiums line the fairways and greens (see our Relocation chapter).

One thing we can't overlook: Though we have done our best to give you the most up-to-date greens fees for 18 holes, 9 holes, and the charge for a cart, fees are subject to change. Confirm the fee when making the reservation.

COURSES

Upper Cape

BALLYMEADE COUNTRY CLUB & ESTATES
125 Falmouth Woods Rd., North Falmouth
(508) 540-4005
www.ballymeade.com
Ballymeade opened in 1987 and immediately became known as one of the toughest layouts on the Cape. Recently redesigned by Chichi Rodriquez, this semiprivate 18-hole course plays to a 139 slope of more than 6,900 yards from its back tees. Ballymeade is obviously not a beginner's course, but the front tees do knock the course down to size for most high- and mid-handicappers. Ballymeade has hilly, rocky terrain, and narrow, tree-lined fairways. The panoramic views are stunning, especially from the par 3 11th hole, which is one of the highest points on Cape Cod and offers fantastic views of Buzzards Bay.

Reservations for tee times can be made up to seven days in advance, and groups of 16 or more can book up to a year in advance. Greens fees in the summer, including mandatory carts, are $80 weekends and $65 weekdays. Off-season fees drop. The course is open year-round and has a driving range and a putting green complete with a bunker so you can practice those pesky sand shots. Ballymeade also has PGA teaching pros and a fully stocked pro shop.

CAPE COD COUNTRY CLUB
48 Theatre Dr., North Falmouth
(508) 563-9842, (508) 563-6109
www.capecodcountryclub.com
This course sets up for everyone, good players and beginners alike. From the tips, this par 71 course measures a moderate 6,400 yards with a slope of 120. There are several elevated greens on this layout, including the par 4 14th hole, where you'll feel like you're trying to land your approach on a mountaintop. A few feet left or right turns into several yards with a kick off the side of the hill. Cape Cod Country Club offers rental carts and equipment, a pro shop, and lunch counter. There is a practice green, and lessons are available. Fees are $42 on weekdays and $56 on weekends for 18 holes. After 3 p.m. rates go down. Tee times are taken up to a week in advance. The course is open year-round.

FALMOUTH COUNTRY CLUB
630 Carriage Shop Rd., East Falmouth
(508) 548-3211
www.falmouthcountryclub.com
Falmouth Country Club is a 6,535-yard, par 72, 18-hole course. It is open year-round and its eccentricities include a pair of ospreys nesting above the 10th hole. The course itself is wide open without many trees and is relatively flat, making it perfect for walkers and beginners, who may want to start on the separate 9-hole, par 37 course. It also has a nice practice range, putting green, and pro shop and offers rental equipment and carts. Greens fees are $45 Mon to Fri, and $60 on weekends for 18 holes. Tee time reservations can be made up to fourteen days in advance.

HOLLY RIDGE GOLF CLUB
121 Country Club Rd., South Sandwich
(508) 428-5577
www.hollyridgegolf.com
Set within a residential community on some 90 acres, Holly Ridge is an 18-hole, 2,952-yard, par 54 public course designed by Geoffrey Cornish. The signature hole here is the seventh, which has a pond to avoid on your tee shot. The course has a driving range, practice green, carts, and pro shop as well as a club restaurant. Holly Ridge is

open year-round and offers an extensive lessons program. Reservations are accepted up to seven days in advance for tee times. In-season greens fees are $34 for 18 holes, $21 for 9. After 3 p.m. the fee drops to $21 for 18 holes. Carts are $10 per person per 18 holes, $6 per person per 9 holes, and $4 for pull carts.

NEW SEABURY CAPE COD
Off Great Neck Road South, New Seabury (Mashpee)
(508) 539-8322
www.newseabury.com
New Seabury is distinguished by its two top-notch courses: the renowned Ocean Course overlooking Vineyard Sound and the Dunes Course. The Ocean Course (formerly known as the Blue Course) has long been considered one of the top 100 golf courses in the United States, earning the nickname "Pebble Beach of the East." The course is 7,131 yards from the tips, has a slope of 133, and a course rating of 75.7 for the par 72. Many think that the course plays even harder than those numbers.

The Ocean's sister course, the Dunes, was entirely redesigned in 2001 by architect Marvin Armstrong. Thanks to its 18 revamped holes, it can no longer be regarded as the Ocean's more boring sister. Once known as the Green Course, 300 yards have been added, making this par 70 course 6,340 yards from the tips. It also gained two additional ponds, numerous strategically placed bunkers, and more waste areas than you will find on any other New England course.

New Seabury charges different greens fees per course, so we recommend that you check greens fees when making your reservation. The Dunes Course is open to the general public year-round, whereas the Ocean Course is only open to the general public from mid-Oct through mid-June. Tee-time reservations are taken two days in advance from the general public.

PAUL HARNEY'S GOLF CLUB
74 Club Valley Dr. (off Route 151), East Falmouth
(508) 563-3454
www.paulharneygolfcourse.homestead.com

Owned and operated by former PGA pro Paul Harney, this 18-hole executive course offers outstanding play with five par 4 holes and 13 par 3s, totaling some 3,600 yards (par 59 if you're counting). The 16th hole is a par 3 with an elevated tee and a pond protecting the green about 230 yards from the tee. There are plenty of ways to get into trouble here, so you'll want to hit your shots long and straight. Greens fees are $35, the rate drops to $25 after 4 p.m. Weekends are busy, and the course does not take reservations; still, it's a good idea to call ahead to see how long the wait might be. This course is open year-round and has a practice green to putt on while you wait for your tee time.

QUASHNET VALLEY COUNTRY CLUB
309 Old Barnstable Rd., Mashpee
(508) 477-4412, (800) 433-8633
www.quashnetvalley.com
Be sure to pack plenty of golf balls when you play Quashnet Valley. Water hazards in the way of rivers, cranberry bogs, and even wetlands come into play on 15 of Quashnet Valley's 18 holes. Set among picturesque bogs, this semiprivate par 72 plays 6,600 yards from the back tees to a slope of 132. If you play conservatively around the water hazards, you'll find smooth sailing on large greens and wide fairways. The sixth is a particularly demanding, 430 yard par 4 that calls for your best drive and approach to a two-tiered elevated green with water on the right and woods on the left. The facilities include a pro shop, driving range, carts, and a practice green. Carts are $18 for 18 holes. Check the Web site for greens fees, as they change seasonally. The course is open year-round. Tee times are taken up to a week in advance.

SANDWICH HOLLOWS GOLF CLUB
One Round Hill Road, East Sandwich
(508) 888-3384
www.sandwichhollows.com
Owned and operated by the town of Sandwich, the club offers an 18-hole, par 71 course. The 120-acre setting features views of Cape Cod Bay, and facilities also include a new driving range with

more than an acre's worth of teeing area, two practice greens, a clubhouse, and pro shop. The 420-yard, par 4 9th hole forces you to hit into the prevailing wind to an elevated green. It's not such a bad idea to ride rather than walk around this hilly course (formed of hollows left by the receding glacier). You can reserve a tee time by calling in advance. The course is open year-round.

Mid-Cape

BASS RIVER GOLF COURSE
62 Highbank Rd., South Yarmouth
(508) 398-9079
www.golfyarmouthcapecod.com

The signature hole on this appropriately named golf course is the sixth, a par 3 right on the tidal Bass River. Views of scenic Bass River are just one of the nice things about this course, one of the busiest in Massachusetts. Playing to 6,129 yards and a slope of 124 from the back, this par 72 has a fully stocked pro shop, snack bar, and practice green. This is a year-round course with summer rates of $58 before 2 p.m., $45 after 2 p.m., and $30 after 4 p.m. Carts are $19. Call (508) 398-4112 to reserve a time. It is strongly recommended to call well in advance.

BAYBERRY HILLS GOLF COURSE & THE LINKS 9
West Yarmouth Road, West Yarmouth
(508) 394-5597
www.golfyarmouthcapecod.com

Known as an excellent public course, this challenging par 72 course has 18 holes, two practice greens, and a large driving range. Designed by Geoff Cornish and Brian Silva, Bayberry Hills goes from almost 7,200 yards from the back "professional" tees to about 5,300 yards from the front. Beware the par 4 fourth hole. Not only did Cornish and Silva hide the green below a hill, they also hid a water hazard. It also has a separate 9-hole links-style course. Peak-season fees are $66 before 2 p.m. for 18 holes, $55 between 2 and 4 p.m., and $33 after 4 p.m. Carts cost $19 and are mandatory until 2 p.m. Fri through Sun. Bayberry Hills accepts tee times no more than four days in advance unless you prepay. Call (508) 398-4112 to reserve a time.

BLUE ROCK GOLF COURSE
39 Todd Rd., off Highbank Rd., South Yarmouth
(508) 398-9295, (800) 237-8887
www.bluerockgolfcourse.com

A favorite of longtime Cape golfers, Blue Rock is rated one of the best par 3 golf courses in the Northeast. *Sports Illustrated* once called Blue Rock the top par 3 course in the country. Well designed and beautifully maintained, this public 18-hole, 3,000-yard course is open year-round and has holes that range from 103 yards to 255 yards. Both the 9th and 18th require you to drive over a river to an elevated green. Facilities include two practice greens and a golf school. The on-site Blue Rock Resort (see our Hotels, Motels, and Resorts chapter) offers play-and-stay packages. Summer greens fees are $49. Tee times can be booked starting seven days in advance. You can book them further out if you pay a 50 percent deposit, and guests of the Blue Rock Resort may book up to 90 days in advance.

COTUIT HIGH GROUND GOLF COURSE
31 Crockers Neck Rd., Cotuit
(508) 428-9863
www.cotuithighground.com

If you're looking for an inexpensive round of golf, then head for the Cotuit High Ground. It's been owned and operated by the same family for 50 years and is a great place to introduce kids to the game. Greens fees are $20 (and just $15 after 4 p.m.). Seniors and juniors pay $15. This is a semiprivate, 9-hole, par 28 course. The 2,580-yard layout is known for its small greens and narrow fairways. On the par 3 fifth hole, you'll need to make sure your drive clears the swamp, otherwise you'll be knee-deep in trouble. Open year-round, reservations are not required during the week; for a weekend tee time, call ahead during the week. A putting green and small pro shop are available, as well as pull carts and three or four riding carts. Individual memberships are $500.

DENNIS HIGHLANDS
825 Old Bass River Rd., Dennis
(508) 385-8347
www.dennisgolf.com
Opened in mid-1984, Dennis Highlands has become a favorite among locals and tourists. Besides a solid 6,464-yard layout from the back tees, this 18-hole par 71 offers a large two-tier practice range, a putting green, and a full pro shop. The 175 rolling acres are dotted with stands of pine and oak. The sixth hole, a tricky par 4, has a very difficult two-tiered green. Reservations are suggested during the summer/fall season; they are accepted up to seven days in advance, or up to six months in advance if you are prepaying. In the summer greens fees are $60. In the spring and fall fees for Mon through Thurs dip to $49. Carts are $17 per person per 18 holes and $12 per person per 9 holes. Dennis Pines (see following entry) and Dennis Highlands are both owned and run by the town of Dennis. Both are open year-round, weather permitting.

DENNIS PINES
1035 Rte. 134, East Dennis
(508) 385-8347
www.dennisgolf.com
From the back tees, Dennis Pines is a tournament-caliber 7,100 yards with a slope of 127. Don't fret though; the front tees chop off more than 1,200 yards, making this par 72 suitable for many tastes. The narrow fairways at this year-round course emphasize accuracy off the tee. Expect to use every club in your bag here, as the holes are a good mix of lengths. As Dennis Pines is one of the busiest Cape courses, you'll need to reserve tee times in season: The course takes them seven days in advance, or six months in advance with prepayment. In the summer season, greens fees are $60. In the spring, fees Mon through Thurs dip to $49. Cart rentals are $17 per person per 18 holes and $12 per person per 9 holes.

HYANNIS GOLF CLUB
Route 132, Hyannis
(508) 362-2606
www.hyannisgc.com
Hyannis Golf Club plays to a 6,700-yard par 71 from its back tees, but wide fairways keep this course from turning into a monster. The second hole, a 420–yard par 4, is a local favorite that features a marsh before the elevated tee. (The marsh is particularly beautiful in autumn.) This course hosts the Cape Cod Open and the Cape Cod Senior Open, two major golfing events on the Cape. Amenities include a golf school, full pro shop, driving range, two putting greens, rental carts, and equipment. In-season greens fees for nonresidents range from $45 on weekdays to $60 on weekends, and carts are $18 for 18 holes. Reservations, which are accepted anytime, are recommended in the summer. On-site is the Iyanough Hills Food and Spirits restaurant.

OLDE BARNSTABLE FAIRGROUNDS GOLF COURSE
1460 Rte. 149, Marstons Mills
(508) 420-1141, (508) 420-1143
www.obfgolf.com
Opened in 1992, this par 71 plays to 6,503 yards and a slope of 123 from the tips. This is a generally flat course with difficult par 5s and tricky contoured greens. The 18th hole is a par 5 with a big holly tree in the middle that comes into play as you consider your second shot. Facilities include a fully stocked pro shop, huge practice ranges, and a putting green. Pull and motorized carts and rental clubs are available. Another nice feature is a full-service restaurant where you can sit on the deck and watch biplanes and gliders take off and land at Cape Cod Airport across the street. The in-season fees are $45 for residents, $50 to $60 for nonresidents. Twilight play is $30. Olde Barnstable Fairgrounds is open year-round. Call up to two days in advance for reservations.

TWIN BROOKS GOLF COURSE
35 Scudder Ave., Hyannis
(508) 862-6980
www.capecodresortandconference.com
Golf Digest rated this course, located on the grounds of the Resort and Conference Center at Hyannis, as the toughest par 54 on the Cape. The resort offers a picturesque 2,621-yard, 18-hole course with five

water holes. The third hole is considered the toughest on the course—the only way you'll ever make par is to hit straight as an arrow. The resort has two putting greens and a fully equipped pro shop with equipment and cart rentals. Greens fees are $28 from Sun through Thurs, and $33 on weekends. Tee time reservations are advisable. Various memberships are available.

Lower Cape

THE CAPTAINS' GOLF COURSE
1000 Freeman's Way, Brewster
(508) 896–1716, (877) 843-9081
www.captainsgolfcourse.com

The Captains' two 18-hole courses—Port and Starboard—regularly draw praise for being two of the state's finest public golf courses. The par 72 Port Course features 6,724 yards and a slope of 130 from the back tees. This challenging but accommodating course has a well-bunkered layout, and all the holes are named for Brewster sea captains. The par 72 Starboard Course is newer but has already become a Cape favorite. It features 6,776 yards and has a slope of 130. There is also an expansive driving range featuring bunkers and rolling terrain and a fully stocked pro shop. PGA professionals are on hand for lessons and clinics. In-season greens fees are $66 daily for 18 holes, $45 after 2 p.m. on weekdays, and $30 after 4 p.m. Cart rentals are $18 per person per 18 holes or $5 for a pull cart. Call to reserve a tee time, or book one online at their Web site.

CHATHAM SEASIDE LINKS
209 Seaview St., Chatham
(508) 945-4774

Nestled among Chatham's beautiful ocean-side community of historic houses and summer homes, the 9-hole Chatham Seaside Links offers an intimate golfing experience, as well as a great view of the Atlantic Ocean from the seventh green. At about 4,800 yards for 18 holes, this par 34 hides its challenge in tiny greens and strong ocean wind. The course sits next door to the magnificent Chatham Bars Inn (see our Hotels, Motels, and Resorts chapter) and is often packed with guests. Tee times

are determined on a first-come, first-served basis. There is a practice green at the course.

CHEQUESSETT YACHT AND COUNTRY CLUB
680 Chequessett Neck Rd., Wellfleet
(508) 349-3704
www.cycc.net

Chequessett is a 9-hole gem hidden away in the charming town of Wellfleet on the Lower Cape. The par 70 reaches 5,168 yards for 18 from its back set of tees. Over the past few years, the club has put a lot into the course by creating new tees for a more interesting back nine and installing irrigation. Chequessett is a short, pretty course. On-site are a pro shop, putting green, and a clubhouse with grill and snack bar. Greens fees during the summer season are $33 for 9 holes and $48 for 18. Off-season rates go as low as $33 for 9 ($25 after 5 p.m.) and $48 for 18 holes. Tee times can be reserved up to three days in advance by phone.

CRANBERRY VALLEY GOLF COURSE
183 Oak St., Harwich
(508) 430-5234
www.cranberrygolfcourse.com

After 17 holes, you are faced with an interesting 18th at Cranberry Valley: a par 5 double dogleg right that looks like a bent-open horseshoe. The first three holes on the back side have water. Cranberry Valley features 6,745 yards and a 129 slope from the back tees. But, like Dennis Pines, this course loses more than 1,200 yards when you move to the front tees, making it suitable for many skill levels. On-site are a driving range, a putting green, a pro shop, and a 6,000-square-foot clubhouse. Tee times are required in season and can be made up to 10 days in advance. Those who prepay can reserve a tee time after March 1 for the rest of the year. Clubs and cart rentals are available. Greens fees are $64 in season and $18 per person per 18 holes for a cart. Off-season greens fees for 18 holes drop to $38 weekdays and $54 weekends ($38 on weekends Nov through mid-Dec). The course is open year-round, but temporary greens are in effect from Dec through the beginning of Mar.

HARWICH PORT GOLF CLUB
South and Forest Streets, Harwich Port
(508) 432-0250
www.harwichportgolf.com
This pocket-size course is a real charmer. Two laps around these nine holes will get you about 5,076 yards and a par 68. Harwich Port offers relatively flat terrain, and a flat greens fee structure as well.

This public course is open year-round, "as long as there's no snow on the ground." Reservations are not needed; it's first come, first served. There are no riding carts here (they're not necessary), but there are plenty of pull carts available. There's a putting green and the most quaint clubhouse you'll ever lace up your golf shoes in.

HIGHLAND GOLF LINKS
Highland Light Road, North Truro
(508) 487-9201
www.truro-ma.gov/html_pages/facilities/golf.php
This is the granddaddy of all Cape courses, where winds offer as much challenge as the wild rough that accents the fairways. Founded in 1892, Highland is the oldest course on the Cape and one of the oldest in America. It takes 5,299 yards to go around this 9-hole layout twice from the back set of tees. Highland has a modest difficulty rating with a slope of 103. But it's not the challenge that has earned this course a spot on golf itineraries for more than a century—it's the appeal of playing one of the few courses in this country that mirrors the rustic charm of the great links of Great Britain. Perched high along windswept bluffs overlooking the Atlantic, Highland is as natural as golf gets on this side of the ocean. The open fairways, deep natural rough and moorlands, wild cranberry, beach plum, and thicket are reminis-

cent of the unkempt look of the Scottish links. At this truly special course, it is not uncommon to spot whales spouting in the Atlantic or fishing vessels fighting the waves as they make their way up and down the coast.

It's almost impossible to walk onto the course in the summer, so call to reserve a tee time up to a week in advance, Greens fees in season are $33 for 9 holes and $55 for 18 holes. Carts are $8 per person per nine holes. Highland is open year-round, weather permitting, and club rentals are available. Annual memberships are $575.

i Cape Cod has more than 120,000 yards of public golf courses—about 68 miles. That's like golfing from the Cape Cod Canal to the tip of Provincetown.

OCEAN EDGE GOLF CLUB
Route 6A, Brewster
(774) 323-6200
www.oceanedge.com
Ocean Edge was recently renovated by Nicklaus Design Group and now has a longer course, rebuilt tees and bunkers, reshaped fairways, and new greens in compliance with USGA specifications. Ocean Edge takes reservations a week in advance. The spectacular Ocean Edge Resort (see our Hotels, Motels, and Resorts chapter), which spans both the north and south sides of Route 6A in Brewster, features a driving range, two putting greens, and a fully stocked pro shop. Although the course is open to the public, resort guests receive preferred tee times. Greens fees are $115 on weekdays and $145 on weekends May through June; $90 on weekdays and $110 on weekends during the off-season. Their on-site golf academy is a great way to stay here and learn to play.

SPORTS AND RECREATION

Some visitors are surprised by the caliber of sports they find on Cape Cod. Yet Cape Cod is well known for its baseball, road races, golf, and even soccer. If baseball is your game, then you'll have plenty to watch with the Cape Cod Baseball League, probably the best non-professional baseball league in the country, playing nightly from mid-June to mid-August. The Falmouth Road Race, along with other top-notch road races, attracts runners from around the world, and the Cape Cod Crusaders bring soccer to the peninsula throughout the summer. In this chapter we have listed some of the major spectator sports events in the area. For exact schedules and dates, check the sports section of the *Cape Cod Times*.

If you're in the mood to play yourself rather than watch someone else, there is a list of locations where you can ride a horse, ice-skate, or skateboard. If you're up for a game of tennis or bowling, we'll point you in the right direction. And if you'd just like to work out, there's a list of fitness centers too. For those of you who prefer to play in the ocean or spend your time on the links, we offer separate chapters on Boating and Water Sports and on Golf.

SPECTATOR SPORTS

Baseball

CAPE COD BASEBALL LEAGUE
449 Braggs Lane, Barnstable Village
(508) 432-6909
www.capecodbaseball.org

Often referred to as a college all-star league, the Cape Cod Baseball League delivers a quality of baseball that will satisfy the most demanding fan. Among the major league players who have graced our fields are Mo Vaughn, who played for the Wareham Gatemen; Jeff Bagwell, who was voted Most Valuable in the National League in 1994 and once played for the Chatham A's; Frank "the Big Hurt" Thomas, who played for the Orleans Cardinals (now the Firebirds after a dustup with Major League Baseball officials over naming rights); and Nomar Garciaparra, who also played for the Cardinals and lit up local baseball diamonds before heading up to Boston.

Like much else on the Cape, the Cape Cod Baseball League is historic. The first game was played about 100 years ago between Barnstable and Sandwich. True baseball purists will appreciate the fact that the league only allows use of wooden bats. Imagine the late-afternoon summer sunlight filtering across the ball field, casting players' shadows upon the grass of the outfield. Here spectators fill wooden benches or throw down blankets on the side of a hill. You can buy a jumbo hot dog with heaps of mustard for the price a hot dog should be. You see future big leaguers play the game with the same enthusiasm, not to mention salary, of little leaguers. The quality of baseball is as good as you will find in many professional ballparks. In fact, on any given night, there probably is a professional scout in the crowd looking to spot the next superstar.

Some 300 ballplayers from colleges and universities across the country are recruited each year to play on the 10 teams of the Cape league. They are hosted by local families, who often enjoy following the career of a young player who ate breakfast at their house for the summer and then made it into the major leagues. It's not all play for the players though. Being able to play in the Cape Cod League does carry some additional responsibilities. Each June, before our public schools let out for the summer, players visit classrooms to talk to the kids and build team support, in some cases creating bonds that will never be forgotten. The Cape Cod Baseball League also sponsors baseball clinics each summer for aspiring youngsters.

The Cape League season runs from mid-June to mid-August. Each team plays a 44-game schedule or 220 games across the Cape each summer. An all-star game is held in mid- to late July, and playoffs are held around the second week of August.

You'll find games at Clem Spillane Field in Wareham, Upper Cape Tech Field in Bourne, Guv Fuller Field in Falmouth, Lowell Park in Cotuit, McKeon Field in Hyannis, Red Wilson Field at the Dennis-Yarmouth Regional High School in South Yarmouth, Stony Brook School in Brewster, Whitehouse Field at Harwich High School, Veterans Field in Chatham, and Eldredge Park in Orleans. Games are typically held at 1, 5, and 7 p.m. Printed schedules are available in many local stores and newspapers.

The Bourne Braves and Brewster Whitecaps joined the league in 1988. At that time it was decided to split the 10 teams into two divisions, East and West, thus setting the stage for playoffs at the end of the season. The top two teams in each division face off, with the winners going to the dramatic best-of-three championship series.

Many of the fields, if not all, offer concession stands, but no one will complain if you pack a meal and make a picnic out of it. Because the league's 10 fields are within a 50-mile radius of each other, it is possible to visit all of them throughout a summer. Admission is far more in keeping with the spirit of the sport than at pro ballparks: Donations are accepted, and a hat is passed during the game. So find a seat on the hillside, and let the cool summer evening settle in around you. As you watch a Cape Cod Baseball League game, you will remember something you had perhaps forgotten: pure sport.

SENIOR BABE RUTH LEAGUE
Cape-wide
www.capecodbaberuth.com
Other baseball events, such as the Senior Babe Ruth League featuring 16-through-19-year-olds, are also on tap Cape-wide. Games are played during June and July at many fields across the Cape

with playoffs held in mid-July. Here's a chance to perhaps see some future members of the Cape Cod Baseball League.

RUNNING

In running circles around the world, the word "Falmouth" means one thing: one of the best non-marathon events anywhere. Cape Cod plays host to many other races as well. Johnny Kelley has attached his name to an annual road race in Hyannis. The Cape Cod Marathon is a qualifying event for the Boston Marathon. And then there's that special kind of race that involves running—and more. The New England Triathlon Series Sprint Race, starting in Centerville's Craigville Beach, puts its participants in Nantucket Sound first. After swimming the first leg of the triathlon, participants bike through the public roads of this Mid-Cape community, then finally run back to Craigville Beach.

We begin with a detailed look at our most famous race, then give listings for annual road races across the Cape. Finally, we take a look at other kinds of races—biathlon, triathlon, and walking races.

FALMOUTH ROAD RACE
Falmouth
(508) 540-7000
www.falmouthRd.race.com
For those who run or who like to watch other people run, Falmouth is a mecca. The streets here are etched with the race's proud history, and we don't only mean the start and finish lines painted on the asphalt or the mile markers that follow the flow of footfalls. Even in the chill of winter, you cannot escape the drama of the race as you walk or drive the fabled route. With the heat of August come the runners and the crowds to cheer them on.

Considered one of the country's best non-marathons, the Falmouth Road Race began in 1973. Today the world-class annual event, which is held on the third Sunday in Aug, attracts more than 9,500 runners from around the world to challenge its demanding 7.1-mile course. Some great names in marathon running who have competed here include Alberto Salazar (he won this race in 1981 and 1982); U.S. gold medalist Frank Shorter; four-time winner of the Boston and New York marathons Bill Rodgers; and U.S. gold medalist Joan Benoit Samuelson. Others of note include Grete Waitz, Lorraine Moller, and Lynn Jennings.

Of course, the thing that sets Falmouth apart from other road races is the incredible Cape Cod scenery, from the course's Woods Hole start to its Falmouth Heights finish. Between those two points, runners pass the refreshing waters of Vineyard Sound and the stoic white column of Nobska Light. The race attracts some 70,000 spectators who line the streets.

If you wish to attend the event, we strongly advise that you make your accommodations reservations well in advance. If you are interested in participating in the Falmouth Road Race, call the number above or send a business-size SASE to Box 732, Falmouth, MA 02541. Applications must be received in the race office by May 15. Accepted runners are determined by lottery. Organizers strongly discourage unregistered runners.

i Even if you don't run yourself or enjoy watching others, you might want to check the schedule of road races anyway. As many cross the major traffic routes of the Cape, you may encounter a nasty traffic jam if you happen to be out on the day of a major race.

Marathons and Other Footraces
Upper Cape
ANNUAL DENNIS ROAD RACE
Dennis
(508) 760-6162
www.town.dennis.ma.us
Three hundred runners compete in this 5-mile road race. Held in late July or early Aug, it begins at Wixon Middle School on Route 134 and winds through Dennis, utilizing the bike path when possible. The entry fee is $15, but $20 on race day. Walkers and wheelchairs are welcome.

CAPE COD MARATHON
Falmouth
(508) 540-6959
www.capecodmarathon.com
In late Oct, the Cape Cod Marathon attracts about 1,200 participants. It is a Boston Marathon–qualifying event and also includes a team relay event. It begins and ends at the Falmouth Village Green and is sponsored by the Falmouth Track Club. Part of the race traces the Falmouth Road Race course. The men's and women's winners each receive $1,500.

CENTERVILLE OLD HOME WEEK 5K ROAD RACE AND WALKATHON
Centerville
(508) 771-0650
This 3-mile race starts at the Centerville Elementary School and finishes at Covell Beach along Craigville Beach Road to the east of Craigville Beach. It usually takes place the second or third week of Aug. More than 150 contestants participate in age groups ranging from 13 and younger to 69. A kids' race and a 3-mile walkathon are also encompassed in the event.

FALMOUTH MAIN STREET MILE
Falmouth
www.falmouthtrackclub.org
Sponsored by the Falmouth Track Club, this 1-mile race always takes place on the Sunday after Labor Day. The emphasis here is more on fun than competition.

HYANNIS MARATHON, HALF MARATHON, 10K, RELAY
Resort and Conference Center at Hyannis
(617) 625-2140
www.hyannismarathon.com
This event, usually held in late Feb, starts and finishes at the Four Points by Sheraton-Hyannis Resort Hotel. Some 300 marathoners, 1,500 half marathoners, 500 10Kers, and 50 relay teams wend their way along a scenic course that passes Craigville Beach, Hyannis Harbor, Lewis Bay, the John F. Kennedy Memorial, and the Kennedy Family Compound. The marathon is a Boston Marathon–qualifying event.

JOHNNY KELLEY ROAD RACE
Hyannis
(617) 625-2140
www.greathyannisRd.races.com
This late July race is for competitive and recreational runners. It's named for the recently deceased legend who ran more Boston Marathons than anyone: Johnny Kelley, Runner's World's "Runner of the Century." Choose the 5K course, or run the double loop for the 10K distance. Both are certified by the USATF. More than 100 awards are given, including those presented to the top three runners overall in male and female divisions in both distances and to the top three runners in the seven age divisions.

PAUL E. WHITE MEMORIAL ROAD RACE
North Falmouth
www.paulwhiteRd.race.org
Held annually in July since 1977, this 5K road race takes place in lovely North Falmouth. Wheelchairs are welcome, but no walkers, please.

Lower Cape
ANNUAL BREW RUN
Brewster
(508) 896-6574
The Brew Run is a great warm-up for the Falmouth Road Race, for both runners and spectators. The 5.2-mile race is sponsored by the Woodshed Bar/Brewster Chowder House to benefit the Brewster Fire and Rescue Department. The race is followed by an awards and raffle party at the Woodshed. To register send a SASE to the Woodshed, Box 967, Brewster, MA 02631. It is held the second Saturday in Aug.

IRISH PUB ROAD RACE
West Harwich
(508) 432-8808
www.capecodsirishpub.com
Sponsored by the Irish Pub in West Harwich, this annual 5.25-mile road race, begun in 1976, takes place the first Saturday in Aug to raise money for the Harwich Ambulance Fund. It begins and ends at the Irish Pub on Route 28, West Harwich, where a post-race party is held with an awards

ceremony and live entertainment. The entry fee is $15; $20 on race day.

TRIATHLONS, BIATHLONS, AND WALKATHONS

Upper Cape

NETT–FALMOUTH SPRINT
Falmouth
(508) 224-3601
www.timeoutproductions.com
The annual Falmouth Sprint, staged alongside Vineyard Sound and run through Falmouth Heights, is a 33-mile swim, 9-mile bike, and 3.1-mile run. The first 4 miles of the bike stage hug the ocean, and the 3.1-mile run takes you along the prestigious Falmouth Road Race course. The event, part of the New England Triathlon Tour, takes place in late July. The entry fee is $50 for ages 17 and under and $75 for pros and those older than 18.

UNITED STATES COAST GUARD AIR STATION DUATHLON
Massachusetts Military Reservation
(508) 434-0123
www.firm-racing.com
Held at Camp Edwards Recreational Center, Massachusetts Military Reservation over Memorial Day weekend, this race features a 2-mile run, 12-mile bike race, and another 2-mile run.

Mid-Cape

NETT–HYANNIS SPRINT I AND II
Centerville/Osterville
(508) 224-3601
www.timeoutproductions.com
Start the season fast at Cape Cod's longest-established triathlon in early June. Staged from beautiful Craigville Beach, this is the ideal race for athletes of every ability. It begins with a 0.25-mile ocean swim in Nantucket Sound, continues as a scenic 10-mile bike loop through Centerville and Osterville, and ends with a 3.5-mile run through the quiet neighborhoods of Centerville Village. Sprint I is held in mid-June, and Sprint II takes

place in early Sept. The entry fee is $50 for those ages 10 to 17; the pro fee is $65; it's also $65 for those older than 18.

SOCCER

CAPE COD CRUSADERS
349 Main St., Hyannis
(781) 891-7900
www.mpsbr.com

Soccer has come to Cape Cod with the Cape Cod Crusaders. All home games are played at Barnstable High School. Game time is 6:15 p.m. The Crusaders, who compete in the Premier Development League, considered the top amateur league in the country, won back-to-back PDL championships in 2002 and 2003.

Players come from as far away as Ireland and England, and others hail from nearby New England colleges. Games can draw as many as 2,000 spectators. Ticket prices are $8 for adults and $5 for children younger than 12. Tickets are sold in packages if you know that you will be attending three or more games during the season. Call for ticket and schedule information.

CAPE COD SENIOR SOFTBALL CLASSIC
Eastham
(508) 255-8206
www.capecodconnection.com/oldtimers/
index.php

For a special treat, check out the Cape Cod Old Timers League in the Mid- and Lower Cape towns. The season runs from late May to the Tuesday before Labor Day. The league wraps up with the annual Cape Cod Senior Softball Classic, a three-day tournament in early Sept. This event features surprisingly entertaining softball from players 55 years and older. Teams come from as far away as Connecticut and New Hampshire, and there are divisions for 65 and 70-plus.

TENNIS

As with golf, it is impossible to list all the Cape's tennis tournaments. It is estimated that the Cape's many private and public tennis courts hold in excess of 100 tournaments, 30 of which are played at Mid-Cape Racquet Club in South Yarmouth. Imagine the number of serves we're talking about! Below is a sampling of the events.

Mid-Cape

CAPE COD COMMUNITY COLLEGE OPEN
Cape Cod Community College, Route 132,
West Barnstable
(508) 375-4015
www.ccccfoundation.org

Held over a two-week period in early July, this tennis tournament at the college features men's and women's singles and doubles matches. Junior and adult divisions are based on age, not experience. Matches typically take place between Wed and Sun over the two-week period.

MID-CAPE OPEN
Mid-Cape Racquet Club, 193 Whites Path,
South Yarmouth
(508) 394-3511
www.midcaperacquet.com

These matches take place over a two-week period in late July and early Aug at various locations around the Cape and feature singles, doubles, and mixed doubles. Semifinals and finals are held at the Mid-Cape Racquet Club. The Open is great fun for competitive as well as club players. There are divisions for all ages and skill levels.

Lower Cape

LOWER CAPE OPEN
Eldredge Park, Orleans
(508) 240-3785

In this Aug tournament, players younger than 11 to older than 70 battle it out in junior, men's, women's, and seniors' divisions at Willy's Gym in Orleans and on private courts located throughout Orleans. Highly competitive tennis buffs come from all over New England representing college level through ranked adults. There are singles and doubles (men's, ladies', and mixed) competitions.

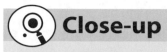 **Close-up**

Public Tennis Courts

If you're looking to hit a ball and just get some exercise, the Cape has many public town courts located in parks and on school grounds. Some of are available on a first-come, first-served basis, and some require reservation. Phone numbers are listed so you can call ahead to determine when the courts are open.

UPPER CAPE

Bell Tower Field
Bell Tower Lane, Woods Hole
(508) 457-2567

Bourne High School
75 Waterhouse Rd., Bourne
(508) 759-0670

Bourne Memorial Community Building
Main Street, Buzzards Bay
(508) 759-0650

Bourne Town Hall Park
Perry Avenue, Buzzards Bay
(508) 759-0621

Chester Park
Monument and Arthur Avenues,
Monument Beach
(508) 743-3003

Clark Field
Clark Road, North Sagamore
(508) 759-0600

East Falmouth Elementary School
33 Davisville Rd., East Falmouth
(508) 548-1052

Falmouth High School
Gifford Street Extension, Falmouth
(508) 540-2200

Forestdale Elementary School/Henry T. Wing School
Route 130, Sandwich
(508) 888-4361

Lawrence School
113 Lakeview Ave., Falmouth
(508) 548-0606

Mashpee Middle School/K.C. Coombs
Elementary School
150 Old Barnstable Road, Mashpee
(508) 539-3600

Nye Park
County Road, North Falmouth
(508) 457-2567

Oak Ridge Elementary School
Quaker Meeting House Road, Sandwich
(508) 888-4900

Sandwich High School
Quaker Meeting House Road, Sandwich
(508) 888-4900

West Falmouth Park
Blacksmith Shop Road, West Falmouth
(508) 457-2567

MID-CAPE

Barnstable Middle School
895 Falmouth Rd. (Route 28), Hyannis
(508) 790-6460

Barnstable-West Barnstable Elementary School
Route 6A, Barnstable
(508) 790-6345

Centerville Elementary School
Bay Lane, Centerville
(508) 790-9890

Dennis-Yarmouth Regional High School
Station Avenue, South Yarmouth
(508) 398-7630

Nathaniel Wixon Middle School
Route 134, South Dennis
(508) 398-7695

Osterville Bay School
West Bay Road, Osterville
(508) 428-8538

LOWER CAPE

Brewster—
four courts are behind the Brewster Police
Department, near the Old Town Hall on
Route 6A, Brewster
(508) 896-9430

Brooks Park
Route 39 and Oak Street, Harwich
(508) 430-7553

continued

Cape Cod Regional Technical High School
Route 124, Harwich
(508) 432-4500

Chatham High School
Crowell Road, Chatham
(508) 945-5175

Depot Road near the Railroad Museum
Chatham
(508) 945-5175

Eldredge Park
Route 28 and Eldredge Parkway, Orleans
(508) 240-3785

Kitty Lane
South Chatham
(508) 945-5175

Mayo Beach
Kendrick Street, Wellfleet
(508) 349-0330

Motta Field
near the Pilgrim Monument, Provincetown
(508) 487-7097

Nauset Regional High School
Cable Road, Eastham (Courts are available
only from late June to Labor Day for a small
fee.)
(508) 255-1505

Prince Street
near the high school, Provincetown
(508) 487-7097

PROVINCETOWN TENNIS CLUB JULY 4TH INVITATIONAL
Provincetown Tennis Club, Bradford St.,
Provincetown
(508) 487-9574

Started more than 20 years ago as a tournament for local year-rounders, the tournament has expanded to include seasonal residents as well as players from outside Provincetown. The fun begins in mid-June with men's and women's singles, doubles, and mixed doubles, culminating in the finals held on the July 4 weekend.

RECREATION

When you've had your fill of competing or watching the pros compete and want to get out there and practice some of those techniques you've admired—or maybe just get some exercise—you'll need to know where you can practice your sport of choice. Turn to our Boating and Water Sports chapter if you have the beach in mind, or to Golf if you're looking for a challenging (or easy) course. Here we provide information on bowling, horseback riding, indoor swimming, ice-skating, tennis, and fitness clubs.

Bowling

Sometimes you just get the urge to bowl a few strings. The Cape can accommodate you with a number of alleys.

Upper Cape

LEARY FAMILY AMUSEMENTS
23 Town Hall Sq., Falmouth
(508) 540-4877
www.learyfamilyamusements.com

Falmouth has plenty of fun spots to explore, and the Leary Family Amusements Center is one of them. It offers good candlepin bowling alleys for leagues as well as for nonleague recreational bowlers. There is a pro shop on-site, and the facility hosts birthday parties.

RYAN FAMILY AMUSEMENTS
200 Main St., Buzzards Bay
(508) 759-9892
www.ryanfamily.com

This popular Upper Cape facility has candlepin bowling, a pro shop, and a game room. Ryan hosts leagues as well as good old recreational bowling and offers birthday party packages.

TRADE CENTER BOWL & AMUSEMENTS
89 Spring Bars Rd., Falmouth
(508) 548-7000

This bowling facility features tenpin with computer scoring. There are leagues for children and high school students as well as moonlight bowling and odyssey bowling where a light show adds to the challenges of the sport. Also on premises are pool tables, video games, a pro shop, and a snack bar.

Mid-Cape
RYAN FAMILY AMUSEMENTS
441 Main St., Hyannis
(508) 775-3411

Ryan Family Amusements' downtown Hyannis location features tenpin, candlepin, and bumper bowling and hosts "Mystic Bowling" parties on Fri and Sat nights.

RYAN FAMILY AMUSEMENTS
Route 28, South Yarmouth
(508) 394-5644

A very busy recreational hotspot, this Ryan Family Amusements Center has both tenpin and candlepin lanes, a pro shop, and a game room. This facility also hosts leagues and birthday parties.

Lower Cape
ORLEANS BOWLING CENTER
Route 6A, Orleans
(508) 255-0636

With 14 lanes, this is an all-candlepin bowling center. Even during league events, there are lanes available for the public. Weekend nights are popular for families.

Horseback Riding

The Cape has a number of good stables for boarding, riding lessons, and trail rides. We will point out that beach riding has been restricted on most of our beaches over the last few years. The Cape Cod National Seashore and Sandy Neck Beach have both decided not to allow riding horses on the beach.

Upper Cape
HALAND STABLES
Route 28A, West Falmouth
(508) 540-2552
www.falmouthvisitor.com/haland_stable
.htm

Located in West Falmouth, Haland Stables provides a guided trail ride through pine woods and cranberry bogs. Only walking and trotting are allowed on the trails, and all riding is English style. Appointments are required, and both private and group lessons are offered.

MAUSHOP EQUESTRIAN CENTER
31 Quashnet Rd., Mashpee
(508) 477-1303
www.maushopequestriancenter.net

Mashpee's Maushop Equestrian Center focuses on riding lessons but will conduct trail rides by appointment. It also offers boarding services, a summer camp, and an indoor arena. Call for rates.

Mid-Cape
HOLLY HILL FARM
240 Flint St., Martsons Mills
(508) 428-2621
www.hollyhillstable.com

Holly Hill offers lessons running from $80 to $100 per hour. This Marstons Mills establishment is a show stable of hunters and jumpers and provides such services as boarding and training. There are no trails on-site.

Lower Cape
MOBY DICK FARM
179 Great Fields Rd., Brewster
(508) 896-3544

This friendly, year-round equestrian center offers instruction and the opportunity to clip-clop through the miles of trails in the wooded Punkhorn Parklands. The staff is specially trained to handle beginners, and the horses here are reliable, steady types. For seasonal fun ask about hayrides, sleigh rides, and carriage rides. On a leisurely trail ride, you'll learn a lot about the natural history of the area and come back to the stable as refreshed and invigorated as only a good trail ride can leave you.

NICKERSON STATE PARK
Route 6A, Brewster
(508) 896-3491
The park has one marked bridle trail and a network of other trails. There is no fee to ride.

PUNKHORN PARKLANDS
Run Hill Rd., Brewster
(508) 896-3701
This maze of scenic trails lends itself perfectly to horseback riding, and there's no charge to ride here. Many of the trails are ancient cart paths still wide enough to ride two abreast, so you can chat with your riding buddies.

Ice-Skating and Hockey

Most people don't associate Cape Cod with ice-skating, yet the Cape is a hot spot on ice. Perennial state high school hockey powers, Cape high school teams have won the state championship at the Fleet Center in Boston (where the Bruins play) and practice at area rinks. Todd Eldredge, a world champion men's figure skater, hails from Chatham, and Olympic medalists Nancy Kerrigan and Paul Wylie have both trained at the Tony Kent Arena in South Dennis. Rentals are available at most rinks. Because times for public skating change frequently, your best bet is to call ahead for hours. Below are some of the Cape's rinks.

Upper Cape
FALMOUTH ICE ARENA
9 Skating Lane, Falmouth
(508) 548-7080
www.falmouthicearena.com
Ice-skating is offered on an 85-by-185-foot rink and includes youth and adult ice-hockey programs, figure-skating programs, and public skating. A pro shop and snack bar are on-site. It is open to the public on weekdays, June through Sept, and on select days from Sept through Apr.

JOHN GALLO ICE ARENA
231 Sandwich Rd., Bourne
(508) 759-8904
www.galloarena.com
Located along the Cape Cod Canal, the Gallo Ice Arena plays host to hockey schools, camps, and clinics, as well as figure-skating camps and public skating. There is a pro shop on-site. The arena is open year-round with free skating Sept to June. There is no free skating during the summer months due to camps and league play.

Mid-Cape
HYANNIS YOUTH AND COMMUNITY CENTER
141 Bassett Lane, Hyannis
(508) 790-6345
www.hyannisyouth.org
Slated to open in the fall of 2009, this facility replaces the now-demolished Joseph P. Kennedy Memorial Skating Park. The new facility will have two ice-skating rinks, a teen center, and a walking track. The $25 million building will also have a basketball court and is close to outdoor basketball courts, ball fields, and the town's skateboard park. A semipro hockey team is expected to play at the new center.

TONY KENT ARENA
8 South Gages Way, South Dennis
(508) 760–2415
www.tonykentarena.com
Olympians Nancy Kerrigan and Paul Wylie have both practiced and performed here. The rink, off Route 134, is home to Dennis-Yarmouth youth hockey as well as figure skating and learn-to-skate programs. The rink also offers a seasonally changing schedule of public skating. Go online or call for a schedule.

Lower Cape
CHARLES MOORE ARENA
23 O'Connor Way, Orleans
(508) 255-5902
www.charlesmoorearena.org
This arena offers ice-skating year-round. Rentals are available, and there is a snack bar.

Indoor Swimming and Fitness Clubs

Most hotels and motels have a pool or two. The resorts around the Cape normally have a couple. And a number of health and fitness clubs also offer indoor swimming facilities. In fact, indoor pools are an excellent resource for those who want instruction, physical therapy, and aerobic exercise as well as an opportunity to continue their favorite form of exercise all year.

Of course the Cape's health and fitness clubs offer more than just the opportunity to swim. You can continue your exercise routine at a club while you're on vacation or visit one for a round of racquetball. Fees and access to facilities vary, but generally fitness centers are open all year.

Upper Cape
BALANCED HEALTH AND FITNESS
133 East Falmouth Hwy., East Falmouth
(508) 540-8896
www.balancedhealthfitness.com
Balanced Health and Fitness Inc. has a StairMaster, treadmill, and NordicTrack equipment and offers body sculpting and core training, Pilates and yoga, Latin dance, and assorted aerobics classes. Monthly memberships are available.

FALMOUTH SPORTS CENTER HEALTH CLUB
33 Highfield Dr., Falmouth
(508) 548-7433
www.falmouthvisitor.com/Falmouth_Sports_Center.htm
The Falmouth Sports Center Health Club offers Nautilus, free weights, and cardiovascular equipment. The club also has a physical therapy department. Daily passes and monthly memberships are available.

MASSACHUSETTS MARITIME ACADEMY
Taylor's Point, Buzzards Bay
(508) 564-5690
www.capecodswimclub.com
Massachusetts Maritime Academy has beginner swimming lessons, lap swimming, competitive swimming, a masters group, and water polo for all ages. And a big plus: Their pool has a giant waterslide.

RMA NAUTILUS RACQUETBALL & FITNESS CENTER
130 MacArthur Blvd., Bourne
(508) 759-7111
www.rmafitness.com
This club has a full complement of Nautilus equipment and free weights plus cardiovascular equipment and racquetball courts. Soothe those aching muscles in the sauna, spa, and steam rooms.

SANDWICH HIGH SCHOOL–SANDWICH COMMUNITY SCHOOL
365 Quaker Meeting House Rd.,
East Sandwich
(508) 888-5300
The Sandwich Community School coordinates public use of the constantly busy Sandwich High School swimming pool. The pool offers lessons, family and lap swims, water aerobics, and a masters program for those interested in improving their water lifesaving skills.

SPORTSITE HEALTH & RACQUETBALL CLUB
315 Cotuit Rd., Sandwich
(508) 888-7900
www.sportssitehealthclub.com
Sportsite offers classes in aerobics, spinning, and body shaping, and has Nautilus and cardiovascular equipment. Children's programs, personal training, and child care are other features here.

WILLY'S WEST WOMAN'S WORKOUT COMPANY
865 Attucks Lane, Hyannis
(508) 771-1600
www.willysgym.com
Willy's West Woman's Workout Company offers a variety of creative alternatives to help members achieve their fitness goals with cross-training workouts. They offer more than 100 aerobics classes per week, a full cardiovascular room, swimming lessons, full dance programs, and a Nautilus and free-weight room. The center also offers babysitting, tanning, a hot tub, steam room, and a beauty shop.

Mid-Cape

MID-CAPE RACQUET & HEALTH CLUB

193 White's Path, South Yarmouth

(508) 394-3511

www.midcaperacquet.com

Mid-Cape is a complete fitness center with Nautilus and free weights and a personal training program. After your workout enjoy the sauna, steam room, and whirlpool. Daily passes are available. The club is a popular choice for Pilates, yoga, and spinning classes. Mid-Cape Racquet Club is open daily year-round.

YMCA

2245 Rte. 132, West Barnstable

(508) 362-6500, (800) 339–9622

www.ymcacapecod.org

The Cape's only YMCA has water exercise, water jogging, lap swimming, and lessons as well as special fitness programs for seniors. The club also has fitness equipment, saunas, and aerobics classes. Three-month memberships are available.

Lower Cape

MUSSEL BEACH HEALTH CLUB

35 Bradford St., Provincetown

(508) 487-0001

www.musselbeach.net

This popular, coed fitness club offers cardio equipment—including rowing machines, treadmills, elliptical trainers, and stair climbers—step aerobics, yoga classes, dry saunas, showers, and free parking. Nonmembers can come and use all the facilities for daily, weekly, and monthly memberships.

PROVINCETOWN GYM

81 Shank Painter Rd., 145 Commercial St. (nutrition outlet), Provincetown

(508) 487-2776

www.ptowngym.com

This club features complete free weights and cardiovascular equipment, classes, and some of the best trainers around. Nonmembers are welcome for a daily or monthly fee.

WILLY'S GYM

21 Old Colony Way, Orleans

(508) 255-6826

4730 U.S. Rte. 6, Eastham

(508) 255-6370

www.willysgym.com

This well-established fitness facility offers a full slate of cardiovascular and toning equipment and an ever-expanding free-weight area. Willy's also offers an encyclopedic menu of classes such as spinning, step aerobics, dance, martial arts, kickboxing, and yoga. There are complete spa facilities, and child care is available. Guests can pay for a daily or weekly membership.

Willy's second location offers Nautilus and Cybex equipment, a 25-yard indoor swimming pool, racquetball and squash courts, six indoor asphalt tennis courts, a basketball court, and spa. Martial arts, aerobics, and yoga are among their class offerings. It also has a 30-foot climbing wall. Clinics offered for both members and nonmembers.

Tennis Clubs

This section lists tennis clubs whose facilities are open to the general public. These facilities can offer you more than just a place to play. There are pro shops, snack bars, racquet repair, instruction, and league play.

Upper Cape

FALMOUTH SPORTS CENTER

33 Highland Dr., Falmouth

(508) 548-7433

www.falmouthvisitor.com/Falmouth_Sports_Center.htm

Open daily, the Falmouth Sports Center has nine hard courts, six indoor and three outdoor. Membership is not required to play. The facility offers leagues, a pro shop, and a ball machine for rent by the hour.

SOUTHCAPE RESORT

50 Falmouth Rd., Mashpee

(508) 477-4700

www.southcaperesort.com

For an hourly fee, you can play on any one of their three hard outdoor and two indoor clay courts. The Southcape Resort is open year-round.

Mid-Cape

KINGS GRANT RACQUET CLUB

Main Street, Cotuit

(508) 428-5744

www.kingsgrantrc.com

An expert professional staff maintains the six clay courts and one hard court. This club, which offers a pro shop and clinics, is open seasonally from early May through Columbus Day.

MID-CAPE RACQUET AND HEALTH CLUB

193 White's Path, South Yarmouth

(508) 394-3511

www.midcaperacquet.com

Centrally located on Cape Cod in South Yarmouth, the Mid-Cape Racquet and Health Club is easily accessed off the Mid-Cape Highway (US 6). If you are looking for a game, the Mid-Cape offers nine well-lit hard indoor courts. Mid-Cape has a pro shop, and racquet stringing is available through their professional staff.

SESUIT TENNIS CENTER

1389 Rte. 6A, Dennis

(508) 385-2200

www.sesuittennis.com

Encompassing two locations (Sesuit Creek and Signal Hill) and a tennis specialty shop, this is the place where the locals get their racquets strung. Seven Har-Tru clay outdoor courts offer fine

league play or instruction, and the staff will find you a match if you are looking for new competition while visiting the Cape. The courts and pro shop are open from sunrise to sunset in season.

Lower Cape

BAMBURGH HOUSE TENNIS CLUB

2022 Rte. 6A, Brewster

(508) 896-5023

Set back off Route 6A, with a small wooden sign at the entrance to the driveway, this club offers four asphalt courts that are available from sunrise to sunset. The tennis club offers court time and lessons and stringing is available.

OLIVER TENNIS COURTS

2183 U.S. Rte. 6, Wellfleet

(508) 349-3330

Clay court enthusiasts, this is your spot. Beautifully maintained red-clay courts highlight this family-owned club. Leagues, lessons, and a pro shop are all available at Oliver, which is open seven days a week, mid-May through Oct.

PROVINCETOWN TENNIS CLUB

286 Bradford St., Provincetown

(508) 487-9574

www.provincetowntennis.com

This private club offers five clay and two hard-surface courts for nonmembers. Daily and weekly memberships are available for nonmembers (in addition to court fees). Games can be arranged, and the club also restrings racquets. The club is open from May through Columbus Day.

RELOCATION

If you've often imagined yourself standing in the doorway of your own Cape or islands home, the sea gleaming in the distance, you're in good company. Thousands of prospective home-buyers pore over the real estate listings every week, hoping to find the perfect saltbox, historic sea captain's home, or contemporary beach house.

People find plenty of reasons to buy on the Cape. The temperate climate, beautiful environment, laid-back lifestyle, and congenial neighborhoods are just a few of those reasons. Odds are that if you are thinking of becoming a "wash-ashore," you already know all about these things. The chapters that follow this one also give you a more complete picture of the services available to year-rounders: Education and Child Care, Health Care, Retirement, Media, and Worship.

During the recession of 2008 and 2009, the Cape was hit hard by foreclosures and even here, in the land of ever increasing home prices, sales of homes dropped off along with prices. While the boom of a decade ago is gone, the chances are property on the Cape will remain expensive, prohibitively so for some. In the past two years, there has been a new focus on providing affordable housing for young families in the hope of keeping them from fleeing over the bridges for more affordable areas. The results of that effort have yet to be fully known.

But if you can foot the bill, there is a wide range of housing available on this desirable spit of land. Inland you'll find neighborhood communities just like those in any town across the country. Old sea captains' homes and other antiquities are available if you prefer historical dwellings. Additionally, there are streets lined with iconic, indigenous "Cape" houses: full-Cape homes, three-quarter Capes, half-Capes, and even some quarter-Capes. There are saltboxes, colonials, Greek Revival houses, and Federal dwellings; there are condominiums, second homes, investment homes, and seasonal cottages.

Be aware that a common Cape concern is that too much of its land has already been developed, to the detriment of its once-rural character. With many other towns showing double-digit growth between censuses, some towns fear that they will reach "build out" (a point at which all available land within a town is developed with residential homes) in the near future. Buildable land is finite on this sandy peninsula, so many towns have reacted by instituting growth-management measures. Barnstable, for instance, has put a cap on the number of building permits it approves each year.

An act of the state legislature formed the Cape Cod Commission, which studies land-use issues and serves as a regional planning body. Polls have affirmed that the majority of Cape residents value protecting their groundwater; encouraging only clean, light industry, cultural facilities, and neighborhood businesses; and restricting the development of new, large hotels, malls, and factory outlets. The commission tries to uphold these values as it reviews the merits of proposed projects. It's a challenge, however, to protect a fragile environment and preserve community character while also meeting the needs of an increasing population, and the commission's decisions often lead to heated debates about the changing face of the Cape. These debates have even led to major changes in the commission itself, including a reorganization over the past two years to refocus the agency on planning rather than on a strict regulatory role.

In Massachusetts, local government is funded primarily by property taxes. Historically Cape towns tended to come in below the state's average tax rate. As more people move to the peninsula, however, towns are facing the need to improve infrastructure and provide more local services, such as police, emergency services, and school facilities, by increasing tax levies and fees.

Also, the Cape is a single-source aquifer, meaning that all of its water comes from one source, and few Cape homes are connected to limited town sewer systems. Residents have recognized the seriousness of protecting their drinking water, so living on the Cape means investing in and maintaining the high standards set by state septic regulations. The condition of a home's septic system is generally the seller's responsibility. Make sure enough time is left for required inspections and any necessary repairs to be made before you close on a property.

Cape Cod towns are currently undertaking massive planning and design to deal with its wastewater as mandated by federal and state laws. The estimated costs are in the hundreds of millions of dollars. While Cape homes are required to have a septic system if they are not on a town sewer system, more towns are looking at the need for sewers and trying to figure out who is going to pay for them. Homeowners are confronting the possibility that they may have to pay for sewers even after they have spent money on expensive septic systems.

In the same vein many Cape homes have private wells, which run off electric pumps, and this adds to the monthly electric bill. Cape residents also pay a fee on their tax bills that goes into the Community Preservation Act, which is used to finance the purchase of open space for various reasons. The CPA has largely taken the place of the Land Bank, which was dedicated to the purchase of open space solely for the sake of preserving the environment. Unlike the Land Bank, the CPA can also be used for historic preservation, recreation, and affordable housing.

Besides primary homes and second homes, the Cape is also known for its rental properties. Many a future year-rounder started out on the Cape by renting a cottage during the summer. A summer rental property close to the beach can fetch $1,000 and more each week during the summer. Over the course of a 10-week season, this can add up to nearly enough to carry a mortgage on a similar property.

The **Cape Cod & Islands Association of Realtors,** 22 Mid Tech Dr. in West Yarmouth (800-442-0006, www.cciaor.com), is a good year-round source of information. For those who are interested in building or remodeling, real estate agencies generally have ample information about local builders.

Another source of information is the **Home Builders & Remodelers Association of Cape Cod,** 9 New Venture Dr. in South Dennis (508-398-3900, www.nvo.com/capecodbuilders). This association represents builders and suppliers throughout the Cape who work on new homes and remodeling projects.

The sections that follow provide you with a good range of real estate professionals available on the Cape.

REAL ESTATE AGENCIES

Upper Cape

CAPE COAST REALTY
4 Barlows Landing Rd., Suite 1, Bourne
(508) 563-3332
www.capecoastrealty.com
This year-round real estate office handles properties in Bourne, Sandwich, Falmouth, and Mashpee, and deals primarily with residential properties, many of which are waterfront.

CENTURY 21 SEASIDE VILLAGE PROPERTIES
877 Main St., Osterville
(508) 477-5200, (877) 477-5200
www.century21.com
Century 21 Regan Realtors is a large office that specializes in waterfront and golf properties from Bourne to Hyannis. The office also deals with new construction, land sales, and condominiums, as well as commercial properties. Because of its affiliation with Century 21, the Mashpee office of

Century 21 Regan Realtors is linked with listings, referrals, and relocation services and general information from 6,000 offices worldwide.

FRANCESCA PARKINSON ERMINE LOVELL REAL ESTATE
881 Palmer Ave., Falmouth
(508) 548-0711
www.francescaparkinson.com
This company deals primarily with properties in Falmouth, Woods Hole, and Pocasset and Cataumet in Bourne. Options include land, waterfront, and residential properties; the company also operates a busy summer rental business.

GREAT BAY ASSOCIATES
77 Cypress St., East Falmouth
(508) 540-3775
They specialize in water-view or near-the-water properties in the East Falmouth area, more specifically on the Maravista, Acapesket, and Davisville finger peninsulas on Little, Great, Green, and Bourne pond inlets, which border Vineyard Sound. Great Bay deals primarily with residential properties—primary homes, second homes, and investment properties, as well as land.

HARRIET DUGAN REALTY
598 Main St., Falmouth
(508) 548-4093
This company handles a full range of properties and services, including commercial land sales and leases, and waterfront property. The office, which also handles summer rentals, specializes in properties in Mashpee and Falmouth.

JACK CONWAY AND COMPANY INC., REALTOR
128 Rte. 6A, Sandwich
(508) 888-2300
www.jackconway.com
The four-decade-old Conway and Company has 45 offices from Boston and the South Shore to the Cape. It deals with residential, commercial, and investment properties and has a financial service division that works with out-of-town buyers. The office has specialists in development, sales, and project making and remodeling. The relocation service provides information and introduction to the community at no extra cost. The company has an in-house insurance company and other offices in Falmouth, Hyannis, Mashpee, and Dennis.

KINLIN GROVER GMAC REAL ESTATE
121 Rte. 6A, Sandwich
(508) 888-3333, (800) 722-0072
www.kinlingrover.com
Kinlin Grover GMAC has more than 150 sales agents plus rental agents. The company has 14 strategically located offices—from Sandwich to Provincetown. Also see the Kinlin Grover listings under Mid-Cape and Lower Cape.

TODAY REAL ESTATE
299 Cotuit Rd., Sandwich
(508) 888-8008, (800) 792-6456
www.todayrealestate.com
Today Real Estate enjoys the distinction of being one of the top locally owned real estate companies on the Cape. Besides being a full-service real estate agency with more than 90 full-time associates and four office locations (Centerville, South Yarmouth, and East Harwich being the others), it also offers its clients the services of Today Mortgage Services, a full-service mortgage brokerage. All offices are open seven days a week, year-round.

VINCENT ASSOCIATES
159 Main St., Town Hall Square, Falmouth
(508) 548-6500
www.vincentassociates.com
This real estate agency offers primarily residential land and dwellings but also deals with commercial transactions and conducts home appraisals. Most of the agency's property listings are in Falmouth, Bourne, and Mashpee, but the office does not restrict itself to sales and rentals only in this area. Vincent also offers summer rentals.

Mid-Cape

THE BUYER BROKERAGE OF OSTERVILLE
874 Main St., Osterville
(508) 420-1804, (800) 290-1804
www.osterville.com
Launched in 1994, this company acts exclusively as a buyer's broker. The five-broker Osterville office specializes in properties in the Mid-Cape area and relies heavily on a team approach.

COLDWELL BANKER/MURRAY REAL ESTATE
3880 Falmouth Rd., Marstons Mills
(508) 420-9955, (800) 254-6701
www.capecodproperty.info
Murray Real Estate has been serving the area from Falmouth to Chatham since 1974, both as an independent agency and Coldwell Banker affiliate. With the addition of an office in Harwich Port, they now offer a wide range of commercial and residential properties all over Cape Cod.

HARRISON & FUHS REALTORS
349 Rte. 28, West Yarmouth
(508) 771-7974
www.harrisonre.com
Harrison & Fuhs deal primarily with residential property in the Mid-Cape area in Barnstable, Yarmouth, and Dennis. The full-service real estate office deals with listing and selling property.

KINLIN GROVER GMAC REAL ESTATE
4 Wiano Ave., Osterville
(508) 420-1130

3321 Rte. 6A, Barnstable
(508) 362-2120, (800) 321-2120
www.kinlingrover.com
Kinlin Grover GMAC has more than 150 sales agents plus rental agents. The company has 14 strategically located offices—from Sandwich to Provincetown. See other Kinlin Grover listings in Upper Cape and Lower Cape sections.

PETER MCDOWELL ASSOCIATES
585 Rte. 6A, Dennis
(508) 385-9114, (888) 385-9114
www.capecodproperties.com

Serving the Dennis, Yarmouth, Barnstable, Brewster, and Harwich areas since 1965, Peter McDowell Associates offers many residential properties for sale in the five-town area.

REALTY EXECUTIVES
1330 Phinney's Lane, Hyannis
(508) 362-1300, (800) 244-1592
www.capecodschoice.com
A national firm, Realty Executives is generally credited with starting the concept of 100 percent commissions, a motivating factor that allows a broker to earn nearly the entire sales commission rather than splitting it with the agency. About 95 percent of calls to the office are generated by agent advertising. The Hyannis office, along with an office at 15 Cape Lane in Brewster (508–896-3200), have hundreds of listings. For regional referrals, Realty Executives has offices scattered throughout Massachusetts.

REEF REALTY LTD.
24 School St., West Dennis
(508) 394-3090, (800) 346-4059
www.reefrealty.com
This firm has won numerous local and regional sales awards. The staff of realtors handles an extensive number of sales properties, both residential and commercial, with a focus on Dennis and Yarmouth properties. Reef Realty Ltd. is also a residential custom-building company and developer with more than 100 years of combined experience.

RE/MAX CLASSIC REAL ESTATE
167 Lovells Lane, Marstons Mills
(508) 428-2300, (888) 428-2300
www.remax-classic-barnstable-ma.com
A national franchise, RE/MAX has a service approach to real estate and handles many of the details that usually fall to the client, such as scheduling the time for inspection of septic systems and smoke detectors. This office focuses on residential and commercial sales and rentals all over Cape Cod and the islands.

STEELE ASSOCIATES REAL ESTATE
1372 Rte. 134, East Dennis
(508) 385-7311
www.steelerealty.com
This full-service real estate agency has developed a specialty of handling beach-area property, particularly along the north section of Dennis. The agency also handles the sale of residential homes, condominiums, land, and commercial properties in the towns of Yarmouth, Brewster, and Harwich.

STRAWBERRY HILL REAL ESTATE
340 West Main St., Hyannis
(508) 775-8000, (800) 882-8586
www.strawberryhillre.com
This agency deals primarily with Barnstable and its villages and with the Mid-Cape area in general. They sell mostly residential real estate—single-family homes, condominiums, estate sales, and waterfront property.

TODAY REAL ESTATE
1533 Rte. 28, Centerville
(508) 790-2300, (800) 966-2448
www.todayrealestate.com
Established in 1985, this large and active real estate company has offices in Sandwich, South Yarmouth, East Harwich, and at the Centerville location listed above. Today's other Mid-Cape office is in South Yarmouth and located at 487 Station Avenue (508-398-0600 or 800-966-0369). Today boasts more than 90 full-time sales associates who specialize in residential property, both owner-occupied and investment properties. Today Real Estate also publishes and distributes its own listings catalog. The office is open seven days a week. (See the Upper and Lower Cape sections for other Today Real Estate offices.)

Lower Cape

AMERICAN HERITAGE REALTY
414 Rte. 28, South Orleans
(508) 255-2202, (800) 420-1776
www.capecodforsale.com
www.americanheritagerealty.com

American Heritage has been one of the leading real estate companies on the Lower Cape for more than 40 years. They specialize in the sale of waterfront and water-view properties in the towns of Orleans, Chatham, Harwich, Eastham, Brewster, and Wellfleet. The professional staff can also assist you with sales of vacation homes, oceanfront properties, condos, and land.

CHEQUESSETT VILLAGE REAL ESTATE
3 West Main St., Wellfleet
(508) 349-3411, (800) 334-0909
www.chequessettvillagerealestate.com
Known as one of the first real estate offices in Wellfleet (and the oldest surviving one in town), Chequessett Village has been privately owned and operated for more than 50 years. It handles Wellfleet properties, commercial and residential, in all price ranges.

COLDWELL BANKER/MURRAY REAL ESTATE
490 Rte. 28, Harwich Port
(508) 432-6600, (800) 775-9980
www.capecodproperty.info
Murray Real Estate has been serving the towns from Falmouth to Chatham since 1974, both as an independent agency and the Coldwell Banker affiliate. The company's listings encompass a wide range of residential and commercial properties, with a focus on the Harwich area.

DUARTE/DOWNEY REAL ESTATE AGENCY
12 Truro Center Rd., Truro
(508) 349-7588
www.ddre.com
This Truro real estate agency first opened its doors for business in 1937. A full-service brokerage with three Realtors, Duarte/Downey offers residential properties, including single-family homes, cottages, and condominiums, in its primary market area of Truro and Wellfleet. The agency also features waterfront homes and land as well as rentals in the Truro area.

GREAT LOCATIONS REAL ESTATE
2660 Rte. 6A, Brewster
(800) 626-9984
www.greatlocationsre.com

This full-service real estate office specializes in vacation homes, golf course properties, and retirement properties in the Brewster, Dennis, and Orleans areas and represents the Ocean Edge Resort properties. Great Locations Real Estate offers expert property management and rental management on the properties it sells, which range from beautiful condominiums to elegant waterfront homes.

HARBORSIDE REALTY
154 Commercial St., Provincetown
(508) 487-4005, (800) 838-4005
www.harborside-realty.com
This agency handles sales and rental properties in Provincetown—from residential homes and condominiums to guesthouses and commercial properties.

KINLIN GROVER GMAC REAL ESTATE
1990 Main St. (Route 6A), Brewster
(508) 896-7000, (888) 316-8533

2548 U.S. Rte. 6, Wellfleet
(508) 349-9800, (888) 349-8800
www.kinlingrover.com
Kinlin Grover GMAC has more than 150 sales agents plus rental agents. The company has 14 strategically located offices—from Sandwich to Provincetown. See other listings for Kinlin Grover in the Upper and Mid-Cape sections.

OUTER CAPE REALTY
5150 U.S. Rte. 6, North Eastham
(508) 255-0505
www.outercaperealty.com
The oldest real estate company in Eastham, Outer Cape was established in 1956. This office features a friendly staff of eight realtors who offer single-family homes, cottages, and beautiful waterfront homes in the Eastham, North Eastham, and Wellfleet area.

i Most homes on the Cape have septic systems. If you're thinking of buying here, you should know that state regulations require the seller to inspect the system and repair or replace it if necessary as part of the sale.

PINE ACRES REALTY
938 Main St. and 509 Main St., Chatham
(508) 945-1186, (508) 945-9450
www.pineacresrealty.com
This company has many exclusive properties along Chatham's waterfront as well as in the towns of Harwich and Orleans. It is an affiliate of Christie's Great Estates, which is a high-end referral network. They also offer rentals.

THE REAL ESTATE COMPANY
207 Main St., East Orleans
(508) 255-5100
www.capecodhomefinder.com
Located on the road to Nauset Beach in East Orleans, the Real Estate Company lays claim to the largest independent real estate agency on the Lower Cape. They also have offices in Chatham and North Eastham and are affiliated with The Rental Company and The Building Company, which focus on—wait for it—rentals and building.

TODAY REAL ESTATE
160 Rte. 137, East Harwich
(508) 430-8288
www.todayrealestate.com
Established in 1985, this large and active real estate company has other offices in Sandwich, South Yarmouth, and Centerville. Today's 90-plus sales associates handle both residential and investment properties from the Cape Cod Canal to the Lower Cape. The office is open seven days a week. (See other listings in the Mid-Cape and Upper Cape sections.)

TRURO REAL ESTATE
U.S. Rte. 6 at Fisherman's Rd., Truro
(508) 487-4225
www.trurorealestate.com
Chuck Leigh founded this company more than a decade ago and offers residential homes, condominiums, and cottages as well as land and commercial sale properties in its primary market area of Wellfleet, Truro, and Provincetown. Many of the properties are in and around the Cape Cod National Seashore.

EDUCATION AND CHILD CARE

Educational opportunities on the Cape abound. From Montessori preschools through colleges, the Cape matches its rich natural environment with an equal wealth of academic offerings. Excellent public schools prepare students for an academic career anywhere in the United States, including at Ivy League or top-ranked state and private colleges. Two private high schools, Cape Cod Academy and Falmouth Academy, also are known for preparing students for higher education. The technical schools here offer a well-regarded vocational education, and several colleges, including Cape Cod Community College in Barnstable offer extension courses. The arts are highly valued on the Cape, and specialized schools offer both residents and short-term visitors exciting classes in the visual arts, theater, and creative writing.

Just about every town on the Cape offers continuing education enrichment classes for adults and stimulating nondegree programs for senior citizens. Community school programs in most towns provide all ages with academic and recreational opportunities, and, befitting the region's maritime tradition, two educational programs dedicated to the sea are located here: Massachusetts Maritime Academy in Buzzards Bay and the Sea Education Association Semester (SEAS) offered at Woods Hole.

For younger learners, there are a number of preschool and child care centers available. We'll begin with a rundown of the Cape's public schools, then move on to private schools, preschools, and child care centers. We'll outline here how many schools and students each town has, but enrollments in many Cape schools have declined sharply in recent years and could continue to do so. For the most detailed, up-to-date information go to the Massachusetts Department of Elementary and Secondary Education's Web site (http://profiles.doe.mass.edu) and search for a particular school. All the data listed below was taken from the department's Web site for 2008 and 2009.

EDUCATION

Public Schools

Each town on the Cape has its own school department, with administration overseen by an elected school committee. The Cape's two regional school systems (Dennis-Yarmouth and Nauset) have both regional and local school committees, and all schools now have advisory councils. Many schools offer after-school programs. Some public schools, such as Barnstable, also offer preschool programs, but most preschools are operated privately; see the end of this chapter for information on preschools and child care.

Upper Cape

Bourne has six schools, including two high schools, one middle school, and three elementary schools. The public school district served 2,443 students in 2008 and 2009. Upper Cape Cod Regional Technical High School (508-563-5515) had an enrollment of 648.

Falmouth had 3,769 students in seven schools during the most recent school year—five elementary, one middle/junior high (for grades 7 and 8), and one high school.

Mashpee has seen tremendous residential growth in recent years, and the town's total school enrollment of 1,818—while off from the most recent years—is almost double the size it was in the mid-1990s. Mashpee has a state-of-the-art high school and two elementary schools: the Kenneth Coombs School, which offers preschool through grade 2, and the Quashnet School for students in grades 3 through 6.

Sandwich has a public high school built in 1975 and three schools for kindergarten through 8th grade in the village, East Sandwich, and Forestdale. One of the fastest-growing towns in the Commonwealth during the 1990s, the Sandwich school system served 3,574 students. The high school is a focus for many activities in the community, including night classes and swimming programs; call (508) 888-5300 for information.

Mid-Cape

The Mid-Cape area has the largest school system on the Cape, located in the Cape's largest, most populated town of Barnstable. The Barnstable School System had about 4,354 students in 10 schools, including a large high school. There wass also a middle school and nine elementary schools in town. Three elementary school buildings were closed down in 2009 because of budget constraints, declining enrollment, and the subsequent need to consolidate.

Barnstable also has a charter school, the Sturgis Charter School (508-778-1782), launched in the fall of 1998. The school (one of the few schools where enrollment is growing), located on Main Street in Hyannis, serves 367 students in grades 9 through 12. Barnstable also has a charter middle school: The Barnstable Horace Mann Charter School served 841 students in grades 5 and 6. Charter schools were created under the state's Education Reform Act of 1993 and are designed to be laboratories of experimental teaching; they offer an alternative to public schools and, at the same time, encourage public schools to become more inventive. Like the other charter schools scattered throughout the state (the first one on Cape Cod was the Lighthouse Charter School in Orleans, listed below), Sturgis is publicly funded and, in choosing its limited enrollment, the school gives priority to those who reside in the host district.

Serving both Dennis and Yarmouth is the Dennis-Yarmouth Regional School District with a total enrollment of approximately 3,461 students in seven schools. The regional high school on Station Avenue in South Yarmouth accommodates students from both towns, each of which have their own middle and elementary schools. The high school is the site of most classes in the region's adult education program. The school district has also seen a decline in enrollment and budget difficulties, forcing officials to shut down at least one elementary school in recent years and lay off a substantial number of staff members.

Lower Cape

Harwich schools served 674 children in preschool through grade 5 at Harwich Elementary School, 302 students in grades 6 through 8 at Harwich Middle School, and 374 students in grades 9 through 12 at Harwich High School. Adult education courses are offered in the fall and winter; call (508) 430-2355 for more information. For updates on courses and activities, check out their Web site at www.harwich.edu.

Harwich is also home to Cape Cod Regional Vocational Technical School, which has an enrollment of 703 students, hailing from towns as far away as Mashpee and Provincetown. The students alternate between attending technical and academic classes, and earn both high school diplomas and certification in such fields as electrical engineering, plumbing, auto maintenance, computer technology, horticulture, cosmetology, and graphic arts. One of only two technical schools on the Cape, Cape Cod VocTech has become so popular that it has had to turn students away in recent years.

Chatham operates three schools, an elementary school with 277 students in prekindergarten through grade 4, a new middle school with 210 students in grades 5 through 8, and a high school with 200 students in grades 9 through 12. The middle school was built adjacent to the high school on Crowell Road, so the two share some core facilities.

The Nauset Regional School District includes the towns of Brewster, Orleans, Eastham, and Wellfleet. Each has its own local elementary

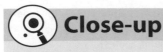 **Close-up**

Libraries

Welcome to CLAMS—Cape Libraries Automated Materials Sharing. Twenty-six libraries, from Falmouth to Provincetown, have joined together to share resources through a computerized system with terminals located in each library. Not only has it made it more convenient to borrow books, it has improved service by providing immediate information on the location of the 1.5 million items—including books, periodicals, and audiovisual resources—available through the system.

Your CLAMS card is easy to obtain; all you need to do is show the librarian a proof of identity and have a local phone number to give them, and you may borrow material from any CLAMS library. It also gives you membership benefits, such as video borrowing or access to a variety of museum passes. These offer a free pass or discount to admissions to some of this region's finest museums, such as the Cape Cod Museum of Natural History, the Heritage Plantation in Sandwich, and the Boston Museum of Science.

Each library has a Friends organization, usually a very active group of community members who support the activities of each library with book sales, authors' luncheons, and lecture series.

For more information on CLAMS and a list of libraries that participate, go online to www .clamsnet.org or call the local town hall.

school. Brewster, which has seen tremendous growth in the last decade, now has two schools: Stony Brook Elementary School (formerly called Brewster Elementary School) and Eddy Elementary School, which opened in 1997. Stony Brook had an enrollment of 260 in kindergarten through grade 2. The Eddy School had 247 students in grades 3 through 5.

Orleans Elementary School had 197 students in kindergarten through grade 5. Eastham Elementary School had 224 students, and Wellfleet Elementary is the district's smallest school with 136 students. Students from all four towns attend Nauset Regional Middle School in Orleans, which has an enrollment of 512 students in 6th, 7th, and 8th grades, and Nauset Regional High School in Eastham, which serves a student population of 1,007 in grades 9 through 12. Adult continuing education courses are held at the middle school; for information call (508) 255-4300.

The Cape Cod Lighthouse Charter School (508-240-2800) in Orleans is an independent public school with open enrollment for grades

6 through 8. The first of its kind on the Cape, it was formed under the state's Education Reform Act and opened in 1994 as one of a handful of experimental public schools across the Commonwealth. The school had an enrollment of 216. Tuition is free; however, students must meet admission requirements. The majority of the students are from the Nauset District, and admission is by a lottery process.

Truro has no middle or high school of its own, but has an excellent elementary school, Truro Central School, which had 141 students in preschool through grade 6. Older students attend either Nauset Regional Middle School and then Nauset Regional High School or Provincetown Junior and Senior High School.

Provincetown's school system comprises two schools with a combined enrollment of about 230. Veteran's Memorial Elementary School served 80 students from preschool through grade 6, and Provincetown High School had 92 students in grades 7 through 12—some of whom, as explained above, come from neighboring Truro.

Private Schools

Upper Cape

FALMOUTH ACADEMY
7 Highfield Dr., Falmouth
(508) 457-9696
www.falmouthacademy.org

A college preparatory school with roughly 210 students, the academy provides a core curriculum for grades 7 through 12, plus an inclusive athletic program and numerous elective courses, including chamber orchestra, volunteer work, and boating. Students come from as far away as Orleans, Martha's Vineyard, and Carver. Situated in the beautiful Beebe Woods property donated to the town by the late Josiah Lilly of Lilly Drug Company, the school has an aggressive financial-aid program; nearly 40 percent of the students receive some type of financial aid.

HERITAGE CHRISTIAN ACADEMY
655 Boxberry Hill Rd., Falmouth
(508) 564-6341
www.heritageccag.com/hca.htm

This nondenominational Christian school offers a Bible-based curriculum and boasts small class sizes with a teacher/student ratio of about 1 to 10. Current enrollment is approximately 50 students in prekindergarten through grade 8. Heritage is also proud of its standardized testing scores, which generally show its students are one to two years ahead of their public school counterparts here. Art, music, and gym are all standard offerings, and the school maintains a financial-aid program.

Mid-Cape

CAPE COD ACADEMY
50 Osterville–West Barnstable Rd.,
Osterville
(508) 428-5400
www.capecodacademy.org

Incorporated in 1976, this private school has an enrollment of about 400 students from kindergarten through 12th grade. Students come from as far away as Wellfleet and Duxbury. The student/teacher ratio is 8 to 1, and the average class size is 15 students. Athletics, the arts, for-

eign languages, advanced placement courses, and computer science for all grades are areas of emphasis. The school, which includes a student activity center with a gymnasium, has a strong financial-aid program.

TRINITY CHRISTIAN ACADEMY
979 Mary Dunn Rd., Barnstable
(508) 790-0114
www.trinitychristiancapecod.org

Opened in 1967 and recently relocated to Barnstable, this interdenominational Christian school has about 105 students in preschool through grade 12. The curriculum is traditional and Bible based. French is taught in grades 1 through 12, and writing skills are emphasized in every grade. The school holds weekly chapel and has a bell choir.

Lower Cape

FAMILY SCHOOL–SALTBOX SCHOOL
3570 Main St., Brewster
(508) 896-6555
www.thefamilyschools.com

Housed in two buildings in a pleasant wooded setting with outdoor play areas and a pool, the Family School offers programs for infants, toddlers, preschoolers, and elementary school students through grade 5, as well as an after-school program and summer camp. Accredited by the National Academy of Schools, the Family School emphasizes nurturing and the developmental stages of each child, and it accepts state-funded voucher programs for tuition.

THE LAUREL DAY SCHOOL
1436 Rte. 137, Brewster
(508) 896-4934
www.laurel-school.com

This private, state-certified school offers programs for preschool through grade 7, with a focus on individualized instruction that encourages children to develop into self-starters and perpetual learners. With an enrollment of about 123 students, Laurel stresses environmental studies, language arts (including French), and creative and artistic expression. The school also offers a series of after-school arts classes.

Higher Education

CAPE COD COMMUNITY COLLEGE
2240 Rte. 132, West Barnstable
(508) 362-2131, (877) 846-3672
www.capecod.mass.edu

Set on 116 acres a few miles from Hyannis, Cape Cod Community College (known as 4Cs) offers both day and evening classes to its 4,000 students. Two-year programs lead to associate degrees in several areas, including the arts, humanities, and sciences, as well as in nursing, hotel and restaurant management, dental hygiene, and criminal justice. The academic programs are organized into two divisions with seven departments: business, health, social sciences, arts and communications, natural sciences and life fitness, mathematics, and languages and literature. The college has a particularly strong communications program.

Opened in 1961 in the building that is now the Barnstable Town Hall, Cape Cod Community College was established as part of the community college system in Massachusetts. One hundred and sixty-three students from 33 communities enrolled during its first year. Outgrowing space quickly, the college moved in 1970 to its current location in West Barnstable, making it the first community college in the state to build a new campus.

MASSACHUSETTS MARITIME ACADEMY
101 Academy Dr., Buzzards Bay
(508) 830-5000, (800) 544-3411
www.maritime.edu

The Massachusetts Maritime Academy is the oldest continually operating maritime academy in the country. Bachelor of Science degrees are awarded in international maritime business, marine engineering, marine transportation, facilities and environmental engineering, and marine safety, environmental protection, and emergency management. Some students use their time to earn a Merchant Marine officer's license or a Naval officer's commission. The four-year coed course of study includes practical experience on the training ship *Patriot State,* which gives stu-

dents an opportunity to visit numerous countries during their semester-at-sea. Nine hundred and fifty students come from across the nation and participate in a full range of activities and athletics. The academic year includes two academic semesters of approximately 15 weeks and a sea term or internship.

i The Academy for Lifelong Learning Inc. is a program offered through Cape Cod Community College. Open to all residents age 50 and older, for $75 in tuition you can take two classes per semester in subjects such as literature, history, language, music, religion, and more. Call (508) 362-2131, ext. 4400, or visit www.allcapecod.org for more information.

SEA EDUCATION ASSOCIATION
171 Woods Hole Rd., Woods Hole
(800) 885-3633
www.seaeducation.org

This unusual college program offers the academic equivalent of a full college semester on board the *Robert C. Seamens* or the *Corwith Cramer,* both 134-foot brigantines. The *Cramer* is named for the founder of SEA, who designed a program for college students that enables them to spend 12 weeks on shore studying oceanography, nautical science, and maritime studies, followed by six weeks at sea practicing oceanography. Each student is also expected to complete an academic project. Students do not need any prior sailing experience, nor do they have to be science majors. The academic complex, a ca. 1889 estate located on a scenic hilltop site, includes a lecture hall, classrooms, a laboratory, student library, computer room, study areas, and faculty and staff offices.

Arts Education
Upper Cape
FALMOUTH ARTISTS' GUILD
311R Main St., Falmouth
(508) 540-3304
www.falmouthart.org

The guild offers classes and workshops year-round in drawing, painting, pottery, silversmithing, and weaving for very reasonable prices (members get a discount). Class offerings vary from season to season, but run the gamut of media from watercolors to colored pencils. There are also classes for children.

Mid-Cape

CAPE COD CONSERVATORY
2235 Iyannough Rd., West Barnstable
Also at Beebe Woods
Highfield Dr., Falmouth
(508) 362-2772, (508) 540-0611
www.capecodconservatory.org
The conservatory's main facility has been teaching music, art, dance, and drama since 1956, and also offers classes at the Beebe Woods Center. The conservatory has about 1,200 students, mostly from the Cape. Dance classes for adults and children include ballet, tap, and jazz. Drama and art are also offered. Adults may take courses in oil painting, monotype, and music instruction in all instruments. High school students make for about 60 percent of the music classes, which are open to all ages.

COTUIT CENTER FOR THE ARTS
4404 Rte. 28, Cotuit
(508) 428-0669
www.cotuitcenterforthearts.org
This thriving arts center offers a wide range of arts classes for all ages. Children as young as 4 can sign up for combined arts and music classes, and teens and adults can sign up for drama, individual or group instruction in drawing and painting, photography, and painting en plein air. There are also computer graphics classes, writing workshops, life-drawing sessions, and more.

Lower Cape

ACADEMY OF PERFORMING ARTS
5 Giddiah Hill Rd., Orleans
(508) 255-5510
www.apa1.org
Associated with the Academy Playhouse (see our Arts chapter), this school offers a variety of performance classes, including dance, acting, voice, and music lesson. Classes are for the young and the young-at-heart and are given in two 18-week sessions. The academy also offers a summer camp. (See the reference in our Kidstuff chapter.)

CAPE COD PHOTO WORKSHOPS
46 Main St., Orleans
(508) 255-5202
www.capecodphotoworkshops.com
www.bobkornimaging.com
Cape Cod Photo Workshops is dedicated to teaching all facets of photography. With an annual array of printing, shooting, and specialty workshops, you can study everything from light meters to photo collage. Now held at the studios of Bob Korn Imagining, there are classes to suit every level, from beginner to advanced. On photo-taking excursions you'll visit some of the most beautiful nature spots in the area.

FINE ARTS WORK CENTER
24 Pearl St., Provincetown
(508) 487-9960
www.fawc.org
Founded in 1968 by a group of visionary artists and writers (including poet Stanley Kunitz and artist Robert Motherwell) as a place where emerging artists are given an uninterrupted seven months to hone their work, this former lumberyard has since become one of the world's leading artistic retreats, nurturing such creative artists as Portia Munson, Jayne Anne Phillips, Dennis Johnson, Tama Janowitz, and Michael Cunningham. More than 1,000 people apply for the competitive Winter Program each year, but only 20 (10 creative writers and 10 visual artists) are accepted. Residencies, which run from Oct through Apr, include room and board plus monthly stipends. The application deadline for writers is Dec 1; for visual artists it's Feb 1.

The open-enrollment summer program is a series of weeklong and weekend workshops in creative writing and visual arts.

The Fine Arts Work Center also hosts scores of readings and exhibitions throughout the year, as well as occasional benefits, including the much-anticipated fund-raising auction, held each Aug (see our Annual Events chapter).

TRURO CENTER FOR THE ARTS AT CASTLE HILL
10 Meetinghouse Rd., Truro
(508) 349-7511
www.castlehill.org

One of the Lower Cape's most respected non-profit educational institutions, Castle Hill has for more than 30 years offered classes with instructors who are both talented and distinguished. Housed in an 1880s barn with an adjacent windmill that contains the school's administrative offices, this unusual school offers a full range of courses in painting, sculpture, printmaking, pottery, poetry, playwriting, and fiction. Course offerings vary from year to year, but are always interesting and challenging. There are classes for children, a lecture series, and artist receptions.

CHILD CARE

One of the top priorities for the local communities on Cape Cod is providing adequate child care for the local workforce. Although the Cape has a large retirement population, it is also filled with young families who live here year-round. As in other areas of the country, working parents sometimes find good day care hard to come by. A number of family day-care providers have sprung up in response to that need, along with a growing number of preschools. This region still lags behind urban areas in responding adequately to the demand, but new centers are being proposed, and state agencies are attempting to find solutions.

In some cases, preschools also offer infant care and toddler programs, but finding the right care often requires an extensive search. A few local businesses now offer on-site day care, and this number continues to grow, so you might want to check into that option.

Preschools and child-care centers must be licensed by the state or show that they are exempt from licensing. You can check the compliance record of any Cape child-care center by calling the **Massachusetts Office of Childcare Services** at its Quincy office at (617) 472-2722.

One important resource for referrals is the **Child Care Network of Cape Cod,** 115 Enterprise Rd., Hyannis (508-778-9470, 888-530-2430 or at www.childcarenetwork.cc/index.html), a nonprofit agency that maintains a list of all preschools and day-care facilities in the area. They know where vacancies are and which centers are licensed to take drop-in students; the agency can also refer families to other services children may need. On the Lower Cape, check with the **Cape Cod Children's Place,** 10 Forest Ave., Eastham (508-240-3310 or at www.capecodchildrensplace .com), a regional family resource center that not only offers child care but also has information about local child-care providers and preschools, and other services that families may require.

Despite the number of preschool and day-care centers that have opened on the Cape, gaps still remain; many Cape residents work at night and rely on family members and babysitters to take care of their youngsters. There are no "tot-drop" places or 24-hour child-care services on the Cape, and no babysitting services, but on Nantucket, there's Nantucket Babysitters Service (508-228-4970 or at www.nantucketbabysitters.com). The Children's Place in Eastham (see above) maintains a list of referrals for babysitters on the Lower Cape. You might also check the bulletin boards at libraries for local babysitters, who often advertise their services there.

HEALTH CARE

Many Cape Codders have chosen to live here because of life-quality issues, and good health is one of them. There are a number of facilities that help us stay healthy; more and more of those facilities have been able to offer us sophisticated health-care services that once required a trip to Boston. Those who live and work here are also concerned with being able to meet the health-care needs of visitors. And the Cape has a relatively high percentage of elderly residents who need access to health care. For those reasons, rescue units in every town are well equipped and well prepared, with extra staff on hand or on call in the busy summer months. Medical clinics as well as many family practices accept walk-in patients.

Cape Cod is also a place where venerable traditions and promising innovations have met in the formation and growth of Cape Cod Healthcare, which began in 1996 with the merger of Falmouth Hospital and Cape Cod Hospital and Cape Cod Hospital. This health system serves all 15 towns along the 70-mile peninsula that is the Cape.

If you have a major medical emergency, dial 911 to reach a rescue unit. For home visits, screenings, and a variety of other services, the Visiting Nurse Association (VNA) is a great resource. VNAs on the Cape, which are all affiliated with Cape Cod Healthcare, may be reached at (800) 631-3900 or www.vnacapecod.org.

CAPE COD HEALTHCARE

Cape Cod Healthcare comprises the following services:

Primary-care physicians: With more than 400 physicians practicing throughout the area, Cape Cod Healthcare has made it easier for Cape Cod residents to get the health care they need, when they need it. Call Cape Cod Healthcare's information line for a referral to a qualified doctor or specialist: (877) 227-3263. To peruse their services and physicians, check their Web site: www .capecodhealth.org.

Emergency care: Two hospital-based emergency departments and the Cape & Islands EMS operate around the clock and treat more than 90,000 emergencies each year. These departments are complemented by urgent-care facilities within each hospital and at locations in Harwich and Sandwich.

Outpatient services: Diagnosis testing facilities and services include mammography services, MRI, CAT scans, and community-based outpatient lab sites around the Cape.

Hospital care: Two acute-care hospitals— Cape Cod Hospital and Falmouth Hospital—offer more than 300 inpatient beds and admit more than 20,000 people per year.

Surgical care: Specialized surgeons conduct more than 12,000 surgeries annually.

Specialty care: Hospital and community-based facilities offer treatment for cancer, arthritis, rheumatic disease, wound care, behavioral health services, physical therapy, speech and occupational therapy, and infectious disease consulting, among other specialized services.

Home care and support services: The Visiting Nurse Association of Cape Cod specializes in community and home health care. Along with specialized nursing care, they offer personal care, dressing, feeding, shopping, homemaker services that include light cleaning and cooking, and companionship. VNA also supervises volunteers from hospice care.

HOSPITALS

Upper Cape

FALMOUTH HOSPITAL
100 Ter Heun Dr., Falmouth
(508) 548-5300
www.capecodhealth.org

Falmouth Hospital, located 45 minutes west of Hyannis, serves the Upper Cape towns of Falmouth, Sandwich, Bourne, and Mashpee. The 95-bed facility offers a full-time emergency room and intensive-care unit, maternity and pediatric units, occupational and physical therapy, catheterization lab, older adult health care services, and a full range of diagnostic testing, including MRI, CAT scan, ultrasound, mammography, and nuclear medicine. The hospital is at the center of a large medical complex that includes the JML Care Center, a 56-unit assisted-living facility known as Heritage at Falmouth, and private medical offices. The hospital includes a new wing, the Faxon Center, featuring an outpatient surgery center, a maternity center, diagnostic imaging, and a Women's Health Resource Center, which offers educational services and a library.

Falmouth Hospital has more than 200 affiliated physicians (62 primary-care physicians and 140 specialist physicians).

Affiliated with the hospital, the Visiting Nurse Association of Upper Cape Cod offers a private-duty nursing service, two adult day health-care centers, and maternal and child home health care. For information on any of the VNA's services, call (800) 631-3900. For a courtesy bus ride to the hospital, call (800) 352-7155.

Mid-Cape

CAPE COD HOSPITAL
27 Park St., Hyannis
(508) 771-1800
www.capecodhealth.org

Cape Cod Hospital, located in Hyannis serves 11 towns of the Mid-, Lower, and Outer Cape. A large medical complex of more than 12 buildings, the hospital offers 24-hour medical care with on-call specialty consultation. The hospital has 225 beds and more than 300 affiliated physicians. It is the largest surgical center on the Cape and islands and the only one with an inpatient/outpatient psychiatric center. It is a regional center for cancer and radiation treatment and features an emergency wing, a maternity unit, and a lab that offers cardiac catheterization—a service that patients previously had to travel to Boston to obtain.

The family-care assisted-living program allows senior citizens and HIV patients to stay at home during treatment. The hospital also has short- and long-term rehabilitative care; two nursing homes, the JML Care Center and the Pavilion, for extended care; and the Heritage at Falmouth, an assisted-living facility.

The Spaulding Cape Cod Hospital Rehabilitation Center and Sports Medicine Complex is an outpatient facility for physical and occupational rehabilitation. An extensive radiation department provides MRI testing. The hospital has numerous support groups for bereavement, cancer, maternity bereavement, smoking cessation, and domestic violence.

CLINICS

Upper Cape

BOURNE HEALTH CENTER
1 Trowbridge Place, Bourne
(508) 743-0322
www.capecodhealth.org

Affiliated with Falmouth Hospital, this year-round, walk-in clinic has a physician on call at all times. Medical services include primary care, physical therapy, lab and X-ray, immunizations, and allergy injections. Major insurance and Medicare are accepted. Call for walk-in hours.

MASHPEE FAMILY MEDICINE
Mashpee Health Center,
3 Industrial Dr., Suite 100, Mashpee
(508) 477-4282
www.mashpeefamilymedicine.com

This family practice sees patients of all ages, from

infants to centenarians. The practice offers daily walk-in care. Mashpee Family Medicine offers both family and urgent care. The office prides itself on offering same-day care.

THE REHABILITATION HOSPITAL FOR THE CAPE AND ISLANDS
311 Service Rd., East Sandwich
(508) 833-4000
www.rhci.org
An independently owned rehabilitation hospital, the Rehabilitation Hospital offers comprehensive rehab treatment for adult inpatients and adult and child outpatients. With 60 beds and a staff of 200, its resources include a therapeutic pool, a home-activities apartment, specialized evaluations (including hearing), state-of-the-art exercise equipment, and orthotics and prosthetics clinics. The hospital provides treatment for a variety of conditions, including stroke, joint replacement, neurological conditions, complex medical conditions, back and neck injuries, amputation, chronic pain, and work-related and sports injuries. The hospital has a branch in Orleans, which provides comprehensive outpatient therapy for children and adults (see subsequent listing).

SANDWICH HEALTH CENTER
2 Jan Sebastian Dr., Sandwich
www.capecodhealth.org
This year-round walk-in clinic is affiliated with Falmouth Hospital. They can lend a hand with stitches, X-rays, infections, insect bites, rashes, sprains, and the like. Referrals are made to the Falmouth Hospital Emergency Room or specialists if more treatment is required. Open daily 8:30 a.m. to 5:30 p.m.

Mid-Cape
CAPE COD ARTIFICIAL KIDNEY CENTER
241 Willow St., Yarmouthport
(508) 362-4535
This is a year-round, outpatient hemodialysis unit. It does not usually have a waiting list. Hours vary but are generally Mon through Sat 8 a.m. to 4:30 p.m. with longer hours in summer.

CAPE COD MEDICAL CENTER
65 Rte. 134, South Dennis
(508) 394-7113
This full-service facility, with one attending physician and a physician's assistant, welcomes walk-in patients. The center accepts most insurance and credit cards.

MID-CAPE MEDICAL CENTER
489 Bearses Way, Hyannis
(508) 771-4092
Open since 1981 for daily year-round health care, this walk-in center has on-duty physicians and provides medical, lab, and X-ray service. It does immunizations for patients age 12 and older, Pap tests and gynecological exams, and routine physicals. The center also treats minor injuries, such as cuts, abrasions, lacerations, and simple fractures. The center, which is about a mile from Cape Cod Hospital, accepts most types of insurance.

MID-UPPER CAPE COMMUNITY HEALTH CENTER
30 Elm Ave., Hyannis
(508) 778-0300
This clinic opened in Feb 2003. It offers family medicine, disease prevention, lab and radiology services, and dental care.

Lower Cape
FONTAINE MEDICAL CENTER
525 Long Pond Dr., Harwich
(508) 432-4100
This medical center provides comprehensive care for everything from fractures to hives. Hours vary seasonally. The center accepts most insurance and major credit cards.

ORLEANS MEDICAL CENTER
Bayberry Square, 225 Route 6A, Orleans
(508) 255-9577
Established in 1984, this center offers walk-in attention for urgent medical needs. It is open all year Mon through Fri from 8 a.m. to 4 p.m. In July and Aug the center is also open Sat from 8 a.m. to 11:30 a.m. It accepts some insurance plans and MasterCard and Visa.

OUTER CAPE HEALTH SERVICES
3130 U.S. Rte. 6 at Briar Lane, Wellfleet
(508) 349-3131
www.outercape.org
Outer Cape Health Services offers a full range of services for acute and chronic medical conditions. It has a lab and X-ray facility, and a team of physicians, nurse practitioners, physician assistants, and nurses. Walk-in care is available on a first-come, first-served basis. The center accepts most insurance plans and credit cards, and also offers a sliding-scale payment plan for low-income patients. The center is open 8 a.m. to 5 p.m. Mon and Tues, 8 a.m. to 7 p.m. Wed and Fri, and 9:30 a.m. to 5 p.m. on Thurs.

OUTER CAPE HEALTH SERVICES
49 Harry Kemp Way, Provincetown
(508) 487-9395
www.outercape.org
The services offered here are the same as at the Wellfleet center (previous listing). The center is open 8 a.m. to 5 p.m. Mon, Wed, and Fri; 8 a.m. to 7 p.m. Tues; 9:30 a.m. to 5 p.m. Thurs; and 9 a.m. to noon Sat.

RHCI-ORLEANS
Orleans Marketplace, 21 Old Colony Way, Orleans
(508) 240-7203
This branch of the Rehabilitation Hospital for the Cape and islands (see our listing in the Upper Cape section) provides comprehensive outpatient therapy for children and adults including physical, occupational, speech, and language therapy. It also offers physician services with board-certified rehabilitation physicians, a gym, and specialized services such as electro-diagnostic testing.

Who to Call in an Emergency

Emergency	911
Battering/Physical Abuse of Women:	
Independence House	(800) 439-6507, (508) 428-4720
Child Abuse (Department of Social Services)	(800) 792-5200
Disabled Persons Abuse	(800) 426-9009
Drug Abuse/Crisis Intervention	(800) 234-0420
Drug/Alcohol Abuse Hotline	(800) 234-0246
Elder Abuse Hotline	(800) 922-2275
Emergency Mental Health Services	(508) 778-4627
Helping Our Women (HOW)	(508) 487-4357
Missing Children Hotline	(800) 843-5678
Parental Stress Hotline	(800) 632-8188
Poison Hotline	(800) 682-9211
Rape Crisis Line	(508) 428-4720
Samaritans Suicide Prevention:	
Cape-wide	(800) 893-9900
Falmouth	(508) 548-8900

RETIREMENT

Cape Cod is clearly a popular place for retirees. Over the decades it has been marketed heavily as the ideal destination to live out the golden years. Many of those who move here and have their grandchildren visit them were themselves first drawn to the Cape in their youth.

Activities abound for the senior set. From golf—nearly 50 public, semiprivate, and resort courses—to the natural beauty of the Cape and the ease with which it can be accessed, retirees are unlikely to want for something to do.

As is outlined in other parts of this book, there is plenty for history buffs to digest: National Audubon Society bird sanctuaries, museums, arts, and music including the Cape Cod Symphony.

Retirees will also find the proximity to Boston a plus, as well as the health-care resources here. There is an abundance of resources for those who need to keep track of their finances: Most Boston banks and brokerage houses are represented here if online banking is not an option.

With the baby boomers arriving at retirement age, the Cape's population is expected to continue to rise. Not everyone sees this as a good thing, but there is a certain inevitability to it. With the current and future trends in mind, every town has an active Council on Aging with a senior center. These centers provide interesting activities and the chance to make new friends.

Many nonprofit organizations also offer a great opportunity to share, with visitors and locals alike, your life experience through volunteer programs. Whether a museum, nature center, or town organization, volunteerism is alive and well on Cape Cod, providing a great way to meet others and get involved with the community.

The Cape also offers a number of assisted-living communities that provide independent-living options coupled with on-site health care and supportive services. And for those who just can't stop working, there are opportunities, including a program by the Cape and Islands Workforce Investment Board designed to match people 55 and older with employers in need of workers.

In this chapter, we offer information about these resources and services for retirees, as well as descriptions of retirement villages.

SENIOR CENTERS

At the Cape's senior centers, retirees can learn a new hobby—perhaps how to knit, quilt, sew, paint, or carve wood. You can learn good health management and have regular medical screenings for high blood pressure, diabetes, hearing and visual impairment, other physical conditions, and mental health concerns. You can take yoga classes; you can get home-delivered or on-site meals; or you can join in any of the councils' dining clubs, cribbage matches, choral groups, bingo games, birthday parties, film festivals, or day trips.

The senior centers are open year-round. Below is contact information for each council on aging. Most offer a range of activities and services. Call for specifics in each town. We have found that the majority of the centers have their own newsletters, and you may want to ask them to send you one so you can see what the center near you is all about. Most councils have Web sites. You may link to them through www.cape andislandscoas.org.

Upper Cape

BOURNE COUNCIL ON AGING
239 Main St., Buzzards Bay
(508) 759-0654, (508) 759-0653

FALMOUTH COUNCIL ON AGING
300 Dillingham Ave., Falmouth
(508) 540-0196

MASHPEE COUNCIL ON AGING
26 Frank E. Hicks Dr., Mashpee
(508) 539-1440

SANDWICH COUNCIL ON AGING
270 Quaker Meetinghouse Rd.,
East Sandwich
(508) 888-4737

i Elder Services of Cape Cod & the Islands coordinates many national volunteer programs for seniors, such as Retired and Senior Volunteer Program (RSVP), the Senior Environment Corps, and America Reads. Interested seniors can join community service projects to address serious local needs. Call (508) 394-4630.

Mid-Cape

BARNSTABLE SENIOR CENTER
825 Rte. 28, Hyannis
(508) 862-4750

DENNIS COUNCIL ON AGING
1045 Rte. 134, South Dennis
(508) 385-5067, (508) 385-8414

YARMOUTH COUNCIL ON AGING
528 Forest Rd., South Yarmouth
(508) 394-7606

Lower Cape

BREWSTER COUNCIL ON AGING
1673 Rte. 6A, Brewster
(508) 896-2737

CHATHAM COUNCIL ON AGING
193 Stony Hill Rd., Chatham
(508) 945-5190

EASTHAM COUNCIL ON AGING
1405 Nauset Rd., Eastham
(508) 240-0164

HARWICH COUNCIL ON AGING
100 Oak St., Harwich
(508) 430-7550

ORLEANS COUNCIL ON AGING
150 Rock Harbor Rd., Orleans
(508) 255-6333

PROVINCETOWN COUNCIL ON AGING
26 Alden St., Provincetown
(508) 487-7080

TRURO COUNCIL ON AGING
346 U.S. Rte. 6, Truro
(508) 387-2462, (508) 487-9247

WELLFLEET SENIOR CENTER
715 Old Kings Hwy., Wellfleet
(508) 349-2800

i *Prime Time,* a free publication put out by the *Cape Cod Times,* is geared specifically for the 50-plus crowd. You may pick up a copy at local libraries or grocery stores throughout the area.

RETIREMENT COMMUNITIES

Retirement communities include three basic types—independent living, assisted living, and independent living with some assistance.

Independent living is aptly named because senior citizens enjoy all the independence of living on their own but with the added advantages of being part of a community. Assisted living is a housing alternative that combines independent living with personalized support service. Healthcare needs are also included, and programs are designed to cater to the individual. Indepen-

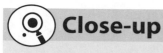

Close-up

Volunteer Opportunities for Seniors

Here's a sampling of volunteer opportunities for seniors offered through several local non-profit organizations:

Council on Aging: Cape-wide with centers in each town.

The Meals on Wheels program is a popular volunteer opportunity, or you can participate in the Senior Dining Program by helping to serve daily meals at senior centers.

Heritage Plantation: Grove Street, Sandwich, (508) 888-3300. Be a volunteer Gallery Guide.

Cape Museum of Fine Arts: Route 6A, Dennis, (508) 385-4477. Lend a helping hand in the museum store.

Cape Cod Museum of Natural History: Route 6A, Brewster, (508) 896-3867. Lead nature walks, answer questions in the marine room, or help in the library.

Senior Service Corps, sponsored by Elder Services of Cape Cod and the islands: 68 Rte. 134, South Dennis, (508) 394-4630.

Volunteers have their choice of more than 100 programs or stations, from the Senior Environmental Corps to helping test Cape homes for the presence of lethal radon gas.

---

dent living with some assistance is somewhere between the two. It is for someone who is largely self-sufficient, but requires assistance from time to time. Here are the retirement community options on Cape Cod.

Upper Cape

ATRIA WOODBRIAR
339 Gifford St., Falmouth
(508) 540-1600
www.atriaseniorliving.com

Woodbriar, opened in 1976, has the distinction of being Cape Cod's first retirement community. Today Woodbriar is an assisted-living and retirement community that includes a nine-hole golf course and indoor heated pool, both of which are available to residents' families at reduced fees or free of charge. Their philosophy is to help individuals remain as independent as possible by providing eight levels of personalized, supportive services, ranging from fully independent to those suffering from memory loss. Located in the heart of Falmouth, Atria Woodbriar also has an entertainment room, four dining rooms, and a sun-filled pond-side common room. Their modern

one-bedroom studio apartments overlook Jones Pond and colorful gardens. Upon request, a van is available to transport residents to shopping centers, medical appointments, and cultural events.

CAPE COD SENIOR RESIDENCES AT POCASSET
100 Dr. Julius Kelley Lane, Pocasset
(508) 564-4474
www.seniorlivingresidences.com

Newly opened in the spring of 2004, Cape Cod Senior Residences at Pocasset offers both independent and assisted living. The 20 independent-living apartments include one-bedroom and two-bedroom units. All apartments include private baths and kitchenettes. A beauty parlor, exercise room, country kitchen, dining room, and general store are all located on this campus-like setting. There are 60 assisted-living studio and one-bedroom apartments.

HERITAGE ASSISTED LIVING
140 Ter Heun Dr., Falmouth
(508) 457-6400
www.heritageatfalmouth.org

Located on the grounds of Falmouth Hospital, Heritage is an assisted-living community offering 56 apartments, including studios and one- and two-bedroom units complete with a private bath and kitchenette. All utilities and maintenance are provided, as are three daily meals, housekeeping, personal care, transportation, and activities including social events, wellness classes, and lectures. Heritage is owned by the Falmouth Hospital Foundation.

Mid-Cape

HARBOR POINT AT CENTERVILLE
22 Richardson Rd., Centerville
(508) 778-2311
www.benchmarkquality.com
Harbor Point is Cape Cod's assisted-living community for the memory impaired. Specially trained staff help residents and others who take part in a day program for those with Alzheimer's or other memory impairment. Private apartments are available for this safe, homelike setting.

HEATHERWOOD AT KINGS WAY
100 Heatherwood Dr., Yarmouthport
(508) 362-4400, (800) 352-0365
www.heatherwoodsenior.com
Located at the beautiful condominium community Kings Way off Route 6A, Heatherwood is one of the Cape's premier retirement communities. It offers 183 one- and two-bedroom independent-living units as well as 14 assisted-living units. Amenities include a meal plan, housekeeping, maintenance, transportation, social activities, and arts and crafts activities. The facilities include a greenhouse and resident storage areas. A doctor visits once a week.

Heatherwood also shares numerous amenities with Kings Way, including walking trails, tennis courts, a swimming pool, and, of course, the Kings Way golf course (see our Golf chapter). Surface and underground parking is plentiful, and each resident has a security and emergency response system.

MAYFLOWER PLACE
579 Buck Island Rd., West Yarmouth
(508) 790-0200
www.mayflowerplace.com
This retirement community has 126 full apartment units as well as an on-site 72-bed skilled-nursing facility. The facility offers support services and a medical clinic staffed 24 hours a day by RNs and certified nurse's aides.

Mayflower Place has an on-site library, post office, chapel, theater, dining room, two craft rooms, pub, greenhouse, beauty parlor, bank, game room, indoor swimming pool, and a complete senior-focused fitness center.

THIRWOOD PLACE
237 North Main St., South Yarmouth
(508) 398-8006, (800) 248-5023
www.thirwoodplace.com
With a total of 214 units, this facility, situated on 45 acres overlooking Flax Pond, offers both assisted and independent living. Amenities include an auditorium, swimming pool, dining room, arts and crafts room, post office, greenhouse, and billiards room. The Village at Thirwood Place is new and features 28 graciously appointed apartments. Many services are provided, including activities programs, transportation, a nurse who is available daily, and emergency-trained personnel who are on hand around the clock. All meals, utilities, housekeeping, and laundering are included in the monthly fee. Pets are welcome.

WHITEHALL ESTATE
790 Falmouth Rd., Hyannis
(508) 790-7666
www.sslusa.com
One of the newest facilities on the Cape, Whitehall Estates opened in the spring of 1999. It is an assisted-living home with 80 units with just the right amount of support so residents can do as they please. It's warm and friendly in every detail, from the cozy fireplace to the inviting pub—perfect for socializing. Choose from a private studio and a one- or two-bedroom apartment.

i Nearly 25 percent of the population in Barnstable County (most of the Cape) is age 65 or older—twice the national average. The median age on the Cape is 46, with Chatham and Orleans claiming the oldest populations in Massachusetts.

Lower Cape

CHATHAM HOUSE
33 Cross St., Chatham
(508) 945-5291, (800) 529-5291
www.wiselivingchoices.com
Chatham House is a 10-unit cooperative apartment complex set in bustling yet beautiful downtown Chatham. Within walking distance are many shops, restaurants, churches, and the impressive Eldredge Library. The one-bedroom apartments share laundry facilities. Meals are served in a common dining room.

EPOCH ASSISTED LIVING OF BREWSTER
855 Rte. 124, Brewster
(508) 896-3252
www.epochsl.com
This assisted-living community provides 68 apartments, each with a kitchenette and private bath. Opened in Nov 1996, it offers independence supported by 24-hour assistance and plenty of personal touches, including a staff nurse. The monthly charge includes three meals a day, housekeeping, personal care needs, utilities, and health programs. Transportation is also provided for local errands. Laundry facilities are on each floor. Brewster Place is next to the Brewster Manor nursing home. Pets are welcome.

HARWICH HOUSE
26 Pleasant Lake Ave., Harwich
(800) 529-5291
www.wiselivingchoices.com
This retirement community, located near the junction of Routes 124 and 39, offers 18 one- and two-bedroom condominium units. The facility provides a dining room where dinner is served for a nominal fee. Staff nurses are available 24 hours a day. Each unit is privately owned. There is a com-

mon room with laundry facilities for those who still enjoy doing their own laundry. For a monthly fee you can choose what additional services you need, such as housekeeping, personalized health care, concierge services, and more.

THE MELROSE
601 Rte. 28, Harwich Port
(800) 529-5291
www.wiselivingchoices.com
The Melrose is built on the same site as the old Melrose Supper Club, which served as a hotel before being converted into a 29-unit housing complex. The building's appearance remains much the same, but inside you will find modern conveniences. All two-bedroom apartments feature full kitchens and private laundry rooms. Meals are provided at a nominal charge in the common dining room. The monthly service fee includes 24-hour assistance.

ORLEANS CONVALESCENT AND RETIREMENT CENTER
60 Daley Terrace, Orleans
(508) 255-2328
www.capecodretirementhome.com
The Orleans Retirement Center, built in 1969, was one of the early pioneers providing supportive living concepts for older adults. It has 19 apartments (with garages and security systems) ranging in size from studio to two-bedroom units. The evening meal, which can be served either in the common dining room or in the privacy of the individual apartments, is included in the monthly fee, as are housekeeping and laundry services. This facility also offers a 50-bed private skilled-nursing facility with 24-hour medical coverage.

MEDIA

The Cape has a daily newspaper, several weekly newspapers, special-interest magazines, a public-access television station, and a range of radio listening choices to keep residents and visitors informed and entertained.

NEWSPAPERS

BARNSTABLE PATRIOT
4 Ocean St., Hyannis
(508) 771-1427
www.barnstablepatriot.com
The oldest newspaper on Cape Cod, the *Barnstable Patriot* was launched in 1830. The *Patriot* is published every Friday and covers the town of Barnstable and its seven villages. Bought by *Cape Cod Times* in 2005, the weekly is now part of the Dow Jones Local Media Group. The paper focuses on county government and local news. Weekly sections deal with such topics as senior citizens, sports, and entertainment.

CAPE COD CHRONICLE
60-C Munson Meeting Way, Chatham
(508) 945-2220, (508) 430-2700
www.capecodchronicle.com
Established in 1965, the *Chronicle* is the Lower Cape's only independent weekly newspaper. The *Chronicle* focuses on Chatham and Harwich and includes news, features, sports, community-service listings, and entertainment news.

CAPE COD COMMUNITY NEWSPAPERS
Sunflower Marketplace, Route 6A,
Yarmouthport
(508) 375-4900
www.wickedlocal.com
Owned by the Gatehouse Media Group, these weekly newspapers include the *Register*, the *Harwich Oracle*, the *Cape Codder*, and the *Provincetown Banner*. Gatehouse also publishes the *Sandwich Broadsider*, *Bourne Courier*, and *Falmouth Bulletin*. All the papers are sold on newsstands and by subscription.

The newspapers are community-oriented, general-interest papers that include news and events along with local features and columns.

CAPE COD TIMES
319 Main St., Hyannis
(508) 775-1200
www.capecodonline.com
The Cape's only year-round daily paper, the *Cape Cod Times*, covers news throughout the area, including Martha's Vineyard and Nantucket, as well as state, national, and world news. It is delivered to subscribers in the morning and available on newsstands.

The *Cape Cod Times* started in 1936 as part of the *New Bedford Standard Times*, and its offices in downtown Hyannis date to 1938. In 1966, the paper was acquired by Ottaway Newspapers Inc. (a Dow Jones subsidary), which has more than 20 daily newspapers. News Corp. bought the Ottoway newspapers along with the *Wall Street Journal* in 2007. The newspaper group's name was changed to Dow Jones Local Media Group in 2009. In the past decade the paper has focused on its online content.

In addition to the daily newspaper, the *Cape Cod Times* also publishes *Prime Time*, a free monthly magazine with an age 50-plus target audience; the *View*, a monthly lifestyles magazine; *CapeWeek*, a weekly events supplement to the Friday edition; and special seasonal and topical editions.

THE FALMOUTH ENTERPRISE
Depot Avenue, Falmouth
(508) 548-4700
www.capenews.net

This biweekly paper has been published since 1895 and has been owned by the Hough family of Falmouth since 1929. Today they publish not only the *Falmouth Enterprise,* but also the *Bourne Enterprise,* the *Mashpee Enterprise,* the *Sandwich Enterprise,* the *Barnstable Enterprise,* and the *Cape Cod Shopper.* These papers include calendars of events, arts and entertainment, and weddings and births. The papers are sold at newsstands and by subscription.

MAGAZINES

CAPE COD LIFE
60 North St., Hyannis
(508) 775-9800, (800) 698-1717
www.capecodlife.com
This glossy magazine comes out 10 times a year and is sold by subscription and on newsstands. The full-color magazine concentrates on local people, historic and current topics, events, and activities. Topics include art, cooking, nature, shopping, dining, and lodging on Cape Cod. The recently launched *Martha's Vineyard Life* and *Nantucket Life* address life on the islands. *Cape Cod Life* also publishes articles covering gardening, interior decorating, house styles, retirement, and a complete list of all the art galleries on Cape Cod in their annual *Cape Cod & Islands Home* and *Cape Cod Arts* magazines.

CAPE COD MAGAZINE
396 Main St., Suite 8, Hyannis
(508) 771-6549
www.capecodmagazine.com
Cape Cod Magazine is a free full-color quarterly that prints features on Cape Cod homes, personalities, gardening, shopping, and dining. Widely distributed on Cape Cod, the magazine offers subscriptions as well as home delivery.

GOLF ON CAPE COD
143A Upper Country Rd., Dennisport
(508) 398-6101
www.golfoncapecod.com
Golf on Cape Cod is a publication written for and about the Cape Cod golf community. The maga-

zine is published four times a year and is available for purchase at most local bookstores, magazine racks, or by subscription.

ON THE WATER
35 Technology Park Dr., East, Falmouth
(508) 548-4705, (800) 614-3000
www.onthewater.com
Published monthly by the *Falmouth Enterprise, On the Water* covers fishing and boating with a focus on the Cape and islands. With a large format, it's filled with photographs and articles by Cape fishermen, among others.

TELEVISION

Although the Cape has only one station of its own, we get lots of others. Most are from Boston; a few are from Providence.

In addition, there's a plethora of cable stations available, depending on the cable package you (or the place where you are staying) pay for.

CAPE COD COMMUNITY MEDIA CENTER/CHANNEL 17
307 Whites Path, South Yarmouth
(508) 394-2388
www.c3tv.org
Formerly known as C3TV, Cape Cod's Community Media Center is a versatile community resource that airs a daily schedule of social, political, and cultural programs. It also has conference and workshop space and a gallery. The station is funded by the towns of Barnstable, Yarmouth, Dennis, Harwich, and Chatham.

Programming covers local sports, selectmen's meetings, and committee meetings as well as original programs produced by local residents.

RADIO

Classical
WFCC 107.5 FM
www.wfcc.com

Community

WOMR 92.1 FM (Provincetown)
www.womr.org

WUMB 91.9 FM (folk, jazz, and NPR)
www.wumb.org

Contemporary/adult/easy listening

106 WCOD 106.1 FM (adult contemporary)
www.106wcod.com

WQRC 99.9 FM (easy listening, jazz)
www.wqrc.com

WRZE 96.3 FM (Top 40)
www.therose.net

WOCN 103.9 FM ("memory music" from 1930s to '80s)
www.ocean104.com

Rock

WPXC 103 FM (classic rock)
www.pixy103.com

WMVY 92.7 FM (adult rock)
www.mvyradio.com

WCIB 102 FM (classic rock)
www.cool102.com

Talk

WBUR 1240 AM (NPR)
www.wbur.org

WCAI 90.1 FM (NPR)
www.wgbh.org/cainan

WNAN 91.1 FM (NPR)
www.wgbh.org/cainan

WCCT 90.3 FM (NPR)
www.wbur.org

WKKL 90.7 FM (Cape Cod Community College)
www.geocities.com/wkkl247

WSDH 91.5 FM (Sandwich High School)
www.sandwich.k12.ma.us/shs/clubs.htm

WXTK 95.1 FM (news talk)
www.95wxtk.com

WORSHIP

Religion has long played a role in the lives of Cape Codders, beginning with the American Indian thanking their Great Spirit for all the life-giving gifts they received each day. The religion of the Wampanoag Indians was the only religion of the area for 10,000 years, until European settlers came at the beginning of the 17th century.

OUR RELIGIOUS ROOTS

This migration commenced with the landing of the Pilgrims in 1620. These 102 hardy souls braved the Atlantic and hardships of the New World so that they could be free to live and worship as they pleased. Half of them did not survive the first winter. The Pilgrims were certainly devout to begin with, and the New World's adversity only caused the Pilgrims to turn more deeply toward their faith. It is against this backdrop that the settlements of the area were built and laws formed.

England's established church at the time was the Church of England. In opposition to this establishment were the Pilgrims, separatists seeking to forge their own church. Their pilgrimage to Plymouth brought more settlers in the following years. These settlers brought a Congregational church with them with more conservative ideas. They established settlements all along the Northeast coast, including the Cape, as early as 1637.

As soon as enough Congregationalists gathered and built a meetinghouse (and encouraged a minister to relocate to their corner of the wilderness to preach to them), they were in line for incorporation. Incorporation brought more settlers to add to the flock. As the flock grew and people began to settle in the outlying areas, east and west parishes and north and south parishes were established. Many of these local parishes would lead to the incorporation of completely separate townships in years to follow. (See our Historic Cape Cod chapter.)

In those days, religion and community meant the same thing. The meetinghouse served as both the religious and political center of the community. Church and state were one and the same (and would be until 1692 when a charter provided religious freedom). All members were expected to contribute to the church that had earned their township incorporation.

Congregationalists were not the only ones settling down during the 17th century. By the mid-1600s, Quakers began to settle in Sandwich, Falmouth, Barnstable, and, later, Harwich. These Quakers, whose religion taught them to tremble or quake at the fear of God's wrath, attempted to gain converts from the Congregationalist flock and, in some cases, succeeded. Despite their efforts, the Quakers were singled out as heretics. Many were forced through repeated persecutions to flee town for other parts. Some, such as John Wing of Falmouth, relocated to a remote wilderness lying between Yarmouth and Eastham to begin the settlement of what would become the town of Harwich. Quakers tended to settle in sparsely populated areas, such as in South Yarmouth, which became a Quaker village. The Quakers were followed by Baptists, who settled at Harwich during the mid-18th century and later spread outward across the Cape.

By the late 18th century, a new religious group arrived on Cape Cod. In England, Methodism had grown from a spiritual awakening of John Wesley in 1738. Great Britain and Ireland saw the spread of this new religion, and by the latter quarter of the 18th century, Methodism made its way across the Atlantic. The first Methodist meetinghouse on the Cape was erected in Harwich in 1792, followed by another in Bourne in 1794. By the early to mid-19th century, Methodism had rattled the Congregational spires, and the latter began to see many divisions and splinter groups emerge.

The middle of the 19th century saw a religious revolution on Cape Cod as small religious sects began to form from factions of the more established churches of the day. During this period, the town of Dennis saw its church separate into a half-dozen groups; in neighboring Harwich no less than 15 divisions formed from the church in that town. Each group had its own issues, its own agenda, and its own particular belief system that set it apart from the others. It was during this time that the Unitarian Universalists came into being. By the end of the century, though, many of these groups were able to resolve their differences, and they came back together.

Meanwhile, Catholicism began to emerge with the coming of Irish immigrants during the 1830s and throughout the 19th century. The first Catholic parish was established in Sandwich 1830 as Irish immigrants were settling there to work in the factories. A second parish was erected in 1869 at Harwich. Portuguese fishermen in Provincetown had already brought their Catholic church along with them. Cape Verde Islanders, who settled in Falmouth as farmers, did the same. As the 20th century arrived and people began to migrate southward from around Boston, the Catholic population of the Cape began to grow. Today this once predominantly Protestant peninsula, settled initially by Congregationalists, is largely Roman Catholic.

WORSHIP TODAY

Despite more than three centuries of change and growth, religion continues to play a major role on this sandy peninsula, as evidenced by the many churches here. Some of the best examples of the Cape's ability to blend its religious tradition with secular festivity are the blessing of the fleet celebrations at the beginning of each summer season.

Recent trends on the Cape reflect the national growth of many conservative congregations.

Here on the Cape you also see many interfaith efforts to address social issues, such as homelessness, domestic abuse, and poverty.

Some of the Cape's private religious schools have significant waiting lists—an indication that young families, like so many Cape Codders before them, place a high value on religion.

The Cape remains largely Christian, but there are two Jewish synagogues and other groups such as Baha'i spiritual assemblies. For a listing of all church locations, consult the Yellow Pages of the local phone book. Most Cape Cod newspapers have information on services. The *Cape Cod Times'* Web site, www.capecodonline.com has a complete listing in its community section. Also, the Cape Cod Council of Churches at 320 Main St. in Hyannis (508-775-5073) is an excellent source of information on places of worship. The council encourages the various religious societies to work together in an effort to provide for the Cape community.

United Church of Christ churches, which grew from the old Congregational parishes, are the largest Protestant sect on the Cape. Five UCC churches can be found on the Upper Cape, eight in the Mid-Cape area and seven along the Lower Cape. The First Congregational Church of Yarmouthport is not a member of the United Church of Christ, retaining its original congregational charter as a member of the National Association of Congregational Christian Churches.

There are some 16 Baptist churches on the Cape—American Baptists, National, and Independent. Five of these churches are in the Upper Cape, seven are in the Mid-Cape, and four are along the Lower Cape.

United Methodists have 14 churches, five in the Upper Cape, two in the Mid-Cape, and seven in the Lower Cape towns of Harwich, Orleans, Chatham, Eastham, Wellfleet, and Provincetown.

Roman Catholic churches account for 21 of the Cape and islands' more than 150 places of worship. Adding seasonal parishes brings the total number of Catholic churches closer to 30. There is at least one Roman Catholic church in each of the Cape's 15 towns. Although the Protestants on the Cape have more church buildings, the average membership of a Catholic parish is larger than that of a Protestant congregation. As a result, the Cape is predominantly Catholic by a ratio of nearly 2-to-1. President John F. Kennedy was a member of the St. Francis Xavier Church in Hyannis, where he and his brothers, Joe, Bobby, and Ted, served as altar boys.

Episcopalians arrived in Woods Hole in 1852 and at Sandwich in 1854. Today they are well represented on the Cape. There are 12 Episcopal churches in Buzzards Bay, Sandwich, Woods Hole, Falmouth, Osterville, Barnstable, South Yarmouth, Harwich Port, Orleans, Chatham, Wellfleet, and Provincetown. Three Assembly of God churches can be found in Hyannis, Dennisport, and Wellfleet.

Lutheran churches are in Falmouth, West Barnstable, East Harwich, and Brewster. Pentecostal churches are in Barnstable, Mashpee, and Dennisport. Two Church of Jesus Christ of Latter Day Saints congregations are on Cape Cod, one in Cataumet and the other in Brewster.

Community Churches can be found in Marstons Mills, East and West Dennis, as well as in South Chatham. For Unitarian Universalist parishes, you'll want to look in the towns of East Falmouth, Barnstable, Brewster, and Provincetown. The Society of Friends has meetings in West Falmouth and South Yarmouth (once known as Quaker Town and Friends Village). In Falmouth and South Dennis, you can find a Church of the Nazarene, whereas Buzzards Bay, Falmouth, Hyannis, Brewster, Harwich Port, Chatham, and Orleans all have Christian Science churches. Jehovah's Witnesses can be found in four locations across the Cape: Hatchville, Hyannis, Dennis, and East Harwich. West Barnstable has a Presbyterian church, and Centerville is home to a Greek Orthodox church with its Byzantine building erected in 1949.

Rounding out the Christian places of worship are two Christian Missionary churches in Buzzards Bay and Brewster, and two Federated Churches in Cotuit and Hyannis. Seventh Day Adventists are in Osterville; Full Gospel churches are in Sandwich, Mashpee, West Barnstable, and Dennisport; and the Church of New Jerusalem (Swedenborgian) was established in 1870 in Yarmouthport. Orleans is home to the chapel of the Community of Jesus, and Hyannis is home to the Salvation Army, which holds services.

Hyannis has a Zion Union church that caters to the black members of the community. Interdenominational parishes are in Centerville and Hyannis; nondenominational parishes are in Sandwich, Mashpee, and Marstons Mills; a Christadelphian Ecclesia parish is in Cataumet; and an Evangelical Covenant church is in Brewster. A Unity church is located in Centerville.

Cape Cod also hosts the Falmouth Jewish Congregation in Hatchville (East Falmouth). It is housed in what was once the East End Meetinghouse of the United Church of Christ, founded in 1797. The Cape Cod Synagogue in Hyannis was erected in 1949. There is also a Lubavitch Chabad Jewish Center in Hyannis.

Last, but by no means least, the Wampanoag Indians of Mashpee hold services at the Old Indian Meeting House on Route 28 in Mashpee. Built in 1684, this meetinghouse is the oldest church on Cape Cod.

NANTUCKET

Nantucket is the only place in the United States that is a town, a county, and an island, and in its entirety, both a State Historic District and a National Historic Landmark. It is a place where nearly half the land is held in conservation, and there are no stoplights, shopping malls, or fast-food franchises.

Nantucket may be an island , but it is readily accessible, so visitors feel that although it's nice to stay for a few days or more, even a day trip here is worthwhile. The trip from Hyannis is a little more than two hours by traditional ferry or just an hour by high-speed ferry and only 15 minutes by air. It is especially nice to arrive by ferry and see the whole town come into view as the vessel rounds the lighthouse at Brant Point and enters the harbor. The first thing you'll notice is the uniformity of the buildings, which are built almost exclusively of gray weathered shingle with white trim, one of the indications that construction and alterations are strictly monitored. In 1970 the entire island was established as a Historic District, which means that all construction must be accepted by the Historic District Commission, the Nantucket Building Department, and the Planning Board. Residents may grumble or joke about the stringent regulations, but there's no arguing with the result: Nantucket has an incredibly unspoiled appearance.

Islanders have also taken care to preserve the land here. More than 12,000 acres—40 percent of the island—are protected from development, much of that through the Nantucket Conservation Foundation, which owns and manages more than 8,700 acres. History, of course, has also been carefully and lovingly preserved. This community, which has a year-round population of more than 10,000 (which swells to 56,000 during the summer and contributes roughly 70 percent of the economic base), maintains more than a dozen museums

The island is 47.8 square miles—3.5 miles deep and 14 miles wide—a bit larger than Manhattan, which is 2.5 by 12 miles.

As islanders, Nantucketers are keenly sensitive to the environment and their quality of life. They are generally friendly and good-humored, but if you sense that your car is not exactly welcome on Nantucket, you are right. Islanders are happier to see visitors arrive without an automobile, largely because traffic has become a real problem here in summer. The truth is, you don't really need a car for a visit. It is very expensive to bring a vehicle to the island, and you can walk or bike just about anywhere. There are also taxis and bus service. Even if you are staying for an extended time, you can rent a car when you need one. You'll find it's actually quite liberating not to have to worry about parking, gas, and navigating the narrow roads. Nantucket forces you to forsake some aspects of modern life, and that is part of its charm.

AREA OVERVIEW

Nantucket Village, the most concentrated part of the island, is situated around the harbor. Most businesses and accommodations are here, so if there is no town named in an address for any of the following listings, assume it is in Nantucket Village. We'll tell you if a business or accommoda-tion is found in any of the outlying villages, which are less populated and more seasonal. The village of Madaket, to the west, consists of residences and a few businesses. The residential village of Cisco is on the island's southern shore. The village of Siasconset, more commonly referred to as Sconset, is a bustling summertime resort on the eastern end of the island known for its excellent restaurants and rose-covered cottages with sweet names such as Little House and Auld Lang Syne, the oldest cottage on the islands. Look for the images of spouting whales cut into privet hedges. The old schoolhouse, now a fire station, was used until 1957.

If you're an artist, bring your sketchpad. Nantucket's air is full of moisture, and it is warmer in winter and cooler in summer than the rest of the area, which results in beautiful flowers and gardens.

Wildlife you may see on Nantucket includes deer, pheasants, rabbits, and squirrels. Today the island is host to several grassland-nesting bird species, including short-eared owls and northern harriers, which are scarce on the mainland but thrive here because there are fewer natural predators. Nantucket is a popular spot for birders, and it's easy to see why: More than 350 bird species have been recorded here. The island abounds with wild blueberries, blackberries, beach plum, and elderberries. The 260-acre Milestone Cranberry Bog is one of the largest in the United States. The highest point of land is Folger Hill, which at 109 feet is a foot higher than Altar Rock.

It's true that much of Nantucket shuts down in the off-season, but even in the quiet months, it's a beautiful place. Nantucketers, however may be less than eager to share that.

HISTORY

Indian legend has it that the giant Maushop created Nantucket and Martha's Vineyard from the sand in his moccasins. The scientific version, though less romantic, is consistent with what we know about the formation of Cape Cod. Prehistoric glaciers deposited sand, rock, and rubble in the area. As the glaciers melted, the water level rose. About 6,000 years ago Nantucket Sound was flooded, separating the Cape from the islands. By roughly 2,000 years ago, Nantucket and Martha's Vineyard had taken the general form they have today.

In the mid-1500s, the island was home to about 1,500 native inhabitants. European explorers first laid foot on Nantucket sand around that time but did not explore it. Credit for the island's "discovery" generally goes to Bartholomew Gosnold, a sailor who in 1602 noted the island in the log of his ship, the *Concord*, even though he did not land. In October, 1641, William, Earl of Sterling, a representative of Charles I of England, executed the deed of sale for Nantucket, granting Thomas Mayhew of Watertown, a merchant who had never visited the island, and his son, Thomas Mayhew Jr., the right to "plant and inhabit upon Nantucket and two other small islands adjacent," meaning Muskeget and Tuckernuck. William also granted Martha's Vineyard and the Elizabeth Islands to the Mayhews in a second transaction. The two Mayhews shortly thereafter settled on Martha's Vineyard, limiting their Nantucket activities to Christianizing the Wampanoags.

In the fall of 1659, Thomas Macy, Tristram Coffin, and Edward Starbuck arrived on Martha's Vineyard from England to escape religious bigotry and persecution. Learning that the Mayhews were willing to dispose of most of Nantucket, these men formed a partnership with the Mayhews and settled the island of Nantucket. Like the Mayhews on Martha's Vineyard, they too raised sheep on Nantucket, taking advantage of the island's lack of predators and the fact that livestock here could not just disappear into the wilderness. As the population on the island grew, sheep raising, spinning, and weaving became the main occupations, and the settlers prospered. In 1671 the town of Nantucket was incorporated, and it became a very important town, very much in the mainstream of colonial America's economy. (Nantucket's physical isolation was not then such a barrier; most mainland communities were isolated too—for lack of roads. Also, rivers and oceans were widely used then as highways for travel and commerce.)

More settlers would arrive over the next quarter century. By 1700, the island population consisted of approximately 800 Native Americans and 300 European settlers, who lived together in relative harmony. During this time Tristram Coffin was considered the patriarch of the island. Benjamin Franklin's grandfather, Peter Foulger, lived on Nantucket and, like his grandson, was a versatile person, respected as a preacher, poet, artisan, Native American interpreter, and Clerk of the Works. Three ships involved in the Boston Tea Party were out of Nantucket.

In addition to raising sheep—at one time, there were 10,000 sheep on the island—and farming, Nantucketers also began whaling, first from offshore and then from whaling boats, and this activity in time became the mainstay of the island's economy. By 1774, 150 Nantucket vessels were plying the Atlantic, producing two-thirds of the whale oil in New England. The island's original town, called Sherborn, was renamed in 1795 and moved to the "Great Harbor," a change reflecting the island's transformation from a farming community to the center of America's whaling industry.

Though Quaker influences kept the island neutral during the American Revolution and the War of 1812, the wars with England were devastating to Nantucket. With enemy blockades and control of the seas, Nantucket was, for the first time, truly isolated from the mainland. Eighty percent of the whaling fleet was destroyed, and many seamen died in prison ships.

After the War of 1812, Nantucket regained its prosperity and once again thrived as a whaling port. New technologies allowed ships to store blubber and remain at sea longer. The economy flourished. Nearly four decades of growth and prosperity produced fine homes and a cosmopolitan atmosphere unique to such a small island. By 1840 the population increased 600 percent to 9,712 year-round residents, and Nantucket became an important source of capital for a growing nation. However, the whaling era was soon to end—this time for good.

Although each year more oil was produced than before the Revolution, 1830 was the last year Nantucket would lead the American whaling industry. In 1846 a fire destroyed Nantucket Village center and, despite a quick rebuilding, the decline in whaling activity had begun. In addition a sandbar across the mouth of the harbor made it increasingly difficult for large whale ships to enter. The railroad connected New Bedford's flourishing whaling industry to a growing American market, and the demand for oil in Europe declined as more people began to use less expensive gaslight. Nine years after the fire, Nantucket's whaling activity was cut in half. The last whaling ship, the *Oak,* left in 1869, and with its departure the whaling industry closed on Nantucket.

By 1875, two-thirds of the population had left Nantucket; only 3,200 remained. With railroads connecting the mainland cities, Nantucket was increasingly isolated. It was decidedly not a practical location for the Industrial Revolution with its factories and jobs. The failing island economy did, however, protect Nantucket's buildings from the dramatic changes that were sweeping the country.

As steam and electric power began making life easier, "vacation mania" sent people in search of places to enjoy their new freedom. Nantucket, with an overabundance of houses and a pleasant summer climate, became a favorite place for increasing numbers of visitors.

Once again economic growth and prosperity returned to Nantucket. At first a mere trickle of wealthy summer people came to enjoy boating and saltwater bathing. But, with the introduction of steamboat service from New Bedford and the construction of its first airport in 1920, vacation travel to Nantucket boomed. Today, 40,000 to 50,000 people visit Nantucket on a busy weekend.

i Sturdy, utilitarian Nantucket lightship baskets originated, not surprisingly, on Nantucket. They were made and used by men stationed on the lightships off the coast. Gradually these baskets, made of rattan woven around wooden ribs, became more ornate. They were fitted with hinged tops, embellished with ornamental carvings, and more. They're still a popular, if pricey, souvenir from Nantucket.

GETTING HERE

There are regularly scheduled trips by air service, aircraft charters, private aircraft, ferry, or private boat to and from Nantucket. Many visitors love to fly in because the aerial views are spectacular. And the speedy flights give you added time to enjoy the island. Bear in mind, however, that it costs roughly two-thirds more to fly to Nantucket than to take the ferry. If you're flying in, you'll arrive at Nantucket Memorial Airport.

By Air

CAPE AIR
660 Barnstable Rd., Hyannis
(508) 771-6944, (800) 352-0714
www.flycapeair.com
Cape Air offers hourly flights, with year-round shuttle service between Hyannis and Nantucket, and regular service from New Bedford, Boston, Providence, and Martha's Vineyard. Seasonal service from Provincetown is available as well. In the peak season, the company offers more than seven flights daily from Boston. Flights from Hyannis leave every hour; these are approximately 15-minute flights. Flights from Boston leave at hour intervals. These are approximately 50-minute flights. Charter service is also available, as are connections to an increasing number of locations around New England.

CONTINENTAL EXPRESS
(800) 525-0280
www.continental.com
This carrier offers non-jet regular seasonal service from Newark, New Jersey; Boston; or Martha's Vineyard to Nantucket.

ISLAND AIRLINES
(508) 228-7575, (800) 248-7779
www.islandair.net
Island Airlines, a Nantucket-owned business, offers approximately 20 scheduled flights daily year-round between Hyannis and Nantucket.

NANTUCKET AIRLINES
(508) 228-6234, (800) 635-8787
www.nantucketairlines.com
Nantucket Airlines, affiliated with Cape Air, flies between Nantucket and Hyannis. Fights leave from Hyannis on the half hour and Nantucket on the hour every day.

NANTUCKET MEMORIAL AIRPORT
14 Airport Rd., Nantucket
(508) 325-5300
www.nantucketairport.com
Off Old South Road, Nantucket Memorial Airport is the second most active commercial airport in Massachusetts. Shuttle service is available from Logan International Airport in Boston, Hyannis, Martha's Vineyard, and New Bedford, all in Massachusetts, as well as from T. F. Green Airport in Providence, Rhode Island, La Guardia in New York City, and Newark International Airport in New Jersey. The facility is open year-round.

The airport's terminal recently underwent a $29 million renovation that included high tech security advances and the installation of a geothermal heating and air conditioning system. The system decreases the carbon footprint of the airport by drawing water up from almost 200 feet in the earth and using a heat exchanger to control the temperature in the building.

Taxi service is available, but if you call ahead to make arrangements, most of the resorts offer shuttle service. The Nantucket Regional Transit Authority shuttle service runs from late May through late Sept and goes from one end of the island to the other.

Nantucket Memorial Airport accommodates anything from twin-engine Cessnas to 19-seat Beechwoods and jets. For private planes, the airport offers servicing and repair facilities; fuel is available 24 hours a day.

The following charter and commercial airlines are at Nantucket Memorial Airport.

OCEAN WINGS AIR CHARTER
(800) 253-5039
www.flyoceanwings.com
Ocean Wings offers 24-hour year-round service to any New England, U.S., or Canadian destination. This company has a private hangar and offers flight instruction. Ocean Wings also has winter service based in Puerto Rico and the Caribbean.

US AIRWAYS EXPRESS
(800) 428-4322
www.usairways.com

This carrier provides daily flights in season to Boston, with connecting flights to La Guardia and also to Martha's Vineyard.

By Sea

Ferryboats

If you'd prefer to spend a few hours enjoying a ride on Nantucket Sound—sunshine, sea breezes, and perhaps a glass of wine on the upper deck of a passenger ferry—you can take advantage of regular ferry service throughout the year from Hyannis. The standard ferry ride takes about two-and-a-quarter hours. The *Grey Lady*, Hy-Line's speedy catamaran, makes the trip from Hyannis in an hour.

(**Note:** Falmouth's ferry service only goes to Martha's Vineyard, not Nantucket.)

FREEDOM CRUISE LINE
702 Main St., Harwich Port
(508) 432-8999
www.nantucketislandferry.com

Sailing from Saquatucket Harbor in Harwich Port, Freedom Cruise Line offers daily passenger service to Nantucket, and you can bring along your bicycle and pet, too. The trip takes about an hour and twenty minutes. A round-trip fare is $68 for adults and $51 for children; one-way fare is $39 for adults and $29 for children; children under two pay only $6 round-trip ($3 one-way), and bicycles are $12 round-trip. *Freedom* is an 80-passenger ferry, so reservations are recommended for day trips. There are also restrictions on how many "overnighters" the line can leave on the island, so reservations are necessary. There is free parking for day-trippers.

HY-LINE CRUISES
22 Channel Point Rd., Hyannis
(508) 778-2600, (800) 492-8082
www.hy-linecruises.com

Hy-Line offers a year-round ferry between Hyannis and Nantucket. It takes less than two hours to journey by ferry from Hyannis to Nantucket.

Round trip fare is $43 for adults and $22 for children. Hy-Line's High Speed Ferry, the *Grey Lady*, makes the crossing from Hyannis to Nantucket in about an hour, and a round-trip ticket costs $75 for passengers 12 and older and $51 for children ages 5 to 12. It's a good idea to call ahead for reservations, especially if you plan to travel during a holiday weekend or during July and Aug. Ferries leave from Dock One, Ocean Street, Hyannis.

THE STEAMSHIP AUTHORITY
Woods Hole Wharf, Woods Hole
(508) 477-8600
(508) 693-9130 for vehicle reservations
(508) 495-3278 for high-speed ferry passenger reservations
www.steamshipauthority.com

The Steamship Authority is the only company offering year-round ferry service from Woods Hole to points on Martha's Vineyard, and from Hyannis to Nantucket. It's also the only ferry that transports cars. Keep in mind that taking your car to the islands can be very expensive, and it's usually not necessary because you can rent one upon your arrival. Better yet, rent a bicycle or moped (see our Martha's Vineyard and Nantucket chapters). We advise you to check the schedule for boat departures as they change seasonally. The one-way fare from Woods Hole to Martha's Vineyard is $7.50 for adults, $4.00 for children ages 5 to 12, and free for children younger than 5. Ferry service from Hyannis to Nantucket costs $14.00 one-way for adults, $7.25 for kids (5 to 12), and is free for those under 5. The Steamship Authority also offers a fast ferry to Nantucket from Hyannis, and the cost is $65 round trip for adults, $49 for kids (5 to 12), and free for those under 5.

Private Boat

The boating crowd will find superb facilities within Nantucket harbor, which has moorings, tie-ups, fuel, and food service. Most of the island's restaurants, accommodations, and attractions are within easy walking distance. For more information call the Town Pier at (508) 228-7261; the Nantucket

Boat Basin at (508) 325-1350 (www.nantucket-boatbasin.com); or Nantucket Moorings at (508) 228-4472 (www.nantucketmoorings.com).

Marine supplies are available at Nantucket Marine, (508) 228–6505 (www.nantucketmarine.com); Madaket Marine, (508) 228-1163 (www.madaketmarine.com); and Nantucket Ship Chandlery, (508) 228-2300, at the harbor.

GETTING AROUND

Nantucket Town is the main part of the nearly 50-square-mile island, which has only a few paved roads. Madaket Road leads to the community of Madaket, about 5.5 miles from town. Hummock Road leads to Cisco Beach, about 4.5 miles away; Surfside Road leads to Surfside Beach, about 2.5 miles from town; and Siasconset is about 9 miles from town along Milestone Road. Take Polpis and then Wauwinet Road to get to Wauwinet, an area roughly 5.5 miles from town. Past Wauwinet is conservation land on Great Point. Nantucket Memorial Airport is about 2.5 miles from town.

By Shuttle Bus

A highly successful means of coping with traffic and transportation has been the use of shuttle buses, which run seasonally. It may even bring romance: a few years ago, a couple who met on the shuttle were married on Nantucket!

NANTUCKET REGIONAL TRANSIT AUTHORITY
(508) 228-7025, (508) 325-9571, (508) 325-7516 (TDD)
www.shuttlenantucket.com
Nantucket Regional Transit Authority has expanded its seasonal shuttle service to serve the entire island, with routes to Sconset and Madaket and loops out to Surfside Beach and Jetties Beach. Downtown shuttle stops are on Washington Street and Broad Street; other stops are on the routes. The Mid-Island Loop bus costs $1, as do the Miacomet Loop buses. Three different routes run regularly to Sconset (one via Polpis Road, one via Milestone Road and Jetties Beach, and one via Old South Road/Nobadeer Farm Road) and cost

$2. Service to Madaket costs $2. One-, three-, and seven-day, as well as monthly and season passes are available. Senior citizens older than 65 and those with disabilities pay half-fare, and children 6 and younger ride free. Buses are wheelchair accessible and have bicycle racks. Service runs from late May to early Oct, seven days a week from 7 a.m. to 11:30 p.m. Park-and-ride lots are at the west end, the elementary school, the Muse, the Chicken Box, Faregrounds Restaurant, and Odd Fellows Lodge parking lot.

There is also a summer beach shuttle service to Surfside and Jetties Beaches from downtown. Fares are $2 each way to Surfside Beach and $1 each way to Jetties Beach.

By Car

One important piece of advice concerning cars: Leave your vehicle behind. Nantucket Town was designed in the 1700s, and its cobblestone streets and narrow lanes are not conducive to high-volume traffic. Streets become congested with traffic, especially during the summer months, and parking can be difficult, if not impossible. You really don't need a car here, particularly for day trips; you can walk to just about anyplace in town and get out of town by bike, bus, and taxi.

If you won't part with your car, be prepared to part with your money, because it is expensive to bring a car to the island (see the Ferry Service section); consider renting a car instead. You'll need a $100 beach vehicle permit to drive on beaches; contact Nantucket Police Department (508-228-1212). A special permit is also required for driving on property managed by the Nantucket Conservation Foundation (508-228-2884).

There are no in-town parking lots, only street parking: it's free, but the one-hour limit is enforced. A final note: Nantucket has many one-way streets, so watch for signs.

Car Rentals and Taxis

Once on the island, transportation is not difficult to arrange. Taxis meet incoming flights at the airport and incoming ferries downtown. Car rental agencies are at the airport and in town.

Many rental agencies offer four-wheel-drive vehicles. You'll want to call Nantucket Windmill Auto (508-228-1227, 800-228–1227) at the airport. This year-round, full-service agency has a fleet of jeeps and SUVs, along with the more traditional sedans, vans, and station wagons, complete with beach vehicle permits. They also provide free pickup service at your hotel or guesthouse or at the Steamship Authority.

Some of the other rental services on the island include Affordable Rentals, 6 South Beach St., (508) 228-3501 and Hertz Car Rental, (508) 228-9421 or (800) 654-3131. Hertz is at the airport.

By Bicycle or Moped

Bicycles are an excellent way to get around, because the island is relatively flat, and there are more than 24 miles of paved bike paths that stretch from Nantucket Town to Siasconset to the east, Surfside to the south, and Madaket to the west. Mopeds are faster, but inexperienced drivers can get in trouble with sand on the roads. To avoid getting ticketed (or hurt), please familiarize yourself with local regulations and observe them. Rental agencies can inform you of the regulations.

Do not ride bikes on sidewalks or mopeds on bike paths, and heed one-way street signs and other street signs. Front and rear reflectors are required.

The following shops have bike and moped rentals (Young's also repairs bikes). All are within walking distance of the ferry dock.

COOK'S CYCLE SHOP INC.
6 South Beach St.
(508) 228-0800

HOLIDAY CYCLE
4 Chester St.
(508) 228-3644

NANTUCKET BIKE SHOPS
Steamboat Wharf and Straight Wharf
(508) 228-1999, (800) 770-3088
www.nantucketbikeshop.com

YOUNG'S BICYCLE SHOP
6 Broad St.
(508) 228-1151
www.youngsbicycleshop.com

ACCOMMODATIONS

Nantucket has outstanding accommodations of all types. With nearly 1,400 rooms to choose from, you can stay in a single cottage on the inner harbor or in a small guesthouse nestled amongst rose gardens. Or perhaps you'd rather be centrally located in one of the many fine bed-and-breakfasts or inns situated in the center of town. Nantucket has no private campgrounds, and public camping is prohibited. The closest you'll get to camping is the hostel, which offers dormitory-style accommodations.

Most places have lower rates in the off-season, which is a nice time to visit anyway. Many of the smaller inns do not allow children, whereas some allow children older than a certain age. Families with children might be better off renting a cottage or staying at a larger resort that accommodates children.

It is always wise to inquire about the specific policies of any facility concerning children, pets, cancellations, and refunds. Most places accept major credit cards; we tell you of those that do not.

Reservation and Information Services

If you're planning a vacation on Nantucket, reserve your accommodations well in advance—many places are booked months ahead of time. Some summer guests often reserve rooms before they leave for the October Cranberry Festival and the Christmas Stroll (see our Annual Events section of this chapter), and then reserve their summer vacation slot while here for the holidays.

However, people's plans do change, and cancellations can easily create the opportunity for you to get a room in a first-rate inn without reserving far in advance. That's when reservation services come in especially handy. Here are a few resources to try.

ROBERTS HOUSE INN
11 India St.
(508) 228-0600, (800) 872-6830
www.robertshouseinn.com
This year-round reservation service represents a group of historic inns, bed-and-breakfasts, and cottages distinguished by fireplaces, harbor views, and antique furnishings.

NANTUCKET ACCOMMODATIONS
4 Dennis Dr.
(508) 228-9559
www.nantucketaccommodation.com
This well-established year-round reservation service represents about 95 percent of the licensed accommodations on the island, including hotels, inns, bed-and-breakfasts, rental homes, and cottages. They will book rooms for you. They also have private house rental listings and cottages.

NANTUCKET CHAMBER OF COMMERCE
48 Main St., Nantucket
(508) 228-1700
www.nantucketchamber.org
Call or write for an extensive brochure that covers everything you could want in the way of accommodations. The office is open year-round.

THE NANTUCKET CONCIERGE
P.O. Box 1257, Nantucket 02554
(508) 228-8400
www.nantucketconcierge.com
Nantucket Concierge books accommodations; makes reservations for airline tickets, dinner, and entertainment; arranges the delivery of everything from flowers to birthday cakes; and can get tickets for anything on the island. They can fix you up with swimming or sailing lessons and tennis court time, too, as well as golf lessons and tee times.

NANTUCKET VACATION RENTALS
15 North Beach St.
(508) 228-2530, (800) 228-4070
www.nantucketrealestate.com

If you have questions about rental houses, cottages, or apartments, give Nantucket Vacation Rentals a call. The office, at Nantucket Real Estate Co., is open all year.

NANTUCKET VISITORS SERVICES AND INFORMATION BUREAU
25 Federal St.
(508) 228-0925
www.nantucket-ma.gov
This town-run bureau, along with the chamber of commerce, has compiled a detailed list of accommodations on a day-by-day basis where vacancies exist; however, the bureau does not make bookings. Lodging information can be found at www.nantucketlodging.org.

The office is open daily year-round.

Price Code
The following key is based on the average cost of a night's stay in a double-occupancy room in the busy season, minus tax and special charges. State and local taxes add about 9.7 percent to a bill.

$................. Less than $75
$$ .... $75 to $110
$$$ .... $111 to $175
$$$$ .... $176 or more

Inns, Bed-and-Breakfasts, and Guesthouses

ANCHOR INN $$$$
66 Centre St.
(508) 228-0072
www.anchor-inn.net
Next door to the historic Old North Church just outside of town, this old sea captain's home retains its original antique paneling and random-width floorboards. The common room has a fireplace, and guests enjoy home-baked muffins, coffee, and other goodies each morning on the bright, enclosed breakfast porch. Each of the 11 guest rooms is named for a Nantucket whale ship and has a private bath; most have queen canopy beds.

BRASS LANTERN INN $$$$
11 North Water St.
(508) 228-4064, (800) 377-6609
www.brasslanternnantucket.com

The inn is charming, but you'll especially love the gardens in the backyard. Some rooms have fireplaces and canopy beds, and you can order room service for breakfast if you wish, but that means you'd have to turn down having breakfast outdoors in the Shakespearean herb garden.

CENTERBOARD GUEST HOUSE $$$$
8 Chester St.
(508) 228-9696, (877) 228-2811
www.centerboardguesthouse.com

This immaculate Victorian-style guesthouse has seven rooms, beautifully decorated with fresh flowers and lace; some have lovely painted murals in pale pastels. One suite has a private Jacuzzi and fireplace, and the fir-walled Houseboat Room accommodates up to five guests. Rooms offer a private bath, telephone, refrigerator, and flat-screen television. Your hosts serve a continental breakfast. The facility is nonsmoking.

CENTRE STREET INN $$-$$$$
78 Centre St.
(508) 228-0199
www.centreSt.inn.com

A close walk from both town and beaches, this inn offers 13 guest rooms with antique brass or canopy beds and private or shared baths. The large common room, where a continental breakfast is served each morning, is especially inviting, and guests can enjoy a cup of coffee or tea there any time of day. The inn, which is a nonsmoking facility and accommodates children in certain rooms, is open mid-Apr through Columbus Day.

THE CENTURY HOUSE $$$$
10 Cliff Rd.
(508) 228-0530
www.centuryhouse.com

Nestled partway up the hill between Cliff Road and Centre Street, this is the oldest operating guesthouse on the island. Built in 1833 by Capt. Robert Calder, it became a rooming house in 1870. Guests are treated to a veritable feast each morning, including homemade coffeecake, bagels, and breads. Guests can relax anytime in the comfortable common room. An interesting touch: all 16 rooms feature lovely and varied paintings by artists who have stayed here. The Century House is open from mid-May through mid-Oct.

HAWTHORN HOUSE $$$-$$$$
2 Chestnut St.
(508) 228-1468
www.hawthornhouse.com

Right in town, this homey, 1849 historic house offers nine guest rooms decorated with antique furnishings, original artwork by local artists, and, in many cases, handmade quilts. A separate cottage is also available. Coffee is offered in the cozy upstairs common room, and guests receive a coupon good for a full breakfast at one of two restaurants in town.

MARTIN HOUSE INN $$$$
61 Centre St.
(508) 228-0678
www.martinhouseinn.net

Polished mahogany, classic paintings, and Oriental rugs characterize this elegant 1803 mariner's home, which became an inn in the 1920s. A piano graces the common room, where window seats beckon, and a continental breakfast is served at a large, beautifully appointed table. Many of the 13 guest rooms have four-poster beds, fireplaces, and private baths. Guests can sit on the veranda in summer or curl up in front of the fire in cooler months. The inn, open year-round, is just a short walk from town.

> **i** Weddings are huge on Nantucket. Inns and hotels fill up with wedding parties, especially during September and October.

THE PINEAPPLE INN $$$$
10 Hussey St.
(508) 228-9992
www.pineappleinn.com

This elegant old home includes modern amenities such as air-conditioning, telephones with voice mail, cable televisions (tastefully concealed in reproduction wardrobes), and computer hook-ups in the 12 guest rooms, which feature marble bathrooms. One room is wheelchair accessible, as is the beautiful brick garden patio, compete with a pineapple fountain. Just outside the busy center of town, the inn is quiet, yet close to shops and restaurants. The hearty continental breakfasts here are a real treat, whether served in the formal dining room or on the patio. Open late Apr through Christmas, the inn is nonsmoking and designed for adults.

SHERBURNE INN $$$$
10 Gay St.
(508) 228-4425, (888) 577-4425
www.sherburneinn.com

Named for the original settlement on Nantucket, this eight-room inn was originally a silk factory and later converted to a lodging house. Its quirky layout includes front and back stairways, so you can get to your room either way, and the floors slope charmingly in places. The rooms are nicely furnished in elegant, yet warm, old-fashioned style, with antiques, lace canopies, luxurious linens, and fresh flowers. Each guest room has central air-conditioning, phone, cable TV/DVD/CD, wireless Internet access, and a private bathroom. Guests are served a continental breakfast in the common room or out in the garden, and there is also a second-floor sitting room with a television. Tucked just outside of town in a quiet neighborhood, it is still close to attractions, shops, and restaurants.

SHIPS INN $$$–$$$$
13 Fair St.
(508) 228-0040
www.shipsinnnantucket.com

Open seasonally, this inn began as the home of Capt. Obed Starbuck, who built it in 1831; many of its rooms are named for the ships he commanded. The antiques-filled home is also distinguished as the birthplace of Lucretia Coffin Mott, the first female abolitionist and advocate of women's suffrage. The inn has a romantic downstairs restaurant and bar that is open to the public for dinner; continental breakfast is available for guests.

THE WOODBOX $$$$
36 Fair St.
(508) 228-0587
www.woodboxinn.com

Built in 1709, this is known as the oldest inn on the island, and the original, unpainted wood paneling; hand-hewn beams; low ceilings; and huge old fireplaces bear witness to its history. Period antiques and reproductions are used throughout. The Woodbox has nine units, which include six suites with one or two bedrooms and three double-bed guest rooms. All rooms have private baths, refrigerators, and television, and all suites have working fireplaces. It is open from May through Christmas. The inn's restaurant serves breakfast and dinner. No credit cards.

Hotels and Resorts

CLIFFSIDE BEACH CLUB $$$$
46 Jefferson Ave.
(508) 288-0618
www.cliffsidebeach.com

This luxury hotel was built on the site of a prestigious beach club, where members once gathered to be assured of having a private stretch of beach with the same umbrella and chairs each day. Today, guests come for the private beach, waterfront rooms, daily maid service, exercise facility, lake, lap and leisure pools, hydro therapy spa, and fine restaurant. Open May to mid-Oct, Cliffside offers hotel units, suites, studio apartments, and a cottage; some rooms have private decks; most rooms have an ocean view, both a queen-size bed and sleeper sofa, and air-conditioning. All rooms have refrigerators, cable television, and phones. Guests get a continental breakfast and have use of beach umbrellas, chairs, and beach towels. *NOTE:* The hotel accepts American Express only.

NANTUCKET ISLAND RESORTS $$$$
10 Amelia Dr.
(800) 475-2637
www.nantucketislandresorts.com
The Nantucket Islands Resorts include some of the most upscale lodging on the island. Choices include the elegant and centrally located Jared Coffin House; the grand 53-room White Elephant; the stately waterfront Wauwinet; the quaint and nautical Cottages at the Boat Basin; and the newest addition, the White Elephant Hotel Residences. There is a lot to choose from here so the best bet is to go online and cruise around their extensive Web site. Then you can decide whether you want to be downtown in the historic Jared Coffin House or on the harbor at the White Elephant. Either way, this looks like it's a case of you get what you pay for: in this case, luxury.

Cottages

THE SUMMER HOUSE $$$$
South Bluff, Siasconset
(508) 257-4577
www.thesummerhouse.com
Ten rose-covered cottages are beautifully situated on a bluff overlooking the ocean, within steps of a main building where one can dine by candlelight to the accompaniment of live piano music. The private beach is never crowded, and its idyllic setting at the base of the bluff also encompasses a luncheon restaurant and the Summer House heated swimming pool. Equally transporting accommodations can be found at the Inn's two satellite locations on India Street and Fair Street. The Summer House is open from late Apr to early Dec.

WADE COTTAGES $$$$
Siasconset
(508) 257-6308, (212) 989-6423
www.wadecottages.com
The grounds of this former estate are delightful, and you'll enjoy the solitude of the private beach.

The accommodations include guest rooms with private or shared bathrooms, apartments with one to four bedrooms, and cottages with three, four, or five bedrooms. The facility is open from mid-May to early Oct.

Hostel

ROBERT B. JOHNSON MEMORIAL HOSTEL $–$$$
31 Western Ave.
(508) 228-0433, (888) 901-2084
www.usahostels.org/cape/hint/index.php
Those who enjoy roughing it can make this their base for biking or backpacking getaways. This hostel, once a historic lifesaving station, has 49 beds, cooking facilities, and beautiful sunset views from its location just across from Surfside Beach. Reservations are required in season (you can call for reservations beginning Dec 1), and dorms cost $32 to $35 per night; private rooms can be had for $178. It's open from mid-May through early Oct.

Vacation Rentals and Real Estate

More and more visitors to Nantucket are choosing the relaxing vacation lifestyle that is best enjoyed in the quiet seclusion of a lovely private home or cottage. Despite the fact that Nantucket has strict building regulations, it has an active and extremely pricey real estate and new-construction market.

The low end of the market is high here. If you can afford it, there are some great listings in the higher end of the market. You can get a classic antique in the heart of the historic district for anywhere from upward of $1 million to $8 million, and a waterfront estate may go for $10 million or more.

Some of Nantucket's larger real estate offices have a rental department, in case the price of buying is out of the question or you're here strictly for R&R.

The Nantucket Listing Service is another resource for prospective buyers.

The following agencies represent the best sources on the island for real estate purchases and rentals.

COFFIN-'SCONSET REAL ESTATE
40 Centre St.
(508) 228-1138
www.coffinrealestate.com
Open year-round, since 1963 this longstanding and experienced real estate office of 19 brokers and agents offers seasonal and vacation rentals, and residential and commercial sales.

CONGDON & COLEMAN REAL ESTATE INC.
57 Main St.
(508) 325-5000
www.congdonandcoleman.com
This full-service company offers sales, appraisals, year-round rentals, and summer rentals by month or season. The office is open year-round.

DENBY REAL ESTATE INC.
5 North Water St.
(508) 228-2522
www.denby.com
With eight brokers and sales representatives Denby can help you arrange a summer rental from a selection of more than 800 homes. The office also does appraisals and subscribes to the Nantucket Listing Services.

ISLAND PROPERTIES REAL ESTATE
35 Old South Rd.
(508) 228-6999
www.islandpropertiesre.com
Island Properties offers both sales and rentals (long- and short-term). Home sale prices are seldom less than $1 million and often much, much more. Rental rates will vary depending on location, size of the house, and proximity to the water. The firm is open year-round.

MAURY PEOPLE SOTHEBY'S INTERNATIONAL REALTY
35 and 37 Main St.
(508) 228-1881
www.maurypeople.com
Maury People Sotheby's International Realty has extensive sales listings throughout the island

and approximately 1,500 rental listings. Open daily year-round (the Sconset office is open June through Sept), the Main Street office has been doing business on Nantucket for more than 30 years.

RESTAURANTS

The caliber of dining facilities on Nantucket makes this an island you wouldn't mind being stranded on. It could take all summer, or possibly longer, to sample all the great restaurants here, and there is plenty of variety. It is not, however, what you would call cheap.

Dinner for two at some restaurants can easily cost $150. But there are less expensive options. One idea: Go out for lunch instead of dinner at your favorite elegant restaurant. And look into more casual places for dinner or restaurants that offer bistro or tavern menus in addition to full dinners.

Although we have given you a great head start on finding your own special place among Nantucket's long list of restaurants, consider yourself morally and gastronomically obliged to do your own research. Most of the places we have included are open year-round, but they may take a much-needed break sometime after New Year's; it's best to inquire about winter hours at any facility.

As a general rule, you don't have to dress up for dinner here; we signal restaurants that require specific dress. Most restaurants accept major credit cards; we'll tell you the ones that do not.

Price Code

We've included the following pricing codes as guidelines in helping you decide where to dine. The key is based on the average price of dinner for two, excluding appetizers, alcoholic beverages, dessert, tax, and tip.

$................. Less than $20
$$ .... $20 to $50
$$$ .... $51 to $80
$$$$ .... $81 and more

ARNO'S AT 41 MAIN STREET $$–$$$
41 Main St.
(508) 228-7001
www.arnos.net

A popular, reasonably priced meeting place for working folk, families, and hungry tourists, Arno's serves a big breakfast (until 2 p.m. on weekdays), lunch, and dinner. Get a window table and people-watch while you enjoy your food. We suggest you try the fried seafood platter. Children have their own menu. Arno's is open Apr to Dec.

BLACK-EYED SUSAN'S $$
10 India St.
(508) 325-0308

There have been some Darwinian scenes on the sidewalk outside this wildly popular BYOB, which accepts reservations only for its 6 p.m. seating and divvies up dining times on a first-come, first-served basis thereafter. The homely storefront conceals a small dining room lit by glass chandeliers, but real gourmets scramble for a seat at the bar, where they can observe chef Jeff Worster at work in his open kitchen. The menu changes every three weeks, featuring global fare ranging from tuna tartare with cucumbers and srirachi aioli to tandoori chicken with green mango chutney. Open for breakfast daily and dinner every day but Sun from Apr through Oct.

i Nantucket has something most parents really appreciate: a babysitting service. Nantucket Babysitters' Service, Inc. (call 508-228-4970 or visit www.nantucket babysitters.com), sends sitters to you—to your home, cottage, hotel, even your boat. Sitters are experienced, carefully screened, and do everything from caring for infants to supervising teens, so you can enjoy some adult time during your stay.

THE BOARDING HOUSE $$$
12 Federal St.
(508) 228-9622
www.boardinghouse-pearl.com

In Nancy Thayer's novel *Belonging*, which is set on Nantucket, the sophisticated, affluent heroine Joanna Jones dines twice at the Boarding House. The lady, however fictional, knows her restaurants. Chef-proprietor Seth Carter Raynor's innovative cuisine has both Mediterranean and Gallic influences; littleneck clams with sweet garlic, cherry tomatoes and white beans and sirloin steak frites are two examples of dishes that appear on the ever-changing menu. Choose from a lighter bistro menu or more-formal fare, and sit in the romantic, smoke-free lower dining room with low-beamed ceilings and fresco walls; in the comfortable bar area; or, in summer, outside on the patio. The Boarding House serves lunch and dinner and is open year-round. If the Boarding House does not suit your tastes, try the Pearl next door ("next door" on the Web site as well), which is also operated by Raynor and his wife.

THE BROTHERHOOD OF THIEVES $$
23 Broad St.
(508) 228-2551
www.brotherhoodofthieves.com

Low, oak-beamed ceilings, wood paneling, and lots of candlelight create a wonderfully warm and cozy atmosphere. The food is terrific, and there's lots of it. The shoestring fries served with burgers and sandwiches are great, and the chowder is hard to beat. It is casual, offers pub fare, and is open daily year-round for lunch and dinner, with evening entertainment. This beloved institution has a downstairs bar and five upstairs dining spaces. There is also an outdoor patio and bar and a schedule of live entertainment.

CAP'N TOBEY'S CHOWDER HOUSE $$
20 Straight Wharf
(508) 228-0836

This moderately priced tavern-style restaurant offers a menu and prices that families can appreciate. The clam chowder is widely and highly recommended. It is open daily for lunch and dinner May through Oct.

CENTRE STREET BISTRO $$

29 Centre St.
(508) 228-8470
www.nantucketbistro.com

You can grow old waiting for a table here in July, one of the few downsides of the fact that some of the island's most gratifying cuisine happens to be served in a space the size of a ship's galley. With its book-laden shelves and punched-tin-lanterns, the atmosphere affects the illusion of dining in a friend's living room. Regulars rave about simple specialties like the warm goat cheese tart, seared salmon with citrus soy and spice glaze, and Bistro pad thai (which features sesame-crusted shrimp and red curry rice noodles). The wine list is short but swell, and the desserts are inspired by seasonal ingredients, with the lemon tart and strawberry rhubarb crisp deserving special mention.

CINCO $$$

5 Amelia Dr.
(508) 325-5151
www.cinco5.com

When your taste runs to tapas, try stylish Cinco, whose walls wear tones of chocolate, mint, and marmalade. Owned by one of the Island's most popular bartenders (Michael Sturgis, formerly of 21 Federal and the White Elephant), this Spanish-American newcomer serves the kind of confident cuisine that goes exceptionally well with sangria. Larger meals include two kinds of paella (one centered on seafood, the other on pork, pancetta, and chorizo), but the real draw lies in small plates like caramelized brussels sprouts and sautéed Nantucket bay scallops with pear brown butter and fresh citrus. Serving dinner only, from Apr through Dec.

i For prime sunset views over dinner, visit the Westender at 326 Madaket Rd. This two-story restaurant has a bar serving "Madaket Mysteries" on the first floor and a cathedral-ceilinged second floor that showcases the evening show over the water.

THE CLUB CAR $$$

1 Main St.
(508) 228-1101
www.theclubcar.com

Near the waterfront with a ringside seat on Main Street, this well-regarded restaurant skillfully combines casual dining and elegant eating. The menu is rich and varied—you may find anything from rabbit to octopus—and the food is consistently excellent. If your budget is tight, have lunch at the bar in season. If, however, rack of lamb is a favorite of yours, just remember that you only live once.

Open seasonally, from May through the Christmas Stroll, serving lunch and dinner.

DEMARCO $$$$

9 India St.
(508) 228-1836
www.demarcorestaurant.com

This restaurant has outstanding Northern Italian food, an absolutely superb wine list (more than 100 Italian selections), and a wonderful atmosphere. If the menu offers swordfish, don't pass it up. Owner Don DeMarco has operated the restaurant for many years. The menu changes regularly, and breads and desserts are made on the premises. DeMarco is open from May through Oct. Reservations are advised.

LE LANGUEDOC $$

24 Broad St.
(508) 228-2552
www.lelanguedoc.com

This family-owned restaurant is known and loved by an appreciative following for its warm, intimate, and comfortable atmosphere; excellent service; and wonderful wine—it's one of the few places you can get superior wines by the glass. You can choose between a more elaborate and pricey menu upstairs and a more casual and affordable but equally enjoyable cafe menu downstairs or on the outdoor terrace in summer. The restaurant is open for dinner daily in season. Lunch and dinner are available in the fall from Sept through Christmas Stroll (the first weekend in Dec; see the Annual Events section), and then it closes until Apr.

ORAN MOR $$$
2 South Beach St.
(508) 228-8655
www.oranmorbistro.com

Though it is named after a rare single-malt scotch, Oran Mor's menu owes more to Nantucket's waters than anything Scotland has to offer. Chef Chris Freeman (who owns the restaurant with his wife, Heather) has a winning way with fresh-caught seafood, serving up specialties like Nantucket lobster bisque (with smoked haddock brandade and morel mushrooms) and sautéed fluke (with soft polenta, littleneck clams, linguica, and smoked tomato broth). Open year-round; call for off-season hours.

PROVISIONS $
3 Harbor Square
(508) 228-3258

This gourmet deli is a popular place among both locals and visitors, who come for hearty soups, salads, and terrific sandwiches. Or you can opt for pâtés or cheese with French bread, and treat yourself to a cappuccino. In fine weather the benches outside are filled with people enjoying lunch. Provisions is open for breakfast, too, and they'll pack picnic lunches for you to take along. It's open Apr to early Nov.

ROPEWALK $$
1 Straight Wharf
(508) 228-8886
www.theropewalk.com

Situated near the wharves, RopeWalk is a convenient place to eat lunch or dinner before or after your ferry ride. You'll find ample indoor seating, or you can eat outdoors at the raw bar. It's very casual, the food is good (especially the crab cakes), and some say the calamari is the best on the island. Open seasonally from May through Oct.

THE SEAGRILLE RESTAURANT $$
45 Sparks Ave.
(508) 325-5700
www.theseagrille.com

The creative and well-prepared seafood, especially the lobster bisque served with dill pastry crust topping, makes the SeaGrille popular with locals, but you can find most any other kind of entree here too. They specialize in local and regional fresh seafood, prepared both traditionally and creatively, as well as the standards—filet mignon, grilled tenderloin of baby lamb, and chicken Provençal. A reasonably priced array of seasonal specials is also offered and includes quesadilla salad. The SeaGrille serves dinner nightly and lunch Mon through Sat year-round.

SOMETHING NATURAL $
50 Cliff Rd.
(508) 228-0504
www.somethingnatural.com

This is a great place to stop on your way out to Madaket. Pack one of their incredible, healthy sandwiches in your bike pack, and you'll have something to look forward to when you stop. Or stay and eat at one of the shaded picnic tables, where you're likely to see a number of locals filling up on their lunch break. The homemade breads alone are wonderful, and if you really want to indulge, try one of their fresh-baked chocolate chip cookies. It's open from Apr to Oct.

THE SUMMER HOUSE RESTAURANT $$$$
17 Ocean Ave., Siasconset
(508) 257-9976
www.thesummerhouse.com

The Summer House Restaurant is open from the Nantucket Wine Festival Weekend in May (see the Annual Events section in this chapter) to Columbus Day weekend from 6 to 10:30 p.m., though the bar stays open until 1 a.m. Reservations are recommended. The casual Oceanside Restaurant, on the grounds, is open from late June until Labor Day serving lunch from noon until 3:30 p.m. in a comfortable beachfront Caribbean atmosphere just feet from the Atlantic Ocean.

TOPPER'S $$$
At The Wauwinet, Wauwinet Rd.
(508) 228-0145
www.wauwinet.com

Accessible either by car, jitney, or boat, Topper's is the world-class restaurant of the Wauwinet (see our Accommodations chapter), a Nantucket Island Resorts property with its own private bay and ocean beaches. Those opting to arrive by sea will approach the "up harbor" establishment aboard the *Wauwinet Lady*, a 26-foot open launch complete with cocktail service. Adding to the restaurant's aura of extravagance is its menu, which morphs the seasonal riches of New England into New American–style cuisine unequalled on Nantucket. Try the butter-basted New England lobster with herbed hand-rolled spaghetti and tempura sea beans, and pair it with a pour from the 1,450-bottle wine list. Closed from Nov through Apr, and open for lunch, dinner and Sunday brunch the rest of the year.

21 FEDERAL $$$
21 Federal St.
(508) 228-2121
www.21federal.com
With polished wood, linen, and candlelight, this place is quietly sophisticated—and the food has the same quality. Entrees such as braised lamb shank and sautéed breast of duck are simply and elegantly prepared, and first courses include some unusual appetizers, such as tuna tartare. Do not skip dessert, which might be hazelnut and raspberry Dacquoise with coffee butter cream or warm berry compote. They are open for lunch and dinner mid-May through mid-Oct and Thanksgiving through Christmas Stroll.

SHOPPING

Just as the island's old-time sea captains traveled the world and brought home exotic wares of distant ports, today's shopkeepers import the best from all over, without neglecting the quality items produced right here on the island. You'll find everything from gold jewelry and pearls to beautiful hand-woven shawls and the lightship baskets for which Nantucket is famous.

Most of the shops listed below are open all year long; we'll let you know when hours are seasonal.

BILL AND JUDY SAYLE'S NANTUCKET LIGHTSHIP BASKETS
112 Washington St. Extension
(508) 228-9876
Beautiful, practical, versatile—and undeniably expensive—the traditional Nantucket lightship baskets that are exquisitely handmade by Bill and Judy Sayle range in size from miniatures as small as thimbles to ones as big as baby's cradles. Woven with fine caning material, the baskets are made with a cherry wood bottom, oak stays, oak handles, and leather hinges, and the lids are decorated with carved ivory or scrimshaw scenes.

The prices vary according to the size, the type of wood used for the tops, and the type of decoration. Miniature baskets can range in price from $195 to $525, and medium-size covered baskets with a carved sperm whale on the lid can start at around $800. The Sayles' shop is open weekdays from 10 a.m. to 3 p.m. and weekends by appointment year-round (unless they take a winter break after the holidays).

CLAIRE MURRAY
11 South Water St.
(508) 228-1913
www.clairemurray.com
Claire Murray's handmade rugs, both finished pieces and kits, fall into a unique class of artwork. Beautiful, colorful, and cheerful, some patterns are simple enough for beginners, others are a challenge to accomplished rug makers, but all are visually exquisite. You can buy a finished rug for $70 to $3,000, and kits average about $130 each. Needlepoint and counted cross-stitch kits, gift items, and cotton throws are also available. Classes are offered with a purchase.

CROSS RIP OUTFITTERS
24 Easy St.
(508) 228-4900
www.crossrip.com
If there's an angler on your gift list, be sure to stop here. In addition to rods and reels, this shop has a collection of fishing-related gifts, including beautiful painted mugs, ties, jewelry, hats, shirts, sunglasses, and even stationery. Cross Rip also

offers fly-fishing instruction, equipment rentals, and guide service.

DIANA KIM ENGLAND, GOLDSMITHS
56 Main St.
(508) 228-3766, (800) 343-1468
www.dianakimengland.com

A fleet of goldsmiths contribute to the elegant handmade jewelry sold here, all of which is produced in the studio upstairs, including earrings, pendants, and bracelets in ivory and 14- to 18-karat gold. Among the most popular pieces are the gold lightship basket pendants with scrimshaw. The shop is open year-round.

ERICA WILSON NEEDLE WORKS
25 Main St.
(508) 228-9881
www.ericawilson.com

This store has lovely original gifts, including quilts and hand-knit sweaters from England and Ireland, contemporary women's petite and children's clothing, and European specialty silk shoes. Erica Wilson Needle Works also displays locally crafted jewelry, Nantucket baskets, and special Nantucket china. Unique needlepoint kits range in price from $20 to $1,500 (for a rug) and work into patterns adapted from famous tapestries and original designs.

THE HUB
31 Main St.
(508) 325-0200

This is the place to go to buy a newspaper—just about any newspaper. The Hub also sells magazines, books, lottery tickets, postcards, and sundries, and offers photocopy and fax service. As its name implies, it's generally a lively place, great for chatting with perfect strangers.

THE LION'S PAW
0 Main St.
(508) 228-3837

Baskets, pillows, hooked rugs, linens, and boldly colorful ceramics make up the bulk of inventory in this delightful, spacious store. There is a terrific selection of tablecloths, beautiful hand-painted furniture, accessories, and unique gift items.

MITCHELL'S BOOK CORNER
54 Main St.
(508) 228-1080
www.mitchellsbookcorner.com

If you love books, you won't be able to resist this corner shop. The Nantucket Room is especially engrossing, with the island's more complete offering of books about Nantucket, whaling, marine history, boating, and nature. Choose from such titles as Nathaniel Philbrick's *Away Off Shore*, deservedly touted as one of the most readable Nantucket histories; *Death in Rough Water* by Francine Matthews; Martha Lawrence's *Lightship Basket*, and John McCalley's *Nantucket Then and Now*. Mitchell's also has a great general inventory and a large selection of quality children's books.

MURRAY'S TOGGERY SHOP
62 Main St.
(800) 368-2134
www.nantucketreds.com

Murray's has just about everything. You'll find shoes, sweaters, hats, and Estée Lauder products, and it is the largest men's clothing store on Main Street. Started by Philip Murray, the popular Nantucket Red menswear line originated here from a type of slacks made in France. It has now expanded to Oxford shirts, coats, jackets, sweatshirts, and caps.

NANTUCKET BOOKWORKS
25 Broad St.
(508) 228-4000
www.nantucketbookworks.com

This year-round store not only has a wonderful collection of books and plenty of room to browse, but a fun assortment of greeting cards, stationery, blank books, and other gifts for writers. It has a great children's section, and gifts for all ages are scattered throughout the store. Nantucket Bookworks keeps long hours, so you can browse after dinner.

NANTUCKET COUNTRY ANTIQUES
38 Centre St.
(508) 228-8868
www.nantucketcountryantiques.com
This store is chock-full of one-of-a-kind pieces and specializes in old quilts and folk antiques. It has a few new items as well, such as hooked rugs and country accent pieces. It's open April 1 through Jan 1.

NANTUCKET GOURMET
4 India St.
(508) 228-4353, (866) 626-2665
www.nantucketgourmet.com
This store has everything for the true or aspiring gourmet, from Nantucket-made jams and jellies to mustards, cranberry marmalade, vinegars, and teas. The pepper gun, an unusual one-handed grinder invented by Tom David of Nantucket, is particularly popular. The shop also has a full deli with a dizzying array of cheeses and other edibles.

NANTUCKET LOOMS
16 Federal St.
(508) 228-1908, (888) 718-8089
www.nantucketlooms.com
Nantucket Looms displays beautiful handwoven throws, mufflers, and shirts and small elegant toiletries, jewelry, and oversize mugs. Local and international craftsmen have contributed to this rich assortment of clothing and gift items, including decorative birdhouses and dog doorstops, handmade sweaters, and hand-painted furniture.

NANTUCKET NATURAL OILS
5 Centre St.
(508) 325-4740, (800) 223-8660
www.nantucketnaturaloils.com
Perfumer John Harding has any name-brand scent you can think of, but with an important difference: There is no alcohol or other additives. These are essential oils, so they have amazing staying power and can even be used by people who find conventional perfumes give them a headache or make them sneeze. And these oils last and last—we can tell you from personal experience that a tiny bottle can easily last a year. The shop also carries lotions, bath gels, shampoos, and soaps that can be scented, along with lovely perfume bottles and other accessories.

NINA HELLMAN MARINE ANTIQUES & AMERICANA
48 Centre St.
(508) 228-4677
www.nauticalnantucket.com
Here is a wonderful collection of marine antiques—everything from old anchors, tools, and ship lanterns to intricate ship models and ships in bottles. The shop also has a great collection of old books on whaling, sailing, and other nautical topics. It's open from Daffodil Weekend to Christmas.

SWEET INSPIRATIONS
26 Centre St.
(978) 526-4843, (888) 225-4843
www.nantucketclipper.com
Chocolate, chocolate, chocolate. Those who love the stuff will find a haven in Sweet Inspirations, where the glass-front display cases are filled with plates of all sorts of positively inspired creations. Try one of their heavenly truffles, chocolate buttercrunch, chocolate-covered cranberries, or our perennial favorite, a simple square of dark chocolate wrapped in foil embossed with a tiny Nantucket Island. Sweet Inspirations has lovely collectible tins to fill with the chocolates of your choice, and they do mail order, too.

WEEDS
14 Centre St.
(508) 228-5200
www.weeds-nantucket.com
A beautiful take on the Nantucket lightship basket is a line of porcelain baskets designed by George Davis, manufactured by Bennington Potters, and sold exclusively through Weeds on Nantucket. Davis, founder and owner of Weeds, also has a beautiful collection of fine bone china, which he designed for Wedgwood, that is still sold worldwide and is available exclusively on Nantucket at his shop. Of course there's a lot

more to see than dinnerware in this year-round shop, which sells antique and reproduction furniture, hatboxes, tins, garden items, and gifts to fit every price range.

ENTERTAINMENT AND NIGHTLIFE

The streets of Nantucket are wonderfully quiet when the stars come out but, if you're a night owl, there are some lively spots. Also consider taking in some of the cultural arts offerings of Nantucket. During the summer season, theater is performed on the island.

Theater

THE THEATRE WORKSHOP OF NANTUCKET
Nantucket United Methodist Church,
2 Centre St.
(508) 228-4305
www.theatreworkshop.com
If you're a fan of community theater, attend a production by the island's year-round community theater company, which has showcased local talent for enthusiastic audiences for more than 40 years.

Movies

Check out the Siasconset Casino in Siasconset (508-257-6661), open seasonally. The Gaslight Theatre on North Union Street (508-228-4435) is open year-round.

Live Entertainment

THE BROTHERHOOD OF THIEVES
23 Broad St.
(508) 228-2551
www.brotherhoodofthieves.com
This cozy eatery has great food, good drinks, and often performances by solo guitarists or folk duos.

CHICKEN BOX
14 Dave St.
(508) 228-9717
www.thechickenbox.com

Heading toward Surfside Beach, you can find this super-casual, year-round bar, better known as the Box. The Box has live bands seven nights a week from Memorial Day to Labor Day and every weekend the rest of the year.

THE MUSE
44 Ave.Surfside Rd.
(508) 228-6873
www.228-muse.com
The Muse is Nantucket's hottest nightclub and concert venue. Here you will find everything from pizza to cool tunes. You might even find yourself competing in the air band competition. The Muse has live entertainment on weekends, usually bands but occasionally DJs. It also offers keno and video trivia games.

i The Nantucket police and the Parks and Recreation Commission show free movies every Friday evening from early July through August at Children's Beach. Movies start at dusk. Call (508) 228-7213 for more information.

ROSE & CROWN
23 South Water St.
(508) 228-2595
www.theroseandcrown.com
In town, the Rose & Crown is a perennial favorite of islanders and visitors, offering a traditional pub atmosphere. They serve lunch and dinner and offer lively entertainment on their stage, varying nightly from rock 'n' roll to karaoke. It is closed in winter.

HISTORICAL BUILDINGS AND MUSEUMS

Nantucket's place in history is richly illustrated in the island's museums and historic buildings. You can visit them for an Insiders' view of the past, including the whaling period that shaped Nantucket's salty character. Be sure to allow plenty of time to see everything, including the three picturesque lighthouses that dot the shoreline.

THE AFRICAN MEETING HOUSE
Five Corners, 29 York St.
(508) 228-9833
www.afroammuseum.org

This small post-and-beam building was built around 1827 by African-American island residents, who used it as a school, church, and meeting-house. The building, which is the only remaining public African-American landmark, is owned by Boston's Museum of Afro-American History, and was restored in 1999. It is open June through Sept. Tours are available by appointment only.

THE COFFIN SCHOOL
4 Winter St.
(508) 228-2505
www.eganinstitute.org

Completed in 1854, this Greek Revival building succeeded the island's first school on Fair Street after the Great Fire of 1846. Around the turn of the 20th century, the school became a center for nautical training and home economics for the Nantucket public schools. It now houses the Egan Institute of Maritime Studies and is open from 1 to 5 p.m. to the public from late May to mid-Oct, offering lectures, exhibits, and history videotapes.

THE HINCHMAN HOUSE
7 Milk St.
(508) 228-0898
www.mmo.org

Wildlife enthusiasts will appreciate the natural history collection of living and preserved variet-ies of wildlife here. The staff conducts children's nature classes and bird and nature walks. The Hinchman House is open for self-guided tours mid-June through Aug, Tues through Sun, 10 a.m. to 4 p.m. Admission is $4 for adults and $3 for children.

THE LIFE-SAVING MUSEUM
158 Polpis Rd.
(508) 228-1885
www.nantucketlifesavingmuseum.com

This is an authentic re-creation of the original 1874 station built in Surfside to assist mariners. It is open daily from mid-June through Columbus Day weekend, 10 a.m. to 4 p.m. Admission is $5 for adults, $3 for children ages 5 to 18, and free for children older than 5.

MACY-CHRISTIAN HOUSE
12 Liberty St. and Walnut Lane
(508) 228-1894
www.nha.org

Built in 1723 and restored in the late 19th cen-tury, this house has furnishings and architecture representative of the colonial and colonial Revival periods. Daily tours are available and admission is covered by the Nantucket Historical Association general admission tickets (see entry below).

MARIA MITCHELL BIRTHPLACE
1 Vestal St.
(508) 228-2896
www.mmo.org

America's first female astronomer, who taught at Vassar College in 1865, is memorialized in her preserved home. The Maria Mitchell Society (508-228-9198) works to preserve her contributions. You can tour the home from June through Aug, Mon through Sat, 10 a.m. to 4 p.m. The admis-sion fee for nonmembers is $5 for adults, $4 for children.

The society also operates the Maria Mitchell Observatory, next door at 3 Vestal Street (508-228-9273), and the Marine Aquarium at 28 Wash-ington Street (508-228-5387).

NANTUCKET ATHENEUM
1 Lower India St.
(508) 228-1110
www.nantucketatheneum.org

The renovated Greek Revival library is one of the oldest continuously operating libraries in the country; Maria Mitchell was the first librarian. It contains some 40,000 volumes as well as paint-ings, ship models, scrimshaw, and sculpture, and also has a wonderful children's room. Be sure to visit the Upper Hall, where such figures as Daniel Webster, Ralph Waldo Emerson, Henry David Thoreau, and Frederick Douglass once spoke.

NANTUCKET HISTORICAL ASSOCIATION SITES
2 Whalers Lane
(508) 228-1894
www.nha.org

The association maintains and operates 24 historic sites, locations, and buildings all over Nantucket. Among them are the Quaker Meeting House; the Old Mill, Mill and Prospect Streets, which has original mechanisms and stones; the Old Gaol, Vestal Street, which is one of the oldest jails in the United States; and the Hadwen House, 96 Main Street, which contains architectural detail and furnishing characteristic of the 19th century. Other sites maintained by the association are the Oldest House and Hose Cart House.

A general pass, good for entry into all the association-maintained sites, is $18 for adults, $15 for seniors, and $9 for children (ages 6 to 17). The association's gift shop (508-228-5785) is next to the Whaling Museum.

THE OLDEST HOUSE
Sunset Hill
(508) 228-1894
www.nha.org/sites/oldesthouse.html

This colonial saltbox was built in 1686, nearly 100 yeas before the American Revolution. It was built for Jethro and Mary Gardner Coffin, as a wedding present from their parents, ending a notorious feud between the two families. Admission is $6 for adults and $3 for children 6 to 17. A Historical Association general pass is also good for admission (see entry above). It is open from late May through Columbus Day.

PETER FOULGER MUSEUM
15 Broad St.
(508) 228-1655

This facility hosts changing exhibits on Nantucket history. Admission is $10 for adults and $6 for children 5 to 14.

THE WHALING MUSEUM
Broad St.
(508) 228-1894
www.nha.org

Originally a candle factory, this superb museum offers displays of whaling equipment, scrimshaw, early records, and the skeleton of a 43-foot finback whale. Don't miss the lively lecture on the history of whaling, presented three times a day. The museum is open Thurs through Mon starting in May and daily late May through Sept from 10 a.m. to 5 p.m. Admission is $15 for adults, $12 for seniors, and $8 for children 6 to 17. A Historical Association general pass is also good for admission.

LIGHTHOUSES

BRANT POINT LIGHTHOUSE
Harbor entrance

Built in 1746, Brant Point Light is the second-oldest lighthouse in the United States. Photographs of its Christmas wreath have graced numerous magazine pages. This is the lighthouse you see when entering the harbor on the ferry.

GREAT POINT LIGHT
Great Point

Destroyed by a storm in 1984 and rebuilt, Great Point Light sits at the northern tip of the island in an area frequented by bird-watchers and picnickers. (See the Natural Areas section of this chapter.)

SANKATY HEAD LIGHTHOUSE
Sankaty Bluff

Picturesque red-and-white Sankaty Head Lighthouse is perched on Sankaty Bluff at the eastern end of the island. It overlooks the sea and a golf course.

ART SCHOOLS AND GALLERIES

Art Instruction

NANTUCKET ISLAND SCHOOL OF DESIGN AND THE ARTS
23 Wauwinet Rd.
(508) 228-9248
www.nisda.org

If the visual arts are your love, contact the school and take some classes. The school offers courses for academic credit and enrichment to both children and adults in such subjects as drawing, painting, photography, clay, textiles, and crafts. The school has accommodations on Washington Street on the harbor.

SHREDDER'S STUDIO
Salros Road off Appleton Rd.
(508) 228-4487
www.madeonnantucket.com
Shredder's offers oil painting, watercolor, jewelry making, and stained-glass classes to adults and young adults and watercolor, ceramics, and other classes for children. It even has a preschool creative workshop for little budding artists.

Galleries

ARTISTS' ASSOCIATION OF NANTUCKET: JOYCE & SEWARD JOHNSON GALLERY
19 Washington St.
(508) 228-0294
www.nantucketarts.org
This small gallery near Straight Wharf features paintings, photography, sculpture, jewelry, and drawings by established island artists and emerging local talent. It hosts a year-round schedule of changing member exhibitions, featured artist shows, juried shows, auctions, fund-raisers, and community-oriented arts events. New shows are usually unveiled at Friday evening opening receptions.

THE GALLERY AT FOUR INDIA STREET
4 India St.
(508) 228-8509
www.galleryatfourindia.com
This gallery is open year-round. It has 19th- and 20th-century oils, pastels, watercolors, sculpture, and bronze work, 80 percent of which is the work of local and regional artists.

i Just a short walk from the bustle of Main Street, you'll find a historic section of Nantucket. Stroll up and down Union and East York Streets while visiting galleries and shops selling antiques, fine arts, and more.

THE NANTUCKET GALLERY & FRAME SHOP
23 Federal St.
(508) 228-1943
www.nantucketgallery.com
This gallery is owned by artist Marshall DuBock, who sells Nantucket scenes.

ROBERT WILSON GALLERIES
51 Main St.
(508) 228-2096
www.robertwilsongalleries.com
While in Nantucket, be sure to visit this gallery, which has exquisite landscape and still-life renderings in oils and watercolors.

TOURS AND EXCURSIONS

On a tour of Nantucket you may get a history lesson, personal insights, or priceless anecdotes. Most tours will meet you at a central location or pick you up. Call for prices. And you may have guessed already that when you're visiting a spot in the middle of the ocean, local tours aren't limited to land. You can choose from among sunset cruises, children's cruises, and—not surprisingly, as Nantucket was once the center of America's whaling industry—cruises that search for whales—just for the joy of sighting them, of course.

Land Tours of Nantucket

ARA'S TOURS
P.O. Box 734, Nantucket, MA 02554
(508) 221-6852
www.arastours.com
Ara's offers a 90-minute tour that covers 30 miles of this unique and beautiful island. Listen to guided commentary in an air-conditioned van. See historic Main Street, the rose-covered cottages of Sconset, and the lighthouses of Nantucket. In season, tours leave at 10:30 a.m., 12:30 p.m., and 2:30 p.m. You can be picked up at your in-town accommodations, boat, or a convenient location in town. Advance bookings for tours are highly recommended. Tours are available on a daily basis from early Apr thorough late Oct. Naturalist and photographer Ara Charger provides the commentary and always stops for photos.

The van tour can accommodate 14 people, and private tours are also available.

BARRETT'S TOURS
20 Federal St.
(508) 228-0174

Barrett's provides narrated one-and-a-half-hour bus tours of Nantucket daily Apr through Nov and also offers shuttle-bus service to Jetties, Surfside, and Madaket Beaches and to Siasconset. A family-owned and -operated business for more than five years, Barrett's also offers tours and transportation for special groups, such as wedding parties, with group rates for 20 or more people.

GAIL'S TOURS INC.
(508) 257-6557
www.nantucket.net/tours/gails

A sixth-generation native, Gail Nickerson Johnson has a wealth of knowledge and a great sense of humor. Her two air-conditioned vans can accommodate a total of 13 people. She offers sightseeing and private tours, including sunset, picnic, or beach excursions. Regular tours depart at 10 a.m., 1 p.m., and 3 p.m.

GREAT POINT NATURAL HISTORY TOURS
(508) 228-6799
www.thetrustees.org

Run by the nonprofit group the Trustees of the Reservations, these two-and-a-half-hour, naturalist-led tours offer a rare opportunity to explore the Coskata-Coatue Wildlife Refuge. Get close-up looks at migrant and nesting shorebirds, learn about wildflowers, see deer tracks crossing coastal heathlands, and visit historic Great Point Lighthouse—you even get to climb to the top. Tours meet at the gatehouse just before the Wauwinet Inn parking lot and are limited to seven people. Only two trips are scheduled a day and reservations are required. Tours are offered from June through Oct.

Cruises and Whale Watching

ENDEAVOR
Straight Wharf, Slip 1015
(508) 228-5585
www.endeavorsailing.com

Since 1982, this Friendship sloop, owned and operated by Jim and Sue Genthner, has been offering daily sails around Nantucket Sound, plus a sunset cruise. The longest operating sailing charter on the island, the *Endeavor* was built by Captain Jim, and if you wish, he will share his knowledge of traditional boat building with you. The sail cruises leave at 10 a.m., 1 p.m., 4 p.m., and sunset.

For children, the Endeavor offers a one-hour special sail each day at 11:30 a.m.. Or ask about the Songs and Stories of the Sea trip, which is fun for children ages 4 to 8, and the Fiddlin' on the Sea trip, which provides whaling-era instrumental music for families with older children.

NANTUCKET HARBOR CRUISES
Straight Wharf, Slip 11
(508) 228-1444

Nantucket Harbor Cruises offers several trips daily in season aboard the *Anna W II*, starting with a 90-minute morning marine cruise in which you pull lobster traps and learn about what's in the boat's touch tank. You must be at least 4 years old to come aboard. Captain Bruce Cowan is a naturalist and very knowledgeable about marine life as well as boats. Bring your own beverages, and sit at the boat's comfortable tables as you watch other boats come in through the fading light on a 90-minute sunset cruise..

SHEARWATER EXCURSIONS
Town Pier
(508) 228-7037
www.explorenantucket.com

On Sundays from mid-June through Sept, take the catamaran *Shearwater* on a six-hour whale-watching trip 15 to 30 miles southeast of Nantucket. Out on the open Atlantic, you are guaranteed to spot humpback, minke, and finback whales—and maybe dolphins and sea turtles—or you get a free ticket for another whale watch. *Shearwater Excursions* also offers two-and-a-half-hour seal cruises and evening cocktail cruise.

BEACHES

When you're on a relatively small island, it's hard to go very far without stumbling onto a beach. Take time to learn the existing swimming conditions before you head into the water. Currents can be very strong along the entire south side of Nantucket, including Cisco, Madaket, and Surfside Beaches. The Parks and Recreation Department (508-228-7213) recommends that people swim only at beaches with lifeguards; beaches are closed when conditions warrant it. Free parking is available at all beaches, and you can usually find a space even in the busy summer months. All of Nantucket's beaches are lovely; here are some of our favorites.

North Shore and In-Town

BRANT POINT
Easton Street
This beach right by the lighthouse has no lifeguards or facilities, but the view of the harbor is always entrancing. An easy walk from town, it's a great place to just sit and watch the boats rounding the point.

CHILDREN'S BEACH
Harbor View Way
Families naturally gravitate toward this pleasant beach; it's on the harbor, an easy walk from town, a lifeguard is on duty, restroom facilities are available, and there is a snack bar. And as you might expect, it has a nice play area for children, as well as picnic tables and a bandstand.

DIONIS BEACH
North Beach Street
This large, popular beach is a long walk from town or an easy bike ride of about 3 miles. Shuttle service is also available. It has lifeguards, restrooms, bathhouses, a restaurant, tennis courts, and towels and chairs for rent.

Keeping the Peace

Nantucket is justifiably proud of its beaches, especially the fact that 80 miles or so of them are largely open to the public, regardless of public or private ownership. Lately, however, the increasing number of SUVs on the island has led to some conflict. More and more people are arriving with SUVs, buying beach permits, and going four-wheeling or holding loud parties on the beach, to the chagrin of many beach owners. To help allay tensions between these owners and vacationing four-wheelers, a town beach manager has been appointed to maintain friendships . . . and open beaches.

FRANCIS STREET BEACH
Francis Street and Washington Street
A five-minute walk from Main Street, Francis Street Beach is on the calm waters of the harbor and ideal for swimming. There is no lifeguard.

JETTIES BEACH
North Beach Street
An easy bike or shuttle ride from town, this beach is great for families. It has lifeguards, restrooms, concessions, a playground, and volleyball nets. Sailboard, sailboat, and kayak rentals are available, and swimming lessons are offered by the Parks and Recreation Commission for children age 6 and older. Call (508) 228-7213 for dates and times.

South Shore and Out of Town

CISCO BEACH
Off Hummock Pond Road
Travel southwest about 4 miles out of town to reach this stretch of shore, which is a popular place for surf casting. A lifeguard is on duty. You

can also take the 4-mile bike path to the end of Hummock Pond Road.

MADAKET BEACH
Madaket Road

As far west on the island as you can go. There is a regular bus shuttle, or you can take the 6-mile paved scenic bike path from town. The surf and currents here are strong and can be dangerous depending on weather conditions. Still, it's a popular spot for surf swimming, and lifeguards are on duty. Restrooms are available at the beach.

MIACOMET BEACH
Miacomet Road

This beach, located at the end of Miacomet Road, has no facilities or lifeguards on duty. The surf is also very heavy and strong. But if you want to get away from it all and find a deserted spot on the beach, this is the place to go.

SURFSIDE BEACH
Surfside Road

Located at the end of Surfside Road, this is one of the most popular Nantucket beaches. The beach is wide—perfect for kite flying—and has a bathhouse, restrooms, and lifeguards. You can also get food nearby at a number of restaurants and convenience stores. It's accessible by shuttle bus, or you can take the 3-mile paved bike path from town.

Eastern Shore and Out of Town

SIASCONSET BEACH
Sconset Village

A regular shuttle bus gets you to this popular area, which is the only public beach on the east shore of the island. There is also a 7-mile paved bike path that you can take. Surf and currents can be heavy. There is a lifeguard, and food is available in nearby Sconset.

NATURAL AREAS

Nantucket's unique natural resources can be shared by all. The Nantucket Conservation Foundation owns many properties that can be used by the public for recreation such as hiking. Other properties are owned by the Nantucket Land Bank or other conservation organizations. The Conservation Foundation owns and manages more than 8,452 acres, about 40 percent of all the land on Nantucket. We've listed a few of our favorite properties; for others, look for their maroon concrete posts decorated with the foundation's gull and waves logo. For a complete map of all Foundation properties and regulations, visit the foundation office at 118 Cliff Road, go online at www.nantucketconservation.com, or call (508) 228-2884. Remember: Vehicles on these properties are strictly regulated or prohibited.

COSKATA-COATUE WILDLIFE REFUGE

This barrier beach that stretches across Nantucket Harbor is actually several protected areas in one: Coatue Wildlife Refuge and the Haulover, 476 acres owned by the Nantucket Conservation foundation; Coskata-Coatue Wildlife Refuge, 792 acres owned by the Trustees of Reservations; and Nantucket National Wildlife Refuge at Great Point, owned by the U.S. Fish and Wildlife Service. Great Point, which is home to the lighthouse of the same name that's a replica of the one lost in a severe storm in 1984, is the island's northernmost point, slicing up between Nantucket Sound and the Atlantic Ocean. Remote and wild, the barrier beach offers breathtaking views and the opportunity to observe nature firsthand. In spring, it's a nesting place for piping plovers, least terns, northern harriers, and other shorebirds.

The area as a whole includes not just beaches and sand dunes, but salt marshes and windsheared oak and cedar forests. Vehicles are strictly controlled here; a pass is required for four-wheel-drive vehicles, and officials advise inexperienced beach drivers not to drive in the very soft sand. This is a place for serious nature lovers who don't care about frills or modern amenities. There are no lifeguards, and some of the beaches are particularly dangerous for swimming. There are no restrooms, concessions, or public buildings within the refuge; come here only if you want to be one with nature and are willing to respect her.

The Trustees of Reservations offers guided natural history tours of the refuge. They take you all the way out to Great Point Lighthouse and back. Call (508) 228-6799 to make reservations (they're required). These tours are very popular, so be sure to plan for your trip in advance. Tours leave at 9:30 a.m. and 1:30 p.m. daily from the Wauwinet Gatehouse on Wauwinet Road. Call for prices.

EEL POINT

A spit of sand on the western end of the island, just north of and bordering Madaket Harbor, Eel Point is a Nantucket Conservation Foundation property that attracts great numbers of birds. The 100-plus acre property abounds in goldenrod, roses, wild grapes, bayberries, and other vegetation. To get there, take Eel Point Road off Cliff Road and park on the dirt road. If you're biking, take a right off the Madaket bike path onto Eel Point Road.

LONG POND

Owned by the Nantucket Land Bank, this 64-acre property is especially good for bird-watching. It features a 1-mile walking path that runs along the pond, past meadows and a natural cranberry bog. To reach the area, take Madaket Road and look for a dirt road on the left across the sign to Hither Creek, near Madaket. Cross the bridge to reach a parking area and the entrance to the trail.

THE SANFORD FARM, RAM PASTURE, AND THE WOODS

These properties total 767 acres of wetlands, grasslands, and forests in the southwest portion of the island. With more than 6.6 miles of roadways and trails to explore, the area includes a panoramic view of Nantucket's south shore from the barn in Ram Pasture. Ambitious hikers can follow a 6-mile round-trip trail that leads to the ocean and travels alongside Hummock Pond. You'll find a variety of wildflowers and may spot such wildlife as ring-necked pheasant, ospreys, red-tailed hawks, rabbits, and deer. The land is accessible from a parking area off Madaket Road, near the intersection of Cliff Road.

RECREATION

Boating and Water Sports

Water sports are big here, and it's a great place to finally learn how to sail or sailboard or try kayaking. Whether you're an old hand or just starting out, look to the following places for equipment and sales.

ℹ Guides from the Maria Mitchell Association know where the most productive birding sites are on the island. They run bird field trips Tuesday and Thursday during the summer at 6:30 a.m. and Saturday at 8 a.m. Trips start at the MMA Science Library courtyard at 2 Vestal St.. Call for prices.

NANTUCKET BOAT RENTAL
Slip 1, Straight Wharf
(508) 325-1001, (508) 524-6528
If the sight of all those beautiful boats in the harbor makes you want to take one out yourself, contact Nantucket Boat Rental. They rent a good selection of well-maintained powerboats (13-foot, 17-foot, 20-foot, or 22-foot) that you can rent by the hour, half-day, day, week, or month.

NANTUCKET COMMUNITY SAILING
Jetties Beach and Polpis Harbor
(508) 228-6600
www.nantucketsailing.com
Community Sailing offers popular youth and adult sailing instruction at levels from beginner to advanced sailor, as well as to those interested in racing, at their Polpis Harbor and Jetties Beach locations. Adult programs include women's sailing clinics, private and group lessons, and racing clinics. NCS also offers sailboat rentals of Sunfish, Rhodes 19s and Marshall Cat 15s. They also have an open sailing program, which allows experienced sailors to "borrow" the NCS sailboats for two-hour periods for sailing within Nantucket Harbor.

SEA NANTUCKET KAYAK RENTAL
Washington Sreet Extension
(508) 228-7499
This seasonal shop can deliver kayak rentals any-where around the island.

Fishing

Fishing has been a way of life for Nantucketers for generations and still provides a healthy and popular form of recreation, not to mention a delicious meal. If you want to go for bluefish or striped bass, you can pick up equipment, bait, and a guide with a four-wheel-drive and head for Great Point, Smith Point, or Surfside Beach.

A four-wheel-drive vehicle is needed for access to Great Point and Smith Point, but you can walk onto Dionis, Surfside, and Pebbles Beaches. These are perhaps the best-known beaches, but keep in mind that Nantucket is rimmed by beaches, so finding a fishing spot is not difficult. Of course, as any angler knows, find-ing fish is another matter. We highly recommend that you contact the local tackle shops for current information about fishing (we suggest several below), because obviously the location of fish and conditions at sea change from day to day.

The Nantucket Anglers Club (508-228-2299 or www.nantucketanglersclub.com) sponsors the Annual Billfish Tournament for offshore fishing. Open to the public, this weeklong tournament takes place in August.

If you don't own a boat, you can go fishing in a head boat (charges by the person) or a charter boat (charges for the boat). Head boats always provide fishing equipment, and you generally do not need reservations, but it is always best to check ahead. The cost is in the vicinity of $30 per person. There are not many big-game fish char-ters out of Nantucket. Ask at local tackle shops for recommendations on big-game fishing charters.

If your kids want to do a little bottom fishing off the wharves, they might catch some scup or flounder, but most people head to the beaches. Nine- to 11-foot spinning rods are prevalent for surf fishing.

Tackle Shops
BARRY THURSTON FISHING TACKLE
Harbor Square at Nantucket Marina
(508) 228-9595
www.nantucket.net/sports/thurston
Open seven days a week, this fishing shop outfits for deep-sea fishing, surf casting, freshwater fish-ing, and shellfishing. It's a licensed Orvis dealer and sells equipment and clothing, offers daily or weekly equipment rentals, and does repairs.

BILL FISHER TACKLE
3 Polpis Rd.
(508) 228-2261
www.billfishertackle.com
Open year-round, this shop has a full line of conventional freshwater and saltwater tackle, spinning tackle, and fly-fishing tackle. It also offers freshwater bait, rental equipment, referrals for guide service, and maintenance and repairs.

> **i** Nantucket's six bicycle paths range in length from 2.5 miles to 8 miles. The paved paths offer scenic routes along Cliff Road, Milestone Road, Surfside Road, Mada-ket Road, and Polpis Road. Pack a picnic, take your swimsuits, and keep your eyes open for the wild blueberries, blackberries, and beach plums that grow near some of the paths.

Golf
MIACOMET GOLF COURSE
12 West Miacomet Rd., off Somerset Rd.
(508) 325-0333
www.miacometgolf.com
Owned by the Nantucket Land Bank since 1985, this is the island's only publicly owned course. It has 18 holes, a par of 74, a driving range, pro shop, and both pull and electric carts. Reservations for tee times are required at least a week in advance; the course turns away about 100 people a day in summer. Call for current greens fees.

SANKATY HEAD GOLF CLUB
Sankaty Road, Siasconset
(508) 257-6655
www.sankatygolfclub.org
This year-round private course is open to the public only from Oct 1 until the first Frid in June, excluding Memorial Day weekend when, as in summer, it's reserved for members. The 18-hole, par 72 course, developed in 1920 and still recognized as one of the country's finest links courses, enjoys water views from just about every hole. Carts are available, and an on-site pro shop offers everything a golfer may need. Call for greens fees.

SIASCONSET GOLF COURSE
Milestone Road
(508) 257-6596
Founded in 1894, this 9-hole, par 70 public golf course is one of the oldest golf courses in the United States. No tee times are required, and club and pull cart rentals are available. Open May through mid-Oct. Call for greens fees.

Tennis
GREAT HARBOR YACHT CLUB TENNIS & SWIM CENTER
23 Wobadeer Farm Rd.
(508) 825-2020
www.ghyc.com/tennis/index.php
This club has eight clay courts, a squash court, two heated swimming pools, and a club pro shop. The Great Harbor Yacht Club bought the former Nantucket Tennis & Swim Club in 2007.

JETTIES BEACH PUBLIC TENNIS COURTS
North Beach Street, Jetties Beach
(508) 325-5334
www.nantucket-ma.gov
These hard-surface courts are free and open to the public.

ANNUAL EVENTS

There's a lot going on here, and not just in summer. Besides the annual events, there are dozens of concerts, craft fairs, and other events to watch for when you come to the island. Check with the chamber of commerce (508-228-1700 or www.nantucketchamber.org) for a current guide.

April
THE DAFFODIL FESTIVAL
(508) 228-1700
Staged in late Apr, the Daffodil Festival heralds spring as the island's millions of yellow daffodils come to life. The road to Sconset is lined with thousands of the brilliant blooms, which the Garden Club and townspeople started planting in 1974. Highlights of the festival include the gathering of antique and classical cars on Main Street, a parade, and a giant tailgate party at Sconset.

May
THE NANTUCKET WINE FESTIVAL
(508) 228-1128
www.nantucketwinefestival.com
Launched in 1997, the annual weeklong Nantucket Wine Festival has become a huge success. More than 150 wineries of international acclaim are represented, and chefs vie to produce the class of cuisine that best enhances fine wines. Participants get to sip wine in private mansions and dine on world-class cuisine. It culminates with a charity gala at the White Elephant Hotel. Call ahead for a program so you can make reservations. Ticket prices range from $40 to $900 per event, and many sell out in advance.

FIGAWI RACE
Hyannis to Nantucket
(508) 420-1400
www.figawi.com
A local tradition since 1972, this sailboat race from Hyannis to Nantucket and back generates as much excitement here as it does on the Cape. It takes place on Memorial Day weekend (see our Cape Cod Annual Events chapter for details).

June
THE NANTUCKET FILM FESTIVAL
(508) 325-6274, (212) 708-1278
www.nantucketfilmfestival.org

Important Numbers

Medical, fire, or police emergencies	911
A Safe Place, 24-hour hotline	(508) 228-2111
Alcoholics Anonymous	(800) 252-6465
Children at Risk	(800) 792-5200
Missing Persons	(800) 622-5999
Alzheimer's Information	(800) 548-2111
Cancer Information	(800) 422-6237

An inspiring inside look at screenwriting for film authorities and fans alike, the five-day film festival is more than a decade old and attracts more than a few celebrities as well as film buffs and fans. It's held around the middle of the month.

ℹ **The best place to get a bird's-eye view of Nantucket is from the tower of the First Congregational Church on 62 Centre St.. The 94-step journey to the top is interrupted by a display of old photographs of the Old North Church, as it is known. Tours offered mid-May through mid-October. A donation of $2.50 is requested (50 cents for children).**

July

INDEPENDENCE DAY

Nantucketers do it up on the Fourth, with a riotous fire-hose contest on Main Street, pie-eating contests, face painting, and more. In the evening, a gala celebration with music and children's games takes place at Jetties Beach. The grand finale, of course, is a fireworks display.

August

SANDCASTLE AND SCULPTURE DAY
Jetties Beach
Nantucket
This popular event, cosponsored by the Nantucket Chamber of Commerce and the Nantucket Island School of Design and the Arts, attracts residents and visitors of all ages who vie for honors sculpting the most creative sandcastle and sand sculptures. The event, held on Jetties Beach, is always held the third Sat in Aug. Entries are judged in five divisions, ranging from Family to Under 10; preregistration is required. You can use tools, but you cannot add any supporting or form devices to the sculpture. There is a minimal registration fee.

September

NANTUCKET ISLAND FAIR
Tom Nevers Navy Base
(508) 228-7213
Held in early Sept, this is a real old-fashioned tradition started in 1992. Baked goods, jams, and jellies vie for ribbons, and an animal tent, hayrides, pet show, pumpkin contest, and flea market are some of the lively activities.

October

NANTUCKET ARTS FESTIVAL
(508) 325-8588
www.nantucketartscouncil.org
This weeklong festival is held in late Sept and early Oct. Island musicians, authors, actors, artists, and dancers come together to celebrate the arts on Nantucket through roughly 80 events. You'll find everything from chamber music concerts and readings to puppet shows.

November

FESTIVAL OF WREATHS AND SILENT AUCTION

Peter Foulger Museum, 15 Broad St.
(508) 228-1894
www.nha.org/specialevents/fow.html

Nearly 100 wreaths decorated by merchants, local artists, and community members adorn the walls of the Peter Foulger Museum during this festival. The wreaths are auctioned off at the end of the festival, for prices ranging from $45 to $1,000. Held in the days before and after Thanksgiving, proceeds from the festival and on suing auction benefit the NHA's educational programs.

December

NANTUCKET CHRISTMAS STROLL

(508) 228-1700

During the first weekend in December, the Christmas Stroll draws tens of thousands of people to Nantucket for the townwide celebration of Christmas. Christmas trees are placed throughout the town and decorated by local businesses, services, and students in a decorating contest. At 12:30 p.m. on Sat, a U.S. Coast Guard cutter (not Rudolph and company) delivers Santa, who is then transported to the stroll in a horse-drawn carriage. Schoolchildren, carolers, and bell ringers in period costume create a joyful atmosphere with holiday song. NOTE: Make your holiday hotel reservations way in advance—a year ahead is strongly advised.

HEALTH CARE

NANTUCKET COTTAGE HOSPITAL

57 Prospect St., Nantucket
(508) 825-8100
www.nantuckethospital.org

The only medical facility on the island, this hospital offers 24-hour emergency care, home health care, chemotherapy, X-rays, mammography, physical therapy, dialysis, and laboratory service.

MEDIA

Newspapers

THE INQUIRER & MIRROR

Old South Road
(508) 228-0001
www.ack.net

The Inquirer & Mirror is Nantucket's oldest newspaper, established in 1821. The publication started as the Inquirer and merged with the competing paper, the Mirror, in 1865. This newspaper operated as an independent until 1990 when it was sold to Ottaway Newspapers Inc., a subsidiary of Dow Jones. Marianne Giffin Stanton, whose parents once owned the paper, is the editor and publisher.

The Inquirer & Mirror, affectionately known on the island as the Inky, is published every Thurs and has a circulation of about 10,000. It has the largest classified section on the island and also publishes Nantucket Today, restaurant and wedding guides, real estate and home improvement magazines, and a monthly vacation guide. Mailed subscriptions reach far and wide, including towns and cities in every state.

THE NANTUCKET INDEPENDENT

15 North Beach St.
(508) 228-1654
www.nantucketindependent.com

Second newspapers on the island have come and gone over the years. The latest contender is this locally owned upstart, which published its first issue in the summer of 2003. It bills itself as the island's "only locally owned weekly newspaper." Reporting focuses on island-related economic news, local business profiles, analysis of town contracts, and listings of property transactions. Reporting also explores standard-of-living and quality-of-life issues that have particular relevance on this isolated isle, such as the economics of environmental preservation, beach erosion, and the eternal complaint that groceries are cheaper on the mainland.

MARTHA'S VINEYARD

Depending on the point from which you measure, the Vineyard, as Martha's Vineyard is known locally, lies only 7 to 9 miles from the mainland. If you are riding on the Falmouth ferries on a clear day, you never lose full sight of either the Cape or the Vineyard. Martha's Vineyard is a convenient respite full of spectacular views, quaint villages, charming gingerbread cottages, and elegant sea captains' homes.

While Nantucket surely has its share of rich and famous, the wealthy and well-known who frequent the Vineyard seem to make more news. Some of the more popular islanders include Carly Simon, actress Patricia Neal, and actors Dan Ackroyd and Jim Belushi (his late brother John is buried on the island). The late political humorist Art Buchwald and the late news anchor Walter Cronkite also lived here. In addition, the island has been a favorite stop for former president Bill Clinton and his family and has been rumored to be part of President Barack Obama's vacation plans.

While you might come to the island in search of film faves and politicos, your gaze will likely be diverted very quickly by the striking charm each town possesses. You may find yourself replacing your search for the stars with a tour of the island's real celebrities: its five unique lighthouses.

If you are wedded to your automobile, you had better do some planning. Only a limited number of vehicles can make it over on the Steamship Authority ferry. You have to make a reservation several months in advance if you hope to take a car over in the summer season. Sometimes you can get a spot at the last minute on one of the first ferries out in the morning, but don't bet your vacation on it. Also, once driving on the island, you'll have to practice a lot of patience as intersections are crowded with pedestrians and bicyclists.

Even though Martha's Vineyard is New England's largest island at 10 miles long and 9 miles wide, you'll find it easy to negotiate on foot or pedal. The island consists of six towns, each with its own personality. Some 15,000 year-round residents call the island home, but, during the busy summer months, that population swells to 100,000. Together with the town of Gosnold on Cuttyhunk Island (the only public island of the Elizabeth Island chain, just west of the Vineyard) and No Man's Island (an uninhabited island off Aquinnah, the island's westernmost community), the six towns of Martha's Vineyard are part of Dukes County. FYI: You can get to Cuttyhunk Island from the Vineyard (see the Excursions section of this chapter).

The island's northernmost town is incorporated as Tisbury, but most call it by the name of its very busy harbor Vineyard Haven. The gateway to Vineyard Haven is marked by two spits of land: West Chop, the northern tip of Tisbury and, directly across the harbor, East Chop, the northern tip of the town of Oak Bluffs. Southeast of Oak Bluffs is the town of Edgartown, which includes the island of Chappaquiddick, known locally by its nickname, Chappy. "Up island" (or sometimes "outer island") refers to the more rural towns of West Tisbury, Chilmark, and Aquinnah. Chilmark includes the fishing village of Menemsha. The term "up island" can be confusing to visitors. Up, in this case refers to longitude. The farther west one travels, the higher the longitude—it's a nautical thing.

You'd expect prices to be a little higher because Martha's Vineyard is a resort but, because it's an island, most of the goods have to be shipped over by ferry or plane, which increases the prices a bit, too. Do your essential shopping on the mainland to help save money for mementos and entertainment.

As far as the weather goes, don't be caught off guard at night. A cool ocean breeze and dropping temperatures can demand an evening sweater, even in midsummer.

HISTORY

Though the legend of Moshaup creating Martha's Vineyard with the sand from his moccasin is fun to relate, Martha's Vineyard was in fact created during the last ice age when the Laurentide ice sheet deposited the boulders and gravel it had carried along on its slow journey southward. As the ice sheet receded, the southernmost deposits became the islands of Nantucket and Martha's Vineyard. The oceans began to rise with the melting ice, thus forming Nantucket Sound between these lovely islands and the equally lovely peninsula to the north known as Cape Cod.

As the climate warmed, American Indians began to migrate to the island, settling here some 5,000 years ago.

Legend has it that Viking explorers discovered the island back around A.D. 1000, but that story is very hard to prove—or disprove for that matter. What is known for sure is that in March 1602, English navigator Bartholomew Gosnold set off in his vessel *Concord* across the Atlantic to arrive months later along the coast of Maine. Farther south, he discovered Cape Cod and, on May 22, he arrived at Martha's Vineyard (Edgartown to be more exact—Cape Pogue, Chappaquiddick to be even more exact), which he named for his daughter, Martha. Gosnold later attempted to establish a settlement on nearby Cuttyhunk Island but abandoned the attempt, citing unfavorable living conditions.

Though there is a story of white settlers arriving as early as 1632, the official settlement of Martha's Vineyard by Thomas Mayhew Jr. would not occur until 1642. During the previous year, in October 1641, his father, also named Thomas Mayhew, a merchant of Watertown, and Thomas Jr. were deeded rights "to plant and inhabit" the islands of Martha's Vineyard, Nantucket, and the

neighboring Elizabeth Islands by William, Earl of Sterling, a representative of Charles I. Thomas Mayhew Jr. brought a group of 80 to settle at Great Harbor, which later incorporated as Edgartown in 1671. The settlement was named by New York Governor Lovelace to honor Edgar, the son of the Duke of York, and was no doubt done to earn the favor of the royal family. Edgar was the 3-year-old nephew of King Charles, and because the King did not have any children of his own, Edgar appeared to be heir to the throne. Unbeknownst to Lovelace, poor little Edgar died a month before the town's incorporation.

White settlers and American Indians quickly learned to live together in this island paradise. As they had at the Plymouth colony, the American Indians shared their farming and fishing skills with the settlers. Hostilities between the two groups were nonexistent, and even during the King Philip War of 1676-77 (which saw white settlers and Indians battling on the mainland), relations on the island remained friendly. Yet this paradise turned into disaster for the American Indians as they began to fall in great numbers to the diseases brought by the white settlers. Around 3,000 Indians lived on Martha's Vineyard when Mayhew and his group first arrived. Within 30 years, the Indian population had been cut in half as a result of disease. Many of the surviving American Indians converted to Christianity because they believed the English settlers' god was protecting the settlers from the diseases that swept through the Native American community.

Very soon the settlers outnumbered the dwindling American Indians. By the middle of the 18th century, there were perhaps only 500 American Indians remaining. Fortunately pockets of them survived, and today half the population of the town of Aquinnah are Wampanoag Indians.

THE TOWNS

The history of each of the Vineyard's towns is as varied as their differing personalities. Though settlement began in Edgartown, people began to settle in different parts of the island. Farming and fishing provided the staples of life early on, but soon each town developed based on its unique characteristics.

Edgartown prospered as a whaling port during the early to mid-1800s. More than 100 whaling captains hailed from this town, and today their stately homes, a majority of them built between 1830 and 1845, line the main road as reminders of the fortunes made harvesting whale oil. The last half of the 19th century saw a rapid decline in whaling when the discovery of petroleum made the pursuit of the leviathan an obsolete profession. Edgartown's prosperity stagnated until tourism restored the town and its many beautiful buildings to their 18th- and 19th-century splendor.

Vineyard Haven, known early as Holmes Hole, is the island's second-oldest town, incorporated in 1671 as Tisbury. Its excellent harbor made it an important port town where the wares of the Vineyard could be readily sold to off-islanders. Oceangoing traffic was so busy in the area that Nantucket and Vineyard Sounds were considered second only to the English Channel for the number of vessels passing through. Today Vineyard Haven maintains its port status, providing a busy harbor connecting the island to the mainland—and to the rest of the world for that matter.

The town of Oak Bluffs, incorporated in 1907, was once part of Edgartown. Its development as a seasonal community began in 1835, when an Edgartown man, Jeremiah Pease, selected the area of Oak Bluffs to hold a Methodist camp meeting. The idea caught on, and each summer the camp meeting grounds were visited by religious folk who pitched tents to spend time worshiping and relaxing beneath the oaks, which grew abundantly in the area. Very soon the tents were replaced by cottages. So many cottages were built when Oak Bluffs broke away from the town of Edgartown in 1880 it was named Cottage Town

(until 1907, when it was renamed). Residents decorated the cottages with ornate woodwork, and today their gingerbread flavor dictates the personality of this quaint resort town.

Up island lie the towns of West Tisbury, Chilmark, and Aquinnah (formerly known as Gay Head). West Tisbury was largely a farming community and maintains its rural personality. It was a part of the town of Tisbury until it broke away as a separate town in 1892. Meanwhile Chilmark, with its fishing village of Menemsha, earned its living from both the sea and the land. Chilmark was incorporated in 1694. Aquinnah, which became an independent town in 1870, is a geological wonder, with its cliffs of clay displaying the fingerprint of the last ice age. The town's roots stem from a Native American settlement, and today Aquinnah is home to more than 100 members of the Wampanoag tribe.

At present Martha's Vineyard's economy is driven largely by tourism. Tourism began in the mid-19th century at Oak Bluffs. In fact the tourism prevalent in Oak Bluffs and then in neighboring Vineyard Haven helped resurrect Edgartown years after the whaling boom of the mid-1800s had gone bust. Islanders seized this new industry by renovating the old sea captains' houses, turning them into inns, bed-and-breakfasts, shops, and restaurants. In the process they also preserved magnificent architecture and irreplaceable history. Today Edgartown is an upscale vacation town where you can stay and dine in buildings that speak volumes about a century when men went to sea to hunt whales.

GETTING HERE

From Woods Hole, Martha's Vineyard appears to be just a good swim away—it seems that close! Well, not quite. It takes a bit more than a brisk breaststroke to get to the islands.

There are only two ways of getting to the island: by air and by sea.

By Sea

Journeying to the island by water, you get a feel for what Gosnold saw and felt upon that May day in 1602 when he first made his discovery. Yet, for a singular treat, make the journey after nightfall and watch as Nobska Light of Woods Hole, West Chop Lighthouse of Vineyard Haven, and East Chop Lighthouse of Oak Bluffs beam across the waves to one another like a triangle of lovers.

Once you've decided that you're going to travel to the island via water, you then have to decide how. Here are your options.

Ferries
FALMOUTH-EDGARTOWN FERRY
278 Scranton Ave., Falmouth
(508) 548-9400
www.falmouthferry.com

As the name implies, this ferry will take you directly to Edgartown (most ferry services take you to Oak Bluffs or Vineyard Haven). Sailing time aboard the *Pied Piper* is roughly one hour. They offer four round-trips daily in summer, with five on Fri. Mon through Thurs round-trip fares are $40 for adults, $25 for children 6 to 12, free for kids 5 and under, and $10 for bicycles. Fri through Sun round-trip fares for adults are $50, $30 for children 6 to 12, and free for children 5 and under. There is an $25-per-day parking charge. Reservations are recommended.

HY-LINE CRUISES
22 Channel Point Rd., Hyannis
(508) 778-2600, (800) 492-8082
www.hy-linecruises.com

Hy-Line offers a year-round high-speed ferry between Hyannis and Martha's Vineyard. The trip takes about an hour, with scheduled departures throughout the day, seven days a week. In season (late May to late Oct), a round-trip fare for Hyannis to Martha's Vineyard costs $69 for adults and $48 for children ages 5 to 12 (free for children four and under with boarding passes). The company also services the Hyannis to Nantucket route and offers interisland service between Nantucket and Martha's Vineyard. It's a good idea to call ahead for reservations, especially if you plan to travel during a holiday weekend or during July and Aug. Ferries leave from Dock One, Ocean Street, Hyannis.

ISLAND QUEEN
75 Falmouth Heights Rd., Falmouth
(508) 548-4800
www.islandqueen.com

For $18 round-trip ($9 for children), you can take the 600-passenger *Island Queen* from Falmouth Harbor to Martha's Vineyard from Memorial Day weekend to Columbus Day. The trip is a leisurely 35 minutes each way, and food service is available on board, along with a full bar. The passenger-only vessel makes seven trips each day in summer, and reservations are not needed. The *Island Queen* is also available for charters. This ferry service does not take credit cards.

i Thousands upon thousands of people visit the Vineyard every summer. Most of the summer population visits between July 4 weekend and Labor Day weekend. You can usually find accommodations—it's the car you have to worry about. You'll need to reserve a space for your car on the Steamship Authority ferry months in advance or rent one on the island.

THE STEAMSHIP AUTHORITY
Woods Hole Wharf, Woods Hole
(508) 477-8600
(508) 693-9130 for vehicle reservations
(508) 495-3278 for high-speed ferry passenger reservations
www.steamshipauthority.com

The Steamship Authority is the only company offering year-round ferry service from Woods Hole to points on Martha's Vineyard, and from Hyannis to Nantucket. It's also the only ferry that transports cars. Keep in mind that taking your car to the islands can be very expensive, and it's usually not necessary because you can rent one upon your arrival. Better yet, rent a bicycle or moped (see Getting Around by Car (or Bike or Moped) and Bicycling in this chapter). We advise you to check the schedule for boat departures as they change seasonally. The one-way fare from Woods Hole to Martha's Vineyard is $7.50 for adults, $4.00 for children ages 5 to 12, and free for children younger than 5. Ferry service from Hyannis to Nantucket costs $14.00 one-way for adults, $7.25 for kids (5 to 12), and is free for those under 5. The Steamship Authority also offers a Fast Ferry to Nantucket from Hyannis, and the cost is $65 round-trip for adults, $49 for kids (5 to 12), and is free for those under 5.

Private Boats

For those of you who captain your own vessel, the island offers four harbors where you can dock. Menemsha offers slips with electricity; the harbormaster (508-645-2846) can provide more details. Edgartown Harbor has moorings available by the day, week, or season. None have plug-in facilities. One pump-out station and one pump-out boat are available. You can reach the Edgartown harbormaster at (508) 627-4746.

Vineyard Haven offers moorings, launch service, and dockage. The harbormaster's number is (508) 696-4249. Oak Bluffs has plug-in slips for sail and motorboats; a small number of moorings are available in the harbor. The Oak Bluffs harbormaster's number is (508) 693-4355. As you can imagine, there is a high demand for slips in season. Be sure to plan ahead.

By Air

Several airlines service the island and can make your businesslike journey to the island more of a pleasure flight of fancy as the landscape of the Vineyard becomes more clear.

The island has two airports: Martha's Vineyard Airport (508-693-7022 or www.mvyairport .com) near the center of the island, and the smaller Katama Airfield in Edgartown (508-627-9018) offering runways of grass. Katama is one of the original Curtiss-Wright fields from back in the early airmail days and is one of the largest turf fields of its type remaining in the Northeast. The following airlines serve the Martha's Vineyard Airport.

CAPE AIR
660 Barnstable Rd., Hyannis
(508) 771-6944, (800) 352-0714
www.flycapeair.com

Cape Air offers hourly flights, with year-round shuttle service between Hyannis and Nantucket, and regular service from New Bedford, Boston, Providence, and Martha's Vineyard. Seasonal service from Provincetown is available as well. In the peak season, the company offers more than seven flights daily from Boston. Flights from Hyannis leave every hour; these are approximately 15-minute flights. Flights from Boston leave at hourly intervals. These are approximately 50-minute flights. Charter service is also available, as are connections to an increasing number of locations around New England.

OCEAN WINGS AIR CHARTER
14 Airport Rd., Memorial Airport,
Nantucket
(800) 253-5039
www.flyoceanwings.com

Ocean Wings Air Charter offers 24-hour year-round charter service to and from airports throughout the Northeast. If it is necessary to travel quickly and on the spur of the moment in and out of Nantucket, Martha's Vineyard, or Cape Cod, Ocean Wings may fit in with your personal demands. This company has a private hangar and offers flight instruction.

US AIRWAYS EXPRESS
(800) 428-4322
www.usairways.com

If you are from the Boston Area, you can take the direct route to the island onboard US Airways.

Getting Around by Car (or Bike or Moped)

No car? No problem. The island is prepared for your arrival in a big way. There are cars, mopeds, scooters, and bicycles for rent. Buses run every 15 minutes during peak season. For $6, the buses will shuttle you to the three towns of Vineyard Haven, Oak Bluffs, and Edgartown and back again. Sightseeing tours and taxis are available as well.

ⓘ **Oak Bluffs and Tisbury are the only towns on Martha's Vineyard that currently offer moped rentals. If you opt to rent one, be careful on the Vineyard's narrow, winding—and during summers, quite crowded—roads. Mopeds are not allowed on bike paths or sidewalks and must follow the same traffic rules as automobiles.**

Depending on your visit, you may not even need any of the above. For instance, if you arrive at Oak Bluffs or Vineyard Haven via ferry for a day trip and don't plan to leave the town at all, your legs alone can get you to nearly all the hot spots. Or a shuttle can take you to an adjoining town for a couple of bucks and your legs can take care of the rest.

This is probably as good a point as any to give you an idea of the distance between the island towns. Vineyard Haven and Oak Bluffs are side by side, straddling the Harbor of Vineyard Haven; it's a 10-minute car ride (if that) from the ferry dock of one, around the harbor, to the ferry dock of the other. Southeast of Oak Bluffs is Edgartown, a good 15-minute car ride along Beach Road. Southwest of Vineyard Haven lies West Tisbury, maybe 10 minutes from Vineyard Haven and about 20 minutes from Edgartown via the Edgartown–West Tisbury Road. From that point in West Tisbury to Beetlebung Corner in Chilmark is about 4 or 5 miles, about 10 minutes of driving. Another 6 miles (10 minutes, perhaps 12) along State Road brings you to Aquinnah. Then to get from Aquinnah back up north to Vineyard Haven, allow perhaps 35 to 40 minutes for the 18-mile trip.

The basic rule of thumb in driving between towns is fairly easy. Once you get in town, traffic slows down considerably, especially when ferries are arriving or departing. The towns of Edgartown, Oak Bluffs, and Vineyard Haven are far more active than West Tisbury, Chilmark, and Aquinnah.

Rentals

Auto rentals during peak season are offered at, of course, peak prices. Call around—and in advance—for the best prices. Larger cars, of course, are more expensive. Jeeps and off-road vehicles cost even more. In Vineyard Haven is Thrifty Rent-a-Car (508-693-8143). Budget Rent A Car (508-693-1911, www.budgetmv.com) is located near the harbors at Vineyard Haven and Oak Bluffs in Edgartown and at the main terminal at Martha's Vineyard Airport. AAA Island Auto Rentals is in Edgartown (800-627-6333, www.mvautorental.com).

For about $50 to $90 you can rent a moped for the day. Daily bicycle rates run $20 and up, depending on the model. As you come off the boat at either Vineyard Haven or Oak Bluffs, these rental outfits are everywhere. In fact, we challenge you to swing a striped bass without hitting a bike rental shop.

By Shuttle Bus

The island's bus service is superb. The drivers, who each probably answer the same dozen questions a couple hundred times a day, do so in such a courteous way that you'd think you were the first person ever to ask, "Does this bus go to Edgartown?"

MARTHA'S VINEYARD REGIONAL TRANSIT AUTHORITY
(508) 693-9440, (508) 627-7448
www.vineyardtransit.com
The VTA offers 13 scheduled routes around the island. A one-day pass costs $7; a three-day pass is $15.

In Edgartown, nothing can beat the Edgartown Shuttle, which you can ride for the cost of the change you might find buried under your sofa at home. From May to Sept, the shuttle runs throughout the historic streets of Edgartown. Edgartown also has an open-air trolley that carries passengers from the center of town to the very popular South Beach every 30 minutes, June to Sept.

ACCOMMODATIONS

If you are here for an overnight stay or for several nights, you'll need to know your different options in the way of accommodations. By the way, if you happen to be glancing at this section on the boat ride over to the island, we hope you've already made reservations. Even in September and October it is common to see the no vacancy signs posted.

If your choice is to stay at an inn or a bed-and-breakfast, you'll be happy to learn that there are many sprinkled throughout the island. Some are quaint places; others are majestic showplaces. Many of them are old sea captains' houses or, in the case of Edgartown, the former abodes of whaling captains.

For those not in with the inn crowd, there are a number of fine hotels, some with spectacular views. More frugal travelers might opt for the hostel with rates starting around $32 a night. Also there is a campground starting at around $49 per night for those who seek oneness with nature.

The peak season generally runs from late May (Memorial Day) to late September—in some cases until Columbus Day in mid-October. During this peak season, hotels, inns, bed-and-breakfasts, and guesthouses charge peak prices. During the off-season, room rates are lowered, in some cases substantially. It is not uncommon to see rates cut in half after Columbus Day and, with the crowds gone, you feel like you own the island.

Unless otherwise noted, all accommodations are nonsmoking and welcome well-behaved children with prior approval. We'll let you know which places accept pets. Most accept major credit cards; we'll let you know those that don't.

Reservation Services
MARTHA'S VINEYARD AND NANTUCKET RESERVATIONS
Box 1322, Vineyard Haven
(508) 693-7200
www.mvreservations.com
For more than two decades this company has been booking rooms in inns, hotels, cottages, bed-and-breakfasts, and guesthouses. The service does not handle vacation rentals, but if you are looking for a room on the island, this is the

number to call. About 95 percent of the islands' inns and hotels work with this service. Although the sooner you book the better, especially for a room in season, the inns and hotels on the island regularly notify the service of cancellations, making this one of the first numbers to call if you are throwing together plans at the last minute. You pay no fee for the service.

Price Code
Our price code is based on the average cost of a night's stay in a double-occupancy room during peak season, minus tax and special charges. (State and local taxes add up to about 10 percent of the bill.) Because this is an average, rooms may be had in some places for more or less than what's reflected in our code.

$.................. Less than $75
$$ .... $75 to $110
$$$ .... $111 to $175
$$$$ .... $176 and more

Bed-and-Breakfasts and Country Inns
Vineyard Haven
HANOVER HOUSE AT THE TWIN OAKS INN $$$$
28 Edgartown Rd.
(508) 696–6099, (800) 696-8633
www.hanoverhouseinn.com
Behind a row of large hedges hides the Hanover House, a cozy, quiet bed-and-breakfast inn located just steps from the harbor. This village inn offers 16 well maintained rooms, each with private bath, two double beds or a queen- or king-size bed, air-conditioning, Internet access, and cable TV. Many of the rooms feature entrances that open onto one of two spacious sundecks. In a separate carriage house are three suites, two of which have full kitchens. Each suite has a private deck or patio. Complimentary breakfast includes homemade waffles, egg dishes, and potatoes and fresh-ground gourmet coffee. Hanover House is open year-round.

MANSION HOUSE $$$$

9 Main St.

(508) 693-2200, (800) 332-4112

www.mvmansionhouse.com

Located at the foot of historic Main Street and just a few blocks from the ferry, the Mansion House rose from the ashes of the Tisbury Inn, destroyed by fire in late 2001. Construction finished on the new building during the summer of 2003. Its 32 rooms feature air-conditioning, cable television, telephone, high-speed Internet connections, and refrigerators. Deluxe rooms and suites offer soaking tubs, flat-screen plasma TVs, fireplaces, and balconies with views of Vineyard Sound. Rooms can be converted into suites complete with kitchens to accommodate larger groups. Guests of the Mansion House enjoy a complimentary breakfast at the on-site restaurant, Zephrus (see our Restaurants chapter). For everyone else, it's open daily for lunch and dinner (remember to BYOB). The Mansion House also has the Vineyard's only 75-foot "spring water" indoor pool, as well as its largest health club.

THORNCROFT INN $$$$

460 Main St.

(508) 693-3333, (800) 332-1236

www.thorncroftinn.com

The Thorncroft is one of the island's premier inns, offering 15 guest rooms (including a private cottage) in two antique-appointed houses on three-and a-half acres of land. Each room features a private bath, central air-conditioning, cable TV/VCR, and complimentary Internet access. Many have canopied four-poster beds, and 10 have wood-burning fireplaces. Three rooms offer two-person Jacuzzis, and two have 300-gallon hot tubs.

A full country breakfast and afternoon tea and pastries are served daily in the dining rooms. This has been cited as one of the 10 best wheelchair-accessible inns in the country, as its private cottage was built with accessibility needs in mind. The entire inn and grounds are smoke-free. Special services include a fire-ready fireplace upon your arrival, a *New York Times* at your door in the morning, turndown service, and continental breakfast in bed. Thorncroft Inn is open year-round.

Oak Bluffs

DOCKSIDE INN $$$$

Circuit Ave. Extension

(800) 245-5979

www.vineyardinns.com/dockside.html

This Victorian inn is painted a combination of cream, pink, and soft pastel blue, as are the chairs that line its front porch. With its second-floor wraparound balcony and its proximity to the harbor, the place has a riverboat feel to it. It's hard to believe that this beauty, with architecture pointing to the mid- to late-19th century, was actually built in 1989. All 22 of the Dockside Inn's rooms have air-conditioning, private baths, and cable TV with VCRs; most rooms have queen-size beds. Five full kitchen suites are also available. The Dockside, convenient to all that Oak Bluffs has to offer, is open from mid-Apr to late Oct.

ISABELLE'S BED AND BREAKFAST $$$$

83 Seaview Ave.

(508) 693-3955, (800) 674-3129

www.isabellesbeachhouse.com

You couldn't ask for a better location: right across the street from the town beach on Vineyard Sound and within easy walking distance of all the sites in Oak Bluffs, including the community of gaily colored gingerbread cottages. It is also within a 5- to 10-minute walk of the ferry dock. This bed-and-breakfast is under new ownership. Where once there were nine rooms, there are now 11.

THE MADISON INN $$–$$$$

18 Kennebec Ave.

(508) 693-2760, (800) 564-2760

(Eastern Massachusetts only)

www.madisoninnmv.com

The Madison Inn is just a short five-minute walk from the island ferry and an even shorter two-minute stroll to Oak Bluffs Town Beach. All of Oak Bluffs, from her fanciful gingerbread cottages to her Flying Horses Carousel, is just around the corner. Each of the inn's 14 rooms is brightly decorated and includes a private bath, flat-screen TV, wireless Internet access, and individualized temperature control. Several of the rooms also feature private entrances. The outdoor patio is a great place to socialize after a day of touring the island. The inn is open from May to the end of Oct.

Edgartown
ASHLEY INN $$$$
129 Main St.
(508) 627-9655
www.ashleyinn.net
Converted to an inn during the spring of 1983, this 19th-century sea captain's home is convenient to the many shops of Edgartown. You can stroll the historic streets of the old whaling port, or simply kick up your feet and relax in a hammock out in the lawn. Each of the inn's 10 bedrooms is beautifully decorated with period antiques and has a private bath, cable TV, phone, and air-conditioning. Also on the property are one- and two-bedroom carriage houses equipped with modern kitchens, living rooms with fireplaces, whirlpool baths, and sundecks. Begin the day with a wholesome gourmet breakfast in the English tearoom or on the garden terrace. Children 10 and older are welcome at this year-round inn.

THE CHARLOTTE INN $$$$
27 South Summer St.
(508) 627-4751
www.relaischateaux.com/charlotte
Like many of Edgartown's inns, the Charlotte Inn began life as a sea captain's home. Built in 1860, it is today one of the premier inns in Edgartown and on the island. Brick courtyards and flower beds accent the grounds. Inside English antiques, fine furnishings, and high ceilings convince you that you're in a very special place.

When the longtime in-house restaurant, L'Etoile, left for a new spot on North Water Street, the Inn replaced it with the equally elegant Terrace Restaurant (see our Restaurants chapter), whose chef specializes in New England contemporary cuisine with a French accent. The Charlotte Inn welcomes children older than 14. It is open throughout the year.

THE EDGARTOWN INN $$–$$$
56 North Water St.
(508) 627-4794
www.edgartowninn.com
Built in 1798 by Capt. Thomas Worth (Fort Worth, Texas, is named for his son, William, a hero of the Mexican War), this colonial inn has had many distinguished guests over the past two centuries. Daniel Webster, Nathaniel Hawthorne, abolitionist Senator Charles Sumner, and John F. Kennedy (while a senator from Massachusetts) have all stayed here. In fact Hawthorne was writing his Twice Told Tales while a guest at the inn.

The inn is small, with 12 rooms in the main inn all with private baths; some have balconies offering harbor views. The Garden House has two spacious rooms with king-size beds, private baths, and balconies overlooking the gardens below; a smaller room shares a bath. Two of the barn's five rooms have private baths; three share a bath and shower. The inn is open Apr through Oct. No credit cards.

THE HOB KNOB INN $$$$
128 Main St.
(508) 627-9510, (800) 696-2723
www.hobknob.com
The Hob Knob Inn features great accommodations just on the outside of the hustle and bustle of Edgartown's center. Begin your day with a full farm breakfast of juice, coffee, and freshly baked muffins, scones, and breads in the sunlit tearoom. In the afternoon enjoy a cup of tea and sample some tasty treats, or relax in the parlor or on the porch sipping complimentary sherry. The Hob Know Inn's 16 rooms feature private baths, ceiling fans, and king-size brass or four-poster beds. This Victorian is elegant yet comfy all at the same time. Its convenient location along historic Main Street makes for a short stroll to the shops along Edgartown's waterfront. The inn welcomes children age 7 and older and is open year-round.

SHIVERICK INN $$$$
5 Peases Point Way
(508) 627-3797, (800) 723-4292
www.shiverickinn.com

This lovely inn was built in 1840 for the town physician Dr. Clement Francis Shiverick. It offers 11 guest rooms, many with fireplaces, two of which are suites. The inn has been lovingly restored to evoke the period in which it was built.

Enjoy a breakfast of breads, cakes, and freshly baked muffins in the garden room. Afterward stroll the grounds or lounge on the terrace. The Shiverick Inn, which is open year-round, welcomes children age 12 and older. Dogs are accommodated in certain guest rooms for a nightly surcharge of $25.

THE VICTORIAN INN $$$$
24 South Water St.
(508) 627-4784
www.thevic.com

Directly across the street from the famous Edgartown Pagoda Tree is the Victorian Inn, built ca. 1820 and listed in the National Register of Historic Places. All 14 guest rooms have private baths and are decorated with antiques and flowers. A number of rooms have four-poster beds, and some have balconies. Some rooms overlook the historic harbor, whereas others overlook the English garden below, where a complimentary gourmet breakfast is served. An informal tea is also served in the afternoon. Children 8 and older are welcome at the inn, and from Nov to Apr pets are allowed. The inn is open year-round.

Up Island
DUCK INN $$$–$$$$
10 Duck Pond Way, off State Road,
Aquinnah
(508) 645-9018
www.gayheadrealty.com

At nearly land's end lies the Duck Inn, with incredible views of the Aquinnah Cliffs and Lighthouse. To get to this cozy five-room, 200-year-old farmhouse, you must take a dirt road. The decor varies from Southwest to Japanese. The Southwest room has pink stucco walls, and the Japanese room is filled with silks. All rooms but the detached cabin (attached by a glass breezeway) have private baths. The cabin's bath is not connected to the room. A ground level suite features

a fireplace, and all guests have access to the hot tub and two house cats. Miles and miles of the most secluded beaches lie outside the door. Duck Inn is open all year long, and children are welcome. Pets are welcome during the summer.

LAMBERT'S COVE COUNTRY INN $$$$
Lambert's Cove Road, West Tisbury
(508) 693-2298
www.lambertscoveinn.com

If you really want to get away from it all, this is the spot. Once a horticulturist's estate, Lambert's Cove is the kind of country inn you dream about. Off Lambert's Cove Road you take an unpaved path through woods to this inn hidden amid towering pines, 150-year-old vine-covered stone walls, gardens, and an old-fashioned apple orchard. The inn comprises fifteen rooms, with seven in the original 1790 main building and four each in the restored carriage house and converted barn. All rooms have private baths, air-conditioning, TV/DVD/CD, Internet access, and some have private sundecks. Other amenities include a heated pool and spa and access to the private Lambert's Cove Beach. A gazebo rests in the yard beyond the inn, and a tennis court awaits you just past that. They provide a full made-to-order breakfast. The inn is also home to one of the island's finest dining rooms (see the subsequent Restaurants section of this chapter).

MENEMSHA INN AND COTTAGES $$$$
North Road, Menemsha
(508) 645-2521
www.menemshainn.com

This complex of 17 shingled buildings is set in the pretty fishing village of Menemsha. The Carriage House features six suites. The inn has nine rooms, six with a view of the water and all with cable TV/VCR, Internet access, private bath, and deck. If you are more in the mood for the independence of a housekeeping cottage, try one of the 11 cottages spread out on more than 14 acres of land. They have kitchens, fireplaces, and outdoor showers. The most luxurious accommodation is the two-bedroom mainstay suite, with its breathtaking water views and two baths. The Menemsha Inn and Cottages are open year-round.

Hotels
Oak Bluffs
ISLAND INN $$$-$$$$
Beach Road
(508) 693-2002, (800) 462-0269
www.islandinn.com

Along the road that connects Oak Bluffs and Edgartown lies the Island Inn. Overlooking the Farm Neck Golf Club, the Island Inn is a short walk to Oak Bluffs Town Beach and Joseph Sylvia State Beach. The inn offers an assortment of 51 rooms, suites, and even a cottage—all sporting fully furnished kitchens, private baths, and cable TV. There are three Har-Tru tennis courts on-site. A full-time tennis pro is available to give you lessons. Families can take advantage of the seven acres of grounds, including a barbecue area, an outdoor pool, and a playground for the kiddies. The Island Inn is open from late Mar to late Nov and has one wheelchair-accessible unit.

WESLEY HOTEL $$$
70 Lake Ave.
(508) 693-6611, (800) 638-9027
www.wesleyhotel.com

The Wesley Hotel, built in 1879, is the last of the grand hotels of Oak Bluffs. Open from early May to mid-Oct, she seems to watch over the town from her knoll facing the harbor, where you can relax and enjoy the views from one of the rocking chairs on the spacious front porch.

Renovations over the years have restored the Wesley to her former greatness. You will feel yourself going back in time as you climb the steps to the veranda, enter the dark oak lobby, and walk up to the old-fashioned registration desk. In two adjacent Victorian-style buildings (the Main Building and the Wesley Arms), the Hotel houses 95 rooms equipped with private baths, individual temperature controls, and satellite TV. There are wheelchair-accessible rooms located on the first floor of the main building, and the Wesley Arms' upper floors are accessible by elevator.

Edgartown
**CLARION MARTHA'S VINEYARD–
EDGARTOWN HERITAGE HOTEL** $$$$
227 Upper Main St.
(508) 627-5161, (800) 922-3009
www.clarionmv.com

Those looking for a modern hotel just a 10- to 15-minute walk from Edgartown's historic waterfront will want to look into the Clarion Martha's Vineyard. Each of the hotel's 34 rooms offer queen- or king-size beds, a private bath, cable TV, microwave, refrigerator, air-conditioning, and a telephone. A complimentary continental breakfast is provided. The Heritage can accommodate groups of up to 50 people for business meetings, social functions, and private parties. This year-round hotel has two wheelchair-accessible rooms available. Children younger than 18 stay free with an adult.

EDGARTOWN LODGE $$$-$$$$
67 Winter St.
(corner of Church and Winter St.s)
(508) 627-1092
www.edgartownlodge.com

Like to get away but not feel isolated? Try the Edgartown Lodge and one of its eight rooms and two suites. Each suite is set up like its own apartment, with a bedroom, living/dining area, full bath, and cable TV. Each suite sleeps two to five comfortably, and you're just a block off Main Street and a few blocks away from the beaches.

THE HARBORSIDE INN $$$-$$$$
3 South Water St.
(508) 627-4321, (800) 627-4009
www.theharborsideinn.com

A complete waterfront resort located right at Edgartown's historic harbor, the Harborside Inn offers seven buildings (some are former 19th-century whaling captains' homes) housing 90 rooms. About half of these rooms have views of the harbor, and some have huge private balconies. A large heated outdoor pool is just steps from the waters of the harbor. You can relax in the whirlpool or in the sauna after a busy day of shopping, swimming, or bike riding. Rooms include color cable TV, refrigerators, private baths, air-conditioning, and Internet access. The resort is open mid-Apr through early Nov and provides full service banquet facilities. If you have children, you'll be happy to learn that children younger than 12 stay at the Harborside Inn free with an adult.

THE HARBOR VIEW HOTEL $$$$
131 North Water St.
(508) 627-7000, (800) 225-6005
www.harbor-view.com

The windows command incredible views of Edgartown Lighthouse, Edgartown Harbor, and Chappaquiddick Island beyond. Dating to 1891 as two separate buildings, today the Harbor View Hotel is one large gem of a grand hotel, accented by a magnificent 300-foot veranda. A multimillion-dollar renovation a few years ago restored all her 130 rooms and suites to their former Victorian splendor.

Guests are pampered by the accommodating staff. Concierge, room service, and the daily newspaper are just some of the extras that set this hotel apart. Seven townhouses on-site feature cathedral ceilings, kitchens, and outside decks. The 12-acre complex includes a swimming pool, a private beach, and all-weather tennis courts.

KELLEY HOUSE $$$$
23 Kelley St.
(508) 627-7900
www.kelley-house.com

Over the past two-and-a-half centuries, since 1742 to be exact, the Kelley House has been open for travelers and vacationers alike. It was formerly a tavern where whalers and sea captains raised their pints, and today all of the inn's 60 rooms maintain the colonial charm that guests a century ago would have enjoyed. Of course, today's guests also enjoy modern-day amenities.

Period antiques, quilts, and an overall early-American personality will make you think you're staying back in 19th-century Edgartown. Some rooms have kitchens and private balconies. A

complimentary breakfast awaits you, as does afternoon tea. Bedtime arrives with homemade cookies and milk. A refreshing outdoor pool offers views of Edgartown Harbor. After a swim you can wander into the Newes from America, an American pub at the Kelley House that offers casual fare (see the Restaurants section in this chapter). Kelley House is open from May through Oct.

WINNETU INN AND RESORT $$$$
31 Dunes Rd., Edgartown
(508) 310-1733, (866) 335-1133
www.winnetu.com

The rare resort that not only allows but encourages children, Winnetu occupies 11 acres just off Katama's South Beach. Built in 2000, it is one of the Vineyard's newer accommodations, yet in style it hearkens back to the days when sprawling, service-oriented lodgings were all the rage in seaside communities. All the units are suites (kitchenettes included), and many overlook the water from private decks or patios. With a heated outdoor pool, a putting green, a fitness room, and 10 tennis courts (a pro is on-site in season), you'll have your hands full without ever leaving the grounds. A complimentary children's program gives parents a break on summer mornings (June to Sept), and the in-house restaurant (Lure Grill, see our Restaurants chapter) has made quite a splash among local gourmets. The inn is open from mid-Apr through late Oct. Several wheelchair-accessible rooms are offered.

Hostel

HOSTELLING INTERNATIONAL–
MARTHA'S VINEYARD $
25 Edgartown–West Tisbury Rd.,
West Tisbury
(508) 693-2665, (888) 901-2087
www.usahostels.org/cape/himv/index.php

If you weren't paying about $32 a night, you'd think you were staying at the quaintest of country inns. This cedar-shake saltbox, now more than five decades old, sits at the edge of the Manuel F. Corellus State Forest. The hostel has a fireplace in the common room, a volleyball court, a sheltered bike rack out back, and a spacious kitchen that awaits budding gourmets. Five dorms house 74 beds; check-in is between 8 a.m. and 10 p.m. daily. The hostel fills up quickly; we suggest you make reservations (especially during the season) at least two weeks in advance. The hostel is open from late Apr through early Oct.

Condominiums

Vineyard Haven

HARBOR LANDING   **$$–$$$**
15 Beach Rd.
(508) 693-2600, (800) 545-4171
www.harbor-landing.com

For families who want to spend an extended period of time on the island, Harbor Landing offers 39 very affordable units, each with a full, private bath, cable TV, air-conditioning and heating, refrigerator, and a common kitchen for guests to share. The efficiency units have fully equipped kitchens. A large sundeck on the third floor offers great views of the harbor, and a five-acre park borders the rear of the building. Complimentary coffee is served each morning. If you're interested in visiting the island during the off-season, check out Harbor Landing's incredibly low $70 rates. High season rates range from $140 for a budget unit to $215 for a double suite. Harbor Landing is open year-round.

Campgrounds

**MARTHA'S VINEYARD FAMILY
CAMPGROUND**   **$**
Edgartown–Vineyard Haven Road
Vineyard Haven
(508) 693-3772
www.campmv.com

Families who enjoy camping will love the time they'll have at the Martha's Vineyard Family Campground, located just a mile or so away from Vineyard Haven center. Each campsite is allowed one motor vehicle and either one large tent or two small tents. Trailer sites are also available. Both types of sites include electric and water hookups; the trailer sites also include sewer. Rates are $49 per night for a campsite and $55 for a trailer site. These rates are for two adults and any children younger than 18. Additional adults are charged $15 per night. Also, there are one- and two-room cabins and even tent trailers available. The grounds include plenty to keep the family busy: table tennis, billiards, biking, baseball, a store, and a playground. Cable TV is available. There are some 180 sites; it's open mid-May through mid-Oct. No dogs and no motorcycles are allowed in the campground.

VACATION RENTALS AND REAL ESTATE

There are a number of real estate companies on the island; unfortunately, space does not permit listing them all. Besides selling properties, many of these companies also handle vacation rentals. Below are a handful that do handle rentals. We encourage you to shop around, but don't wait too long to decide, as it's best to reserve a rental at least 10 months in advance. Otherwise there may be nothing left.

Vineyard Haven

ISLAND REAL ESTATE
107 Beach Rd., Suite 203
(800) 287-4801
www.islandrealestatemv.com

Island Real Estate offers rentals throughout the island. Island Real Estate offers hundreds of properties in a wide spectrum of prices. The six agents can show you every land, home, and condo listing on the island.

MARTHA'S VINEYARD VACATION RENTALS
107 Beach Rd., Suite 107
(508) 693-7711, (800) 556-4225
www.mvvacationrentals.com

The agents at Martha's Vineyard Vacation Rentals personally inspect each of the privately owned homes they offer for rent. Their varied inventory includes vacation homes and waterfront properties in every price range. They can also connect you to bike, boat, linen, and baby-equipment rental services.

i Heading "up-island" means traveling in a southwesterly direction toward Aquinnah. "Down-island" refers to the easterly towns of Tisbury, Oak Bluffs, and Edgartown. These terms are nautical in origin: Sailing west means crossing increasingly higher degrees of longitude, hence going "up," and sailing east means going "down" in longitude.

Edgartown

LINDA R. BASSETT REAL ESTATE
201 Upper Main St.
(508) 627-9201, (800) 338-1855
www.mvseacoast.com
Located in Edgartown, this company handles both the sale of properties and vacation rentals throughout Martha's Vineyard. In the area of sales, it deals primarily in private year-round homes, cottages, condominiums, and estates, with many of its properties being either waterfront or water view. On the rental side, Linda R. Bassett offers more than 650 properties from around the Vineyard.

MARTHA'S MANAGEMENT REAL ESTATE RENTALS
P.O. Box 2866, Edgartown, 02539
(508) 627-5005, (888) 481-9504
www.marthasmgmt.com
On a cozy island like Martha's Vineyard, you may want to try a smaller rental agency like Martha's Management Real Estate Rentals. Martha's covers about 150 properties around the island, and the owners and employees are very familiar with each property, many of which they also maintain. In most cases they will also escort you to your rental, which is a great service if you happen to be unfamiliar with the island.

MARTHA'S VINEYARD LANDVEST
19 South Summer St.
(508) 627-3757
www.mvlandvest.com
Martha's Vineyard Landvest specializes in waterfront properties and in-town historical homes for rent. The properties they handle are worth the price.

SANDCASTLE REALTY
256 Edgartown–Vineyard Haven Rd.
(508) 627-5665
www.sandcastlemv.com
This agency deals in rentals only. They offer more than 500 homes all over the island that range from simple cottages to elegant estates. Prices range from $1,000 to more than $10,000 per week, to $100,000 per month.

SANDPIPER RENTALS, INC.
60 Winter St.
(508) 627-6070, (508) 627-3757
www.sandpiperrealty.com
Whether you're in the market for a small seaside cottage or a sprawling 200-acre waterfront estate, Sandpiper Rentals can fulfill your order from their list of more than 700 rental properties.

RESTAURANTS

As you might expect, the Vineyard offers the fare one would expect from an island—plenty of seafood. But the offerings do not end there. Across the island there are a number of specialty restaurants serving the finest in Italian, French, Indian, Chinese, and Mexican dishes. There are also plenty of casual dining establishments serving your basic chow. Yet even basic chow tastes so much better when you have an ocean view.

Below is a listing of some of the restaurants located throughout the towns, but we encourage you to be like Bartholomew Gosnold and explore. You'll be fascinated at the wonderful discoveries you'll make. For instance, there are a number of fine dining establishments in Edgartown, but sometimes there is nothing better than wandering into a local pub and ordering the special off the chalkboard along with a pint of beer to wash it down. What these places lack in cloth napkins and unpronounceable entrees they make up for in honest, down-home Yankee cooking and atmosphere.

Something to keep in mind: Every town but Edgartown and Oak Bluffs remains "dry" (no alcohol can be served in restaurants) as of the publication of this guide. There continue to be debates over whether the other towns should convert to allow alcohol to be served in restaurants, but progress to that end has moved forward in fits and starts. This does not mean you have to go without, only that you have to bring your own bottle.

Price Code

The price code used here is intended as a guide in helping you decide where to dine. It is based on the average price of dinner entrees for two, excluding appetizers, alcoholic beverages, dessert, tax, and tip. Most restaurants accept major credit cards; we note the ones that do not.

$. . . . . **Less than $20**
$$ . . . . **$20 to $35**
$$$ . . . . **$36 to $50**
$$$$ . . . . **$51 and more**

Vineyard Haven

THE BLACK DOG TAVERN $$$
21 Beach St. Extension
(508) 693-9223
www.theblackdog.com

After seeing all the T-shirts and hats, you have to be at least a little curious about the Black Dog Tavern. While the Black Dog's Labrador silhouette logo has ventured well beyond New England, the menu at this landmark is down-home seafood with plenty of dishes for landlubbers as well. Just yards from the waters of Vineyard Haven Harbor during low tide and just a few feet away when the tide is high, rusted iron chains and anchors, weathered wooden barrels, and a tavern sign swaying in the salty breeze all provide a wharf atmosphere.

There are no reservations here and, considering its renown, arrive very early if you want to even have a shot at a window table. The Black Dog is also BYOB (Bring Your Own Booze) if you want a drink with dinner. Also on the grounds are the Black Dog General Store and the Black Dog Bakery (see the subsequent Shopping section of this chapter). The Black Dog Tavern is open year-round and serves breakfast, lunch, dinner, and Sunday brunch.

LE GRENIER $$$$
96 Main St.
(508) 693-4906
www.legrenierrestaurant.com

If you're going to open a French restaurant on Martha's Vineyard, it helps to hail from France. Le Grenier chef/owner Jean Dupon is a native of Lyon who keeps his menu steeped in such traditional French cuisine as shrimp Pernod, frog legs Provençale, steak au poivre, and lobster Nomande flambé with Calvados apples. Le Grenier is open for lunch and dinner nightly year-round. Reservations are suggested.

ZEPHRUS $$$$
9 Main St., Vineyard Haven
(508) 693-3416
www.mvmansionhouse.com

The elegant Mansion House Inn (see our Accommodations chapter) operates an equally appealing restaurant, where you can bring your own bottle (Prohibition is still in effect in Vineyard Haven) to enjoy with visionary dishes like calamari bruschetta and honey dill roasted Atlantic salmon. Named for the mythical God of the West Wind, Zephrus also seduces sweet tooths with its decadent dessert offerings (pumpkin mousse parfait, anyone?).

Oak Bluffs

GIORDANO'S RESTAURANT $$
Lake Avenue and Circuit Avenue
(508) 693-0184
www.giosmv.com

On summer weekend evenings, patrons line up to get into Giordano's. Inside is an Italian dinner like your grandma used to make—that is, if your grandma was Italian. People have been waiting in line to get in ever since the Giordano family opened the Italian restaurant in 1930. The food here is hearty and wholesome; expect heaping plates of cutlets and cacciatore, pizza, pasta, fried clams, and seafood. There is a noisy ambience about the place, but it's all part of the charm of this family dining experience. Children's meals are offered at substantially lower prices.

Lunch and dinner are served daily from mid-May through mid-Sept. Reservations are not accepted. No credit cards.

JIMMY SEAS PAN PASTA $$$
32 Kennebec Ave.
(508) 696-8550

Expect to receive your food in large portions, and expect to receive it served right in the pan in which it was cooked. The restaurant has a comfortable atmosphere, and the staff is very friendly. Jimmy Seas is a favorite spot of President Clinton when the former First Family is on the island. The restaurant does not accept reservations (although, for some reason, we can't see the Clintons waiting in line for a table). It's open nightly for dinner from Apr through Columbus Day, and on weekends (Sat and Sun) from Columbus Day through Nov.

LINDA JEAN'S $-$$
34 Circuit Ave.
(508) 693-4093

If breakfast is your bag, then you'll definitely want to check out Linda Jean's on Circuit Avenue. Fluffy pancakes made from scratch are as good a way as any to start the day on the island. A year-round family-owned restaurant, it is a favorite spot for locals and visitors alike. Linda Jean's also serves lunch and dinner—check out the seafood platter with a full plate of clams, scallops, shrimp, haddock, fries and cole slaw. Open year-round, it has been an Oak Bluffs fixture for more than 25 years. No credit cards, no reservations.

LOLA'S RESTAURANT $$$
Beach Road
(508) 693-5007
www.lolassouthernseafood.com

There's something to be said for the fact that when the locals and island regulars go out to eat, most of them hit Lola's. Open year-round, Lola's is a wonderful, family-style restaurant where the emphasis is on seafood prepared in southern style, including some great New Orleans dishes in its pub and main dining room. The pub offers a more moderately priced menu and live entertain-ment nightly in season (on weekends in the off-season). You can also catch an occasional gospel brunch on Sundays during the summer. Lola's is open for lunch and dinner.

MAD MARTHA'S $
117 Circuit Ave.
(508) 693-9151

This is the place for ice cream on the island. With more than two dozen flavors from which to choose, there's something here for even the pickiest tastes. Established in 1971, Mad Martha's can be found at several other locations through-out the island: Dockside Market Place in Oak Bluffs, Lake Avenue in Oak Bluffs, Union Street in Tisbury, and North Water Street in Edgartown. Besides serving ice cream, Mad Martha's also offers burgers and grinders (sandwiches made with hard rolls) from May to Columbus Day.

OCEAN VIEW RESTAURANT AND TAVERN $$
Chapman Avenue
(508) 693-2207

The Ocean View serves great tasting food at very reasonable prices. Its menu features everything from pizza to prime rib and lobster. Shrimp is a local favorite, and you'll definitely want to try the fillet of sole almandine. The lounge has a large hearth with a fire crackling on cooler days with a popcorn maker built into the hearth. There is an informal tavern, along with two dining rooms complete with a mural of the harbor and a large fish tank. The clientele is a mix of locals and visitors. Lunch and dinner are served daily year-round.

OFFSHORE ALE $$
30 Kennebec Ave.
(508) 693-2626
www.offshoreale.com

Offshore Ale is a favorite Vineyard establishment as an upscale brewpub with good food. There is live entertainment nearly every night during the summer months and less often during the slower months. The menu features a mix of seafood and typical fare such as pizza and burgers. Offshore Ale is open year-round.

SEASONS EATERY & PUB $$–$$$
19 Circuit Ave.
(508) 693-7129
www.seasonspub.com

Seasons is located halfway down busy Circuit Avenue. The menu contains an encyclopedic array of moderately priced items, such as scallop and shrimp plates for seafood eaters, and a full sushi selection for those who don't necessarily like it hot. The entertainment schedule encompasses acoustic acts, karaoke, and DJs. Seasons is open year-round for breakfast, lunch, dinner, and brunch.

Edgartown

ALCHEMY BISTRO AND BAR $$$–$$$$
71 Main St., Edgartown
(508) 627-9999
www.alchemymv.com

You'll see few signs of the humble grocery shop that once occupied Alchemy's spot on Edgartown's main drag, so thoroughly have the owners effected the transformation from dross to gold. With its aged wooden floors and papered white tablecloths, Alchemy is every inch the Parisian bistro it aims to be. It's a great place to emulate Hemingway as you peruse the exhaustive menu of wines, beers, and spirits ranging from cognac to grappa, but the real attraction lies in edible offerings like oyster brie soup and lobster shepherd's pie.

AMONG THE FLOWERS $$$
17 Mayhew Lane, Edgartown
(508) 627-3233
www.mvol.com/menu/amongtheflowers

Friendly service and reasonable prices form the philosophy behind this dockside cafe, where you can watch boats come and go over comfort food creations like cinnamon and walnut waffles (at breakfast), lobster salad rolls (at lunch) and shellfish bouillabaisse (at dinner).

ATRIA $$$$
137 Main St., Edgartown
(508) 627-5850
www.atriamv.com

Named for a navigational star in the Southern Triangle constellation, Atria has become something of a star in the Vineyard dining scene. Set in an 18th-century sea captain's house, its wraparound porch and candlelit interior have served as the setting for many a special occasion. Fusion-oriented regional cuisine fuels the seasonal menu, which exploits the freshest local ingredients for dishes like island lobster mac 'n' cheese, grilled swordfish with watercress and preserved lemon, and an innovative spin on surf and turf featuring seared Georges Bank scallops and red wine–braised short ribs. The downstairs Brick Cellar Bar is a big draw for singles.

DAVID RYAN'S
RESTAURANT CAFE $$$–$$$$
11 North Water St.
(508) 627-4100
www.davidryans.com

As you're hitting all the shops along North Water Street in Edgartown, you may want to hit the brakes and stop for a bite at David Ryan's. How about seafood mac 'n' cheese with Gruyère, scallops, shrimp, and lobster? Or perhaps butter-poached lobster with warm fennel in a lobster saffron broth? Nothing like native seafood to give you a real feel for the island. David Ryan's also serves satisfying sandwiches and choice meats and has a full liquor license. After dinner you can either continue shopping or mosey on down to the wharf and just take in the sights. David Ryan's has a casual cafe and an elegant upstairs. It is open every day, serving lunch and dinner.

DÉTENTE $$$–$$$$
Nevin Square, off Winter St., Edgartown
(508) 627-8810
www.detentewinebar.com

Whether you sit at the soapstone bar or on a sleek banquette in the dining room, you'll appreciate the elegance of Détente. Tea-stained draperies swath the windows and black and white photographs adorn the walls in the dining room, where the seasonal menu features ingredients from island farms and markets. Depending on the month, your meal may consist of pan-crisped trout on fresh corn and apple wood-smoked risotto, Niman Ranch pulled pork Bolognese, or island lobster ravioli. Open from Apr through Jan; reservations strongly recommended.

L'ETOILE $$$$
22 North Water St.
(508) 627-5187
www.letoile.net

A stand-alone now after years of affiliation with the Charlotte Inn, L'Etoile is an exquisite French restaurant featuring the culinary artistry of chef/owner Michael Brisson. Begin with an appetizer of sautéed, spice-crusted duck foie gras with honey-roasted Seckel pears and poire brandy-muscat sauce, or roasted corn and seafood chowder.

Your choice of entrees includes sautéed fresh Dover sole fillets with champagne and sweet parsley risotto and citrus-caper beurre blanc, or perhaps Harissa-spiced Australian lamb paired with herb-rubbed rack chops. The incredible desserts are sure to break even the most determined diet. Dinner is served daily in season; call for off-season schedule. Reservations are required.

LURE GRILL $$$$
Winnetu Inn and Resort, Katama,
Edgartown
(508) 627-3663
www.winnetu.com/dining.htm

"Native, casual, coastal cuisine" is the emphasis at the Winnetu Resort's (see our Accommodations chapter) extraordinary eatery, where Boston transplant Ed Gannon (formerly of Aujourd'hui at the Four Seasons) is winning fans among island foodies. Dazzling sunsets can be seen from a window seat or deck table, and in season you can up the ante by taking the complimentary water taxi at dusk. Gannon's expertise lies in enhancing (rather than smothering) the flavor of fresh local ingredients, and his style can be seen in dishes like seared foie gras (with roasted stone fruit, hazelnuts, and rhubarb-sangria syrup) and poached lobster with pea ravioli.

MAIN STREET DINER $–$$
65 Main St.
(508) 627-9337

This is your classic—right out of a Norman Rockwell print—diner. It's a bit hard to find, but the journey is worth it. You approach from Main Street by following a long, well-lit, and flower-wallpapered walkway. Along the way you'll pass American memorabilia. On the wall at the end is an American flag with 36 states. Turn left, and then take a quick right, and there you are. Open the door, and you enter a museum of early 20th-century stuff. The food is the good old-fashioned American variety, and the smells are delicious. Most of the entrees are under $10. As you look at some of the pictures on the walls, you'll be amazed at who else has found this spot: Kevin Costner, Patricia Neal, Bill Pullman, even a Kennedy or two. Main Street Diner serves breakfast, lunch, and dinner year-round.

NEWES FROM AMERICA PUB $–$$
23 Kelley St.
(508) 627–7900
www.kelley-house.com/dining

You almost expect to see Captain Ahab limp through the door into this classic whaling port pub. Brick walls and rustic wood planking on the walls and ceiling provide its character. Housed in an 18th-century building, the Newes is a famous gathering place for visitors and locals in search of good food at a good price. The beers served here have become legendary. If you can't make up your mind which beer to have, why not order the Rack of Beers, which allows you to sample five different brews. Regulars who consume in the neighborhood of 1,000 short drafts, or 500 talls, receive their own personal bar stool for a full year.

The food served here is old American pub chow—hamburgers, grilled sandwiches, and hot soups to burn away the thickest fog. It's the kind of food that tastes great with a pint of beer and a salty sea tale. The Newes is open for lunch and dinner year-round.

i For more than 50 years, Humphrey's on State Road in North Tisbury has been the place for your morning coffee and breakfast. They're known for their belly bombs—huge, perfect jelly-filled dough-nuts. Enjoy your apple or cherry turn-overs, huge cinnamon rolls, lemon cookies, bagels, and pies at the picnic tables outside. They also offer sandwiches and quiche for lunch.

Up Island

THE AQUINNAH SHOP $$
Cliffs of Aquinnah, Aquinnah
(508) 645-3867

The views from the restaurant's open porch are incredible, courtesy of the Cliffs of Aquinnah and the ancient glaciers that created them. An Aquin-nah landmark since 1949, the Aquinnah features plenty of great seafood and plenty of crowds. Patrons are offered both inside and outside seat-ing with take-out windows catering to those sit-ting outdoors to enjoy the awesome views. You can also buy clams and scallops by the pint and quart. The Aquinnah serves breakfast, lunch, and dinner while it's open from May to mid-Oct.

BITTERSWEET $$$$
688 State Rd., West Tisbury
(508) 696-3966

This West Tisbury BYOB is a bit off the beaten path, but its up-island locale can't stop the crowds from coming to sample Job Yacubian's Mediterranean-accented American cuisine. The downscale facade belies a stylish interior that showcases the work of local artists.

HOME PORT RESTAURANT $$-$$$
512 North Rd., Menemsha
(508) 645-2679
www.homeportmv.com

Since 1931, the Home Port Restaurant has been offering spectacular views along with great sea-food. It is at the Menemsha fishing port with its weathered shanties lining the harbor, the very fishing port used as Quint's homeport in the movie Jaws. In fact, as you dine on lobster here,

you can look out across the water and see the remains of Quint's boat ORCA on the opposite shore. The Home Port is open for dinner starting at 5 p.m. from mid-Apr to mid-Oct.

LAMBERT'S COVE COUNTRY INN $$$$
Lambert's Cove Rd., West Tisbury
(508) 693-2298
www.lambertscoveinn.com

Housed in a 1790 building, this restaurant offers a romantic country setting featuring beautiful pastoral views far removed from the hustle and bustle of the more populated town centers. Besides offering an elegant dining room, an outside deck is also available if you wish to look out over the apple orchard. Seafood lovers will want to try the locally harpooned swordfish or sea scallops. Landlubbers may wish to sample the pan-roasted duck breast or the braised veal cheeks. The restaurant is open year-round: seven days a week during the summer months for dinner only; during the off-season you should call ahead for days and hours of operation. Res-ervations are suggested, though walk-ins are always welcome. Lambert's is a nonsmoking establishment and, since West Tisbury is a dry town, guests are encouraged to bring their own alcoholic beverages.

i The West Tisbury Farmer's Market is a lovely Vineyard tradition. It's held at the historic Grange Hall on State Road on Saturday from 9 a.m. to noon. This is where many island farmers sell their pro-duce, great greens, flowers, jams, herbs, and more.

ENTERTAINMENT AND NIGHTLIFE

The Vineyard can kick up its heels as well as any resort destination. However, the island also is a haven for artists and performers, lending more than just a touch of culture to this island paradise.

For those in the 21-plus crowd, bars close at 1 a.m. Many places have live entertainment in season. You'll find most of the action in Oak Bluffs and Edgartown. Unlike the Cape mainland, you'll generally find a good supply of public transportation and cabs to help you plan a fun and safe evening.

Here's a list of island spots where you can enjoy a well-rounded assortment of entertainment and nightlife.

Vineyard Haven

ISLAND THEATRE WORKSHOP
(508) 693-2769

www.itwmv.org

This is the island's oldest year-round theater company, presenting original plays as well as musicals and dramas. The group presents several shows a year at various venues. They also offer classes for children and adults. It is associated with the Young Director's Studio, Apprentice Players, the Theatre Guild, Family Classics Theatre, and Children's Theatre.

OWEN PARK
Off Main Street, Vineyard Haven

Ocean Park

Seaview Ave., Oak Bluffs

Music fans will appreciate the free Sunday night summer concerts alternately given at Owen Park off Main Street in Vineyard Haven and at the gazebo in Ocean Park on Seaview Avenue in Oak Bluffs. The events are quite festive and, as you lie back on your blanket, the music provides the starry night sky with a soundtrack.

TISBURY AMPHITHEATER
Tashmoo Overlook

State Rd.

(508) 693-6450

Summer Shakespeare takes the stage at the natural Tisbury amphitheater every Wed through Sat at 5 p.m. from mid-July through mid-Aug. Call for ticket prices. Tickets are sold at the amphitheater before shows, and they accept cash only. A helpful hint: It's Shakespeare outdoors, so you may want to bring along a blanket and some mosquito repellent.

i While on the island, call 311 for nonemergencies from any landline. All calls will be directed automatically to police stations in the town where the call originated. This is the line to call if your car gets stuck in the sand, to report noise complaints, graffiti, illegally parked cars, and the like. If it's an immediate emergency, call 911.

THE VINEYARD PLAYHOUSE
24 Church St.

(508) 693-6450

www.vineyardplayhouse.org

The Vineyard Playhouse is a nonprofit community center professional theater that puts on shows throughout the year. Tickets cost anywhere from $20 to $35 during the summer season. The Playhouse offers educational programs for both adults and children as well as children's shows, staged on summer Saturdays at Tisbury Amphitheater, with tickets around $6. The Playhouse stages about four different presentations (not including their outdoor Shakespeare selection, see above) each summer, between mid-June and early Sept.

Oak Bluffs

LAMPOST
111 Circuit Ave.

(508) 693-4032

www.lamppostmv.com

This is a club for the under-30 crowd. Eclectic live bands and DJs pack the dance floor in season for a modest cover charge (free to $10). The Lampost is open from Apr to Oct.

LOLA'S
Beach Road

(508) 693-5007

www.lolassouthernseafood.com

This hot spot is next to the Island Inn on the Beach Road on your way to Edgartown (or if you're coming from Edgartown, it's on your way to Oak Bluffs). It's jazz, blues, funk, soul, R&B, and the occasional DJ every night in July and Aug and weekends in the shoulder seasons (Apr through June and Sept through Oct). Look to their Web site for a calendar of entertainment. Lola's is open year-round.

SEASONS EATERY & PUB
19 Circuit Ave.
(508) 693-7129
www.seasonspub.com
This busy pub offers acoustic guitar, rock, DJs, or karaoke most evenings. There is a Sunday afternoon happy hour.

TABERNACLE
Campgrounds
(508) 693-0525
The Tabernacle on the campgrounds in Oak Bluffs often hosts free band concerts and shows by big-name performers. Also, if you like sing-alongs, tune up your vocal chords and set aside an evening or two for communal music making. Every Wed at 8 p.m. in season, the Tabernacle hosts a community sing-along. A songbook is provided for a small donation.

Edgartown
THE OLD WHALING CHURCH
89 Main St.
(508) 627-4442
The Old Whaling Church is often used for live performances. The day we stopped by, there was a concert by the Martha's Vineyard Chamber Music Society. Performers such as Livingston Taylor visit regularly.

Up Island
CHILMARK COMMUNITY CENTER
Beetlebung Corner, Chilmark
(508) 645-9484
www.chilmarkcommunitycenter.org
Beetlebung Corner's Chilmark Community Center is a spot where outside concerts often take place. The center also holds dances and other social events for all ages, including an end-of-July talent show.

MARTHA'S VINEYARD CHAMBER MUSIC SOCIETY
Chilmark, Edgartown
(508) 696-8055
www.mvcms.vineyard.net
The MVCMS has been committed to brining outstanding music to islanders year-round for nearly 40 years. Winter concerts fill the cultural yearning of year-round residents, and the summer series is always a highlight for vacationing music lovers. Call or check their Web site for a schedule and ticket prices. Monday concerts are held at Edgartown's Old Whaling Church, and Tuesday concerts at the Chilmark Community Center.

OUTERLAND
Martha's Vineyard Airport, West Tisbury
(508) 693-1137
www.outerlandmv.com
From the ashes of the Hot Tin Roof, perhaps the island's most iconic nightspot, rises Outerland, a fledgling club hoping to create a few legends of its own. Nostalgic locals of a certain age can still remember catching acts from reggae star Peter Tosh to wry comic Steven Wright on the Hot Tin Roof's storied stage, and new owner Barry Rosenthal has added an international wine list, an eclectic menu, and a smaller, lounge-like performance space to accommodate a new generation of music fans.

THE YARD
Middle Road, Chilmark
(508) 645-9662
www.dancetheyard.org
This is a 110-seat theater in a renovated barn off in the woods of Chilmark. A professional dance troupe, the Yard stages various theatrical events and dance previews throughout the summer season. Designed to sharpen the skills of professional artists, the Yard supports original works. Located near Beetlebung Corner, it is culture out amongst the trees. Tickets range from $10 to $75 for general admission, less for seniors and those 30 and under.

ATTRACTIONS

Martha's Vineyard is an island rich in history. Settled just decades after the Pilgrims arrived in Plymouth, the island has grown, prospered, and suffered over the years.

The Vineyard is a natural playground with its miles and miles of beaches and beautiful country settings, which might make you forget that colonists, patriots, whaling ship captains, and Civil War soldiers once called this sandy island home. Today their homes and churches and even gingerbread cottages stand as reminders of the grand lives they lived, lives that helped put Martha's Vineyard on the map as an important American port.

Many of the attractions listed below are historical sites that have, over the years, played a role in the island's development. The island's five lighthouses are listed according to location.

Vineyard Haven

ASSOCIATION HALL AND CEMETERY
Spring Street
Originally a Congregational and Baptist church built in 1844, this building is now the town hall and is also home to the Katherine Cornell Memorial Theater. Behind the building is an old cemetery with stones dating back to the 18th century.

THE MAYHEW SCHOOLHOUSE
110 Main St.
(508) 627-4440
www.mvpreservation.org
Owned by the Martha's Vineyard Preservation Trust, the island's first schoolhouse dates back to 1828. In 1776, a Liberty Pole stood in front of this building. When the British decided they would take it down for use as a spar on one of their vessels, three Vineyard Haven women blew up the pole with gunpowder rather than let the patriotic symbol fall into enemy hands. To commemorate their patriotism, a new pole was erected in 1898. Owned and operated for half a century as a nautical museum by the DAR, the schoolhouse is now occupied by Sail Martha's Vineyard, a nonprofit

committed to educating local children about sailing and maritime history.

SEA CAPTAINS' HOUSES
William St.
The largely residential William Street boasts many sea captains' houses, some of them now inns. Spared by the great fire of 1883 that engulfed much of the waterfront, William Street is now part of the official Historic District, in which buildings are protected from alteration.

SEAMEN'S BETHEL
15 Beach St.
Bethels are chapels used by seamen. This one has been catering to the needs of visiting sailors since 1893 and houses a display of maritime artifacts, including carved ivory and old photographs—gifts of seafarers in appreciation of the bethel's work and hospitality.

WEST CHOP LIGHTHOUSE
Main St.
Follow Main Street westward to its end, and there you will discover West Chop Lighthouse, the island's first lighthouse site. The light was initially constructed of wood in 1817. This was replaced, in 1838, by the present brick structure. In 1848 it was moved back from the eroding 60-foot cliff, only to be moved again in 1891. It stands 84 feet tall and emits a white light that can appear either red or pinkish depending on your vantage point. This is due to red-tinted glass on one side of the tower.

Oak Bluffs

CIVIL WAR MEMORIAL STATUE
Seaview, Lake, and Ocean Ave.s
At the busy intersection across the street from the Oak Bluffs ferry stop is a peculiar monument, and like most things in Oak Bluffs, it's the color scheme that is its peculiar attribute. This Civil War memorial dating to 1892 reads: "Erected in honor of Grand Army of the Republic by Charles Strahan, Co. B. 21st Virginia Reg." Yes, you read correctly, it was erected by a Confederate soldier—way up

here in Yankee territory. In 1980, the town of Oak Bluffs repainted the Union soldier atop the memorial in Confederate gray colors to pay homage to Strahan.

THE COTTAGE MUSEUM & SHOP
One Trinity Park
(508) 693-7784
www.mvcma.org/museum.htm
This museum allows you a rare glimpse at the inside of a gingerbread cottage. It is representative of the more than 300 fancifully designed and painted cottages that line the narrow streets of the 30-acre-plus campground community. The architecture of these cottages was modeled after the Newport, Rhode Island, Victorian style, but these have special (could we say, revolutionary) touches and colors that helped create a style unique to Oak Bluffs. Plan to take a better part of an hour just to stroll through the cottage community and examine the architecture and the many colors.

DR. DANIEL FISHER HOUSE
99 Main St.
(508) 627-4440
www.mvpreservation.org
This fine example of Federal period architecture was built in 1840 as the home of town physician and whaling mogul Dr. Daniel Fisher. Fisher was also the founder of the Martha's Vineyard National Bank. The building was recently restored by the Martha's Vineyard Preservation Trust. For more information or to arrange a guided tour, call (508) 627–8720. Combination tours are offered. Call for current rates. The Dr. Daniel Fisher House is also available for weddings and receptions; call (508) 627-8017.

EAST CHOP LIGHTHOUSE
Tall atop the bluff it stands, some 80 feet above the sea, casting its lonely beam across the waves of Nantucket Sound below. This cast-iron lighthouse was built in 1876, replacing a wooden light erected in 1828 that burned down. Originally brown-red in color, it was known as the Chocolate Lighthouse until it was painted white in 1988. It emits a green light, marking the port side of Vineyard Haven Harbor and balancing West Chop's red beam marking the starboard side.

FLYING HORSES CAROUSEL
Circuit Avenue
(508) 627-4440
www.mvpreservation.org
This is the oldest operating platform carousel in the United States. It features 20 wooden horses sporting real horse hair and glass eyes. It was constructed in New York City in 1876 and arrived at Oak Bluffs in 1884. Open from Easter Saturday through Columbus Day (schedule varies), it is listed as a National Historic Landmark. Rides are only $1.50. It's great entertainment for the kids, and yes, you do get to grab for the brass ring!

TABERNACLE
Trinity Park
At 100 feet high, 130 feet wide, and with seating for more than 3,000, this open-air auditorium is considered one of the largest wrought-iron structures in the United States. A uniquely beautiful piece of architecture combining the seemingly unlikely mixture of stained-glass windows and corrugated metal, it was built in 1879 amidst the

Oak Bluffs campground community. It replaced a one-ton tent used by the Methodists, who congregated at this spot for their religious summer gatherings. The Martha's Vineyard Camp Meeting Association, (508) 693-0525, offers a free schedule of events open to the public, including concerts (James Taylor has played here), flea markets, and interdenominational services.

UNION CHAPEL
55 Narragansett Ave.
(508) 627-4440
www.mvpreservation.org
When it was built in 1872, this was a non-denominational church. The octagonal-shaped building is now used for summer concerts and a jazz series, as its acoustics are quite good. The church building, owned by the Martha's Vineyard Preservation Society, features some interesting architecture, including a three-tiered roof.

Edgartown
CAPE POGUE LIGHTHOUSE
Chappaquiddick Island
By far the toughest of the island's lighthouses to visit, the Cape Pogue Lighthouse is at the northernmost tip of Cape Pogue on the island of Chappaquiddick. Built as a wooden lighthouse in 1801, it was destroyed by the sea and replaced in 1838. The second light lasted for about 50 years until it too was destroyed and was replaced by a third light, which was replaced by a fourth in 1892 (do you see a trend developing here?). This fourth lighthouse, which stood 33 feet high, was replaced by the present structure in 1922. This present lighthouse has earned its place in the Lighthouse Hall of Fame by being the only one ever moved in one piece by helicopter. The feat took place in 1985, when the structure was moved 300 feet back from the water because—you guessed it—it was in danger of being destroyed by the ocean. It stands 55 feet tall. Located at the farthest reaches of Chappaquiddick, the lighthouse is not accessible by road. For information on touring the lighthouse, contact the Trustees of Reservations at 508-627-3599.

EDGARTOWN LIGHTHOUSE
Off North Water Street
Originally constructed on an artificial island in Edgartown Harbor in 1828, the Edgartown lighthouse is now connected to the beach by a bar of accumulated sand. But before the sands filled in, there was a long wooden walk that led out to the lighthouse. This was called the Bridge of Sighs because it was a popular place for young whalers to bring their girlfriends or wives before heading out on a long journey. In 1938 the lighthouse was replaced by another that was floated to this spot from Ipswich (a town on Massachusetts's North Shore).

FERRY TO CHAPPAQUIDDICK
Dock Street, Edgartown Harbor
(508) 627-9427
We don't know if you would actually consider this a point of interest, but it does meet the criteria of a must-see when visiting Edgartown. Two simple ferries, *On Time II* and *On Time III,* make the daily runs between downtown Edgartown and Chappy, transporting you and your car, bicycle, or moped in the process. By the way, the ferries have never been late, thus earning their names. Round-trip fares are $10 for a car and driver, $3 for each passenger, and $6 for a bicycle and rider. Open daily from June to mid-Oct, the on-time ferry runs from 7 a.m. to midnight.

OLD WHALING CHURCH
89 Main St.
(508) 627-8017, (508) 627-4440
www.mvpreservation.org
This is an absolutely massive structure, with six gigantic wooden columns supporting the weight of the centuries and a 92-foot clock tower whose four-pointed spires seem to challenge the heavens. Since 1843, this soaring tower has been a landmark for sailors approaching Edgartown by sea. Built as sturdy as the old whaling ships, with 50-foot hand-hewn pine beams joined with wooden pegs, today the church is a 500-seat performing arts center. Summer church service is still held here on Sundays, as are weddings and receptions.

PAGODA TREE
South Water Street

A visit to Edgartown would not be complete without a visit to the famous Pagoda tree along South Water Street. The tree was planted during the mid-19th century by Capt. Thomas Milton, who carried it as a seedling from China. It is considered perhaps the oldest and largest specimen of its kind in America.

THE VINCENT HOUSE MUSEUM
Off Main Street
(508) 627-4440
www.mvpreservationtrust.org

This gem of a full Cape was built in 1672 and is considered to be Martha's Vineyard's oldest residence. It is behind the Old Whaling Church and the Fisher House. Interestingly sections of the interior walls of this museum have been left open and unfinished so you can observe its original colonial construction. Individual or combined tours are offered. Call for current rates. Tours are held at 11 a.m., noon, 1 and 2 p.m. Mon through Sat.

VINEYARD MUSEUM
59 School St.
(508) 627-4441
www.marthasvineyardhistory.org

This museum complex consists of four buildings that form 1 square block. The 1765 Thomas Cook House was once a customs house and now houses antiquities of the island, including tools and folk art. Exhibits to honor the whaling industry, such as scrimshaw and ship models, can be found in the Francis Foster Maritime Gallery, and Native American and island geophysical exhibits can be found in the Pease Galleries. The Gale Huntington Library is a must for those interested in genealogy. The carriage shed houses a whaleboat and a fire engine dating back to 1856. If you're a lighthouse enthusiast, be sure to get a look at the original Fresnel lens from the Gay Head Lighthouse. The lens, now installed in a lighthouse tower on the museum's front lawn, was installed in 1856 and removed from the lighthouse in 1952. It is illuminated a few hours

each evening during the summer months. The museum is open from 10 a.m. to 5 p.m. Mon through Sat in the summer; call for hours in the off-season. Admission for adults is $7 ($6 fall and spring) and $4 for children 6 to 15. Children under 6 enter for free.

WHALE MEMORIAL
Across from Memorial Wharf

A fitting memorial to the whales and the whalers is the Whale Memorial located down near the harbor in Edgartown. The memorial features a sculptured whale diving into the ground with its flukes raised and a whaleboat in pursuit. It was erected in 1995 and says it is "Dedicated to the whales and the whalers who pursued them."

Up Island

AQUINNAH LIGHTHOUSE
Aquinnah

High atop the Aquinnah Cliffs is the red brick Aquinnah Lighthouse, built in 1844 to replace its wooden sister. The original lighthouse was built by order of President John Adams. Due to a mingling of two tides, one from the north and one from the west, this stretch of ocean is considered to be very treacherous. Devil's Bridge off Aquinnah has wrecked many a ship over the centuries, including the City of Columbus in 1884, with the loss of 120 lives. The Fresnel lens of the second lighthouse, which for the better part of a century warned sea captains of the hazardous cliffs, was removed in 1952 and is now on display at the Vineyard Museum in Edgartown.

CLAY CLIFFS OF AQUINNAH
State Road, Aquinnah

Travel up to Aquinnah and you'll think you've landed on an entirely different island. Aquinnah Cliffs, at the westernmost reaches of Martha's Vineyard, are the island's most popular and most photographed tourist attraction. Its clay cliffs cause you to catch your breath in awe of that which only nature herself could possibly create.

These 150-foot-high clay cliffs were originally named Dover Cliffs by explorer Bartholomew

Gosnold, who first discovered the island in 1602. The Wampanoag Indians of the area have their own name for this place—Aquinnah. Gay Head, the cliffs' other name, came from British soldiers who sailed past this the area in the 17th century.

Today the cliffs are owned by the Wampanoag Indians of the area. Formed during the ice age, the cliffs are a geological treasure chest as well as a paleontologic gold mine with the numerous fossils unearthed here. The cliffs also had some practical uses. For instance, early islanders used the cliffs' clay to make paint and bricks. The high cliffs were also a prime vantage point—a high ground, you might say—and a perfect place to put a lighthouse (see below). The cliffs, now a national landmark, are protected in an attempt to reduce erosion. Only the Aquinnah Wampanoag Indians are allowed to remove clay from them.

MAYHEW CHAPEL AND INDIAN BURIAL GROUND
Off Indian Hill Road, West Tisbury

This area known as Christiantown, known to the Wampanoag Indians as Manitouwattotan, can be found off Indian Hill Road in West Tisbury. You follow a dirt road to this historic site hidden deep in the woods. Here stands the small Mayhew Chapel, built in 1829, and the adjoining Indian Burial Ground. The chapel is scarcely 20 feet by 15 feet, and yet it contains a dozen pews and a small altar. Early settler and minister Thomas Mayhew Jr. preached here, converting many native inhabitants in this area to Christianity. In the nearby cemetery nameless stones, perhaps as many as a hundred, mark Indian graves. It is a unique historical location, moving in its simplicity.

ℹ️ Nestled back in the woods, the Chicama Vineyards (pronounced Chi-cay-ma) are located on Stoney Hill Road, off State Road in West Tisbury. Started in the early 1970s, these vineyards produce chardonnay, cabernet, merlot, and more. Visit for a tasting or a tour. They also offer mustards, vinegars, jams, and salad dressings.

MENEMSHA FISHING VILLAGE
North Street, Menemsha

A classic fishermen's harbor, Menemsha was the site chosen to represent Quint's home port in the movie *Jaws*. There are some unforgettable shots of the harbor in the movie, notably as Quint's vessel ORCA is chugging out of the fishing port to hunt down the 25-foot great white shark. In fact a local told us that until recently one of the fishermen's shacks still had the name "Quint" painted on the door from the days when the movie was shot here. Furthermore, another local told us that the ORCA itself lies wrecked across the harbor at the mercy of the elements two decades after the mechanical beast staved her.

Beyond this bit of Hollywood, Menemsha is everything you expect from a salty fishing port: piles of lobster traps, heaps of discarded quahog shells, men wearing yellow waders bathed in fish blood, their faces aged by years at sea. Along the docks are little weather-beaten fishing shacks with shingles either warped with salt breezes, painted with gull droppings, or else missing altogether.

Menemsha also is home to one of the best sunset venues anywhere. From Menemsha Public Beach you're facing due west, giving you a great opportunity to watch the golden sun melt into the Atlantic.

TOURS AND EXCURSIONS

Boating excursions are popular throughout the island. We'll let you in on a few of our favorites.

There are a number of companies presenting narrated tours. Gay Head Sightseeing (508-693-1555), Island Transport (508-693– 0058), and Martha's Vineyard Sightseeing (508-627-8687) all have buses waiting as you come off the ferries at Oak Bluff and Vineyard Haven. Tours run from mid-Apr to Nov. All three tour companies offer two-and-a-half-hour tours of the six island towns; the cost is $29 for adults, $10 for children.

THE ARABELLA
Menemsha Harbor
(508) 645-3511
www.outermostinn.com/htboat.htm

This 50-foot catamaran sails out of Menemsha Harbor twice a day in season. Captain Hugh Taylor will take you to Cuttyhunk (or the town of Gosnold)—the only public island in the isolated Elizabeth Islands chain. Or you can take a sunset cruise to the Aquinnah Cliffs. The day sail to Cuttyhunk leaves at 10:30 a.m. and returns by 4 p.m. It costs $75 per adult or teen, $40 for children younger than 12. The sunset sail leaves at 6 p.m. (or thereabouts) and returns after the sun has totally set. The sunset cruise costs $50.

AYUTHIA CHARTERS INC.
13 Beach St., Coastwise Harbor, Vineyard Haven
(508) 693-7245
This truly classic 48-foot Gaff Ketch yacht sails out of Coastwise Harbor offering half- and full-day sails and overnight trips to Nantucket and the Elizabeth Islands. Master Captain Tom Grew offers one trip a day from 1 to 4 p.m. It's well worth packing a picnic, perhaps a bottle, and joining him as the experienced captain takes you on a traditional sailing experience.

i Public libraries located in each town on the island offer public Internet access, though we recommend you try to get through your vacation without logging on.

MAD MAX
Edgartown Harbor
(508) 627-7500
www.madmaxmarina.com
Mad Max leaves Edgartown to cruise along Chappaquiddick and past Oak Bluffs. A 60-foot-long by 25-foot-wide catamaran, it departs twice a day at 2 p.m. and 6 p.m. daily. Rates are $55, with children under 10 paying $50. An Insiders' tip: You get $5 off per person with a cash payment.

THE BLACK DOG TALL SHIPS: *SHENANDOAH* AND *ALABAMA*
Vineyard Haven
(508) 693-1699
www.coastwisepacket.com

Now affiliated with the Black Dog Tavern (and sailing from the newly named Black Dock Wharf, just steps from the iconic restaurant), this pair of towering schooners offers children, young adults, and more seasoned sailors an immersion course in the "thrilling power of sail." From day and sunset sails to kids' cruises and private charters, the *Alabama* and *Shenandoah* aim to initiate guests to the challenges and camaraderie of schooner sailing.

BEACHES

We hope you brought along your bathing suit, because Martha's Vineyard has 125 miles of coastline offering some of the most memorable beaches you'll ever encounter. And we hope you wear your swimsuit, because sunbathing in your birthday suit, or swimming in it for that matter, is against the law in all six Vineyard towns, even if you do happen to be the only bather for miles and miles and miles.

That having been said, to avoid surprises, visitors should know there are a few private beaches near the base of the Aquinnah cliffs that have built a reputation for their relaxed views toward bathing suits or the lack thereof.

Many of the beaches on Martha's Vineyard are private. In fact, we only count a little more than a dozen public beaches out of all those 125 miles.

Below we've listed our favorite public beaches. To park at some of these beaches, you'll need to get a parking and/or beach permit, which can be obtained by contacting the local town hall. (Vineyard Haven/Tisbury, 508-696-4200; West Tisbury, 508-696-0100; Chilmark, 508-645-2107; Oak Bluffs, 508-693-3554; Aquinnah, 508-645-2300; Edgartown, 508-627-6110.) Of the beaches below, all but Aquinnah and East Beaches are free. For current fees for these two beaches, call the Aquinnah Town Hall.

So get your permit, pack a lunch, bring along a book, and head off to the beach.

Vineyard Haven
LAKE TASHMOO BEACH
Herring Creek Road

Sunbathers, swimmers, surf casters, and shellfish seekers flock to this beach on the island's north shore, where the lake meets the ocean. This teeny stretch of sand is also known as Herring Creek Beach. You'll find lifeguards here, but no bathhouses or concessions.

OWEN PARK BEACH
Off Main Street
Here you'll discover a small, sandy, quiet harbor beach that offers great sunbathing, swimming, boat-watching, and lifeguards. It even has a separate kiddie play area. Bathhouses and concessions are nearby.

SOUTH BEACH
Off Edgartown–West Tisbury Road
The 633-acre Long Point Wildlife Refuge Center preserve boasts this half-mile-long deserted beach where swimming and surf fishing are allowed in freshwater and saltwater ponds. Better get there early; there are only 55 parking spaces available. South Beach has bathhouses but no concessions or lifeguards.

TISBURY TOWN BEACH
Owen Little Way
Sitting on the sand at Town Beach is the closest thing to being on a yacht, as this beach is right next to the Vineyard Yacht Club. Lifeguards are on duty here, and concessions and bathhouses are close at hand.

Edgartown
FULLER STREET BEACH
Fuller Street
This section of beach, not far from Lighthouse Beach, is a popular hangout for the younger crowd. It looks out across the water at Cape Pogue and Cape Pogue Lighthouse. There are no lifeguards, concessions, or bathhouses at the Fuller Street Beach.

JOSEPH SYLVIA STATE BEACH
Beach Road, Edgartown and Oak Bluffs

This lovely beach is framed with grassy dunes and wild roses and marked by calm, shallow waters. It is also known as the Edgartown–Oak Bluffs State Beach because it stretches along 2 miles of those towns. (The Edgartown section of the beach is known as Bend-in-the-Road Beach because of its unusual shape.) The beach, which has lifeguards and nearby concessions but no restrooms, is quite popular.

KATAMA BEACH
Katama Road, Katama
Also known as South Beach, this 3-mile-long barrier strand is the island's largest public beach. It's a favorite among surfers, who challenge heavy wave action of the mighty Atlantic pounding at its doorstep. (Watch for riptides, and check for swimming conditions!) In contrast to the Atlantic waves is a calm salt pond to the north of the beach. A shuttle bus runs between the beach and the center of Edgartown. Lifeguards are on patrol and bathhouses are available, but there are no concessions.

LIGHTHOUSE BEACH
Starbuck's Neck
Lighthouse Beach is a perfect place to watch boats entering and leaving the harbor. From here you get a nice view of Chappy and Cape Pogue. At night it's an ideal spot for sunsets and stargazing. There are lifeguards at this beach, but no bathhouses or concessions. It's called Lighthouse Beach because it's right there beside the Edgartown Lighthouse.

Oak Bluffs
EASTVILLE BEACH
Beach Road
If you're looking for a quiet stretch of shoreline along the harbor, you've found it. You can find Eastville Beach at the bridge between Oak Bluffs and Vineyard Haven. When you're not being lulled by the gently lapping surf, you can watch the sails billowing in the breeze as the boats go tacking by. There are no lifeguards, restrooms, or concession stands.

OAK BLUFFS TOWN BEACH
Seaview Avenue
Oak Bluffs Town Beach straddles both sides of the ferry wharf, and its calm surf makes it ideal for families with small kids. It's also a great spot to sit and wait for the ferry to come in. This beach has lifeguards on duty. Public restrooms are available nearby on the ferry dock, and various concessions are close by as well.

Up Island
AQUINNAH BEACH
Off Moshup Trail, Aquinnah
A wooden boardwalk winds alongside the famous cliffs, through cranberry bogs and beach plum bushes, down to the surf. Below is Aquinnah Beach, a 5-mile-long stretch that is actually four beaches in one. From north to south they are Aquinnah, Moshup, Philbin, and Zack's Cliffs. The last two beaches are private. The farther south you walk, the more isolated you find yourself. Fortunately, there are restrooms and concessions located at the head of the cliffs, though you won't find any lifeguards out here. Be careful in the tricky surf. *NOTE:* The parking out here is a bit expensive—up to $15 a day.

MENEMSHA PUBLIC BEACH
Menemsha Harbor, Chilmark
Resting right beside the stone jetty at the entrance to Ditcher's Dock, Menemsha Public Beach is a quiet place with a gentle surf and surprisingly few people. Sit and watch the fishing boats go in and out, or just kick back and catch some rays. Lifeguards, restrooms, and nearby concessions provide all the comforts.

Chappaquiddick
EAST BEACH
Chappaquiddick Road
Wasque Reservation and Cape Pogue Wildlife Refuge are adjoining beaches, known as East Beach, that run along the eastern coast of the island of Chappaquiddick. Even on the hottest day, you may find yourself the only one basking in the unspoiled glory. Because the beach sits at the end of a bumpy dirt road, it's accessible only by boat or four-wheel-drive vehicle. There are no bathhouses, concessions, or lifeguards. To get to Chappaquiddick Island, you'll need to take your car across on the On Time ferry. You will also have to pay a nominal fee to the Trustees of Reservations, which maintains and preserves the area. The beautiful beach is worth it, though.

NATURAL AREAS AND TRAILS
The island offers a mixture of natural settings, and as you travel through, say, Chilmark, you will see a number of her settings all in the same eyeful. Turn a corner, and you get a vista of rolling fields dampened by small ponds and ending in a vast sweep of ocean blue. Look the other way, and you see painstakingly erected stone walls vanishing off into the distance, beyond a swaying marshland carrying the island to sea.

Nature and humanity share the island, although in the Up Island area it seems that nature has the upper hand. Wildlife is ever apparent, including turkeys, which seem to have taken over parts of the island in recent years.

More than a fifth of the island is protected from development, and there are several sanctuaries and parks you can explore. You may have to pay a nominal parking fee.

CAPE POGUE WILDLIFE REFUGE AND WASQUE RESERVATION
Chappaquiddick Island
(508) 627-7689
www.thetrustees.org
These two adjoining parcels of land (516 acres and 200 acres, respectively) bordering Katama Bay on the southeastern corner of Chappaquiddick Island form the perfect escape from crowds. Even on the hottest summer day, you'll find few people here.

Salt marshes, tidal flats, ponds, cedars, barrier beaches, and sand dunes are everywhere. A myriad of shorebirds such as ospreys, snowy egrets, kestrels, great blue herons, and the endangered least terns and piping plovers populate this haven. Swimming, fishing, and picnicking are

Herring Bonanza

Many of the Vineyard's great ponds are occasionally opened (naturally, or with help from a backhoe) to the sea. This allows herring to return to freshwater to spawn and improves pond conditions for growing oysters. Predators—osprey, stripers, and bluefish—gather for an easy meal. Fishermen show up to this rich fishing opportunity too, as soon as they catch word of an opening. These openings typically happen in the spring and fall, and there is no set schedule. Local tackle shops are the best place to pick up word of these fishing bonanzas.

permitted. The Trustees of Reservation own and manage this property and offer several guided tours during the summer season. Check their Web site or call for specifics. All tours depart from the Mytoi parking area and run from Memorial Day through Columbus Day weekend. Reservations are recommended. Call (508) 627-3599 for ticket prices and reservations. The areas are open year-round.

CEDAR TREE NECK WILDLIFE SANCTUARY
Off Indian Hill Road
(508) 693-5207
www.sheriffsmeadow.org
This 300-acre natural habitat and living museum is tucked among the unspoiled woods of West Tisbury. It's a varied environment where freshwater ponds, brooks, scrub oaks, beech trees, bayberry bushes, rocky bluffs, and bogs all compete for your attention. The wooded color-coded trails offer many a delight: One leads to secluded North Shore Beach, another to a bird refuge, still another (the one starting at the parking lot) to the sanctuary's summit and breathtaking views of the Aquinnah Cliffs. It is open year-round.

FELIX NECK WILDLIFE SANCTUARY
Off Edgartown–Vineyard Haven Road
(508) 627-4850
www.massaudubon.org/felixneck
Situated 3 miles outside of Edgartown and run by the Massachusetts Audubon Society, Felix Neck is a nature-lover's dream come true—350 acres of open fields, woods, beaches, and marshlands inhabited by reptiles and other wildlife. In the summer, visitors can hike 6 miles of meandering, marked trails; be sure to look for the osprey nesting platforms. Throughout the year, professional naturalists offer various demonstrations and expeditions, including snake and bird walks, and stargazing and snorkeling sessions.

An exhibition center features displays of fish, snakes, and turtles and also has a library and gift shop. Felix Neck also offers summer camps for kids during the season.

LONG POINT WILDLIFE REFUGE
Off Waldron's Bottom Road, West Tisbury
(508) 693-3673
www.thetrustees.org
Long Point is the best spot for bird- and duck-watchers, provided, that is, you can deal with the very bumpy roads that get you here. This 633-acre area of open grassland and heath is bounded on the sides by salt and fresh water. The trails here wind their way through pine and oak forests and will take you to either idyllic Long Cove Pond (look for the river otters) or the lovely, but crowded, South Beach, where you can swim.

MANUEL F. CORRELLUS STATE FOREST
Airport Road
(508) 693-2540
www.mass.gov/dcr
This forest sits smack-dab in the middle of the island. It's a 5,145-acre spread of scrub oak and pine laced with paved bike, nature, horse, and hiking trails. You can pack a picnic basket and bask in the cool shade of majestic trees. A hostel is located at the southwest corner of the forest (see the previous Accommodations section of this chapter). There is no parking fee.

MENEMSHA HILLS RESERVATION
North Road, Chilmark
(508) 693-3673
www.thetrustees.org

This 211-acre Trustees of Reservations property includes trails that meander through distinct coastal ecosystems and offers stunning views. The Harris Trail curves through wetlands where red maples, cinquefoil, beech, and black cherry trees grow. Eventually you'll climb to the top of Prospect Hill, one of the highest points on Martha's Vineyard, with views of Menemsha village, the Elizabeth Islands, and Aquinnah Light. Turn around there, or follow the Upper or Lower Trails down to the rocky coast. At the overlook along the bluffs, you should be able to spy the remains of a 19th-century brickyard, a tall brick chimney.

MYTOI
Off Dike Road, Chappaquiddick
(508) 627-7689
www.thetrustees.org

This 14-acre Japanese garden is an astounding profusion of azalea, dogwood, iris, daffodils, rhododendron, wild rose, Japanese maple, holly, and sweet gum. We could sit all day and stare at the koi and goldfish, innocently swimming in their picturesque creek-fed pool beneath an ornamental bridge. Mytoi is open year-round.

WASKOSIM'S ROCK RESERVATION
North Road, Chilmark
(508) 627-7141
www.mvlandbank.com

The Martha's Vineyard Land Bank Commission acquired this unique 185-acre property in 1990 from a developer who planned on building scores of houses on it. Now it remains an unspoiled preserve of rolling hills, wetlands, oak, and beetlebung woods; it even has the ruins of an 18th-century homestead. As for Waskosim's Rock, it was deposited by a retreating glacier and, some say, looks like a breaching whale. The rock sits on a ridge from which you can soak in panoramic views of the Vineyard Sound foothills and the Mill Brook Valley.

RECREATION

The island is really one big playground. Surrounded as it is by the sea and the sounds, water sports and fishing abound. Meanwhile, on land there is plenty to do and discover.

Bicycling

Perhaps the best way to explore Martha's Vineyard is by bicycle. Just waiting to be explored are several superb bike paths that traverse the island. The island terrain is not known for its smoothness. The east side of the island is flatter than the west side, which rises well above sea level in some places. The more level bike paths are those connecting Vineyard Haven to Oak Bluffs, Oak Bluffs to Edgartown and to South Beach, and State Road between North Tisbury and Vineyard Haven. Middle Road in Chilmark has little traffic and is a wonderful country jaunt.

If you do enjoy scaling hills, follow the circular trail that begins at the Aquinnah Lighthouse. The views are incredible. There are also several paved bike paths in the Manuel F. Correllus State Forest, off Edgartown–West Tisbury Road, and in Oak Bluffs, West Tisbury, and Edgartown.

Many people bring their own bikes across from the mainland on the ferry, but you can lease bikes and riding equipment at a number of rental shops throughout the island.

ANDERSON'S BIKE RENTALS
Oak Bluffs
(508) 693-9346

EDGARTOWN BICYCLES
Edgartown
(508) 627-9008
www.edgartownbicycles.com

MARTHA'S BIKE RENTALS
Vineyard Haven
(508) 693-6593, (800) 559-0312
www.marthasvineyardbikes.com

R. W. CUTLER BIKES/EDGARTOWN BIKE RENTALS
Edgartown
(508) 627-4052, (800) 627-2763
www.edgartownbikerentals.com

Fishing

Perhaps one of the most popular recreational activities on the island is fishing, especially in the fall, when the Vineyard hosts its annual fishing derby. You don't have to be Quint, or Ahab for that matter, to catch the big one. You just have to be at the right place at the right time with the right equipment.

Fishing is superb at any of the beaches, so you'll notice plenty of surf casters. You'll also spot anglers casting their lines over the island's various bridges and stone jetties.

Insiders head to the Chappaquiddick shore at Cape Pogue and Wasque and to Lobsterville Beach in Aquinnah to reel in bluefish and bonito. Scup is common in the waters almost everywhere. Cod and striped bass are best caught during the spring and fall; head over to the entrance of Menemsha Harbor to find them.

If you're into surf casting, try the beaches at Aquinnah or any beach facing south. Remember, the tides in the Atlantic Ocean can be tricky; for instance there is an eight hour difference between high tides at Cape Pogue and Aquinnah. The *Vineyard Gazette* prints a tide chart each Friday on the Fishing page.

Equipment and Guides

Several stores offer fishing rod, tackle, bait, and other equipment. Many stores also offer guide services. Tackle shops and guides also are the best places to find out about local limits on size and numbers of fish you can keep. Here are some of our favorites:

DICK'S BAIT AND TACKLE
New York Avenue, Oak Bluffs
(508) 693-7669

CAPTAIN PORKY'S BAIT & TACKLE
Dock Street, Edgartown
(508) 627-7117
www.captporky.com/baitandtackle.shtml

COOP'S BAIT AND TACKLE
147 West Tisbury Rd., Edgartown
(508) 627-3909
www.coopsbaitandtackle.com

LARRY'S TACKLE SHOP
258 Upper Main St., Edgartown
(508) 627–5088
www.larrystackle.com

Charter Fishing

Looking for tuna, shark, and white marlin? Consider taking a fishing expedition; you'll find them offered at all of the island's harbors. Here are several of the local tried-and-true charter services.

Banjo's Captain Robert Plante (508-693–3154, www.banjocharters.com) offers half- and full-day charters out of Oak Bluffs.

The party boat *Skipper* (508-693-1238, www.mvskipper.com) leaves from Oak Bluffs for fluke and scup.

Great Harbour Sport Fishing Charters (508-627-3122, www.vineyardfishing.com) leaves from Edgartown Harbor.

Conomo Charters (508-645-9278) out of Aquinnah, offers half- and full-day charters. Captain Brian Vanderhoop offers spin or fly fishing.

Golf

Every vacation should include a little driving, chipping, and putting. To help you out in that area, Martha's Vineyard has two fine public golf courses.

Courses
FARM NECK GOLF COURSE
Farm Neck Way, Oak Bluffs
(508) 693-2504

This challenging 18-hole, par 72 championship course is open from early Apr to late Dec. You may find a few golf balls with the Presidential Seal on them, as this is where President Clinton spent most of his daylight hours while on the island. Simply, Farm Neck is one of the best courses in New England. Call ahead for reservations (though no more than 48 hours in advance) and current greens fees. This beautiful course follows Sengekontacket Pond and overlooks the beach. It features a driving range and pro shop with rental equipment.

Minigolf

ISLAND COVE MINIATURE GOLF COURSE
State Road, Vineyard Haven
(508) 693-2611
www.islandcoveminigolf.com
If you're not up to the challenge of a full 6,000-plus yard course, then bring the kiddies over to Island Cove for some family adventure golf. This Vineyard Haven course offers 18 holes and waterfalls to boot. The first 9 holes are wheelchair accessible.

MINK MEADOWS
320 Golf Club Rd., Vineyard Haven
(508) 693-0600
www.minkmeadowsgc.com
Mink Meadows is an intimate course with 9 holes and great ocean views. In fact, the views are so awesome that you might not be able to keep you eyes on the ball. The facility also has a pro shop and driving range. Greens fees are $55 for 9 holes, $80 for 18 holes in season.

Horseback Riding

Enjoy the scenery of the island while in the saddle of a horse trotting down a country lane.

ARROWHEAD FARM
Indian Hill Road, West Tisbury
(508) 693-8831
www.arrowheadfarm.net
This farm provides lessons, boarding, an outdoor and indoor ring, and offers pony rides. There are beautiful woods to ride in. Arrowhead Farm welcomes visitors and offers a day riding camp during the summer.

CROW HOLLOW FARM
Tiah's Cove Road, West Tisbury
(508) 696-4554
www.crowhollowfarm.com
Located near the state forest and a network of trails and lanes, Crow Hollow's guided trail rides roam through the varied terrain of old farmland and conservation land. The farm also offers lessons, clinics, and a summer riding program.

MISTY MEADOWS HORSE FARM
Old Country Road, West Tisbury
(508) 693-1870
Misty Meadows is a trail farm that is only open during the summer. It offers family-oriented trail rides in the forest behind the farm.

Ice-Skating

MARTHA'S VINEYARD ICE ARENA
Edgartown–Vineyard Haven Road,
Oak Bluffs
(508) 693-5329
www.mvarena.com
This arena is open for skating, lessons, and hockey games from the beginning of Aug through mid-Apr. Summer camps are offered in hockey and figure skating.

Tennis

Public tennis courts are available at the following locations to the residents or vacationers of each town.

Edgartown: Town Courts, Robinson Avenue
Oak Bluffs: Town Courts, Niantic Avenue
Vineyard Haven: Town Courts, Church Street
West Tisbury: Town Courts, Old County Road

Water Sports and Boating

Equipment Rentals
MARTHA'S VINEYARD OCEANSPORTS
Dockside Marina, Oak Bluffs
(508) 693-8476
www.mvoceansports.com

This business rents Jet Skis and will take you out for an afternoon of waterskiing or for the ride of your life—parasailing. The instructors are Coast Guard licensed and insured. Call ahead for reservations.

VINEYARD SCUBA
110 South Circuit Ave., Oak Bluffs
(508) 693-0288
www.vineyardscuba.com
The waters around the Vineyard were unlucky for many a sailor in the 18th and 19th centuries. With the help of Vineyard Scuba, you can now visit these sunken ships and lost schooners. They offer equipment rentals so you can explore the Vineyard's undersea world.

WIND'S UP
199 Beach Rd., Vineyard Haven
(508) 693-4252
www.windsupmv.com
Sailboarders will find the waters around the Vineyard to their liking. Wind's Up offers lessons and rentals of sailboards, wet suits, body boards, sailboats, surfboards, sea kayaks, and canoes. Ask for a free copy of their brochure listing the best places to catch the wind. Wind's Up is open until Christmas, reopening in Mar.

Boat Rentals
If your plans include hoisting your own sail, then you'll be happy to learn that there are many boat rental establishments on the Vineyard. Keep in mind many renters limit how far you can go in their crafts. Here are a few of our favorites.

ISLAND WATER SPORTS
100 Lagoon Pond Rd., Vineyard Haven
(508) 693-7767, (508) 693-5884 (off-season)
www.boatmv.us
Island Water Sports rents powerboats, sailboats, skiffs, inflatables, dinghies, kayaks, outboard motors, and water skis. They also have fishing rods for rent. Must be 21 to rent a boat.

MARTHA'S VINEYARD OCEANSPORTS
Dockside Marina, Oak Bluffs
(508) 693-8476
www.mvoceansports.com

Hourly, daily, weekly, and seasonal rentals of Boston Whalers. You may also rent parasailing, waterskiing, wakeboarding, Jet Skiing, and tubing equipment. Professional instruction is available.

WIND'S UP
199 Beach Rd., Vineyard Haven
(508) 693-4252
www.windsupmv.com
This is the place to go for catamarans, Aqua-Finns, American 14.6 centerboard sloops, sailboards, and boogie boards.

Boat Ramps
Those who bring their own boat to the island or buy their own boat on the island can launch it at several boat ramps.

In Vineyard Haven: Beach Road, on the Vineyard Haven side of the lagoon drawbridge, into the lagoon or at Lake Street into Lake Tashmoo.

In Oak Bluffs: At East Chop Drive, along the north side of the Harbor, into the harbor or at Medeiros cove, on the west side of town, into the lagoon.

In Edgartown: Anthier's Landing into Sengekontacket Pond or at the south end of Katama Bay Road into Katama Bay.

In Aquinnah: Aquinnah-Chilmark town line at Hariph's Creek Bridge into Nashaquitsa Pond or at Lobsterville, West Basin, into Menemsha Pond.

ANNUAL EVENTS
There's always something happening on the island, especially during the summer months. Whether it's fireworks, fairs, festivals, road races, concerts, or fishing tournaments, you are bound to find something of interest. And the events don't end on Columbus Day weekend. Edgartown celebrates an old-fashioned Christmas with a host of festivities, and there's even a First Night event on the first night of the new year. So get out your calendar and pencil in some dates.

January

WMVY ANNUAL CHILI CONTEST
Atlantic Connection, Oak Bluffs
(508) 693-5000
www.mvyradio.com

This fund-raiser held in late Jan (usually on Sat the weekend before Super Bowl Sunday) and sponsored by WMVY radio station is sure to warm you up. One category involves the island's top chefs, and the other is for amateurs. A fee, usually about $20, will get you in the door to sample all the chili you can eat.

May

OAK BLUFFS MEMORIAL DAY 5K ROAD RACE
Oak Bluffs
(508) 693-7887

Memorial Day weekend kickoffs the new tourist season here on the island. It is also the weekend for the annual Memorial Day 5K Road Race, held on Sunday. You can sign up at the Wesley Hotel.

June

OAK BLUFFS ANNUAL HARBOR FESTIVAL
Oak Bluffs
(508) 693-2892
www.oakbluffsmv.com

This is a festive waterfront celebration that attracts both locals and tourists in large numbers. Bands fill the air with sound while seafood fills the air with aroma. There are games and arts and crafts booths to keep kids and adults entertained. Admission is free. Sponsored by the Oak Bluffs Association, this event takes place in mid-June from noon to 5 p.m. with a rain date of the next day.

A TASTE OF THE VINEYARD
Edgartown
(508) 627-4440
www.mvpreservation.org

Sample food and drink from the island's finest eateries and beverage merchants on Thurs night and be wined and dined at the live auction featuring various goods and services on Sat night. It is held in mid-June under a tent next to the Old Whaling Church. Tickets for Thurs night are $125 and $150 Sat night. All money raised benefits the Martha's Vineyard Preservation Trust.

FARMERS' MARKET
West Tisbury
(508) 693-0085

Held at the old Grange Hall on Saturdays from June to Oct and on Wednesdays from June to Aug, this farmers' market offers fresh locally grown vegetables, homemade baked goods, and artisans selling arts and crafts.

July

VINEYARD HAVEN AND OAK BLUFFS BAND CONCERTS
(508) 645-3458
www.vineyardhavenband.org

Now this is an island vacation—music on a summer night! Sunday night is the night for band concerts, alternating between Owen Park in Vineyard Haven and Ocean Park in Oak Bluffs. You might want to bring your own lawn chair or blanket. The band is the Vineyard Haven Band Inc., and the admission is free.

TISBURY BIRTHDAY AND STREET FAIR
Vineyard Haven

Tisbury is the second-oldest town on the island, incorporated in 1671 just after Edgartown. To celebrate its incorporation, the town throws itself a party in early July, and you are invited. Festivities include games, live entertainment, and craft booths. Of course, food is available as well.

EDGARTOWN REGATTA
Edgartown Yacht Club
(508) 627-4364
www.edgartownyc.org

This 80-year-old regatta is one of the largest amateur sailing events in the area, usually beginning the third Thurs in July and running throughout the weekend. Races include anything from smaller boats to large cruising vessels. The race weekend attracts large crowds to Edgartown, so you may want to make your room reservations months in advance.

PORTUGUESE HOLY GHOST FEAST
Vineyard Ave., Oak Bluffs
(508) 693-9875

Portuguese first arrived on the island in the early to mid-18th century as merchant seamen or on whaling vessels. Portuguese-American heritage is the focus of the Holy Ghost Feast—a festival of games, entertainment, and some of the greatest food on the planet. The festival is held in mid-July at the Portuguese-American Club.

MONSTER SHARK FISHING TOURNAMENT
Oak Bluffs
(781) 834-2899
www.bbgfc.com

This controversial shark tournament has drawn the ire of the Humane Society of the United States and the late Peter Benchley, the author of *Jaws*, and later his widow. Despite, or perhaps because of, the controversy, this three day tournament held toward the end of July remains popular. Local charters and anglers alike vie to land the largest shark. Registration is held at Oak Bluffs' Wesley Hotel. Call the Boston Big Game Fishing Club for more information.

August

ALL ISLAND ART SHOW
Oak Bluffs
(508) 693-0525

The famed Tabernacle at the Methodist campgrounds in Oak Bluffs is the site of this art show in early Aug. The event is well attended, as the work is of the highest caliber. Admission is free.

POSSIBLE DREAMS AUCTION
Edgartown
(508) 693-7900
www.possibledreamsauction.org

This Aug event at the Harborside Inn gardens is a fund-raiser that was hosted by a Vineyard legend, the late Art Buchwald, for 29 years. Although Buchwald died in Jan 2007, the auction

he reigned over lives on. Donations are raised for Martha's Vineyard Community Services by auctioning off experiences like cocktails with Ted Danson and Mary Steenburgen. Anything is possible, so bring your checkbook.

CHILMARK ROAD RACE
Chilmark
(508) 645-9484, (508) 645-2100
www.chilmarkRd.race.org

This 5K road race takes place in mid-Aug. It benefits the Chilmark Community Center. The race starts at 10:30 a.m.

AGRICULTURAL FAIR
West Tisbury
(508) 693-9549
mvas.vineyard.net

This old-fashioned country fair is anchored by an old dairy barn where you'll find agricultural exhibits featuring fruits and vegetables, and arts and crafts—all judged. In the livestock barn different farm critters are judged daily throughout the four days. The fair takes place the third week in Aug on Thurs, Fri, Sat, and Sun. Admission is $8 for adults, and $5 for seniors and children 5 to 12 years old. Rides and food cost extra, but the dog and horse show, ox pull, and music do not. The fair prompted Bonnie Raitt to write Stayed Too Long at the Fair. (She probably had too much cotton candy.) The Agricultural Fair is sponsored by the Martha's Vineyard Agricultural Society.

FIREWORKS AT OCEAN PARK BY THE SEA
Oak Bluffs
(508) 693–0077
www.mvcma.org

This traditional end-of-summer fireworks show takes place the third weekend of Aug. The event is free; bring along your own lawn chairs and blankets. Sponsored by the Oak Bluffs Firemen's Civic Association.

ILLUMINATION NIGHT
Oak Bluffs
(508) 693-0525
www.mvcma.org

Tradition abounds as each of the gingerbread houses of Oak Bluffs' old Methodist campground twinkles with Japanese lanterns and candles as they have each year for the past century. Illumination Night marks the end of yet another summer season and is a free event.

September

VINEYARD ARTISANS FESTIVAL
West Tisbury
(508) 693-8989
www.vineyardartisans.com
Local artists display their work amidst West Tisbury's country setting. Sounds like a fun afternoon to us. It all takes place at the Agricultural Hall the first weekend in Sept from 10 a.m. to 5 p.m. The festival is free.

DUKES COUNTY SAVINGS BANK GOLF CLASSIC
Vineyard Haven
(508) 696-0785
www.mvsbclassic.com
The Vineyard golf course is the site of this annual tournament. It is held in mid-Sept to benefit the Vineyard Nursing Association.

TIVOLI DAY FESTIVAL
Oak Bluffs
www.oakbluffsmv.com or e-mail obainfo@ yahoo.com
Tivoli is a city in Italy, just northeast of Rome. Closer to home, the Tivoli used to be the old dance hall in Oak Bluffs and is now a festival of music, arts, crafts, and food held from noon to sundown on Circuit Avenue. Admission is free to the event that usually falls on the second Sat after Labor Day.

MARTHA'S VINEYARD STRIPED BASS AND BLUEFISH DERBY
Edgartown
www.mvderby.com
This fishing tournament is a monthlong competition with more than $100,000 worth of prizes for those who catch the largest bass, bluefish, bonito, and false albacore. Running from mid-Sept to mid-Oct, there are daily, weekly, and grand prizes awarded.

The weigh station is at the Edgartown Junior Yacht Club, although Derby Headquarters can be reached by writing 1A Dock Street, Edgartown, MA 02539.

COLUMBUS DAY 5K ROAD RACE
Oak Bluffs
(508) 693-7887
The air is a little cooler for this 5K race every year the Sunday before Columbus Day. The event usually draws a good field of runners and an enthusiastic crowd of onlookers.

HAPPY HAUNTING WEEKEND
Edgartown
(508) 627-4711
www.colonialinnmvy.com
Ghosts and goblins and a devilishly good time come together in this traditional Halloween weekend. There is a pumpkin-carving contest, face painting, and trick or treating at participating stores.

November

VINEYARD ARTISANS HOLIDAY FESTIVAL
West Tisbury
(508) 693-8989
This annual holiday festival is held on Thanksgiving weekend. Local artists display their work amidst West Tisbury's country setting (a reprise of the August show). This festival takes place at the Agricultural Hall, and admission is free.

TISBURY'S COME HOME FOR THE HOLIDAYS
Tisbury
(508) 693-0085
From Thanksgiving through the First Night Celebration, the town of Tisbury holds a variety of events. There are horse-and-buggy rides, chowder festivals, and performances at the Vineyard Playhouse. For a listing of all events, check the calendar section of either the *Vineyard Gazette* or *Martha's Vineyard Times,* or call the chamber

of commerce at the above number. Most of the events are free, except for the performances.

December

ANNUAL GREAT CHOWDER CONTEST
Vineyard Haven
(508) 693-0085

There's nothing like good "chow-dah" to keep you warm on a brisk Dec day. Your taste buds will be dancing as you sample the many delicious chowders made by area restaurants competing for the coveted title of "Best Chow-da on the Island." Held at the mini-park on Main Street, the event raises money for the Red Stocking Fund, a charity that buys gifts for families in need.

CHRISTMAS IN EDGARTOWN
Edgartown
(508) 693-0085

This old-fashioned Christmas celebration, full of fun and festivities, is held over three days, typically on the second weekend of the month. There are trolley tours, festival of lights tours, church Christmas fairs, horse-and-buggy rides, musical events, and holiday concerts at the Old Whaling Church. There's a Christmas parade and of course all the shops are open for business to cater to all your Christmas shopping needs. Many offer free eggnog and tea to get you warm and toasty as you walk the brick sidewalks of the perfect Christmas village.

Many of the inns and hotels offer special rates for the weekend. Call ahead for reservations.

FIRST NIGHT CELEBRATION
Island-wide
(508) 693-0085

First Night was first held in 1994. Activities abound, including lantern-making classes for kids, acoustic acts, improvisational comedy, ballet performances, dancing, and a fireworks display over Vineyard Haven Harbor. The majority of activities are held in Vineyard Haven. Recent First Night celebrations attracted as many as 2,500 spectators and more than 200 performers.

HEALTH CARE

MARTHA'S VINEYARD HOSPITAL
1 Hospital Rd., Oak Bluffs
(508) 693-0410
www.mvhospital.com

This full-service hospital has an emergency room, inpatient/outpatient service, operating rooms, a day surgical suite, a radiology department, a three-bed dialysis unit, a psychiatry department, and a cardiac rehabilitation program—basically all the services available at the mainland hospitals. There are 45 staff physicians available at the hospital. A new $50 million hospital on Beach Road was expected to be complete in 2010.

MEDIA

Being on an island is no excuse to lose touch with the outside world. Besides the Boston Globe, the Cape Cod Times, and many other mainland newspapers, the Vineyard has a couple of newspapers of its own. You'll be able to pick up the many Cape radio stations, as well as those from Providence, Rhode Island, and Boston. There is also 92.7 WMVY for truly local radio: the station plays adult-oriented rock. You can hear local news and weather, as well as entertainment, concert reports, steamship sailing updates, and music.

Newspapers

MARTHA'S VINEYARD TIMES
30 Beach Rd., Vineyard Haven
(508) 693-6100
www.mvtimes.com

Started in 1984, the *Times* is the island's other newspaper. It comes out on Thurs.

VINEYARD GAZETTE
34 South Summer St., Edgartown
(508) 627-4311, (877) 850-0409
www.mvgazette.com

Founded in 1847, the *Vineyard Gazette* is one of the oldest papers in the country. It publishes twice a week from Memorial Day to Columbus Day (on Tues and Fri) and once a week throughout the winter (Fri only).

INDEX

ABOUT THE AUTHOR

Patrick Cassidy is a reporter for the *Cape Cod Times*. Prior to working for the *Times,* he spent two years as a Peace Corps volunteer with his dog Fogo in Cape Verde off the west coast of Africa. He lives on Cape Cod with his fiancé and their two fish, Bleu and Tiger, not to mention Fogo.